THE SHOCHET

A Memoir of Jewish Life in Ukraine and Crimea

Pinkhes-Dov Goldenshteyn

Touro University Press Books

Series Editors
MICHAEL A. SHMIDMAN, PhD (Touro University, New York)
SIMCHA FISHBANE, PhD (Touro University, New York)

THE SHOCHET

A Memoir of Jewish Life in Ukraine and Crimea

Pinkhes-Dov Goldenshteyn

Volume One

Presented and Translated by Michoel Rotenfeld

Preface by Israel Singer

Library of Congress Cataloging-in-Publication Data
Names: Goldenshteyn, Pinkhes-Dov, 1848-1930. | Rotenfeld, Michoel, 1964- translator.
Title: The shochet : a memoir of Jewish life in Ukraine and Crimea / by Pinkhes-Dov Goldenshteyn; presented and translated by Michoel Rotenfeld.
Other titles: Mayn lebens-geshikhṭe. English | Memoir of Jewish life in Ukraine and Crimea
Description: New York: Touro University Press, 2023. | Complete in two volumes--Publisher. | Includes bibliographical references and index. | Contents: v. 1 -- v. 2.
Identifiers: LCCN 2023024382 (print) | LCCN 2023024383 (ebook) | ISBN 9798887193007 (v. 1 ; hardback) | ISBN 9798887193557 (v. 1; paperback) | ISBN 9798887193014 (v. 1; adobe pdf) | ISBN 9798887193021 (v. 1; epub)
Subjects: LCSH: Goldenshteyn, Pinkhes-Dov, 1848-1930. | Jews—Europe, Eastern—History—19th century. | Jews—Europe, Eastern—History—20th century. | Hasidism—History. | Habad—History. | Jews—Ukraine—Tiraspol—Biography. | Jews—Ukraine—Crimea-Bakhchisaray—Biography. | Jews—Eretz Israel—History—1917-1948, British Mandate period. | Israel—Petaḥ Tiḳvah—Biography. | Shehitah. | Slaughtering and slaughter-houses. | Kashering of meat. | Autobiography. | Providence and government of God—Judaism.
Classification: LCC DS135.U43 G65 2023 (print) | LCC DS135.U43 (ebook) | DDC 940.5318092--dc23/eng/20230627

LC record available at https://lccn.loc.gov/2023024382
LC ebook record available at https://lccn.loc.gov/2023024383

Copyright © Touro University Press, 2023
Published by Touro University Press and Academic Studies Press.
Typeset, printed and distributed by Academic Studies Press.

ISBN 9798887193007 (hardback)
ISBN 9798887193557 (paperback)
ISBN 9798887193014 (adobe pdf)
ISBN 9798887193021 (epub)

Touro University Press
Michael A. Shmidman and Simcha Fishbane, Editors
3 Times Square, Room 654,
New York, NY 10036
press@touro.edu

Book design by Kryon Publishing Services
Cover design by Ivan Grave.
On the cover: Issachar Ber Ryback, *Reznik* (1917)
(Source: Wikimedia Commons)

Academic Studies Press
1577 Beacon Street
Brookline, MA 02446, USA
press@ academicstudiespress.com
www.academicstudiespress.com

FIGURE 1. Pinkhes-Dov "Pinye-Ber" Goldenshteyn (1848-1930) in the early 1900s, when he first started to write his autobiography. At that time, his beard was still mostly red. He is wearing a *yarmlke* (skullcap worn by Jews) used by cantors, since he served as the *shoykhet* and cantor of Bakhchisaray. Taken in Feodosiya, Crimea, where his oldest two children resided at the time. Courtesy of Shifra Bernfeld.

Contents

Volume One

Foreword	xiii
Acknowledgements	xvii
A Note about the Translation	xxi

Introduction. The Autobiography of Pinkhes-Dov (Pinye-Ber) Goldenshteyn—A Traditionalist's Unique Depiction of Nineteenth-Century Jewish Life in Tsarist Russia — 1

An Exceptional Autobiographer: Pinye-Ber's Status, Motives, and Choices	1
Pinye-Ber in Contrast to Modern Jewish Autobiographers	4
How Did Pinye-Ber Come to Write an Autobiography?	11
Pinye-Ber's *Alltagsgeschichte*: Traditional Jews in Tsarist Russia	18
Common Life and Incidental Observations	18
Work, Family Life, and Social Struggle	23
The Rebbe as an Inspirational Light	35
Anti-Fanaticism and Anti-Corruption	38
Religious Self-Realization	41
Pinye-Ber's Sense of Divine Providence	47
A Divine-Providence-Centered Consciousness	47
Hasidism and Divine Providence	53
A Life Seen as God's Will	61
Dates in the Autobiography	67
Pinye-Ber's Language	71
Conclusion	73
Bibliography	74

The Shochet: A Story of Jewish Life in Ukraine and Crimea   83
  In Lieu of a Preface   84
Part I. My Family and Youth   87
  A. My Parents and Siblings   88
    Chapter 1: My Parents   89
    Chapter 2: The Deaths of My Parents, Brother-in-Law, and Brother, 1854–1857   97
    Chapter 3: Tragedy in the Lives of Three of My Sisters, ca. 1857–1864   107
  B. My Early Years, 1848–1864   127
    Chapter 4: My Early Childhood, 1848–1855   129
    Chapter 5: A New Set of Parents, 1856   137
    Chapter 6: With Grandfather in Groseles, 1857–1858   147
    Chapter 7: Shuffled Around, 1858–1860   157
    Chapter 8: Sent Off to an "Uncle," 1860   165
    Chapter 9: My Dream of a Celestial Palace, 1860   177
    Chapter 10: Working as a House Servant for Shulem Tashliker, 1860–1863   181
    Chapter 11: Beyle's Fiancé, 1863   191
    Chapter 12: Gaining Admittance to the Yeshiva in Odessa, 1863   194
    Chapter 13: In Odessa, Tiraspol, and Romanovke, 1863–1864   205
Part II. Engagement, Marriage, and Seeking a Livelihood, 1864–1873   215
  Chapter 14: My Unexpected Engagement, 1864–1865   217
  Chapter 15: Obtaining a Romanian Passport and Traveling to Lubavitch, 1865   237
  Chapter 16: The Lubavitcher Rebbe and Studying in Shklov, 1865–1866   247
  Chapter 17: Delivering an *Esreg* to the Lyever Rebbe, 1866–1867   265
  Chapter 18: My Wedding and a Fiery Pursuit, 1867–1868   291
  Chapter 19: In Search of a Livelihood, 1868–1869   319

Chapter 20: Studying to be a *Shoykhet* and Searching for Uncle Idl, 1870–1872   343

Chapter 21: Receiving Certification as a *Shoykhet* and Returning to Lubavitch, 1872–1873   365

Volume II, Contents   389

Foreword

During the past year, followers of world events have had a crash course on the conflict-ridden Ukraine and Crimea. Looking back in history, we find that life in these regions was also turbulent over one hundred years ago, as illustrated in *The Shochet*, the newly translated (from the original Yiddish) and fascinating memoirs of Pinkhes-Dov Goldenshteyn (1848-1930). At one time, the towns, villages, and cities of Goldenshteyn's native Ukraine were home to hundreds of thousands of Jews. For centuries, Jews were part and parcel of the area's landscape. In this land rich in woes and wars, the Jews suffered—sometimes together with their neighbors and sometimes at the hands of their neighbors. Antisemitism was rampant; the region was the site of some of the largest number of murders committed against the Jewish people. Goldenshteyn's portrayal of his youth and early adulthood tells the story of Ukrainian Jewry—their traditional way of life and their struggle for survival.

Goldenshteyn was born in 1848 in a Ukraine ruled by the Russian tsars, and that was where he spent his formative years. Orphaned at the age of seven, he was shuttled from relative to relative. His travels took him throughout Ukraine, Romania, and Lubavitch and Shklov in Belarus. He was hired as a *shochet* in the Crimea in 1879, and finally, after working there for decades, he immigrated to the Land of Israel in 1913, where he remained until he died in 1930. The streetwise Goldenshteyn is a natural storyteller, and he tells his story—the story of life in those lands during those years—in a delightful and captivating manner.

I believe that autobiographies are anthropological treasure troves of history, and few sources of history are as trustworthy. Goldenshteyn, in particular, serves as an honest and accurate source of a vast amount of historical data, much of which he mentions unwittingly. In the course of telling his own story, he touches on almost every realm of life. As the translator writes in the Introduction, he gives us clear glimpses into the relationships between adults and children, men and women, Jews and non-Jews, feudal lords and serfs, communities and their leaders, craftsmen and apprentices. Through his vivid depictions, we experience the life of a Jewish child—the *kheyder* (traditional Jewish elementary school), children's games, and the differences between city and *shtetl* children. Having worked in various occupations, he describes the lives of *shochets* (kosher slaughterers), house servants, cantors, *melamdim* (teachers in traditional Jewish elementary schools), grain merchants, melon farmers, tavern keepers, and storekeepers. He recalls hiding from the *khapers* (snatchers) who seized Jewish children for forcible conscription into the Russian military and seeing the wrenching sight of a battalion of cantonist children-soldiers. He recounts his interactions with various Hasidic Rebbes and their Hasidim including the Tolner Rebbe and the Tzemach Tzedek of Lubavitch; the great Sephardic rabbi, the Sdei Chemed; *mitnagdim* (non-Hasidim); Karaites; and even informers and apostates. His depiction of a cholera pandemic describes the quarantining of cities and towns and the primitive efforts used to save the lives of the stricken. He describes town fires—which were constant sources of danger, baking *matzohs* for Pesach, purchasing *etrogs* for *Sukkot*, building *mikvehs*, petty synagogue politics, assimilation, and immigration to America and Palestine.

Indeed, *The Shochet* may be rightfully labeled the Glikl of Hameln of Ukraine. Just as Glikl's memoirs give us a picture of life as a Jewish woman in the seventeenth century that no history book can describe, Goldenshteyn's depiction of traditional Jewish life in Ukraine is unmatched by any other method of historical description.

A terribly important hole is filled by this authentic and vital document, for Goldenshteyn's is the first book-length memoir I know of that depicts the life of a religious Jewish functionary (*klei kodesh*) in Eastern Europe. It offers a unique opportunity to examine the reactions of a traditional Jew during a time when religion was being undermined all over the globe, particularly in the Jewish world when Jews were inclining more and more towards secularism and leaving Jewish religious practice. Goldenshteyn's portrayal of this conflict, at times in an agonizing manner, gives us insight into the effects of modernization on traditional Jewish life. His pain in confronting these radical changes makes Goldenshteyn's memoirs a compelling historical and personal description of a tumultuous period of transition.

For many years Goldenshteyn lived in the Crimea, where he lived and worked in a Muslim society. His vivid recollection of the local Karaites—a breakaway Jewish sect originating in eighth-century Babylonia—and the relationships between them, the Jews, and their Muslim and Christian neighbors, makes fascinating reading.

Goldenshteyn's recollections of his move from the Crimea to Palestine in an age where travel was prohibited and prohibitive, his suffering there during the First World War amid the battles between British and Ottoman-Turkish forces, and his description of the fledgling Jewish settlement serve to round out this unique memoir. His decision to go to Israel, a move he made many years before the idea became popular, is the ultimate reflection of the courage and resourcefulness he displays time and time again throughout his life.

Michoel Rotenfeld's superb annotated translation of this unique work allows the English-speaking reader to learn—for the first time in such granular detail—about daily life in Eastern Europe at a time when the traditional Jewish world was falling apart, hundreds of thousands of Jews were about to be killed in pogroms in the Russian Civil War, communism was at the threshold, and Ukraine and Crimea were poised to become part of the Soviet nightmare. The focus on life in Israel at the end of the book is a consolation. It is comforting to know that our *shochet*, after everything he went through, made it out of Eastern Europe before all hell broke loose. Foreshadowing the experience of the Jews of Europe as a whole, he manages to survive, if only barely at times, and by the grace of God he establishes a new life in the Land of Israel.

The Shochet is a magnificent new contribution to Jewish and Eastern European history. Kudos to Rotenfeld for shedding light on this extremely significant primary source which was known until now only to a small circle of Yiddish-speaking scholars. With its folksy style, it invites a broad audience to go back in time and take a long look at a vanished world.

Dr. Rabbi Israel Singer
Vice-President of International Affairs and
Professor of Politics at Touro University
Secretary General & Chairman of the
World Jewish Congress, 1985–2005

Acknowledgements

I would like to express my tremendous gratitude to God Almighty for granting me the opportunity to be able to translate and annotate this remarkable work.

My becoming the translator of the autobiography of Pinkhes-Dov "Pinye-Ber" Goldenshteyn came about in an unusual manner. In 1988, I was fascinated to read an article in Hebrew about this work by the late outstanding Chabad historian Yehoshua Mondshine, and I hoped one day to find the original Yiddish work. In 1997, I was fortunately able to find a copy of Pinye-Ber's book to purchase. Wanting to find out more about the author, I contacted Yehoshua Mondshine for assistance in finding his descendants. He had met someone who had known the author's great-granddaughter Tsviya Gelbshtein (1944–1992), who had become religious and connected to the Chabad movement. After a phone call or two, I located Tzviya's mother (and Pinye-Ber's granddaughter) Aliza Goldenshteyn Bernfeld (1921–2008) of Petakh-Tikva. Aliza proved to be a fountain of information about her grandfather and the extended family, and she gave me the contact information for some of her relatives in America. Among these, both Cynthia Unterberg and her sister Muriel Casper (Pinye-Ber's great-granddaughters) were very receptive and arranged to meet me right away. During our first meeting, Cynthia told me that she had been looking for someone to translate Pinye-Ber's book and thought I had been heaven-sent to do so. I was reluctant to undertake such a large translation project and consulted with two knowledgeable friends: Max Apple, who strongly encouraged me, echoing my feeling that this autobiography of the traditional everyman of the *shtetl* was an entry into a world rarely depicted; and the late George Greenberg, who believed that I would be the perfect person for the job, given my background and capabilities. Buoyed by their enthusiasm, I contacted Cynthia to tell her I would do it.

In his autobiography, Pinye-Ber traces the divine providence in his life; certainly it was by divine providence that I discovered so many connections between my ancestors and the author. My first research trip for the translation was in 2001 to Israel, where the author had lived for the last seventeen years of his life. I immediately went to interview Aliza and her daughter Shifra. In one of my interviews with Aliza, I learned that Pinye-Ber had frequented Petakh-Tikva's Great Synagogue, where both of my father's grandfathers had prayed. My father, a native of Petakh-Tikva, told me that, in the early 1920s, when the population was less than 4,500 people, all the adults knew each other. On a trip to Petakh-Tikva's Segulah Cemetery with Aliza, we were amazed to see that my great-grandmother and her mother are buried right across from Pinye-Ber's wife Feyge. And only after working on this project for several years did I recall that my grandfather, who died before my birth, had managed one of Petakh-Tikva's only two book stores in the late 1920s and early 1930s; he would have likely sold the original Yiddish edition of this book when it was published in 1928–1929. He was said to have been a voracious reader and would likely have read it.

Parenthetically—but also providentially—important information about my own family emerged as a result of my research for this book. During my perusal of Uriel Gellman's annotated bibliography appearing in *The Heder: Studies, Documents, Literature and Memoirs* (2010), when I was looking for sources that would help me better understand the life and times of Pinye-Ber, I noticed an entry for the autobiography of an A. S. Melamed, who had lived in the Crimea as Pinye-Ber did. With great difficulty, I obtained scans of Melamed's two-volume work and was startled to find that he was raised in the same small Ukrainian village where my paternal grandfather's family had originated. In reading it, I was excited to see that he mentions at length my own great-great-grandfather, along with his wife, father, and other relatives, beginning in the 1870s. With some research, I located Melamed's elderly great-great-niece in Israel who sent me the unprinted manuscript of the third volume, which turned out to mention my great-grandfather and my great-aunts. I can't help but feel that I was directed to this family treasure—an autobiography no less—as a result of my devotion to the translation of Pinye-Ber's autobiography.

This project would not have been possible without the unflagging commitment of Cynthia Unterberg and generosity of her daughter Kara Unterberg to bring this translation to the light of day. A very refined soul, Cynthia has inherited her great-grandfather's spiritual sensitivities and concern for the spirituality of her family. During the first few years of this project, Cynthia kept turning up one important document after another in her basement, including a copy of S. Niger's 1930 review of Pinye-Ber's book, her grandmother's engagement contract handwritten by Pinye-Ber, and ten handwritten letters by Pinye-Ber from the 1920s. I am also grateful to Cynthia's daughter Lisa and her husband Michel Delafontaine for their constant encouragement and great interest.

Pinye-Ber's descendants and extended family with whom I have been in contact have been wonderfully supportive as they shared their family memories, photographs, and documents. In particular, I would like to thank Shifra Bernfeld, Christopher T. Blue, Michael Budiansky, Muriel Brockman Casper,

Myriam Pozwolski Cronin, Virginia "Ginny" Starr, and Nancy Merenbach Zuniga, as well those who have since passed away, Samuel Solis Goldeen, Jr., Dvora and her husband Meir Gavrieli, Yosef "Yoske" Grinberg, Abraham Solomon "Sol" Levitt, Hadassa Perlkvort Levitt, and Henry P. "Hank" Starr.

I cannot thank my close friend Rabbi Yitzchok Stroh enough for generously sharing his vast knowledge of European Jewish life throughout the entirety of this project. He referred me to scores of important sources and suggested multiple areas of research. He reviewed every page of my translation and compared it to the original Yiddish. His insights and criticism were invaluable. I was particularly humbled by his patient attention to detail in editing the Introduction, much of which is based on my notes from our conversations about the book over the years. His assistance in deciphering the author's handwritten letters was also essential.

Without help, no single person could possibly adequately translate such a difficult and large work—which is written in an unpolished Yiddish, with little punctuation and numerous typographical errors, especially in regard to its Slavic components. For clarifications and elucidations, I reached out to experts, too numerous to mention, in various fields. Thankfully, I started this translation when the older generation of Eastern European Jews, who were able to explain certain words and phrases, was still alive. I also feel privileged to have met and corresponded with the last few individuals to have known Pinye-Ber. Naturally, I alone am responsible for all errors.

Among the experts in Yiddish linguistics with whom I have been in contact were Paul (Hershl) Glasser and Yitskhok Niborski. Among those who have already passed away were Joshua A. (Shikl) Fishman, Marvin (Mikhl) Herzog, and particularly Mordkhe Schaechter, with whom I discussed the project at length.

I am also indebted to Zalman Alpert, David Assaf, Robert P. Evans, Hershl Hartman, Rabbi Yisroel Shimon Kalmenson, Rabbi Eliezer Katzman, Rabbi Yosef Yitzchok Levertov, Rabbi Eliyohu Matusof, Rabbi Moishe Traxler, and Rabbi Sholom DovBer Levine, chief librarian of the library of Agudas Chasidei Chabad in Brooklyn.

I want to express my heartfelt thanks to my dear friend Todd Berliner for his guidance in writing the Introduction and throughout the publishing process. Likewise, I am grateful to Glenn Dynner and Joshua M. Karlip for their assistance in helping me formulate the Introduction. Thanks, as well, to Andrew Escobedo, Pearl Lam, and Rivka Schiller for their editorial assistance.

In 2016, the JewishGen Bessarabia SIG announced that they were looking for sponsors for the transcribing of the recently located supplement to the

1858 *revizskie skazki* (revision list) of the Jews of Tiraspol, the author's place of birth, in the State Archives of Kherson Oblast (fond 22, inventory 1, file 72) in Kherson, Ukraine. A revision list was a poll-tax census for taxation and conscription. Unlike US censuses, each revision updated the previous revision with births, marriage, and deaths. Cynthia Unterberg generously sponsored the transcription and translation of this revision list, which has since been posted to the JewishGen Romania-Moldova Database. This supplementary revision list turned out to include the author's maternal grandfather and several other individuals mentioned in the text. No nineteenth-century metrical records have yet been located for Tiraspol. For their assistance in translating other Russian-language documents, much thanks is owed to my relative Denis Krol, who was instrumental in seeking out numerous Ukrainian documents, and Lyudmila "Lucy" Schwartz.

I am also indebted to the librarians at the Library of Congress's Geography and Map Reading Room for their expert assistance in helping to identify some of the elusive villages mentioned by the author.

Mrs. Bashe Simon, Director of Touro University Libraries, was encouraging and supportive throughout the lengthy process of bringing this book to print. The dedicated work of the following Touro University Library staff members helped me obtain materials from libraries across America and Europe: Carol Schapiro, Edward Schabes, and the late Sarah Nakar.

I offer my sincere thanks to the editors at Touro University Press, Michael A. Shmidman and Simcha Fishbane, and to the president of Touro University, Alan Kadish, MD, for their support of this project. I am also deeply grateful to Israel Singer, vice president of international affairs at Touro University, for his insight into the value of this work and for his encouragement. I would like to thank the staff at Academic Studies Press, particularly Kira Nemirovsky, Ilya Nikolaev, and Ekaterina Yanduganova, for their professionalism and high standards.

Most of all, I owe tremendous gratitude to my family, who have accompanied me enthusiastically on this journey: my father Benjamin, of blessed memory; my mother Joan; my brother David L. Ronn; my father-in-law Murray Kirschner, of blessed memory; my mother-in-law Chaya Kirschner. I am grateful beyond words to my wife Rivka Leah and my daughter Basya, who treat stories about Pinye-Ber like family lore and who have been excited participants in this long-running project.

Lastly, I would like to express my heartfelt appreciation of the Lubavitcher Rebbe זי"ע from whom I have learned so much and who has been a source of inspiration and direction for me.

A Note about the Translation

The romanization of Yiddish words and phrases follows Uriel Weinreich's system in his *Modern English-Yiddish/Yiddish-English Dictionary* (1968). For the unfamiliar, this system concerns itself solely with conveying the pronunciation; hence, it does not attempt to indicate the Hebrew-character spelling of its Hebrew and Aramaic components. Although based on the Northeastern (Lithuanian) Yiddish dialect, Weinreich's system provides a uniform manner of romanizing Yiddish words and place names in all Yiddish dialects, as done by Mordkhe Schaechter in *Yiddish II* (1995:443–446). Yiddish words and phrases have been transliterated using the Southeastern (Ukrainian) Yiddish dialect, the author's subdialect of Southeastern Yiddish, and the Northeastern (Lithuanian) Yiddish dialect. Stressed syllables are indicated by accent marks directly over the stressed vowels, the first time a word or place name is used. For details, see the Introduction to the Glossaries and the Romanization/Transliteration Schemes.

The author uses certain Yiddish words as they were once commonly used, though their usage has changed. For example, Jews in certain areas, including the Ukraine, used the word *fraynt* (or as the author writes *fraynd*) to mean a relative, while a *guter-fraynd* meant a friend. Another example is *mistome*, which was formerly used to also mean "certainly," though today it is exclusively used to mean "probably." *Lang* (and its inflected form *langer*) was formerly used, in some areas of Eastern Europe, to denote "long" and "tall," though today it is exclusively used to denote "long." Similarly, *sibe* (סיבה) was formerly used to also mean a "mishap" or an "accident," though today it is exclusively used to mean a "cause" or "reasons." And *geveyntlekh* was formerly used to mean "of course," while today it is used to mean "normally" or "usually." With the Hebraization of Yiddish over recent decades, some speakers of Yiddish will be unfamiliar with the traditional Yiddish pronunciations of certain Hebrew and Aramaic components of Yiddish, for example, *Yontef* instead of *Yomtov* (meaning a Jewish holiday). Since not all such words (not even all of those listed above) have been noted in the footnotes, if the reader notes such discrepancies between the original Yiddish (the digitized version can be accessed at https://archive.org/details/nybc206510) and today's usage of certain Yiddish words, an appropriate first resource would be Beinfeld and Bochner's *Comprehensive Yiddish-English Dictionary* (2002).

Similarly, the Yiddish pronunciation for certain words or names might be different from that to which the reader is accustomed. For example, the name Joseph is transcribed in Yiddish as Yosef (not Yoysef) being that Yosef (with a short "o") is the traditional Yiddish pronunciation of this name.

Personal names in the text have been romanized according to their Yiddish (or Ashkenazi-Hebrew) pronounciation and have been used similarly when mentioned in the footnotes or introduction, for the sake of consistency (see the Glossary of Jewish Personal Names). On the other hand, some names mentioned exclusively in the translator's footnotes and appendices are transliterated using a Modern Hebrew scheme. Nonetheless, sometimes the names of well-known personages are spelled as commonly rendered into English. See also the Glossary of Jewish Personal Names.

It is important for the reader to understand that many of the author's actions were conducted in accordance with *halakha* (binding and sacred Jewish legal statutes) and were not matters of optional tradition or personal preference. Hence, when the author mentions aspects of Jewish life associated with *halakha*, the specific section in the *Kitsur Shulkhan Arukh* (*Abridged Code of Jewish Law*) has been noted. The translators of similar works such as Aronson (1983), Kotik (2002), and Shapiro (2002) also cite the *Kitsur Shulkhan Arukh* at times. The *Kitsur Shulkhan Arukh* has become the classic guide to practical observance in all Orthodox Jewish circles and is readily available in English translation in several printed editions and freely accessible online. If a particular *halakha* is not found in the *Kitsur Shulkhan Arukh*, then the relevant place in the *Shulkhan Arukh* (*Code of Jewish Law*) or other Hebrew halakhic works has been cited.

The chapter titles and their year spans were provided by the translator, with the exception of those of chapters 14 and 32. All comments in square brackets and footnotes were added by the translator, including the section headings in chapters 1–3. Regarding the author's chapter summaries at the beginning of most chapters, sometimes the entries in the original Yiddish are not in order or even appear at the beginning of the wrong chapter. Though amended in the translation, not all such discrepancies have been noted. The beginning of chapter 4 has been removed and attached to the end of chapter 3 in order to separate the story of the author's parents and siblings from that of his own life. When the author writes "as you already know" or the like, a footnote indicating the incident's location in the text only appears when occurring in a different chapter. For the sake of clarity, the translator at times changed the order of the sentences (in less than a dozen places) and changed the order of the paragraphs (in a handful of places).

Unless otherwise indicated, Hebrew calendar dates are footnoted with their corresponding dates according to the Gregorian calendar and not according to the Julian calendar, which was still is use in Tsarist Russia until 1918.

Jewish personal names mentioned in Russian-language metrical documents and revision lists cited in the footnotes have often been slightly altered to be consistent with their presentation in the text, for instance, Mirke instead of Mirka.

I have attempted to identify the current name and location of every geographic location mentioned. See the Glossary of Geographic Places in Eastern Europe. I have transliterated places in Israel according to the Modern Hebrew pronunciation and not according to the author's Ashkenazi pronunciation, for example, Petakh-Tikva instead of Peysekh-Tikve, and Zikhron-Ya'akov instead of Zikhren-Yankev.

Information readily available in popular dictionaries and encyclopedias has not been cited.

Map of Ukraine, Moldova, and Romania

- The place names used on the map are those used in the text, which are often their Yiddish names. When differing from its current name, its current name follows in parenthesis.
- Current borders are indicated by black lines, and current country names are noted. For more details about each location see Glossary 3: Geographic Locations in Eastern Europe in volume 2.

Map of Tiraspol and Its Environs

- The place names used on the map are those used in the text, which are often their Yiddish names. When differing from its current name, its current name follows in parenthesis.
- Current borders are indicated by black lines, and current country names are noted. For more details about each location see Glossary 3: Geographic Locations in Eastern Europe in volume 2.

Introduction

The Autobiography of Pinkhes-Dov (Pinye-Ber) Goldenshteyn—A Traditionalist's Unique Depiction of Nineteenth-Century Jewish Life in Tsarist Russia

An Exceptional Autobiographer: Pinye-Ber's Status, Motives, and Choices

A *shoykhet* (kosher slaughterer) named Pinkhes-Dov Goldenshteyn (1848–1930),[1] commonly called Pinye-Ber,[2] printed his unedited 510-page autobiography in Petakh-Tikva in the British Mandatory Palestine in 1928–1929.[3]

---

1   Though the word *shoykhet* has been spelled in the text according to the academic standards of transliterating Yiddish words (see "A Note About the Translation"), the popular spelling of *shochet* has been used in the title.
2   In his autobiography, the author rarely mentions his formal name Pinkhes-Dov, while he mentions his nickname Pinye-Ber dozens of times. Pinye is a Yiddish nickname for Pinkhes. Before the twentieth century, Hebrew personal names such as Dov (bear), Tsvi (deer), and Zev (wolf) were rarely used in vernacular life, except for religious purposes or when written. Instead, their Yiddish translations were used, namely Ber (bear), Hersh (deer), and Volf (wolf), respectively. Hence, the author was called Pinye-Ber. Before the First World War, Jews in Tsarist Russia generally used surnames only for official purposes and not among themselves (Beider, 2008:1:11), which is why this introduction refers to him by his first name. In truth, he only refers to himself by his surname a few times in regards to his interactions with the government and in crossing the border.
3   Pinye-Ber's autobiography was printed in three parts with an addendum. From the "In Lieu of a Preface" and his private letters, it seems that part I was printed in August or September 1928; part II in March 1929; part III including the addendum in June or July of 1929. In a private interview with Pinye-Ber's granddaughter Aliza (Goldenshteyn) Bernfeld of Petakh-Tikva in 2001, she related that 500 copies of each of its three parts and addendum were printed and paperbound separately; 400 copies were sent to New York and 100 remained in Palestine. In New York, Pinye-Ber's son Refuel had the parts hard bound in a single volume and added the author's photograph. Without the financial assistance of his sons Yosef and Yankl in America, printing his book would have been impossible. See Appendix A7 for more

A privately printed book, particularly a work written by an unknown author, would rarely draw the attention of a leading literary critic, yet the foremost Yiddish literary critic of his day, Shmuel Niger, wrote a lengthy review on March 2, 1930 in the Yiddish daily *Der Tog*. Though Niger was evidently motivated to write a review by a visit from Pinye-Ber's son Refúel (Raphael Goldenstein), who brought him a copy of the autobiography, the very fact that Niger reviewed a relatively unknown work at such length, and found such significance in it, indicates its importance.[4] He writes that the author, an average poor and pious Jew in the Ukraine, portrayed "the typical life of yesteryear at greater length and more thoroughly than those who initially took it upon themselves as a goal to be the historians of those eras and environs," and that he had done this "unwillingly and unknowingly." Niger was not the only important reviewer to take notice of this autobiography: the renowned Yiddish scholar Yudl Mark wrote a lengthy linguistic review of Pinye-Ber's work in the journal *Yidishe Shprakh* (The Yiddish language) in 1943.

These reviews, penned by two major Yiddish figures of the twentieth century, only hint at the exceptional significance of this largely overlooked work.[5] Pinye-Ber's autobiography is distinct due to its anomalous nature. Nineteenth-century Jewish autobiographies were generally written by middle-class *maskilim* (followers of the Haskalah, the Jewish Enlightenment Movement) reflecting

---

   details. As late as 1920 he did not think that it would be printed in his lifetime, as implied by comments in his Hebrew ethical will (Appendix B2).

4 In the Archives of YIVO Institute for Jewish Research in New York City in the S. Niger Collection (RG 360, Box 75, Folder 1634) are two Yiddish-language letters from Refuel to Niger: one dated February 11, 1930, three weeks after their meeting, asking Niger for a prompt response explaining the reason he had not kept his promise to write a review; and the second dated March 5, 1930, three days after Niger's review was published, expressing his heartfelt thanks.

   Niger's review evidently made waves in Warsaw. The April 1930 issue of *Ortodoksishe Yugnd Bleter* (Orthodox youth newspaper), published by Agudath Israel, reported that Pinye-Ber's book "has generated much interest." On August 8, 1930, a favorable English-language book review by the writer Abraham Shinedling appeared in an unknown newspaper. The text of both reviews appears in Appendix A7.

5 The dissemination of this work has faced several hurdles. In the 1930s, the author's son Shloyme in Petakh-Tikva wanted to print more copies, but his cousin Yankl Grinberg threatened to sue if he did so since he felt that he and his wife had been unkindly portrayed in it. In 2002 Yankl's only surviving children, Dvora Ben-Ya'akov and Yosef ("Yoske") Grinberg, granted permission to include their father's surname in this translation. The paperbound copies remaining in Palestine did not hold up well over time, which, apart from its being written in Yiddish, certainly contributed to the omission of Pinye-Ber's account of his experiences in Petakh-Tikva and Kfar-Saba during the First World War from virtually every work on that subject. This omission of Pinye-Ber's work is particularly glaring in the five-volume study by Rubinshtein (1990), which pertains specifically to this period in Petakh-Tikva.

on traditional Jewish life, a life they abandoned decades earlier, and were written in the languages of scholarship, Hebrew or at times German or Russian.[6] Pinye-Ber, on the other hand, remained a traditionalist his entire life, a product of the predominating impoverished class of Jews, and he wrote in the Jewish vernacular, Yiddish. As his work was virtually completed by 1909, it is actually one of the first known Yiddish-language autobiographies written. He is also arguably the first traditional Jewish religious functionary to write a book-length life story.[7] These factors combined make Pinye-Ber's autobiography unique, though ironically his life story is more characteristic of the life stories of the vast majority of nineteenth-century Eastern European Jewry. His work is presented here in English translation under the title *The Shochet: A Story of Jewish Life in Ukraine and Crimea*.[8] It offers a rare, authentic glimpse of traditional nineteenth-century Jews in Tsarist Russia mostly untouched by modernity and secularism.

Pinye-Ber in Contrast to Modern Jewish Autobiographers

Until the late modern period, Jews produced few autobiographies, and the reasons for this have been debated by historians (Bar-Levav, 2002:45; Stanislawski, 2004:10–17). Modern Jewish autobiography has its beginnings in the 1860s, and autobiographies written in Hebrew became a major genre of the Haskalah literature. Nineteenth century Jewish autobiography was overwhelmingly a

---

6   My comments in this Introduction concentrate on book-length Jewish life histories in which most of the narrative occurs in the nineteenth century. Most of these autobiographies were written by Jews raised in Eastern Europe. Pinye-Ber's life story reaches the turn of the nineteenth century in the middle of chapter 28 (out of thirty-four), which covers eighty-two percent of his autobiography. The term *maskilim* here is used to refer to Jews in the Tsarist empire who abandoned their traditional upbringing to become followers of the Haskalah and lead a secular lifestyle. The Haskalah movement waned in the 1880s and 1890s, overtaken by other cultural and political movements in Jewish society, such as Jewish socialism, various forms of Zionism, and Yiddishism.

7   Two Western European rabbis wrote their life stories, but they were not rabbis in the traditional mold. Rabbi Leone Modena (1571–1648) served as a rabbi in Ferrara and Venice, Italy, but he pursued many other occupations and is considered by many to be the first modern rabbi. First published in the original Hebrew in 1911, it was translated into English in 1988. Joseph Samuel Bloch (1850–1923) first served as a rabbi in several small communities, but by 1884 he had moved into journalism to combat antisemitism and carried on the fight in the Austrian parliament. First published in German in 1922, it was translated into English in 1923.

8   The title of the original Yiddish version is *Mayn lebens-geshikhte: Farshidenartige pasirung'n un epizod'n fun a yosem* (My life story: Various events and episodes of an orphan).

secular pursuit written by secular Jews at a time when traditional Judaism was still the norm.[9] These autobiographies tell the stories of those who broke away from traditional Jewish life, rather than the stories of those who remained dedicated to it.[10] They typically describe a confined and oppressive childhood; the clandestine reading of secular books; the severance of ties with family, community, and Judaism; overcoming the authors' ignorance of the local non-Jewish vernacular and the deficits in their secular education; and, finally, the attempt to forge a secular lifestyle for themselves. In short, these authors were describing their secular self-realization. And often, the maskilic autobiographer had the aspiration for his work to join the ranks of literature and be a contribution to secular culture. As Shulamit S. Magnus (2010:25) writes, "The very articulateness of the *maskilim* against the silence of the vast majority of Jews, and their enormous cultural influence, made their writings conspicuous, which has led to the presumption of normativeness; we have before us dramatic, explicit tales of 'the odyssey' from Jewish traditionalist to modernity. Somehow, the contradiction between the justified emphasis on the specificity and uniqueness of the maskilic product and the assertion that this product is normative, has been missed."

David Assaf (2002b:22) notes that most of these maskilic autobiographies are either disparaging critiques or sentimental post-destruction romanticizations of Jewish communal life. On the one hand, as critiques, they belittle traditional Jewish education, dismiss Talmudic studies as mere sophistry, disparage Yiddish, and discredit Jewish law and traditions as superstition and myths. In their zeal to influence the traditional Jewish masses to shed their distinctive culture and appearance, acculturate linguistically, and change their traditional educational methods, they emphasize the negative aspects of *shtetl* life, portraying it as more backwards and primitive than it actually was. On the other hand, as romanticizations, Jewish autobiographies tend to be sentimental and nostalgic depictions of a destroyed world, particularly after the devastation wrought to Eastern European Jewish life by the First World War and incomparably more so after its annihilation during the Second World War. Childhood and *shtetl* memories were sweetened and embellished because that world, due to mourning, became to some extent off limits to criticism (Pinchuk, 2001:169–179).

---

9   Jews who maintained traditional observance continued to be the majority in Eastern Europe at least until the First World War (Katz, 1986:3).

10 Few maskilic women wrote their autobiographies. Tova Cohen (2008) points out that it was the male *maskilim* who were the breakaways from their families and traditional Jewish society, while Jewish women usually pursued Haskalic literature under the encouragement of their families.

Many of these writers are so engrossed in either disparaging or prettifying the traditional Jewish society they have left behind that they focus on the external circumstances of their lives without any discussion of their personal experience. In his monograph on nineteenth-century Hebrew autobiography, Mintz (1989:18, 20) writes, "In these works the events witnessed are more important than the mind and soul of the autobiographer; at most his individual experience is presented as paradigmatic of the ordeal of some larger collective. . . . [I]t is surprising in how many examples of the genre the focus falls on the many things other than the inner life of the narrator: the times, the folkways of a culture, scholarly controversies, other family members, professional accomplishments, and so on." These writers are eager to describe what happened around them, but less inclined to reveal how they felt about it.

Many nineteenth-century Jewish autobiographies were written in America, Western Europe, or Palestine, in environments greatly removed both culturally and religiously from their authors' communities of origin. In addition, they were written many decades after their authors left those communities. Writing in their old age in a language other than Yiddish, the language in which all the events of their youths were impressed on their memories, we may have before us a skewed picture of Jewish life as it was. In his monograph on the emergence of the autobiographical genre among Jews, Moseley (2006:209–210) writes regarding the author Berdichevsky, "distance—geographic, temporal, and cultural—provided Berdichevsky, the 'Jew without beard or *peyes*' with the possibility of entering into an autobiographical relationship with his Eastern European past. . . . With the passage of years, however, and the geographical and intellectual migration of Berdichevsky, retrieval of the lost world of [his youth] is almost entirely dependent upon the tenuous thread of memory. . . ." It is no wonder that Miron (2000:28) writes that the maskilic writer "cannot help but blunder as he goes back to the world of his childhood." After being separated from traditional Jewish life for decades, it is not surprising that maskilic autobiographies err in regard to some common practices of Judaism.[11]

---

11   The following are a few examples: Aronson (1983:289n24) cites a phrase from the Jewish prayer book that he attributes to the wrong blessing—a mistake that a traditional Jew would not have made. Pauline Wengeroff (2010:137) confuses practices of the days of *Sfira* with mourning customs of the first nine days of the Hebrew month of *Av*. Wengeroff (2010:171, 310n204) also incorrectly relates that in her youth Jewish men doffed their hats in deference to each other, which is a retrojection of a social custom that she would have only known in her assimilated circles as an adult. And Kotik (1922:1:92) incorrectly describes a Jewish wedding with the groom reciting a Hebrew blessing under the *huppah* (wedding canopy). For an English translation, see Kotik (2002:180).

In contrast to the almost ubiquitous perspective of the defector from Jewish tradition, Pinye-Ber's autobiography provides the rare description of Jewish life in nineteenth-century Eastern Europe as seen through the eyes of a traditionalist. Pinye-Ber cannot be accused of being disdainful of traditional Jewish life. And Pinye-Ber has no desire for his autobiography to be considered literature; as Niger writes, "[T]here is no mix of literature here. It is a human (and therefore a historical) document, not the work of a writer." And his ungarnished portrayal of the suffering and poverty experienced throughout most of his life is unencumbered by sentimentalism and written without pretensions. A skilled storyteller, Pinye-Ber is quite expressive of his thoughts and emotions and readily shares his inner world with the reader, for he has no social agenda. His very typicality as a traditional Eastern European Jew of his time makes his autobiography stand out. In contrast to those writing their works decades after abandoning their communities, Pinye-Ber began his Yiddish-language autobiography while relatively young, and, as Pilowsky (1986:292) notes, he wrote about his entire life in Tsarist Russia while still living there.[12]

As few traditionalists engaged the genre, modern Jewish historiography has become distorted into a simple, unidirectional secularization narrative while the traditionalist masses have been filtered out. Even among the relatively few nineteenth-century Jewish autobiographies written by traditionalists, Pinye-Ber's is a rarity in making no mention of the Haskalah, *maskilim*, Modern Hebrew or Yiddish literature, or modern political or social movements. Mark (1943:33) even comments that it is apparent from Pinye-Ber's Yiddish that he was as good as untouched by modern Yiddish literature. The autobiography of a traditionalist who was virtually unaffected by modernity is truly a rare and much-needed perspective, as our sense of Jewish history has become skewed owing to our reliance on modern-oriented genres like autobiography.

In his review of Pinye-Ber's work, Niger writes that all Jewish autobiographers prior to Pinye-Ber wove portraits, episodes, and entire chapters describing Jewish life into their personal reminiscences. Attempting to recreate Jewish life as it was, they viewed themselves as the custodians of the vanishing *shtetl* culture. Influenced by their transformed consciousness, they attempted to document historical, social, and cultural phenomena through the lens of one who is aware of history's effect upon them, a historical consciousness. They

---

12   Pinye-Ber evidently wrote the chapters of his autobiography sequentially (see p. 67, footnote 95). Chapter 28 includes indications that Pinye-Ber wrote it while still in Tsarist Russia in 1913, while he notes at the beginning of chapter 29 (the last chapter regarding his life in Tsarist Russia) that he wrote it shortly after arriving in Petakh-Tikva in November 1913.

considered their life histories to be ethnographic documents, gifts to posterity, which would preserve the memories of a way of life on the verge of extinction. In *Zakhor: Jewish History and Jewish Memory*, Yerushalmi (1982:86) writes, "The modern effort to reconstruct the Jewish past begins at a time that witnesses a sharp break in the continuity of Jewish living and hence also an ever-growing decay of Jewish group memory. In this sense, if for no other, history becomes what it had never been before—the faith of fallen Jews."

Pinye-Ber's autobiography is an exception in this respect. His story lacks any and all historical context; he concentrates solely on his own experiences. History does not concern him. He is not building a written monument to a vanishing traditional Jewish way of life. He does not have grandiose ideas of crafting an autobiography that encapsulates Jewish life in Eastern Europe, a memorial to a bygone era. Unless a historical event directly impacts him, Pinye-Ber does not mention it. As Niger observes,

> I wondered what was pulling me through the hundreds and hundreds of often quite trivial "events and episodes of an orphan."[13] Why did I not want to put it down while in the middle of reading it? . . . Is it that it touches only on the most important historical, moral, or psychological issues? No, this is clearly the history of a person who simply fought for his own existence, took care of his own family and almost never devoted himself, apart from his later years, to communal matters. No outstanding events occurred during his lifetime. He met no particularly interesting people and took no part in any significant historical events. His life is that of an average poor and pious Jew in southern Russia . . .[14] It is a complete portrayal of a single individual's life, practically without any pretext of introducing us to the spheres of a certain lifestyle, environment, or era. . . . He does not attend to history. He is not a historian. He is solely involved with himself and his own life. And that which he wrote is an autobiography—nothing more. But an autobiography it is, and, as stated, an authentic, 100% one at that. The one who reads it feels and knows that he is being pulled into a very narrow stream, into the life-stream of one person from one family. But regardless of this (or actually because of it), the reader is doubly rewarded: the

---

13 This quotation is a translation of part of the original Yiddish subtitle of Pinye-Ber's autobiography.
14 In Yiddish, "southern Russia" (*dorem-Rusland*) refers to the Ukraine.

reader's curiosity to experience another's path of life is gratified, and the reader recognizes that life was actually lived that way by many, if not by everyone, in those times and surroundings.[15]

For Niger, the very narrowness of Pinye-Ber's story, focusing only on his own life and that of his family, itself opens a fresh vista into nineteenth-century Jewish life. Unencumbered by historical consciousness, the autobiography imposes minimal distance between the reader and the way of life described.

Uninterested in social context, Pinye-Ber does not note many major historical events that occurred during his lifetime, even when they affected close members of his family. For example, he makes no mention of the Russo-Turkish War (1877–1878); the pogroms of 1881–1882; the Kishinev pogroms of 1903 or 1905, in which his niece was injured;[16] the wave of pogroms throughout the Ukraine in 1905, which affected Feodosiya where Pinye-Ber's two oldest children resided;[17] the Beilis Affair (1911–1913), which attracted international attention;[18] and the Russian Civil War (1917–1922), which directly affected several of Pinye-Ber's children and grandchildren. He also makes no mention of the enormous difference in lifestyle he encountered upon moving to Bakhchisaray in the Crimea in 1879, where the population was almost entirely Muslim Crimean Tatars, and the women wore white burqas revealing only their eyes. As one visitor to Bakhchisaray noted (Hadas, 1896), "Those coming from the northern cities could forget that they are on Russian soil and could think that they are in Turkey."

Pinye-Ber likewise is disinclined to mention local events. For example, Pinye-Ber says nothing of the collapse of the building that housed Bakhchisaray's only synagogue in 1896, causing its thirty-two Jewish families to hold prayer services in private homes until the completion of a new, stone synagogue four years later (Keren, 1981:89; Rabinovits, 1900). He also does not mention the

---

15 In the years after Niger's article was published in 1930, two slim nineteenth-century Jewish autobiographies were published also without historical context, namely those of the prominent rabbi, Rabbi David Eliyahu Rabinovits-Teomim (1843–1905), and the well-known *magid* (an Eastern European Jewish religious preacher) and author, Rabbi Bentsion Alfes (1851–1940), though both differ substantially from Pinye-Ber's work. For example, Rabbi Alfes's account centers on his public life and his communal work.
16 Pinye-Ber mentions his niece's injury in a private letter dated the 21st of *Tamuz* 5686 (July 3, 1926). See Appendix B3.
17 For details of the pogrom in Feodosiya, see the autobiography of Nathan Merenbach (1977:17–19), who was married to the author's granddaughter.
18 Pinye-Ber left Tsarist Russia for Palestine a few days before the jury declared its decision of not guilty on October 29, 1913, while all of Russian Jewry was in fear of the notorious Black Hundreds' threat to instigate massive pogroms if Beilis was found guilty.

huge sendoff in Sevastopol for Rabbi Khayim Khizkiyahu Medini (1833–1904), better known by the name of his monumental encyclopedic work *Sdei Khemed*, upon his departure for Palestine in 1899, in which Pinye-Ber participated.[19] In fact, Pinye-Ber almost never relates anything about anyone's background or subsequent life, with the sole exception of his enemies in Bakhchisaray, as will be discussed later.[20] Even when describing his own Hasidic Rebbe, Rabbi Menakhem-Mendl Schneerson (1789–1866) of Lubavitch, Pinye-Ber makes no mention that he wrote many highly regarded *halakhic* and Hasidic works or that he had tens of thousands of Hasidim. In short, Pinye-Ber leaves out many of the historical details that were the bread and butter of Jewish autobiography at this time.

Heschel (1946:34) describes the ahistorical consciousness of Eastern European Jews in terms of living not horizontally (chronologically) but vertically, in a fusion of past and present. He writes that these Jews lived with the great sages of the past in their emotions and dreams; every Jew felt a kinship with Rabbi Akiva and the Talmudic sages, the *ushpizin* visited their *sukah*,[21] and the prophet Elijah visited their Pesach *seder* and circumcision ceremonies.

Graupe (1978:142) discusses the difference between the traditional Jewish view of history and the modern view of history:

> The new approach is to see history as a process, as *development*. This process leads into and culminates in the present. But for the actual present, for the reflecting historian, the previous ages are past and gone. They have fulfilled their task of bringing about the present and now a new relation exists between them—that of *distance*. What is missing here is the inclusion of the past in the present, whereby the Jewish scholars of the old school held past and present actively together. *Development* and

---

19   In both his 1916 thesis on the Krymchaks and in his 1925 Hebrew-language article about Rabbi Medini in *Ha-Toren*, Pinye-Ber's son Refuel (aka Raphael Goldenstein) mentions that his father joined the thousands who had come from all over the Crimea to see him off. See Appendix C2 for complete excerpts.
20   At the beginning of his autobiography, Pinye-Ber does describe his parents, sisters, and inept brothers-in-law, but this is done to provide the circumstances of his orphanhood and the abject poverty in which he was raised.
21   According to the *Zohar* (Emor 103a), the souls of the seven great biblical leaders—Abraham, Isaac, Jacob, Moses, Aaron, Joseph, and King David—visit each Jew in his *sukah* during *Sukes*, one guest for each of the seven days of the festival. Collectively, they are known as *ushpizin*, the Aramaic word meaning "guests."

distance came to be criteria in the modern historian's view of history and method of working.

A historical consciousness is indeed a sign of the modern age; Yerushalmi (1982:82–84) shows that a historical conscience was first introduced to Jews by the *Wissenschaft des Judentums* (Science of Judaism) movement, an offshoot of the Haskalah, in their first publication in 1821.[22]

Furthermore, just as Pinye-Ber does not set out with the historian's aim to document a fading culture, so too he does not focus on philosophic or broader societal and political issues. Maskilic autobiographies often contain descriptions of the intellectuals that the autobiographers had met, such as authors, speakers, and social activists, along with accounts of their philosophical, political, and societal discussions. In reading nineteenth-century Jewish autobiographies, the reader may come under the mistaken notion that most Jews of those times were concerned with modern social activism. Not so with Pinye-Ber's autobiography: Niger (1930) comments in his book review that Pinye-Ber met no particularly interesting people. True, Pinye-Ber does describe his interactions with eight Hasidic Rebbes—some renowned—as well as famous rabbis such as Rabbi Meir Leibush Malbim (ch. 19). In October 1867, he became the only individual in two years to meet privately with the Lyever Rebbe, Rabbi Dov-Ber Fridman (ch. 18), who a year later abandoned his position as a Hasidic leader, thereby becoming the center of one of the most controversial Hasidic episodes in the late nineteenth century. Yet in his descriptions of these interactions, Pinye-Ber mentions no philosophical or societal discussions. His daily life is lived following God's will, fulfilling the Torah and its commandments, not in pursuing a modern social agenda.

Mark (1943:62) describes Pinye-Ber as a "Jewish folk intellectual," suggesting that he was neither secularly educated nor philosophically trained but, instead, was an intellectual of and for the common folk. Though learned in Torah and clearly a thinking man, Pinye-Ber was in many ways a simple Jew— "simple" in the sense that he did not elaborate his story with analytical observations. Even when explaining the philosophical notion of divine providence to Kizilshteyn, a former apostate, where he has the opportunity to state his philosophy and cite Jewish philosophic works, he chooses instead to explain this concept non-conceptually by telling a story about a famous Rebbe (ch. 29). As

---

22 Of course, Funkenstein (1993:16–17) argues that there are traditional Jewish sources that have a sense of accurate historiography, for example, rabbinical responsa that preserve the whole intellectual history of the Jewish legal tradition in historical context. Nonetheless, historical consciousness is an awareness of the process and its causes in social, cultural, and other realms, which was clearly lacking among traditional Eastern European Jews.

Niger writes, Pinye-Ber's "life is that of an average poor and pious Jew." Pinye-Ber resembles most traditional Jews of his age cohort, who were neither philosophical as the *maskilim* were nor involved in the social or political movements of their times, after the demise of the Haskalah.

How Did Pinye-Ber Come to Write an Autobiography?

Although the details of Pinye-Ber's life are rich, it has a relatively simple and straightforward outline. The author was born in 1848 to a father who was a Bersheder Hasid in Tiraspol in the Tsarist Russian province of Kherson, in the historical region of the Ukraine. After his parents' deaths, he was shuffled around from one relative to another, until he left to study in 1863 in a yeshiva in Odessa where he spent some eight months. He made his way back to Tiraspol where he became engaged in 1864 at the age of sixteen. He traveled to Lubavitch in Belarus, arriving in August 1865, and the Rebbe advised him to study in the yeshiva in nearby Shklov, where he studied for five and a half months. Compelled by the Tsarist Russian government to leave the yeshiva and go to Romania (for he had earlier acquired a Romanian passport), he found employment for a year as a *melamed* (a traditional teacher in a *kheyder*). In May 1867, he crossed the border back into Tsarist Russia, where he continued to work as a *melamed* in Kalarash in the province of Bessarabia, some eighty miles from Tiraspol. He married in November 1867 in the village of Buter, near Bender in Bessarabia. He returned to Lubavitch a second time in December 1872, and upon his return obtained his first position as a *shoykhet* in Slobodze, near Tiraspol. In early 1876, he began working as a *shoykhet* in Buzinove, Ukraine, and in March 1879 he moved to Bakhchisaray in the Crimea, the location in which he wrote his autobiography. In 1913, he moved to Petakh-Tikva, where he died in 1930.

The life story outlined above raises a number of questions. How is it that one of the earliest modern-day Yiddish-language autobiographies in book form, written when the genre of Jewish autobiography was overwhelmingly secular, was authored by a Hasidic *shoykhet*? Where would a *shoykhet*, who traditionally would be quite distanced from secular culture, have been exposed to such a genre? Additionally, why did Pinye-Ber write his work in Yiddish at a time when traditionalists were publishing their books in Hebrew? And finally, how did it come about that this early autobiography by a traditionalist was written in the Crimea, an area that was physically and culturally removed from the traditional Jewish centers of Eastern Europe?

Orthodox Jews in general have been reluctant to write their autobiographies, and this is particularly true of Hasidim. As noted, Jewish autobiography in the nineteenth century was almost exclusively a secular vehicle of self-expression. The distinguished Jewish historian Jacob Shatzky (1925:484) reports that he knew of only one autobiography written by a Hasidic Jew, namely the autobiography of Rabbi Nathan Shternharts (1780–1844) of Nemirov published in 1876. Pinye-Ber's autobiography, the second Hasidic autobiography to appear in print, was published about half a century later, in 1928. Pinye-Ber apparently began writing his autobiography shortly after 1901 and had written most of it by 1913, placing it among the first book-length Yiddish autobiographies to be written.[23] The first five book-length autobiographies published in Yiddish were an autobiographical novel by Mendele Moykher-Sforim (New York, 1901); a pure autobiography by the celebrated Yiddish *badkhn* and songwriter Eliakim Zunser (New York, 1905); the autobiography of the Yiddish writer and folklorist Samuel Hurwitz, also known as A. Litvin (Vilna, 1908);[24] Rokhl Feygenberg's *Di kinder-yohrn* (Warsaw, 1910);[25] and Yekhezkel Kotik's memoirs (Warsaw, 1913).[26] As a genre, Yiddish autobiographies first began to gain popularity in the 1920s.

As to how Pinye-Ber knew of the autobiographical genre, it is possible that he was aware of the few rabbinic autobiographies published by that time: the autobiography of Rabbi Yomtov Lipman Heller (1579–1654), first published in 1818 and republished numerous times; the autobiography of Rabbi Jacob

---

23 In a 2001 private interview with Pinye-Ber's granddaughter Aliza (Goldenshteyn) Bernfeld, she recalled her father Shloyme (born 1889) relating that he remembered "as a boy" awakening at night and seeing his father diligently working on his autobiography. This suggests that Pinye-Ber began writing it in the 1890s or early 1900s. We can probably narrow down that period to sometime after 1901, since according to his narrative Pinye-Ber was struggling financially and working very hard up until three years after his remarriage in 1897 (ch. 28). By 1909, he had written most of it, since he mentions (ch. 23) that it was then *Rosh-KhoydeshTamuz* 5669 (June 19–20, 1909). Shortly after arriving in Petakh-Tikva in November 1913, he had written up to chapter 29 (out of thirty-four), as noted in that chapter.

24 The title of Hurwitz's work, *Fun'm kheyder'ishn pinkes: ksovim fun a Litvishen yungel* (From a Kheyder notebook: Writings of a Lithuanian boy), http://www.worldcat.org/oclc/41454650, apparently presents it as a work of fiction. Nonetheless, the last chapter makes it evident that it is an adult's recollections of his boyhood, as corroborated by its listing in Gellman (2010:530) as an autobiography.

25 Remarkably, Rokhl Feygenberg (1885–1972) wrote her autobiography at the age of sixteen, and it was first published in the periodical *Dos lebn* in 1905 (Khinits, 1973:291). She later wrote in Hebrew under the surname Imri.

26 Though Kotik's work bears 1913 as the year of publication, Assaf (2002a:37, 90n54) has determined that he wrote his memoirs in 1912 and that it was published by December 1912.

Emden (1697–1776), published in 1896 in Warsaw; and the memoirs of Rabbi Nathan Shternharts of Nemirov, published in 1876. Nonetheless, it is more likely that Pinye-Ber was exposed to the autobiographical genre through the Hebrew and Yiddish press and their serialization of various autobiographies. Not only does Pinye-Ber incidentally mention newspapers in his autobiography, but it is apparent from his language that he read the Yiddish newspapers.[27] A few examples of autobiographies serialized in Hebrew and Yiddish newspapers in the 1890s and early 1900s are as follows:

- the Hebrew-language newspaper *Ha-Melits* serialized the memoirs of the writer Elazar Shulman (1837–1904) entitled "Zikhronot ir moladeti" (Memoirs of the town of my birth) in 1894–1895;
- The memoirs of Glikl of Hameln (1646–1724) were summarized in Hebrew by F. H. Vetshtein in *Ha-Magid* in 1896 (nos. 28, 29, 33, 34);[28]
- The Yiddish weekly *Der Yud* (Warsaw and Krakow) serialized the first eleven chapters of the autobiographical novel *Shloyme Reb Khayms* by Mendele Moykher-Sforim (pseudonym of Sholem-Yankev Abramovitsh) in 1899 in its first nineteen issues;
- From February to April 1900, *Der Yud* serialized "Erinerungen fun kindishen lebn" (Reminiscences of a childish life) by the popular Yiddish author Yankev Dinezon.

Yet, even though Pinye-Ber was aware of the autobiographical genre and decided to write one, the question remains: Why would he write in Yiddish at a time when traditionalists were writing almost exclusively in Hebrew? In the early 1900s, the only books traditionally published in Yiddish were religious works for women or the semiliterate. Hebrew enjoyed greater prestige. Every traditional Jewish male who did not want to appear as an ignoramus would endeavor to write private letters and even business letters in Hebrew, even if they did not write it well. Before Yiddish began to be regarded as a respectable literary form

---

27   Yudl Mark (1943:33) notes that it cannot be ruled out that Pinye-Ber had seen a novel by Shomer, the pseudonym of Nokhem-Meyer Shaykevitch (ca. 1849–1905), whose popular Yiddish novels were geared toward an unsophisticated readership. Yet the writer of this introduction is under the opinion that Pinye-Ber probably did not read secular books since he does not mention them even in passing, and he writes about practically every aspect of his life, including newspapers.

  It is unlikely that Pinye-Ber personally subscribed or purchased newspapers on his occasional visits to large Jewish communities; after all, few had money for such a luxury, and subscribers, as a matter of course, would allow their newspapers to be circulated in their communities.

28   Glikl's memoirs were first published in 1896 in Frankfurt in its original Old Yiddish along with a German translation. It was first translated into Hebrew in 1929.

in the 1880s, maskilic writers generally dismissed Yiddish as merely a jargon—even as some of them used the language as a means of disparaging traditional Jewish life. In his Yiddish-language "In Lieu of a Preface," Pinye-Ber, as many authors of his day, includes a justification for writing in Yiddish.[29] He states that even though he greatly values and cherishes the Holy language, he is writing in Yiddish so that his message and moral lessons could be read by those who did not know Hebrew, particularly his children, family members, and those who persecuted him in Tsarist Russia. Such a statement excusing his use of Yiddish would have been expected of a *shoykhet* like himself, who was learned and able to write in Hebrew.[30]

Yet, despite Pinye-Ber's explanation that his choice to write in Yiddish was for the benefit of his progeny and adversaries, the reader of the original work senses Pinye-Ber's affinity for his mother tongue. It is in Yiddish that he can best express the nuances of his emotions and experiences. Hebrew would not have served him as well in this regard, since it had not been used as a colloquial language since Late Antiquity. Pinye-Ber would not have been able to recount the details of his inner life so vividly, and the result would have been a somewhat stilted and stifled work.[31] Pinye-Ber uses his best and richest Yiddish in his autobiography, as is evident from comparing it to his handwritten personal letters, which are written in a much simpler, less idiomatic Yiddish.[32] If he entertained any hope that his words would have their desired effect on his children, his primary intended audience, he knew that he had to write from the heart, and what better way to do so than in *mame-loshn* (mother tongue, that is, Yiddish).

And here we come to Pinye-Ber's primary motive for writing his autobiography. He wishes to convey a spiritual message to his progeny: that they maintain

---

29 Many authors justified writing in Yiddish by including a preface (usually in Hebrew) or a statement on the title page claiming that it was to benefit those who did not know the holy tongue (Weinreich, 2008:1:274–276).

30 Pinye-Ber's mastery of the complexities of rabbinic Hebrew is clear from his 1897 handwritten engagement contract for his daughter Nekhame Brockman (formerly Brakhtman) and from his Hebrew ethical will written in 1920. His great-granddaughter Cynthia (Brockman) Unterberg allowed me to examine the engagement contract, and his late granddaughter Aliza (Goldenshteyn) Bernfeld provided me with a copy of the typewritten Hebrew ethical will. See appendices B1 and B2 for translations of both.

31 For example, Vilf (2017), a Hasidic Jew whose nineteenth-century autobiography was written in Hebrew, produced a stylistically pallid narrative. It is the translator's opinion that Vilf, who does not have Pinye-Ber's "very fine talent for storytelling and a sense for the dramatic" (Mark, 1943:33), may not have appreciated the advantage of writing in the Yiddish language.

32 Pinye-Ber's great-granddaughter Cynthia (Brockman) Unterberg allowed me to examine Pinye-Ber's ten handwritten letters written from 1926 to 1930 from Petakh-Tikva to his daughter Nekhame in America. See Appendix B3 for translations.

the traditional Jewish mode of life and remain true to God and His Torah. He knew that some of his children were straying from the ways of their forefathers, and was determined to influence his progeny to return to traditional Judaism. He felt so strongly that his life story was the best means to achieve this goal that he chose autobiography, at least initially, over the traditional Jewish method of moral instruction for one's heirs, namely, a Hebrew ethical will. Pinye-Ber only wrote a Hebrew ethical will many years after beginning his autobiography, and its writing was motivated by several circumstances in his later years: the welfare of his third wife whom he had recently married; his desire to stipulate which of his children would inherit the Torah scroll he had recently completed; and the completion of his autobiography, whose manuscript he willed to his son Refuel, who had promised to have it printed.[33] Thus he considered the story form of autobiography, rather than an ethical will, the primary way to convey his message of divine providence to his progeny. Furthermore, perhaps the concept of autobiography had intrigued the natural-born storyteller within him to such an extent that he began to write his own.

Pinye-Ber put much time and labor into his autobiography, which was one of several ways in which he was trying to encourage his children to return to the ways of their forefathers. He was not willing to give up on his offspring, although so many Jews of his generation became resigned to the fact that their children would lead non-traditional Jewish lives. One of the first Lubavitcher activists to arrive in America, Rabbi Yisroel Jacobson (1972:11), writes that upon his arrival in 1926 practically all of even the staunchest observant immigrants in America "had given up hope as far as the Yiddishkeit [Judaism] of their children was concerned. They were resigned to the complete estrangement of their children ... [They] felt helpless to insist that their children withstand the bitter tests and trials that the New World presented, in making a living, in Shabbos observance, in every facet of Jewish life." With three of his sons in America, Pinye-Ber was in a similar situation, but he refused to lose hope and consistently used a very Hasidic (that is, positive) approach throughout his autobiography in attempting to impact his children's lives. In his Hebrew ethical will written in 1920, he also attempts to entice his children to move to the Holy Land by promising him or her the inheritance of the Torah scroll, which he had just completed. No doubt, he was trying to encourage their move to the Holy Land because he saw that there they had a better chance than elsewhere of eating kosher, having their children marry Jews, and remaining connected to Judaism. By contrast,

---

33   At that time, Pinye-Ber did not imagine that his autobiography would be printed in his lifetime. After several years, he added several concluding paragraphs.

one of his grandsons in America had married a non-Jew the previous year. And, when writing about his son Refuel's enrollment in Hebrew Union College in Cincinnati, Pinye-Ber does not focus on the negative and lament that his son was studying to become a Reform rabbi rather than an Orthodox one. Instead, he offers his blessings for his son's success in having "enrolled in the rabbinical seminary to become a *rabiner*" (ch. 28), though he likely did not realize the extent of Reform's departure from tradition.[34]

Finally, why did Pinye-Ber write his autobiography in the Crimea, a region by no means saturated with traditional Judaism? Though far from the Jewish centers of Eastern Europe, the Crimea, where Pinye-Ber lived, was perhaps the perfect place for one of the first Hasidim to write an autobiography. The decline of traditional Jewish society is linked to the development of the Jewish autobiographical genre (Bar-Levav, 2002:57). Traditional Jewish life was slowly deteriorating in Eastern Europe in the late nineteenth century due to secularization, urbanization, and rural exodus. In the nineteenth century, Jews in the Ukraine were generally less observant of and learned in Torah than the Jews of the territories of Lithuania, Belarus, Poland, Galicia, and Hungary.[35] As the author comments about Jewish life in 1866 in the Kherson province of Tsarist Russia and Eastern Romania where he resided, "The same type of Torah study was available in both places—and neither were places of Torah" (ch. 16). In 1879, a year after the end of the Russo-Turkish War (1877–1878), Pinye-Ber moved to Bakhchisaray in the Crimea. He had hoped that there was less corruption in the Crimea, but he was shocked to find the Crimea much worse; the Jews there were even less learned and less observant than those in the Ukraine. Jews first began settling in large numbers in the Crimea in 1881 due to the wave of pogroms ravaging the Ukraine (Keren, 1981:68). The Crimea, distant from traditional Jewish centers, lacked rabbis, teachers, and other spiritual functionaries, and was populated by simple, ignorant Jews (Keren, 1981:65–66). Shortly after Pinye-Ber's arrival in Bakhchisaray, the community leader Simkhe

---

34 Pinye-Ber was apparently under the impression that Refuel was studying to be something like a *rabiner*, which in Tsarist Russia denoted a crown rabbi whose job was to record Jewish vital statistics and deliver addresses in Russian on various occasions but who lacked any real religious jurisdiction. Though most crown rabbis were not observant of Jewish tradition, some were, and it was certainly not a contradiction for them to have been so. Hebrew Union College, under Reform auspices, which Refuel attended, produced no graduates who were traditionalists due to their belief that Torah was merely divinely inspired and was not God's word.

35 Nineteenth-century Hungary included Transylvania, which is now part of Romania; Maramureș, which is now divided between Romania and Ukraine; and Carpathian Ruthenia, which is currently mostly located in Ukraine with smaller parts in Slovakia and Poland.

Mayster warned Pinye-Ber at length of the debauched character of Crimean Jews, himself included (ch. 24). The Jews of Bakhchisaray were so unlearned that Pinye-Ber had to lead all prayer services on the High Holy Days, read the Torah, and blow the *shofar*, with no one capable of relieving him (ch. 25). This situation never occurred in any of the small communities in the Ukraine in which he had previously served. Whereas in Slobodze in the Ukraine Pinye-Ber had recourse to Hasidic Rebbes to turn to for help in his conflicts with corrupt community leaders, in the Crimea, where there were no Hasidic Rebbes, the corrupt community leaders answered to no one.

In his discussion of the Jews in the Crimea in 1883, Avraham Shlomo Melamed (1922:1:253) mentions that only in the Crimea did he find Jews who would eat non-kosher meat if kosher meat was not readily available or if too expensive. Hadas (1896) writes regarding the state of Jewish education in Pinye-Ber's town of Bakhchisaray, "There is no Talmud Torah, no *kheyder*, no *melamed* . . ." By the mid-1890s, the Jewish youth in the city of Feodosiya in the Crimea generally spoke Russian rather than Yiddish, when most Jews in Eastern Europe considered the abandonment of Yiddish to be a grave breach of tradition (Merenbach, 1977:35). It is apparent that the great disaffection of large numbers of Eastern European Jews with traditional Judaism between the two world wars started even earlier in the Crimea.

As mentioned, the disruption of the traditional Jewish mode of life in the Crimea had its effect on some of Pinye-Ber's children. Pinye-Ber began to write his autobiography after his children began to stray from Jewish observance. His sons Yosl, Refuel, and Yankl were already transgressing some Jewish laws as early as 1899 (ch. 28). All three immigrated to Portland, Oregon in 1905–1906 where they no longer remained Sabbath observant. Only two of Pinye-Ber's surviving children remained so, and he had little hope at that time that even the children of his oldest son, who was a *shoykhet* in Feodosiya, would be raised as Orthodox Jews.[36] Since Jewish autobiography emerges where traditional Jewish life is in decline, it is only reasonable that the Crimea was the most well-suited place in Eastern Europe for an autobiography of a Hasidic Jew to be written.

In summary, the decline of traditional Jewish life was a signal to numerous *maskilim* that it was necessary to document the disappearing world of their

---

36 In fact, none of Pinye-Ber's grandchildren remained Orthodox Jews, though several remained traditional. His great-granddaughter Tsvia Bernfeld (1944–1992) became religious and followed her great-grandfather Pinye-Ber's example by becoming a follower of the Lubavitcher Rebbe. Her second husband was even a descendant of Rabbi Shneur Zalman of Lyadi. After Tsvia became observant, her parents also began to observe the Sabbath. Tsvia's only child, a son named Shlomo Zilbershtein, studied in the Lubavitcher yeshivas in Kfar-Chabad, Israel, and Brooklyn.

youth, which they themselves had helped to bring about through their efforts to radically alter traditional Jewish life. In contrast, the decline of traditional Jewish life brought Pinye-Ber to the realization that he had failed to convey to his children his deep-rooted belief in divine providence, a belief that he felt would have automatically resulted in their leading traditional Jewish lifestyles. He realized that his deep and natural consciousness common to Jewish traditionalists, which he had assumed would be transmitted to his children as it had been transmitted to him, had not reached them. He decided to address this issue in the form of an autobiography. In his own words: "[I] hope [my autobiography] will affect my children and grandchildren by strengthening their trust in God so that they will go on along the right path and believe in God and divine providence, as their aged father has in his life" (ch. 34).

Pinye-Ber's *Alltagsgeschichte*: Traditional Jews in Tsarist Russia

Common Life and Incidental Observations

Prior to the mid-twentieth century, only the autobiographies of famous and influential people (politicians, actors, and prominent military figures) were regarded as worthy of being written or read. When we examine modern Jewish autobiographies written between the dawn of the genre in 1860 and 1940, we find authors who had attained some degree of prominence as writers and social activists. Yet, as important as such authors are, their stories generally do not shed the same direct light on daily life afforded by autobiographies of the working class. As Niger observes in his 1930 review of Pinye-Ber's autobiography,

> It is a mistake to believe that one needs to be famous or a celebrity to write the history of one's life. On the contrary, a great person is rarely well suited to write his own biography. A great person often has a small life. What is the daily existence of a historic figure in comparison with his heroic accomplishments? A poet, a leader, a hero lives (for us) in his poetry, in his leadership, in his heroic deeds. His weekdays are consumed by his Sabbath. ... Tolstoy was correct in saying that a writer gives away the best that he has to his work and his life remains empty. ... The everyman, though, gives us his life in his autobiography. These simple,

ordinary human beings reveal to us their simplicity in their mundaneness, and the history of their days and years is truly human history, human fate.

Indeed, Pinye-Ber's autobiography is even more representative than Niger appreciates. When we compare him to some other autobiographers whom Niger describes as "ordinary, non-literary persons," we realize that they had actually achieved a degree of influence far exceeding that of Pinye-Ber, who throughout his life remained a *shoykhet* in small Jewish communities of some thirty to sixty families.[37] Pinye-Ber took no part in any significant historical events and his autobiography includes no outstanding events, rather his life is simply, in Niger's words, "the history of his hard and bitter fight for a piece of bread." But, as Niger writes, in exclusively describing his own quite ordinary life, he has "told the reader about the typical life of yesteryear at greater length and more thoroughly than those who initially took upon themselves as a goal to be the historians of those eras and environs." It seems counterintuitive that, by not consciously describing anything but his own life, Pinye-Ber produced a work that describes Jewish life in those regions more thoroughly than those who made deliberate attempts to document it. The answer to this paradox lies in Pinye-Ber's natural storytelling style, which is detailed, descriptive, and extremely unpretentious; hence, he unwittingly includes much granular detail about the typical life of yesteryear not found elsewhere.

Though containing little significant historical information, Pinye-Ber's densely written story is steeped in quotidian details. He describes the relationships between adults and children, men and women, Jews and non-Jews, feudal lords and their peasants, the community and its leaders, and artisans and apprentices. In his vivid depiction of the life of a Jewish child, he describes the *kheyder*, children's games, and the difference between city children and *shtetl* children. Having held a variety of occupations, he describes the lives, particularly the economic aspects, of house servants, cantors, *melamdim* (plural of *melamed*), storekeepers, grain merchants, melon farmers, tavern keepers, and

---

37 The ordinary autobiographers mentioned by Niger were, in reality, social activists: Yekhezkel Kotik founded or was closely involved in the formation of every Jewish welfare society or federation in the metropolis of Warsaw, where he also ran a café, which became a vibrant center for young intellectuals, Yiddish writers, and workers' activists (Assaf, 2002a:25–26, 30–31); Yisroel-Iser Katsovitsh was the co-editor of the monthly periodical *Yidisher Farmer* published by the Jewish Agricultural and Industrial Aid Society; and Isidore Kopeloff was a prolific writer who published articles in the Yiddish press and helped found a number of Yiddish periodicals. (Katsovitsh's autobiography was translated into English under the English spelling of his surname, Kasovich, in 1929.)

shokhtim. Raised in and around Tiraspol in the Tsarist Russian-ruled Ukraine[38] on the border of the Tsarist Russian province of Bessarabia (most of which is in today's Moldova), he depicts the *khapers* who seized Jewish children for forcible conscription into the Russian military, and the tear-wrenching sight of a battalion of cantonist children soldiers. Not only was he familiar with many places in his native Ukraine, but he also resided in Romania, Belarus, and the Crimea, where he encountered different types of Hasidim and their Rebbes, *misnagdim* (non-Hasidim), Krymchaks, and Karaites, as well as informers and apostates. He depicts the fourth pandemic of cholera of the nineteenth century, including the quarantining of cities and towns and the primitive efforts used to try to save the lives of the stricken. He discusses using flint for indoor lighting; town fires—constant sources of danger at the time; baking *matses* for Pesach; purchasing *esroygim* for *Sukes*; building *mikvehs*; and petty synagogue politics. He discusses immigration to America and Palestine and assimilation. Though Jewish autobiographies have tended to focus on life in small towns, which perhaps has contributed to the impression that Jewish life was more authentic there, certainly everyday Jewish life in Eastern Europe took place in cities, towns, villages, and rural hamlets, all of which are described in Pinye-Ber's autobiography.

In their reviews of Pinye-Ber's autobiography, both Niger (1930) and Pilowsky (1986:291) use the Talmudic expression *mesiakh le-fi tumo* ("mentioning unwittingly"), which refers to someone who is unaware of the significance of his or her casual remarks. Such casual remarks are considered extremely trustworthy and have the validity of testimony in a rabbinical court. As Niger writes, "There is practically not one sphere of life, not one institution that is not clearly characterized through one fact or another, one episode or another, in Goldenshteyn's life," much of which is mentioned "unwillingly and unknowingly." As discussed earlier, most nineteenth-century Jewish autobiographers attempt to place their lives in historical context. No matter how

---

38 For the purposes of this introduction, "the Ukraine" refers to the ten Tsarist Russian provinces (*guberniyas*) into which it was then divided, excluding the Crimea, which took up forty-two percent of the province of Taurida. The territory of the Ukraine under Tsarist Russia is different from that of modern Ukraine, which includes areas that belonged to Austria-Hungary before the First World War. Though Pinye-Ber was born in Tiraspol, which was then in the Ukraine, he never mentions the word "Ukraine" since it was not widely used until after the First World War. He simply refers to the Tsarist provinces in the Ukraine by their names. In Yiddish, the Ukraine was referred to as *dorem-Rusland*, meaning southern Russia, or *Male-Ros*, a variant of the Russian Malorossiia, meaning Little Russia. Before the First World War, a Jew from the Ukraine or Bessarabia was specifically called a *Risisher Yid* in Yiddish. In today's Yiddish, the term *Risisher Yid* no longer exists, while a *Rusisher Yid* can refer to any Jew from the former territory of the Soviet Union.

objective autobiographers strive to be, they cannot escape their own viewpoints or biases in writing history, particularly their own social, political, or religious outlooks. More often than not, these biases result in the past being reconstructed to meet the goals of the present. Miron (2000:8) notes that the autobiographical novel by the classic Hebrew and Yiddish writer Mendele Moykher-Sforim (pseudonym of Sholem-Yankev Abramovitsh) virtually omits any mention of Hasidim and hardly mentions Torah study, though he was raised in a society dominated by both of these realities. On the other hand, the large amount of historical information mentioned by Pinye-Ber would seem to have an unusually high degree of credibility based on the Talmudic logical principle of *mesiakh le-fi tumo*. And this is particularly exceptional in a genre noted for both disparaging and romanticized portrayals of traditional Eastern European life. In his singular devotion to relating the narrow path of his own story down to every minor detail, Pinye-Ber has inadvertently provided an encyclopedic *Alltagsgeschichte* (history of daily life) of traditional Jewry in entire regions of Tsarist Russia, despite being unaware that he was doing so.[39]

Following are a few examples of Pinye-Ber's incidental comments, which provide an insight into daily life in Tsarist Russia.

- *The custom of interfirers*. The *interfirers* are the married couple who lead the bride or the groom to the *huppah*. These are customarily the groom's or bride's parents if they are alive. Nonetheless, although his bride's parents were alive, Pinye-Ber mentions that her *interfirers* were her aunt and uncle (ch. 18). In fact, the Jewish custom is that other relatives generally act as *interfirers* only when the mother of the bride or groom is pregnant in order to avoid an evil eye (Zinner, 1998:1:112). That is, why should the bride's or groom's parents draw attention to their ample good fortune of being both expectant parents and marrying off a child at the same time, causing people to be jealous? Hence, the reader unwittingly learns of this Jewish custom, which is rarely if ever mentioned in the autobiographical literature.[40]
- *Daily Torah study*. Though it is not generally discussed in autobiographical literature, learned traditional Jewish men normally study the Torah at set times during the day and during their free moments. Pinye-Ber describes how his adversaries in Slobodze began seeking

---

39 Perhaps an indication of the scope of Pinye-Ber's work is the inclusion of over 350 entries in the Glossary of Words and Phrases, despite my efforts to keep the number of such terms to a minimum.
40 See also Rabbi Menachem M. Schneerson, *Likutei Sikhot* (22:56–64).

out his faults and transgressions to publicize them in an effort to oust him from his position as the *shoykhet*. One "sin" that they uncovered was that he would hold his baby in his arms while praying or studying when his wife was out of the house. For his adversaries, this was a sin since, according to Jewish law, one may not study Torah or pray in the presence of excrement, including that of an infant. From this incidental comment the reader learns that Pinye-Ber was studying the Torah whenever able, as required by Jewish law.

- *Alteration of surname usage.* Though Jews in Tsarist Russia had surnames since the turn of the nineteenth century, they only used them for official purposes and did not start to use them among themselves until after the First World War (Beider, 2008:1:11). Until then, Jewish neighbors often did not know each other's surnames. Upon moving to the Crimea in 1879, Pinye-Ber suddenly starts to refer to the Jews there by their surnames. This subtle indication of the early deterioration of traditional Jewish life in the Crimea is noted unwittingly by Pinye-Ber.

- *Russian infrequently spoken in the Crimea.* Unlike most of Tsarist Russia, hardly any Russian could be heard in the Crimea since the non-Jewish population was almost exclusively comprised of Crimean Tatars who spoke their own Turkic language. Pinye-Ber inadvertently reveals this fact when he describes encountering a Jewish father and son from the Ukraine, just arrived in Bakhchisaray in the Crimea. Upon making their way to Pinye-Ber's door, they exclaimed, "*Oy*! Thank God! We were barely able to find our way to a fellow Jew. We walked from the train station through the entire city without coming across a single Jew—only Tatars. And when we asked them where the Jews live, we couldn't understand their answers" (ch. 24). This is Pinye-Ber's sole indication that Russian was not spoken in Bakhchisaray, where he served as *shoykhet* for thirty-four years.

- *The traditionalists' indifference to the local language.* Regarding the above point, Pinye-Ber's silence seems to speak for itself: it was of no particular interest to him which language the non-Jews were speaking. From this incidental comment regarding some visitors, the reader learns of the traditional Jew's total indifference to the language spoken by the local non-Jews. This attitude stood in sharp contrast to that of the *maskilim*, many of whom were enamored by enlightened Russian culture and eager to become well-versed in its language and literature. They had no interest in the Crimean-Tatar language for they also considered the Muslim Crimean Tatars to be ignorant and primitive. A passing maskilic journalist (Hadas, 1896) decried the Jews of Bakhchisaray for being fluent in Crimean Tatar and unfamiliar with Russian.

Work, Family Life, and Social Struggle

As a result of Pinye-Ber's focus on quotidian life and the incidental nature of his observations, his autobiography yields a rich and authentic view of traditional Jewish society in the later nineteenth century. He describes in detail the nature of his chosen profession, the poverty that afflicted his community, the anti-Semitic restrictions on Jewish travel, as well as the shortcomings of *shtetl* life and dogmatism among some Hasidim that he tried to address as a community leader. Crucially, he represents these issues as someone who has lived through them, taking them as genuine components of existence rather than as backward traditions to be recorded and discarded.

Pinye-Ber worked as a *shoykhet*, a highly trained practitioner of *sh'khita*, the slaughtering of animals according to Jewish law, which traces its tradition to Moses on Mt. Sinai: "[Y]ou may slaughter of your cattle and of your sheep, which the Lord has given you, as I [that is, God] have commanded you" (Deuteronomy 12:21). The *sh'khita* method involves cutting the animal's throat with an exceedingly sharp knife in one uninterrupted sweeping motion. In Judaism, slaughtering an animal is not merely a stage in the process of preparing meat but is a sacred act. As Berman (1941:8) writes, "It is felt that the flame of animal life partakes of the sacred, and may be extinguished only by the sanction of religion, and only at the hands of one of its sensitive and reverential servants." Jewish law forbids meat from an animal not slaughtered by a *shoykhet*; hence, before refrigeration, every substantial Jewish community had to employ at least one *shoykhet*, if not more.

Jewish tradition demands much from the *shoykhet*: elaborate training, sensitivity, and compassion. He is required to have studied intensively and been tested, in theory and practice, in the laws of *sh'khita*, animal anatomy, and pathology. He must have served as an apprentice to an experienced *shoykhet* before receiving certification permitting him to practice *sh'khita*. Furthermore, while the non-Jewish slaughterer is conventionally depicted as coarse and beefy, the *shoykhet* is "characteristically mild-mannered, refined, and sensitive" (Berman, 1941:139). Even the socialist *Jewish Daily Forward* ("Pictures of Jewish Life and Characters," 1923) could not help but bestow the following caption on a photograph of an elderly *shoykhet* in Eastern Europe: "Strange how Jewish Kosher slaughterers have the mildest eyes and most cherubic faces." Leading rabbis through the ages have considered it obligatory for a *shoykhet* to be a person of exceptional character and compassion (Greenwald, 1955:111). In point of fact, Judaism considers *sh'khita* to be an act of compassion for the animals since it is deemed the most painless method of slaughtering, which minimizes any suffering. Perhaps the epitome of compassion for animals that a *shoykhet* can reach is exemplified in a story about the founder of modern Hasidism, Rabbi Israel Baal Shem Tov (Kahan, 1990:3:148), who as a young man served as a *shoykhet*. After he had left the position and the community had hired a replacement, a Jewish villager had a non-Jewish worker take a chicken to the new *shoykhet* for slaughter. Yet the worker returned with the chicken still alive, asking, "Do you really want me to have such a *shoykhet* slaughter your chicken? Yisruel the *shoykhet* [the Baal Shem Tov] used to sharpen his knife using a whetstone dampened with his tears, while the new *shoykhet* uses ordinary water. Do you think I'd let such a *shoykhet* slaughter for you?"

In the traditional Jewish community, the *shoykhet* was among the most respected members of the community. As the Lubavitcher Rebbe, Rabbi Y. Y. Schneersohn, writes (*Igrot kodesh*, 8:132), "I have mentioned it often in many of my letters that the position of a *shoykhet* in a Jewish community is a noble position among Jewish religious functionaries. The rabbi of a community is its head, and the *shoykhet* is its heart, because a *shoykhet* is not just a man with a knife in his hand who provides kosher meat to his community. He is charged with being aware of his community's moral and ethical standing and to establish regular classes in Torah, etc." The Lubavitcher Rebbe, Rabbi M. M. Schneerson (1902–1994), once told a *shoykhet* that *sh'khita* affords him the opportunity to draw his fellow Jews closer to Judaism: the Hebrew verb *shokhat* does not only mean "slaughter" but also to "draw close." In other words, by providing Jews with nourishment in the manner decreed by God in His Torah, the *shoykhet* is strengthening their spiritual connection to their Maker. In another letter from 1926, Rabbi Y. Y. Schneersohn (*Igrot kodesh*, 2:513) describes the *shoykhet*'s role in a Jewish community at great length:

> [A] *shoykhet* is not merely an artisan or a tradesman, but he should be considered among the leaders of the Jewish community. From time immemorial, a *shoykhet* took an interest in every aspect of the community including the establishment of fixed times for Torah study. There were *shokhtim* who themselves gave regular classes to the public, were involved in all positive

matters, and assisted the communities in which they were serving. This is the hierarchy in a Jewish community: the rabbi, the *shoykhet*, the *melamed*, the wealthy community member, and then the rest of the townsmen. The rabbi has the greatest say, followed by the *shoykhet*, and after him the *melamed*, for these three are the pillars of the Jewish people, and in every generation they have been the leaders of their Jewish communities. We see clearly that in any community that had a proper *shoykhet* or *melamed*, their influence was apparent in every aspect of the community. . . . [H]e needs help and support so that when he speaks about building a *mikveh* he is not coming empty-handed but has cultivated outside sources of support. . . . [H]is primary work is to implant words of inspiration in the people of his town, to speak to their hearts, and to vitalize them with both guidance and encouragement.

Yet, despite his communal importance, the *shoykhet* is not excluded from the category of common men. No matter how poor a Jewish household was, virtually every traditional Jewish family tried to purchase meat, or at least chicken, in honor of the *Shabes* (the Jewish Sabbath) meals. This demand brought each household in direct contact with the *shoykhet* on a weekly basis. Poultry was not purchased at the butcher shop, rather, each Jewish family purchased or raised the fowl it needed and then brought it to the *shoykhet* for slaughtering. Unlike the rabbi, who is held in high esteem but not in constant contact with all members of his community, the *shoykhet* was one of the people. In point of fact, catalogues of Who's Who have been published listing rabbis, but no such directory of *shokhtim* has ever been compiled. The common-man status of a *shoykhet* is perhaps best depicted by the words of an elderly rabbi in Petakh-Tikva of whom I asked some questions in conjunction with my research on Pinye-Ber. During our brief conversation, he kept exclaiming, "All this for a *shoykhet*?!"

Every substantial Jewish community had at least one *shoykhet*, with large cities having numerous *shokhtim*. Pinye-Ber's book is the only autobiography to describe at any length this occupation that is so central to traditional Jewish life.[41] The *shoykhet* was in fact the most indispensable individual in a Jewish

---

41 The following is a list of the few nineteenth-century autobiographers who were *shokhtim*. Moshe Wassercug (1910:92–96), who wrote a short autobiography, briefly describes his position as a *shoykhet*. Though published sources do not state any specific dates for him, his 1832 death record (no. 64) from Plock, Poland, is located in the State Archives in Poznan and states that he was ninety years old and worked as a Hebrew-language translator, which

community, as indicated by smaller communities, which engaged a *shoykhet* but not a rabbi, since they could not afford both. Needless to say, today's centralized kosher slaughtering and meat-packaging facilities have largely removed the *shoykhet* from yesteryear's essential role in each and every Jewish community. Until the early twentieth century, there was essentially no kosher poultry industry.

Pinye-Ber dedicates entire sections to discussing every aspect of his training and work as a *shoykhet*, including the certification process, his efforts at finding employment, the deliberations regarding the terms of his contracts, and his grueling daily schedule. He discusses the economic, business, and monetary aspects of his positions, including his interactions with his clientele, his collection of the kosher-meat tax, his difficulties in dealing with the kosher-meat tax farmer,[42] the removal of forbidden fats and his sale of them, and his encounters with an encroaching *shoykhet*. And, just as Rabbi Y. Y. Schneersohn's letter above described a *shoykhet* broaching the topic of building a new *mikveh*, so too, Pinye-Ber single-handedly initiated the purchase of a building for a much-needed new *mikveh* in Bakhchisaray (ch. 29). Pinye-Ber provides an excellent picture of the dynamics between a *shoykhet* and his community: he plays a leading role in the towns of Slobodze and Bakhchisaray where his fellow Jews come to accept his guidance.

Another vital position in the Jewish community was the *khazn* (cantor), who led prayers, read from the Torah, and officiated at Jewish life-cycle events. Jewish communities often engaged one individual who could serve as both *khazn* and *shoykhet*. Many smaller towns and villages that could not afford both a rabbi and *shoykhet* made do with one individual who served as both *khazn* and

---

is a rarely listed occupation. Gurwitz (1935:2:17–22, 186–188) briefly mentions working as a *shoykhet* for a few months in around 1877 and again later in Texas after immigrating to America in 1910. (An English translation of his memoirs was published in 2016.) Melamed (1922:1:202–204, 232–234) briefly describes his work as a *shoykhet* for two and a half years beginning in 1880 before becoming a *maskil*. Rabbi Levi Glicman (1934), who served as a rabbi and a *shoykhet*, spends a few pages on the strife that his father experienced as a *shoykhet* but does not mention his own experience. Though he never worked as a *shoykhet*, Gordon (1952:123–125) describes his four-month apprenticeship as a *shoykhet* in 1889–1890 in Zagare, Lithuania. Zicherman (1966), a *shoykhet* and a son of a *shoykhet*, in his fifty-two-page autobiography appearing at the end of his book *Nakhalat Ya'akov*, writes very little about his profession. Bernhard Cahn (1793–1871), a *shoykhet* in Germany, kept a diary from 1817 to 1871 consisting of over 3,800 pages in Judeo-German; excerpts have been published in English translation, though only a few pages touch on his position as a *shoykhet*.

42 A kosher-meat tax farmer bought the rights to collect taxes levied on both the slaughtering and the sale of kosher meat, some of which was sent to finance Jewish communal institutions, though the tax farmers tended to abuse the taxpayers.

shoykhet (called a *khazn-shoykhet*) to fill all their religious needs. A *shoykhet* was deemed absolutely necessary for every small town; on the other hand, when a serious halakhic issue arose, a rabbi in a nearby large community could be contacted.[43] The life of a *khazn-shoykhet*, once so common throughout thousands of small Jewish communities (see Berman, 1941:137–139), is not depicted in any other autobiography. Pinye-Ber discusses all the particulars regarding the cantorial aspect of this position, including the duties, renumeration, and various conflicts associated with it.

Yet, although Pinye-Ber found success in his profession, his narrative does not ignore the economic distress that his community suffered, and that he himself suffered as a child. In fact, it would be difficult to find another nineteenth-century autobiography that depicts the severe poverty and trying circumstances of Eastern European Jewry in such detail as Pinye-Ber's does. At a time when the majority of Jews in Tsarist Russia were poverty stricken, maskilic autobiographers were primarily from the middle ranks of Jewish economic society (Magnus, 2010:25). As result, they did not appreciate the extreme poverty suffered by many of their brethren.

Even before his parents' deaths, Pinye-Ber's family was so impoverished that they did not own a samovar to heat water for tea, and Pinye-Ber did not lay his eyes on one until the age of seven (ch. 5). After his parents' deaths, his sisters could barely earn enough money to feed themselves, let alone their seven-year-old brother, so as a destitute orphan he was shuttled from one relative to another. When just shy of his twelfth birthday, he was handed over to a relative to work as a house servant where he toiled at menial jobs for almost three years, while receiving almost nothing in return. Pinye-Ber describes his duties as a lowly house servant, along with the harassment and indignities he endured. He also mentions that he was refused any education (ch. 10). Even though being a house servant for a relative was considered more respectable than being apprenticed to an artisan, it was not an enviable position. To my knowledge, no other autobiographer mentions working as a house servant, though it was once a position commonly held by the impoverished children of Eastern Europe.[44]

---

43 A *khazn-shoykhet* also sometimes acted as a rabbi, as a passing journalist named Hadas (1896) noted regarding Pinye-Ber. Of course, this does not mean that the *shoykhet* made halakhic rulings, but it simply means that he was considered the authority regarding Jewish religious matters.

44 An indication that a house servant (*shtub-meshores*) was once commonplace is its appearance in Lifshits's Yiddish-Russian dictionary (1876:210) as שטיב-משרת (*shtib-meshures* as pronounced in Southeastern Yiddish) and in Harkavy's Yiddish-English-Hebrew dictionary (1928:494).

No discussion of poverty among the Jews of Tsarist Russia would be complete without mentioning the oppressive laws against them, which exacerbated their economic plight. This body of discriminatory legislation emanated from the tsar down to the provincial governors, mayors, police chiefs, and lowest officials in the remotest villages. The Jews were treated as enemies of the state, and sadistic, draconian laws aimed at tormenting and embittering their lives were regulated and enforced. Levanda (1874) documented 1,073 anti-Jewish laws in Tsarist Russia up until 1873, and much anti-Jewish legislation was passed in the following years. There were numerous taxes, penalties, and fines levied against Jews, including the enormous 300-ruble fine imposed on the family of a Jew who evaded military recruitment, while the family of a non-Jew was not held liable at all for the evasion of a family member. There was a kosher-meat tax on both the slaughtering and the sale of kosher meat; subsidiary taxes on the rental of houses, shops, and warehouses owned by Jews; subsidiary taxes on the profits of breweries, industrial establishments, and other trade enterprises carried on by Jews; a candle tax for Sabbath lights totaling 230,000 rubles a year; and a tax on Jewish printing offices for each type of printing press they owned. Jews were not allowed to purchase a landed estate anywhere and were prohibited from opening their businesses on Sundays and the main Christian holidays, though no such restrictions existed for Muslims and other non-Christians. Jews were not allowed to serve as mayors or generally to hold any civil service positions, even of the lowest ranks. In 1876, Jews were officially declared to be aliens, whose social rights were regulated by special ordinances. Under penalty of criminal prosecution, houses of prayer could only be started in places where there were no less than thirty Jews (Johnpoll, 1995). This discriminatory legislation caused a much greater percentage of poverty and joblessness among Jews than non-Jews, resulting in large bands of Jewish beggars, including children, to roam the streets (Schneersohn, 1968:222–224). As Kofman (1955:43) writes in his autobiography, "It's difficult to describe the fear and consternation that clenched the Jews in Russia."

Perhaps the severest aspect of Tsarist Russia's discriminatory policy was the legislation in effect from 1791 until the fall of the monarchy in 1917, restricting Jews to permanent residence in the western provinces, referred to as the Pale of Settlement, which included Moldova, Lithuania, Belarus, much of present-day Ukraine, part of eastern Latvia, and small parts of present-day western Russia. It comprised only some 20% of the territory of European Tsarist Russia and 5.7% of Tsarist Russia as a whole. Aggravating the situation were the laws forbidding Jews in some provinces to reside in peasant villages. These laws deprived millions of Jews of the freedom of movement, one of the most essential personal rights enjoyed by all other subjects of Tsarist Russia.

These anti-Jewish statutes included draconian documentation requirements and travel restrictions. Pinye-Ber's is the only autobiography I am aware of that discusses the great hardships resulting from the harsh registration mandates, which plagued Jews over decades, if not throughout their entire lives. Like tens of thousands of Jews in Tsarist Russia, Pinye-Ber's parents never registered his birth with the local Jewish community of Tiraspol in order to avoid his conscription into the deeply anti-Semitic military, and they did not register their family either in order to avoid the double poll-tax imposed on Jews (Avrutin, 2010:133; Braver, 1955:42; Freeze, 1999:8–9). As a ten-year-old, Pinye-Ber was forced to hide from *khapers* (snatchers) who had come from the province of Podolia, where his father had been registered, to kidnap him so they could fill the military recruitment quotas; had he been registered locally he might have been able to avoid that threat. When he was twelve, as mentioned earlier, his sisters sent him off to a relative who had promised to register Pinye-Ber as his son. This relative never fulfilled his promise, even though he kept Pinye-Ber as his house servant for three years (ch. 10). Without being registered, Pinye-Ber could not obtain an internal passport and therefore was not permitted to travel beyond a radius of thirty *verst* (thirty-two kilometers) from his permanent place of residence. Anyone caught without proper documents away from his permanent place of residence could be fined and forcibly returned home (Avrutin, 2010:91; Matthews, 1993:7–8).

Several months after Pinye-Ber's arrival at the yeshiva in Odessa, the government began to crack down on Jews without proper documentation, causing him to leave the yeshiva. Out of fear of being denounced by non-Jews to the authorities, who monetarily rewarded such informants (Matthews, 1993:8), Pinye-Ber hid in a synagogue for several weeks and narrowly escaped being captured. He then fled to Tiraspol, but the danger of non-Jewish informants was even worse there (ch. 13). He fled to Romanovke, where he was able to remain for some time, since no non-Jews resided there. Subsequently, Pinye-Ber served as the *gabbai* (attendant) of the rabbi of Romanovke on his trip to the surrounding towns and villages, but Pinye-Ber's lack of an internal passport "created many problems along the way . . . and we were miraculously rescued more than once" (ch. 13). Upon returning to Tiraspol, people were afraid to let Pinye-Ber spend the night in their home since anyone harboring unregistered residents could be fined (ch. 14).

When Pinye-Ber became engaged, he did so on the condition that within three months his future in-laws would have him registered illicitly as their son and then obtain an internal passport for him. Since his fiancée's father was a former soldier, Pinye-Ber would have been exempt from conscription if he were registered as this man's son. Nonetheless, his fiancée's parents soon reneged on their promise, for his mother-in-law was afraid that he would abandon their daughter once he received his internal passport (ch. 14). But Pinye-Ber needed an internal passport in order to travel freely to a yeshiva where he would study until his wedding, which was planned to be at least two years later.

To solve this problem, Pinye-Ber stole across the Romanian border, obtained a Romanian passport, and returned to Tsarist Russia while posing as a foreign citizen (ch. 15). With his Romanian passport, he was able to travel to Lubavitch where the Rebbe advised him to go to Shklov to study in a yeshiva. Sometime before his Romanian passport expired, he naively sent it in to the Governor General of the province with the expectation that it would be exchanged for a Russian provincial passport, which would be valid for one year. By doing so, Pinye-Ber caused his own misfortune: the Governor General refused to exchange his foreign passport but instead ordered him to return to Romania within two months. If Pinye-Ber would not have sent in his Romanian passport, it is unlikely that the authorities in Shklov would have ever known that it had expired, and, in the worst case, he would only have had to pay a ten-ruble fine (ch. 16). Back in Romania, he obtained a new Romanian passport, worked as a *melamed* for a year, and then returned to Tsarist Russia. Half a year later, he returned to Romania to consult with the Lyever Rebbe, obtained a new Romanian passport, and quickly returned to Tsarist Russia, where he posed for many years as a Romanian citizen (ch. 17).

Russian officials were not the only source of threat for someone lacking proper documentation: even fellow Jews who harbored hostility could use this circumstance against an individual. Years later, when notice arrived in Bakhchisaray that all foreign subjects had to return to their native countries, Pinye-Ber's enemies quickly denounced him. The authorities informed him that he had to liquidate all his possessions and return to Romania within three months (ch. 25). With the deadline approaching, his enemies feared that their allegations would not hold, so they upped their charges and falsely denounced Pinye-Ber as a fugitive recruit who had evaded serving in the Russian military, a serious crime that they hoped would land him in exile in Siberia. Miraculously, he located the exact town where his father was registered and obtained the required official transcript of his father's entry in the poll-tax census, although initially all he knew was that his father was from the province of Podolia. With great effort and cost, Pinye-Ber was issued a Russian internal passport, evidently as proof that he was now a Russian subject and an official resident of Bakhchisaray.

Obtaining foreign passports, as Pinye-Ber had done, was common among the Jewish poor in Tsarist Russia. In the early 1890s, there were 150,000 Romanians, Turks, and Austro-Hungarians residing in Tsarist Russia, many of them Jews who, although born there, had been obliged to acquire foreign passports. In 1891–1892, thousands of them were forcibly expelled from Odessa alone, which resulted in many dying of cold and starvation (Errera, 1894:38–41). Pinye-Ber's is perhaps the only first-person account of a Jew in Tsarist Russia struggling to obtain a foreign passport and the perils he endured posing as a foreign citizen.[45]

Pinye-Ber also provides detailed descriptions of the difficulties he had in traveling long distances as a poor person, much of which he did on foot. At one point, he walked for thirteen days non-stop on unpaved roads, filled with mud and rivers of water (ch. 16). He describes his methods of hitching rides and how he raised funds along the way to be able to purchase food and continue his journey. He vividly describes his travels during the winter: "I ended up waiting outside for some two hours and became so permeated by the freezing cold that I felt that my bones were breaking.... I felt that in a short while I would become frozen since I could barely move my feet by then" (ch. 21).

Pinye-Ber's poverty also allows him to shine a distinctive light on the experience of *esn teg* (literally "eating days"), the once-widespread practice of yeshiva students eating each day of the week with a different local family. The more common account of this experience comes from maskilic autobiographers, who express embarrassment or dismay at the meager meals they often received in poor households.[46] These autobiographers, coming from the middle ranks of Jewish society, were unaccustomed to this paltry fare, for they did not know what it was like to live without money or food, nor could they appreciate the sacrifice made by their hosts, who often had barely enough food for themselves. In contrast, Pinye-Ber was all too familiar with poverty: he appreciated the meager food he was given, recognizing both the sacrifice made by his hosts and their joy in helping an impoverished yeshiva student. The maskilic autobiographer may have looked down upon the poor householder and his family, but

---

45 In his autobiography, Schoenfeld (1946:9, 10, 25, 28, 29) briefly mentions that his father had traveled from Tsarist Russia to Constantinople to obtain a Turkish passport to avoid conscription in the Tsarist Russian military. In 1891, his parents were one of over 1,000 Jewish families in Odessa bearing foreign passports who were expelled from Tsarist Russia. They were given seven months to liquidate their business.
46 For example, Abrahams (1953:60, 67–71) in his autobiography describes a considerable variety of embarrassing and demoralizing situations during his *esn teg* as a yeshiva student in Lithuania in the 1890s.

Pinye-Ber identified with their plight since he came from the poorest ranks of society. Indeed, he had not always eaten so well and so regularly as he did during his *esn teg* as a student in the yeshiva. Pinye-Ber goes out of his way to praise this Jewish practice:

> The poorest, even the water carrier and the woodchopper, would also have a *yeshiva* student eat at his home once a week. If you would have seen with what type of honor the poor man took a *yeshiva* student, you would say, "And who is like Your people, like the people of Israel?"[47] for such poor people, who barely made it through the week on dry bread, managed to save food from their own portion to feed a young student for a day, making sure that on that day a piece of meat was cooked for lunch. They would also give the *yeshiva* student a few *kopeks* so that he would be able to buy something for breakfast and dinner. Everything was done with such honor and joy so that the *yeshiva* student marveled at how nicely he was welcomed by the poor man.... But it was amazing to see how precious the *mitzvah* [commandment] of strengthening Torah study and supporting Torah scholars was to the poor. (ch. 16)

Here in this autobiography one finds perhaps the only positive first-person account of this widespread Jewish practice, which was undoubtedly greatly appreciated by untold numbers of unrecorded yeshiva students from similarly distressed backgrounds.

Finally, Pinye-Ber's account of his life in Tsarist Russia intimately includes his sense of himself as a parent. No other nineteenth-century Jewish autobiography discusses raising a traditional Jewish family as his does. He devotes practically two entire chapters to this matter, apart from mentioning his children at length elsewhere (chs. 27 and 28). Numerous maskilic autobiographies are devoted to their authors' formative years and the manner in which they were raised, but they do not discuss raising their own children whom, in any event, they did not attempt to raise in a traditional Jewish manner.

Pinye-Ber and his wife had thirteen children, seven of whom lived to adulthood. He describes hiring *melamdim* for his children, including his daughter. He later describes the heartache of having to send his sons away to yeshivas at the tender age of nine, something he was forced to do since there were no yeshivas

---

47 Samuel II 7:23.

in the Crimea. He writes how either he or his wife would accompany them out of town, make arrangements for their room and board, and even help them adjust to the food. He writes of his and his wife's anguish in not seeing their oldest son Isruel for six years while he was at a yeshiva, and he explains, "We underwent all of this—I am not even including the large expense this incurred—because we wanted our son to be a pious Jew." He writes about arranging and paying for relatives to bring his sons from one town to another and to making regular visits to check up on them. Pinye-Ber describes his son Refuel's return home from yeshiva one Pesach and the conflicts that ensued between the returning yeshiva student and his less religious siblings.

Pinye-Ber writes about the distress that he and his wife endured in contemplating turning two of his sons into artisans, which was stigmatized among many Jews. He relates that he specifically avoided the finer crafts, such as jewelry making and watchmaking, which required one to work on *Shabes*. Instead, he chose coarse crafts for them, specifically cabinetmaking and tinsmithry, where that was not a requirement. When his sons come of age, he discusses his efforts to have them exempted from conscription in the Tsarist Russian army, which not only often treated Jewish recruits brutally but made it impossible to observe even the most basic precepts of Judaism. Despite his efforts, two of his sons were conscripted, but he spent 300 rubles and succeeded in having one of them who had a medical condition discharged. He describes trials and tribulations in marrying off his two eldest children Isruel and Nekhame, who remained Sabbath observant.

Pinye-Ber's autobiography indicates how a traditionalist coped with the changing values and beliefs of his children. Against his wishes, his daughter Rukhl first studied in *gimnaziya* (an advanced institute of secondary education). She then wanted to continue studying in a university. Though Pinye-Ber was against these pursuits, he did not want to be overbearing and eventually acquiesced.

Naturally, he mentions aspects of parenting not necessarily associated with religious life, such as saving his children from a nearly fatal accident, caring for his children when they were extremely ill, and a heartrending description of his son Shulem's death at the age of three and a half. Though other autobiographers mention the deaths of their children, they usually describe these tragedies in one or two lines. When his first wife died and he still had young children at home, he mentions his decision not to marry for beauty or money, though he was heavily in debt, but only for his children's welfare.

Perhaps Pinye-Ber's deep religious consciousness is most powerfully revealed in that which he does not write, that is, in the aspects of his children's lives that were too painful for him to mention explicitly. He omits mentioning that most of his offspring were no longer religious by the early 1900s, although it is implicitly understood from his stated purpose of writing his book, namely, to prove God's existence to them and convince them to follow traditionalist ways.[48] Pinye-Ber generally avoids expressing his deep disappointment and heartache over most of his children having become non-traditionalist. Only in a private letter penned in 1926 to his daughter Nekhame, who had just immigrated to Oakland, California, do we read of the tremendous grief this caused him:

> Please write me more often and with detailed descriptions of your brothers' lives and from your [son] Moyshe's life, and whether he is far, far removed . . .[49] And about his wife and children . . . I understand that my children have *treyf* [non-kosher] homes there, and that you will also have to eat *treyf* because there is no *shoykhet* and no synagogue. Write me everything in detail. It grieves me—tremendously. Woe to me that I have lived to see my children conduct themselves in this manner and that you, my beloved, pious daughter, also have to conduct yourself like this. Write about everything and at least let me truthfully know how my children are living. I imagine that you will conduct yourself as a Jew there also, and God will assist you in your needs.[50]

These parenting experiences were common to thousands upon thousands of traditional Jewish parents at that time. Pinye-Ber's autobiography details the daily struggles that religious parents faced while trying to educate and raise their children in a difficult and rapidly changing environment.

---

48 Still other issues with his children were too painful to even be implied, such as his daughter Rukhl's relationship with a non-Jewish Frenchman, which resulted in the birth of a son, Boris Blondin, in 1911. Pinye-Ber offered to raise her son, but Rukhl declined, saying that she had already chosen a secular lifestyle for herself and her child (correspondence with Boris's granddaughter Agnès [Montelle] Louvrier of Pontarlier, France in 2017).

49 Nekhame Brockman's son Moyshe (known as Martin Brockman) had married a non-Jew in 1919 in Portland, Oregon. Pinye-Ber is possibly subtly asking if Moyshe had apostatized to Christianity, which a Jew in Tsarist Russia had to do to marry a non-Jew from a Christian family.

50 Translation of a Yiddish letter dated the 21st of *Tamuz* 5686 (July 3, 1926).

The Rebbe as an Inspirational Light

Pinye-Ber's autobiography includes another practice distinctive to traditionalist Jewish life in the nineteenth century but almost never mentioned in Jewish autobiographies: the surreptitious observation of respected Rebbes. This practice will no doubt seem curious to many modern readers. In 1865, Pinye-Ber made the long trek to Lubavitch, Belarus, where he met with the Lubavitcher Rebbe, Rabbi Menakhem-Mendl Schneerson (1789–1866), who is posthumously referred to as the Tsemakh Tsedek, the name of his published rabbinical responsa (ch. 15). Pinye-Ber writes a rare, early description of the ongoings in the Hasidic court of Lubavitch.[51] Perhaps the most remarkable aspect of Pinye-Ber's work is his account of his hiding in the large study hall and peeking through the keyhole of the door leading to the study of the Tsemakh Tsedek to observe him when he was by himself, an observation that would inform his decision about whether he would become a Hasid of the Tsemakh Tsedek. And Pinye-Ber writes about all that he observes: the Rebbe's unassuming conduct, his constant studying, the comings and goings of the Rebbe's attendant, and the appearance of the furniture and the bookshelves. Pinye-Ber was greatly impressed with the Rebbe's simplicity, noting the strong contrast with the flourish and pomp at the courts of the Hasidic Rebbes back in his own region of the Ukraine. For Pinye-Ber, the Tsemakh Tsedek clearly conducted himself just as devoutly and unpretentiously in private as he did in public. Again, in the winter of 1872–1873, Pinye-Ber made the long journey to Lubavitch to see the Rebbe, Rabbi Shmuel Schneerson, and he describes attending a festive meal on Saturday night at which the Rebbe was present (ch. 21). Not being able to see the Rebbe through the crowd and being on the opposite end of a long table, Pinye-Ber crawled under the table until he was positioned at the Rebbe's feet where for a couple of hours he "could hear the Rebbe speaking words of Torah, mundane matters, and clever remarks among his inner circle," which "made my entire trip worth all the effort." Clearly his surreptitious observations of these two Rebbes carrying out their daily lives were the experiences that made the deepest impressions on him on both of his trips.

Pinye-Ber's stealthy observations of his Rebbes were apparently not such an unusual practice among Hasidim. At one time the Hasidim had made so many holes in the wall of the Tsemakh Tsedek's private study to secretly observe him that it had to be draped with a blanket to cover up the

---

51   Since Mondshine (1986) translated Pinye-Ber's accounts of his trips to Lubavitch into Hebrew, the section about the Tsemakh Tsedek has been included in practically every substantial Hebrew-language biographical work regarding the Tsemakh Tsedek.

holes (B. S. Schneerson, 2001:77). Moreover, the Tsemakh Tsedek himself, at the age of nine or ten, hid in a heating oven one Saturday night to hear his grandfather, Rabbi Shneur Zalman of Lyadi (1745–1812), expound upon the *Zohar* to his sons (Rabbi Y. Y. Schneersohn, 1989:98–101). Apart from Hasidim of the Tsemakh Tsedek, Hasidim also peeked through holes in a door to observe Rabbi Shneur Zalman of Lyadi in prayer (Rabbi Y. Y. Schneerson, 1936:23–24). On another occasion, Rabbi Shneur Zalman arrived at an inn in Radomysl, Ukraine (now Radomyshl), entered his room, and immediately instructed that the holes in the door and roof be stopped up to prevent unwanted observers, though the twelve-year-old future Rabbi Peretz Kheyn (1797–1883) remained hidden above the wardrobe where he was able to secretly observe Rabbi Shneur Zalman while he prayed ("Gan Eden ha-elyon," 2019).[52] The tremendous effect of these observations on generations of Hasidim is eloquently expressed by the Lubavitcher Rebbe, Rabbi Yosef Yitzchok Schneersohn (1986:162), in describing those who surreptitiously observed his father, Rabbi Shalom DovBer Schneerson (1860–1920), in prayer at the gravesite of his predecessors:

> Certainly, there are those who merited to peer through the cracks in the wall surrounding the *ohel* and see [my father's] holy countenance shining with extraordinary radiance while wrapped in a world of the essence of Godly light.[53] And the elder Hasidim, who toiled in self-refinement, transmitted to their students that which they received from their teachers, namely that these and similar memories can uplift one to a lofty and purified realm at any time and any place.

Such activities were not limited to Hasidim. Rabbi Israel Lipkin (1810–1883), also known as Rabbi Israel Salanter, would watch—while unobserved—his teacher Rabbi Yosef-Zundl (1786–1866) of Salant (Glenn, 1953:19). Rabbi Israel Meir Kagan (1838–1933), known by the name of his magnum opus, the *Khafets Hayim*, once hid under a bench in the synagogue to observe his teacher

---

52 Laine (2014:77–78) mentions different accounts of Rabbi Peretz Kheyn that might imply that this incident actually occurred when Rabbi Kheyn's father brought him at age four to see Rabbi Shneur Zalman in Lyadi. See also Duchman (1990:82), Levine (1998:1), Shmuel (1994:62–63), and Zaltzman (2015:447) for accounts of surreptitious observations of the Lubavitcher Rebbes by their Hasidim.

53 An *ohel* (literally "tent" in Hebrew) is a structure built around a Jewish grave as a sign of prominence of the deceased.

Rabbi Nakhum Kaplan (1812–1879) of Harodne, also known as Grodno (Shvadron, 1990:343).

Such conduct actually dates to Talmudic times, when an incident is recorded of students covertly observing the personal conduct of their rabbi (Babylonian Talmud Brakhot 62a). This conduct has lasted until the present day and the following are just a few examples. In the early 1990s in Brooklyn, a few Hasidic yeshiva students were caught climbing a tree to observe the Bobover Rebbe, Rabbi Shlomo Halberstam (1907–2000), while he recited prayers before retiring at night. Another instance involves a photograph circulating among Lubavitcher Hasidim of the Lubavitcher Rebbe, Rabbi Menachem Mendel Schneerson (1902–1994), studying without his hat and *kapote* (a long double-breasted frock coat); he would never have appeared dressed in that manner in public. The photograph is purported to have been taken about 1963 through the keyhole of his office door. In 1968, two yeshiva students were caught in an attempt to furtively record the Lubavitcher Rebbe's melodious voice while he was praying privately in his office.

According to one intriguing Hasidic story, surreptitious observations of one's Rebbe are not limited to the physical world. Rabbi Yehuda-Leyb of Zaklików, Poland, a Hasid of the Seer of Lublin (ca. 1745–1815), related that a Jewish purveyor to the Russian army named Makitoner would not make any business decisions without consulting the Seer of Lublin. Makitoner passed away and he found himself in a spiritual netherworld, where he continued to conduct business. At one point, he remembered that he needed to consult with his Rebbe, who, as he remembered, had also passed away. Makitoner began to cry out that he wanted to be with his Rebbe, until he pushed his way through to his Rebbe in Heaven. He began to complain to him that he was caught in a netherworld and did not know what would become of him. The Seer of Lublin replied that he could now remain there with him. Rabbi Yehuda-Leyb concluded, "See how Makitoner merited to be with the *Rebbe*. If only we could at least merit in Heaven to observe the *Rebbe* through a keyhole" (Preger, 197?:195–196).

The reason that the practice of observing the private conduct of their leaders is found only among traditional Jews and not non-traditionalists is because Jewish traditionalists consider the conduct of their great rabbis to be closely aligned with the Divine Will, and so their daily actions—and even their very countenance—are worth observing and noting. Orthodox Jewish writings are replete with accounts of the lofty, daily conduct of their exalted rabbis and Hasidic Rebbes, while maskilic writings do not include such observations about their leaders. Jewish traditionalists observe their spiritual leaders' conduct to obtain a glimpse into how a Talmudic scholar steeped in Kabbalah and Hasidic teachings conducts himself, to get a view of a person who has reached such exceptional spiritual heights. By contrast, *maskilim*, often eager to reform traditional Jewish life, engage their leaders in philosophical and social discussions. Jewish traditionalists look to their most esteemed rabbis for inspiration in their inner lives and daily conduct, while the *maskilim* were not concerned with their leaders' personal behavior; it was their ideas and social outlook that they sought to follow. Pinye-Ber is the rare autobiographer who includes his surreptitious observations of his Rebbes' daily conduct. This is solely found among traditionalists and occurred more frequently than is generally recognized.

Anti-Fanaticism and Anti-Corruption

Yet, for all his affirmation of traditional Jewish life, Pinye-Ber by no means claims that his community was perfect. Orthodox Jewry is frequently perceived as a group that denies any and all failings of those faithful to its traditions. Reading the autobiographies of maskilic Jews, one might conclude that traditional Jews were completely unaware of the problems plaguing their society. In their writings, the *maskilim* give the impression that only they were aware of these issues, and they had to take it upon themselves to point out the flaws in traditional Jewish society. Yet in their zeal to reform Jewish life, many early maskilic autobiographers were overly critical of many aspects of traditional Jewish life, perceiving them as archaic, backward, and flawed. They castigated traditional Jewish education, traditional marriage patterns, the Yiddish language, distinctive Jewish garb, the authority placed in the hands of the rabbis, the actions of community leaders, the exclusive study of Talmud, and the negative attitudes of traditional Jews toward European culture. And Hasidim, who in their eyes personified uncompromising traditional Judaism, were considered to be the ultimate enemy of their progressive goals.[54]

Yet, some of these criticisms can be found in the writings of traditional Jews as well. Pinye-Ber's autobiography expresses sentiments that in fact resemble a number of these maskilic complaints. He criticizes a number of aspects of traditional Jewish life. He criticizes the administration of corporal punishment customary in the *kheyder*. He finds fault with the system of *kest*, where many young married men were being supported by their fathers-in-law,

---

54 See Etkes (2005:7–8) for an explanation of the *maskilim*'s intentional campaign to denigrate the Baal Shem Tov and Hasidism.

and points out that many of the young men did not actually spend their time studying. He is critical of the norm where young women were encouraged to marry young men under the pretext that they were marrying Torah scholars when, in fact, these young men were often unwilling or incapable of earning a living. He decries the excessive drinking among certain Hasidim and the fanaticism found among them in its various forms.

It is interesting to read how a Hasidic Jew refers to other Hasidic Jews as fanatics. In the original Yiddish, Pinye-Ber conveys this idea with the international words *fanatizm, fanatizmus,* and *fanatish* (fanaticism, fanatical). He comments that "no record of my birth existed because it was not common to register births in those times, particularly for such fanatical parents as my own" (ch. 25), and refers to his maternal grandfather's *shtetl* of Groseles as a place where "fanaticism raged . . . unbounded" (ch. 1). He discusses the fanaticism of his brother-in-law Shloyme-Leyzer, who was raised by "fanatical Hasidic parents," and believes that this fanaticism was partially the cause of his sister Tsipe's early demise (ch. 3). Reminiscing about a childhood teacher, Reb Shloymele, he writes that he "understood me well and was very sympathetic, despite the fact that he was a fanatical Jew of the old school" (ch. 7). Pinye-Ber was a devout Hasid, yet he wanted his wife to become more sophisticated and culturally advanced (ch. 18). Pinye-Ber was upset when his son Refuel returned home after yeshiva and refused to acknowledge his siblings because of their open violations of Jewish law and refers to him as a "Polish-Jewish fanatic" (ch. 28). Yudl Mark (1943:37–38) suggests that Pinye-Ber renounces the fanaticism of the Ukrainian Hasidim because he was a Chabadnik (that is, a Chabad Hasid, a Lubavitcher) who are known to be moderate.[55] Perhaps his becoming a Lubavitcher was a factor in his developing a disdain for fanaticism. Nonetheless, Pinye-Ber traveled to Lubavitch to receive the Rebbe's blessings, leaving his pregnant wife for one-and-a-half months without notifying her in advance (ch. 21). Decades later, he writes,

---

55 The Chabad branch of the Hasidic movement, today synonymous with Lubavitch, was founded in the late eighteenth century by Rabbi Shneur Zalman (1745–1812) of Lyadi, the author of the *Tanya*, a seminal Hasidic work. He was a disciple of Rabbi Dov-Ber, the *Magid* of Mezritsh, the heir to the Baal Shem Tov, the founder of Hasidism. Chabad is a Hebrew acronym for *Chochmah, Binah, Da'at,* meaning "Wisdom, Understanding, and Knowledge." It is known as the intellectual branch of Hasidism.

Rabbi Norman Lamm (1989:113) comments that the Chabad Hasidic movement in Tsarist Russia was comprised of "moderate Hasidim." In describing the Chabad Hasidim of Konotop where she lived from her marriage in 1850 until 1856, Pauline Wengeroff (2015:74–76) writes in her memoirs, "Most of the Jews in Konotop were Hasidim. . . . For all of their devout practices, we must note that the Lithuanian Hasidim are far more temperate and practical than the Polish."

"Obviously my fanaticism at that time was spurring me on and making it so that I could not have possibly done anything but travel to Lubavitch, disregarding anything that might have disturbed my plan including my compassion for my wife."

Like many *maskilim*, Pinye-Ber criticizes the community's leadership when it is corrupt, and he campaigns to modify longstanding practices maintained by the establishment. He repeatedly suffered abuse from scheming, unethical community leaders. Nonetheless, he did not see any of this as a cause to lose faith, rather it served to strengthen his resolve to improve the Jewish communities in which he lived. In 1873, Pinye-Ber obtained his first position as a *shoykhet* in the village of Slobodze where he signed a contract which included "terms that had been used from time immemorial" (ch. 22). Eventually, he realized that he needed to abolish these terms, which compelled him to personally collect his weekly stipends from door to door, often without much success. After two and a half years in Slobodze, he devised a new payment plan, which abolished the weekly stipends and established a fee for *sh'khita*, which was to be paid before slaughtering. The residents of Slobodze were concerned that he was "altering the order of the world since time immemorial—all the way back to Slobodze's very beginnings," yet most people were pleased when they realized that the new arrangement actually saved them money. While in Slobodze, Pinye-Ber successfully brought down an unscrupulous community leader and prominent Tolner Hasid, who illegally hired a competing *shoykhet* and insisted that Pinye-Ber could not slaughter unless he obtained a letter of recommendation from the Tolner Rebbe. Pinye-Ber realized that if one did not have money to tip the Rebbe's *gabbaim* (attendants), one could wait days to see the Rebbe. Having no money for tips and no time to waste, he ingeniously dodged two *gabbaim* and was in front of the Rebbe shortly after his arrival, thereby preventing the unscrupulous community leader from sabotaging the meeting. Impressed with Pinye-Ber, the Rebbe realized the community leader's unethical ambitions and brought them to a halt. Pinye-Ber continued his anticorruption efforts years later, in Bakhchisaray, where he fought the corrupt community leaders' control of kosher-meat production and their embezzlement of portions of the kosher-meat tax.

Unlike the *maskilim*, who saw their criticisms of Jewish life as a reason to forsake it, Pinye-Ber criticized out of a desire to make Jewish life better. His activities throughout his life show how committed he was to this project of improvement. He single-handedly arranged the purchase of a building to house a new *mikveh*, replacing an older, dilapidated one. Many local Jewish women who had forsaken this essential aspect of traditional Jewish married life due to the conditions of the old *mikveh*, now began to use the *mikveh* regularly. The full story of one of Pinye-Ber's greatest accomplishments is actually not found in his autobiography. In the early 1910s, Pinye-Ber befriended a crotchety, wealthy, former apostate named Kizilshteyn whom he succeeded in convincing to amend his will to ensure that his wealth and large estate, worth 200,000 rubles (equivalent to $2,774,092 in 2021), would be donated to the Jewish community of Feodosiya (ch. 29). Shortly after Pinye-Ber left for the Holy Land in 1913, Kizilshteyn died and his former estate served as a Jewish community center and a Jewish hospital ("Inyane ha-Yehudim," 1914; Keren, 1981:138, 203–204).

Although Pinye-Ber's autobiography is critical of various traditional Jewish institutions and leaders, even sounding at times like some of the maskilic autobiographers, he always remained a traditionalist. A Hebrew-language newspaper article about Bakhchisaray, by a passing maskilic journalist, mentions that the *shoykhet* of that community (that is, Pinye-Ber) was not a *maskil* (singular of *maskilim*). In fact, he deprecates Pinye-Ber for his lack of interest in secular knowledge and maskilic literature (Hadas, 1896). Only someone unaware that Hasidism has always had its internal critics would think that Pinye-Ber had maskilic tendencies. Certainly other traditionalists have had the same issues with their communities as Pinye-Ber did, but there is a reluctance among traditionalists to put such criticisms in print. Ongoing problems in a community do not necessitate abandonment of Jewish practice as the singular solution. The defining difference between Pinye-Ber's criticism and that of the *maskilim* is in their intention to record their distaste of traditional norms. When maskilic writers criticized traditional society, they were justifying their decision to abandon Jewish tradition, while Pinye-Ber's criticisms were aimed at building up and strengthening local traditional Jewish society while also weeding out corruption.

Religious Self-Realization

As has been observed, practically all nineteenth-century Jewish autobiographies are stories of secular self-realization. They tell the story of a traditionalist residing in an insular community who transitions and adopts the mores of the Haskalah, breaks away from his family and community, and eventually leads a secular life. Pinye-Ber's autobiography is also a story of self-realization, but in the opposite direction: he experiences a religious self-realization, which serves to strengthen his connection to the traditions, values, and mores of his family and community. The first and primary experience of Pinye-Ber's self-realization revolves around his renewed awareness and connection to his family's strong ethos of Torah study (ch. 5). As we shall see, Pinye-Ber describes this emotional experience and a dream, which is the prelude to his self-realization.

Pinye-Ber came from a family devoted to Torah study, and he was related to the rabbi of Tiraspol. His father was a *melamed* though "above all … an accomplished Talmudic scholar," and his mother's "entire motive in life lay in her sons growing up to be rabbis and spiritual leaders of their generation" (ch. 1). His maternal grandfather was the "first Talmudic scholar in the entire region," and his older brother "outshone all other Torah scholars [in town] with his mastery of the Talmud and the major halakhic works" (ch. 2). By the time he was eight, his parents and older brother had died. His older sisters could barely provide for themselves, so they tried to find a relative who would take Pinye-Ber in and provide him with a traditional Jewish education. Yet this plan did not work. Over the next few years he was so rambunctious that his relatives sent him back, or, in other cases, his relatives' ruthless treatment caused him to run away. When he was eleven, his sisters gave up on providing him with a Jewish education and turned him over to someone who could teach him a means of earning a living. They farmed Pinye-Ber out to a stranger from an isolated hamlet who had promised to teach the boy a trade, but this stranger merely had him do menial tasks. At the first opportunity, Pinye-Ber ran away and returned to his sisters (ch. 8). At about that time, Pinye-Ber dreamed that he met his departed father while walking on the Ukrainian steppe. His father led him to a splendid palace, which turned out to be a yeshiva, when suddenly his father disappeared. He was initially refused entry into the yeshiva, but he was finally admitted and seated at a table. At that moment, everything vanished, and he was back on the steppe (ch. 9). This dream planted a seed of hope in the young orphan that he would one day reconnect with his family's dedication to Torah study.

Back in Tiraspol, Pinye-Ber began to frequent a local *bes-medresh* (Torah study hall), but all he succeeded in learning was the art of petty larceny in which he received ample instruction from the local impoverished youth (ch. 9). At that point, his sisters pleaded with a relative who lived in a village to make something of the boy. Though this relative had agreed to employ him as a house servant and to hire a *melamed* for him, Pinye-Ber received no education and was never renumerated for his services (ch. 10). After spending three years with this relative, Pinye-Ber realized one day that he no longer remembered the meaning of the Hebrew words he was reciting in his prayers. He picked up a volume of Talmud and was shocked to find that he no longer understood the meaning of the words and barely recognized the Hebrew letters. Panic stricken, he prayed to God that he not remain an unlettered boor. Then, "A light went on in my head, and I remembered what I was and who I was"—a member of a pious family devoted to Torah study. Pinye-Ber became consumed with the idea that he could in no way remain an ignoramus and shortly afterwards fled to seek out a place to study the Torah. He made his way to a yeshiva in Odessa and, after great effort, was admitted.

Pinye-Ber's flight from his position as a house servant to find a yeshiva is the primary turning point in his life. It is the moment where he takes his destiny into his own hands. When fleeing, he avoids the towns where his sisters lived for he feared that they would compel him to learn a trade. He writes about his servitude in biblical terms: "But God had pity on me and sent me a liberating angel in the form of a bright idea that brought me to my senses and would not let me rest until I was delivered from my exile, as were the Jews from the Egyptian exile through Moses our Teacher" (ch. 10). As the Jews were redeemed from Egypt to receive the Torah at Sinai, so Pinye-Ber escapes servitude to reclaim his heritage of Torah study. Indeed, he often sees his life story in biblical terms. Like many Jewish traditionalists of his time, Pinye-Ber expresses a deep, personal identification with the biblical forefathers of the Jewish people. In the course of his narrative, Pinye-Ber quotes the Five Books of Moses, Rashi's classic commentary on them, the Psalms and other parts of the Hebrew Bible, the Talmud, and the Mishna. For example, he describes working as a house servant for his relative Shulem: "Now it is necessary for me to describe this related family who used me in every possible way and whom I served like Joseph did in Potiphar's house in Egypt.... All that was missing was to have Potiphar's wife fall in love with me" (ch. 10). After describing an incident where he fought an arrogant nobleman (ch. 23), Pinye-Ber writes, "Upon entering my house, I lay down and cried over my bad luck, over my encounter with Esau.[56] I personally had wrestled with Esau—and not with his angel as Jacob, our forefather, did."[57] And regarding his move to Bakhchisaray, he writes, "I imagined how I would live a tranquil life now, but as Rashi comments, 'Jacob wanted to settle down in tranquility, and then the trouble of Joseph and his brothers' hatred toward him was thrust upon him'" (ch. 23).[58] One generally does not hear Orthodox Jews today talk or write in this manner, which is at least partially connected to the inroads made by a modern historical consciousness and the breach of experiencing divine providence as described by Haym Soloveitchik, discussed below. Yet, Pinye-Ber's inclination to think

---

56 In Yiddish, a brutal non-Jew is sometimes referred to as Esau.
57 According to Jewish tradition, the man with whom Jacob wrestled was Esau's angel; see Rashi's commentary on Genesis 32:25.
58 Rashi's commentary on Genesis 37:2.

in these terms illustrates a habit of thought likely typical of nineteenth-century traditional Jews.

Pinye-Ber's is arguably the only nineteenth-century Jewish autobiography that emphasizes the responsibility and the drive to reclaim the tradition of one's family and one's people. It is important to point out its historical distinctiveness in this regard. Although some maskilic autobiographies describe a return to Torah study and tradition, it usually amounts to only a fleeting moment in the author's life. For example, after having read much Haskalah literature, Kalman Marmor (1959:346–349) developed doubts about his life's direction, so in 1897, at the age of twenty-one, he returned to Torah study for almost a year in an attempt to obtain clarity. Similarly, after losing his father in 1878 at the age of twelve, Milch (1946:146,151) was removed from *kheyder*, which his mother could no longer afford, and was apprenticed to a woodcarver in Warsaw for five years. At one point, Milch missed the *bes-medresh* so much that he fled his apprenticeship for a full two months. Yet neither Marmor nor Milch came from families with a strong ethos of Torah study, and despite their brief returns to this discipline, they ultimately became ardent *maskilim*.

Pinye-Ber's account of his religious journey in many ways charts an inverse course to the accounts recorded in the autobiographies of secularized Jews. While the turning point in the latter is the author's break with the spirit of his faith and family, in Pinye-Ber's account the turning point is a break with the mundane life of a servant and the return to the core of his faith and family, the spirit of Torah study. Furthermore, just as maskilic autobiographies portray secular realization as an ongoing process taking place in phases over many years, Pinye-Ber's religious self-realization is a pathway. After six months in the yeshiva in Odessa, he was forced to leave due to his lack of documents. Returning to his family in Tiraspol, he became engaged and, posing as a Romanian citizen, lived undisturbed in Tsarist Russia. At about seventeen years of age, he became disenchanted with various aspects of Hasidic life in and around Tiraspol. Since he had been impressed with the Lubavitcher Hasidim whom he had met at age fifteen in Romanovke, he decided to explore Chabad Hasidism and travel to the Rebbe in Lubavitch.[59] The 700-mile trip to Lubavitch, some of it made on foot, lasted over four weeks. This journey was another critical juncture on his lifelong

---

59   Romanovke (Romanovka in Russian) was in the Tsarist Russian province of Bessarabia and is now called Basarabeasca, Moldova. It is not to be confused with Romanovka, Ukraine, formerly in the province of Kherson, whose rabbi was Rabbi Avraham David Lavut (ca. 1815–1890), a maternal ancestor of the Lubavitcher Rebbe, Rabbi Menachem Mendel Schneerson (1902–1994). Though both Romanovkas began as Jewish agricultural colonies, they are some 200 miles apart.

path to religious self-realization. The Lubavitcher Rebbe's simple and straight-forward style and strong emphasis on Torah study impressed him greatly. He had found what he had been seeking and was tremendously inspired.

Yet, although Pinye-Ber considered himself a Lubavitcher Hasid, he was far from a typical one. The majority of Lubavitcher Hasidim lived in eastern Belarus and spoke the Belarussian dialect of Yiddish; the learned among them were steeped in Chabad philosophy. In addition, they were in contact with the Rebbe's court, receiving copies of the discourses delivered by the Rebbe through his emissaries.[60] Pinye-Ber, on the other hand, was a native of Tiraspol far from Belarus, and spoke the Southeastern (Ukrainian) dialect of Yiddish.[61] Pinye-Ber also makes no reference in his autobiography to Chabad philosophical works. Even his basic terminology in describing the Rebbe's court is that used in and around his native home of Tiraspol, which differs from that used by Lubavitcher Hasidim.[62] Only a small number of Lubavitcher Hasidim lived in the area of Pinye-Ber's native Tiraspol, and other than the few Lubavitchers he met before his trip to Lubavitch, he makes no mention of any contact with any Lubavitcher Hasidim.

Even though Pinye-Ber was an atypical Lubavitcher, he was not unique. Unlike followers of other Hasidic Rebbes who tended to live close to each other and in relatively close proximity to their Rebbes, Chabad Hasidim were frequently found living in isolation and quite a distance from the Rebbe. The Yiddish writer and journalist Shloyme Bikl (1949:13) comments,

> The author of the *Tanya* and his successors have in some way imparted to the Chabad Hasid a moral task that is not connected to any Rebbe nor a Rebbe's court. In this way, Chabad had the power to spread itself over all areas of Jewish settlement.... Can

---

60   For a depiction of a typical pious Chabadnik of Belarus of approximately Pinye-Ber's generation or a bit earlier, see "Reb Abe," a series of monologues (first published in 1910) written by Zalman Yitskhok Aronsohn (known by the pseudonym of Anokhi). Aronsohn would read these monologues in the character of Reb Abe in presentations across Eastern Europe and later elsewhere, including South America (Kariv, 1960:viii).

61   Southeastern Yiddish (so-called "Ukrainian" Yiddish) was spoken before the Second World War in most of the Ukraine and Romania (Bessarabia, Moldavia, Bukovina) and the easternmost part of Galicia. In terms of pronunciation, Southeastern Yiddish can be considered to occupy an intermediate position between the two other major Yiddish dialects, Northeastern (so-called "Lithuanian") Yiddish and Central (so-called "Polish") Yiddish. For details, see Schaechter (1995:443–446).

62   See the footnotes in ch. 15 regarding Pinye-Ber's use of the following terms: "conducting a tish," *kvitl* (instead of *tsetl*—petitionary note to a Rebbe), and *gabbai* (instead of *meshores*—the Rebbe's attendant).

you imagine a Rizhiner Hasid living in a town in the area exclusive to Lubavitchers? No, under no circumstances. Chabadniks resided in Bessarabia, Romania, and even Galicia. Though the town of Lubavitch was far away, the Chabad literature (*Tanya*, *Likutei Torah*, and other works) was close at hand. They could be acquired and brought home.

The significance of Pinye-Ber's identifying himself as a Lubavitcher was that he had found a branch of Hasidism that attracted him and he was able to identify with its Rebbes, followers, and philosophical outlook. Thus, becoming a Lubavitcher Hasid enabled him to reclaim his Hasidic heritage, as opposed to abandoning it, which seems to have been the norm among other autobiographers from Hasidic backgrounds. Apart from his descriptions of the Hasidic court in Lubavitch during his two visits there in 1865 and 1873, his daily life does not differ greatly from the many Ukrainian Hasidim who were not attached to a particular Hasidic Rebbe. In nineteenth-century Eastern Europe (as in today's Hasidic centers), there were many Hasidim who lived a Hasidic lifestyle but were not closely associated with any particular Hasidic Rebbe. When a Hasidic Rebbe would come to town, they would seek his blessings or counsel but did not count themselves among his Hasidim. In sum, Pinye-Ber's Hasidism is primarily apparent in his consciousness (as discussed below) rather than in the quotidian details of his life story.

While in Lubavitch, the Rebbe advised Pinye-Ber to study in a yeshiva in Shklov and recommended that he not marry before the age of twenty. Being almost seventeen at the time, he was thrilled at the thought of finally having the opportunity to devote over three years to Torah study. Unfortunately, after only six months of fruitful study in Shklov, Pinye-Ber was forced to leave. Yet, those few months in yeshiva where he studied diligently gave him a fine grasp of the Talmud, which served as the basis for further advancement in his spiritual self-realization. Having obtained a strong background in Torah study, he was able to study to become a *shoykhet* and later served in that capacity in various small communities that were too small to hire both a rabbi and a *shoykhet*. He attended to most of the spiritual needs of these communities, which included, among other things, leading the services during the High Holidays and throughout the entire year, serving as the sole reader of the Torah, serving as *gabbai* (warden) and *moyel* (a Jew who is specially trained to circumcise Jewish boys according to Jewish law) in the region, and assisting the community in obtaining the religious articles they needed, such as *esroygim* for *Sukes*.

And this pathway of religious self-actualization continued even after his move to the Holy Land in 1913. The Talmud (Kidushin 69a) states that the Land of Israel is spiritually elevated over other lands, meaning that a Jew can connect to God there on a deeper level through Torah study and the observance of God's other commandments. Pinye-Ber was eager to pursue this deeper spiritual connection in his life. And once he reached the Holy Land, his self-actualization culminated in his studying the intricate laws of writing a Torah scroll, which he eventually put into practice, and which he continued to do throughout the battles between the Ottoman Turks and the British during the First World War during his exile from his home in Petakh-Tikva.[63] Had he not pursued the path of Torah study, he would not have become a *shoykhet* or a *moyel*, or have been involved in other communal activities.

Pinye-Ber's Sense of Divine Providence

A Divine-Providence-Centered Consciousness

Pinye-Ber, as noted, wrote about his life in practical terms, focusing on daily life and including details of Jewish life in the late nineteenth century, as well as on his work and his religious self-realization. He did not write as an historian commenting on social change, and he did not write as a philosopher espousing theological concepts. Yet his writing is imbued with a key concept from Jewish thought that permeates his consciousness throughout the autobiography. He describes it early in the narrative (ch. 2):

> From such an extraordinary autobiography, one can fathom God's wonders: how He is the Father of orphans, oversaw a forlorn child, and, in his parents' merit, guarded their beloved son, the only survivor of all of their children. From my account one can deduce the following principles: there is a God in the world,

---

63 The author's Torah scroll remains until this day at the Nakhalat Yisrael synagogue in Petakh-Tikva. Though no living member of the Goldenshteyn family had seen it in some seventy years and no member of the Nakhalat Yisrael synagogue knew of its existence, the translator successfully located it there in 2002 and arranged for it to be scanned and computer checked. The author's Torah scroll passed the inspection with excellent results. Since then, it is used regularly, since it is their only older Torah scroll that has been computer checked and the readers enjoy the relatively large size of its letters.

"God does not withhold the reward of any creature,"[64] He protects all of His creations with His divine providence, He unceasingly safeguards all who seek His protection, and those who trust in Him are never disgraced. You yourself will be convinced of all of this upon reading how this orphan endured misery and suffering and was often in danger and mortal fear, yet God constantly guarded and protected him from every evildoing and evildoer in the world. Upon reading all of this, you will certainly say, "How great are Your works, O Lord; how very profound Your thoughts."[65]

Pinye-Ber mentions the concept of divine providence (*hashgakha pratit*) not only here but throughout his autobiography. Likewise, he concludes his book with his fervent hope "that my autobiography will affect my children and grandchildren by strengthening their trust in God so that they will go on along the right path and believe in God and divine providence, as their aged father has in his life." Early readers of the autobiography appear to have noticed the prominent role in it of divine providence: Niger mentions Pinye-Ber's strong belief in this idea in the opening sentence of his review.

Divine providence forms a bedrock for Pinye-Ber's consciousness. Throughout his narrative, wherever Pinye-Ber sees divine providence he considers it a personal revelation of Godliness, a palpable encounter with God's divine presence, and proof of His existence. Pinye-Ber is making a bold and essentially unique statement for an autobiographer—in relating the instances of divine providence occurring over the course of his life he proves that God exists. He is not only encouraging trust in God but is offering a proof of His existence—specifically the existence of the one true God, Creator of the world, Redeemer of the Jews, and the source of revelation at Mt. Sinai. For Pinye-Ber, once a Jew is convinced that there is a God, all aspects of Jewish observance follow—the sanctification of *Shabes* and the Jewish Holidays, a kosher home, a daily regimen of Torah study, and so on.

From the Bible, Talmud, and midrashic texts, a view emerges of God Who, in His omniscience, guides and determines every aspect and event in a person's life. The classic early Jewish philosophers, writing from the eleventh to the fifteenth centuries, discuss divine providence. There are divergent views as to its exact nature, and a comprehensive discussion of this subject would overstep

---

64 Talmud (Pesakhim 118a).
65 Psalms 92:6.

the bounds of this introduction. Nonetheless, it can be summarized as God's knowing, engaging in, and supervising every aspect of human life. In traditional Judaism, divine providence is a benevolent providence, for God is considered to be the essence of goodness; He desires to do good and no evil emanates from Him. The belief in divine providence is by definition more specific than a general belief that God directs the world through the laws of nature, that everything is for the best, and that there is reward and punishment.[66]

Divine providence is no mere philosophical issue. Its effect on those who believe in it can be tangible. A deeply ingrained belief in divine providence enables one to live more in the moment; it allows no room for brooding about the past or being anxious about the future, for these are realms over which man has no control. For the believer in this concept, there is no serendipity, happenstance, or accidental occurrences, and nothing occurs by mistake because all is divinely orchestrated.

Naturally, Pinye-Ber particularly recognizes divine providence in his life at times of adversity, missed opportunities, and when saved from harm's way. He sees the hand of providence when he arrives in time to save his young nephew Duvid from starvation: "But divine providence had led me to come along with my sister Súre to take Duvidl" (ch. 18); when happening upon his children just in the nick of time to thwart a horrible accident: "I thanked God for sending me there at that precise moment, thereby saving them" (ch. 24); and when, during a momentary break he takes while writing his Torah scroll, a cannonball falls on the exact spot where he had been sitting: "God not only saved me then, but divine providence saved me constantly. Bombs landed near me many times, but I was not injured, God forbid" (ch. 33). When his young son Shloyme falls and injures his kidney (ch. 28), Pinye-Ber recognizes that God is the cause of the numerous factors that enable his life to be saved:

> We did not think that he would live, but when a person has years and it is destined for him to live then everything needed to save his life occurs at the right time. For example, if I would not have examined him thoroughly, I would not have known the danger of his illness. Furthermore, if we would not have found the doctor at home, a lot of time would have passed until his arrival

---

66 The term "divine providence" used here differs from its use by a number of historians who use it as one of the defining characteristics of *Haredi* (fervently Orthodox) historiography. See, for example, Karlinsky (2007) and Caplan (2005). These historians use this term merely when referring to any allusion to the influence of a higher power on the Jewish people in *Haredi* works of history.

and every minute was precious. In addition, ice [to place on the area of his kidneys] is unobtainable in Bakhchisaray, but it just happened that ice was then available.

In the face of seemingly undesirable events, a Jew who believes that even negative experiences are divinely orchestrated will not only survive them but will be uplifted by them. This is the story of Pinye-Ber; the stronger he remains in his faith under the most trying of circumstances, the sooner he realizes that it was no more than a test. As Pinye-Ber writes regarding overcoming hardships, "But, if God wills it, anything can happen, and everything falls into place when one trusts in God. And that is precisely what happened. God helped me and took care of everything" (ch. 27). As mentioned, in 1917–1918 during the First World War in Palestine, Pinye-Ber was almost killed by bullets and cannonballs flying between the battling Ottoman Turks and British forces. He survived the many illnesses, such as typhus, malaria, and cholera, which were raging at that time and killing off so many (ch. 30). His description of these experiences is prefaced with the words, "May they [my children] take a lesson from this that one must never lose faith in God. He who trusts in God is always helped. So is it with the Jewish people and with the individual as well, as it states, 'He who has faith in God will be enveloped in kindness.'"[67]

Pinye-Ber examines his own world and sees divine providence in it. By emphasizing the divine providence in his life, he practically elevates his seemingly unending series of challenges and hardships to an art form. In fact, his autobiography includes an impressive array of Yiddish words meaning "suffering," "suffer," and "endure." His strong belief in divine providence gives Pinye-Ber a sense of serenity: since everything is meant to occur precisely as it does and is being intentionally orchestrated by God, Pinye-Ber has a diminished sense of indignation and entitlement. Pinye-Ber's awareness that every aspect of God's creation is meaningful makes any and every undesirable event bearable and less disquieting. Instead of becoming enraged at his relatives' mistreatment of him as their house servant, he sees that "God had arranged it so that my unfortunate experience ... had driven me to a source of blessings," namely, it motivated him to leave to study in a yeshiva (ch. 13). His profound sense of divine providence places him in the moment; he does not try to recreate the past nor does he even attempt to relate life as it was, rather he tells it as it is.[68]

---

67 Psalms 32:10.
68 In point of fact, Pinye-Ber uses the present tense—often mixed with the past tense—in the original Yiddish. For the benefit of readability and clarity, this translator changed the verb tense for the most part to the past or the past imperfect. Other translators have dealt with

A natural consequence of Pinye-Ber's focus on the divine providence in his life is his sole concentration on his own experiences to the exclusion of all else. Since his goal is to prove God's existence from the events of his own life, it would be a distraction to provide historical background to periods of his life or to recount the background or fate of anyone else. He has no historical consciousness and is not interested in providing historical context, because his goal is solely to trace the trajectory of divine providence in his personal experiences. Rather than being viewed as egocentricity or obliviousness, the singular concentration on his own life can be viewed as a direct result of his spiritual orientation and of the lofty goal he has set for himself. Pinye-Ber has a message, and he will not be diverted from it.

Nonetheless, Pinye-Ber's belief in divine providence does not encourage a passive philosophy of sitting back and watching as God unfolds the future. Judaism requires constant and active participation in one's destiny and a sense of agency, as stated in the Mishna (Avot 1:17), with which Pinye-Ber was quite familiar: "The essential thing is not study but deed." The paradox of acceptance and proaction in Hasidic life can be seen in the act of prayer and other spiritual practices which acknowledge divine providence but also attempt to influence God's will.[69] In this respect, Pinye-Ber, although convinced that his life is an expression of God's will, does not hesitate to take the action necessary to improve his life and that of his children. An obvious example is found in his numerous endeavors to earn a living. In addition to his grueling schedule in his official position as *shoykhet* and cantor in Bakhchisaray, he had several sidelines to supplement his meager earnings. He slaughtered animals for the Muslim Crimean Tatars, he sold the tail fat of the sheep he slaughtered, he performed circumcisions, he dabbled in matchmaking, and he engraved tombstones on the mountain of Chufut-Kale for the Karaites.

In his overview of Pinye-Ber's book, the Hasidic historian Mondshine (1986:66) comments on the especially deep belief in divine providence found in his accounts of his interactions with the Lubavitcher Rebbes. Pinye-Ber personally meets with two successive Lubavitcher Rebbes; nonetheless, he thinks

---

similar issues of tense in memoirs of this kind including Assaf (2002a:85–86) and Polen (2002:xlvii–xlviii).

69 Quietism in Hasidic philosophy has been discussed in the academic literature: see Uffenheimer (1993). Pinye-Ber's life story provides insight into quietism and pro-activism as lived by a Hasidic Jew. The paradox in Hasidic life of accepting everything as God's will and trusting that everything is meant to be, while, on the other hand, being proactive and exerting energy to actively influence the course of events, is also relevant in the spiritual realm by accepting God's will and attempting to influence His will through prayer and other spiritual means, that is, seeking the intersession of a *tsadik*.

that he has failed to listen carefully enough to their words, thus implying that, had he done so, his life may have turned out better. Nonetheless, he also sees the divine providence in the actions he did perform. When meeting with the Lubavitcher Rebbe, Rabbi Menakhem-Mendl Schneerson, in 1865, the Rebbe tells him to study in a yeshiva in Shklov (ch. 15). Due to circumstances detailed in his autobiography, which he felt were his own fault, he had to leave Shklov. He believed that had he continued studying in Shklov for three years, he would have become a great scholar, as the head of the yeshiva there had anticipated. Feeling extremely dejected on his way to Romania at having lost this opportunity, he writes, "I would constantly advise myself... 'Such is the will of God, so it has to be good. And so it will be good. Don't worry. You don't need to have any heartache over this.' And no matter how bad I was feeling then, I would calm down right away."

Unable to find a position as a *shoykhet*, Pinye-Ber made the long trip to Lubavitch a second time in the winter of 1872–1873 (ch. 21). Shortly after his arrival, the Lubavitcher Rebbe, Rabbi Shmuel Schneerson, told him to return home immediately, but he could not bring himself to leave until some three days later. Before Pinye-Ber left, the Rebbe inquired as to why he had not left earlier, adding, "No matter, God will help you." He only realized why the Rebbe had told him to leave immediately when he returned home and learned that men from Petrovke had been seeking him three days earlier to offer him a position as a *shoykhet*. Nonetheless, Pinye-Ber traveled to Petrovke where he found that the position had already been filled, though he cleverly managed to obtain their new *shoykhet*'s former position in Slobodze. Sensing that life in Slobodze would be easier than in Petrovke, Pinye-Ber sees the divine providence in his delay, "how God did not abandon me." He sees the fulfillment of the Rebbe's after-the-fact blessing of "No matter, God will help you" in his successfully obtaining the position in Slobodze.

Pinye-Ber's conviction in divine providence illustrates a longstanding Jewish mindset that was soon to diminish. Haym Soloveitchik (1994:67, 70, 96) writes how Orthodox Jewish society has undergone a transformation that began at the end of the nineteenth century and continued and solidified approximately between the mid-1950s and the 1970s. Up to then, Judaism followed a dual tradition: laws and mores of life as codified in rabbinic literature, on the one hand, and life the way it was lived in actuality, generation after generation, on the other. During a period of approximately one hundred years (1870–1970), a living traditional Jewish society changed into an orthodox, text-based society. Religious conduct became a self-reflective, conscious behavior instead of being the product of social custom, as it had been.

Soloveitchik continues: "What had been lost . . . was precisely a 'culture.' A way of life is not simply a habitual manner of conduct, but also, indeed above all, a coherent one. It encompasses the web of perceptions and values that determine the way the world is assessed and the posture one assumes towards it." And Soloveitchik (1994:101–103) particularly sees a breach in experiencing divine providence:

> I think it safe to say that the perception of God as a *daily, natural* force is no longer present to a significant degree in any sector of modern Jewry, even the most religious. Indeed, I would go so far as to suggest that individual Divine Providence, though passionately believed as a theological principle—and I do not for a moment question the depth of that conviction—is no longer experienced as a simple reality. With the shrinkage of God's palpable hand in human affairs has come a marked loss of His immediate presence, with its primal fear and nurturing comfort. With this distancing, the religious world has been irrevocably separated from the spirituality of its fathers, indeed, from the religious mood of intimate anthropomorphism that had cut across all the religious divides of the Old World.

Pinye-Ber lived at the very end of a period when many Jews still experienced divine providence as a daily presence, before the development of a modern historical consciousness where God's immediate presence is no longer palpably felt among the masses of Orthodox Jewry. Pinye-Ber's autobiography provides an unusually clear depiction of one experiencing his daily life with divine providence as a simple reality. Perhaps Pinye-Ber's pronounced and distinct appreciation of divine providence in daily life is an outcome of a deeper Hasidic interpretation of divine providence, which we examine next.

Hasidism and Divine Providence

It would appear that the changes in the place that divine providence occupied in the consciousness of European Jewry, described above, can be discerned in the Jewish autobiographical genre. Even though we, unfortunately, do not have a plethora of autobiographies upon which to base our analysis, for until the late modern period Jews produced few such works, it is nevertheless telling that in the few Jewish autobiographies written before the advent of Hasidism, such as those of Rabbi Yomtov Lipman Heller (ca. 1579–1654), Ascher Levy of Reichshofen (1598–1635), and Glikl of Hameln (1646–1724), we find practically no mention of divine providence.[70] We may cautiously garner support for our contention that, prior to the times of the Baal Shem Tov, *hashgaḥah pratit* was not yet imbedded in the consciousness of the traditional Jew. Modern Jewish autobiography, a major genre of the Haskalah literature, was overwhelmingly a pursuit of secular Jews and is virtually bereft of the concept of divine providence. The same holds true for the nineteenth-century autobiographies of non-Hasidic Orthodox Jews—we find little or no references to divine providence.[71] By contrast, in the few nineteenth-century autobiographies written by Hasidim, the divine providence in their lives is emphasized.[72] A consciousness centered on divine providence constitutes a distinctive part of Hasidic experience. As Louis Jacobs (1972:7:1404) has noted,

> As a corollary of hasidic pantheism (more correctly, panentheism) is the understanding in its most extreme form of the doctrine of divine providence. The medieval thinkers limited special providence to the human species and allowed only general

---

70 Although the term *hashgakha pratit* (literally "detailed supervision") is used among Orthodox Jews to mean divine providence, Glikl (2006:394,422) uses the term *hashgakha pratiyot* twice to refer to someone supervising another person. Glikl (2006:374) only uses the term once to refer to God and only as He relates to humans—not in the sense of absolute divine providence.

71 Examples include the autobiographies of Rabbi Eliyahu David Rabinovits-Teomim (1843–1905), Rabbi Barukh Epshtein (1862–1942), and Rabbi Meir Berlin (1880–1949). The exception is the autobiography of Rabbi Bentsion Alfes (1851–1940), which frequently mentions divine providence. Rabbi Alfes was a well-known *magid* and a prolific writer of religious literature, primarily in Yiddish. He lived in Petakh-Tikva for about two years, during which the first volume of Pinye-Ber's autobiography was published (Alfes, 1940:96; "Yerushalayim," 1929). Rabbi Alfes and Pinye-Ber clearly knew each other since they both frequented Petakh-Tikva's Great Synagogue whose main sanctuary seats some 250 men (Rabbi Pinto, "Rabbi Ben Zion Alfes"; interviews with Pinye-Ber's granddaughters Aliza Bernfeld and Dvora Gavrieli in 2001). Since the translator heard from older residents of Petakh-Tikva that in the mid-1930s all the adults there knew each other, then certainly the older generation all knew each other in 1928 when Petakh-Tikva had an even smaller population of 6,500 individuals (Trofe, 1949:70). Perhaps Pinye-Ber's autobiography influenced Rabbi Alfes to frequently mention divine providence in his own autobiography.

72 Other nineteenth-century Hasidic autobiographers, besides Pinkhes-Dov Goldenshteyn, who frequently mention divine providence are as follows: Rabbi Nathan Shternharts (1780–1844) of Nemirov, the leading disciple of Rabbi Nakhman of Breslov; Shmuel Kofman (1855–1925); and Refael Vilf (ca. 1857–1929). Regarding Kofman (1955:133–134, 437), his identification as a Hasid began to wane in 1888, but he reverted to Hasidism to some extent years later in Jerusalem.

providence so far as the rest of creation is concerned. It is purely by chance that this spider catches that fly, that this ox survives, the other dies. For the Hasidim there is nothing random in a universe that is God's "garment." No stone lies where it does, no leaf falls from the tree, unless it has been so arranged by divine wisdom.

Avraham Yaakov Finkel (1994:xxii) concurs: "A chasid recognizes Hashgachah (Divine Providence) in everything that happens. Nothing occurs by chance; the most trivial incident is predetermined from Above...."

The classical Jewish philosophers maintain that God manifests His providence in two distinct ways: 1) a general divine providence through which God cares for animals, plants, and inanimate objects; and 2) a specific divine providence through which God knowingly engages in supervising every aspect of human life. These philosophers posit that *divine providence* over animals and plants is non-specific; God concerns Himself, so to speak, merely with individual species of animals and plants but not with each member of the species. God's involvement in matters relating to human beings is specific to each and every individual, or, according to some opinions, only to those leading a pious intellectual life.[73] The upshot of this philosophy is that it allows for a random element in nature, while only humankind receives individual divine care.

The interpretation of divine providence of Rabbi Israel Baal Shem Tov differs from these classical Jewish philosophers. The Baal Shem Tov (ca. 1700–1760) was a deeply spiritual leader who is said to have breathed new life into the Jewish nation and renewed Jewish fervor in the observance of Judaism. This increased fervor was the result of the Baal Shem Tov's emphasis on sincere prayer, joyous optimism, an unlimited love of all Jews, and an absolute and implicit belief in divine providence. His interpretation of divine providence, however, differs from the interpretation of the classical Jewish philosophers and is directly related to the fundamentals of Hasidism in thought and in practice. Although the Baal Shem Tov's teachings were met with strong opposition from much of the traditional Jewish world, the effects of his teachings transformed

---

73 Maimonides, in his *Guide for the Perplexed* (3:17–18), limits specific divine providence to human beings and believes that it is only extended to individuals who lead intellectual and pious lives. Gersonides, in his *Wars of the Lord* (part 4), discusses the question at length and arrives at a similar conclusion.

traditional Judaism in Eastern and Central Europe and his influence continues to be felt today.[74]

Based on his interpretation of Talmudic passages, the Baal Shem Tov extended specific divine providence to every occurrence and to all of creation; we shall refer to this interpretation as absolute divine providence.[75] One of the foremost students of the Baal Shem Tov, Rabbi Pinkhas Shapiro (1988:179) of Korets, taught that a person ought to believe that even a strand of straw lying on the ground is there by heavenly decree and even its exact orientation on the ground is by divine providence.

Louis Jacobs (2005:6), a noted theologian, writes, "Because God's presence is all-pervasive, Hasidim refuse to accept Maimonides's view that there is only divine Providence for species. . . ." According to the Baal Shem Tov, not only is the fate of each species divinely ordained, but each and every detail in all species and everything in the natural world occurs with the direct knowledge and providence of God. Every aspect of life is orchestrated by God for an immediate purpose. A strong belief in divine providence seems to be the natural result of one of the basic ideas of Hasidism, for Hasidic teachings elaborate the myriad ways in which this world is intrinsically connected to a higher spiritual realm (Gurary, 1997:93–122). Hence, a Hasid tends to see all aspects of the physical, mundane world as a reflection of a higher realm, giving any and every event meaning and purpose.[76] The Hasidic view of the purposeful nature of the world strongly impacted Pinye-Ber's sense of his own life. He is acutely aware of the Baal Shem Tov's unique interpretation of divine providence: early in his autobiography he writes that God's divine providence affects not only every particular occurrence involving man but "all of His creations" (ch. 2), which includes animals, plants, and inanimate matter.

According to Rabbi Nochum Grunwald, a noted Hasidic scholar, the Hasidic emphasis on divine providence does not emerge as much in formal exposition or theology as it does in Hasidic storytelling.[77] Storytelling is a charac-

---

74 For more about the spread of the Baal Shem Tov's expanded view of divine providence to the rest of the Jewish world, see Rotenfeld (2022).

75 The terminologies of "absolute" and "partial" divine providence are borrowed from Gross (2015:250–280). Orthodox Jews often refer to absolute divine providence as individual or specific divine providence—or simply as divine providence. Though the Baal Shem Tov did not personally write down any of his teachings, some of his disciples did. Grunwald (2009) and Leibowitz (2012:85–87) list some of the earliest printed sources citing the Baal Shem Tov's interpretation of the concept of divine providence.

76 For more on the Baal Shem Tov's expanded view of divine providence, see Rabbi M. M. Schneerson (1998) and Gurary (1997:139–157).

77 Private correspondence with Rabbi Grunwald, who is the editor-in-chief of *Heikhal ha-Besht*, an in-depth journal of Hasidic thought and scholarship.

teristic feature of Hasidim; the Baal Shem Tov himself taught that relating tales of *tsadikim* (righteous Jews) is as praiseworthy as meditating on the mysteries of the Divine Chariot which contains many deep kabalistic concepts (Carlebach, 1990:233; Kliger, 1989:309–325). In fact, miraculous stories regarding the Baal Shem Tov were being told by his disciples shortly after his death, if not beforehand. One such account appears in the story of the Baal Shem Tov, which Pinye-Ber relates in his autobiography (ch. 29). The tale begins with the Baal Shem Tov, shortly before his death, instructing a close disciple to support himself by means of relating stories of the Baal Shem Tov. This disciple later heard that there was a man of means in another country who paid handsomely for each story he was told about the Baal Shem Tov.

Although Hasidic stories often have a miraculous element to them, their underlying motif is that God controls the world in all its detail. Stories of divine providence remind the believer that the particulars of life are orchestrated from on High and serve to strengthen a person's faith and religious resolve. As Rabbi Menachem M. Schneerson (1902–1994), the future Lubavitcher Rebbe, wrote in 1932, "[Hasidic stories] elevate the soul and create a desire to rise, if even slightly, above the mundane. These stories have the power to transform even the simplest of souls and elevate individuals who are in a state of spiritual decline" (Schneerson, 1994:11).

Significantly, when Pinye-Ber wishes to explain the concept of divine providence to another, he does so by telling a story (ch. 29). The centrality of this story—which is about Rabbi Israel Baal Shem Tov—to Pinye-Ber's consciousness seems obvious as it is the only diversion of any length from the story of his life.[78] Indeed, in his very telling of this story Pinye-Ber experiences divine providence. Pinye-Ber goes to introduce himself to a wealthy former apostate named Kizilshteyn who chases Pinye-Ber out of his house. At a later date, Pinye-Ber returns, convinces him to sit and talk, and explains how he bears no animosity towards him for being ill-treated: "We know that no one is in complete control of himself and everything is caused by divine providence. That's how it was destined to be, and you're not to blame. It had to be that way." Pinye-Ber then tells him a lengthy story of divine providence regarding a Jew who had apostatized to Christianity, eventually becoming a cardinal, whom Rabbi Israel Baal Shem Tov succeeds in returning to Judaism. Pinye-Ber relates that the cardinal's initial motivation to return to Judaism came from a dream-like vision in which his departed grandfather and the Baal Shem Tov urged him to return. Suddenly,

---

78 Of interest is that the Hasidic discourse that Pinye-Ber heard in 1865 from the Lubavitcher Rebbe, Rabbi Menakhem-Mendl Schneerson (1994:2:721–725), in fact mentions divine providence several times, a concept not often mentioned in such discourses (ch. 16).

Kizilshteyn interjects that he also began to return to Judaism through a dream. The divine providence of telling a story so similar to Kizilshteyn's own experience was not lost on either of them, and Pinye-Ber was able to form a deep friendship with Kizilshteyn and influence his complete return to Judaism.

Despite the fact that Pinye-Ber, after moving to the Crimea in 1879, does not provide details of Hasidic life or tell Hasidic stories (aside from the one described above), we know that he considered himself a Hasidic Jew his entire life.[79] The Hasidic concept of divine providence played a crucial role in the way he understood the problems he faced. For example, an extension of the Baal Shem Tov's view of divine providence is his teaching that one ought to learn from every occurrence that he or she encounters (Schochet, 2004:394–397). Self-examination becomes the reaction to life's events, and mundane actions become permeated with significance. Pinye-Ber practiced such introspection. For example, in his lengthy description of his harrowing and unsuccessful trip to borrow funds from a supposedly wealthy uncle, he concludes that one must put one's trust only in God and not in men (ch. 26). In other words, he concluded that his trip had failed because he had placed too much hope in his uncle instead of in God. For Pinye-Ber, life is filled with divine messages; God is constantly guiding mankind, sometimes through revealed positive experiences and other times through seemingly negative ones.

As a Hasidic Jew, Pinye-Ber strives to serve God with joy, which is a cardinal principle taught by the Baal Shem Tov, and this seems to be a natural consequence of his divine-providence-centered consciousness. Regarding the belief in divine providence, the Lubavitcher Rebbe, Rabbi Menachem Mendel Schneerson (1998:451), writes, "[W]hen one reflects on the reality of God's constant watchfulness and care, there is no room for anxiety at all. Afterwards, one can proceed to serve Him with joy and gladness of heart." Pinye-Ber remarkably experiences a seemingly unending series of tribulations throughout his long life; nonetheless, his indomitable spirit and joyous determination to press onwards shine forth. Being conscious of the divine providence in his life serves to remind Pinye-Ber that behind all adversity and challenge lies divine purpose, a concept that enables him to transcend the hardships of this physical world and serve God with joy. Despite his complaints, he is a cheerful person,

---

79 Private interview in 2001 with Pinye-Ber's granddaughter Aliza Bernfeld. The main reason for his not mentioning Hasidism, particularly after 1879, is because that year he moved away from Hasidic environs (first to the Crimea and then in 1913 to Petakh-Tikva, which was primarily populated by non-Hasidic Jews) where there had been much internal Hasidic strife regarding the Hasidic orientation of the *shoykhet* (see below for more regarding this topic). Hence, from that point forward, Hasidism was no longer a source of strife for him and was therefore not noteworthy in recounting the divine providence in his life.

a happy complainer, who skillfully relates his troubles and engages his reading audience. Pinye-Ber certainly is aware that "Happiness writes in white ink on a white page";[80] extended descriptions of happiness are vapid and boring.[81]

In his tale of woe, the extent of the joy he felt might elude the inattentive reader, but it is clear from oral accounts of those who knew him. When he would visit his children and grandchildren in Feodosiya in the early 1900s, his grandson Victor Brockman (1904–1985) would bring home his friends to listen to Pinye-Ber, who would sing and tell captivating stories; these occasions were some of the highlights of Victor's life in Feodosiya.[82] Another such encounter occurred while Pinye-Ber, along with 1,500 other Jews, was exiled for half a year in 1917–1918 by the Ottoman Turks from his home in Petakh-Tikva to shacks in Kfar-Saba, which were on the front line between the fighting Ottoman and British forces (ch. 32). Amid the cold, hunger, suffering, and death from typhus, malaria, and cholera, Pinye-Ber raised the spirits of the children during those trying times by gathering them together to sing and play.[83] For his grandchildren in Petakh-Tikva and abroad, he used to whittle *dreydlekh*, dice, and walking sticks with whimsical animal heads as their handles. His granddaughters Aliza and Dvora remembered him in Petakh-Tikva as a happy person who enjoyed laughing and laughed easily. All their friends would come over to their house where their grandfather would play with them in the yard. He loved children very much, and his pocket was always filled with candies; a child approaching him for a piece of candy was first caught and stroked on the cheek or given a pat on the head. The local children believed him to be the prophet Elijah. He was highly regarded in Petakh-Tikva, so much so that upon his death children came over to Aliza to tell her that their teacher had announced that one of the thirty-six hidden *tsadikim* on whose merit the world exists had died and that his name

---

80 This literary maxim was coined by the French novelist Henry de Montherlant.
81 Though easy to overlook, Pinye-Ber experienced tranquil, happy periods in his life, for example, when he studied in the yeshivas in Odessa and Shklov. The reader of Pinye-Ber's autobiography, which is so filled with one episode after another of trials and tribulations, might be surprised to read his brief statement regarding his three-year position as a *shoykhet* in Buzinove in the late 1870s: "I never heard a harsh word from the Jews there. On the contrary, they liked me and appreciated me—and I felt the same toward them. It was difficult for me to part from them because I was fond of them. The only problem was that I did not earn much there, which was not their fault since they paid according to their means" (ch. 23).
82 As related by Cynthia Unterberg, as heard from her father Victor Brockman (originally Brakhtman).
83 In a 2001 private interview with Pinye-Ber's granddaughter Aliza (Goldenshteyn) Bernfeld of Petakh-Tikva, she related that she heard this from a number of people who had been in exile as children in Kfar-Saba with her grandfather.

was Goldenshteyn.[84] Aliza remembered never having seen seeing a larger crowd at any funeral she attended.[85]

In his autobiography, it is clear that Pinye-Ber's joyousness is his conscious choice. He describes at times his concerted efforts to serve God joyously, such as in the following section (ch. 19): "[My wife] knew my situation and was aware of the hunger I endured. Even when others heard me singing joyously, she knew that I was just singing to bring myself some relief. Only by exerting myself to be joyous was I able to cast away the horrible worry from my heart." And at the end of that same chapter, he writes, "I lived solely on hope and accepted everything with love, so when things were the worst they could possibly be I sang a lot and made myself happy. Outsiders thought that I had it good and that I sang out of contentment. Those who knew my bitter situation and saw me in such a happy mood very likely considered me to be out of my mind or an irresponsible husband whose family did not concern him." The latter excerpt shows that Pinye-Ber's efforts to remain joyous are connected with accepting suffering and hardship with love, a Talmudic concept (Brakhot 101a) that he mentions a number of times.

I have found only one other nineteenth-century Jewish autobiographer who writes about his efforts to be joyous, namely Rabbi Nathan Shternharts (2009:1:115, 2:70), the leading disciple of Rabbi Nakhman of Breslov. The verse "Serve God with joy" (Psalms 101:2) is widely known to be a fundamental element of the Hasidic way of life, as emphasized by the Baal Shem Tov and his disciples. Rabbi Shneur Zalman of Lyadi, the founder of the Chabad philosophy of Hasidism (more regarding this below), devotes an entire chapter (ch. 26) in the *Tanya* to joy and considers it an essential element in the spiritual battle each person wages between his evil and good inclinations. Regarding the effort to be joyous and cleanse one's heart of all sadness and worry about mundane matters, Rabbi Shneur Zalman advises accepting misfortune with joy, since misfortune emanates from a "hidden spiritual world," which is higher than this "revealed" physical world. This advice on being joyous involves keeping in mind that seemingly negative events or conditions are part of an incomprehensible, spiritual plan; in other words, they occur by divine providence.

Another Hasidic concept is the significance of each and every Jew, no matter how unlearned or seemingly unconnected to Judaism he or she may be.

---

84   The concept of the thirty-six hidden *tsadikim* is mentioned in the Talmud (Sanhedrin 97b; Sukah 45b).
85   This account of Pinye-Ber's attitude toward children comes from private interviews in 2001 with Aliza (Goldenshteyn) Bernfeld of Petakh-Tikva and her sister Dvora (Goldenshteyn) Gavrieli of Givat Khayim.

There are numerous stories detailing the Baal Shem Tov's efforts to help the simplest, poorest, most unlettered Jews both physically and spiritually. In contrast, Adler (1951:602) writes in his article describing the non-Hasidic Jews of Lithuania that this deep regard for every individual Jew found in Hasidism is completely foreign to Lithuanian Jews, who reserve their respect and appreciation for Talmudic scholars alone. And this Hasidic concept is a direct result of a strong belief in divine providence: since every leaf matters, then certainly every single person has a divine mission to fulfill. Hasidic teachings are focused on spiritual purpose; everything operates according to a plan beyond what the eye sees. According to limited, human perspective, the rabbi is doing much more for the community than the shoemaker. But when one looks at the world from a spiritual perspective, recalling that everything was created with a purpose, then the shoemaker's life might have as great a purpose as the rabbi's. Not only the elite serve a purpose, but everyone in his or her own way has meaning.

Pinye-Ber's autobiography shows his strong belief in this Hasidic concept of the importance of every Jew. This is apparent in his great efforts to arrange the purchase and building of a new *mikveh* for the Jewish community of Bakhchisaray right before leaving Tsarist Russia. He did not consider this community, which included its fair share of corrupt and coarse individuals, to be beyond redemption. After his wedding, he did not despair of his wife Freyde upon discovering that she was lacking communication skills and any sophistication. But after much effort on his part, her character developed to the point that others wondered how a *shoykhet* like Pinye-Ber had managed to marry such a sophisticated and intelligent woman (ch. 18). He did not consider it too late for himself to write a Torah scroll despite cannonballs flying overhead during the First World War (ch. 32). Pinye-Ber also did not consider it too far-gone for the elderly Kizilshteyn, as we have seen, to fully return to Judaism after decades of living as an apostate (ch. 29). Just like in the Hasidic story that Pinye-Ber told Kizilshteyn, where the Baal Shem Tov did not consider it too late to assist a hateful Jewish bishop to return to the faith of his forefathers, it was certainly not too late for Pinye-Ber to attempt to influence his children to strengthen their Jewish observance by means of writing an autobiography.

A Life Seen as God's Will

Pinye-Ber thus steered his life according to the Hasidic precepts of self-introspection, joyous service to God, and a conviction in the value of every Jew. He did so because, according to his account, he had absolute faith in the Hasidic doctrine that God has charge of every nuance of existence. Pinye-Ber relied on the reality of divine providence to describe two difficult aspects of his story, his orphanhood and his conflict with his enemies.

After describing his family background, Pinye-Ber introduces the story of his own life with the words, "This autobiography of an orphan shows God's wonders, how He directs the world, and how He is truly a Father of orphans" (ch. 4). Moseley (2006:458–461) points to the prominence of orphanhood, or more exactly the bereavement of a parent, in Jewish autobiographies.[86] He notes the remarkably larger ratio of this occurrence among Jewish autobiographers in comparison with their non-Jewish counterparts and "the centrality that the theme assumes in this literature." Pinye-Ber was bereaved of both parents, by his mother at age five and his father at age seven. In desperately pleading with the administrators of the yeshiva in Odessa for poor children to be allowed admittance, he poignantly describes the pain he felt at being an orphan (ch. 12):

> I responded, imploring and sobbing . . . "I won't leave here, even if it means my death, until you admit me to the yeshiva. I don't have anywhere to spend the night, nor do I have a kopek to my name with which to buy a bit of bread. Don't you see how lost I am and how poor and alone I am? Don't you see that I'm orphaned?!" My last words apparently touched their hearts, and I saw them wiping their eyes.

His deeply felt loss of both parents motivated Pinye-Ber to mention orphanhood in the title of his autobiography, the only purely autobiographical work written by a nineteenth-century Jewish author to do so.[87] In fact, he still refers to himself as "the misfortunate orphan" when he was a twenty-four-year-old father (ch. 22).[88]

---

86   Unlike in English, the word "orphan" in both Yiddish and Hebrew can indicate a child who has lost only one parent.

87   The title of the original Yiddish version is *Mayn lebens-geshikhte: Farshidenartige pasirung'n un epizod'n fun a yosem* (My life story: Various events and episodes of an orphan). The subtitle of Peretz Smolenskin's famous work *Ha-Toeh be-darkhe ha-khayim* (1876) is *Toldot Yosef ha-yatom me-ir madmenah* (The history of Yosef the orphan . . .), yet it is not a regular autobiography but rather a novella based on his life.

88   Yudl Mark (1943:33) suggests a reason for Pinye-Ber's writing his autobiography: "Only with great difficulty was the author able to find a means of earning a living, and thus is he permeated with a certain pride in what he succeeded in doing in his life's journey. And it can be that this very feeling pushed the *shoykhet* of Bakhchisaray to become a writer of his memoirs." Yet Mark fails to mention that much of his "great difficulty" was a result of the tremendous hardships associated with being orphaned. Though Mark posits that

Writing about the typical maskilic autobiographer, Moseley (2006:459) comments, "The existential predicament of loss of faith translates well in to the image of the fatherless children. . . ." Sholem Aleykhem has the eight-year-old protagonist of his Yiddish novel *Motl-Peyse dem khazns: Ksovim fun a yingl a yosem* (Motl, Peyse the Cantor's Son: The Writings of an Orphan Boy) proclaim, "*Mir is gut—ikh bin a yosem*" ("I'm doing fine—I'm an orphan").[89] This is a declaration of freedom, since after his father's death he is the subject of much sympathy and forbearance and is free from his father's discipline. Sholem Aleykhem even uses this line as the title of the second chapter. Miron (2000:231–232) explains this oft-quoted, oxymoronic phrase as an expression of Motl's newfound freedom from Jewishness and Jewish law, which had died for him with his father's death. For Pinye-Ber, by contrast, orphanhood is not a reason to lose faith and abandon tradition, but rather shows the workings of divine providence in his life all the more clearly: "You yourself will be convinced of all of this upon reading how this orphan endured misery and suffering and was often in danger and mortal fear, yet God constantly guarded and protected him from every evildoing and evildoer in the world" (ch. 2). Pinye-Ber uses the original biblical Hebrew phrase "Father of orphans" (Psalms 68:6) several times, which itself indicates God's providence over the most vulnerable and helpless.

Pinye-Ber takes a similar attitude regarding his various enemies, imagining their sufferings in terms of divine providence. Modern readers might take umbrage at the approving tone with which he describes the vengeance (in his view) that God took on his enemies. Yet Pinye-Ber's attitude offers insight into the consciousness of nineteenth-century Hasidic Jews who lived with a profound sense of absolute divine providence.

In general, Pinye-Ber uses the word "enemy" to refer to those who made concerted efforts to deprive him of all or part of his source of livelihood, harass him, or otherwise embitter his life. Pinye-Ber is not referring to petty adversaries in synagogue squabbles from whom he could simply walk away. Corrupt local community leaders in cahoots with community members, due to their greed for money and power, tormented Pinye-Ber and tried to have him driven out of town and even expelled from the country. At that time, being expelled from Russia to Romania cost many Jews their lives (Errera, 1894:38–41).

Pinye-Ber's motivation for writing his autobiography was out of pride and Niger (see p. 66) suggests that he devotes a chapter to the bitter fates of his enemies out of egoism, I disagree and suggest that Pinye-Ber's motivation for both was to impart his message of divine providence to his progeny, as will be discussed.

89 Sholem Aleykhem was the pen name of one of the founders of modern Yiddish literature Sholem Rabinovitz (1859–1916). *Motl Peysi dem khazns* was first published in serialized form in 1907.

Unfortunately, his position as a *shoykhet* pitted him against the desires of corrupt community leaders regarding control of the kosher-meat tax, thereby placing him at the center of *shtetl* politics. As Berman (1941:73–74) writes, whenever a Jewish community "was rent asunder by factional strife, the probability was strong that the controversy would involve the management of Shehitah [kosher slaughtering] ... Intra-communal strife involving Shehitah affairs was common in Eastern Europe during the eighteenth and nineteenth centuries." And the combination of Pinye-Ber's integrity and unwillingness to back down from a fight only served to aggravate these situations.

Regarding his enemies, Pinye-Ber writes in his "In Lieu of a Preface," "I also want those who plagued and tormented me and are currently in Russia to read this in order to learn the moral lesson that there is a God in the world who protects the harassed and oppressed and repays every one according to his deeds."[90] In subsequent chapters, he writes that he will eventually devote a separate chapter to the bitter fates exacted by God upon his enemies, and comments in chapter 24, "That separate chapter will teach you the lesson that everything is repaid. God waits long and pays well. Nothing is overlooked. At times, He delays that payment because He is waiting for repentance—perhaps the person will regret his actions and repent."[91]

It is human nature to want to take revenge on one's enemies. In popular culture, vengeance is ubiquitous and even celebrated. Nonetheless, the Bible (Leviticus 19:18) strictly forbids a Jew from doing so, "You shall neither take revenge from nor bear a grudge against the members of your people; you shall love your neighbor as yourself." In fact, Pinye-Ber not only never exacts revenge on his tormentors, he even expresses his compassion for those who treated him cruelly and attempts to help them. Though his wife's wealthy Uncle Yankev refuses to lend him anything beyond one ruble, Pinye-Ber goes out of his way to help him obtain a release for his son from conscription into the Russian army: "Anyone else in my position would have immediately pointed out his past injustices—and cursed him out as well. But being that I like to do everything rationally, I saw that refusing to do his son a favor would not be proper" (ch. 26). When being persecuted by a wealthy community leader in a town where he served as *shoykhet*, Pinye-Ber did him many favors without his

---

90 Alas, copies of Pinye-Ber's autobiography never reached the Soviet Union. His son Yosef of California attempted to send some copies to the Soviet Union, but they were confiscated by the authorities, as indicated in a private letter from Pinye-Ber to his daughter Nekhame dated 26 *Sivan* 5690 (June 22, 1930).

91 Nonetheless, Pinye-Ber did not end up writing a separate chapter regarding the fate of all his enemies, but only devotes a part of chapter 34 to just those in Bakhchisaray, omitting his earlier enemies, particularly those in Slobodze.

knowledge (ch. 22). After another influential community leader stopped persecuting him and had become impoverished, Pinye-Ber hired him as his son's *melamed* and made a point of paying him well (ch. 24). In Bakhchisaray, a drunken community member tried to wrestle Pinye-Ber away from the lectern in the synagogue, but after the police commissioner heard about it, Pinye-Ber said that he forgave him and did not want to press charges (ch. 26). Not only did Pinye-Ber never pray for misfortune to befall his enemies, he even wished for them to undergo a change of heart, as he writes regarding his enemies, "If God wanted to, He could turn those who hated me for no reason into friends," which is exactly what later transpired (ch. 22). Pinye-Ber also forgives his enemies upon their expressing regret for their cruelties towards him in the past, as he writes regarding one of his nemeses, "According to what I was told, before he died he expressed his remorse and repented for having caused me pain. If it is true, I forgive him" (ch. 29).

Pinye-Ber's outlook on his enemies and revenge can best be understood by examining the traditional Jewish perspective in the mishnaic tractate of Avot, which is studied by Orthodox Jews during the summer months. Upon seeing a skull floating on top of the water, the great Jewish sage Hillel, who lived during the first century BCE, famously taught (Avot 2:6), "Because you drowned others, you will be drowned." In other words, the world is not lawless. A day of reckoning and renumeration will come from on High for evil deeds. The elements in the Hebrew Bible about God's revenge, including prayers in Psalms for God to take revenge on enemies, are often misunderstood. Jewish belief in God's vengeance, as viewed by traditional Jews, is closely connected to human non-violence, the rationale being that people's attempts to remedy injustice usually brings about more violence. This concept is expressed in a well-known traditional story about a rabbi who was once asked by a European monarch, "Why is the Old Testament filled with descriptions of God as being jealous (Exodus 32.13), as a God of war (Exodus 15:30), a God of vengeance (Jeremiah 51:6), and so forth, while God's character in the New Testament is depicted in terms of love?" The rabbi explained, "In our tradition, when it comes to hate, war, vengeance, and revenge, those are God's responsibility, while ours is to love, embrace, and respect. You say that God is love, so therefore all the hating, murdering, killing and abuse is left to man."

Thus, traditional Jews believe that, since man does not know his fellow man's intentions, he cannot judge him. And, since the believer trusts that the all-knowing God knows everyone's intentions, he refrains from violence against his perceived enemies and leaves it in God's hands to avenge injustice and punish the wicked. When the believer sees that God holds evildoers accountable and responsible for their wicked deeds and that justice is carried out, his faith that God controls the world is strengthened. Hence, Pinye-Ber finds comfort in seeing the bitter fates of those who harmed him for it indicates to him that there is justice in this world and that bad people get their due. This also reinforces his belief that every aspect of the world is under God's watchful eye. It is likely, in fact, that Pinye-Ber's enumeration of his tormentors' bitter fates actually stems from his conviction in divine providence. Of the three arguments for divine providence listed by the classical Jewish philosopher Gersonides (1288–1344), two of them involve the punishment of evildoers (Bleich, 1973:35).[92]

Pinye-Ber focuses on the workings of divine providence in his own life, which means, naturally, that he spends much of the narrative talking about himself. If we underestimate how seriously he took divine providence, we might be tempted to see his self-focus as a sign of egoism and his complaints about his enemies as a persecution complex. In fact, this is how Niger understood it: "Being an orphan serves him well in awakening sympathy for himself and also justifies his seeking vengeance on his enemies. (The egotist constantly thinks that he is being persecuted, that others want to harm him, and that he has an unlimited number of enemies.)" Of course, it was difficult for Niger to know with any degree of certainty whether his analysis of Pinye-Ber's personality was correct and that Pinye-Ber's enemies were not real but the workings of an egotistical psyche. But more significantly, research has unearthed an archival document confirming that Pinye-Ber was indeed unjustly beleaguered by enemies, namely an incriminating letter dated November 1879 from the renowned Rabbi Khayim Khizkiyahu Medini to the leaders of the community of Bakhchisaray in which he reproaches their efforts to oust Pinye-Ber, "a man with whom no fault can be found."[93] Rather than egoism, then, it makes more sense to see Pinye-Ber's emphasis on divine reward and punishment vis-á-vis his enemies as a manifestation of the overall theme of divine providence that informs his book.

---

92   As a classical Jewish philosopher, Gersonides proceeds to rebut these arguments.
93   The original Hebrew letter is found in the Klau Library—Hebrew Union College-Jewish Institute of Religion in Cincinnati, Ohio (Acc 477, 12v–13r). A translation can be found in Appendix C1. A transcription of the original was printed, with a few minor transcription errors, in the published collection of Rabbi Medini's letters, *Igrot Sdei Khemed* (2006:1:11). Pinye-Ber apparently gave the letter to his son Refuel, and either Refuel (1885–1933), a graduate of Hebrew Union College, or his widow Claire (1910–1994) donated it to the Klau Library along with two certifications in sh'khita (kosher slaughtering) that Refuel received in Tsarist Russia (see Appendix C2 for translations). Pinye-Ber does not mention this letter in his autobiography, though he does mention an even more incriminating letter, which Rabbi Medini wrote to the leaders of the Jewish community of Bakhchisaray on his behalf in February 1880 (ch. 24).

Dates in the Autobiography

Though much relevance is attached these days to exact dates and documentation, particularly with the advent of computers, it was not that way in the not-so-distant past. Traditionally, Eastern European Jews did not place much importance on their dates of birth, and it was not the practice to include ages or birth years on tombstones.[94] Researchers who make regular use of historical censuses and census-type records are aware that as people grew older, the tendency to overstate their ages increased. In the 1980s, in speaking with an elderly relative who had two great-grandfathers who were said to have lived to the age of 110, I asked her about the veracity of this claim. She replied, "Well, they didn't count years then like we do," which is an intriguing explanation of this phenomenon. I later located the 1885 death record of one of these great-grandfathers, which states his age as 92; and according to his entry in an 1858 revision list (poll-tax census), which seems to be the most reliable document, he would have been 78 at the time of his death. And that is the general rule in this aspect of historical research: the ages stated on the earliest documents in an individual's life tend to be the most accurate.

This pattern of error tends to afflict Pinye-Ber's dating of events in his life. Although he appears to have written the chapters of his autobiography sequentially,[95] his account of his own age varies from chapter to chapter. At the beginning of his autobiography, he writes that he was born in 1842,[96] yet a close examination of chapters 15 to 18 makes it abundantly clear that he was actually

---

94 In many Orthodox Jewish circles, it is still not the practice to note ages or years of birth on tombstones.
95 In chapter 23, he writes that it is currently *Rosh-Khoydesh Tamuz* 5669 (June 19–20, 1909). Chapter 28 contains two indications that it was written in 1913. (A slight exception appears at the beginning of chapter 29 where he writes that he is now living in Petach-Tikva, where he moved at the end of 1913. Yet later in chapter 29 there appears his long-planned section about his enemies, which he evidently wrote earlier that same year back in Bakhchisaray.) The beginning of chapter 32 is dated *Adar* 5678 (February 1918). In chapter 34, there are sequential sections dated *Heshvan* 5680 (early 1919), *Iyar* 5685 (April 1925), and *Iyar* 5689 (May–June 1929).
96 In his "In Lieu of a Preface" and at the beginning of chapter 18, Pinye-Ber notes that he was born shortly after *Sukes* of the Hebrew year 5603, which corresponds to September-October 1842. He also notes in ch. 2 that he was five when his mother died in *Adar* 5608 (March–April 1848), implying that he was born in 1842. Using this mistaken year of birth, he then calculates the years of his father's death (ch. 2), his brother Isruel's death (ch. 2), and his marriage (ch. 18). Yet, even by using his mistaken year of birth of 1842, he miscalculated the year of his brother's death, which he writes occurred a year and five months after his father's, to be 5612 (1852) instead of 5611 (1851).

born in 1848.⁹⁷ In examining various documents along with his autobiography, a similar pattern of age inflation over the years can be discerned in the autobiography and in documents pertaining to Pinye-Ber, of which only a sample are listed below.

- Pinye-Ber's July 1897 marriage record in Odessa states that he was sixty-one, that is, born approximately in 1836, which makes him twelve years older than his actual age. In his autobiography, he writes that in 1884 he filed a delayed birth record that made him out to be ten years older than he actually was (ch. 25). By deducting the ten years from the twelve, one can conclude that in 1897 Pinye-Ber was under the mistaken impression that he was born in 1846, two years before his actual year of birth (ch. 25).
- By the time Pinye-Ber began writing his autobiography in the early 1900s, he thought that he was born in 1842 (see p. 67, footnote 96), which was six years before his actual year of birth.
- On the back of a photograph of himself dated *Shvat* 5687 (January–February 1927) sent to his daughter Nekhame in Brooklyn, Pinye-Ber notes that he was eighty-six years old, that is, born approximately in 1840, some eight years before his actual year of birth.

Although, as noted, this tendency toward date miscalculation increased as one aged, it is rarely encountered in nineteenth century Jewish autobiographies. Perhaps the paucity of such errors is due to the fact that most Jewish autobiographies in this period were written by *maskilim* modeling themselves on the educated classes of non-Jewish society, which relied on documentation. Pinye-Ber's errors in calculating his age are actually an indication of the authenticity of his autobiography, for unlike maskilic autobiographies, which tend to include dates and descriptions of events from outside sources, Pinye-Ber relies on his memory alone, a memory that is in general quite reliable. On the other hand,

---

97   Pinye-Ber's age is actually a central aspect of several chapters. During an audience with the Lubavitcher Rebbe, Rabbi Menakhem-Mendl Schneerson (1789–1866), the Rebbe tells him not to marry before the age of twenty (ch. 15). A year and four months afterwards, Pinye-Ber wonders if the Rebbe had meant for him to wait to marry until after beginning his twentieth year (that is, turning nineteen) or until after turning twenty. As the Lubavitcher Rebbe had since passed away, he seeks out three different Rebbes to whom to ask this question, and all replied that he should only wait to marry until he begins his twentieth year (that is, turns nineteen). Immediately after turning nineteen in October, he marries and then mentions the secular date of January 1, 1868 as occurring a couple of months afterward (ch. 18) and a bit later mentions the Hebrew date of *Iyar* 5628 (April 1868). Hence, he was clearly born in October 1848.

a writer who confirms his memory with outside sources might be influenced by those sources; hence, the authenticity of his own recollections would be diminished.

Even though Pinye-Ber rarely identifies the correct year of any given event, he is very precise in relating the sequence of the events in his life from one Jewish holiday to the next, from one season to the next, while noting the number of months he stayed in any given place or the number of months that had elapsed since the last incident. Obviously, a lack of historical consciousness in no way indicates that he does not have a sense of chronology. Remarkably, he always provides just enough detail to enable the dating of nearly every event, without any gaps, during the first thirty-one years of his life.[98] In dating the events in those thirty-one years, outside sources attest to the exceptional accuracy of his chronology, which supports the contention that the information that he mentions incidentally is exceptionally accurate.[99]

Occasionally, the proper dating of the events in Pinye-Ber's autobiography revealed interesting aspects of daily life. For example, Pinye-Ber writes, "I had already become a bar mitzvah; I had begun putting on *tefillin* [phylacteries] during the first winter after my arrival there [in Tashlik]" (ch. 10). Through dating the events in Pinye-Ber's autobiography, it can be determined that he is referring to the winter of 1860–1861, which was shortly after his twelfth birthday. It was once a widespread custom that a child bereaved of one or both of his parents began to don *tefillin* during the morning prayers at the age of twelve instead of at the customary age of thirteen in order to provide merit for his deceased parent (Rabbi Gavriel Zinner, 2002:226–229). In their autobiographies, Milch (1946:123) and Bonchek (1955:107) explicitly mention that, since they had been bereaved of one of their parents, they began to don *tefillin* at

---

98 Pinye-Ber's ability to precisely chronicle the events in his life was undoubtedly helped by his constantly moving from place to place, which provided him with numerous milestones. Naturally, he no longer tracks his life in chronological order to the same extent once settling in Bakhchisaray in the Crimea in 1879, where he remained for the next thirty-four years.

99 Using Pinye-Ber's correct birth year of 1848, his chronology of the following events in his life, among others, can be corroborated using outside sources. 1) The death of his brother-in-law Ershl Teplitsky in 1854 in Tiraspol is corroborated by his date of death listed in the Supplement to the 1858 revision list (poll-tax census) of Tiraspol (ch. 2). 2) Though the cantonist legislation was legally stopped in 1856, the author's account dates its actual end to 1859 (ch. 6), which is corroborated by Petrovsky-Shtern (2010). 3) Pinye-Ber notes the death of Rabbi Hillel Malisov ("Hilke Paritsher") as taking place in August 1864, which corresponds to the date in published sources (ch. 13). 4) He recalls the coronation of Karl as Prince of Romania in April 1866, which corresponds to the date in published sources (ch. 17). 5) Finally, he recalls Rabbi Borukh-Sholem Schneerson's visit to Iassy in late 1866 (ch. 17), which corresponds to the date of this event given in Heilman (1903:3:24).

the age of twelve, which they also refer to as their *bar mitzvah*. Though it is clear from the Mishna (Avot 5:21) that a Jewish male becomes a *bar mitzvah* (obligated in fulfilling the *mitzvahs*—commandments—of the Torah) at age thirteen, Pinye-Ber and the other two autobiographers are only informally referring to their early start in donning *tefillin* as their *bar mitzvah*, since that is the primary new daily obligation incumbent upon a Jewish boy at his *bar mitzvah*.

Pinye-Ber's dating errors have caused historians and scholars who cite his work to err in attempting to date various episodes in his life. Who would imagine that not a single year in his autobiography can be assumed to be correct and that an accurate dating of any event in his autobiography would necessitate a thorough analysis of the chronology of most of his book?[100] The following is a list of such errors incurred by historians in attempting to date Pinye-Ber's encounters with well-known rabbinical figures.[101]

- Pinye-Ber mentions meeting Rabbi Borukh-Sholem Schneerson in late 1866 during his visit to Iassy, Romania (ch. 17), a visit that is also mentioned by Heilman (1903:3:24). Based on their miscalculations of the author's year of birth, Bloy (2020:65) and Luria (2006:48) erroneously conclude that Pinye-Ber was referring to an earlier trip made by Rabbi Borukh-Sholem Schneerson to Romania; Bloy gives the year as 1862 and Luria as 1861, at the latest.
- Pinye-Ber describes his visit to the Lubavitcher Rebbe, Rabbi Shmuel Schneerson, in January 1873 (ch. 21), which Mondshine (1986: 64–65) mistakenly dates as December 1871. Mondshine calculates this date based on the last year mentioned by the author at the beginning of chapter 20, namely *Tamuz* 5631 (July 1871), which is clearly an error, as explained in my footnote there, and should state *Tamuz* 5632 (July 1872).
- Based on Mondshine's miscalculated date of December 1871 as Pinye-Ber's date of arrival in Lubavitch, the Hasidic discourse that Pinye-Ber heard from the Lubavitcher Rebbe was incorrectly identified by the editors of the two volumes of the Hasidic discourses that Rabbi Shmuel Schneerson (2003:218–219) recited in honor of weddings.[102]

---

100 The translator spent dozens of hours attempting to accurately date each and every event mentioned in the autobiography. The results have been noted in the footnotes to the text.
101 Assaf (2012:410) credits this translator for his assistance in determining the correct dates of Pinye-Ber's encounters with the Lyever Rebbe in chapters 17 and 18.
102 Since Pinye-Ber was evidently in Lubavitch on *Shabes*, January 18, 1873 (19 *Teyves*, 5633), he, in fact, heard the Lubavitcher Rebbe, Rabbi Shmuel Schneerson, recite the Hasidic discourse based on the verse in Songs of Songs (5:1), "I have come into my garden, my

Pinye-Ber's Language

Much of Pinye-Ber's unpolished writing style is not apparent in this translation, which has striven for clear and natural-sounding English. His writing is so vague in places that the translator was compelled to read some passages dozens of times to arrive at his intended meaning. Though the original Yiddish work reads naturally, it comes across as being from a bygone era, which is likely due to a combination of his vocabulary, expressions, and writing style, which is not the case in regard to Yiddish autobiographies written by modernized *maskilim* of that same era.

Yet the unpolished nature of Pinye-Ber's prose is part of the autobiography's linguistic importance. In his eleven-page linguistic analysis of Pinye-Ber's autobiography in the journal *Yidishe Shprakh*, Yudl Mark (1943:34, 42) describes Pinye-Ber's autobiography as having significance from the standpoint of language research, though his Yiddish is quite unsophisticated and never transcends literary primitive.[103] After providing an overview of Pinye-Ber's life, Mark reproduces sample paragraphs of his writing style followed by examples of his wry and humorous comments. Mark then cites numerous examples of Pinye-Ber's language, including lists of his phraseology and word usage rarely encountered nowadays; idioms and folksy figures of speech; different types of his grammatical constructs;[104] dialectal words and spellings; and some of the numerous Slavisms

---

sister, my bride," apparently in honor of his niece's wedding of the previous day. It is printed in his published Hasidic discourses for that year in *Likute Torah—Torat Shmuel . . . 5633* (1994, 1:101–111). See ch. 21, p. 378, footnote 36, regarding the identity of the Rebbe's unnamed niece whose wedding was being celebrated.

103 The fact that no other lengthy article about an autobiography was ever published in the pages of *Yidishe Shprakh*, which ran for decades, hints at the distinctive linguistic importance of Pinye-Ber's text.

104 Mark (1943:41–42) writes that some grammatical aspects of Pinye-Ber's language are often more typical of a Lithuanian Jew although he was among Northeastern (Lithuanian) Yiddish speakers for only two short periods in his life. In truth, Pinye-Ber spent two weeks in Lubavitch followed by six and a half months in nearby Shklov in 1865 (chs. 15 and 16), and his second visit to Lubavitch in 1873 (ch. 21) was only for five days. In addition, he spent a third lengthy period among Lithuanian-Yiddish speakers of which Mark was seemingly unaware, namely the seventeen years from 1913 until his death in 1930 when he resided in Petach-Tikva, which has been described as being like a Lithuanian *shtetl* (Kressel, 1953:282; Yakobzon, 1986:13). In addition, though Pinye-Ber does not comment on their origins, research has shown that his second wife Feyge, whom he married in 1897 in Odessa, and his third wife Bashe, whom he married in 1920 in Petakh-Tivka, were both originally from areas where the Northeastern (Lithuanian) dialect of Yiddish was spoken. An analysis of possible alterations in Pinye-Ber's Yiddish grammatical constructs after his arrival in Petakh-Tikva lies outside the purview of this introduction.

and international words he uses. Towards the end of his article, Mark (1943:62) comments, "Such a complete document of the life of a Jewish folk intellectual gives us insight into the actual, living, spoken language in a certain area and from a certain social class of Jews.... It is a treasury of the simple, unaffected, and rich Yiddish of the Jews of the provinces of Kherson and Bessarabia. Eternalized in this book is the spoken Yiddish language."[105]

In the middle of his analysis, Mark (1943:37), who wrote the review under the name M. Rekhtman,[106] comments, "Understandably, it is difficult to say whether all was taken 'as is' from his environs or whether there are his own creations here. Some words sound quite modern, like neologisms." Having emigrated from his native Lithuania to America in 1936, Mark was evidently unfamiliar at that time with the Yiddish of the older generation of Jews from the Ukraine. Some Yiddish linguists and lexicographers have used this statement as cause to doubt the authenticity of Pinye-Ber's language without having noticed a letter to the editor (Verlin, 1943:154), which Mark, as the editor of the journal, printed in the next issue to dispel this very statement:

> Please let me reassure Mr. M. Rekhtman [that is, Yudl Mark] and the readers of *Yidishe Shprakh* that as a native of the district of Kanyev in the province of Kiev,[107] I saw no new words mentioned. It seems to me that Reb Pinye-Ber simply used a thoroughly pure idiomatic Yiddish commonly spoken in our region, though he did not originate or live in our towns. The style of the long citations brought by M. Rekhtman is like an echo of the old language of my youth, which I have not stopped using until this very day.

---

105 Of course, Mark's article is not exhaustive. In his *Food and Beverages: A Study in History of Culture and Linguistics*, Kosover (1958:139) finds it noteworthy to mention Pinye-Ber's variant for the word *knish*, namely *knishkelekh*. There are also words not mentioned by Mark, which are not listed in any dictionaries, as noted in footnotes to the text, for example, *arman*, meaning a threshing floor (ch. 20); *treybitshkes*, denoting the forbidden fats that need to be expertly removed from slaughtered cattle according to Jewish law (ch. 27); and *motuske* (מטותקע), meaning a teacher's pet (ch. 7), which evidently derives from the Aramaic מטותא meaning "favor," that is, a teacher's favorite. *Motuske* is particularly significant, for it is not mentioned elsewhere in the rich, extant *kheyder* literature.

106 Yudl Mark wrote his review under the pseudonym of M. Rekhtman, as noted in "Indices to *Yidishe Shprakh*" (1977:12). As editor of *Yidishe Shprakh* from 1941 to 1968, Mark wrote articles under various pseudonyms to avoid the appearance that he alone was writing so much of its content.

107 Kanyev, Ukraine is now called Kaniv.

At one point, Mark comments that Pinye-Ber writes like he speaks: "One can say that this book is a document of the spoken language, and therein lies the curiosity of this book for the linguist." He then proceeds to cite a number of sentence constructions typical of the spoken language but not normally found in the printed word. There is often little or no punctuation, with sentences sometimes continuing for an entire page.[108] In fact, Pinye-Ber's narrative is written in the regional Yiddish vernacular of his youth and was self-published without editorial revision, thereby preserving the author's own authentic voice. At that time, no established Yiddish publisher would have printed such a work without standardizing the orthography and thoroughly editing it. In order to possibly find similar material, a researcher would need to search archives for handwritten Yiddish letters, which would generally be limited in length, content, and scope. Naturally, had Pinye-Ber written his autobiography in Hebrew, the linguistic aspects discussed in Mark's article would have been lost.

Conclusion

The autobiography of Pinye-Ber Goldenshteyn, a Hasidic *shoykhet*, is an outlier in a sea of nineteenth-century maskilic autobiographies. His ahistoric, God-oriented consciousness led him to trace the sequence of divine providence throughout his trying and difficult life, to the exclusion of all else, granting rare insight into the consciousness and religious self-realization of a Hasidic Jew of those times. Paradoxically, his ahistoric perspective has provided us with a real historical document.

---

108 Both Mark (1943:39) and Niger (1930) comment that Pinye-Ber created his own, unique orthography in Yiddish (which is even apparent in the full Yiddish title) by placing an apostrophe where one would normally see the letter *ayin* (equivalent to /e/) when it has no sound. For example, he writes *d'rvust* (ד'רוואוסט) instead of *dervust* (דערוואוסט), meaning "find out"; and *trink'n* (טרינק'ן) instead of *trinken* (טרינקען), meaning "to drink." Though Pinye-Ber's book was never edited, his handwritten letters (to which Mark and Niger had no access) reveal that this orthography was not his innovation but that of the typesetter. In addition, the typesetter misspelled most Slavic components appearing in the book, while Pinye-Ber's spelling of such elements in his letters appear without error. (The typesetter was likely a young native of Palestine, which would account for his unfamiliarity with such words.) Despite the typographical errors, the translator feels fortunate in having deciphered, sometimes with great effort, every word in the text; the most elusive words have been noted in the footnotes. Nonetheless, the typesetter did improve upon the author's orthography by removing the numerous superfluous silent letters no longer generally used by Yiddish publishers.

Recorded contemporaneously, Pinye-Ber writes at length about every episode in his life, thereby unwittingly making mention of a wide array of aspects of Jewish life in the areas of Tsarist Russia and Romania in which he lived. His autobiography provides numerous quotidian details regarding the Jews in Eastern Europe, which cannot be found in other nineteenth-century autobiographies. Many of these aspects of daily life seem so commonplace that it is surprising that they are not mentioned at length elsewhere in the autobiographical genre, while other aspects at first seem obscure but upon investigation turn out to have been more common than presumed. Pinye-Ber provides the reader with information about all aspects of the daily life of a Jew in the nineteenth century, including details of the life of a *shoykhet*, a traditionalist raising his children, the inner-workings of local Jewish institutions, a real taste of Hasidic life, the deep connection of a Hasid to his Rebbe, and his unparalleled descriptions of the oppressive poverty of the Jews in Tsarist Russia and its effects on the financial, cultural, and social aspects of Jewish life. It is a resource we should treasure.

Bibliography

Abrahams, Bernard. *Mayne zibetsik yor.* Johannesburg: Kayor Publishing House, 1953.

Adler, Moshe Khayim. "Khsides un misnagdes." In *Lite: bukh eyns*, edited by Mendl Sudarsky and Uriya Katsenelenbogen, 599–603. New York: Kultur-gezelshaft fun Litvishe Yidn, 1951.

Alfes, Bentsion (Rabbi). *Ma'aseh Alfes: Toladah ve-zikhronot.* Jerusalem: Beit ha-yetomim Diskin, 1940.

Anokhi (Aronsohn), Zalman Yitskhok. *Reb Abe un andere ksovim.* Buenos-Aires: Tsentral-farband fun Poylishe Yidn in Argentine, 1953.

Aronsohn, Zalman Yitskhok: see Zalman Yitskhok Anokhi.

Aronson, Chaim. *A Jewish Life under the Tsars: The Autobiography of Chaim Aronson, 1825–1888.* Translated by Norman Marsden. Totowa, NJ: Allanheld, Osmun & Co., 1983.

Assaf, David. "Life as it Was"—Yekhezkel Kotik and His Memoirs." Introduction to *Journey to a Nineteenth-Century Shtetl: The Memoirs of Yekhezkel Kotik*, translated by Dena Orden, 16–98. Detroit: Wayne State University Press, 2002.

Assaf, David. Introduction to *My Town Motele* [Hebrew], by Hayim Chemerinsky, 7–30. Jerusalem: Hebrew University Press and Magnes Press, 2002.

Avrutin, Eugene M. *Jews and the Imperial State: Identification Politics in Tsarist Russia.* Ithaca, NY: Cornell University Press, 2010.

Bar-Levav, Avriel. "'When I was Alive': Jewish Ethical Wills as Egodocuments." In *Egodocuments and History: Autobiographical Writing in its Social Context since the Middle Ages*, edited by Rudolf Dekker, 45–59. Hilversum: Verloren Publishers, 2002.

Beider, Alexander. *A Dictionary of Jewish Surnames from the Russian Empire: Revised Edition.* Bergenfield, NJ: Avotaynu, Inc., 2008.

Berlin (Bar-Ilan), Meir (Rabbi). *Fun Volozin biz Yerushalayim: Epizoden.* New York: n.p., 1933.

Berman, Jeremiah J. *Shehitah: A Study in the Cultural and Social Life of the Jewish People.* New York: Bloch Publishing Co., 1941.

Bikl (Bickel), Shloyme. *Yidn davnenen: Nyu Yorker reportazhen.* New York: R. Y. Novak, 1948.

Bleich, J. David (Rabbi). *Providence in the Philosophy of Gersonides.* New York: Yeshiva University Press, 1973.

Bloch, Joseph Samuel. *Erinnerungen aus meinem Leben.* Vienna: R. Löwit, 1922.

———. *My Reminiscenses.* Vienna: R. Löwit, 1923.

Bloy, Amram, *Bene ha-Tsemakh Tsedek.* Jerusalem: Mayanotekha, 2020.

Bonchek (Bontshek), Samuel. *Vi es gedenkt zikh.* New York: Schulsinger Brothers, 1955.

Braver, Mikhael, and Avraham Ya'akov Braver. *Zikhronot av u-beno.* Jerusalem: Mosad ha-Rav Kuk, 1966.

Cahn, Bernard. *The Diaries of Bernhard Cahn,* translated by Arline Sachs. Bergenfield, NJ: Avotaynu, 2003.

Caplan, Kimmy. "Innovating the Past: The Emerging Sphere of the 'Torah-True Historian' in America." *Studies in Contemporary Judaism* 21 (2005): 270–287.

Carlebach, Eliyahu Chaim (Rabbi), ed. *Shivkhei ha-Baal Shem Tov.* Jerusalem: Mekhon Zekher Naftali, 1990.

Cohen, Tova. "Portrait of the Maskilah as a Young Woman." *Nashim: A Journal of Jewish Women's Studies and Gender Issues* 15 (2008): 9–29.

Duchman, Shneur Zalman. *Likut le-shema ozen: zikhronot, sipurim u-fitgamin kadishin.* Brooklyn: n.p., 1963.

Emden, Jacob (Rabbi). *Megilat sefer.* Warsaw: Bi-defus he-akhim Shuldberg ve-shutafam, 1896.

Epshtein, Barukh (Rabbi). *Mekor Barukh: Zikhronot yeme khayav.* Vilnius: Romm, 1928.

Errera, Leo. *The Russian Jews: Extermination or Emancipation?* London: David Nutt, 1894.

Etkes, Immanuel. *The Besht: Magician, Mystic, and Leader.* Waltham, MA: Brandeis University Press, 2005.

Feygenberg, Rokhl. *Di kinder-yohren.* Warsaw: ha-Shakhar, 1910.

Finkel, Avraham Yaakov. *Contemporary Sages: The Great Chasidic Masters of the Twentieth Century.* Northvale, NJ: Jason Aronson, Inc., 1994.

Freeze, ChaeRan Y. "Following the Paper Trail: Genealogical Resources in the Ukrainian and Moldovan Archives." In *Jewish Roots in Ukraine and Moldova: Pages from the Past and Archival Inventories,* 7–17. Secaucus, NJ: The Miriam Weiner Routes to Roots Foundation, and New York: YIVO Institute for Jewish Research, 1999.

Funkenstein, Amos. *Perceptions of Jewish History.* Berkeley: University of California Press, 1993.

"Gan Eden ha-elyon: or khadash: Reshimot she-katav . . . he-khasid R. Alter Simkhovits. . . ." *Tekhayenu* (Brooklyn) 10 (2019): 86–103.

Gellman, Uri. "The Heder in Eastern Europe: An Annotated Bibliography." In *The Heder: Studies, Documents, Literature and Memoirs,* edited by David Assaf and Immanuel Etkes, 525–566. Tel-Aviv: Tel-Aviv University Press, 2010.

Glenn, Menahem G. *Israel Salanter: Religious-Ethical Thinker*. New York: Bloch Publishing Co., 1953.

Glicman (Glikman), Levi. *Zikhronot bet Levi*. Chișinău: Tehnic, 1934.

Glikl of Hameln. *Zikhronot: Marat Glikl Hamil.* . . . Frankfurt am Main: Kaufmann, 1896.

———. *Zikhronot Glikl* [Hebrew]. Translated by A. Z. Rabinovits. Tel-Aviv: Dvir, 1929.

——— (Glikl of Hamelin). *Glikl: Memoires 1691–1719* [Hebrew]. Translated by Chava Turniansky. Jerusalem: Zalman Shazar Center for Jewish History, Ben-Zion Dinur Center for Research in Jewish History, The Hebrew University Press, 2006.

Goldenstein (Goldenshteyn), Raphael. *The Krimchaks: Their Life and Origin in the Crimea*. Unpublished thesis for a rabbinical degree, Hebrew Union College, Cincinnati, 1916.

———. "R. Khayim Khizkiyahu Medini." *Ha-Toren* (New York) 11, no. 6 (September 1925): 13–20.

Goldenshteyn, Raphael: see Raphael Goldenstein.

Gordon, Benjamin L. *Between Two Worlds: The Memoirs of a Physician*. New York: Bookman Associates, Inc., 1952.

Graupe, Heinz Mosche. *The Rise of Modern Judaism: An Intellectual History of German Jewry, 1650–1942*. Translated by John Robinson. Huntington, NY: R. E. Krieger, 1978.

Greenwald, Leopold (Yekutiel Yehuda). *Ha-Shokhet veha-shekhitah ba-sifrut ha-rabanut*. New York: Philip Feldheim, Inc., 1955.

Gross, Chaim. *The Paths of Providence: Does GD Control Everything?* Jerusalem: Targum Press, 2015.

Grunwald, Nochum. "Hashgakhah pratit al-pi shitat ha-Baal Shem Tov." *Mayanotekha* 23*Kislev* 5710 [November–December 2009]). http://www.yeshiva.org.il/midrash/12930. Accessed February 27, 2023.

Gurary, Noson. *Chasidism: Its Development, Theology, and Practice*. Northvale, NJ: Jason Aronson Inc., 1997.

Gurwits (Hurvits), Aleksander-Ziskind. *Seyfer zikhroynes fun tsvey doyres*. New York: n.p., 1935.

——— (Gurwitz, Alexander Z.). *Memories of Two Generations: A Yiddish Life in Russia and Texas*. Translated by Amram Prero. Tuscaloosa: The University of Alabama Press, 2016.

Hadas, Tsvi-Hirsh. "Bakhchisaray." *Ha-Melits*, June 3, 1896, 3.

Ha-Kohen, Refael Nakhman: see Refael Nakhman Kahan.

Harkavy, Alexander. *Yiddish-English-Hebrew Dictionary*. New York: Hebrew Pub. Co., 1928.

Heilman, Hayim Meir. *Beit Rebbi*. Berdichev: H. Y. Sheftil, 1902.

Heller, Yomtov Lipman (Rabbi). *Megilat evah*. Ashdod: Mifal moreshet ha-Tosfot Yom Tov, 2005.

Heschel, Abraham Joshua. *Der Mizrekh-Eyropeyisher Yid* (The Eastern European Jew). New York: Schocken, 1946.

Hurvits, Aleksander Ziskind: see Aleksander Ziskind Gurwitz.

Hurwitz, Samuel (A. Litvin). *Fun'm kheyder'ishn pinkes: Ksovim fun a Litvishen yungel*. Vilna: n.p., 1908.

"Indices to *Yidishe Shprakh*: 1941–1974." *Yidishe Shprakh* (Yiddish Scientific Institute-YIVO, New York) 36 (1977): 1–152.

"Inyane ha-Yehudim." *Ha-Zeman* (Vilna), April 20, 1914, 3.

Jacobs, Louis. "Hasidism, basic ideas of." *Encyclopedia Judaica*, v. 7: 1403–1407. Jerusalem: Keter, 1972.

———. *Their Heads in Heaven: Unfamiliar Aspects of Hasidism*. London: Vallentine Mitchell, 2005.

Jacobson, Yisroel (Rabbi). "The History of Chabad in America: Agudas haTmimim of America: Part IV." *Di Yiddishe Heim* (Brooklyn) 14, no. 2 (Autumn 1972): 9–14.

Johnpoll, Bernard K. "Why They Left: Russian-Jewish Mass Migration and Repressive Laws, 1881–1917." *American Jewish Archives* 47, no. 1 (1995): 17–54.

Kahan (ha-Kohen), Refael Nakhman. *Shmuot ve-sipurim mi-rabotenu ha-kedoshim*. Brooklyn: n.p., 1990.

Kariv, Avraham. "Z. Y. Anokhi." In *Reb Abe un andere ksovim*, by Zalman Yitskhok Anokhi (Aronsohn), iv–x. Buenos-Aires: Tsentral-farband fun Poylishe Yidn in Argentine, 1953.

Karlinsky, Nahum. 'The Dawn of Hasidic-Haredi Historiography." *Modern Judaism* 27, no. 1 (2007): 20–46.

Kasovich, Israel. *The Day of Our Years: Personal and General Reminiscence (1859–1929)*. New York: Jordan Publishing Co., 1929.

Katsovitsh (Kasovich), Yisroel-Iser. *Zekhtsig yohr leben: Erinerungen: Eygeyen un algemeyn-Yidishe (1859–1919)*. New York: Max N. Maisel, 1919.

Katz, Jacob. "Orthodoxy in Historical Perspective." In *Studies in Contemporary Jewry*, v. 2, edited by Peter Y. Medding, 3–17. Bloomington: Indiana University Press, 1986.

Keren, Yekhezkel. *Yahadut Krim me-kadmutah ve-ad ha-shoah*. Jerusalem: Rubin Mass, 1981.

Khinits, Nakhum. "Rakhel Feygenberg-Imri z"l." *He-Avar: Rivon le-divre yeme ha-Yehudim veha-Yahadut be-Rusiyah* 20 (1973): 291–293.

Kliger, Iser, *Tiyul ba-parde"s be-ferek Ein Dorshin*, Israel, 1989, pp. 309-325, [Otzar HaHochma Online, accessed February 27, 2023].

Kofman, Shmuel. *Zikhronot*. Tel-Aviv: n.p., 1955.

Kopeloff (Kopelov), Isidore. *Amol iz geven*. New York: M. N. Mayzel, 1926.

Kosover, Mordecai. *Food and Beverages: A Study in History of Culture and Linguistics* [Hebrew]. New York: YIVO Institute for Jewish Research, 1958.

Kotik, Yekhezkel. *Mayne zikhroynes*. Warsaw: A. Gitlin, 1913.

———. *Mayne zikhroynes*. Berlin: Klal Verlag, 1922.

———. *Journey to a Nineteenth-Century Shtetl: The Memoirs of Yekhezkel Kotik*. Translated by Margaret Birstein and Sharon Makover-Assaf. Detroit, MI: Wayne State University Press, 2002.

Kressel, Getzel. *Em ha-moshavot Petakh-Tikva*: 1878–1853. Petakh-Tikva: Iriyat Petakh-Tikva, 1953.

Laine, Eliezer. *Avnei Chein*. Brooklyn: Kehot Publication Society, 2014.

Lamm, Norman. *Torah Lishmah: Torah for Torah's Sake in the Words of Rabbi Hayyim of Volozhin and his Contemporaries*. Hoboken, NJ: KTAV Publishing House, Inc., 1989.

Leibowitz, Aryeh. *Hashgachah Pratis: An Exploration of Divine Providence and Free Will*. Jerusalem: Targum Press Book, 2012.

Levanda, Vitalii Osipovich. *Polnyi khronologicheskii sbornik zakonov i polozhenii kasaiushchikhsia evreev*. S. Petersburg: Tipografiia K. V. Trubnikova, 1874.

Levine, Sholom DovBer (Rabbi). *Toldot Avraham Khayim: toldotav... shel Rabi Avraham Khayim Rozenboym mi-Pleshtsenits.* Brooklyn: Kehot Publication Society, 1998.

Levy, Ascher. *Die Memoiren des Ascher Levy aus Reichshofen.* Berlin: Louis Lamm, 1913.

Lifshits, Y. M. *Yudish-Rusisher verter bikh.* Zhytomyr: Y.M. Baksht, 1876.

Litvin, A.: see Samuel Hurwitz.

Luria, Ilia. "Education and Ideology: The Beginnings of the HaBaD Yeshivah." In *Let the Old Make Way for the New,* edited by David Asaf, v. 1: *Hasidism and the Musar Movement* [Hebrew], 185–222. Jerusalem: The Zalman Shazar Center for Jewish History, 2009.

Magnus, Shulamit. Introduction to *Memoirs of a Grandmother: Scenes from the Cultural History of the Jews of Russia in the Nineteenth Century,* by Pauline Wengeroff, v. 1, 1–75. Stanford: Stanford University Press, 2010.

Marmor, Kalman. *Mayn lebns geshikhte.* V. 1. New York: Yidisher Kultur Farband, 1959.

Matthews, Mervyn. *The Passport Society: Controlling Movement in Russia and the USSR.* Boulder, NC: Westview Press, 1993.

Mark, Yudl: see M. Rekhtman.

Medini, Khayim Khizkiyahu (Rabbi). *Igrot Sdei Khemed.* Makhon Shem Olam, Ed. Shimon Hirshler, Bnei Brak, Israel, 2006.

Melamed, Avraham Shlomo. *Khayim kemo she-hem: avtobiografiya mefaretet . . . .* V. 1. Istanbul (Kushta): L. Babok u-vanav, 1922.

Mendele Moycher-Sforim. *Shloyme Reb Khaym's: A bild fun Idishen leben in der Lita. . . .* Brooklyn, NJ: The Hebrew American Publishing Comp., 1901.

Merenbach, Nathan. *Grampa: The Autobiography of Nathan Merenbach.* San Francisco: n.p., 1977.

Milch (Milkh), Yaakov. *Oytobiografishe skitsn.* New York: Yidisher Kultur Farband, 1946.

Mintz, Alan L. *"Banished from Their Fathers' Table": Loss of Faith and Hebrew Autobiography.* Bloomington: Indiana University Press, 1989.

Miron, Dan. *The Image of the Shtetl and Other Studies of Modern Jewish Literary Imagination.* Syracuse, NY: Syracuse University Press, 2000.

Modena, Leone (Yehudah Aryeh) (Rabbi). *The Autobiography of a Seventeenth-Century Venetian Rabbi: Leon Modena's Life of Judah* (translated by Mark R. Cohen), Princeton: Princeton University Press,1988.

Modena, Leone (Yehudah Aryeh) (Rabbi). *Khaye Yehudah: kolel avtobiografiya.* Kyiv: n.p., 1911.

Mondshine, Yehoshua. "Ekhad be-ekhad yigashu." *Kerem Khabad* 1 (*Tishre* 5747 [1986]): 60–66.

Moseley, Marcus. *Being for Myself Alone: Origins of Jewish Autobiography.* Stanford: Stanford University Press, 2006.

Moykher-Sforim, Mendele: see Mendele Moykher-Sforim.

Niger, Shmuel. "Nayntsig yohr leben." *Der Tog,* March 2, 1930, 7.

Petrovsky-Shtern, Yohanan. "Military Service in Russia." *YIVO Encyclopedia of Jews in Eastern Europe.* September 2, 2010. http://www.yivoencyclopedia.org/article.aspx/Military_Service_in_Russia. Accessed February 27, 2023.

"Pictures of Jewish Life and Characters." *The Jewish Daily Forward,* December 16, 1923, section 3, [3].

Pilowsky, Arye Leyb. *Tsvishn yo un neyn: Yidish un Yidish-literature in Erets-Yisroel, 1907–1947.* Tel-Aviv: Veltrat far Yidish un Yidisher Kultur, 1986.

Pinchuk, Ben-Cion. "Jewish Discourse and the Shtetl." *Jewish History* (Dordrecht) 15 (2001): 169–179.

Pinto, Chaim (Rabbi). "Rabbi Ben Zion Alfes: "The Author of *Maase Alfes*." https://hevratpinto.org/tzadikim_eng/145_rabbi_benzion_alfes.html. Accessed February 27, 2023.

Polen, Nehemiah. "Some Words about the Translation." In *The Rebbe's Daughter: Memoir of a Hasidic Childhood,* by Malkah Shapiro, translated by Nehemiah Polen, xlvii–xlviii. Philadelphia: The Jewish Publication Society, 2002.

Preger, Yosef Aryeh. *Kitve R. Yoshe Shub: Amarot tehorot, shivatayim mezukakot. . . .* Jerusalem: n.p., 197?.

Rabinovits, Y. L. "Bakhchisaray." *Ha-Tsefirah*, August 20, 1900, 3.

Rabinovits-Teomim, Eliyahu David (Rabbi). *Seder Eliyahu: Avtobiografiya shel ha-gaon ha-Aderet.* Jerusalem: Mosad ha-Rav Kuk, 1983.

Rekhtman, M. [Yudl Mark]. "The Language of the Memoirist P. Goldenshtain." *Yidishe Shprakh* (Yiddish Scientific Institute-YIVO, New York) 3 (1943): 32–43.

Rotenfeld, Michoel. "The Baal Shem Tov's Expanded View of Divine Providence and Its Unacknowledged Impact on World Jewry." *Hakirah: The Flatbush Journal of Jewish Law and Thought (forthcoming)*.

Rubinshtein, Shimon. *Mashber u-temurah: Petakh-Tikva be-tekufat ha-ma'avar meha-shilton ha-Turki la-Briti.* Jerusalem: n.p., 1990.

Schaechter, Mordkhe. *Yiddish II: An Intermediate and Advanced Textbook.* New York: Yiddish Language Research Center, 2005.

Schneersohn, Isaac. *Lebn un kamf fun Yidn in Tsarishn Rusland, 1905–1917.* Paris: Les Editions Polyglottes, 1968.

Schneersohn, Yosef Yitzchok (Rabbi). "Ketae reshimot meha-yoman shel . . . admor mi-Lyubavitsh shlit"a mi-shenat 5658–72. . . ." *Kovets ha-tamim* 8 (5696 [1936]): 20–25.

———. *Igrot kodesh.* Brooklyn, NY: Kehot Publication Society, 1982–2011.

———. *Sefer ha-ma'amarim 5710.* Brooklyn, NY: Kehot Publication Society, 1986.

———. *Sefer ha-sikhot 5696khoref 5700.* Brooklyn, NY: Kehot Publication Society, 1989.

Schneerson, Barukh Shneur. *Reshimot ha-Rabash.* Brooklyn, NY: Kehot Publication Society, 2001.

Schneerson, Menakhem-Mendl (Rabbi) (1879–1866). *Or ha-Torah: Devarim.* Brooklyn, NY: Kehot Publication Society, 1994.

Schneerson, Menachem Mendel (Rabbi) (1902–1994). *Reshimot: Khoveret 138.* Brooklyn, NY: Lahak Hanochos, Inc., 1994.

———. *Led by G-d's hand: The Baal Shem Tov's Interpretation of the Concept of Hashgachah Peratis Based on the Works of the Lubavitcher Rebbe, Menachem M. Schneerson.* Translated by Eliyahu Touger. Brooklyn, NY: Sichos, 1998.

Schneerson, Shmuel (Rabbi). *Likutei Torah—Torat Shmuel . . . 5633.* Brooklyn, NY: Kehot Publication Society, 1994.

———. *Likutei Torah—Torat Shmuel: Sefer drushe khatuna.* Brooklyn, NY: Kehot Publication Society, 2003.

Schochet, Jacob Immanuel (Rabbi), ed. *Keter shem tov ha-shalem: ve-hu likut divre . . . R. Yisrael ha-Ba'al Shem Tov.* Brooklyn, NY: Kehot Publication Society, 2004.

Schoenfeld (Sheynfeld), Samuel, *Zikhroynes fun a shriftzetser*, Bibliotek fun YIVO, New York, 1946.

Shapiro, Pinkhas (Rabbi). *Imre Pinkhas: Ha-shalem*. Ramat-Gan: Mishor, 1988.

Shatzky, Jacob. "Idishe memuaren literatur." *Di Tsukunft* 30 (August 1925): 483–488.

Shmuel, B. *Meore Yisrael*. Jerusalem: Mekhon Ohale Yosef, 1994.

Shneur Zalman (Rabbi) of Lyadi. *Likute Amarim: Tanya*. Brooklyn, NY: Kehot Publication Society, 1973.

Sholem Aleykhem. *Motl Peyse dem khazns*. New York: Varhayt, 1918.

Shvadron (Schwadron), Shalom Mordekhai. *She'al avikha ve-yagedkha*. Jerusalem: Makhon da'at, 1990.

Smolenskin, Peretz. *Ha-Toeh be-darkhe ha-khayim: O toldot Yosef ha-yatom me-ir madmenah. . . .* Vienna: Y. Shlossberg, 1876.

Soloveitchik, Haym. "Rupture and Reconstruction: The Transformation of Contemporary Orthodoxy." *Tradition: A Journal of Orthodox Jewish Thought* 28, no. 4 (Summer 1994): 64–130.

Stanislawski, Michael. *Autobiographical Jews: Essays in Jewish Self-Fashioning*. Seattle: University of Washington Press, 2004.

Shternharts, Nathan (Rabbi). *Yeme Macharna"t*. Lviv (Lemberg): U. W. Salat and J. M. Nik, 1876.

———. *Yeme Macharna"t*. Beitar Ilit: Makhon Even Shetiyah, 2009.

Trofe, Eliezer. *Yesodot le-toldot Petakh-Tikva*. Petakh-Tikva: n.p., 1949.

Uffenheimer, Rivka Schatz. *Hasidism as Mysticism: Quietistic Elements in Eighteenth-Century Hasidic Thought*. Translated by Jonathan Chipman. Princeton, NJ: Princeton University Press, 1993.

Vasertsug, Moshe: see Moshe Wassercug.

Verlin (Werlin), Yankev-Ber (Jacob Baer). "Me shrabyt undz." *Yidishe Shprakh* (Yiddish Scientific Institute-YIVO, New York) 3 (1943): 154–155.

Vilf, Refael, *Netivot Refael: Pirke yoman ve-sipurim mi-tokh ketavav shel he-khasid R' Refael Vilf . . . mi-Yerushalayim*. Jerusalem: n.p., 2017.

Wassercug (Vasertsug), Moshe. "Korot Moshe Wasertsug u-nedivat lev aviv ha-manoakh R. Iserl. . . ." *Jahrbuch der Judisch-Literarischen Gesellschaft* 8 (1910), edited by Henrich Loewe, 87–114.

Weinreich, Max. *History of the Yiddish Language*. Edited by Paul Glasser, translated by Shlomo Noble and Joshua A. Fishman. New Haven, CT: Yale University Press, 2008.

Wengeroff, Pauline. *Memoirs of a Grandmother: Scenes from the Cultural History of the Jews of Russia in the Nineteenth Century*. V. 1. Translated by Shulamit S. Magnus. Stanford: Stanford University Press, 2010.

———. *Memoirs of a Grandmother: Scenes from the Cultural History of the Jews of Russia in the Nineteenth Century*. V. 2. Translated by Shulamit S. Magnus. Stanford: Stanford University Press, 2015.

Yakobzon, Khayim. *Petakh-Tikva be-reshit ha-meah*. Petakh-Tikva: n.p., 1986.

"Yerushalayim," *Doar ha-yom*, January 31, 1929, 4.

Yerushalmi, Yosef Hayim. *Zakhor: Jewish History and Jewish Memory*. Seattle: University of Washington Press, 1982.

Zaltzman, Hillel. *Samarkand: The Underground with a Far-Reaching Impact*. Brooklyn, NY: n.p., 2015.

Zicherman, Jacob. *Nakhalat Ya'akov*. New York: n.p., 1966.

Zinner, Gavriel (Rabbi). *Nite Gavriel: hilkhot nesuin*. Brooklyn, NY: Cong. Nitei Gavriel, 1998.

———. *Nite Gavriel: halakhot ve-halikhot bar mitsvah*. Brooklyn, NY: Cong. Nitei Gavriel, 2002.

Zunser (Tsunzer), Eliakim. *Tsunser's biografye: Geshriben fun ihm aleyn*. New York: Tsunzer Yubileum Komite, 1905.

The Shochet:
A Memoir of Jewish Life
in Ukraine and Crimea

Volume One

In Lieu of a Preface

This narrative is divided into three parts: The first two consist of life events and episodes from my birth in 5603 [*sic*] until 5674, when I moved to *Erets-Isruel*.[1] Although I thought that I would be able to live a peaceful life here, I found myself in the midst of the World War and endured much here. It was here where I wrote the third part.

FIGURE 2. Pinkhes-Dov "Pinye-Ber" Goldenshteyn (1848–1930), taken in January or February 1927 in Petakh-Tikva. It was printed on the page opposite the title page in the hardbound copy of his autobiography. Courtesy of Shifra Bernfeld.

---

1 The author writes here that he was born in 5603 and in chapter 18, p. 291, that he was born shortly after *Sukes*, hence that he was born in September or October 1842. Nonetheless, he was in fact born in October 1848 (see Introduction, pp. 67–70). Based on his mistaken year of birth, he apparently miscalculated the years of death of his father, mother, and brother (ch. 2) and the year of his own marriage (ch. 18). The author moved in 5674, more precisely November 1913, to *Erets-Isruel* (*Erets-Yisroel* in Northeastern Yiddish), meaning the Land of Israel, as mentioned at the beginning of ch. 30.

This book is written in Yiddish for a few reasons. Though I greatly value and cherish the Holy language, I wrote this book for my children and relatives who are spread throughout numerous countries where Hebrew is not readily understood. Hence, I wanted them to be able to understand what their father endured during his lifetime and how God always helped him and never abandoned him. I also want those who plagued and tormented me and are currently in Russia to read this in order to learn the moral lesson that there is a God in the world who protects the harassed and oppressed and repays every one according to his deeds.[2]

May they repent.

P. D. Goldenshteyn
Petakh-Tikva, *Rosh-Khoydesh Elul* 5688[3]

---

2   See Appendix A7 for details regarding his unsuccessful attempt to ship his printed book to the Soviet Union.

3   August 16–17, 1928. *Rosh-Khoydesh Elul* denotes the beginning of the Hebrew month of *Elul*.

Part I

My Family and Youth

A. My Parents and Siblings

CHAPTER 1

My Parents

The City of Tiraspol • The Dniester River • Commerce in Tiraspol • Names and Nicknames • *Melomdim* in Those Times • Sons-in-Law on *Kest* • Reb Itse, the Gróseler *Melómed* • His Wife Ester-Khaye, a Woman of Valor • Making a Living • God is Right

In the city of Tiraspol, which lies on the Dniester River, the houses are built along the length of the low banks of the river.[1] Occasionally, when the ice melts and the resulting flow streams off into the river, the water level of the river rises, overflows its banks, and fills the nearby streets with water. When its floodwaters rise all the way up to the houses, one has to go from street to street and from house to house by boat or dinghy.[2] Tiraspol is in the province of Kherson (in Russia) and lies ten *versts* from Bendér, sixty *versts* from Kishinev, and ninety *versts* from Odessa.[3]

Tiraspol is a large city of commerce. The main products of trade are bread and fruit. The large surrounding district is filled with wealthy villages and

---

1 Tiraspol was in the Tsarist Russian province of Kherson in the Ukraine. In 1924, the Soviet Union created the Moldavian Autonomous Soviet Socialist Republic (MASSR) from a territory previously administered as part of the Ukraine. The MASSR encompassed the modern territory of Transnistria, a narrow strip of land on the right bank of the Dniester River, which included Tiraspol. In 1940, the Soviet Union dismantled the old Moldavian ASSR and formed the Moldavian Soviet Socialist Republic (MSSR), which included parts of Romania, namely Bessarabia and Bukovina. In 1991, the MSSR declared independence from the Soviet Union and took the name Moldova; hence, Tiraspol is currently in modern-day Moldova.
2 In 2003, Leva (Khotskl-Leyb) Zeltser of Brooklyn, a native of Tiraspol, related that he also remembered using small boats as a boy in the 1930s whenever the "Nester" (the Yiddish name for the Dniester) would overflow.
3 A *verst* is an obsolete Russian unit of length equivalent to 1.067 kilometers or 0.6629 miles.

colonies of Germans, Romanians, and Old Believers.⁴ Tiraspol has 15,000 inhabitants, with Jews being practically its largest component and who play in it the greatest role.⁵ Apart from its many businessmen, who are well known in the world of commerce, are tremendous Talmudic scholars, Hasidim of a variety of *tsadikim*, and also pious and God-fearing laymen of distinguished lineage and prominence.⁶

My Parents, Itskhok-Refúel and Ester-Khaye

In this very same Tiraspol lived a *melómed* by the name of Reb Itskhok-Refúel Goldenshteyn.⁷ In the times of which we are speaking, no one was referred to by his surname—not even businessmen and the wealthy—and especially not a *melomed*.⁸ So he was called "Reb Itsye the Gróseler *melomed*" because, in those days, one could not get away by being called by merely one name. For example, if someone was named Nokhmen and his mother was named Dvose, he was called Nokhmen-Dvoses.⁹ If he married someone from another city and

---

4   In the seventeenth century, the Russian Orthodox Church undertook a major reform of its liturgy and rituals to bring it in line with the Greek and Ukrainian Orthodox practice. Those who rejected the reforms and supported the "old rite" were known as Old Believers and were severely persecuted. In the eighteenth century, many were forcefully exiled from European Russia to Siberia, where they have secluded themselves and shunned much of Western innovation.
5   In 1870, Tiraspol's official population was 16,692 including 3,614 Jews ("Tiraspol," 1892).
6   *Tsadikim* literally means "righteous people" and refers here to Hasidic Rebbes, that is, Hasidic grand rabbis.
7   *Melamed* is pronounced as *melomed* in the author's Yiddish dialect, which is spoken in the southernmost part of Southeastern Yiddish (see the Introduction to the Glossaries). A *melamed* is a teacher in a *kheyder*. "Reb" is an honorific used before a man's first name; it does not denote that the person was a rabbi.
8   The implication is that businessmen and the wealthy were later called by their surnames, while all other Jews were not. This practice lasted to around the First World War. Before the First World War, Jews living in *shteytlekh* in Tsarist Russia were often unaware of their own neighbors' surnames, which were generally used only for official purposes. After all, surnames among Eastern European Jews are generally no older than the turn of the nineteenth century. See Beider (2008:1:11).
9   Nakhmen is pronounced as Nokhmen in the author's Yiddish dialect, which is spoken in the southernmost part of Southeastern Yiddish. Also, in that region Dvose is pronounced as Dvosye, just like the author's father was called Itsye instead of Itse or Itshe, all nicknames for Itskhok, as the name Yitskhok is pronounced in Southeastern Yiddish. From the author's handwritten letters, it is apparent that the typesetter omitted many of these subtleties.

then lived with his in-laws on *kest*,[10] he would be called "Nokhmen-Dvoses of Tiraspol." Now if this Nokhmen became a *melomed*, yet another name would be tacked on: "Nokhmen-Dvoses the Tiraspoler *melomed*." Similarly, one can understand that Reb Itsye was called "Reb Itsye the Groseler *melomed*," because he came to Tiraspol from the small *shteytl* of Gróseles, where he was married.[11]

The *shteytl* Groseles is fifty *versts* from Tiraspol. It was a rich *shteytl* and, in those days, was very religious; fanaticism raged there unbounded.[12] Residing there was my maternal grandfather, a tremendous Torah scholar and God-fearing Jew, the elderly Reb Yankev Gredenitser.[13] He had one daughter and two sons, who were God-fearing and perfectly pious. Since this Reb Yankev took my father, Reb Itsye, as his son-in-law for his one and only daughter Ester-Khaye, one can easily understand how worthy and virtuous this Itsele was—as well as devout, handsome, and respectable. And above all, Itsye was an accomplished Talmudic scholar. Reb Yankev was the first Talmudic scholar in the entire region

---

10 *Kest* is a prearranged agreement to provide the son-in-law with food and board for a specified number of years after marriage so he could continue his Torah studies in peace. Heschel (1978:48–49) writes, "The ambition of every Jew was to have a scholar as a son-in-law, and a man versed in the Torah could easily marry a well-to-do girl and obtain kest for a few years or even permanently, and thus have the good fortune of being able to study in peace . . . [F]ew institutions have done more to promote the spiritual development of larges masses of people."
11 *Shteytl* (*shtetl* in Northeastern Yiddish) is the Yiddish word for a town and generally refers to a market town with a substantial population of Jews in Eastern Europe before the Second World War.
12 Groseles is the Yiddish name for Grosulovo, Ukraine. In 1897, it had 1,201 Jewish residents out of a general population of 2,088. In the eighteenth century, the area consisted of merely a few hamlets, including two called Boguslavka and Mikhailovka. In 1792, the Tsarist Army Lieutenant Ivan Grosulu (whose surname derives from the Moldovan word meaning "fat") purchased the surrounding land and additional people as serfs and called the entire area Grosulovo. The Yiddish name, Groseles, evidently derives from the area being called Grosulu's. In 1946, the Soviet Union changed the name from one honoring a non-proletarian to Velikaya Mikhailovka, meaning Great Mikhailovka (Cherednichenko, 1978:389; *Evreiskaia entsiklopediia*, 6:802). Little is known of nineteenth-century Jewish life in Groseles except that the head of the rabbinical court there was Rabbi Yosef Katsenelenboygn, whose wife was the aunt of the Bendérer Rebbe, Rabbi Itschok Vertheym (ca. 1848–1911), mentioned in chapter 21 (Grosman, 1989:67).
13 Gredenitser denotes "one from the village of Gredenitse," apparently referring to Grădinița, Moldova (46°40'N, 29°37'E), which is only eleven miles from Tiraspol. Grednitser is misprinted in the original instead of Gredenitser, as spelled in the author's letter from the 8th of *Heshvan* 5691 (October 30, 1930). Though called Yankev Gredenitser in Yiddish, his official surname was Gredenitsky, as indicated in the 1858 additional revision list (poll-tax census) of the Jews of Tiraspol and other sources. The use of such double surnames was not uncommon among Jews in Eastern Europe. He is not listed in the 1796 revision list of the Jews of Tiraspol.

and was also a merchant.[14] He owned his own home, store, cow, and two goats, which he kept near his home.

This Reb Itsele, as Reb Itsye was endearingly called in honor of his good reputation and fine demeanor, was a poor young man and an orphan from his youth. He was raised by an uncle in Tiraspol called "Reb Shoyl the Good"[15] and by other relatives residing in Tiraspol,[16] such as the rabbi, Reb Shmiel, of blessed memory, who was called "Reb Shmiel the Rabbi,"[17] and by an aunt who was called "Ester the change provider."[18] Reb Itsele was born in the small *shteytl* Kódeme, which is not far from Bolte. He was a son of a certain Reb Khayem Kódemer, who was renowned throughout the area for his piety.[19] Until today, people speak of Reb Khayem's tremendous breadth of knowledge in the Talmud and the major halakhic works as well as of his piety.[20] But since Reb Itsele was orphaned at the age of fifteen and was fearful of being conscripted into the military in his small *shteytl*, he left for his relatives in Tiraspol, whom he notified that he would be coming.[21] He was raised by them until his marriage. When the previously mentioned Reb Yankev Gredenitser went to Tiraspol and met this eligible young man, he took this prize catch as his son-in-law, the husband of his one and only daughter, Ester-Khaye. As generally done, the young couple remained for a few years on *kest* with Reb Yankev in Groseles. So what became of such a young married man after *kest*? He most likely became a *melomed*. But being a *melomed* in such a small *shteytl* did not provide him with enough income to

---

14   In a letter dated the 8th of *Heshvan* 5691 (October 30, 1930) to his daughter Nekhame Brockman in Brooklyn, the author writes that his grandfather "was God-fearing, a tremendous Torah scholar, and his memory evokes blessing and brings to mind his good name."
15   "Reb Shoyl *der Giter*" in the original Yiddish.
16   In a number of areas of Eastern Europe, including the Ukraine, the Yiddish word *fraynt* (spelled by the author as *fraynd*) denoted "relative(s)" while *gute-fraynd* denoted "friends" (Schaechter, 1986:182–184).
17   "Reb Shmiel *der Ruv*" in the original Yiddish. He was evidently the rabbi of Tiraspol.
18   A change provider denotes someone who, for a fee, changed larger units of Russian money into smaller units. Since banks were not accessible to the general populace and the poverty was great in Tsarist Russia, storekeepers could generally not provide change when purchases were made. In the original Yiddish, *Ester di manilke* is misprinted instead of *Ester di menyalke*; *menyalke* is the Yiddish feminine form of *meniala*, the Russian word for a change provider. A *menyalke* indicates the wife of a change provider or possibly a widow who inherited the occupation from her deceased husband.
19   Denotes "of Kodeme."
20   Halakhic works are the entire body of Jewish legal works.
21   In Yiddish, being orphaned can refer to the loss of even one parent. Jews first began to be conscripted into the Russian army in 1827, including children less than twelve years of age. Fatherless children were particularly preyed upon in filling Jewish conscription quotas. For details regarding cantonists, see ch. 6, p. 152, footnote 17.

support a whole family with several children, for he and his wife began being on *kest* as two but left as six. Therefore, Itsele left Groseles for Tiraspol to become a teacher of Talmud for young boys, thereby acquiring the title of "Reb Itsye the Groseler *melomed*."

In Tiraspol, Reb Itsye became acclaimed as the greatest, kindest, and most devout *melomed*. He was so esteemed that it was considered a privilege to have one's son study with the Groseler *melomed*. Torah scholarship was held in high esteem in those days, and children would leave his tutelage brimming and permeated with knowledge of the Talmud and Jewish law. All was as it should have been; more children kept being born to them, and their oldest four children grew up. Nonetheless, a *melomed*'s wages would not support a family of ten. So understandably this Reb Itsye and his family suffered great want, which compelled his wife to become a wage earner—a storekeeper. Since her father could not bear to see and hear about their destitution, he set up for her a store of pots and all types of basic dishware—also axes, shovels,[22] rakes, and plain glassware. The entire value of the stock of the store probably added up to less than 100 silver rubles.[23] That was when Reb Yankev's one and only devoted daughter—Ester-Khaykele—acquired the name "storekeeper" and began working tremendously hard because the store demanded much more work than simply selling. She also had to display the glassware, pots, and plates in front of her store and lift the axes, shovels, and rakes. Whenever a customer would come in and misplace the merchandise, she would then need to put everything back in its place. And finally, every evening she had to carry everything back inside the store. In truth, the children used to come to help out, but they broke more than they helped. So Ester-Khaye, poor woman that she was, made certain that they did not come to help her; she was able to do everything more quickly herself. Now we cannot forget that she had a home with a husband, who himself devotedly labored bitterly hard from dawn until dusk and worried and grieved over his students whom he wanted to make into scholars, though they had no such desires for themselves. And her children also wanted to eat. Upon returning home from her store in the evening to cook dinner, the genteel Ester-Khaye needed to do and arrange everything herself. When she left for her store in the morning, she took along breakfast and lunch for her husband and children.

---

22 In the original Yiddish, *opides* was mistakenly printed instead of *lopites*, meaning "shovels," as is apparent from other lists of items in the store appearing in chapter 1 and elsewhere in this chapter.

23 The silver ruble coin circulated in Tsarist Russia simultaneously with the paper ruble, which was worth less.

On top of all of this, she would have to travel every two weeks with her wares to the fair in a German colony called Silts, thirty *versts* from Tiraspol; all the storekeepers would go to the fair there.[24] The entire trip would take her two days, and she would be up to her ears in work. Both in the heat of the summer and the cold of the winter, Ester-Khaye unfortunately had to travel to the fairs. Apart from the fair in Silts, Tiraspol itself held two or three fairs a year close to town. She toiled away like this and assisted her beloved husband in his exhausting labor. She used to bemoan how hard he worked, thereby ignoring her own strenuous labor, which was possibly much more difficult than his, particularly being the genteel and weak woman that she was. Although her circumstances were certainly more lamentable, her pity was reserved for him. As she would say, "Well, I work bitterly hard, but at least I'm able to see the outdoors and be in the open air a whole day. But my unfortunate husband, who is such a scholar and a refined person, must sit in a pent-up room and slave away an entire day with a bunch of loafers. Some small task—making dolts into . . . learned Jews! And this comes at no small cost to his health? And how much health does he lose when he sees me working so deathly hard, especially when he knows that I'm not used to such work and my strength fails me. And that's why he tries in any way he can to ease my workload when he has some free time." In this selfless manner she would speak to herself, feeling sorry for him alone. She tried to hide from him her onerous toil in order not to cause him any heartache.

Being earnest, pious, and devoted, Ester-Khaye believed that with her husband's Torah scholarship and fear of Heaven, she would merit life in the World to Come and their children would grow up to be God-fearing and perfectly devout, illuminating the world with their Torah learning and piety. Because the devout and kind woman Ester-Khaye thought this, it is clear that no undertaking was too difficult or large when it came to her home or the raising of the children. Her entire motive in life lay in her sons growing up to be rabbis and spiritual leaders of their generation and in her daughters' marrying scholars of the same caliber. She was certain that her husband, her Itsele, would raise their children this way with his tremendous abilities and under his tremendous moral instruction, piety, and devotion. With this vitality, so to speak, she lived and had the fortitude to work so tremendously hard while, at the same time, everything appeared to her to be so easy and sweet. Not only did she not feel her poverty-stricken condition but she was also practically unaware of it. She was always in good humor and happy, was never worried, and did not permit any

---

24 Evidently referring to the Germany colony Selts, now called Lymanske, Ukraine, which is 28.5 *versts* (30.4 kilometers) from Tiraspol.

worry to reach her dear and devoted husband nor her dear children. She strove with all of her strength to embed good character traits in the young hearts of her children and primarily strove to implant faith in them. This matron, Ester-Khaye, acquired the reputation in town of being the most pious woman in all of Tiraspol and was considered to be a *tsadeykes*.[25]

The poverty of the Groseler *melomed* grew from day to day. Their children grew up, and the family continued to increase with the birth of each newborn that God bestowed upon them. Both the Groseler *melomed* and Ester-Khaye the Gróselerin worked extremely hard day and night yet barely earned enough to buy dry bread.[26] They suffered like this their whole lives and, unfortunately, never lived to see their children established nor had any joy in the world. Both he, the pious Reb Itsye the Groseler *melomed*, and the devout and kind Ester-Khaye the Groselerin died young. She died before him because her strength gave out earlier, and then he died a year and seven months later because he could not bear the poverty and the pain of his loss. The light of his life extinguished before its time, and his strength left him. His world ended in his fortieth year. How young he was when he died, but his wife was even younger when she died—only thirty-eight.[27] They suffered in this world as much as if they had lived to be twice their ages. But who can ask God, "What are You doing?" God certainly knows what He is doing for He is always right![28] Everyone in town took his death so to heart that they asked: "Where is God's mercy? Why did they deserve to die so young and leave so many impoverished and forlorn orphans—big, little, and in-between? What will the orphans do? Who will raise them? Who will feed them? God, God, where is Your mercy? Where is the merit of their parents' good deeds?" Though the townsfolk questioned and protested, it stayed at that and God once again remained right as always.

---

25 Denotes an extremely righteous woman.
26 Having lived in Groseles before moving to Tiraspol, the author's father and mother were known respectively as the Groseler *melomed* and the Gróselerin (pronounced "Gróselern").
27 If the author's mother was thirty-eight when she died, that means that she was fourteen when she gave birth to Tsipe-Rukhl approximately in 1830. The 1858 additional revision list (poll-tax census) of the Jews of Tiraspol includes several women who were born in the 1810s and had their oldest child at age fourteen. Only in 1835 did Tsarist Russia pass legislation forbidding Jews from marrying early (Dubnow, 1918:2:40, 112). In chapter 15, p. 245, the author writes that both of his parents died in their forties.
28 Though *mistome* (*mistama* in Modern Hebrew) and *minastám* (pronounced *min ha-stam* in Modern Hebrew) are today both used in Yiddish and Hebrew to mean "probably," these words could also mean "of course" or "certainly" in the Yiddish of those times. See Harkavy (1928:306, 307). It is the latter meaning that the author uses, as is clear from numerous examples further in the text.

CHAPTER 2

The Death of My Parents, Brother-in-Law, and Brother, 1854–1857

Divine Providence • A Lofty Soul • An Eternal Source of Pain • Six Orphans • Matchmaking in Those Days • A Remarkable Housewife • A Disgusting Blemish • Isruel the Diligent Scholar • A Groom Obtains a Dowry • The Romanovker *Shoykhet*[1] • Death • Left Without Any Means of Support • A Young Storekeeper • The Death of an Orphan

I know that the reader will be strongly interested in knowing how many children the Groselers had during their lifetimes and how many orphans—boys and girls—were left behind after their deaths. Also, did the unfortunate and impoverished orphans ever find any happiness for themselves? Who raised each of them? Certainly, all of this must be of interest to every reader. So I will oblige you by relating everything. Though I will not be remiss in relating the fate of each child, I will do so succinctly and with the utmost brevity. Yet regarding the youngest orphan, their five-year-old son, I will relate all that occurred to him from the age of five until now, when he is already old and gray, because I know that it will be very interesting to read. From such an extraordinary autobiography, one can fathom God's wonders: how He is the Father of orphans, oversaw a forlorn child, and, in his parents' merit, guarded their beloved son, the only survivor of all of their children. From my account one can deduce the following

---

1   The original Yiddish states "The Romanenker *Shoykhet*." Romanenko was an alternate name for Romanovka. For consistency, "Romanovker" has been used since the author refers to it as Romanovke in all other instances.

principles: there is a God in the world, "God does not withhold the reward of any creature,"[2] He protects all of His creations with His divine providence,[3] He unceasingly safeguards all who seek His protection, and those who trust in Him are never disgraced. You yourself will be convinced of all of this upon reading how this orphan endured misery and suffering and was often in danger and mortal fear, yet God constantly guarded and protected him from every evildoing and evildoer in the world. Upon reading all of this, you will certainly say, "How great are Your works, O Lord; how very profound Your thoughts."[4]

Returning to our subject, I promised to oblige the reader by relating the number of children that they had, and so on. I can tell you that the pious and good couple, Reb Itsele Groseler and his beloved, devout wife Ester-Khaye, gave birth to eight children—three boys and five girls. Two children, a girl and a boy, died in infancy. They did not mourn their daughter, who died at a few years of age, as intensely as they did their little two-year-old son, who they were utterly convinced would eventually illuminate the world with his Torah knowledge, as a light appeared to emanate from him when he was born. Understanding that he must have been a lofty soul and would have grown up to be a great personage, they continued throughout their lives to grieve for and weep over their not having merited raising such a child. Yet, his two and a half years in this world provided them enough to relate about him for their entire lives: his handsome appearance, his cleverness, his expressions, his crying, his laughter, and his purity. In short, he was exceptional in comparison with other children. Even stubborn skeptics also had to admit that this child was something exquisite, a wunderkind. Consequently, he was not shown to strangers,[5] and that is also the reason that the heartache his death caused his parents actually remained an eternal source of pain for them.

The remaining six children, the surviving two boys and four girls, were brought up by their parents until they became orphaned—poor, unfortunate, motherless orphans. The tragedy and pity were not equal for each child, but whichever one of them was looked upon, one's heart rent in pain. The oldest daughter was named Tsipe-Rukhl; the second, Ite; the third, Khone; and the fourth, Súre.[6] Regarding the two orphaned sons: one was called Isruel, and the

---

2 Talmud (Pesakhim 118a).
3 This is the Baal Shem Tov's interpretation of the concept of divine providence. See the Introduction, pp. 53–61.
4 Psalms 92:6.
5 He was not shown to strangers out of fear of the evil eye.
6 Khane (Hannah in English) is pronounced as Khone in the author's Yiddish dialect, which is spoken in the southernmost part of Southeastern Yiddish (see the Introduction to the

youngest, was called, out of pity, Berele, the diminutive of his name, as if this nickname made him seem happy.⁷

My Oldest Sister—Tsipe-Rukhl

Tsipe-Rukhl was very attractive, kind, and an outstandingly skillful housewife. Her father made a match for her with a young man from a small *shteytl* near Tiraspol by the name Zarivke (Zakhárovka in the non-Jewish vernacular). As matches were generally made in those days, particularly among such pious people, the young man and woman neither saw nor spoke to each other before the wedding. In this manner, they were married. Nonetheless, after the wedding, Tsipe-Rukhl did not want to continue living with her husband. Though he came from a wealthy home, which was truly fortunate for her and would have enabled her to live happily and to move out of her impoverished parents' home, she did not care for him. She could in no way convince herself to continue living with him because he had a tremendous blemish; he would go to sleep dry and wake up . . . wet.

Owing to her impoverished condition, others attempted to coax her into continuing to reside with him, but she was predisposed to returning to her parents rather than continuing to live with such a husband. Understandably, he was not too quick in granting her a divorce. After dragging it out a few years, he was finally, through rabbinical intervention, compelled to divorce her. Hence, she ended up a divorcée living with her impoverished parents.

My Sister Ite

The second daughter, Ite, was even more attractive than Tsipe-Rukhl and also a very pious young woman. She married someone from Tiraspol by the name of Ershele, who was a serious student, a devout young man.⁸ He was the only son

---

Glossaries). Note that Khone is not to be confused with the masculine name of Khone in Northeastern Yiddish (pronounced Khune in Southeastern Yiddish).

7   Before the twentieth century, Hebrew personal names such as Dov, Arye, Tsvi, and Zev were rarely used in daily life, except for religious purposes or when written. Instead, their Yiddish translations were used, namely Ber (bear), Leyb (lion), Hersh (deer), and Volf (wolf), respectively. Hence, the author was called Ber or its diminutive forms Berl and Berele (as mentioned later) as a child.

8   The name Hershele is pronounced as Ershele in the author's Yiddish dialect, which is spoken in the southernmost part of the Southeastern Yiddish territory. Ershele's surname was Teplitsky, as noted in the 1858 additional revision list (poll-tax census) of the Jews

of Reb Simkhe the *shoykhet*.⁹ After the wedding, she and her husband lived on *kest* with her in-laws.

My Only Brother Isruel's Marriage and My Mother's Death

Their son Isruel was kind and devout. He studied the Torah for its own sake and with great diligence, so much so that he would not come home from the *bes-medresh* from *Shobes* to *Shobes*.¹⁰ His diligence was without limit: when food was brought to him in the *bes-medresh*, he ate; otherwise, he thought that it was just as well not to eat. His sisters would take pains to bring him food, and, from what has been said before, one might guess the kind of meager sustenance it was. But since he was very dear to his parents, they devoted all of their energies, despite their poverty, to providing him with food from which he could derive strength to strenuously labor in prayer and study the Torah. This son was the only pleasure in their lives and served to comfort them in the loss of their little son who died in infancy. Their true aspiration was that he would grow up to be a tremendous Torah genius. In actuality, they were not mistaken in their assessment of him because his reputation as the greatest Torah scholar in town began to spread and he outshone all other Torah scholars with his mastery of the Talmud and the major halakhic works. He knew both volumes of *Yoreh*

---

of Tiraspol (where he is referred to as Gershko) and on the genealogical chart made by Bernard Budiansky and his son Michael based on an interview with Bernard's grandfather Israel Chaplick in the mid-1960s. Israel's wife Feyge was the daughter of Ershele's daughter Ester-Khaye Apatshevsky. See Appendix D2 for a genealogical chart of the extended Teplitsky family.

9 "Simkhe *shoykhet*" in the original. The author also refers to other *shokhtim* (plural of *shoykhet*) in a similar manner, meaning without an article (for example, Simkhe the *shoykhet*), which is how *shokhtim* were referred to in that area; Carmel (1975:265) refers to his father, who was a *shoykhet* in nearby Bender, in a similar manner. A *shoykhet* is one who slaughters animals in accordance with Jewish law. The 1858 additional revision list (poll-tax census) of the Jews of Tiraspol indicates that Simkhe's full name was Itskhok-Simkhe (referred to as Itsko-Simkha), the son of Meyer Teplitsky (born ca. 1812). It also indicates that his wife Feyge—mentioned later—was born ca. 1815.

10 In those times, a *bes-medresh* denoted a Torah study hall where no formal instruction took place but where students studied independently and where prayer services were also held, as opposed to a *shul* (synagogue), which was established solely for prayer services. Today the *bes-medresh* and *shul* have merged together. *Shabes* (the Jewish Sabbath) is pronounced as *Shobes* in the author's Yiddish dialect, which is spoken in the southernmost part of the Southeastern Yiddish territory.

Deah practically by heart.[11] Above all, he was very pious and handsome, so he was strongly praised and people would bless the local children that they should be like him. When he was eighteen years old, he was taken as a son-in-law by a certain *shoykhet* who was an outstanding Torah scholar from a small *shteytl* near Kishinev called Romanovke. Understandably, he put money into Isruel's father's wallet, paid his son-in-law a dowry, provided him with *kest*, and gave him expensive gifts; nothing was too expensive or too difficult for him, as long as he achieved the goal of having this young man as his son-in-law. Even though his father-in-law was a *shoykhet*, a scribe of Torah scrolls and *mezuzahs*, a devout Jew from a large family, and a bit wealthy as well, he nonetheless considered himself quite fortunate in obtaining such a precious groom for his daughter.[12] The entire world was envious of the match, and, in truth, their envy was actually justified. Unfortunately, his precious, kindhearted, devout mother did not live to have any pleasure beyond seeing the girl engaged to her dear Srulik, for she did not live to escort him to the *huppah*.[13] The same year that he became engaged and several months before he was to be married, she took ill, lay sick in bed a few months, and died on the 20th of *Adar* 5608 [*sic*].[14]

After her death, five orphans remained at home: Tsipe-Rukhl (age twenty-four), a divorcée; Ite (age twenty), who was still living with and being supported by her in-laws; the engaged Srulik (age eighteen); Khone (age twelve) [*sic*]; Sure (age eight); and [myself,] Berl, the youngest (age five).[15] Reb Itsele the Groseler *melomed* was now a widower and began to take his tremendous loss—the loss of such a precious wife and devoted mother—to heart and to

---

11   *Yoreh Deah* is one of the four sections of the *Shulkhan Arukh* (*Code of Jewish Law*) and deals with various prohibited and permitted subjects, such as dietary laws, interest, purity, and mourning.
12   The original states that Isruel's father-in-law was a "*shoykhet* and *boydek*," the latter denoting an examiner of the lungs of slaughtered animal. Jewish law necessitates the checking of the lungs of slaughtered cattle, goats, and fowl to ensure that no holes or scar tissue have rendered the animal forbidden to eat (Berman, 1941:7–8). Since this is an essential part of the slaughtering process, the word *shoykhet* is used in the translation whenever the words "*shoykhet* and *boydek*" appear.
13   Srulikl is a diminutive form of Isruel. A *huppah* is a canopy under which a Jewish couple traditionally stands during their wedding ceremony (Kaplan, 1983:133–148).
14   As mentioned in his "In Lieu of a Preface," p. 84, footnote 1, the author mistakenly thought that he was born in 1842 instead of 1848, from which he calculated his mother's year of death. Hence, she did not die on the 20th of *Adar* in 5608 (1848) but rather in 5614 (March 20, 1854). For more regarding the author's erroneous dating, see the Introduction, pp. 67–70.
15   The author states that five orphans lived at home and then enumerates six siblings. He might not have originally included Tsipe-Rukhl since she was married at the time and living with her in-laws. Khone died in the winter of 1860–1861 at the age of twenty-one, which the author mentions twice (ch. 3, p. 124, and ch. 15, p. 245); hence, she was approximately fourteen (not twelve) at the time of her mother's death in 1854.

deeply feel her absence. His strength began to wane from day to day yet no one had time to pay him any attention. Tsipe-Rukhl and Khonele were preoccupied with the store that their mother, may she rest in peace, had maintained and also watched over the small orphans.[16] Since some merchandise remained, the two oldest daughters struggled to ensure that the store would provide them with some income so as to relieve their father of the burden of paying for all the household expenses. And their father, poor soul that he was, toiled away, saw to it that his son Isruel was prepared for his wedding, and lived to marry him off.

My Sister Ite Becomes a Widow

Upon returning from his son's wedding, Reb Itsele found his daughter Ite's husband Ershl quite ill, thereby marring the only bit of joy he had from Ite, whom he had hoped would live happily. After lying in bed about three months, Ershl died at the age of nineteen, leaving his infant daughter, Ester-Khaye, a tiny orphan only a few months old.[17] When their father saw what had become of his precious progeny—Tsipe-Rukhl's becoming an impoverished divorcée and the young, beautiful Ite, right at the prime of her life, a widow with an orphaned infant—he became heartbroken and ill. When he was seriously ill, he understandably received no payment for teaching. Since their entire sustenance was then earned solely from the store, its stock quickly became depleted until nothing was left. When he died, nothing was left even for one meal.

My Father's Death

Reb Itsele's death was as follows: he recovered from being dangerously ill and in *Elul* was already up and walking about.[18] He expected to once again arrange to teach a group of boys after the High Holy Days. With the arrival of Rosh Hashanah, his condition worsened while praying. He was taken from the *besmedresh* and carried to the home of the rabbi, Reb Shloymele, who lived next to

---

16 Khonele is the diminutive of Khone.
17 The author's mother died in March 1854 (p. 101, footnote 14), a few months before Isruel's wedding; hence, he married in 1854. Ershl died a few months after Isruel's wedding, also in 1854. Ershl's year of death (1854), his age at the time of his death (nineteen), and the year of birth of his daughter (1854) are all confirmed by the 1858 additional revision list (poll-tax census) of the Jews of Tiraspol.
18 August–September 1855. *Elul* is the Hebrew month preceding Rosh Hashanah.

the *shul*.[19] Since his condition did not improve there, the rabbi permitted carrying him home by wagon.[20] At home, he lay in bed for three days and died on the fifth of *Tishre*—eighteen months after his wife's death.[21] "May his soul be bound up in the bond of eternal life."[22]

My Sister Ite and Her Mother-in-Law Feyge

Their mother's death was not as great a tragedy for the orphans as their father's death appeared to be. The three small orphans—two girls and a boy—were now left without any means of support. Besides them, there were the oldest, Tsipe-Rukhl, a divorcée; the son Isruel who was just married; and the young widow Ite who did not have the best relationship with her in-laws. Ite's *kest* had quickly ended because she unfortunately had a mean mother-in-law, a nuisance, known in town as Feyge the *shoykhet*'s wife. Even while Feyge's son Ershele was alive, Feyge made her daughter-in-law Ite's life miserable.[23] Disregarding that Ershele was her only son, Feyge nagged Ite the whole day when Ershele was not at home; he was, of course, studying Torah in the *bes-medresh*. When Ershele would come home, his mother would become kind and devoted. When Ite once complained to Ershele, he almost could not believe his ears and he then rebuked his mother. Later that day, Ite was repaid for that dearly. Ite would secretly go to her impoverished father and cry, but how could he help her beyond consoling her that this would eventually pass and that a time would come when her mother-in-law would also become kind? "Suffer, my child, suffer," he used to say. "Patience and time change everything." From these circumstances alone one can already understand how much consideration Ite received from her mother-in-law after the death of her two champions, her father and her husband. Although she still had her in-laws, Ite was no better off than her earlier-mentioned orphaned siblings.

And, in the end, that is exactly what happened.

Upon weaning her daughter, Ite left her with her wicked mother-in-law, because Ite decided that it was better to be at home like all of her orphaned sisters and brothers and to eat together with them merely a dry piece of bread

---

19 In chapter 3, p. 112, the author writes that Reb Shloyme was the rabbi of Tiraspol.
20 Although a wagon is generally prohibited to use on the Sabbath (*Shabes*) and major Jewish holidays, the rabbi permitted carrying him home due to his ill health. See *Shulkhan Arukh* (*Orakh Khayim* 329).
21 September 17, 1855.
22 Samuel I 25:29.
23 Ershele and Ershl are both diminutive forms of the name Hersh.

every third day than to be among snakes and eat of the best. But we will relate more about this matter later. We now need to relate what happened to the littlest orphans and to the older daughter Tsipe-Rukhl, who was called Tsipe.

My Sisters Tsipe and Khonele at Work

When their grandfather from Groseles, their mother's father Reb Yankev Gredenitser, learned that his son-in-law Reb Itsele had also died and that his grandchildren were left without any means of support, he disregarded his advanced age, came to Tiraspol, and made a tumult among relatives and friends. It was decided that Tsipe-Rukhl would be given merchandise—sewing notions—and would set up a booth next to a textile store. By standing alongside her booth of sewing notions, she would sell and thereby earn a living. In those times, many poor people supported themselves from such booths, and those who were lucky to find a good place earned a living.

At the same time, Khonele was placed with a storekeeper who ran the type of store that sells pots, axes, shovels, and the like, with which Khonele was familiar when she used to help her mother. This storekeeper was a devout Jewish woman, who continued to keep Khonele employed and teach her until she became a full-fledged merchant. This storekeeper later set up another store in partnership with Khonele, whose total income was barely enough to support Khonele alone. Nonetheless, after a while, Khonele was able to begin to assist the household financially as well, and their situation became a little easier. Until then, the burden of supporting the family was completely upon Tsipe, who made a living by selling sewing notions and darning socks. But things were not to be easy for long.

My Brother Srulik's Death

Exactly a year after their father's death, Srulik suddenly arrived from Romanovke for the High Holidays to visit his parents' graves. When he returned from the cemetery, he took to his bed ill. One can easily understand how miserable the orphans were now that their dear Srulik lay in bed. He must be saved, but there were no medical means to do so. His wife would have come, but she was then in labor with their first child, a daughter.[24] When the child was a month old, his wife came, but Sruel's condition was still not improving. The town was in

---

24   Isruel's daughter's name was Freydele, as indicated in chapter 22.

turmoil: they wanted to save him, but they were powerless to do so. He died at the age of twenty on the 2nd of Adar 5612 [*sic*]—a year and five months after his father's death.²⁵ "May his soul be bound up in the bond of eternal life."²⁶

One can understand the orphans' grief, but the whole town also ended up in mourning. The story behind this was as follows: Isruel's rebbe in Tiraspol was called Reb Yosef the Elder,²⁷ who would study day and night, fast every Monday and Thursday, and would not leave the *bes-medresh* from *Shobes* to *Shobes*.²⁸ In town, he was considered a tremendously God-fearing and holy person. Eight days before Isruel's death, he learned that his cherished student was dangerously ill and went to visit him. Afterward, he returned to the *bes-medresh*, where he suddenly became ill. He returned home to lie down and died the same day and at the same moment that his student Isruel died.

In one day, the town lost two great personages. Since Torah was then important, all the stores closed and all went to pay their last respects to those two important people. The two funerals were talked about for many years, even very far from Tiraspol. Thousands of people followed the funeral procession and both, student along with teacher, were interred beside each other in the cemetery.²⁹

Though the town forgot the pain, the orphans could not forget the tremendous loss of such a precious brother and being left so poor and alone. Before his death, they could have hoped that their brother would become a rabbi somewhere and then take in a couple of the orphans, thereby helping them. What would now become of the orphans without his help? It is difficult to relate the

---

25 As mentioned in his "In Lieu of a Preface," p. 84, footnote 1, the author mistakenly thought that he was born in 1842 instead of 1848. Yet, even by using his mistaken year of birth, he miscalculated the year of his brother's death as 5612 (1852) instead of 5611 (1851). His brother Isruel actually died on February 26, 1857, which was a year and five months after his father's death, as noted here and implied in chapter 5, pp. 137–138. Since Isruel was eighteen when his mother died in 1854 (p. 101), he was twenty years old upon his death, which is also explicitly mentioned in chapter 15, p. 245. See also the Introduction, pp. 67–70.
26 Samuel I 25:29.
27 The term "rebbe" here means a rabbinical teacher. The only Yosef listed in the 1858 additional revision list (poll-tax census) of the Jews of Tiraspol as having died in 1857 is Yos (son of Shmiel) Mirkhinik at the age of thirty-eight. Despite Mirkhinik's young age, he could have been called "the Elder" to distinguish him from a younger Yosef (possibly a nephew) in his family or from a younger Torah scholar also named Yosef in Tiraspol.
28 Though not as common today, many pious Jews used to fast every Monday and Thursday, which are considered especially favorable days for supplication and prayer (*Kitsur Shulkhan Arukh* 22:9).
29 Leva (Khotskl-Leyb) Zeltser of Brooklyn, a native of Tiraspol, relates that the Soviet Union had Tiraspol's pre-Second World War Jewish cemetery destroyed and built houses and factories in its place.

details of their individual fates. After *shivah*,[30] Isruel's widow returned home and took along the little boy Berele, since a Jewish woman is prohibited from traveling alone with a non-Jewish wagoner.[31] When she brought the little orphan to her father, he took a strong liking to Berele. Perhaps compassion was instrumental in his agreeing to raise the little orphaned boy until adulthood.

---

30 *Shivah* is the seven-day period of mourning that Jews observe after the death of a close relative. This practice is often referred to as "sitting *shivah*."
31 To avoid the halakhic prohibition forbidding seclusion between a man and a woman (known as *yikhud*), it was common practice for a Jewish woman traveling with a non-Jewish wagoner to take along a minor (Zinner, 2001:117).

CHAPTER 3

Tragedy in the Lives of Three of My Sisters, ca. 1857–1864

A Girl for a Boy • Surele's Husband—A Tall *Melomed*[1] • Tsipe—The Lady of the House • Ite's Heartache • Jobs for the Orphans • Tsipe's Prospects for Happiness • Tsipe's Second Husband • A Proper Jew • All Envy Tsipe • A Biography of a Son-in-Law • A Lazy *Melomed* • Shloyme-Leyzer—A Coward • Jewish Life • An *Eynikl* of a Rebbe • The Walls Tremble • Miracles and Wonders • Divine Inspiration • Ite Marries • Supported by a Wealthy Man • Reb Alter's Star Performance • Good Business Dealings • Like Before • Ite—A Divorcee • Mother and Child • Khonele • Tsipe the Sufferer • Khonele's and Tsipe's Bearing Children before Their Deaths[2]

My Being Sent Home from Romanovke

Shortly afterward, the women in Romanovke deliberated among themselves as follows: "What's the use of our keeping a little boy for whom we need to pay his *melomdim*—apart from our getting no use out of him. If we already have the *mitzvah* of taking in an orphan, wouldn't it be better to take in a little girl? A little girl wouldn't need to cost us anything for her education, and we could get

---

1 The original Yiddish states "*a langer melamed*." Lang (and its inflected form *langer*) was formerly used, at least in some areas of Eastern Europe, to also denote "tall," though today it is exclusively used to denote "long."
2 The translator has moved the beginning of chapter 4 to the end of chapter 3 to separate the story of the author's parents and siblings from that of his own life. See ch. 3, p. 120, footnote 41.

some use out of her as well.³ As soon as she arrives here, she could be a nanny to her brother's child, a little orphan only a few months old. And afterward, her sister-in-law could use her to help out in the house." In short, they concluded that returning the boy and taking the girl would be better in every way. She was three years older than he was—he being seven and she being ten—and she would therefore also be more mature. In short, the elderly Reb Tsvi the *shoykhet*, Isruel's father-in-law, was persuaded to make the exchange: he sent the little boy Berele back and took the little girl Súrele.⁴

This decision irked the older orphans because they considered it more important for the boy to be raised in Romanovke. They would have then known that Berele would grow up to be a Torah scholar and a pious Jew. Yet back in Tiraspol with them, what would become of him? But what could they do since it was not up to them? They thought about not giving up Surele, but they could not afford to do so since sending her away would relieve them of another mouth to feed. Additionally, they knew that Surele would be raised in Romanovke until she would be of marriageable age and would then be married off there. On that account, they agreed to give up Surele, whom they sent to her brother's widow and her father. Surele was raised there as their own daughter, and they married her off to a fine young man, giving her a dowry and a trousseau. The young man was a *melomed* from a fine family. He was no professor—just a simple *melomed* of very young children.⁵ Though his name was Leyb Vaynberg, he was called "*Leyb-Itsl-der-Bube-Ites der melomed*."⁶ Though he was called by such a lengthy

---

3   At that time, most Jewish girls in Eastern Europe did not receive a formal education outside of the home.

4   Before the twentieth century, the Hebrew name Tsvi was rarely used in everday life, rather someone named Tsvi (meaning deer) was called by its Yiddish translation of Hersh (or the dialectal Ersh), which is how he is referred to in chapter 13. See ch. 2, p. 99, footnote 7. His surname was Itskovitsh; see ch. 13, p. 210, footnote 30, for details. Surele is the diminutive of Sure.

5   *Dardeker melamed* in the original. Yudl Mark (1943:41) refers to the author's use of *dardeker melamed* here and in chapter 4 instead of the proper *dardeke melamed* (*dardeke* means "child" in Aramaic) as a folkism, though it might be one of the many mistakes made by the typesetter. A *dardeke melamed* was the name used for a beginning-level *melamed*, who taught his students the Hebrew alphabet, as the author explains. For a detailed overview of the *kheyder* of the *dardeke melamed*, see Shtern (1950:7–32).

6   Meaning "Leyb the *melomed*, the son of Itsl, the son of the midwife Ite." In Southeastern Yiddish, a midwife is called a *bube* and a grandmother is a *bobe* (Schaechter, 1991:xxxiv). The 1854 and 1859 additional revision lists (poll-tax censuses) of the Jews of Romanovke (aka Romanenko) indicate that Leyb was born approximately in 1845 and that his father Itsl (born ca. 1822)—referred to as Itsek—was the son of Kelman (ca. 1798–1850) and Ite (born ca. 1800). (The 1854 revision list mistakenly refers to Itsl's mother as Eta, and the 1859 census mistakenly refers to them as Voynberg.) These censuses are housed at the Moldova State Archives in Chișinău (134/2/330, p. 63, registration no. 61, and

title, he was even lengthier . . .[7] But we will discuss Surele's married life later. Meanwhile, let us return to Tiraspol to see what happened with the orphans, the Groselers' children, after the departure of their sister-in-law.

The orphaned children all lived together in a tiny, little dwelling. The oldest sister, Tsipe, served both as the lady of the house and as their mother. She rented a place for them fairly close to her sewing-supplies store so as to easily give proper attention to the household. The little orphan Berele would spend the entire day either in *kheyder* or engaged in playing with friends.[8] Khonele was busy with her dishwares store. Their sister Ite was then still with her in-laws. Understandably, their expenses could barely be met. More than once they did without food or drink to at least have money for heating so they would not freeze; but even so there was not enough money for heating.

My Sister Ite's Struggle with her In-Laws over Her Daughter

All of a sudden, a new hardship came along. As soon as Ite's daughter Ester-Khaykele was weaned and no longer yearned to be breastfed, the unfortunate Ite was compelled to leave her child and take her own clothes and few items of bedding to escape her mother-in-law, that witch, who had for so long been doing everything in her power to torment her. Ite went to her sister Tsipe's and lived in the little room where all the orphans lived—better said, cried—because a sob now arose from the wretched orphans regarding their dire condition.[9] But how could they ever improve their lot? Now, Ite was back staying with them, so the question arose, "How will we survive?" Perhaps feeding Ite the first day was not a problem because her fervor for her child was so great that she ate nothing that day.

Ite would run to her in-laws every day to see her daughter. Her mother-in-law's cruelty is impossible to describe. Just imagine, when her mother-in-law would see Ite coming, she would not let her in. Ite was only allowed inside after desperately making a commotion in the street, but her child had already been removed to another location. All of Ite's crying, yelling, and fainting in

---

134/2/501, p. 18/86, registration no. 61). Extractions of these records were obtained from the JewishGen Romania-Moldova Database.
7   Meaning that Leyb was tall.
8   A *kheyder* was a one-room traditional Jewish religious school, usually for boys of a similar academic level in which the teaching is carried on by a *melamed*.
9   The author is making wordplay on the similar-sounding Yiddish words, *voyn* (live) and *veyn* (cry).

desperation to be shown her daughter were to no avail. Her mother-in-law's pretext was that she wanted her granddaughter to become accustomed to living apart from Ite, and only then would she let Ite see her. In short, Ite, the ill-fated mother, had to resign herself to stop her efforts to see her daughter and become used to living apart from her. Eventually, Ite calmed down and began to think about sustenance and earning a livelihood.

Tsipe-Rukhl did not earn enough from her glasswares store, even when combined with Khonele's income. After all, Khonele was now a big girl and had her own needs apart from her contributions to the household. In short, the situation was miserable and saddening. No matter how hard they tried, they still did not have a *kopek* to their name.

Ite made her way to the elderly woman in whose store Khonele once worked and obtained a place near her. The elderly woman was already old and could no longer travel to the fairs. She hired Ite on a percentage basis, and Ite thereby earned from her either one or one and a half silver rubles a week. Ite suffered like this for two years until a lucky coincidence arose. A certain wealthy person—Reb Khaym-Shloyme,[10] as he was called—wanted to open a store to sell pots, shovels, axes, and glassware.[11] In other words, he wanted to open exactly the same kind of store with which Ite, but not he, was familiar. He took Ite as his partner, and Ite ran the store together with his wife, while he attended to other business endeavors. At that point, Ite's life became a little brighter, and she could then hope to make a better life for herself and to take back her daughter. But nobody advised Ite to take her back since she would be given a better upbringing at her grandparents. She would be able to live a calmer life and would not have a stepfather upon Ite's remarriage.

And that is exactly what happened:

Ite's daughter was raised with her grandparents and was actually married off by them. Nonetheless, Ite would constantly see her, and her daughter would visit her and knew her to be her mother. Being with her grandparents was actually good for the child. She married and her grandparents were satisfied with her as a constant remembrance of their son. Though we will relate more about this matter later, let us now discuss Tsipe-Rukhl and Khonele. Since there is much to relate about Pinkhes-Berele [that is, the author], who was called Berl, we will leave him for last.

---

10 In the original Yiddish, his name is written as "Reb A. Khaym-Shloyme." Apparently the "A." (א.) is a typographical error. Not all such errors have been noted.

11 The only Khaym-Shloyme listed in the 1858 additional revision list (poll-tax census) of the Jews of Tiraspol is Khaym-Shloyme (son of Gedalye) Moldavsky (born ca. 1820). Perhaps Moldavsky was the surname of Ite's business partner.

My Sister Tsipe's Marriage to Shloyme-Leyzer

Tsipe ran the household and all were living together. The light of day drove them outside and the dark of night brought them home again, when everyone would relate their daily trials. All would then go to sleep so as to have energy to endure the sufferings of the next day.

Two years passed like this.[12] All of a sudden Tsipe was presented with some good fortune: a scholarly and God-fearing Jew, a widower, from Poland, from the city of Olt-Konstantin.[13] Upon being described to her as a great Torah scholar and a pious Jew, she immediately agreed to meet him, though he had no money. She was especially satisfied with him upon his consenting to let her younger siblings live with them. I knew quite well, though, how she had snubbed a number of marriage proposals only because the prospective grooms were not Torah scholars and not religious enough, despite their wealth and distinguished rabbinical ancestry. For Tsipe was religious, and a pious, respectable Torah scholar was of great importance to her. That was Tsipe.

One thing, however, deterred her from marrying this widower—he was said to have several children. But upon his giving his word that his children were already grown and no longer dependent on him, everything became all right. A match was made, and they were wed. Tsipe now had a husband . . . and the beginning of a new life.

Everyone in town envied Tsipe's good fortune. "How's it possible," they exclaimed, "that such a poor woman could attain such an important person as a husband?" Nonetheless, she knew the blunder that she had made and how unfortunate she actually was. Due to her piety and respectability, she buried the pain in the depths of her heart and comforted herself in the knowledge that it was certainly her destiny, and that his Torah learning would protect them all. She worked even harder for she now had a husband who sat in the *bes-medresh* and studied, and his food had to be prepared on time so as not to keep him from his studies. She served him with a certain holiness and awe, because she was pious and respectable, and showed him honor only because of his Torah scholarship. She worked and hoped that between terms he would arrange to teach

---

12   Two years passed since their brother Isruel's death in 1857 (ch. 2, pp. 104–105); hence, it is now 1859.
13   Though Olt-Konstantin was in the Volhynia Province of Tsarist Russia, the Tsarist Russian provinces of Volhynia, Podolia, and Kiev (in contemporary Ukraine) were also referred to as Poland by many Jews in Tsarist Russia, since these areas had been a part of the Commonwealth of Poland whose sovereignty ended in 1795 with the Third Partition of Poland. Botoshansky (1942:1:34) mentions that the Jews in Bessarabia even referred to the Jews of the province of Kherson as *Poylishe* (Polish Jews).

a group of boys and that his teaching would pay for everything. Sure enough, between terms, she put together a *kheyder* of older teenagers and young men of marriageable age who were the offspring of the well-to-do. Even Moyshe, the son of Reb Shloymele, the rabbi of Tiraspol, became his student. That term he earned a total of 150 silver rubles from six students, which at that time was a large sum, even for someone who was not a *melomed*. He could have lived nicely if he would not have been . . . himself. His students were already old enough to understand that their parents were paying in vain since he was too lazy to teach and was of no benefit to them. He ended up with only two students from his original group during the second term, and he could not put together a *kheyder* at all during his third term. He could have taken little boys, but he would not and could never permit himself to teach at such a low level.

He then sat without work for an entire term. Seeing that Tiraspol was no place for him, he left for Kishinev, where he ran into a wealthy fellow, Reb Ide Poloner, who wanted him to teach his son privately. This was very appropriate for him: little work, a lot of money, and good food and drink. What more could he ask for? And this was certainly good for Tsipe! She would now not have an additional mouth to feed for he would not be around, and he would certainly send her his wages, plus she earned some money herself. So she certainly was happy! But if anyone thought that this is what would occur, they certainly would have been gravely mistaken for they did not know this fellow, this unique character. His laziness, lack of devotion, and fanaticism caused my unfortunate, impoverished, and innocent sister Tsipe to leave this world so miserably and resulted in his children being so unfortunate.

For this, he can never be forgiven.

Tsipe's husband was called "Reb Shloyme-Leyzer, the *melomed*, the Olt-Konstantiner." He was thirty-six years old when he married Tsipe. He was of short stature, with a large, broad, curly blond beard. His *peyes* resembled small bottles as was then the style in Poland.[14] He spoke quickly, and his speech was chock-full of Torah and Hasidic lore. When someone would stop to talk to him in the *bes-medresh*, a circle of people immediately formed around them and continued to grow until a large crowd soon formed. Why? Because everyone wanted to hear what Shloyme-Leyzer was saying. Meanwhile, someone would ask him a question about a passage in the Talmud or about a commentary by the *Maharsho* and he would respond right on the spot.[15] When the conversation

---

14 Botoshansky (1942:1:278), who was from nearby Bessarabia, also describes someone as having "long *peyes* twisted like small bottles."

15 *Maharsho* is a Hebrew acronym referring to the classic Talmudic commentator, Rabbi Shmuel Eideles (1555–1631).

turned to *tsadikim*, he was able to show his expertise in this subject matter as well.[16] Understandably, it comes as no surprise that Tsipe was envied for having such a outstanding husband.

It was also no surprise that such an attractive young woman of twenty-five [sic],[17] who was very learned in *Tsene-verene*,[18] *Menoyres ha-Moer*,[19] and in all Yiddish ethical books, should agree to marry a poor widower so much older than herself. In actuality, he did not own more than what he regularly wore: a *kapote* and a hat for *Shobes*, and another *kapote* and a hat for the weekdays.[20] Nonetheless, everyone was startled: "How can it be? She was offered matches with well-off, prominent layman who didn't have children and were younger than him, yet she did not want them. So why is she consenting to marry him?" But, as I previously mentioned, since everyone in the *bes-medresh* was impressed with him and his great knowledge of Torah and Hasidic lore, it was actually no surprise that Tsipe, with her love of Torah scholarship, consented to marry him and did not listen to the words of the common person. Afterward, when she fully contemplated her situation and saw how she had deceived herself regarding him, it was already too late since she did not want to divorce yet another time. She used to say that she realized that she had no luck with husbands and who knew if she would do any better in choosing a third. On the other hand, she did not want to remain unmarried for she was eager to have children. So she was willing to bear him in poverty and want, as long as she would at least have children with him. She assumed that when he would have children he would try to do everything he could to feed his family and no longer spend most of his time in uselessness among the idlers in the *bes-medresh*, where they licked their fingers and lapped up his stories while his family sat at home in the dark, suffering from hunger and cold.

---

16 *Tsadikim* here refers to Hasidic Rebbes.
17 Tsipe is mistakenly noted as being twenty-five years old, that is, being born ca. 1824, instead of twenty-nine (see ch. 1, p. 95, footnote 27).
18 *Tsene-verene* is a Yiddish paraphrase with commentary of the *Five Books of Moses*, the Haftorahs, and the Five Scrolls, which was widely used by women in pre-Second World War Europe since many of them did not know Hebrew. Written at the end of the sixteenth century by Rabbi Ya'akov Ashkenazi, the title is taken from *Song of Songs* (3:11) and literally means "Come and see." The late Dr. Mordkhe Schaechter said that speakers of Southeastern Yiddish refer to this work as *Tsene-verene*, though it is generally referred to as *Tsene-rene* in Yiddish.
19 This popular ethical work (*Menorat ha-Maor* in Modern Hebrew) was written by the fourteenth-century rabbinical author Yitskhak Abuhav (Aboab) of Toledo, Spain. Its Yiddish translation made the work popular among women.
20 A *kapote* is a long double-breasted frock coat.

"Reb Shloyme-Leyzer *melomed*," as he was called, was born in Olt-Konstantin and was raised by extremely fanatical Hasidic parents. He studied well and was clever, but only in the study of Torah. Apart from the realm of Jewish law, he was a complete fool. His parents married him off at a young age to someone from the city of Litin, and his and his wife's parents supported him on *kest*. He lived for only one or two years on *kest* with his own parents, and he remained on *kest* with his wife's parents for thirteen years. Throughout the fifteen years after his marriage, during which he had four children, he had still not tried to earn a sou on his own. He only knew how to sit in the *bes-medresh* and tell miracle stories of *tsadikim*. In general, he was a loafer who was used to others preparing his food for him, cleaning his clothes, and giving him a *groshn* on the side for his small expenditures: giving charity in *shul*; providing *tikn* for the congregants; and entry to the bathhouse.[21] But who cared about his wife and children's expenses? He had no interest in that! At that time, the convention of young sons-in-law on *kest* was as follows: during the period of *kest*, they had nothing to do with household expenses. Nonetheless, all the young married men sat and studied Torah on *kest* for four years, at the most, after their weddings, but he was an exception. He remained on *kest* for fifteen years. Understandably, Shloyme-Leyzer had to cease living on *kest* when his father-in-law died because his mother-in-law had become a poor widow. What does such a fellow do? He becomes a *melomed*. But he was not accustomed to hard work and the burden of supporting a family. So after a few terms, no parent wanted to send their children to him. Exactly what happened to him in Tiraspol had previously happened to him in Poland, only that Polish Jews are more particular regarding Torah study and he was not willing to work hard.[22] And that is what devastated his first wife, poor woman that she was, until she died and left four orphans, who were scattered among her relatives. Like this, the proper and religious Tsipe also suffered and bore the pain and regret in the recesses of her heart, unknown to anyone. She told no one of her bitter heart, even the orphans—her younger, helpless sisters.

---

21 A *groshn* is a half-*kopek* coin. *Shteln tikn* refers to someone providing liquor (often accompanied by food) for the congregants after weekday morning-prayer services on the *yortsayt* (anniversary of death) of a departed relative or Hasidic Rebbe and other special occasions. The *tikn* affords the congregants the opportunity to make a blessing over the liquor (and/or the edibles) in the merit of a departed soul, thereby serving to elevate (*tikn*, or *tikun* in Modern Hebrew, means "to repair" or "to elevate") the soul. For a slightly variant definition, see Wertheim (1992:223–240).
22 So while absolutely no one would hire him in Litin, there were always a few in Tiraspol willing to hire him.

Shloyme-Leyzer's daily schedule was astonishing to observe. Upon arising in the morning, he would yawn a bit and then began to smoke his pipe: puff, and then puff-puff, and puff-puff-puff, and again puff-puff-puff-puff, and then finally the pipe would light up. His preparations for and his use of the privy lasted a few hours and were followed by an hour-long *Asher Yotser*.[23] After reciting the morning blessings, he would drink something hot and then go to *shul* to pray.[24] He would then eat, then study, then eat, and then eat once again. Such was the manner in which he always conducted himself, never—absolutely never—altering his routine.

To the extent that he was well versed in Yiddish, he was ignorant of other languages and did not know even one word of Russian. When he would see a nobleman or a constable approach him on the road, he would flee in a very strange manner.[25] Hence, I have described this unique character, Tsipe's intended one, on whose account Tsipe was the envy of all and thought to be very happy.

In pondering Shloyme-Leyzer's teaching position with the wealthy fellow in Kishinev and the pittance of money his wife received from the whole affair, it is difficult to understand how people survived in those times. During the entire two terms that he was in Kishinev, he did not send Tsipe even one *kopek*.[26] Letters written beseeching him for money were to no avail. At the end of the two terms, after having eaten his full at the home of his wealthy employer and no longer having anything further to do, he wrote a brief letter to Tsipe that she should expect . . . his coming home for *Yontef*.[27] His wife was elated for now that he was coming home, he would certainly bring money with him, and she would then be able to restock her little store. So with her last few coins, she prepared, with all of her energy, a wonderful *Yontef*. And then this unique character arrived.

Upon entering the house, he asked her, "Tsipe, do you have some money? Pay the driver seventy-five *kopeks* and take down my package from the wagon." At the same time, he was greeted by his friends from all sides, for everyone

---

23 *Asher Yotsar* is a relatively short Hebrew blessing thanking God for a functioning body, which is recited after relieving oneself.
24 Upon rising, Orthodox Jews recite the morning blessings, which are a series of Hebrew blessings listed before morning-prayer services in their prayer books.
25 He fled apparently because he did not know how to greet them properly in Russian.
26 In this area of Eastern Europe, there were two terms per year: the winter term started after *Sukes* (in late September or October) and lasted until before Pesach (in late March or April), and the summer term started after Pesach and lasted until a week before Rosh Hashanah (usually in September). See chapter 17, p. 266, footnote 7.
27 *Yontef* (*Yom Tov* in Modern Hebrew) denotes a major Jewish holiday.

considered him to be an important guest. Meanwhile, Tsipe thought to herself that he did not pay undoubtedly because he did not have any change, so she shook out her last few *kopeks*, paid the driver, and took his package off the wagon. Later, after the initial excitement of his arrival died down and everyone dispersed, he asked her for a *gildn* to enter the bathhouse, for he had arrived not long before *Yontef* began.[28] Her heart began pounding and she asked him with irony, "And where is your money?!" "Oh, my money? I'll tell you about it later. Meanwhile, give me fifteen *kopeks*. It's late, and I must go to the bathhouse." She gave him fifteen *kopeks*, he left, but she could not believe that he had absolutely no money. Tsipe thought, "It can't be. Can it be?! He taught for two terms. He didn't send one *kopek* for two whole terms, and he now arrives without any money. It can't be." Her heart, though, pained her with the following thoughts, "Perhaps, though, that is what truly happened. Perhaps he brought home absolutely no money." What would she do? She had indebted herself tremendously, bought so much for *Yontef* for him, and had practically no merchandise left in her little booth. What would she do now? She was so unfortunate. Pondering her predicament, she burst into tears. Her sisters Ite and Khone then entered, found her crying and asked, "What's wrong, Tsipe?"

She told them.

They consoled her. "No," they said, "it can't be that he has no money. You're crying over nothing." "If only I was crying over nothing," Tsipe replied. "Children, you should know that a person's heart is a prophet. My heart tells me that he has truly brought home absolutely no money." Meanwhile, he returned from the bathhouse, and she confronted him directly. "Did you bring home any money? Why aren't you showing it to us? We must have it!" He replied, "I am up to my ears in debt! I don't even have one *kopek*. And you can believe me; I didn't even have any money to pay the driver. If you hadn't paid him, he wouldn't have let me take my package." Upon his uttering of these words, the grieving in their home truly began—Tsipe fainted and the children revived her. By the time she came to, he had already dressed for *Yontef* and left to pray in *shul*.

Upon returning from *shul*, everyone was already calm and quiet, Tsipe had already buried her pain deep inside her heart. Shloyme-Leyzer said the "*Git Yontef*" greeting joyously,[29] made *Kiddush*, washed his hands, went to the table,

---

28 A *gildn* is a fifteen-*kopek* coin. It is customary to bathe before the beginning of the Jewish Sabbath and major Jewish holidays (*Kitsur Shulkhan Arukh* 103:2).
29 *Git Yontef* means "Good Holiday."

and began to eat.[30] Everything was already prepared and the table was all set. She and the orphans sat themselves down as well, and a discussion followed. "Just tell me, how did you lose your money? I know that you don't gamble and that you didn't lose it through any business ventures. You don't give your children any money. If I at least knew that you gave the money to your children, who are staying with others, it wouldn't bother me. Nevertheless, I know that you didn't give it to them, and you didn't send me the money. I'd like to know where's your money?" Tsipe asked all of this tenderly and with tears in her eyes. Only then did he answer that he knew that she was correct and her complaints against him were legitimate, but upon hearing the reason she would also admit that he was not to blame. His bad luck was to blame, and God's providence ordained it to be so. He then concluded, "And now let's eat. We should at least enjoy what we eat. It's *Yontef*, isn't it?!"

He was very particular in fulfilling the "laws" of eating and drinking.

After eating and saying the Hebrew blessings after eating, he related the following episode: "As you know, my *Shobes* clothes were worn out. Being in such clothes at the dining table of such a wealthy person wasn't nice, particularly when I myself couldn't stand them. So I took payment in advance for a term and a half and bought a nice, new *kapote*, a velvet *kartuz*, a nice, silken *gartl*, a pair of pants, and a vest—all new and of good quality.[31] After paying for these items, I was left with only twelve silver rubles from the first term's tuition. And what are a mere twelve silver rubles? Only half a year's expenses for someone. You can understand that it still wasn't enough for me and I was still a few silver rubles in debt until the next term. During the second term, a new mishap[32] (so

---

30 *Kiddush* refers to the blessing recited over a goblet of wine (or some other quality drink) after the evening and morning prayer services thereby sanctifying the Sabbath (*Shabes*) and Jewish holidays. Until it is recited, nothing may be eaten or drunk (*Kitsur Shulkhan Arukh* 77:1–15). When *Kiddush* is recited in a person's home (as opposed to in synagogue) it is traditionally followed by a large meal. Jewish law directs washing one's hands in a prescribed manner before eating bread (*Kitsur Shulkhan Arukh* 40:1–5).

31 A *kartuz* is a type of a cap which was worn by many Jews in Eastern Europe. The Jewish *kartuz* differs from the non-Jewish cap by the same name, which was widely worn from the sixteenth to the early twentieth century in Northern and Eastern Europe, mostly among the Germans, Dutch, and Russians. It is now considered part of the Russian folk costume. A *gartl* is a black cloth belt, often made of silk, worn primarily by Hasidim especially during prayers (Wertheim, 1992:113–114). A pair of pants might be referring to the knee-length pants worn with long socks traditionally worn by Jews. Nonetheless, after a comprehensive set of Tsarist decrees against traditional Jewish attire was passed between 1844 and 1851, many Jews began wearing long pants.

32 In the original Yiddish, the author uses the word *sibe* (סיבה) to mean a mishap. Though it only means "cause" or "reason" in Modern Hebrew, it was formerly also used to mean a "mishap," "accident," or "adventure" in Yiddish. See Harkavy (1928:338).

FIGURE 3. The author mentions here the Jewish cap called a *kartuz*. This photograph includes three Jewish men wearing such caps in the southeastern Ukraine in 1910. The Jewish *kartuz* differs from the non-Jewish cap by the same name which was widely worn from the sixteenth to the early twentieth century in Northern and Eastern Europe, mostly among the Germans, Dutch, and Russians. It is now considered part of the Russian folk costume. Courtesy of Michoel Rotenfeld.

called when one has no luck) unfortunately occurred to me. Listen, Tsipe, and you yourself will admit that I am right!"

Tsipe sat there looking totally crushed as she listened to his absurd explanations, his crazy... And she cried in pain and disappointment. "Come on," she said, "let me hear your second misadventure already! Perhaps your orphaned children somehow found you and, with the help of those that raise them, wrenched the money from you. But if that was the case, it wouldn't bother me at all."

"No," he said, "God forbid. They wouldn't have been able to find me, especially since I asked any acquaintance whom I ran into not to reveal my current whereabouts. The mishap was a simple one. Someone stole my *talis* and *tefillin* from the *shul* where I prayed daily.[33] Not only my own but many *taleysim* were stolen (and among them, understandably, my own as well).[34] So I had to buy a new *talis* and two new pairs of quality *tefillin*,[35] a *gartl*, a Book of Psalms, a

---

33 *Tefillin* are generally kept with the *talis* (prayer shawl) in the same bag, which is often permanently kept in one's synagogue for use each morning.
34 *Taleysim* is the plural of *talis*.
35 Many Hasidim customarily don two pairs of *tefillin* (referred to as Rashi's and Rabeynu Tam's) instead of the standard one pair (Rashi's) during the weekday morning prayers,

Sha'are Tsion,³⁶ and a *sidur*.³⁷ As you can well understand, I now watch over my *talis* and *tefillin* better and don't leave them lying about in the *shul* as I did before. All of this cost me thirty silver rubles. I also happened to buy a silver snuffbox, which cost me only three silver rubles.³⁸ How could one pass up such a fantastic bargain? And then another mishap occurred to me just a month before *Yontef*."

And he proceeded to tell her: "I went to, you'll pardon my mentioning it, the bathhouse on Friday—it wasn't my first time there, and I had never experienced any mishaps before. But this time, upon leaving the bath, I couldn't find my clothes. I searched and searched, and they're hopelessly missing until this very day. I had to sit in the bathhouse until they brought me my *Shabes* clothes from the wealthy man's home, thereby liberating me as if from a jail. If my student, the wealthy man's son, wouldn't have been with me in the bathhouse, I might have remained sitting there for who knows how long. It was simply a miracle that my pupil was with me. He went home and brought me, understandably, my clothes. I then had to have a new weekday *kapote* made for me, along with practically all of my clothes. The total cost was twenty silver rubles—apart from a new *talis-kutn* that cost one silver ruble.³⁹ In addition to various small expenditures for myself, I also had three new shirts, two pairs of pants, socks, and a new hat made for me. It took all the money I had, down to the last *kopek*. Now, knowing all the expenses I had, would you still have expected me to send you money from time to time and return home with money too? I told you, didn't I, that once I told you everything, you would also concede that I am not to blame. Yes, Tsipe, tell me yourself, was I not right?"

After hearing all his outrageous tales, Tsipe told him that the miracle would have been much greater if his student had not been there and he had remained in the bathhouse until *Shobes* morning thereby causing his *Shobes* to be as dark and desolate as her *Yontef* was now. But since he was quickly able to arrive at the wealthy man's *Shobes* table, sit alongside everyone that Friday night, and eat and drink well, that was a very small miracle in her opinion.

---

because of an ancient rabbinical dispute regarding the order in which the four passages written on parchment are placed in the leather tefillin boxes (Wertheim, 1992:120–123; Zinner, 1998:73–81).

36 *Sha'are Tsion* is a book of prayers and meditative passages based on kabbalistic writings. Before the Second World War, it was very popular and underwent dozens of printings, having first been printed in Prague in 1662.

37 He had kept all of these objects in his *talis* and *tefillin* bag, which had been stolen.

38 The inhalation of nasal snuff is primarily used on *Shobes* when smoking is prohibited.

39 A *talis-kutn* is a poncho-like shirt-sized *talis* worn constantly by Orthodox Jewish men and boys.

So what do you say about his shenanigans? What do you say about such a breadwinner? And does Tsipe's life appeal to you? Nevertheless, I know that she was not the only unhappy wife. In those days, there were many such unfortunate women in every city and small town, because fanaticism reigned everywhere. Those parents who raised their children in a fanatical Hasidic lifestyle wished for no better happiness than to obtain a prize catch of a son-in-law, a Torah scholar, who never saw the face of a coin nor knew the meaning of earning a livelihood.[40] And that was how life was for those couples whose marriages were arranged, unbeknownst to them and without their consent. More than one such marriage ended in divorce, but that was how it was. And so it was with Tsipe: she married, divorced, married again, but did not want to divorce again.

After Shloyme-Leyzer's antics in Kishinev, he remained in Tiraspol where he taught little children, while Tsipe worked all of her years eking out a livelihood from her little store.

My Sister Ite's Unfortunate Remarriage[41]

After three years of widowhood, Ite became engaged, a real stroke of luck, so to speak.[42] Her husband was practically just like Tsipe's, except with more flair. But listen closely as to how she became engaged and what occurred afterwards, and you will learn something of the nature of Jewish life.

An *eynikl* came to Tiraspol.[43] He was a Slaviter *eynikl* if I recall correctly.[44] He himself was from Vinnitsa, was a Torah scholar, and an eloquent speaker. Shloyme-Leyzer, with all of his Torah scholarship, was nothing in comparison to him. He was extremely good-looking, dressed in silk and velvet,[45] carried

---

40   Though the author remained a Hasid his entire life, he felt that certain mores of Hasidic life had negative consequences for many of its participants.
41   The section beginning here, to the end of the chapter, was transposed from Chapter 4 in the original Yiddish. It has been moved to form the end of chapter 3 so as to separate the story of the author's parents and siblings from that of his own life.
42   Approximately 1867.
43   Referring to a descendant of a Hasidic Rebbe who is considered to be a bit of a Hasidic Rebbe himself.
44   This is a reference to any descendant of Rabbi Moyshe Shapiro, the founder of the printing press in Slavite in 1791. Rabbi Moyshe Shapiro (died 1839) of Slavite (Slavuta, Ukraine) was a son of the renowned Rabbi Pinkhes (1726–1791) of Korets. In the 1830s, Rabbi Moyshe Shapiro's two sons were libeled, convicted, and tortured, which shook world Jewry (Ginsburg, 1991).
45   "Dressed in silk and velvet" refers to the silken *kapote* or *bekeshe* (a silken robe-like coat) with *strokes*, that is, velvet trimming along the edges of the cuffs and collar of the *kapote* (or *bekeshe*), often worn by Hasidic Rebbes.

a silver-handled cane,[46] and during morning services wore a *talis* with a wide, silver *atore*.[47] Such a Jew was given a seat in the pew along the eastern wall of the *shul*.[48] During prayers, he would scream so that the walls trembled, shake, and clap so that sparks flew. He would pray in the mornings from eight until twelve.[49]

In Tiraspol, he obtained the reputation of being a *Giter-Yid*, even though he himself said that he was merely an *eynikl*.[50] With the spread of his wonder-works, it was not surprising that he was considered to be a *Giter-Yid* and he regularly took *kvitlekh* and *pidyoynes*.[51] The sisters Tsipe and Ite went to him for a blessing, and he took a strong interest in Ite, and he requested that she be suggested as a match for himself since he had been widowed earlier that year. He claimed to have had an inspired vision that his future wife would be from the area of Tiraspol, and he searched until he found her. He merely had to breathe a hint of his thoughts and his agents were already carrying stories of his miracles throughout the city, and telling everyone how he possessed divine inspiration, and had predicted that he would find his future wife in the area—and find her there he did.

They began to attempt to convince Ite that she should marry him, but she absolutely refused. Meanwhile, he acquired a following and Hasidim, who spoke of his greatness day and night. Actually, Ite's own relatives, who had her benefit in mind, as well as their own, began to try to convince her to marry him for they wanted to improve their own family's standing. After all, it was no trivial matter to have such a scholar in the family! In short, one of his Hasidim, a wealthy Jew called Zolmen-Sukher-Kopls, was instrumental in arranging the match.[52] Since this *eynikl* had a room at Reb Zolmen's, Reb Zolmen let himself become involved in the match and affected it by promising to give the couple an apartment, lighting, and heating for a year. Ite had the groom promise her that

---

46 A silver-handled cane was a common article of Hasidic Rebbes.
47 A band of cloth made of silver thread and sewn onto the edge of the *talis* draped over the head.
48 The seats along the eastern wall (that is, along the front wall of the synagogue) were generally reserved for distinguished or wealthy members of the community. In most synagogues, every married person had their own permanent seat in the synagogue.
49 Four hours of prayer during morning services is considered to be quite lengthy.
50 A *Giter-Yid* (literally meaning a "good Jew" in Yiddish) denotes a Hasidic Rebbe, though this term is generally no longer used since the Second World War.
51 *Kvitlekh* are written notes petitioning a Hasidic Rebbe for his blessings. Accompanying the *kvitlekh* are *pidyoynes* (literally "redemptions" in Hebrew), which refer to the monetary donations given to a Hasidic Rebbe to redeem one's soul (Wertheim, 1988:241–248).
52 The name Zolmen-Sukher-Kopls can denote one of the following: 1) Zolmen-Sukher was the son or son-in-law of someone named Kopl; 2) Zolmen was the son or son-in-law of a Sukher-Kopl; or 3) Zolmen was the son or son-in-law of Sukher, who in turn was the son or son-in-law of a Kopl.

he would discard his Hasidic-Rebbe *shtik*.[53] She also requested that he should arrange to teach a group of two or three students, because that meager income would have been more than satisfactory for her. On her part, Ite would then settle her accounts with her partner with whom she shared a store. With her half of the money from the store, she would set up her own glassware stand near Reb Zolmen's store, so as to always be near their home and to be a housewife.

And Ite was married. The entire town was astonished. How could a man of such prestigious rabbinical ancestry take such a poor young woman? It was truly dumbfounding!

Reb Zolmen-Sukher-Kopls was wealthy at that time and had, God forbid, no ulterior motives. Since he highly esteemed the *eynikl* and had heard from his mouth that Ite was his match as decreed in Heaven, Reb Zolmen believed that the match was holy and utilized all of his energy to achieve Ite's consent. He believed that, in the merit of his efforts, God would bless him with fine children, which he was lacking, to accompany his wealth. Since he knew Ite's piety well, he felt it would be a good match. She fasted every Monday and Thursday and was careful to pray the three daily prayers that are only obligatory for Jewish men.[54] The match would be wonderful for Ite too, for alas she was a common widow. Reb Zolmen treated her as a daughter and promised her an apartment, lighting, and heating for a year—as long as the match would come to fruition, which it did.

Ite's husband, Reb Yankev, who was called "Reb Alter the Vinitser," could barely constrain himself from remaining at home until after Pesach.[55] He then picked himself up and left without saying what, when, or where. Only much later did he send letters revealing that business was going well: he already had two

---

53 The original states "*Gite-Yidishe shtik*." In other words, Tsipe asked him to drop his pretenses of being a *Giter-Yid*, that is, a Hasidic Rebbe.

54 Regarding fasting every Monday and Thursday, see chapter 2, p. 105, footnote 28.

55 According to the Hebrew inscription on the 1907 tombstone of his son Itskhok-Refúel (later Isaac Goldstein) in the Neveh Zedek Cemetery in Portland, Oregon, his name was Azriel. Perhaps he had two names, like Azriel-Yankev, and his tombstone only noted one while the author only remembered the other. "The Vinitser" denotes that he was from the city of Vinnitsa, Ukraine. The name Alter denotes "old" and was often given as a nickname to a boy whose birth was preceded by the death of one or more siblings in the hope that he would live to an old age; nicknames like Alter do not appear on tombstones. Reb Alter's surname was "something like Berman or Bertman," according to his grandson Samuel Goldeen (1895–1984), as related by Samuel's son, Samuel S. Goldeen, Jr. in 2008. Isaac Schneersohn (1968:33) mentions that his grandfather Fishl Breytman of Kómenets (Kamianets-Podilskyi, Ukraine)—not far from Vinnitsa—was a descendant of the rabbinic Shapiro family of Slavite, as was Reb Alter, as mentioned earlier. Upon mentioning this to Samuel S. Goldeen, Jr., he replied that Breytman would certainly have been included in his father's description of the possibilities of their original surname. Hence, Alter's surname may have been Breytman.

gabbaim and his own horse and wagon.⁵⁶ He hoped to return with a large fortune and would then settle down to a domestic life—a thief makes similar promises yet remains a thief! Apparently, he was recognized for the fraud that he was, and people stopped bringing him *pidyoynes*. After some time, he returned home with nothing—no *gabbaim*, no attendants. He even had to sell his horse and wagon and returned with only the whip.

Once again, Reb Zolmen let Reb Alter stay with him, but he did it more for Ite than for Reb Alter. For a year, Reb Alter refrained from traveling and remained at home, though he very much wanted to travel again. But the child that Ite bore in the meantime, Itskhok-Refulikl—named after her father—delayed him another half a year.⁵⁷ Only then did he try to convince Ite that she should travel with him to Vinnitsa, where he had a house and some minor possessions. After expending much effort, she finally agreed to accompany him. Ite went with him to Vinnitsa but returned a few months later barely alive. The story behind this was as follows: Arriving in Vinnitsa, he immediately left Ite and traveled elsewhere, not even letting her know his destination. Understandably, she was not able to remain there for long and returned to Tiraspol, where Reb Zolmen gave her a room and allowed her to stand with her glassware outside of his textile store. When her "devoted" husband returned to Tiraspol, the community pressured him, and he was forced to divorce her.

Now Ite was a divorcée. Her son, Itsele, was a nice bright boy; her whole life centered on him. She kept him neat and clean, like a prince.

My Sister Khonele's Death

Regarding Khonele, who worked for the elderly man in his dishware store, there is also a story to tell. She married the son of Tsipe's husband Shloyme-Leyzer from his first wife. This son came to the fair in Tiraspol with merchandise and stayed. He then became a partner in a store that sold sewing notions and small wares, and Khonele remained working where she was. They lived together very nicely and happily, but Khonele was not destined to live long—they were only

---

56 *Gabbaim* denotes here the managers of the affairs of a Hasidic Rebbe.
57 Refulikl is a diminutive of the name Refuel. He was generally called Itsl or Itsele (see the next paragraph). He went by the surname of Goldshteyn (and was known as Isaac Goldstein in the United States), which was a slightly shortened version of his mother's maiden name of Goldenshteyn. He was born in 1862, as confirmed by the New York passenger manifest of the *S.S. Gellert* of December 24, 1889, which lists him as being twenty-seven years old; the 1900 federal census of Portland, Oregon; and his 1907 tombstone in the Neveh Zedek Cemetery which states that he was born on September 3, 1862.

married two and half years before she died. Her death came about as a result of difficulties giving birth. She was having great difficulties during labor and gave birth to a son, who died two months after her. No progeny even remained from my precious Khonele. At the age of twenty-one, the life of a suffering, poverty-stricken orphan ended.[58]

My Sister Tsipe's Death

Now we will return to Tsipe. How was she managing now? Where was she living and what had occurred to her in the last few years? After some time, Tsipe's husband Shloyme-Leyzer's oldest daughter, Reyzl, came to her father in Tiraspol. She was the daughter of his first wife, and was raised by relatives in Kishinev. Reyzl pleaded with her father to at least supply her with a dowry.[59] She maintained that since Shloyme-Leyzer had not helped her like a father in the past, he should at least let her stay with him now. Reyzl's pleas awakened Tsipe's memories of being a lonely orphan, and Tsipe was moved to take Reyzl into their home. Tsipe treated Reyzl as her own child and consoled and comforted her like a mother. After living with them for three years, Reyzl was married off to a fine young man who was seeking to marry a girl from a learned and esteemed family. Reyzl and her husband settled down into their own quarters.

After Khonele's death, Tsipe and her husband moved from Tiraspol to Kovishón—a small *shteytl* near Tiraspol—where Shloyme-Leyzer arranged a nice teaching position for himself. And God blessed Tsipe with a daughter, whom she named Ester-Khaye after her mother.[60] Her child was a comfort to her after all of the suffering that she bore until then. Tsipe had hoped and waited for a child for twelve years but would, nonetheless, not keep quiet.[61] Wherever a *Giter-Yid* or a *tsadik* might have been, she would go to him and give up her last coin as a *pidyen*.[62] Though several promised her that she would have a child, their promises did not help. In time, when she had practically lost all hope of having children, God found her worthy and gladdened her with the birth of a daughter, Ester-Khaye.[63] How happy Tsipe was!

---

58 Khonele died in the winter of 1860–1861 (ch. 3, p. 124, and ch. 10, pp. 185–186).
59 Without a dowry, Reyzl would have had slim chances of ever marrying.
60 Chapter 14, pp. 223–224, notes that Tsipe's son Duvid was born in October 1864 and that his older sister Ester-Khaye was three years older (born 1861).
61 Twelve years had elapsed since marrying her first husband.
62 *Tsadik* is the singular of *tsadikim* and was used by Hasidim to denote a Hasidic Rebbe. *Pidyen* is the singular of *pidyoynes*.
63 She is later referred to as Khayele.

After living for two years in Kovishon, Tsipe and her family then moved to Bender, where Shloyme-Leyzer again arranged to teach a group of boys and taught for a year. During that year, Tsipe bore another child, a boy named Duvid, who would say *Kaddish* for her after her death.[64] In Bender, though, her strength waned, and she died, leaving two young orphans, a three-year-old girl and a son aged three months. And that is how Tsipe's life ended.[65]

---

64 *Kaddish* is the Jewish mourning prayer recited for eleven months during all three daily prayer services following a Jewish person's death and in the three daily prayers on the anniversary of their death, often called "saying *kaddish*" (*Kitsur Shulkhan Arukh* 26).
65 Tsipe died in approximately November 1864 (ch. 14, p. 227).

B. My Early Years, 1848–1864

CHAPTER 4

My Early Childhood, 1848–1855

A Poverty-Stricken Child • The Fairgoer • Falling from a Sled • Exposed to the Elements • The Screaming at Mother's Death • My Good Fortune • My First Journey • Longing for Home[1]

Now we will speak about the youngest child, Berele, who unfortunately never had a good day since the day he was born.[2] His impoverished parents, who were so encumbered with children and were barely able to feed themselves, were nonetheless happy with the birth and survival of an additional child, Berele. After all, poor people's greatest pleasure is their children, may they all live and be well. Nonetheless, the child born to the poor does not have as much pleasure as the parents, as in the case of our Berele!

If he had been lucky, he would have been born to rich parents. Having no luck, he was born to poor parents surrounded by naked, barefoot siblings, large and small. Furthermore, his mother was a shopkeeper and had to mind her store, thereby leaving her baby at home in the care of a sister. And his sister, who would rather have been playing, did not rock him as devotedly as his mother would have; she rocked him with only one foot, knocking him and the cradle over with the other. More than once was his life miraculously saved by being pulled out from under the overturned cradle and all the rags used as his bedding just before suffocating. In addition, his father was a *melomed*, after all. Just as Berele would fall asleep, his father's students would begin a heated discussion of

---

1 The last two entries in this chapter summary were mistakenly placed at the beginning of the summary for chapter 5. Not all discrepancies in the chapter summaries have been noted.
2 The translator has moved the beginning of this chapter to the end of chapter 3 to separate the story of the author's parents and siblings from that of his own life. See chapter 3, p. 120, footnote 41.

their Torah lesson and would begin debating and shouting loudly. Berele would awake, and, in the manner of babies who do not sleep their full, would begin crying. Father would then scream, "Take him away to his mother. He's not falling asleep. He keeps screaming. I can't study with the children!" And he was then brought to his mother. As soon as he was calmed down, the devil would bring in a customer, and she would need to put down the baby and rip her breast out of his mouth. Of course, the baby would then again awake with a shriek and could not be calmed, which made speaking with the customer impossible. Mother would then become angry and yell, "Why did you bring this affliction of mine here? Take him right back home, stuff his mouth, and wrap him up well until he falls asleep once and for all!" And the same cycle of events occurred practically every day. At the age of one month, the baby felt that he was born to suffer.

By the time he was a month old, he had already become a fairgoer for his mother took him along when she traveled to the fairs. Twice a month a fair was held in Selts, which is not far from Tiraspol. The merchants of Tiraspol traveled to that fair and would stop on the way back at another fair near Linoye.[3] Berele's mother also needed to be at the fairs; if not, certainly the *Goles* would have been even greater.[4] She would generally take her nursing child along with her on her travels, but whether it was a good fair or not was of no concern to him; he was only concerned with the "good fair" that he was forced to endure.[5] He would constantly return home hoarse and coughing from shouting and crying; he suffered quite a bit.

During one such trip, a miracle occurred! While traveling to the fair on *Rosh-Khoydesh Shvat*, when the frost was strong and there was much snow, his mother was holding him in her arms in the sled.[6] In the meantime she fell asleep and did not feel herself letting go of the child. He fell from the sled onto the ground and remained there in the snow. When the mother awoke and realized that her baby was gone, she fainted. They revived her, and she shouted and cried out to Heaven. Her baby was gone! All of the sleds stopped. The entire party shook with dread. What would be if, God forbid, the baby had been ridden over

---

3   In the original, an extra Yiddish letter was apparently mistakenly inserted by the typesetter, thereby making the town Linoye appear as Linvey.
4   *Goles* denotes the Jewish Diaspora, the divinely ordained spiritual darkness in which the Jewish people find themselves since the destruction of the Holy Temple in Jerusalem. The author is commenting sarcastically that if his mother had not been forced to drag herself to the fairs, God's plan for the world would have been, no doubt, impaired.
5   A "good fair" refers here to the miserable situation he endured at these fairs.
6   The beginning of the month of *Shvat* occurs in January.

by a sled, had frozen to death, or was devoured by a wolf?[7] Everyone had different thoughts as to the baby's bitter fate. They returned a few *versts* and heard the child crying. They found him on top of some snow near the road and lying in the rags in which he had been wrapped. His mother danced with joy. He was found completely unharmed, may God protect us, and immediately began nursing for he was hungry. The entire fair and all of Tiraspol resounded with the news, and all said that he was a lucky child who needed to be well watched and loved. From then on, he was particularly watched over and loved, but we will hear and see later if this led him to good fortune.

At the age of five, Berele was orphaned by his mother's death. Since he was a discerning child, with a good head on his shoulders, including a good memory, I can rely on him to relate everything and not to leave out any detail of his entire life that happened to him until now.

This story of an orphan shows God's wonders, how He directs the world, and how He is truly a Father of orphans. If anyone is interested in all of this, then listen well to this little orphan's story, including his elaborations upon every detail and occurrence in his life—and he will see that it is so.

When Mother died, I was elated, delighted, and jumped in the air.[8] I am relating this to let you know that it was impossible for it not to be so in those times when a child was locked in *kheyder* as in prison and the rebbe was no better than a Spanish inquisitor.[9]

"Reb Shmiel the children's blind *melomed*" was how our rebbe was called.[10] He was the *melomed* with whom I began to study upon turning four. Almost 150 little boys between the ages of three and six studied under this *melomed*. No children older than six studied with him because that was already the age to study under the *melomed* who taught Talmud. Under Reb Shmiel, the children began to learn the Hebrew alphabet, they then learned the pronunciation of Hebrew words, the translation of the verses of Torah,[11] and then Torah with Rashi's commentary, and no more.[12] Reb Shmiel had eight assistants who would go to the homes of the three- and four-year olds, recite with them *Moyde Ani*,

---

7   A baby being accidently dropped from a sled and being devoured by a wolf was a real concern. Eliakum Zunser (1836–1913) writes in his autobiography that his infant son's wetnurse accidently fell asleep and the baby fell out of the wagon, which resulted in the child's death in this horrible manner (Zunser, 1905:32).
8   Berele, namely the author, starts speaking here in the first person.
9   "Rebbe" here denotes the children's *melamed*.
10 "Reb Shmiel *der dardeker blinder melamed*" in the original. See chapter 3, p. 108, footnote 5, regarding the term *dardeker melamed*.
11 When the Torah is mentioned in conjunction with children or with Rashi's commentary, it usually refers to the Five Books of Moses.
12 At that point, the children were ready to begin studying under a more advanced *melamed*.

bring them to *kheyder*, and then return them home before nightfall.[13] When the streets turned to mud, the children were carried like sacks on the assistants' shoulders. When the streets were dry, the children were led by their hands. During the day, the assistants would bring the children the food provided by their parents, because the children had to be kept in *kheyder* the entire day. The assistants already had certain baskets in which they would put the food given to them by the parents and would remember what was whose using only their memory. These assistants needed to have tremendous memories to remember which food was whose, whether it was dairy, meat, thick, or thin. Upon arriving with the children at the *kheyder*, the assistants then taught *Moyde Ani*, the *Shma*, and *Kiddush* to the children.[14] They would also take the children to women after childbirth to recite the *Shma* next to their newborns.[15] In addition, they would also go to the children's parents to collect *Rosh-Khoydesh gelt*.[16] They would teach the children the proper pronunciation of Hebrew, review with them their studies of the Torah, test their knowledge of the Yiddish translations of the Hebrew words, etc.

Reb Shmiel the blind *melomed*, who was blind in one eye and saw way too much with the other, taught the Torah with Rashi's commentary to the highest class.[17] He was a severe *melomed*, before whom the children shook and shuddered out of fear of his severe punishments. A child was forbidden to leave the room to relieve himself without his knowledge. When a child wanted to urinate, he had to show one finger; when taking care of his needs would take longer, he had to show two fingers. But he was severely punished if he tried to deceive Reb Shmiel, dallied, or played around outside. Though but little boys, they felt freer

---

13 Such assistants were generally called *belfers* in Yiddish, which the author refers to as *bahilfers*, which Mark (1943:39) points out is a dialectal variant. *Moyde Ani* is the name of a short prayer said upon first awakening in the morning.

14 *Shma* is the first Hebrew word of the verse, "Hear, O Israel; the Lord is our God, the Lord is One" (Deuteronomy 6:4) and is used to refer to the three sections of the Hebrew Bible (Deuteronomy 6:4–9, 11:13–21, and Numbers 15:37–41) that are the centerpiece of the morning and evening Jewish prayer services. The *Shma* is a daily declaration of faith and is considered to be the most important prayer in Judaism, and its recitation twice daily is a Biblical commandment incumbent on Jews. The first line of the *Shma* is often recited at times of danger. See also *Shma Yisruel*.

15 It is customary to have children recite the *Shma* at the bed of an infant male on the evening prior to his circumcision.

16 *Rosh-Khoydesh gelt* was gift money given at the beginning of every Hebrew month, apart from tuition (Rivkind, 1959:237–239).

17 Though the Torah can mean the entire body of Jewish religious works, it refers to the Five Books of Moses when the mentioned in conjunction with Rashi's commentary.

to breathe outside than in the dark room among so many children. When it would happen that a boy failed to return quickly enough, he would then receive his just desserts. The punishment was without mercy. When a child could not, or did not, understand his lessons well, he would bear the brunt of each and every one of Reb Shmiel's slaps, pulls of the ear, and hard pinches on the cheek, so much so that the boy's soul wanted to leave him then and there. Apart from the *melomed*, every assistant also had the right to punish. So the child felt like he was in a prison rather than in a *kheyder*. It is no wonder that all the children feared the *melomed* like the Angel of Death.

Another punishment in practice at that time with the five-year-old boys, who by that age already had some intellect, was the *kine*.[18] After receiving this punishment, a stigma would remain for a while and one would be teased often for having had to undergo the *kine*.

The concept of *kine* was as follows: A hat with feathers was placed on the child's head. A broom was put in one hand and in the other a fire poker, upon which he had to ride. His pants were removed, and his shirt rolled up. On his chest would be placed a piece of paper with his name on it and the name of the transgression for which he was being punished. Like this, he was driven through two rows of children. From behind, one of the assistants would drive him forward with a cat-o'-nine-tails and all the children would have to follow him and spit at him, saying, "Phooey! Phooey! Shame on you! You should be ashamed, *kine*-boy. . . ." Afterward, the child would have to stand in place until the good-hearted rebbe would have mercy on him by telling him to wash up. The rebbe also made the child promise that he would not tell his parents. You were never to tell anyone what went on in *kheyder*![19] And all the other children were also warned.

I was a student of Reb Shmiel the blind *melomed*. More than once was I punished for practically nothing, just like other children. But one specific time I will never forget and it happened as follows.

---

18 *Kine* (pronounced in Northeastern Yiddish as *kune*) is used to denote the corporal punishment described by the author above. Shtern (1950:29) and Braver (1966:234) recount variants of the same punishment as described here. The name *kine* is taken from the eighteenth-century punishment used in some Jewish communities which involved a cell usually near a town's main synagogue where the community could lock up one of its members for a brief punishment or a pillory or iron collar on a chain cemented near the entrance to a synagogue (Asaf, 1943:78–79). This Yiddish word derives from the Polish word *kuna*; the Jews apparently adopted this form of punishment from their Christian neighbors (Rosenthal, 1906).

19 "You were never to tell anyone what went on in *kheyder*" is a common Yiddish expression used regarding anything that is to remain a secret.

The streets would quite often flood from rain and snow, but one could take a boat from one street to another at certain places or circle around and around to find a place to be able to cross over. Boating from one street to the other cost money, which I certainly did not have. Therefore, I would seek out unflooded far-off routes and alleyways and would often be late to *kheyder*. Upon arriving late once, the rebbe gave me a fine welcome by having me put in *kine*. He did not want to hear any of my excuses for being late.

The assistants, those demons, pounced upon me, ignoring my supplications and entreaties. I promised that I would be a good boy and would never do anything wrong again—but it did not help at all. I would rather have been buried alive than suffer such embarrassment—embarrassment and resentment together.

Unexpectedly, I was suddenly redeemed. My salvation came from God Himself, some good fortune from the One on High. Just when they were about to lead me around in the "procession" between the boys, a girl barged into the room, approached the rebbe, asked him to step outside to talk with her, and then returned to the room crying silently. The rebbe approached me and told me to go home, "Today you can now go home, Berele. Wash up and go home!"

The girl carried me in her arms and cried and cried—and I was happy and laughing. She said to me, "Your mother died, Berele! You understand that you no longer have a mother!"[20] I practically did not hear what she said and thanked her in my heart for coming to *kheyder* and redeeming me from the *kine*.

When we came home, I figured that I would run inside with great joy. But my joy was immediately disturbed, and I understood what was going on. When I entered my home, the crying and shrieking became even louder. Everyone shouted, "Berele, you no longer have a mother!" and only then did I begin to cry because everyone else was crying. I cried along like a child who imitates those around him. Only when I saw my mother lying on the ground with burning candles placed around her head—only then did I really begin to cry with all the emotions of my tender age.[21] Returning from the cemetery, all began sitting *shivah* and I was told that I was released from going to *kheyder*.

After *shivah*, Father sat and studied Torah with me, and I was elated that I would no longer have to look at my rebbe, that inquisitor. Father studied Talmud with me and went with me to shul in the morning and evening for prayer services until he himself took ill and eventually died between Rosh Hashanah and Yom Kippur, on the fifth day of *Tishre*, a year and a half after Mother's death.[22]

---

20 The author's mother died on March 20, 1854. See chapter 2, p. 101, footnote 14.
21 Jewish law prescribes that the deceased be laid on the floor (*Kitsur Shulkhan Arukh* 194:8).
22 The author's father died on September 17, 1855. See chapter 2, pp. 102–103.

FIGURE 4. Like his father before him, Pinye-Ber Goldenshteyn carved objects out of wood, like this intricate Hanukah *dreydl* (1.6"W x 4.7"H) made for his grandchildren. Photograph courtesy of Myriam Pozwolski Cronin.

My mother! I barely remember her. Her appearance is hidden from me, though I often remember something that I will never forget. Once when I returned from *kheyder*, she gave me her portion of milk, saying, "The child is tired from studying and weak from toiling all day in *kheyder*."

I remember my father much better. He was handsome with a broad, blond beard. He used to shave his head and had long, curly *peyes* and would wear a *kapote* that reached the ground. I remember when he once took me to the public bath and had my head shaved there in a similar manner; he wanted to educate me as a Hasid.[23] He himself was a Hasid of the Bersheder Rebbe.[24] He could whittle and paint well, and his paintings and whittle work hung on the wall in our house.

Our furniture consisted of a large white table, four chairs, a bench that served as a bed at night, a couch, and a bed. Apart from two long benches for my father's students, there was no other furniture in my father's home.

---

23 Evidently, barbers worked at the public bath. In Hasidic communities it is still customary for men to have their hair cut before the Sabbath (*Shabes*) or Jewish festivals, and this is usually done by the *mikveh* attendant in an adjacent room.

24 The Bersheder Rebbe, Rabbi Refuel (ca. 1751–1827), was an outstanding disciple of the renowned Hasidic Rebbe, Rabbi Pinkhas Shapiro (1726–1791) of Korets, Ukraine (Huberman, 1942; Shapiro, 1993:2:502–520). After his death in 1827, his Hasidim remained for some time a distinct group without a Rebbe, a rare occurrence in the history of Hasidism, with an extreme example being the Hasidim of Rabbi Nakhman of Breslov, who died in 1810 (Sharot, 1980:332).

Right after Father's death, my siblings did not know what to do with me. A little boy has to study Torah also, apart from his needing to eat. Even though Torah was an absolute priority, who was going to pay his tuition? And who would watch him, particularly since the child was wild and did not want to listen to or obey his sisters. In short, my sisters decided to send me to Romanovke to my brother Isruel. Storekeepers who travel to the fair in Antshekrák, which is only fifteen *versts* from Romanovke, took me and promised that they would hand me over to storekeepers from Romanovke, who would be coming to the fair. My departure occurred with much fanfare. On the one hand, my sisters cried over me, and kissed and blessed me, yet, on the other hand, the women shook their heads and wiped the tears from their eyes out of pity. But I was happy and laughing at them. I did not understand why they were all crying because my interest in traveling was greater than anything else—primarily my being seated next to the driver and being able to touch the reins and the whip . . . Three days later, I was in Romanovke, but on the way I cried plenty because I had already satiated my curiosity in traveling, and was already sick of being on the road, and began to miss home, my friends, and my dear sisters—but more than anyone else, more than anyone else . . .

CHAPTER 5

A New Set of Parents, 1856

The Leader of the Local Kids • Without My Brother • A Head on My Shoulders • Saying *Kaddish* • Migration • A Second Set of Parents • Surke the *Rebetsn* • The Plot against Me • Shoylikl • The Rebbe's Anger • My Flight from *Kheyder* • A Night under a Barrel • In the Cemetery with My Parents • In the Gravedigger's Home • Found • Back at My Sisters'

I was now in Romanovke. My brother, who noticed me from afar, was overjoyed to see me. Everyone treated me as an honored guest and it was not long after that that I became acquainted with the kids there. I let them know just who I was and that I was tougher than they were. One of them quickly learned it the hard way, and word of it soon reached my brother. It was immediately made clear to me that this was not Tiraspol; here one had to be a quiet little boy and not fight. It was understood that this time I would be excused, but next time I would face punishment; so my brother told me and often made good on his threat. My name was soon known throughout the *shteytl* and every boy around came over to acquaint himself with me. I became the leader, just as at home in Tiraspol. Everyone called me "Berele, Isruel's little brother." In short, I stayed with my brother for eight months, from *Kislev* until *Rosh-Khoydesh Av*.[1] In the third week, he took me with him on his trip to Tiraspol to visit our mother's grave and for our father's first *yurtsayt* on the 5th of *Tishre* 5610 [sic].[2] A tragedy

---

1 From November 1855 until August 2, 1856.
2 The actual year was 5617. The author's calculation is based on his mistaken year of birth of 1842 instead of 1848. See the Introduction, pp. 67–70. Hence, his father's *yortsayt* was October 4, 1856. The author writes that he stayed in Romanovke until *Rosh-Khoydesh Av* (August 2, 1856) but that he left "in the third week of the month." Perhaps he actually left in the third week of the month of *Elul* (mid-September 1856), which was only two to three

occurred upon our arrival in Tiraspol: he became ill and remained bedridden until the second of *Adar*, when he died at the age of twenty.[3]

So now I remained bereft of my dear brother too. Upon his death, I now understood quite well that I needed to mourn. I comprehended fully that I would miss him and that my life without him would be no life. Had he lived, I would have stayed with him and would have been a better Talmudic scholar than he; he always said I had the better mind. True, he would hit me for my mischievousness and frivolity, but he loved me very much for my mind, which absorbed everything I was taught. What I would learn in an hour would take another boy two days—and even then he would not have really understood it. That was why he often forgave my boyish sins; he would say that it was not my fault, rather it was the result of my little mind racing nonstop. Since I had to say *Kaddish* at the *bes-medresh* for my father, I never missed a prayer service, God forbid. When I would come there, people would come over to me to question me about my learning, I would answer all their questions and they would pinch my cheek and say that I was a good little boy. My *Kaddish* and my *Borukh hu uvorukh shmoy* was much appreciated; I had a ringing little voice and used to shout at the top of my lungs.[4] Jokesters would deliberately urge me on to shriek even louder, and I would obey them because I myself enjoyed the fun. In return, I earned many a slap from my brother. While he led prayers, I would screech loudly "*Borukh hu uvorukh shmoy*" or "Amen." He would then become confused and shout at me lovingly, not in cruelty, God forbid. If he had lived, I am certain that after a while I would not have felt that I was an orphan.

After *shivah*, my widowed sister-in-law had to return home with her baby girl, who had been half-orphaned at only a few months of age. So she took me along as a caretaker; perhaps her father would take me back in.[5] But I was not there for long. After a brief period of time, I was sent back to Tiraspol and replaced by my sister Surele, who was three years older than me. Meanwhile, I remained in Tiraspol, bouncing around from place to place. More than once was I relocated—always to new persons and new environments. By this time, I had already been moved around twice, and I was but a child of seven.

Now I began to face new hardships, new incarnations.

---

weeks before their father's *yortsayt* and around the time that the summer term normally ends (see ch. 17, p. 267).

3   February 26, 1857.

4   *Borukh hu uvorukh shmoy* ("Blessed is He and blessed is His Name") is recited upon hearing the leader of prayers invoke God's name in reciting a blessing, of which there are many in the Jewish prayer services.

5   Before his brother Isruel's death, the author lived with him and his father-in-law.

In Tiraspol lived Reb Elye the Vinegar Maker, as he was called. He was a Hasid, a prominent person, and the son-in-law of the rabbi of Tiraspol, Reb Shloymele.[6] The whole town considered Reb Elye to be pious and learned. He was a very respectable person and owned his own home as well as several hundred rubles, in ready cash; he lacked for nothing except children. God had not granted him any children. The *tsadikim* of those times had promised him that he would have children but their promises had not helped! Ten years had passed since his marriage and his wife had not borne children, so he hit upon an idea; he would seek out an orphaned boy or girl in town to take in and raise as his own, and so he did. Since he knew me well because we were distant relatives to his father-in-law, the rabbi, I caught his eye and appealed to him.[7] So he and his wife visited my sisters and made their proposal. My sisters did not find it necessary to appear reluctant for long and quickly agreed, considering it a great stroke of luck. Before I knew it, I was at Reb Elye's.

They brought me into their home, which had every comfort imaginable and was beautifully decorated—with just "slightly" better furniture than at my sisters'. And there was even a samovar; tea was prepared at my sisters' with a little pot heated on the oven or prepared with hot water brought from an eatery—but mostly from a little pot.[8]

Before the age of seven, I had never seen a samovar. But when I turned seven, I visited a friend of mine and watched as he poured himself tea from a beautiful samovar; he also offered me a glass of tea.[9] That was the first time in my life that I drank tea from a samovar, and now, upon coming to my new parents' home, I again had tea made in such an elegant utensil. This time, however,

---

6   Hasid is the singular of Hasidim.
7   Hence, the author was related to Reb Shloymele, the rabbi of Tiraspol. In chapter 1, p. 92, the author writes that his father was partially raised by Reb Shmiel, who was an earlier rabbi of Tiraspol. Perhaps Reb Shloymele was a son or son-in-law of Reb Shmiel. Unfortunately, no further information about these rabbis could be found in outside sources, and his exact relationship to the author is unknown.
8   Since starting a fire from scratch using flint and kindling took considerable time and effort (as mentioned in chapter 6, p. 154), people would often go with their pot to a local eatery to purchase some hot water to take back home and make tea. I am indebted to the late Dr. Mordkhe Schaechter for elucidating this passage.
9   The author was seven in 1855. Originating in Russia, a samovar is a metal container traditionally used to heat and boil water and traditionally heated with coal or kindling. Paperna (1923:86–87) writes that in 1846 his father, a wealthy merchant, was the first Jew to bring a samovar to their town of Kapulye (now Kapyl, Belarus), and he also introduced them to tea. Though they had known of the existence of a samovar, which they had even seen at the commissar's office, to own one was an unheard-of luxury.

it made no impression on me, even though it was now my own samovar and I knew that I would always be drinking from it.

I was now with rich parents. They had a new little *kapote* made for me, and bought me new shoes and a hat. Dressing me well, they sent me off to study with a good *melomed*, where his brother-in-law Shoylik, the son of Reb Shloymele, studied. Altogether, the *melomed* had few students—six, including me. It seemed to me that I was finally living the good life. I was studying, living in a fine home, and provided with clothing. Everything would have truly been good if my luck had been good, but since I had no luck things turned out poorly for me again.

At my new *melomed*'s, where I suffered much, quite a few of the children were older than me, from eleven to twelve years old. Though all of eight, I was sent to that *melomed* because I was an unruly child and the *melomed* was strict and quite adept at punishing. The *melomed* was called "Reb Duvid *melomed*." He was told to beat me for everything and anything, and he naturally followed this order; I was beaten for the slightest of gestures. By nature, I was happy; if I chuckled or simply had a happy expression on my face, I would earn a blow of the strap across my face or back. It made no difference where the strap struck, as long as it hit me well. I was never beaten on account of my learning, because I knew the sections of Talmud and the *khimesh* with Rashi's commentary as soon as I reviewed them once on Monday.[10] So I was left with nothing to do all week except to listen to the others constantly reviewing Sunday's lessons and still not mastering them by Thursday. Naturally, I had to laugh at them. But since they were the children of the well-to-do, I was slapped because they were blockheads. I was slapped so much that I became disgusted with the *kheyder* and the *melomed*. If only things would have gone well at home—but things were no good there either.

My new father, Reb Elye, was involved with his business all week long so that I did not see him for days on end until the arrival of *Shobes*. While *Shobes* was a pleasure for others, for me it was utter hell. The more I distinguished myself with my Torah learning on *Shobes*, the more I suffered during the week. My misery was compounded by Surke the *Rebetsn*, Reb Elye's mother-in-law,

---

10 *Khimesh* (*khumash* in Modern Hebrew) refers to the Five Books of Moses in Hebrew, which usually also includes such classic commentaries as Rashi. A new lesson was taught each Sunday, which was then reviewed the entire week until all the students knew it perfectly.

who was my new mother's mother and was known throughout the area as a wicked woman.[11]

It was Reb Elye's custom to extend the meals on *Shobes*. Upon returning from *shul*, I had to assist him in the loud singing of *Sholem Aleykhem* and the entire long and lengthy *Riboyn Kol ha'Oylomim* along with *Eyshes Khayil* and *Askinu Seudoso*.[12] Even afterward, I had to wait a long time until he finished saying all sorts of other prayers, until he was ready for *Kiddush*. When all the neighbors were already finished eating, he was just beginning *Kiddush*. But thank God, right after *Kiddush*, it took no time for everyone to wash their hands and sit down to eat.[13] As soon as the fish was served, the questioning began.[14] He wanted to know what I had been taught this week and if I knew it. He would test me on my knowledge of a verse from the Torah with Rashi's commentary. Naturally, I never ate any fish because I was exhausted from my long day and from staying up so late at night. I would rather have slept than eaten, or rather eaten than slept; had I been able, I would have eaten and slept simultaneously— but he insisted on asking me more about my studies. If I answered, he would ask more, and if I answered correctly, he would want to ask still more, so that my eyes would close and I would start to doze. Suddenly, he would stop asking questions and angrily order me to eat. "One sleeps at the table? Sleepyhead!" When I would start eating, he would mention another word in *khimesh*, and the same business started up again. Afterward, I had to sing all the *zmires*.[15] By the time everyone else was asleep, we had just finished the blessings after a meal.

Such were my Friday nights.

On *Shobes* during the day, the situation was really remarkable. The premeal preparations were even longer than on Friday nights. After making *Kiddush* and finally sitting down to eat, the questions would begin regarding my lessons in Talmud. At night, I was questioned about the Torah with Rashi's commentary, and by day about the Talmud. "Now Berele, do you know your Talmud lessons from this week? You certainly aren't sleepy now!" In short, I would say that I knew it and would show my acuity by repeating my lessons by

---

11 *Rebetsn* (often rendered into English as "rebbetzin") denotes here the wife of a rabbi, in this case Reb Shloymele the rabbi of Tiraspol.
12 *Sholem Aleykhem* is the liturgical poem usually sung upon returning home from synagogue on Friday night. The last three titles mentioned are often chanted or sung prior to the Friday evening *Shabes* meal and are found in most traditional prayerbooks.
13 Jewish law prescribes washing one's hands in a prescribed manner before eating bread (*Kitsur Shulkhan Arukh* 40:1–5).
14 Fish is traditionally served as the first course of each *Shabes* meal.
15 *Zmires* are Hebrew songs sung during the *Shabes* meals and at the close of the *Shabes*, which are printed in many prayer books.

heart. I thought that this would make things better for me, but it only resulted in causing me much trouble. He would immediately find that volume of the Talmud, look inside while I was reciting it by heart, be greatly amazed with my memory, and then demand still more and more.[16] The *Shobes* meal would last two to three hours, without exaggeration. We would sing some *zmires*, then study again, and study some more, and still more, until he himself would finally take pity on me and let me go. He would say that a Jew must speak words of the Torah and does not need to have any enjoyment in this world. Having seen that I was a good little boy with a good head on my shoulders for learning, he instructed the rebbe to study with me more because I could absorb more. And so the rebbe began to extend his studies with me.

This resulted in arousing Surke the *Rebetsn*'s jealousy and hatred. She would come to the table and hear me recite from memory my Talmud lessons with Rashi's commentary, while her Shoylik sat there knowing nothing. An envious fire burned in her heart and she began to plot against me. She said to her daughter, "Do you have to support a stranger? Support your own brother. If you paid as much for him, he'd also be able to learn well!" She belittled and chastised me in front of her daughter, so that, even during the week, I would be punished by not being fed.

It was customary in *kheyder* that when one boy did not know the section of Talmud being studied, another boy who knew it was to study with the former. In addition, the rebbe instructed the boy who knew his lessons to hit the other boy if he did not learn well! Generally, when I would teach Shoylik, he would catch some solid, stinging slaps from me, and I would get my comeuppance at home from his grandmother, Surke. Things reached a point that after six months of this, I returned to my impoverished sisters, preferring to eat a dry piece of bread with them than a good lunch there. My foster parents, Reb Elye and his wife, after learning the real reasons for my departure, quarreled with her mother and came to beg me to return, promising me mountains of gold: that Surke would no longer come to their home and that I would not be tested at the *Shobes* table. Having prevailed on all accounts, I agreed to return on the third day after I had left them.

---

16 Regarding the traditional testing during the Sabbath (*Shabes*), see Scharfstein (1943:118–119). Deutsch (1972:15) also notes that his father tested him on the Five Books of Moses on Friday night and in Talmud during the meal the next day. *Khimesh* and Talmud are the principle subjects of children that age. Since children are usually tired by the time the Friday-night meal is served, one can readily understand why the Five Books of Moses was the preferred subject to review at night since it is much easier than the Talmud. Once rested, a child could then be tested on the Talmud during the following day.

The first two weeks after my return were tolerable, and I thought that it would continue in that vein. But nothing is allowed to go well with me! Since Surke the Rebetsn could not endure the situation, she reconciled with her daughter and resumed visiting the house. When she would see me, she would shoot arrows at me with her angry, evil glare so that I would become frightened. Shoylik also began coming around and things quickly became what they had been before. Once, when the tailor delivered a new suit for me and Surke saw how well I looked in it and how her daughter was so pleased, she again began to rant at and argue with her daughter, and once again proceeded with her own grievances, "Why don't you take your brother Shoylik into your home? Why should strangers be your heirs and benefit from your worldly goods?" Ultimately, she again began to bombard me with curses and I ran off to *kheyder*.

From that moment on, Surke was forbidden to enter her daughter's home. So she turned to my *rebetsn*, in other words, the wife of Reb Duvid, my *melomed*.[17] Through her, Surke arranged to have the *melomed* make my life miserable. I noticed that the *melomed* began beating me for everything and anything, though I was in no way guilty. His accusations against me became constant: once I was not sitting properly, another time I was laughing at a boy who did not know his lessons, and yet another time he saw me eating in the street.[18] In short, he found every reason to torture me.

At first, my boyish logic could not understand why this was happening to me. Afterward, I perceived that it was originating from Surke and she was using my *rebetsn*; they were conspiring together to torment me. I then reported at home the entire story of how I was being tortured. Crying profusely, I showed my foster parents the marks on my body from the *melomed*'s blows. I said that I was not being hit for any deficiencies in my learning but for entirely imaginary fabrications generated to embitter my life.

Surke and my *rebetsn* then found new grievances in their defense: "Since you're an orphan, a forlorn child, it is incumbent upon us, pious women that we are, to teach you and raise you properly. The rebbe's beatings are only for your own good in order that you should merit the World to Come..."

Then another opportunity arose in which the *melomed* could remain justified in his harsh treatment of me.

At that time, they began to add on to the structure of the large *bes-medresh* by digging a deep foundation. We children would go there to play by jumping over the pits, and sometimes it would happen that children would fall in,

---

17 *Rebetsn* can denote the wife of a rabbi or, as it does here, the wife of a *melamed*.
18 Eating in the street is compared in the Talmud (Kidushin 40b) to the behavior of a dog.

not managing to jump all the way across. This also happened to Shoylik, the *rebetsn*'s brat: he jumped . . . right into the pit! The boys burst out in laughter, and I was among them. Upon hearing his screams of "*Mome! Mome!*" the *rebetsn* came running.[19] She pulled him out of the pit and took him directly to the *melomed* to report me so as to be rid of me once and for all. And the *melomed*'s wife put in her two cents: "How can it be, Duvid, that you haven't seen to it that he becomes a *mentsh*? After all, he's an orphan, and who knows what will become of him if you don't teach him some respect!"

My sentence had been decided, though I knew nothing of it. The next morning, I arose and went off to *kheyder*. When Shoylik entered, all angry, with a bandaged cheek and a battered nose, laughter arose from all the children. Everyone had a different question regarding his fall: "What happened, Shoylik? Where were you? With whom did you wage war, Shoylik? With a billy goat or a nanny goat?! . . ." When the rebbe entered, I was laughing along with everyone else. "What's causing you to be as happy as a songbird? Why are you laughing with such gusto? Have no fear," the rebbe said to me, "I know all about it. You'll soon have your just desserts, you impudent boy!" The rebbe grew furious, and I was ready for anything, even to flee for I could see in his eyes that I was in for it.

Sure enough, the rebbe began to make preparations for his disciplinary task and ordered me to let my pants down and lie down on the chair. No pleas helped, and I saw that I would not emerge alive from his hands. I decided to take a step of which the rebbe himself would never have dreamed: I decided to flee.

When I saw that I must do the rebbe's will and that nothing would help me, I suddenly tore out of his hands and leaped through the window. Before the rebbe could make a move, I had already disappeared out of sight and gone into a courtyard. From there, I went into a shed, hid behind a barrel of sugar, and covered myself with some straw. I lay there for a while until I fell asleep. When I awoke, it was already daylight, and I decided to leave before I was found. I was already quite hungry and thirsty, yet I did not want to go home. Instead, I decided to go to a friend of mine who lived outside of town and planned to spend some time there. But upon arriving at my friend's house and finding them asleep, I sat down on the ledge surrounding the house to wait.[20] I then realized that my plan was no plan at all. "What am I doing?" I asked myself. "When my friend tells his rebbe and his rebbe tells my rebbe, he will then come and really

---

19 *Mame* (mother) is pronounced as *Mome* in the author's sub-dialect of Southeastern Yiddish (see the Introduction to the Glossaries).
20 *Prizbe* in the original. The foundations of older houses in the Ukraine often used to reach higher than ground level and were wider than the houses built upon it. This ledge-like portion of the foundation surrounding the entire width of the house is called a *prizbe* in Yiddish.

take vengeance on me." And then another thought came to mind, "Since it isn't far from here to the cemetery where my parents and my brother lie, I'll go there and pour out my heart to them and tell them that they didn't do well by leaving me here in this evil world."

And I went off to the cemetery. Here was where my sisters would come during difficult times of loneliness and hardship to cry out their hearts to our parents. Here I too had come to plead and cry for my parents to somehow help me and make my life easier. And I was then all of eight years old.[21]

As I arrived at the cemetery, the Jewish woman there was milking her cow. Seeing me approach, she began asking me from a distance, "Little boy, little boy! Where are you going and whom are you seeking here?" I told her that I was looking for my parents and my brother who are buried here and resting their eternal rest. She asked again: "If they're dead, why do you need to look for them?" I replied with a question, "Why then do my sisters come here? I am begging you to unlock the gate and let me into the cemetery. I'm an orphan and have many troubles. Let me in!" And I began to argue with her. The woman even began to cry seeing such a little boy who already knew how to speak about feelings and tragedy. Meanwhile, her children arrived and encircled me joyfully saying, "Little boy, come play with us!" I was still standing outside the fence when the woman's husband also emerged and a heated debate arose between us. He said to me, "A little boy mustn't enter a cemetery!" I said to him, "A little boy may enter a cemetery!" He said to me, "No!" I said to him, "Yes!" After a short while, they finally opened the little gate, and, before you knew it, I was standing inside the fence.

When I found my father's grave and began to weep out loud, all of them, from the youngest to the oldest, sobbed along with me, shedding bitter tears. My contention was that since my life was so very bad, my father should take me to be with him. Things would be good for me with him. I would not be an orphan, no one would beat me, and no one would rule over me. I slowly lowered my head onto the gravestone and fell asleep out of weakness and hunger, not having eaten in almost twenty-four hours. Seeing my condition, they took me into their home, fed me bread and milk, and I became revitalized. I felt unburdened, as if a heavy stone had been lifted from upon my heart. Tears, it seems, are heavy!

That Jewish man, the gravedigger, had another source of income: he sold little knishes in town. He asked me to accompany him to town, but I replied that I would like to play a little more with his children. He left me alone and went off

---

21 Summer of 1857.

to town by himself. I played with the children the entire day. Their mother fed me and I felt quite good.

The next day, the gravedigger was again going to town and told me to accompany him. He explained that since he and his wife had barely enough food for themselves, they could not feed me. He continued that he, for his part, could not afford to raise me, so I must accompany him to town to my sisters where all would be well, "Come. I'm telling you, come!" But I did not go with him. I assured him that I would not eat his food anymore and only asked of him to be allowed to play with his children. He left without me.

Upon coming to town, he heard that they had been searching for a little boy for the past two days and he could not be found. He asked for particulars, and they described the child to him. "In that case," he said, "go to his sisters and tell them that the little boy is playing at the cemetery." There was no lack of volunteers to carry the message to the sisters, and the sisters ran off at once to the cemetery. As I saw Ite and Khone approaching, I began to tremble out of great fright and fell into a faint.

When I opened my eyes, I found myself in my sisters' arms—being embraced, kissed. They asked me if I recognized them. "Yes, I recognize you, my sisters. You are my dear sister Ite and you," pointing to Khone, "are my dear sister Khonele." Hearing these words, they began once again to cry and to comfort me. I revealed to them my apprehensions: my fear of being beaten, my not wanting to go to that rebbe anymore, and my not wanting to be with my foster parents anymore. In response, they promised to honor all of my requests. Only then did I agree to go home with them. Nonetheless, my fears did not leave me.

Coming to town and hearing all the advice that good people gave my sisters about what should be done to me, I tore out of their hands and went dashing off through the streets, not knowing where or why. When I was caught and brought to my sisters' home, Reb Elye and his wife came and asked me to return to them, but I did not want to hear of it and remained with my sisters.

CHAPTER 6

With Grandfather in Groseles, 1857–1858

At Grandfather's in Groseles • Small-Town Old Folks • Questions and Answers • Back to Tiraspol • Rebuke from My Sisters • Old Buddies • An Amazing Child • Astonishment • The Leader of The Gang • Games • Before the High Holy Days • Seeking Transgressions • One Misdeed • The Little Apple • Piousness • A Fervent Prayer • The Cantonists • Rescued • In the Attic • God's Help • "Israel is a Scattered Sheep"[1]

My sisters lived in great poverty in a tiny, little house. Tsipe was still married to Shloyme-Leyzer, who taught children, so the little house also included a *kheyder* of six children. Consequently, since there was not enough to survive upon each day, they again began to think of what to do with me and decided to send me to our grandfather in Groseles. And so they did.

Now I was at Grandfather's. Grandfather lived to be more than a hundred years old, and, when I arrived, he was certainly ninety-six, if not older.[2] Grandmother was not my mother's mother, but Grandfather's second wife

---

1 Jeremiah 50:17. This verse refers to the Jewish people being scattered, though the author slightly misquotes it by using the Hebrew word for "dispersed"—instead of—"scattered." He is referring to his being sent away to his Aunt Rosye's.
2 In previous eras, the elderly were often assumed to be much older than they actually were, as exemplified by the author who thought in his later years that he was some six years older than he actually was. (See the Introduction, pp. 67–70.) Often, those who were in their eighties were assumed to be much older. Yet, the 1858 additional revision list (poll-tax census) of the Jews of Tiraspol indicates that his grandfather, Yankev Gredenitsky, would have been seventy-two at the time of his death. On a visit to the Jewish cemetery in Groseles in 2004, a few dozen tombstones were still intact, but none pertaining to the author's family. In Chapter 34 and in a letter from the 8th of *Heshvan* 5691 (October 30, 1930), the author writes that his grandfather lived to be 105. Nonetheless, when he visited his uncles in Groseles in 1859

whom he married when he was about sixty and with whom he had two sons: one named Pinkhes and the other Idl.³ Uncle Pinkhes already had a family of his own and lived with his in-laws in the village of Baranev.⁴ When I arrived at Grandfather's, Idl was on *kest* with his father. My elderly grandparents had their own place of residence and a hardware store that sold rope, regular and cheap rustic tobacco, scythes, whetstones, iron and iron boxes, nails, chalk-based whitewash, and many other things.

By that time, Grandfather could no longer hear, and Grandmother Khontse was still quite able to assist him. It was remarkable to see the energy with which this couple managed to maintain themselves and their children, that is, their son and daughter-in-law, who lived with them on *kest* but did not even put a hand in cold water. The house was divided into two: one half was occupied by a neighbor and the other by the old couple and the young one. This was how they lived.

I was in no way pleased with the village of Groseles. It was small and narrow and in one minute I could walk from one end to the other. Also, the boys appeared to be wild compared with the town-boys I knew. Half-naked, barefoot, and filthy, they surrounded me like madmen. One or two of them even indulged in pinching me and asked me my name. "What is it? What is it? Berele?!" They repeated this several times and always called me Berele there.

In the morning, I went with Grandfather to *shul*. And here began another round of introductions: "What are you doing here, little boy?" "What's your name, little boy?" "What Talmudic tractate are you studying, little boy?" I responded in an orderly fashion, point by point. Everyone praised and beamed at me with joy. Meanwhile, I made new friends and kept then entertained with my chatter. My good name spread throughout the *shteytl*, and I developed a reputation as an exceptional boy.

A few days later, I began to study in *kheyder*, where I learned well. Everyone had something to say about me. I understood that here I could become a *mentsh* and grow up to be a respectable person.

I felt that things would go well for me now.

(ch. 7, pp. 160–161) and in 1864 (ch. 13, p. 209), he makes no mention of the grandfather, which might be an indication that his grandfather was deceased by that time.

3   The 1858 additional revision list (poll-tax census) of the Jews of Tiraspol refers to her as Khaye though she is called Khontse (a nickname for Khone) below; perhaps she had two names, most likely, Khaye-Khontse. It also indicates that she was thirty-eight years old and that her sons Pinkhes and Idl—referred to as Yudka—were aged twenty-three and eighteen and were married to Feyge and Beyle, respectively.

4   "Baronve" appears in the original, which is evidently a typographical error for it is spelled as "Baronev" several times in chapter 23.

But here, too, I did not last long, no more than half a year—a winter—from after Yom Kippur until after Pesach.[5] Right after Lag Baomer, I found myself suddenly in Tiraspol.[6] The story behind this was simple. I was quite undisciplined and no one had authority over me. I had no fear of my elderly grandparents and used to make trouble in the *shteytl*. I beat up one kid and bloodied his nose, causing the locals to complain about me to my grandfather. And what could Grandfather do to me? Before he even made a move, I had already fled, hiding behind a fence, and burying myself in the grass. When testing me in my studies, he would look in the Talmud and I would have to repeat it by heart, shouting while motioning with my hands in accordance with the subject matter.[7] He understood at once whether I knew the Talmud properly or not by the movement of my hands. If I would fail even once to move my hands to the proper rhythm, I would be slapped. When I realized that this was not a good arrangement, I began to hide the shank of his pipe and tobacco; he would spend so much time searching for them that our study time passed before we even began. When he realized that this was one of my machinations, he began to specially prepare for me by making sure that one pipe-shank was locked up so that he would have it when he studied with me. But I still managed to wiggle out from under him. Once he chased me all the way into the street and pleaded with his neighbors to catch me. Sympathetic people were around and gave chase ... and I gave them a good chase, indeed! Once caught, I hit them with my hands and feet and threw street-dust into their eyes. In short, I had the time of my life in that little *shteytl*; all the boys were afraid of me and the rebbe of the *kheyder* was very kind to me—he was compassionate toward me because I was growing up without any parents.

Meanwhile, my grandparents came to a decision to rid themselves of me and sought an opportune time.

I remember that there was a wagon heading for Tiraspol. Grandmother set me on it and sent me off to Tiraspol. I very much enjoyed the trip—and felt completely invigorated. I imagined how I would now appear to my friends in Tiraspol and prepared for their welcome. In short, I arrived safely at my sisters'

---

5 Yom Kippur was on September 28, 1857, and Pesach ended on April 5, 1858.
6 May 2, 1858. Lag Baomer is the thirty-third day of the counting of the *Omer*, which is counted from the second day of Pesach until *Shvues*. On this day, a plague killing 24,000 disciples of Rabbi Akiva (ca. 50–135 CE) came to an end. It is also the anniversary of the death of one of Rabbi Akiva's most eminent disciples, Rabbi Shimon bar Yokhai. It is a minor festival and a day of rejoicing.
7 The Talmud is traditionally studied with the accompaniment of various hand motions, which help clarify the rapid flow of questions, answers, logical arguments, and varying opinions.

and found them in good health and in great poverty as before. When my sisters first saw me, they were overjoyed since they had not seen me for some half a year or seven months. When they later read the note that Grandfather had sent along with me, they began to rebuke me and said: "You see, Grandfather couldn't keep you because you caused him so much trouble and he couldn't live in peace. That's why he sent you back, though he knows that there's no one you can be sent to. But he can't follow you and watch over you. What's to become of you, you murderer, you butcher? What can we do with you? Why don't you have any mercy on us? We ourselves don't even have enough to get by from day to day!"

I stood there all the while as though I were truly concerned, edging out of the house to the street to see my old friends and tell them news from the outside world. I was joyful and forgot about everything.

Returning home late that evening, I ate with my sisters a dry, poor "supper" and lay down to sleep in my place—above the oven.[8]

My sisters were apparently very troubled in trying to figure out what would become of me. More than once did I hear them talking while glancing at me from a distance. They were wondering how it was possible for me to appear so lively and joyful. "What does the kid live on?" they would ask each other. "What causes him to be so cheerful—the dry piece of bread that he eats with us? Tell me, what? Take for instance the rich man's son; though he has every comfort that money can buy, he's as thin and green as a church. And Berele, *kenehore*, is handsome, lively, and joyful.[9] And from what—a dry piece of bread? Simply amazing. Blessed be He and blessed be His Name who conducts the world with such kindness."

In this vein of excitement and sorrow my sisters would talk among themselves. It would have been self-denigrating, God forbid, had strangers been there—something they never ever would have done! But I could not have cared less. I was still the same rambunctious kid and the leader of a whole pack of boys, especially on *Shobes* when we turned the world upside down.

---

8   The flat tops of the broad brick ovens used in those times were often used for sleeping. The ovens of those days served not only for preparing food but also for heating the entire dwelling.

9   *Kenehore* is the common Yiddish pronunciation of the words *keyn ayin hore* (literally "no evil eye"). It is customarily added after saying words of praise or commenting on something desirable (i.e., a large crowd), thereby expressing the wish that the evil eye should have no effect.

There were various games: *malkhes pletselekh*;[10] *kamer, kamer, hoyz*;[11] and more and more. And the more children there were, the greater the excitement, the greater the fun. I was the "commander" and the head of all the games and was envied for my energy and talent. But upon returning home to my sisters, they would again resume their complaints of "What's to be done with you?" and "What's to become of you?" And along with the dry bread, I would receive a few dry slaps—and I would then forget the games and grow serious for a while.

The summer passed like this. *Rosh-Khoydesh Elul* arrived; very soon would be Rosh Hashanah and Yom Kippur, and you needed to recall your transgressions.[12] But no matter how hard I tried, I could not find any. Missing praying— no. Missing *Asher Yotser*—no.[13] Missing the Hebrew blessings recited after a meal—no. Even in the midst of playing a game, if thunder rolled or lightning struck, all of us would shout in a loud voice the blessing of "whose power and might fill the world."[14] I searched and searched and could not find anything. Perhaps I had thrown a stone at a boy's head? That was no sin; the kid should not have been where he was not wanted! But, still, I did manage to find one sin.

If you search hard enough, you will find something.

During the summer, I once went to *kheyder* and had two little apples, bought for a *groshn*. One looked delicious and I really wanted to eat it, but what was I to do since it was before morning prayers?[15] But my evil inclination was working doubly hard . . . so I just took one bite. A good little apple—actually very good. And . . . I ate it all up. Suddenly, I felt an ache in my heart. What

---

10 Denotes "royal *pletselekh*"—*pletselekh* being flattened rolls of bread strewn with poppy seeds, chopped onion, and coarse salt. Shtern (1950:24) describes other children's games similar to tag named after various foods.
11 Literally meaning "chamber, chamber, house." Shtern (1950:59–60) describes this game as follows: While the other players hid, one player faced a wall and sang a twelve-word nonsensical rhyme. He then turned around and sought the hiding players while closely guarding his beginning position. Upon spotting a player, he went and tapped the player's hiding place and said, "Chamber, chamber, house, Pinye (that is, the boy's name), come out from your hiding place." The last player found took the seeker's place. If a player managed to seize the seeker's beginning position without being noticed, the usurper shouted, "Chamber, chamber, house, one, two, three," and the game started over again, with the seeker resuming his position and role.
12 *Rosh-Khoydesh Elul* (the beginning of the month of *Elul*) occurred on August 10–11, 1858. The month of *Elul* is traditionally a thirty-day period of repentance directly preceding the High Holy Days (*Kitsur Shulkhan Arukh* 128:1). Rosh Hashanah and Yom Kippur occurred on September 9–10 and September 18, 1858, respectively.
13 *Asher Yotser* is the Hebrew blessing thanking God for a functioning body recited after relieving oneself.
14 This blessing praises God "whose power and might fill the world" and is recited upon hearing thunder.
15 Jews generally do not eat before morning prayers (*Kitsur Shulkhan Arukh* 8:2).

have I done? Before prayers—eating?! Now I would surely die. I was certain that my days were numbered. Fear gripped me—I very much did not want to die so young. I felt the transgression burning inside me and leaving me no rest. Rosh Hashanah arrived, and I beseeched God and sobbed before Him to forgive me for my misdoing and that I should sin no more. And suddenly . . . a commotion broke out in *shul*; a mortal fright overcame the entire congregation. As everyone pushed to look out the windows, they saw entire regiments of soldiers surrounding the synagogues—standing guard to prevent the children from escaping. The snatchers entered, seized boys, and handed them over to the soldiers.[16] Mothers dashed about like poisoned wolves and their cries reached the seventh heaven.[17]

I was there too, and they were searching for me.

But I was miraculously rescued. It seems that my prayers were so fervent that God had mercy upon me.

This was how it happened: As soon as the commotion started, my sisters came into the men's section of the *shul* and took me with them into the women's section. There, Ite told me to crawl under her dress and to stay there without saying a word or else I would be doomed. She let down her dress a bit and told me to crawl along with her—she warned me not to stop sooner or later than her—but to keep abreast of her pace. And that was how we walked home. As

---

16 In the original, the snatchers are referred to by the Hebrew word *khoytfim*, rather than the more commonly used Yiddish word *khapers*. See the following footnote for further explanation.

17 In 1827, a statute was passed under Tsar Nikolay I introducing compulsory military service for Jewish males in Tsarist Russia between twelve and thirty-five years of age for a period of twenty-five years (reduced to fifteen years in 1859); non-Jews were also required to serve twenty-five years but had to provide conscripts between the ages of eighteen and thirty-five. Such young Jewish recruits were conscripted with the intention of integrating them into Russian society by alienating them from their coreligionists and coercing them to convert to Christianity. Since Jewish communal leaders were made responsible for meeting the quotas, they often preyed upon the most vulnerable elements of their communities, that is, orphans and the children of the poor. When not able to fulfill their quotas, Jewish snatchers forcibly seized men and children, sometimes those younger than twelve. Until the age of eighteen, they were placed in barracks (cantonments), from which the word "cantonists" was derived. The child recruits were generally forbidden to observe any tenets of Judaism, to talk their native Yiddish, and were forced to attend Christian religious instruction. They often displayed tremendous self-sacrifice in enduring torture rather than submitting to baptism. At the age of eighteen, the cantonists then began their twenty-five years of military service, a slightly less severe form of the same type of prison. Though the cantonist system of conscripting those younger than eighteen was legally stopped in 1856, Petrovsky-Shtern (2010) points out that it actually lasted through 1859, thereby giving credence to the author's encounters with snatchers here in the summer of 1858. (See Ginsburg, 1937:3:3–127; Mendelevich, 2011; and Stanislawski, 1983:13–34.)

soon as we arrived home, I was hidden in a neighbor's attic because they were still searching hard for me. At first I was afraid to be there alone, fearing evil spirits—so Khonele had to stay with me. But later I became so accustomed to the attic that I was no longer afraid to be there alone. Finally, the period of recruitment passed and I was completely freed. Everyone wondered how I was saved. They did not know that it was God who had helped me.

For a time, my sisters did not want to reveal the clever manner with which they had saved me. They made sure I would not reveal it either by threatening me with death, of which they knew I was very afraid; they said they would tell the soldiers to shoot me if I breathed a word. In short, this remained a secret and I was rescued, thank God. I returned to *kheyder* to study, live with my sisters, and sleep on top of the oven. And life proceeded as usual. But something happened that I will never forget. In fact, whenever I recall it, it always seems as vivid as real life, my eyes become filled with tears, and the hair on my head stands up in fright.

This was what happened: One evening two months after the horrible raid on Rosh Hashanah—around Hanukah time—as I was walking home at dusk from *kheyder*, I saw a large crowd of people running, so I ran along with them.[18] Suddenly, I saw little soldier-boys walking—many, many of them . . . I say walking, but they were not quite walking but rather dragging themselves along; actually, they were not quite dragging but crawling in the mud, while many grown soldiers marched alongside and drove them mercilessly while the area resounded with their cruel shouting. The children screamed as well, and their voices reached the heavens.

Tiraspol was a regional center and it was here that they herded together all the young boys from the surrounding towns and villages before driving them farther along to be quartered with non-Jews.[19]

Many unfortunate parents traveled after them, or to be more precise, walked behind them. The sobbing of their parents and of others at the scene was extraordinary. It was impossible to observe the scene and not be moved to tears over the tragedy. Even I, a small child, who could not understand the great misfortune befalling my unfortunate little brethren, sobbed aloud.

As I stood there and observed the heartrending and horrible scene, my sisters came running up to me in horror, "Why are you standing here, you bandit?

---

18 Hanukah lasted from December 2 to December 9, 1858.
19 Sometimes the young cantonists were sent to distant Russian farmsteads, where they were maltreated. Upon reaching eighteen, their formal military service of twenty-five years began. See p. 152, footnote 17, earlier in this chapter.

Run quickly home and don't dare to come out. May God protect you. Don't you see what's going on here?"

And I remained at home.

Later I was told what had happened to the young boys; how they had been led off to distant towns, how their mothers had followed them, and how many had died on the road due to their pain and weakness, their suffering and sorrow.

This was how the despotic rulers treated the Jewish people at that time, and so they continue to treat us to this day—in different guises and in different manners.

So I suffered through that winter. I was constantly forced to hide in various places that my sisters would think up for me: at times in a cellar, at other times in an attic, and many times simply with a good friend. I remember that once in the middle of the night my sisters heard heavy steps. Before a light could be lit—in those days, lights were still lit by striking flint—one of them grabbed me and took me during the night to a neighbor's house. I was once again miraculously saved, for the heavy steps were those of the snatchers who had come from Poland to find me since my father was registered in the little *shteytl* of Kodeme in the district of Bolte.[20] If they had found me, I would have been their ready victim.[21]

At that point, my sisters thought about sending me still farther away. They decided to send me to Chechelnik. An aunt of mine, my father's sister, lived there, so they took advantage of the opportunity when they heard that a local resident was traveling there. He was going to visit the Chechelniker Rebbe, and they promised him a portion of the World to Come for performing the mitzvah of saving an orphan, because they were afraid that I would eventually, God forbid, fall prey to the snatchers. That fellow brought me to Chechelnik with a letter of recommendation for my aunt. Upon my arrival the fear of the snatchers was over, because the conscription law had been abolished.[22] Had we known this earlier, they would not have sent me off so far. Chechelnik is fifteen *versts* from Tiraspol, if not more, and was a long journey for so small a child.

In short, there was nothing to be done since I was already there in Chechelnik with my Aunt Rosye, whom my sisters did not even know, nor had they realized that she was such an elderly woman who was residing with her

---

20 Kodeme was located in the Tsarist Russian province of Podolia in the Ukraine, which was also referred to as Poland in Yiddish (see chapter 3, p. 111, footnote 13).
21 The snatchers (*khapers*) came to find the author to meet the recruitment quotas in Kodeme.
22 Though the cantonist legislation mandating the recruiting of Jews under the age of eighteen was legally stopped in 1856, Petrovsky-Shtern (2010) indicates that it actually lasted through 1859, which is corroborated by Goldenshteyn's account here of it being abolished in the spring of 1859.

children. In the end, after reading the letter I had brought and having a good cry, she said to me: "To whom did those fools send you? To me?! I'm certainly your aunt. My heart hurts for my flesh and blood, but how can I help you? I am a widow myself, an old woman, and I reside at times with one of my children and at times with another. So how can I help you? If it was a short distance to Tiraspol, I would take you and send you right back, but it's so far. How can I find someone to take you back?" Meanwhile, her children gathered to see the guest that had been brought to their mother, and they calmed her: "Don't cry, dear Mama, don't cry. As of now, he's just a child, so if God helps us and we can manage, we will keep him. If not, we'll send him back."

CHAPTER 7

Shuffled Around, 1858–1860

Boarding at Etye-Yoyls • A New Shoylikl • Squabbles • My Rebbe's Plan • Winter at the Crack of Dawn • Tsipe's Illness • A Dream • A Heavenly Cure • In a New Dwelling • Dancing and Hopping • Off to Groseles • Among Fiery Hasidim • A Learned Boy • A Bloody Game • In the Deep Grass • Escape • The Good-Hearted Rebbe and His Wife • A Strange Visit • A Friend • Upheaval

Aunt Rosye had two sons and two daughters. The oldest son, Avrúm, was poor and had a houseful of children. The other son, Itskhok, was just as poor but had fewer children. A daughter, Khaye, lived outside of the town, ran a tavern and had no children. The other daughter, Rukhl, lived in a village, was mean, and also had many children. It fell to Khaye to keep me, but she lived so far from town and how could a child walk so far to attend *kheyder*? In addition, she was very stingy. On the other hand, Avrum was not stern and was milder than all the others. So it was decided that I would stay with him, and the others would pay my tuition. My aunt would sometimes stay with her daughter and sometimes with her son Itskhok across from the *hoyf,* as the Rebbe's house was called.[1] The Rebbe held her in great esteem because she was one of the Hasidim of the old Savráner Rebbe.[2] Since Reb Moyshele, the present *tsadik*, practically

---

1 *Hoyf* literally means a "courtyard" in Yiddish.
2 The Chechelniker Rebbe at that time was Rabbi Moyshe Giterman (ca. 1838–1870). He was the son of the "old Savraner Rebbe" (as the author refers to him), Rabbi Shloyme Giterman (died 1848), who is often called the Savraner-Chechelniker Rebbe since he had moved from Savran to Chechelnik. Rabbi Moyshe Giterman was married to Sheyne-Reyze, the daughter of the well-known Rebbe of Rakhmestrivke (Rotmistrivka, Ukraine), Rabbi Yoykhenen Tversky (1802–1885). (Hager, 2002:111–128; Hager, 2006:85–90; Shapira, 1990:2:178–179.)

grew up in her arms, she was considered to be among the most honored women in Chechelnik. When she entered the *hoyf*, she was treated with great respect.

I began to attend *kheyder* and they were pleased with me. Every *Shobes*, I went with my uncle Avrum to the Rebbe's *hoyf*, where they sang and were joyful.[3] I sang too (I had learned a few little songs) and the Rebbe was pleased with my voice. He blessed me, saying that I should be a pious Jew and be able to study Torah as well as I sing.

Once I became acquainted with the local boys and began to spend time with them, I became bored with going to the Rebbe and found various excuses for not going there. I preferred meeting some friends at the barracks, where we would hear military music being played. This displeased my uncle Avrum and he doled out to me a good thrashing. I was also displeased with his behavior, so I began moving from one uncle to the next, from one aunt to the next, until they packed me off, with great pleasure, and sent me back to my sisters.

So, at the age of ten, I was back with my "rich" sisters in Tiraspol.

Now I was once again living with my sisters. Shloyme-Leyzer was still teaching, and his wife, my sister, Tsipe was selling glassware near Etye-Yoyls's market stand.[4] But here I must tell something about Etye, since it relates to an important period of my childhood.

Etye had been widowed for quite some time, had saved money, and had managed to accumulate some capital. She then remarried but did not want to live with her husband, so she was once again alone. He would travel about as a prestigious person and earned money doing so.[5] I caught Etye's eye as one who might say *Kaddish* for her after 120 years, so she took me in.[6] I was now living with her and had everything a person could want. Nonetheless, my good fortune did not last very long. Her husband returned during *Sukes*, and, upon hearing that she had taken in an orphan, he was thunderstruck. He began to argue that his little Leyzerl was also an orphan and that she should have, if she had

---

3   Referring to the author's Aunt Rosye's son Avrum.
4   Referring to a woman named Etye who was probably the wife or widow of a man named Yoyl.
5   "A prestigious person" is a translation of "*a sheyner Yid.*" A step above the average downtrodden beggar was the individual claiming to be the son of a prominent rabbi or family who collected alms to sustain his family and himself. Such an individual did not simply go from house to house asking for alms but might enter a synagogue in full rabbinical regalia, seat himself at the front of the synagogue along with the prominent members of the community, and then approach the rabbi, explaining his prominence and relating his sob story. After services, the rabbi might then make an appeal for funds for the unfortunate victim. Such was the manner of a person making a living by simply being a prominent person, *a sheyner Yid.*
6   "After 120 years" is a euphemistic manner of saying "after her death."

been fair, chosen his son. He then began to work toward making peace. Others intervened in the matter and the couple reunited.

So now, I once again had a new little brother, another Shoylik, and no end of trouble. For a month, all was quiet, but then the squabbles began. Leyzerl would complain to his father: Etye gave me "this" while he had gotten "that"; Etye fed me aches and him pains.[7]

There were charges and accusations with hearings before my rebbe, before my sisters, and even before Etye herself.[8] It all made me very upset; I spit at the whole affair and returned to my sisters.

I did continue my learning, because Reb Shloyme, my rebbe, liked me.[9] Even when he was not paid, he did not throw me out. In addition, he proposed a plan so I could study with him more. Since I was more capable than all the other children, but he would be uncomfortable studying more with me in their presence, I should arrive at the crack of dawn and wake him up, and he would then study with me. And I then began to arrive before dawn when the rebbe was still asleep, waiting outside in the freezing cold until he awoke and let me in.

I remember that once, as I was running barefoot to *kheyder*, a rich man's wife saw me and took pity on the orphan before her. She told me to enter her house and showed me a bunch of old shoes and galoshes, from which I was to select and put on a pair.

I was delighted by that event.

A short while later, my sister Tsipe began to feel very weak and was unable to arise from her bed. Ite and Khonele ran to the *bes-medresh* and fell upon the Holy Ark with great sobbing, pleading for God to have mercy on them and cure their sister, since they could not even afford to pay a doctor.[10] They went home, but Tsipe was still no better. Suddenly . . . she fell asleep but soon awoke and pointed to the large chest, indicating with her hand that it be moved away from the wall. Since they did not understand her, she began to speak a few words, saying that under the chest was a small radish that they should take, shred, and squeeze out its juice for her to drink. And so they did. That very day, she began to feel better and quickly regained her health.

Later, she told the following story: "When I fell asleep, Mother came to me and asked me how I was doing. I answered her: 'You see for yourself that

---

7   Meaning that Etye treated both the author and Leyzerl exactly the same.
8   "My rebbe" is referring to the author's *melamed*, Reb Shloyme (see below).
9   This Shloyme and his wife are not to be confused with Reb Shloyme, the rabbi of Tiraspol, and his wife Surke of chapter 5.
10 The Holy Ark is a decorated cabinet in the synagogue in which a Torah scroll(s) is kept. It is usually located along the wall that faces Jerusalem.

I'm not well and that I'll probably die soon. Who'll take care of the orphans?' Mother calmed me down and told me not to cry. She said that I would live and be well because she had brought me a remedy from Heaven. She then told me about the small radish lying beneath the chest, what was to be done with it, and that I would get well." Indeed, Tsipe grew stronger and prettier than before, and everyone marveled at the miracle that had occurred.

Once again I found myself in a new place. This was at Reb Duvid-Boye-Yóykhenens.[11] The Boye part of his appellation was in reference to his brother, who was rich while Duvid was not, so the reference was to the prestige of his brother. I never saw any business dealings taking place and of what use I was to them I still cannot understand to this day. Apparently, I was of service in the errands that I performed. Duvid's wife, Dvoyre, would constantly be sending me around, "Berele, hop over here," and "Berele, dash over there." And Berele hopped and dashed all over the place and was happy to do so.

They had a son who frequently traveled to and from Odessa, until he finally settled there and sent for his parents to live with him. So I was again back at my old spot, at Tsipe's, because in the interim both Ite and Khonele had married, leaving Tsipe living alone.

But I did not live with her for long. She began to urge me to go to Groseles to live with my Uncle Pinkhes and even showed me a letter from him asking me to come. So I mounted a coach and rode off to Groseles.

My uncle and aunt accepted me as a guest, and the group of boys there was especially delighted to see me. I recognized some of them, but some I could no longer recognize since they had changed completely in their strange attire. Boys aged thirteen wore little *kapotes* and *gartln*, à la Hasid, so that they looked at me as if I were a heretic.[12] But I had a good excuse for not dressing as they did—I had not yet reached the age of thirteen, so I was permitted to dress as I did.

Walking into the *bes-medresh*, I realized how strange the younger and older Hasidim there were. For hours on end they would run about in pairs, like horses, to and fro, talking and whispering instead of studying. I just stood there, pondering what I had fallen into and what sort of world this was. Then I realized how much of a "heretic" I was. Two days later, my uncle "overjoyed" me with

---

11 Yóykhenen was apparently the name of the father of the two brothers, Duvid and Boye. Boye might be a nickname for Burekh. In fact, Rabbi Burekh Shimshon Hager (the son of Vizhnitzer Rebbe of Monsey, New York, Rabbi Mordche Hager) was called Boyele in his youth. His mother was the daughter of the Skverer Rebbe, Rabbi Ya'akov Yosef Twersky (1899–1968), who lived in Kalaráҫ́ sh, near Tiraspol.

12 In his linguistic review of the use of Yiddish in Goldenshteyn's autobiography, Yudl Mark (1943:39) found it curious to discover such an international term as *à la* in conjunction with the word Hasid: "Did such an *à la* come from his children or the newspapers?"

the good news that he had hired a good rebbe for me and that this rebbe would finally teach me how to be a *mentsh*.

I arrived at *kheyder*, and the rebbe greeted me warmly and asked me whether I was the mischievous kid whom the whole town was talking about. He told me to sit and to listen to what was being taught, and that if I did not know it this week, he would not be angry with me. (It was a Wednesday, and the pupils were expected to know the week's studies by Thursday.) But he was truly amazed that the others did not know it after a week's study, while I recited it practically by heart. The rebbe quickly understood that he would only have to discipline me for my disrespectful conduct because Torah subjects I mastered easily. And actually, after *Shobes*, he slapped me a couple times for my frivolity, and I was quite angry about it.

At home, too, it was not all milk and honey. My blind aunt was very stingy and begrudged me everything, while my uncle was also angry with me, though I did not know why.[13]

And then *Shobes* arrived. All the kids, with me at their head, went out to play in the fields. I ordered them about just like an officer with his troops. If someone did not please me, I threw him out of the game: "Good riddance and don't bother others!" It happened that I threw out a little boy, a teacher's pet, who went off to tell the rebbe—and I knew nothing about it.[14] The next day, the rebbe gave me a real piece of his mind. He told me not to dare play any games until he awoke, after which he would hold a trial. But as soon as he lay down to sleep, we all went out again to play and the teacher's pet also wanted to join in, but I was wary of him and would not allow it. But when he kept on trying to push his way into the game, he got a slap from me, and then another one. When he tried once again, he got another slap, Tiraspol style, and was bloodied. All the boys grew frightened, the boy ran home, and a commotion ensued.

And I was gone!

I was hiding in the deep grass from where I saw and heard everything that was going on. I comforted myself by telling myself that as soon as things quieted down, I would know what I would have to do. When things grew quiet and night had fallen, I came out of my hiding place and headed off on foot to Tiraspol. In

---

13 Often those blind in only one eye were called "blind" in Yiddish, as in the case of "Shmiel the blind *melomed*" mentioned in chapter 4, p. 132.

14 The author uses the word *motuske* (מטותקע) and its diminutive *motuskele* (מטותקעלע) to indicate a teacher's pet. This word evidently derives from the Aramaic מטותא meaning "favor," that is, a teacher's favorite. Though some Yiddish speakers called a teacher's pet a *gets* (Beinfeld & Bochner, 2013:215), the word *motuske* is not documented elsewhere in the rich *kheyder* literature that is extant.

the village of Plosk lived a Jew who was called in the surrounding area Reb Leyb Plosker.[15] He recognized me from afar, "What are you doing here, Berele? What brings you here to Plosk at night?" So I told him that my sister was sick and that I wanted to go to see her. Since he was traveling to Tiraspol that night, he took me along so that I was at Tsipe's before dawn. She was very frightened at seeing me, and, after hearing my fine story, berated me severely. But her reproof had little effect on me, and I soon fell sound asleep as though I had just come out of a steam bath.

The next day, someone from Groseles arrived with a letter inquiring whether I had returned here. The letter stated that my uncle was losing his strength, the rebbe was losing his mind, and no one knew where I was. I was nothing short of overjoyed that I had been able to "accommodate" them all and let them know how to deal properly with a child. I then remembered hearing, while lying in the tall grass, how they each blamed the other: the rebbe had blamed my uncle for advising him to terrorize me and treat me without mercy; my uncle had blamed the rebbe for torturing me from his first day. They were both guilty, of course, and I could not have cared less which one was guiltier.

After Tsipe's reproach, I replied that I would go to my former rebbe, Reb Shloymele, and ask him to teach me.

And that is just what happened.

Reb Shloymele, the rebbe, still treated me mercifully as before and pitied the fact that I was wasting such great talent and that he could not be of any help. The rebbe understood me well and was very sympathetic, despite the fact that he was a fanatical Jew of the old school. I am certain that if he had been able to help me in any way, he would have determinedly done so. But, alas, what could he have done for me when he himself had so many troubles and knew only one thing—studying the Torah, praying from morning until evening, and teaching big blockheads. This robbed him of all his vitality about which he complained more than once.

"The Almighty has created one thing opposite the other."[16] As good as the rebbe was to me, so I experienced excruciating pain and suffering at the hands of his wife, the *rebetsn*. She would find ways to send me off to the ends of the earth. Once, in the most freezing weather, she took the liberty of sending me to the *shoykhet* to have a chicken slaughtered. When I refused, pointing at my torn shoes, she seized a piece of wood and threw it, almost hitting me in the head.

---

15 Plosk, Ukraine (now Velykoploske) is a village ten miles southwest of Groseles, on the way to Tiraspol.
16 Ecclesiastes 7:17.

When I ran outside, she followed me and threw it at my feet. And that's how, she would claim, she taught me the rules of respect.

Many years later, after I was married, when I came to visit the rebbe so that he might take pride in his once impoverished pupil, the *rebetsn* boasted to one and all with these very words: "Do you see this fine young gentleman? It was I who taught him respect!" and told the story of the piece of wood. The rebbe, who truly enjoyed my visit, pointed out to her that her conduct could only have corrupted my character, not improved it.

In any case, I used to get even with her—as much as my conscience at that age could bear. I would constantly pull out the knitting needles from the sock she was knitting, tangle up the cotton thread, douse the fire, drench the firewood with water, and hide the snuffbox. She would go crazy searching for everything that I hid, which gave me great pleasure. I recall that on my later visit, I told her all this, and she admitted that she had treated me badly. I forgave her.

I had a friend named Shimen, a son of Reb Itsye *der Poylisher*, a rich man's son, whom many in those days already called Itsye Erlikhman.[17] When Shimen grew up and also became quite wealthy, he too was known as Shimen Erlikhman.[18] But at that time, he was simply Shimen, and so he was called. This Shimen needed me because he was weak in his studies, and I helped him a great deal in understanding the *khimesh* with Rashi's commentary and the Talmud and its commentaries. Over time, we became fast friends and shared whatever we had to eat, down to the last bite. Our love and devotion was so strong that it was impossible to believe that we could live without each other. Yet we did part upon my being suddenly transported to another place, where trouble began to rain down on me. By then I had completely forgotten that I once had such a dear friend and that there was no one around to even remind me of him.

The entire winter and more than half the summer had gone by, and I was already twelve years old and life for me was not bad.[19] I studied with the rebbe and ate at my sister's. All of a sudden, everything turned so topsy-turvy for me that I did not return to the rebbe and was completely divorced from the *kheyder*.

---

17 Meaning "Reb Itsye the Polish Jew," which could refer to a Jew from the Tsarist Russian provinces of Podolia, Volhynia, or Kiev. (See chapter 3, p. 111, footnote 13, regarding the term "Poland.")

18 Though Itsye Erlikhman was already referred to by his surname, the Jews in Tsarist Russia at that time did not usually call each by their surnames—not even businessmen and the wealthy—as mentioned in ch. 1, p. 90.

19 Referring to the winter of 1859–1860. Though the author writes here that half the summer had passed, the beginning of the next chapter (ch. 8, p. 165, footnote 2) is dated late May of 1860. He was actually almost twelve; the author is not precise in mentioning ages.

CHAPTER 8

Sent Off to an "Uncle," 1860

A Brand-New Uncle • A Two-Wheeled Wagon • My Sisters' Worry • Expectations of Golden Mountains[1] • Blessings for the Journey • Robbers in the Forest • A *Kiddush* Over Tears • Feudal Servitude • "What's a *Shul*?" • No Jews Around • At a Windmill • A Supervisor over a Non-Jew • The Blades Turn Round as the Years Fly By • A Companion • Without Any Goodbyes • Good Riddance • On the Way to Tiraspol • Necessity Breaks Iron

Upon emerging from *kheyder* on a Thursday right after *Shvues*,[2] I found a *bidke* near a horse in the courtyard outside of our home. (A *bidke* is a two-wheeled cart.) The horse was unharnessed and was eating hay from the *bidke*. At home, I saw a man of about thirty years of age sitting down. My sisters Tsipe, Ite, and Khone were also sitting there looking worried and engaged in conversation, which was interrupted by my entrance. The stranger's eyes suddenly pounced on me, looking me over from head to toe. I wondered about his glare, but my sisters interrupted my thoughts with their headshaking, crying, and nervousness. One of them could not control herself and went into the other room to sob. This caused me to wonder even more about the stranger. "What's going on?" I thought. "Why did he have to look me over?" In short, I went right over to my sisters and asked them why they were so worried and why they were looking at me that way. They told me that an uncle of ours had arrived and that they were telling him some of our troubles. Understandably, there was not much to be joyful about. "Say hello to your uncle, Berele," they said, while they themselves arose and went into the other room to cry.

---

1 The author is referring to his high expectations the night before traveling with his uncle.
2 May 27–28, 1860. *Shvues* is the Jewish holiday celebrated fifty days after Pesach and usually occurring in late May or June. It is the anniversary of the day that God gave the Torah to the Jewish people on Mount Sinai.

I quickly made my acquaintance with this uncle and greeted him. He replied with welcoming money—a genuine five-*kopek* coin.³ He questioned me and I questioned him. I answered his questions, and he answered mine, from which I learned that the *bidke* and the horse were not hired but were his own. He then asked me to ride with him to the village where he lived. Of course, he did not have to ask me more than once—as long as we would be taking a ride, especially in a privately owned *bidke* and horse, and particularly since I had never ridden in a *bidke* of any kind. For such luck to come my way—of course I agreed. My sisters returned as we were talking and also asked: "Will you go with Uncle, Berele?" I told them that I would. "But you'll stay with Uncle, you won't come right back?" I said: "No! Our other uncle didn't have a *bidke* or a horse. I'll have more fun with this uncle!" So the evening passed, and I could hardly sleep that night; it seemed as long as a winter's night to me. I was eager to ride in the *bidke* as soon as possible. It was hardly daybreak when Uncle arose to pray, and I prayed with him. After prayers, he greased the *bidke*'s wheels and watered the horse. He filled a sack with oats and attached it to the horse's head. He then went into the house for a glass of tea and a bite to eat. I was already seated in the *bidke* and refused to budge. They barely managed to drag me out of it and into the house so that I, too, could have tea and a bite to eat.

My sisters showed me so much affection now. They fussed over and doted on me—I cannot recall their ever having showered me with so much love before. In short, they finished packing my bundle and started to bid me farewell. They kissed me and told me 10,000 times that I should remain with our uncle and that I should obey both our uncle and aunt, so that things would go well for me; if not, I should not even bother to return. They also talked endlessly to our uncle out of my hearing, sobbing, but I could not understand what their talk was about. Uncle goaded the horse and my sisters shouted blessings and good wishes after us, and I was on my way. It was still so very early that not even one of my friends saw me leave. Even Shimen *der Poylisher*, my best friend, did not know of my leaving, and I was not able to say goodbye to him, which bothered me very much. But I could not help it since I left when it was so early, when everyone was still asleep.

In any event, I was delighted to be traveling, especially as I was sitting right next to my uncle and was holding one of the reins in my hands. When the horse sneezed, Uncle said in Russian, "Bless you." The horse trotted along and I was happy. Uncle promised me that I would eventually be able to drive the *bidke*

---

3 Welcoming money (*sholem-aleykhem-gelt* in the original) was generally given to children when adults arrived (or returned) from out of town (Rivkind, 1959: 227, 276).

myself and even to ride astride the horse. This was a major event for me, something I had long yearned to do. Until then, I had been unable to muster up the strength to do so because I was afraid to touch a horse, much less ride one. How I had envied other boys as they rode horses and drove their horse-drawn carts on their own. In short, I was joyful about the trip and its promises. But as we drove on a few *versts*, I began to think "Where in the world am I? Where am I going and to whom? What sort of an uncle is this? I've never heard any mention of this uncle! Why were my sisters so worried, and why had they been sobbing so? Why did they show me so much affection before my departure?" In thinking about all this, I began to worry. I started to cry, but inside so that Uncle would neither see nor hear—until I fell asleep. I woke up—everything around me was steppe—only earth and sky. I asked Uncle, "Is it still a long way to your home?" "Hoo-hah," he says, "what a question? It's still plenty far."

I was weary of the ride and even of the *bidke* and the horse, and Uncle himself also did not please me to some extent. I began to observe the road behind us and to memorize landmarks that might be useful to me later. We rode all day and evening approached. There was intermittent rain and the road became more difficult. The horse was tired and stopped every once in a while: we could ride no further. Both of us made our way on foot and the road led into a little forest. I was afraid of robbers—robbers hide in the forests!

"Uncle, is it still far?" I asked in fright. "Is it still far, Uncle?"

"Very soon, Berele! We're almost home."

"What? You live in the forest? Robbers live in the forest!"

He bursts out laughing, "I don't live in the forest, and this isn't a forest—it's a patch of woods. We'll soon pass through it and then we'll be home."

We drove on, that is, the horse moved along with the *bidke* in tow, and we went on foot until Uncle called out with joy, "You see there, Berele? There's a light burning, and that's my house!" I was joyful, too, and thought, "In just a minute, I'll be in Uncle's house and will finally have a place." After a bit, we rode up to the house, and a young woman and two little girls—one ten and the other six—emerged smiling. They exclaimed, "*Tote*[4] has arrived!" Then his wife asked him, "Why did you arrive so late? Who is this little boy you've brought?" He replied briefly, "The horse got tired, the road was long and hard, and besides, it rained a bit," which explained why he was late. And as to who the little boy was, he said, "I'll tell you later." At that point, I realized that he was not a real uncle. He was a fake. Otherwise, why did he not respond, "Why this is Tsipe's

---

4 *Tate* (father) is pronounced as *Tote* in the author's sub-dialect of Southeastern Yiddish (see the Introduction to the Glossaries).

little brother" or "This is Ite's little brother, our little nephew!" This made me quite suspicious. My suspicion grew particularly strong when he came into the house and whispered to her for quite some time about me, and, after all, that she did not come to kiss me as an aunt would do to a visiting nephew but looked me over and glared at me. I said my prayers and then sang *Sholem Aleykhem*. When he made *Kiddush*, I did so as well. But in the midst of making *Kiddush*, I broke down, sobbing so bitterly that the little children, seeing me, began to sob as well. Uncle and Aunt were unable to calm me. I kept on sobbing. I thought, "What have I done? Where have I come? How and why am I here?"

After a good cry, I sat down to eat. I ate, swallowing the tears that flowed uncontrollably down my cheeks. Everything about all of this bothered me: my uncle, my aunt, the house. With a heavy heart, I fell asleep—after all, I was tired from traveling—and slept soundly through the night. When I awoke, I saw the girls standing around me, waiting for me to wake up; the poor things were glad to see another child and have someone to play with. I quickly went out with them to the courtyard around the house, began to observe its surroundings, and was very frightened by what I saw: there were no other houses to be seen near ours—the house was completely isolated. It was surrounded on all sides by steppe and more steppe . . . Not far off, on a hill, was a windmill, which the girls pointed out as belonging to them. Far-off, to the left of the house, appeared little huts, the homes of non-Jews, half buried in earth, half above ground, but covered with earth. They are called *zemlyankes*, because they are truly earthen graves inhabited by the poor non-Jews who worked for the nobleman.[5] To the right of our house in the distance appeared a large, attractive courtyard. I was overjoyed, "There, children! There's the *shul*, the *bes-medresh*!" Wonderingly, they asked, "What's a '*shul*'? And what's that other thing you said?" They were not even capable of repeating the word *bes-medresh*, because they had never heard of it. So I told them, "The place where all the Jews pray together is called a *shul*; the place where they study and pray—a *bes-medresh*." "No!" they said, "No! There are no other Jews here except for our father. He prays at home. There, in that large, attractive courtyard that you see, lives the nobleman. We're never permitted to go there."

Meanwhile, I heard a voice shouting and crying bitterly from the direction of the nobleman's house. I asked the children, "What's the meaning of that?" They told me that those were the cries of people being beaten for having come late to work, and that this was a daily occurrence. If someone was late, he was

---

5   The word *zemlyanke* (*zemlianka* in Russian) derives from the Russian word *zemlia* meaning "earth."

beaten and whipped with thorny twigs, which caused those unfortunate souls to cry bitterly. I said, "*Oy*, such a pity! Why do they keep quiet about the abuses of the nobleman? Why are they forced to work for him?" I did not understand this until my uncle explained feudal servitude to me. This was news to me, as I had never encountered it in the city. I became somewhat apprehensive that the nobleman might force me to work. I was even afraid to look in the direction of his house. My heart grew dark knowing that this was a rural settlement where no other Jews lived here but us—no *shul*, no friends, only poor non-Jews, and a nobleman with thorny twigs that whipped until blood flowed.

I had already begun to think of freeing myself from this place, although I still did not know why my uncle had brought me here and what my sisters' intentions were in sending me here. Upon learning of the "wonderful objective" for which I had been brought here, I kept thinking of ways to free myself from my uncle and his great ideas. I barely survived *Shobes*. It was a total disaster; there was no *shul*, no *bes-medresh*, and no other Jews in sight. I was not used to any of this. It seemed to me that I was in the desert. If it had not been for the two young girls who pranced around me—because it seemed that they, too, were overjoyed to see another living soul—if it had not been for them, I would have gone out of my mind from agony, God forbid.

Early the next morning, meaning Sunday, my uncle led me to the windmill. I was afraid to go, because I had heard that a windmill's blades could kill a person: a blade could yank a person up high and then throw him to the ends of the earth. So I absolutely refused to approach the mill, but he slowly persuaded me to go near it. He illustrated how all one needed to know was how to enter and that one did not need to go near the blades. He explained that if you did not go near the blades they could not harm you, God forbid. "Make sure, Berele, not to go near the blades," he warned me. "I'm actually pleased that you're afraid of the blades. Now I'm certain that you won't go near them, but you must also not put your hands near the wheel, or the millstone, or near this, or near that." And he pointed out all the paths I should follow and how to enter and leave the mill. Upon asking why I needed to know all this and why he was telling me all of it, he replied, "You understand, Berele, that you won't be returning to *kheyder* to study, so you need to have some sort of trade. You'll be here at my mill and learn to be a miller. But since you're still a little boy, your work will be to watch Prokopy, the non-Jew whom you see here, to make sure he doesn't steal. You see," he said pointing to a little measure called a *myertshuk*, "when grain is brought in for milling, I get as payment one *myertshuk* for each pail (pointing to the measuring pail).⁶ For example, this sack contains five such pails of wheat or rye, so Prokopy needs to scoop off the five *myertshukes* that belong to me. Those are mine! So you need to make sure that he's not stealing by taking off only three or four *myertshukes* instead of five and later taking the rest for himself. You only need to count the number of *myertshukes* that I'm owed and how many he takes—that's your job. If you see him stealing, you must tell me." He repeated himself over and over again until I understood my task well. He departed, leaving me at my job.

I immediately began to weep over my bitter fate, "Where on earth am I? How does one escape from this prison?" But I did not know the road by which I had come because we had arrived at night and it had been dark. And I could not speak *goyish* to ask directions.⁷ So how could I run away? Which road would I take to run away? Horrible and outrageous! I had been well deceived and had no way out!

Later, a non-Jew arrived with a sack of wheat. I watched him as he went into the mill. I even watched him as he whispered to Prokopy off to the side as they prepared to play their game, but Prokopy apparently explained to him that the time was not right. So they measured honestly and took the *myertshukes* honestly. I watched quite closely as they poured the wheat into the basket for the milling. Prokopy attached an empty sack to the receiving box so that the flour would pour into it. Upon completing its milling, he brought over another sack of wheat; the mill did not cease its operation. Though few non-Jews lived here, there were many hamlets in the surrounding area and this was the only mill, so they would all come here. And that is how I spent the entire week.

My day consisted of getting up very early, praying, eating something, and then going off to the mill and staying there until lunch. Right after eating, I returned again to the mill until evening. If there was no wind and the mill was still, I could remain at home. And if Prokopy rotated the mill into the wind and it began to run, I immediately had to run back to the mill.

After a few days of this, I was completely frustrated. I kept worrying and yearning for home. I cried almost constantly. Prokopy would empathize with

---

6   *Myertshuk* is the diminutive of the word *mera*, a pre-metric unit of dry measurement once used in most Slavic lands. Though a *mera* is equal to 26.24 liters, a *myertshuk* must have been considerably smaller. *Mera* is also the origin of the Yiddish word *meyre*, that is, a batch of dough kneaded in the making of *matses*, a term still used in many *shmure-matse* bakeries today.

7   Though the Yiddish word *goyish* literally means "the non-Jewish vernacular," Jews in ethnic Ukrainian areas used it specifically to refer to the Ukrainian language (Harshav, 1990:xiii). Nonetheless, the author is evidently referring here to Russian since he later quotes a few Russian phrases.

me and try to console me, but I could not understand what he was saying (though he would mix in Yiddish words), because he knew as much Yiddish as I knew *goyish*. Between the two of us, there developed an interesting language—a brand-new one.

During the second week after my arrival here, I was liberated from my bondage. God took pity on me and showed me a way to free myself. Right after my second *Shobes* there, my uncle prepared to travel to his brother's for a wedding and rented a wagon in which he loaded his wife and two daughters and then rode off. So as to make me more comfortable, they brought a teenaged companion, an eighteen-year-old from the next village—five *versts* from here. My uncle's parents lived there, and they, too, had gone off to the wedding. Since they had many children, they had enough hands to manage things at their place and still provide one to help my uncle. The teenager was called Lebke. Upon their leaving, I heard my uncle tell Lebke to keep an eye on me and not let me go hungry. My uncle told him to bring me food from his house every day so Prokopy could cook *mamaliga*, which we could then eat with milk from the cow here.[8] My uncle and his family then drove off.

I became extremely frightened and cried copiously. Lebke, the teenager, would not let me cry, saying: "Get a grip on yourself. Anyway, there isn't any work at the mill. There's no wind." He led me to the nobleman's estate and showed me how the serfs labored: non-Jewish men, women, and even children. And there were elders too who walked about with whips in their hands to ensure that everyone worked diligently. Anyone seen working poorly or lazily quickly caught a couple of lashes. I recalled the Torah's accounts of our toil in Egypt, and how the taskmasters would stand over us.[9] I felt horrible. I could not bear to watch, and I began to cry over their unfortunate situation. I asked Lebke, "Do they work every day?" He replied that each had to work his assigned time. There were days when they were free to do things for themselves at their homes, but the arrangement was such that each day there were non-Jews working at the estate.[10] Work at the nobleman's was never interrupted, even for a single day; if some were busy, then others came in their places. For example, some of them worked Sunday, Monday, and Tuesday, and some worked the remainder of the week while the others went home to do their own work.[11] The non-Jews,

---

8 *Mamaliga* is cornmeal cooked into a thick solidified porridge. It was a staple food in Bessarabia (the bulk of which is currently part of Moldova) and Romania.
9 Exodus 1:1–13.
10 In his *The Abolition of Serfdom in Russia*, Zaionchkovsky (1978:5) confirms that under Russian serfdom "[t]he peasants received a parcel of land for their use but not in ownership."
11 "Generally, labor obligations" for Russian serfs "occupied three or four days a week and sometimes more" (Zaionchkovsky, 1978:11).

their wives, and their children were forever indentured to the nobleman. "*Oy!*" I said, "theirs is an awful, miserable life. This was how we Jews suffered in Egypt!" Lebke replied, "It must have been worse for the Jews. If non-Jews treat other non-Jews this way, then we can imagine how non-Jews treated Jews."[12]

We went home from there. When we arrived, he said, "I'll get on a horse and ride home to our village Shishken. It's not far—just four or five *versts* away. I'll eat there and bring some food back for you." Unwillingly, I let him depart, and he went off on the horse and returned in the evening, bringing me dinner. It tasted as good as my misery, but it was still better than nothing. The next morning, Lebke decided to ride off very early and he did not return until the following evening, bringing nothing. All that time, I bemoaned my fate and my birth, while Prokopy attempted to console me. Though I did not know what he was saying to me, I understood that he was speaking words of comfort and solace, but what those words were I did not know. He fed me *mamaliga* and milk that he had cooked quite early in the day and it sufficed until the following morning. I ate it cold, and it upset my stomach severely. When I saw Lebke, I started crying, "You had no mercy on me and left me here all alone." He justified his actions by saying that the other children would not let him go. He stayed the night with me. Early the next morning, he told me that he needed to go back home, "But if you wish, you can ride along with me. I'll get another horse for you to ride." I asked him, "How can I go along with you. I don't even know how to ride a horse." He replied that he would teach me, and I allowed myself to be persuaded.

Actually, I was eager to know how to ride a horse. He set me on the horse. Once on the horse, it seemed to me that I was about to fall off, so I began screaming that I was afraid, that I did not want to ... Lebke laughed, "What are you afraid of, idiot? I'm holding you and the horse, too!" I kept on screaming: "*Oy, oy!* I'm afraid!" He did not listen to me and led me until I was somewhat used to it, sitting there with difficulty. Meanwhile, Lebke's horse tore away and ran off. Lebke ran off to catch it, leaving me on my own. When my horse noticed that Lebke's horse had escaped, it also began to run off. Lebke was not holding on to my horse anymore, and the horse had no respect for me. I screamed with all my might until I fell off and bruised myself badly. Lebke had already caught both horses and was standing near me, laughing at my debacle. He exclaimed, "*Nu!*[13] There's a rider for you. And what a rider!" I cried and held my aching sides, and he laughed, holding his sides with glee. In the end, I had to remain again with

---

12   This incident in June 1860 occurred seven months before the official emancipation of Russia's serfs in February 1861.

13   The Yiddish word *nu* is a multipurpose interjection often analogous to "Well?" or "Come on!"

Prokopy while Lebke rode off alone. Lebke only returned the next morning and told me that they would be coming back from the wedding at dusk or later in the evening. So he would be with me until the evening, when he would ride back to his village not to return here again.[14]

I eagerly awaited Lebke's departure because I had formed a plan to leave this wonderful "profession" of mine, the mill, Prokopy, the estate, and even the *mamaliga* and milk. I had learned that the man was not my uncle, but a stranger; Lebke had made that clear to me. Lebke told me that he, my fake uncle, had simply taken me in to become his own little steward. I was sickened and insulted by this. I had also learned from Prokopy that the road I could see leading down the hill from the mill and continuing over another hill into a little patch of woods led to the *shteytl* of Tumanov. I asked Prokopy in my version of *goyish*, "Where does this path lead?"[15] and he answered in his Yiddish: "This path ... Tumanov, yes, yes." In any event, I was convinced that this was the path to Tumanov and that I must head there before my so-called uncle returned. That was why I was anxious to have Lebke leave quickly. But, as if in spite, he did not manage to leave; it was already the middle of the day and he still had not left. I began to become apprehensive: Uncle would arrive any minute and I would not be able to do anything. But as evening approached, Lebke was finally ready to ride off and told me to tell them that he had waited until evening for their arrival but they had not arrived. "Be well, Berele. Come visit us sometime," and with those words he left.

Silently I shouted after him "good riddance" and immediately began to carry out my plan. I was afraid to lose a minute lest they arrive. I did not know on which road they would be returning—perhaps it would be on the road that I planned to take? That would be a fine mess, I thought. But whatever happened, I needed to put an end to this, once and for all.

Prokopy's presence disturbed me. He would be able to see me running down the hill and going up the next hill to the patch of woods. Once I reached the woods, there would be no reason to fear him. I decided to wait until he went home. I ran home and let the calf out of the shed. I then ran over to Prokopy to show him that the calf was loose; since our cattle were returning from grazing with the communal herd, the calf might go suck the milk out of our cow. He

---

14 The original Yiddish mistakenly states that Lebke returned "in the evening," which is incorrect since the author writes below that he was eager for Lebke to leave before the evening when his "uncle" would return. The original also states that Lebke would be with him "until the morning," which is an error as clarified in the next paragraph.

15 The original states "*Kuda yedit doroshka?*," which is a corrupted form of the Russian "*Kuda vediot dorozhka?*"

obeyed me and went off to catch the calf. But I knew that he would not catch the calf so easily, and, by the time he did, the cow would arrive and he would have to milk her and then heat up the milk.[16] So I started to get ready for my journey and took off. I ran down the hill at full tilt with all my might so that I would reach the woods before Prokopy returned to the mill. Once in the woods, I caught my breath and stood under a tree, looking back to see if the mill could be seen, if Prokopy could see me or if I was being chased. I considered everything carefully. Since I could not see any danger around me, I headed off down the road. I walked for about half an hour and came out of the patch of woods; I could see the sun already setting. Nonetheless, to my delight, I could also see houses in the distance; these were the houses of the *shteytl* of Tumanov.

As I reached the *shteytl* outskirts, I was attacked by dogs and was frightened a bit, but they were quickly noticed and driven away, and I entered the *shteytl* safely. I soon went to the *bes-medresh* and was simply overjoyed to see Jews praying *Minkhe* and *Marev*; boys like me and younger were praying and everyone regarded the stranger in wonder.[17] After prayers, they came at me from all sides, assailing me with questions: "Who are you, little boy? How did you come here? Whose child are you?" and so on. I replied and told them that I was from Tiraspol and had traveled with a wagoner from Bolte who left me here. That started it: "Which wagoner? What's his name? What were you doing in Bolte?" And I quickly came up with responses to all of their questions. The end was that they took me to a guesthouse, where wagoners who traveled to Tiraspol spent the night. The *shteytl* of Tumanov was on the highway between Bolte and Tiraspol, so there were always wagons going back and forth. They asked a wagoner to take me along, and they paid him twenty *kopeks* for me. The innkeeper gave me something to eat, and I ate greedily because I had not even had *mamaliga* that day. My wagoner gathered his passengers, myself included, and departed quite early, before dawn. By ten in the morning, I was already back in Tiraspol.

Upon seeing me suddenly appear at her house so dirty and disheveled, Tsipe became very frightened. In her fright, she began to shriek, "How did you get here? Why have you changed so much?" Looking at her, I also became frightened and began to cry. When she calmed down, she asked me why I looked so bad and how I had made my way home. I told her everything and how awful it had been.

---

16 It is not clear why Prokopy needed to heat up the milk as this was certainly before the advent of pasteurization. Perhaps he needed to do so in preparing dinner for the returning family.

17 *Minkhe* and *Marev* are the afternoon and evening prayers.

Meanwhile, my sisters gathered to see the new arrival and there was general crying over our bad fortune. They were very sorry for me and confessed that he was not our uncle but a stranger; they had given me to him to be his servant because he had promised them that he would make me into a *mentsh*.

I can only imagine what sort of *mentsh* I would have become there!

Who was to blame and what caused them to do it? It was necessity. As the saying goes, "necessity breaks iron." Need broke my sisters' hearts and caused them to give me away as a servant to a stranger.

CHAPTER 9

My Dream of a Celestial Palace, 1860

Like a Hammer Blow to the Head[1] • Half a Dream • "Sh! Don't Ask!" • In a Celestial Palace • Thousands of Children Studying There, But No Place for Me • Heavenly Aromas • I'm Led Out onto the Steppe • In the Merit of My Ancestors • An Artisan Is an Embarrassment to the Family but a Servant Is an Honorable Position • Just Like Thieves: One Bargains, the Second Steals, while the Third Waits • A Practical Vocation

As my sisters' guest and because of their sympathy for me, I spent the first few days after my return indoors. My sisters were quite busy with me; they had to clean me up and wash me because I had become very dirty during the time of my absence. So I rested the whole first day at home and fell asleep soundly at night. Before dawn, I had a very sweet dream that still remains with me and that I remember as though I dreamt it today. When I awoke an hour before dawn in the middle of a dream, I was very upset that I had not slept a bit longer. I tried to fall asleep again so that I might learn the end of the dream, but I was unable to do so. I remained awake, and the dream remained unfinished.

And this was the dream: I saw an open, green steppe, in which I walked and wandered, not knowing where in the world I was or where I was supposed to be going. I started to cry profusely, and sat down on the grass alongside the road because my legs were tired from the long walk. I then saw my deceased father walking toward me. He asked me, "What are you doing here, my child?" I immediately realized that he was my father. I began weeping and said, "*Tote, Tote*! Where have you been for so long? Things are very bad for

---

1 Evidently referring to the author's sleeping soundly upon his return.

me. I am suffering from hunger, thirst, and cold, and I have nowhere to stay. My sisters can't keep me with them!" And I told him many more things. My father listened to all of this calmly, appearing handsome and glowing. It was a pleasure to look at him. He asked me where I was headed now, and I told him that I myself did not know. I was wandering and did not know where I was or where I was going. He said, "Come with me," and he took me by the hand and led me.

He walked with me over beautiful mountains and valleys more wondrous than I had ever seen in my entire life. Father kept walking along with me. I asked him, "*Tote*, where are we going?" He said to me, "Sh! Don't ask!" We went on in this way until we came to the steppe. All around was an aroma that was quite refreshing. And far away, a fair distance away in the midst of the steppe was shining a large, beautiful palace. The steppe was flat, without a single hill. The sun was just beginning to rise.

I remember the scene as though it were today. We were coming from the west, and the rising sun, with its rays enchanting the entire area, was directly behind the palace. It was simply delightful to gaze upon the splendid panorama. I wanted to remain there forever. "*Oy, Tote*, it's wonderful here! Who lives in that regal palace that I see there?" Father said, "Yes, my child! It is truly wonderful to be here, but not everyone can be here. You see, I've had plenty of trouble leading you here. Enter the door I'm showing you and tell them that you want to study here. Tell them you wish to join them." I wanted to tell Father that he should come in with me, but he was no longer there. I remained near the palace crying and yelling, "*Tote! Tote!* Where did you go?" But Father was gone, and I remained alone near the palace. I heard voices—wonderful, vibrant voices. There were hundreds of thousands of voices, all in the same pitch—none higher, none lower. It sounded like fine music. I very much wanted to be inside, and I decided to do what my father had told me. I opened the door and stepped into a beautiful vestibule which led to a large, bright corridor, in which well-dressed young men with shining faces and garbed in silken *kapotes* were walking to and fro. I stood like a beggar at the door, afraid to cross the threshold. I saw what was happening in the corridor and heard the sounds of their studying. But I was neither seen nor heard. I decided to enter.

As I entered, everyone took notice of me, and they all disappeared into the back hall. One person, however, remained in the corridor and warned me to go no further. On my request that I be allowed to study since my father had brought me here exactly for this purpose, he replied that I could not study here but only over there, pointing to another door. He then took me by the hand and led me out.

As I approached the other door, someone, apparently a dean of students at the yeshiva there, came over to me and said, "Go, little boy. Leave here! No one may enter here!" I began to cry and begged to be let in. I was allowed inside. I saw that there were thousands of children there and enjoyed seeing everyone engaged in Torah study. But there was no room for me until someone took pity on me and seated me at a table. And just as I was beginning to feel happy, I suddenly saw myself back on the steppe—no palace to be seen, no students, only a large field. I wandering aimlessly seeking my father who had been there a short while ago. I walked and wept . . . and sought my father!

After that dream, I never saw my father again, but many, many of the things in that dream later actually happened to me.[2] I must thank the merit of my ancestors for my father's efforts, from the other world, preventing me from remaining an ignoramus. His merit, after all, has protected me and my children and safeguards them from all evil.

***

After I had rested and recuperated, the questions began anew, "What are we to do with the boy? What will become of him? Should we have him trained to be an artisan? God forbid! One must not even entertain such a thought. It would bring shame to the entire family. But what would be good? A servant! Now, that's an honorable position!" If anyone had wanted to take me on as a servant, my sisters would have immediately agreed, even if it had meant working in a tavern. But no one wanted to take me on. I did not please this one and was not suited for that one; I was too old for one and too young for the other. My sisters continued to seek out a practical vocation for me. They did not know what to do with me, and I began going to the *bes-medresh*.

Those unacquainted might think that in a *bes-medresh* people sat and studied constantly, but in truth that was not the case. The young married men on *kest* and the elderly men who had already retired from their business affairs went to the *bes-medresh* to study. There were also boys from *kheyder* who were studying on their own. Hence, upon entering the *bes-medresh*, you heard a cacophony of all kinds of voices, both young and old, and a tremendous clamor rose to the ceiling. Yet in reality nothing was being accomplished; it was only worthy of jeering. In particular, boys like myself certainly studied no Torah. During prayers when others were around, things were fairly reasonable: the volumes

---

2   The author specifically mentions parts of his dream coming true in chapter 12, p. 201.

of Talmud were held open and everyone was looking into them, but as soon as those who had come to pray began to leave, the fun started.³ Some fellows hit each other with wet towels, others roasted potatoes and others turned over lecterns. It was lively and joyful...

The young married men used the boys there for various chores. If a boy attempted to disobey, he would get his due. Among the *bes-medresh* habitués on *kest* were also the sons-in-law of the rich who spent money on truly useful things such as poppy-seed rolls, apples, plums, and watermelons. With the latter, we kids used to do our best business. When I began to attend the *bes-medresh*, I also became a servant to the rich sons-in-law at the *bes-medresh* and needed to serve them along with all the other kids. Once, I was sent to buy watermelons. Three of us went: one did the bargaining while the other pushed away a melon with his foot so that the third could freely pick it up and carry it away. The Jewish saleswoman, whom the dear customers had just awakened from her nap, had no idea that she had just been robbed in broad daylight. Those boys from the *bes-medresh*, whether they really intended to be or not, were market thieves in the making. The kids would do this one day at one Jewish woman's market stall, the next day at another's, and the day after at a third's. And I was also taught to do as the others. Such an education would have instructed us to become fine gentlemen, the equal of all. Such were the lessons for these boys, the *kheyder*-boys, in the *bes-medresh*.

There was another craft there which was almost our specialty—silvering money. That involved turning copper coins into... silver ones! And this is how it was done: We would take a one *kopek* coin and coat it with mirror-silvering, turning it into a brand new twenty-*kopek* silver coin. We would search out some blind or sleepy Jewish lady who had a little market stall from which she barely eked out an income, and we pushed that "valuable" coin into her hand. She would then give us the merchandise and our change, however much was due us, not realizing that the coin might have been a fake. We continued to steal like this in broad daylight, yet no one saw us.

My sisters apparently saw that there was no productive purpose in my becoming an unemployed *bes-medresh*-goer, a loafer, and thought about some sort of business for me. And they found one.

After three weeks, I left the *bes-medresh*.

---

3   As is common, a number of prayer services were held in this *bes-medresh* each morning. Hence, many of those who studied in the *bes-medresh* had finished praying and were studying while others were praying in the services held later in the morning.

CHAPTER 10

Working as a House Servant for Shulem Tashliker, 1860–1863

A Long Displacement • Under Protest • The Great Fire • Compresses and Pepper • *Zmires* by Heart • Like a Slave in Egypt • An Idea Redeems Me like Moses Redeemed the Jews! • At Potiphar's • Hate instead of Love • A Girl Harasses Me • The Hebrew Letters Seem Upside Down • Anything but a Boor • Bitter Tears • Complaints to the Master of the Universe • "May the Devil Take You!" • "Thanks for the Bread and Salt. Farewell, Tashlik!" • The Foot-of-the-Mountain Village • "The Beginning of Wisdom is Fear of God"[1]

I wound up in a new place where my stay was lengthy and lasted far longer than those I had experienced until now.[2] This stopover lasted a few years.[3] This time, I wound up in a village with my relative, Reb Shulem Tashliker.[4] My sisters had begged him to take me to his village to make something of me—a respectable person—and Reb Shulem had agreed. To this day, I do not know what conditions were agreed upon with my sisters, and I am not interested in knowing. They only told me that our relative Shulem, Aunt Ester's son, would be taking me with him to his village.[5] He had no sons, only two daughters, "So he's taking

---

1 Psalm 111:10. The author is likely referring to his being God-fearing by praying in the morning following his departure from Tashlik before setting out on his journey to pursue Torah wisdom.
2 The summer of 1860.
3 The author stayed in Tashlik almost three years until the beginning of the summer of 1863. See p. 188, footnote 19, later in this chapter.
4 Tashliker denotes "of the village of Tashlik."
5 Aunt Ester was apparently the author's father's aunt, "Ester the change provider," mentioned in chapter 1, p. 92.

you as his son. There's a *shoykhet* there who'll teach you.[6] If you don't stay there then don't ever show your face to us again. We'll kill you. You're almost *bar mitzvah*, you keep getting older, and you're not registered either, so what's to become of you?"[7]

This was Thursday evening after my return from the *bes-medresh*. Since I was not pleased with the behavior of those in the *bes-medresh*, I joyfully and readily agreed to my sisters' proposal of traveling to Reb Shulem's village. I promised my sisters everything, as long as it meant being rid of the *bes-medresh*. Now, even though I was the youngest in the *bes-medresh* and I had no more of a desire to study than those older than me, I did not care for the bad behavior that I was driven to. I had no talent for such things, was often slapped by the young married men there for my disobedience, and was threatened with being expelled from the *bes-medresh*. So despite it being shortly before *Shobes*, I left Tiraspol on Friday for the village so that I could begin doing something useful and practical.

I remember as though it was yesterday. Friday morning at ten I had my belongings packed and was ready to go. Our relative Reb Shulem led me to a wagon driven by a non-Jewish villager, set me into it, and told me to wait until he returned. As I sat in the wagon counting the minutes until we left, the bells of the churches suddenly began ringing the signal for a fire. All the non-Jewish villagers took to their wagons and fled the city.

Since the major fairs in Tiraspol are held on Fridays and Sundays, many wagons from the nearby villages gather there on those days. Whenever a fire breaks out in town, all the non-Jews are recruited to help fight the fire, which the villagers avoid by running back to their homes. This also occurred on that Friday. When the villagers heard the church bells, they made haste to leave. My driver also sped off, not waiting for Shulem. When we left the city, I saw that the fire was quite large, and I began to cry out of fear and terror. The wagons dashed by, the dust was thick, and my driver drove his horses like a madman, while my innards were trembling as if I were sitting on a volcano . . .

By three o'clock, I arrived in the village, at Shulem's family. I was a near-corpse, bruised on all sides, screaming in pain with all my might, and clutching my stomach. This apparently alarmed them greatly. They treated me with compresses and pepper, which actually relieved the pain a bit, and I fell asleep.

---

6   Meaning that Shulem would hire the *shoykhet* to study Torah with the author. In a small village, the *shoykhet* was usually the only one learned enough to be able to teach Talmud.

7   Since the author was unregistered, Shulem would take him to be his son, as it states above, meaning that Shulem would register the author as his son. Yet, he never did so, probably due to the effort and expense involved.

When I woke up after some time, I was already feeling fine and noticed that Reb Shulem had arrived and was relating details about the fire. I was particularly overjoyed to learn that the fire had not reached the street on which my sisters lived and did not, God forbid, harm them.

I was now in this village with a relative. The village was cheerful and lively. It lies alongside a highway, and wagons were constantly traveling back and forth so that one often saw fresh faces. In addition, there was another village nearby in which some more Jews live. On *Shobes*, the communal prayers were held together in the next village and one was able to feel true Jewish flavor. It was a far cry from the "uncle" with the mill in the field, where one saw nothing but the earth and the sky.

It was because of the existence of some Jewish life there that I was not surprised that my stay there lasted longer than all the others during my childhood.

On my first Friday evening there, I sat among my own—with those who had saved me from great physical pain upon my arrival. I sat at the table as an equal among all the others, and I felt good. They welcomed me warmly, for which I truly felt grateful. In quiet joy, I begin to sing aloud.

I sang the *zmires* of *Shobes* evening by heart, and everyone regarded me in wonder, "How can it be?! How does this boy happen to know these so well by heart?" They were very pleased with me, and we sat there singing late into the night.

The next morning, Shulem went with me to the next village to the *minyan*.[8] There I ran into two old friends with whom I had studied in Tiraspol, Mordkhe and his brother Avrum; they were overjoyed to see me, and I was even more pleased to see them. So I had friends with whom to spend my time for quite a while. Having two good friends nearby and a horse and wagon at my disposal encouraged me to enjoy and be satisfied with my "prominent" position, though I later grew bored of it and it no longer interested me. This was how it was: at first I agreed to work for Shulem of my own free will, but later I was forced to work, yet by that time I was unable to get myself out of my situation. I was living proof of the Talmudic phrase "At first by will and in the end by force."[9] I remained in Tashlik as a common house servant. If not for God's compassion on me, I would have remained eternally a slave, a boor, an ignoramus, and a wretch. But God had pity on me and sent me a liberating angel in the form of

---

8 *Minyan* denotes here the locale where Jewish prayer services were held. In villages like these, prayer services were often held in private houses.

9 Though this exact phrase appears in the Jerusalem Talmud (Sota 4:4), it is not well known. The author was probably adapting the common Talmudic expression, "At first by force and in the end by will."

a bright idea, which brought me to my senses and would not let me rest until I was delivered from my exile, as were the Jews from the Egyptian exile through Moses our Teacher. And I became a free person rather than a permanent slave.

Now it is necessary for me to describe this related family who used me in every possible way and whom I served like Joseph did in Potiphar's house in Egypt.[10] The family consisted of three people: Shulem, his wife Khaye, and a girl of about fifteen named Beyle. Their income came from a tavern where they sold liquor, wine, and other alcoholic beverages. They had a house with a large courtyard surrounded by a fence which was always closed. The house was located alongside the highway so that guests desiring food and drink came often. Understandably, their business required a great deal of work, and I had to work diligently and vigorously. Over time, I became better and better at it, and the running of the entire house and even of the kitchen fell upon me. They exploited me to no end.

After a short while, I learned to speak Walachian because the village was populated entirely by Walachians.[11] Once I learned how to speak it, I truly became a big shot like Joseph at Potiphar's. All that was missing was to have Potiphar's wife fall in love with me. But Khaye was too old for that, and their daughter Beyle did not have any sense yet. Instead of love, Beyle exhibited tremendous hatred toward me and persecuted me as much as she possibly could.

After some six months, they were using me in every aspect of the business: "Berl, bring this inside," "Berl, serve that non-Jew some liquor," "Berl, hitch up the horse and ride into town." I can say that I did not have a minute's rest, except for *Shobes*. On *Shobes*, I was off and rested from the week's work. The household also did not sit idly. Shulem worked hard enough, and Khaye, his wife, worked too—there was enough for everyone, especially during Shulem's frequent travels. He found his world too confining; he would seek additional sources of income and, most often, would come up short, so that what was earned at home he would lose outside. Things were easier for me when he was at home since he would then attend to the tavern and the store. His wife had to tend to the house, and the girl—who considered herself both delicate and

---

10 Genesis 39:1–19.
11 The Walachian language and Wallachians refer here to the Romanian language and Romanians. The United Principalities of Moldavia and Walachia, which were autonomous but still vassals of the Ottoman Empire, were only officially named Romania in 1866. When mentioning a person as being Walachian, Romanian, Bulgarian, Russian, Greek, or the like, the author is referring to a member of those non-Jewish ethnicities and not to nationalities (a modern concept). A Jew could be considered none of these and was solely of Jewish ethnicity.

important—would not do a thing except order others about. She sought out easy work for herself: sewing and the like.

The neighboring Jews in the village were impressed with my abilities and figured that Shulem would certainly not let me go but would take me as his son-in-law. I once went over to the neighbor who lived directly across from Shulem, a fine Jew named Reb Moyshe-Ersh, who had fine, married children.

He said to me, "You're Shulem's relative and are of the same family. You're a fine boy. Why doesn't Shulem provide you with some Jewish education? Why doesn't he take you as his son-in-law instead of making you a house servant?"

I was shamed by those words and replied, "How should I know?!"

"Yes, you don't know, but he does though. After all, he's meticulous in his religious obligations and can study the Talmud well too, so why doesn't he know that it's written, 'Do not hide yourself from [the suffering of] your own flesh.'[12] Of course, it would be better for him to do this. He would save you from being an ignoramus and make his daughter happy. You could then grow up to be a great person!"

Reb Moyshe-Ersh would constantly put forth arguments in the same vein, not only when he spoke to me but whenever he spoke to anyone. I do not know if this was out of loyalty or decency or perhaps it was out of envy and enmity for Shulem and he just could not begrudge Shulem such a loyal person in his household. I do not know any of this, but I do know one thing—that when this talk reached Shulem, he pretended not to hear it and swallowed it calmly. But when Beyle learned of it, she felt deeply insulted, "How come I'm held in such little regard that people would think that I would marry a house servant?!" From then on, she began to despise me. She began to find very lowly work for me such as plucking chickens, sweeping the house, and the like. She saw to it that I did such work, with the intention of denigrating me thereby showing how foolish Moyshe-Ersh's words were.

Reb Moyshe-Ersh would storm about this, which did not help at all. His favors caused me suffering, and I cried over this more than once. But I could not help the situation. I was already torn away from the *kheyder*; I had already become a bar mitzvah; I had begun putting on *tefillin* during the first winter after my arrival there.[13] I heard that my sister Khone had died; she had borne

---

12   Isaiah 58:7. "Your own flesh" in the verse is referring to one's relatives.
13   Hence, the author started to put on *tefillin* in the winter of 1860–1861, which was shortly after his twelfth birthday. There was once a widespread custom that a child bereaved of at least one of his parents began to put on *tefillin* at the age of twelve instead of thirteen to provide merit for his deceased parent (Zinner, 2002:226–229). This is the reason that the author refers to his starting to put on *tefillin* shortly after turning twelve at his bar mitzvah, as do Milch (1946:123) and Bonchek (1955:107) in their autobiographies. Nonetheless,

a son that winter and died a few weeks later.[14] To whom could I have gone? Working for strangers would have made me truly a servant. There with Shulem, I was ostensibly working for a relative who had said that he was going to raise me as his own child. Hence, I had to remain there, and I stayed there and suffered from all sides. But I mostly suffered from the girl. A couple of times, I heard her parents rebuke her on my account, even though they always backed her up in my presence.

Shulem's elderly mother, my Aunt Ester, may she rest in peace, came to visit for a short time. She quarreled with her granddaughter in my favor and berated her children for letting their daughter have such power over me. She actually shed tears over my bitter fate. She even supported Moyshe-Ersh's idea, saying that if Shulem were a considerate relative he would raise me as a son, arrange for me to get a Jewish education, and turn me into a Torah scholar instead of having me pluck chickens and grease cart wheels. But her words were to no avail. Since my aunt was very smart and pious and was afraid that God might punish her children on behalf of the orphan, she took up my cause with all her might in order that they might treat me better and consider whose child was suffering so at their hands, "Reb Itsele Groseler's one and only *kaddish*![15] 'This is the Torah and this is its reward?'[16] Where is the merit of his father's Torah learning? *Oy*, children, my dear children! I fear that God may punish you." Despite the fact that Beyle was her grandchild, she cursed her in my presence, demanding that she stop being so cruel toward me because no one is the master of his own destiny. "You can't know what may happen to you and especially to the children that you will have some day."

My elderly aunt departed.

On her departure, she kissed and blessed me, wishing that God might deliver me from them in the merit of my pious parents: "Don't worry and don't cry. God will take pity on you and will soon come to your aid."

---

it is clear from the *Mishna* (Avot 5:21) that a Jewish male becomes *bar mitzvah* (obligated in fulfilling the *mitzvahs*—commandments—of the Torah) at age thirteen. In short, these instances of twelve-year-old boys donning *tefillin* were clearly only informally referred to as *bar mitzvahs* because the primary new obligation incumbent upon a Jewish boy at his *bar mitzvah* is the donning of *tefillin*.

14 Hence, Khone died in the winter of 1860–1861. See chapter 4, pp. 123–124, for more details regarding her death.

15 Though not common today, parents used to refer to a son in Yiddish as their *kaddish* (or *kaddishl*), since a son's recitation of the *Kaddish* prayer for his departed parents' souls during the eleven months following their deaths has great spiritual significance.

16 Talmud (Brakhot 61b).

For a brief time afterward, things were a bit quieter. Beyle did not harass me as much as before and did not assign me any loathsome tasks. But these good times did not last long. In a couple of weeks, she returned to her old ways. She despised me and tortured me in every way. She complained that I was praying for too long and that I was constantly wasting time. She kept on digging and searching for my failings, wanting to be rid of me entirely and have me out of her sight for good.

When Beyle would hear and see how people praised me and how I found favor in their eyes, she would become fearful that her father might reconsider and be willing to follow the suggestions of Moyshe-Ersh and others—that Shulem should marry her to me. She was as scared of being forced to marry me as of death itself. She was frightened, and she let her fright out on me.

Later, after her father made a match for her and she already knew that she had a fiancé, a well-off boy and a good catch, she changed her policy toward me for the better and became good and pious and regarded me with compassion. A new Beyle had arisen before me completely unlike the one I had known just the day before, but I did not want to know her because of her falseness and baseness.

For over two years I worked and suffered like this for nothing except for my food and Shulem's hand-me-down clothes, which consisted of a torn jacket, a pair of boots that had to be made smaller, and a pair of pants that had to be turned inside-out and mended before they could be reused.

I became accustomed to my situation and accepted everything with love.[17] I thought, "This is certainly how things must be," because I knew no different.

My situation continued like this until I once remembered something that caused my heart to grow heavy and tears to begin to choke me. A light went on in my head, and I remembered what I was and who I was. I remember that it happened like this: Once, while praying, I stopped at a few words, not knowing their meaning, and my heart stood still. I grabbed a volume of the Talmud, which I had once known well, and the same thing happened! I understood nothing and saw nothing; the letters turned upside down, and I did not recognize them. Fear gripped me, a hidden fear, and I prayed with hot tears to God that He should have mercy on me that I might not remain a boor because He had already punished me enough. Afterward, whether I was resting or not, eating, or going to sleep, this idea that I could not remain an ignoramus would not leave me for a moment and would not let me live.

---

17 The Talmud (Brakhot 5a) discusses the merit of accepting suffering with love.

Others in the house noticed that I was going about worried and distracted. I was reprimanded for this and was told that Beyle had been correct in her complaints against me, but by now she was simply tired of having anything to do with me and left me to my own means.

At times, when I went off to some place that I had been sent, I would spend many hours on the road where there was not a soul to be seen. I would then think deep thoughts of redemption, beg mercy of God, and cry out in sorrow and pain.

And God heard my plea.

That year, Shulem leased grazing fields, thereby gaining the right to collect money from the *chumaks* for permits to graze: five *kopeks* for every pair of oxen.[18] In addition to all my work in the store and in the tavern, I often needed to ride out to the steppe to see if a *chumak* had stopped somewhere to graze his animals and to collect the fees from him. More than once, I needed to awake before dawn to look out for the *chumaks*.

The *chumaks* who stopped to graze their oxen on that fateful Friday could be seen easily from the house.[19] So I was immediately sent to collect money from them. Since I approached without a horse, they did not want to give me even one *kopek*. They quickly hitched up their oxen, drove off, and totally ignored me. Although I chased after them and shouted that they had better pay because they would be much worse off if my boss had to come, they just laughed at me and continued on their way. Since I could not do anything, I returned home.

My heart was heavy, and I felt devastated. Once again, ominous thoughts filled my mind; thoughts that my mind and my strength were not able to bear. I felt a need to sit down and pour out my heart to Him who knows all and is all powerful. As soon as I sat down, I heard Shulem's voice. He was saying to me, "What? Are you just sitting there? May the devil take you! Weren't you sent after something?!" And he himself went to pursue the *chumaks*. I remained standing there numb as if someone had removed my head.

"The time has now come," I said loudly, talking to myself. "I'll now be redeemed from my exile!" I ran down the hill right into the house. It was still early, and Khaye had just gotten up.

---

18 The *chumak* (pronounced *tshumak*) vocation was a historic occupation of wagoners and traders common in the Ukraine. Via ox-drawn wagons, they transported salt and dried cured fish. Sometimes traveling in huge caravans, they prospered until the advent of railways in the second half of the nineteenth century (Kubijovyč, 1984:467–468).

19 As indicated earlier in this chapter on p. 181, footnote 2, the author arrived in Tashlik in the summer of 1860 and he stayed "for over two years," as found on p. 187. Since he left Tashlik on the Friday before *Shvues* (ch. 11, p. 191), it was now May 22, 1863; hence, he was in Tashlik for almost three years.

I said to her, "Khaye, give me the shirts that I have here. I have no interest in staying with you any longer!"

She asked in fright, "What? What are you saying, Berl? Are you crazy?"

"No," I said. "I'm not crazy. I don't want to be here any longer! If you want to give me my things, fine. And if not, I'll leave without them. You can keep them all." I grabbed my prayer book and *tefillin* and began to leave.

When she saw that I was leaving, she ran after me shouting, "Here! Here they are! What good are your old rags to me here? Here, take them! But just tell me, why did you suddenly get such an urge to leave? Wait until Shulem returns. He'll give you a few *kopeks* for the road. You probably don't have anything to travel with?"

I replied, "No, no! I don't want to wait for him, and I have my own *kopeks*!" So saying, I turned my pockets inside out and showed her that I had thirteen *kopeks*, a tip that I had received from some merchant who had passed through. "Here, see my possessions," I said to her. "See that I have not, heaven forbid, taken anything from you. I hope that God will continue to protect me. Thank you for the bread and salt, Khaye. Be well and don't think ill of me."

And I left.

I truly did not know how to answer all her questions about where and to whom I was going. But one thing I knew—I was leaving Shulem.

When I was outside the village, I sat down on a stone to consider my situation. Where was I going, to whom was I going, and what would I be able to accomplish somewhere else? Yet I continued walking and arrived at the next village, where the *minyan* gathered, but from the other side, which is called Foot-of-the-Mountain Village.[20] The village is called Buter and is divided into two parts; one part is situated along the base of the mountain and the other is some distance away from it.[21] I knew a Jew who lived there, and it was to his house that I went to pray.

---

20 In Yiddish, it was referred to as *Intern-Borg Dorf* (*Untern-Barg Dorf* in Northeastern Yiddish). This second half of Buter lies along the Dniester River and has been called India since the beginning of the twentieth century ("Butor," 2000; "India," 2007).
21 An additional description of this village appears in chapter 18, p. 299.

CHAPTER 11

Beyle's Fiancé, 1863

Shulem-Itsye the Soldier • Respectable People • From Tashlik to Bender • In a Coach with Non-Jews • In Town • With Shulem's Daughter Beyle's Future In-Laws • Greetings from a Bride-to-Be • An Ugly Fiancé • A Golden Watch on a Chain • My Curse Materialized • Man Thinks and God Laughs[1] • "Always Be a *Mentsh*"[2]—Say It, don't Spray It • Wandering • In an Unfamiliar *Shteytl*

I must elaborate about the family with whom I stayed.

After leaving my relative Shulem in Tashlik, and finally being freed from bondage in that Egyptian exile, I was now praying on the Friday morning before *Shvues* at the home of a tenant innkeeper.[3] He was called "Shulem-Itsye the Soldier," and his wife was called Dvoyre-Itsyes and other nicknames...[4] When Itsye had arrived in the village three years earlier and it became known that he had been a "Nikolayevian soldier," it was obvious that he had to be called by the

---

1   The author evidently uses this popular Yiddish expression (similar to the English expression "Man proposes, God disposes") to refer to Chaye's hopes that her husband Shulem had chosen a handsome groom for their daughter Beyle when he was, in fact, quite unattractive.
2   "*Le-olam yehe adam*" in the original, which is part of a Hebrew phrase found towards the beginning of the morning prayers, meaning, "A man should always be [God-fearing in the innermost recesses of his heart]. . . ." By omitting the end of the phrase, the author has humorously altered the meaning of these words to mean, "Always be a *mentsh*," that is, have some common decency—a reference to Beyle's husband spraying spittle in his face while speaking. Since this phrase appears at the beginning of the morning prayers, the author is also implying that common decency comes first and foremost before anything else.
3   A tenant innkeeper is referred to as a *rendár* in the original (a more usual form of this word is *arendár*). That Friday was May 22, 1863. *Shvues* was on May 24–25, 1863.
4   Dvoyre-Itsyes denotes "Dvoyre, the wife of Itsye."

nickname "Soldier"![5] Itsye tried to hide and cover up the embarrassment of his past as a soldier as best as he possibly could through his good deeds.[6]

When I was still in Tashlik, I remember Shulem's wife's brother returning from his service in the military. Having spent so much time among non-Jews, he did not know a word of Yiddish. His presence caused his family such painful embarrassment that they had to take him across the border so that he might no longer be seen and that no one, God forbid, might learn of this stain on the family's reputation.[7]

Itsye was truly a respectable person, gave much charity, and would often contribute a great deal of money for communal affairs. He was God-fearing, treated others with respect, and was particularly conscientious in fulfilling the obligation of opening one's home to wayfarers. His wife Dvoyre wore the pants in the house and used to make parties all the time: she would invite large numbers of guests and dispense generous portions to all. But still, the nickname "Nikolayevian soldier" endured forever.[8]

Shulem would often come to Reb Itsye for an interest-free loan, and he was never refused. More than once, the loan came through my hands, since I was sent with a repayment, to change money, or to borrow some money. If one needed change for a 100-ruble note, it was also obtained from Reb Itsye. He was considered to be richer than was actually the case.

That was how I became familiar with this Reb Itsye, his wife Dvoyre, and his little boy Léyzerke, which was practically their entire family and whom

---

5   *Nikolayevsky soldat* in the original Yiddish. This term can refer to: a Jewish child who was conscripted into a cantonist battalion until the age of eighteen, whereupon he then served in the Russian military under Tsar Nikolay I (1796–1855) for twenty-five years; or a Jew who was conscripted at eighteen years of age or older and served in the Russian military for twenty-five years. The twenty-five-year term of military service was reduced to fifteen in 1859. Evidently, Shulem-Itsye was of the latter type, while Shulem Tashliker's brother-in-law, mentioned in the next paragraph, was of the former, as indicated by his forgetting Yiddish. For more about cantonists, see ch. 6, p. 152, footnote 17.

6   Due to Jewish soldiers having been generally unable to fulfill even the basic laws of the Torah during their years of military service, such as eating kosher food and observing the Sabbath and Jewish holidays, their familiarity with Jewish law and custom greatly diminished, a fact that caused them and their families much embarrassment.

7   Chaye's brother would have been taken across the border into the United Principalities of Moldova and Walachia (later renamed Romania), which was the closest foreign country to Tashlik at the time. Domnitch (2003:119–123) includes the biography of a former cantonist soldier and the suffering he endured upon finally returning home. As his mother said to him upon realizing that he disliked his fiancée, "You're nothing but a soldier! Is the daughter of a respectable family given to a soldier?"

8   Vilk (2017:137) from Skole, Eastern Galicia (now in Ukraine) also mentions the stigma borne by Jews who had served in the Austrian army and their difficulty in finding brides.

I would see every *Shobes*.⁹ But they had another child—a little girl named Freydele. Now was only my second time to see her. The first time was when I had brought a 100-ruble note to change, but since they were not able to do so they sent me to a rich Walachian with their Freydele to show me where he lived and to say that it was for them. At that time, she was a ten-year-old child, a very pretty child, but silly. She did not make the slightest impression on me.

Now, when I stopped off to pray, I saw her for the second time. She pranced around me, "What are you doing here? Changing money again? Come, I'll show you where. Wait here awhile. Don't go away. We'll play together!" It was obvious that the girl was eager to see a new person and to chatter with him. Her little brother was a dolt; he stood there and stared at me with his two eyes wide open and his finger in his mouth.

When Dvoyre saw me coming into her house carrying a bundle in my hands, she asked me, "What are you doing here? Do you need something?" I said that I did not need anything, but that I wanted to pray the morning services. "What's that you're carrying in your hand?" I said, "My shirts—all my possessions!" "What does that mean?" she asked in wonderment, "What does this mean?" So I told her that I left Shulem. "So!" she cried out, "you're leaving Shulem! Why, all of a sudden?" I told her that the time had come for me to leave him. She said, "Why, why?" I replied, "That's my business. I don't want to be with him anymore." "A pity, a pity," she said. "Perhaps you'd like to stay with me? I'd treat you more loyally than Shulem, though he is your relative. I'd also pay you money." I said, "What are you talking about? I should be your servant? God forbid! It's beneath me!" "But you were a servant for Shulem." "At Shulem's," I replied, "I was with my own. That was apparent by my not having taken wages from him. It's not my fault that he treated me like a stranger. If he considered me to be a house servant, then he is no relative at all, and I'm leaving him." Reb Itsye also came in and tried to persuade me to stay at least for *Shobes*. But I had only one reply, "No."

The pretty little girl, Freydele, stood there the entire time, listening to what was said. I did not know if she understood or not, but when she heard I was invited to spend *Shobes*, she also began to beg, "Stay here. Be with us for *Shobes*. All three of us will then play together. Won't you?" I did not answer her. I said, "So long!" and started to leave.

But Dvoyre did not let me leave. "Drink something, at least, and eat a piece of bread," she said to me. "After all, you'll be hungry." I could not keep

---

9   Leyzerke was about eight years old here in May 1863, since he is later mentioned as being ten years old in April 1865 (ch. 14, p. 230).

on declining, so I sat down to eat. The children stood around me and stared down my mouth as though they would have liked to swallow me up just to keep me from leaving. Their mother, too, stood at a distance, and looked at me with compassion and asked me, "Where are you going from here? Do you at least know where you're going?" I answered her by saying that I was going to Bender and asked her to tell that to Shulem at the *minyan* tomorrow. I bade them farewell and left them.

When I climbed up the hill and started walking toward the road leading to Bender, a wagon of non-Jews who were traveling there caught up to me. For ten *kopeks*, they took me up into their wagon. All along the route, they kept poking fun at me, and I regretted the whole affair. I was afraid that they might kill me. When I arrived, with God's help, at Perkón, a village not far from Bender, they stopped to drink at a tavern, and I got off the wagon and went on to Bender on foot.

But where would I go?

That's what I was thinking as I entered the town of Bender. "Where should I go to spend *Shobes*?" Just then I reminded myself that I did have somewhere to go. I remembered that the parents of Shulem's future son-in-law lived in Bender and that I could go there to spend *Shobes*, bringing regards to him from his bride-to-be, the pretty Beyle, Shulem's daughter.

And I went off to his future son-in-law's parents for *Shobes*.

I once met the parents when they came to Shulem's house to draw up the engagement contract, but I did not meet the groom-to-be. They had not brought him along to the writing of the engagement contract. Instead of him, they brought a gift for the fiancée—a gold watch on a chain.

At the time, the groom's absence puzzled me. But when I later saw him, I understood everything.

Arriving at Reb Olter-Avrúm-Azriels, Beyle's future father-in-law, I conveyed Shulem's regards and asked to meet her fiancé.[10] They were overjoyed to see me and treated me as though I were Shulem himself. Meanwhile, he arrived. When I saw him, I stopped dead in my tracks. I was shocked and could not comprehend how Shulem could have agreed to select such an ugly fiancé for his pretty little daughter, his princess! But she would have to agree to the match. After all, would she have any other option?! I remembered that she had once called me "Satan" and spat at me.[11] I had answered her, "You've no reason

---

10 Olter-Avrúm-Azriels refers either to an Olter who was the son, son-in-law, or close relative of an Avrúm-Azriel, or to an Olter-Avrúm who was the son, son-in-law, or close relative of an Azriel.

11 The original states *Satana*, which means "Satan" in Russian.

to spit at me, but God will send you a husband who deserves your spit!" And now, looking at her fiancé whom she had not yet met, I thought about how one should never let a curse out of one's mouth.[12] I remembered what I had said to her then with my mouth and what I had wished for her in my heart, and I now regretted what I had done.

Shulem had been taken by the match because the boy's father was rich and had promised a dowry of 400 silver rubles in addition to *kest*. The boy was a fine fellow and a good student. That is what Shulem said when his wife asked about him. "Just tell me, please," she would ask, "is he handsome? What does he look like? Tell me something about him." And Shulem would reply, "Not bad, a fine fellow, a learner. And when he returns here with Beyle after being on *kest*, I'll make him into a merchant. He'll be a good merchant."

I sat with Beyle's fiancé and looked directly into his eyes and saw that he was enjoying himself immensely, almost indulging himself. He asked me everything about his future wife, what she looked like, and if she yearned for him as he did for her. I realized with whom I was dealing—with a Hasidic teenager who was no better and would be no better than all the other sons-in-law at that time. In addition to being short and thin with thick lips and buck teeth, he sprayed one's face with spittle when he talked. He was still studying in *kheyder* and was ugly as death.

This was Beyle's fiancé.

At the table on *Shobes*, they asked me how I came to be there and why I needed to be in the area. I replied that I had to visit my sisters in Tiraspol, and, since it was on the way, I rode into Bender to visit the groom-to-be and convey regards. From there I would travel to Kovishon to Shulem's other daughter who was with her father-in-law on *kest*, and then I would return home.[13]

Sunday morning I went on foot from Bender to Kovishon, a distance of twenty *versts*, and arrived there at midday. Tired and broken, I asked the way to the *bes-medresh* and went there to rest.

One may wonder why I preferred to go to an unfamiliar *shteytl* where no one knew me rather than to my sisters in Tiraspol. But I had a good reason for this. I knew that my sisters would not allow me to start studying Torah now, especially since it was already over two years since I had been torn away from Torah learning. They would surely not allow me to study and my plans would be completely foiled. I chose to go elsewhere for this reason and also because I was afraid of Ite. For my having left Shulem's, Ite might beat me and send me

---

12 Talmud (Brakhot 19a).
13 Her father-in-law was supporting his own son and daughter-in-law, while his son continued his Torah studies.

off as a servant so that I could learn something practical. Anywhere would do as long as I would not meet up with them.

In Kovishon, no one knew me—not even Shulem's daughter who lived there with her father-in-law on *kest*. Though I knew her, I still thought it was best not to go see her and introduce myself, especially since she had been described to me as someone very bad—even worse than her younger sister, the pretty Beyle.

Yet it was destined that I would not completely avoid my sisters by escaping from their charge and authority to an unfamiliar *shteytl*.

CHAPTER 12

Gaining Admittance to the Yeshiva in Odessa, 1863

In the *Bes-Medresh* • A New Idea[1] • Groups in the *Bes-Medresh* • Lots of Talk, But in Whispers[2] • A Poor Supper • "From Where Will My Help Come?"[3] • An Old Familiar Face • All My Cleverness Was of No Help[4] • The Meeting • Now Mature • Good News • In Odessa • Such Noise • The Realization of My Dream • A Thousand and One Nights[5] • A Beardless Jew • In the Yeshiva • At the *Gabbai*'s House • Looking at Me • A Ray of Hope • "Get Outta Here!" • A Fellow Townsman's Protection • Among High Society • A Visiting Card

Having rested well after my journey, I sat down to study in the *bes-medresh*. I picked up a *khimesh* and began to struggle over that week's Torah portion.[6] I could not translate a single word into Yiddish. Meanwhile, a young man came up to me and asked me: "Where are you from and where are you headed?" I said that I was not headed anywhere, but that I came there because I wanted to study. "Where have you come from?" I said, "From a village." "What's its name? Are

---

1 This is apparently referring to the author's request for someone to teach him some Torah.
2 Though the Yiddish expression "*Me redt un me redt un me shishket zikh*" (literally, "People talk and talk and whisper") figuratively denotes talking a lot without reaching any useful results, the author is using its literal meaning since people in the *bes-medresh* were talking quietly about him.
3 Psalm 121:1.
4 The author is describing the failure of his plan to avoid his sisters by studying in an unfamiliar place.
5 Referring to the author's holding to his principles in speaking with his sister, Tsipe.
6 The Five Books of Moses are divided into fifty-two weekly portions, which are read consecutively throughout the year from a Torah scroll. Each Torah portion is named using one of the Hebrew words in its initial verses.

you a village boy?" I said, "Actually, I'm from Tiraspol, but I was in a village and deprived of study, and now I want to study. If you'd like, please teach me some of the Torah portion with Rashi's commentary." As I spoke, several teenage boys and young married men approached and looked me up and down. Finally, the first young man began to teach me a section of the Torah along with Rashi's commentary. The young man was somewhat of a stutterer and his speech was difficult for me to understand, but I struggled greatly to comprehend him. I quickly repeated to him the section of Torah and commentary that he taught me and I knew it well. He then went off to his spot to study on his own, but he kept a sharp eye on me and what I was doing. When he saw that I continued to study, he asked me, "Well, do you know it? If you don't, ask me and I'll repeat it." I said that I now knew that section with Rashi's commentary well. Said he, "If so, let's hear it!" I immediately repeated the lesson, and he was immensely pleased. "In that case," he said, "I'll teach you another section!" And he studied that with me, and I learned that well too. Meanwhile night had fallen. A crowd assembled to pray *Minkhe* and *Marev*. They gathered in groups where they talked quietly about me; I noticed that everyone kept glancing at me.

After *Marev*, I went and bought a hard roll with my three *kopeks*, ate "supper," and lay down to sleep in the *bes-medresh*. I woke up quite early and took a volume of the Talmud in my hand. The young man arrived, asked me if I knew well the Torah with Rashi's commentary that he had taught me, so I repeated it for him. "We can make a respectable fellow out of you," he said to me. "I'll teach you a bit of Talmud, and another young man will teach you the Torah with Rashi. You'll be able to study as long as you want. But what will you eat? This is a poor *shteytl*. Who can support you?" I said, "I don't expect any food. All I want in life is to study Torah! A bit of dry bread will be enough for me."

At morning prayers, he raised six *kopeks* for me. The money allowed me to survive the day: a roll in the morning and a roll at night, and I spent the entire day studying.

The young man, my guardian angel, was named Yosef-Khayem-Gites.[7] He was engaged to be married and was a Talmudic scholar, who was pious and studied Torah for its own sake.[8]

---

7   Yosef-Khayem-Gites either refers to a Yosef-Khayem who was the son, husband, or close relative of a woman named Gite, or to a Yosef who was the son, husband, or close relative of Khayem, who in turn was the close relative of Gite.

8   "Studying Torah for its own sake" refers to someone who studies Torah to fulfill his religious obligation and not for money, honor, or some other ulterior motive.

This young man taught me the Torah with Rashi's commentary and Talmud. I reviewed them and also struggled to study on my own. Then it happened that I suddenly spotted my brother-in-law, Shloyme-Leyzer. "What are you doing here?" I asked. "Me? I teach here! But what are you doing here? Does Tsipe know that you're here?" I said, "How would she know? I didn't come from Tiraspol." He said, "But Tsipe is here, too. I've been living here with my family since after Pesach."[9]

I was overjoyed, yet I was fearful that she might, God forbid, weaken my resolve to study.

"Come home with me," he said. "Come so I can show you where we live because I must go off already to the *kheyder* to teach."

I went with him. He led me into his house, saying, "Tsipe, you see! You have a guest!" and off he went.

Tsipe grabbed me, kissing and crying, "How did you get here? Berele, what are you doing here? Have you been here long?" I replied to all of her questions and briefly described my plan to her: that I have been here for three days, that I am studying, am very happy that I'm beginning to recall my Torah studies, and am beginning to become a refined boy, so I will no longer be an ignoramus. She cried copiously over me and started with her usual arguments: "How will this help you earn a living? Who'll support you?" And she continued to ask similar questions. I replied, "Don't argue and don't cry. It will do you no good. I won't bother you. I know that you're poor. By now I am mature enough to understand your poverty. I am no longer that child who was totally oblivious to your plight."

So she said to me, "If you're really mature, then why don't you understand that it's too late to start studying now? You'll never really be able to learn properly! Go and be a servant. If you do not want to be with Shulem, then go to someone else and you'll grow up to be a merchant and be able to earn money!"

I said, "I've already heard your plans for me. I know what they are and have had a taste of them. I'm not looking for a means to earn a living. I only want to study and study some more, and if one wants to then it's never too late. I won't, God forbid, come to you for anything. I didn't even know you lived here. Had I known, I would've moved to another *shteytl* so that you couldn't interfere with my plan and you would be spared any and all pain."

I convinced her, and she conceded that it was definitely better to be a refined person and it would certainly be more honorable for her and the family. Nonetheless, she had a hard time believing that I would be able to accomplish my plan and she could not understand how I would achieve this without any

---

9 Pesach ended on April 11, 1863.

help. I told her that the Almighty God could help and would certainly provide the means as well. All one needed was faith and confidence. And with that, I began to leave.

She called me back. "Come in," she said, "and you'll have something to eat!" I said that I would not eat at her house, but would only come to her to spend the night on the ground because it was summer and one could sleep directly on it without any bedding. And so it was. I spent all day studying in the *bes-medresh*, ate two rolls a day, and went to Tsipe's to spend the night.

The depth of Tsipe's poverty is impossible to describe. Things were far worse for her in Kovishon than in Tiraspol. At least in Tiraspol she had her booth of sewing notions, from which she derived a bit of income. But there in Kovishon, she was entirely in his hands, dependent on his "great" earnings, on his... And his earnings were best wished on all the enemies of the Jewish people!

Her little girl, Ester-Khaykele, was by now a child of three and was smart and pretty as could be. There was, though, nothing to feed her with, and my heart went out to both mother and child. I would run to the *bes-medresh* to pour my tears out before God.

Tsipe would often excuse herself for not being able to offer me even a bite to eat and would cry with bitter tears that she could not help me. Her crying

FIGURE 5. Seated in the middle of the photograph are the author's niece Ester-Khaye (born 1854) and her husband Yankev Apatshevsky (called Yankev Kaushaner) ca. 1905 in Tiraspol. Ester-Khaye was the daughter of the author's sister Ite. Standing on the left is the couple's daughter Ite Vitenshteyn. Seated in front of her is probably their grandson Simkha Apatchevksy (1895–1965). Standing on the right is their daughter Feyge (1875–1922), her husband Israel Chaplick (1875–1971), and their daughter Reyzl (aka Rose Budiansky Carmel, 1899–1998). Courtesy of Christopher T. Blue.

would make me feel so much worse. I would make sure to come home late at night when she was already asleep so that she could not force me to eat something. I knew well that I could not accept anything from her because it belonged to the child—the impoverished child. If I had eaten anything, the child would have gone hungry.

I sat in the *bes-medresh* and studied. I had been there already for two weeks. During my third week, I heard that a new yeshiva had opened in Odessa where poor children studied and were fully supported, and that it was wonderful there.[10] I began to ask the young married men in the *bes-medresh* to raise some money for me to make the trip; if not, I would go on foot to Odessa because I heard that one could study well there and I knew that I would devour all that they would teach me.

Hearing such talk from me, the young men thought it over and raised sixty *kopeks* for my expenses. A few days later, one of the local Jewish men was leaving for Odessa in his own carriage, so they asked him to take me along and gave him fifty *kopeks* as a contribution for the oats needed for his horse during the trip. They gave me bread for the journey and ten *kopeks* as spending money. I ran off to Tsipe and bade farewell to my hapless, suffering sister and to her one and only child, and to all those in the *bes-medresh*. They wished me blessings and success and saw me off in good style. And off I went to Odessa.

Three days later, on Thursday afternoon, we arrived safely in Odessa, my last stop. The size of the city made a tremendous impression on me. I felt as though I was in a chaotic world: large houses and broad streets the likes of which I had never seen before in my life. People were running to and fro, and there was so much commotion that my head spun around until . . . I remembered my former dream in which my father led me to a place of study: I had seen high stone buildings in my dream similar to those in Odessa. If I would be accepted in the yeshiva and if it was located in the same type of attractive stone building, I would take that as a sign that my dream had come true.

---

10 The author is evidently referring to the *Talmud Torah* in Odessa, which was apparently founded in 1795, close to the establishment of the Jewish community there. In Eastern Europe, a *Talmud Torah* denoted a traditional Jewish elementary school, but it differed from the privately funded *kheyder* in that it consisted of several grades, was financed by the community, and often primarily served the children of the poor. The author was admitted in June or July of 1863. In 1857, it had been reorganized with the assistance of both the maskilic and more Orthodox elements as part of the Jewish educational reforms that were so novel in Odessa (Zipperstein, 1985:92). Similarly, a yeshiva was founded in Odessa in 1866 by the *maskilim* and Orthodox together, which was unique in Tsarist Russia (Polishchuk, 2002:39–40). Since much of the reform was in pedagogy rather than in subject matter, it makes sense that the *Talmud Torah* still taught traditional texts with traditional commentaries, as described by the author below.

I dashed about the streets of the city, searching for and asking about the yeshiva for poor boys that had recently opened. But all were darting about and going their own way and, in their haste, could not understand my question.

As I walked and searched for the yeshiva, I encountered someone and asked him in my own version of Russian: "Where's the yeshiva?"[11] He turned angrily to me and shouted, "Why are you speaking to me in Russian? I'm a Jew!" and he walked away.

How should I have known that someone without a beard could also be a Jew?[12]

With great difficulty, I managed to find the yeshiva. I climbed the stairs and saw boys milling about, talking among themselves, and spending time together. As soon as they saw me, they asked: "What are you doing here, little boy?" When I told them what I needed and why I had come, they all answered in unison, "Go to the *gabbai*, little boy.[13] And if he so desires, you'll study here. But if not, you won't be able to enter here." And while they were talking, they pointed toward the *gabbai's* house.

I was very hungry and told them that I had been running around all day and had not yet eaten anything. When they learned that I had not eaten all day, they embraced me, sat me down on a bench, and gave me bread and something to have with it. Upon finishing eating and resting up a bit, I went off to the *gabbai's* home.

As I approached the door, I became terrified. I slowly opened the first and second doors and found myself in a large room where the entire family was sitting around a circular table, having tea. When they saw me standing at the door, they asked, "What are you doing here, little boy?" I answered them, "Does the *gabbai* of the yeshiva live here? I need the *gabbai*." The *gabbai* himself spoke up

---

11 The author writes "*De tat yeshiva?*" The proper Russian would be "*Gde eta eshiva?*"
12 In Tsarist Russia at that time, the rare Jew who shaved or even trimmed his beard was considered to be committing a grave breach of Jewish society as a whole. In his autobiography, Melamed (1922:1:185) mentions the uproar in 1879 over his brother's having shaved off his beard—the first from his community to do so. (By the 1890s, most students of the Lithuanian yeshivas were removing their facial hair using a sulfuric compound to avoid the Biblical prohibition of shaving with a blade.) Today, in general, the only Jews who never shave or trim their beards are found among Hasidim. For a halakhic discussion of this subject matter, see Wiener (2006). It is worth noting that Odessa's Jewish community served as the maskilic center of Tsarist Russia and had a reputation for being irreligious, a matter to which Rabbi Meir Berlin (1932:2:320–329) dedicates an entire chapter in his memoirs. According to some accounts, already by the 1870s, ninety percent of Odessa's Jewish-owned shops were open on the Jewish Sabbath which is a severe violation of Jewish law (Zipperstein, 1985:131).
13 *Gabbai* is the singular of *gabbaim*. It denotes here the warden of the yeshiva.

and told me that he was the *gabbai* and asked why I needed to speak with him. I raised my voice pleadingly and told him that I was an orphan and wanted to study Torah. He asked me, "Do you know how to study Torah a little bit?" I answered him, "If I knew how, I wouldn't have had to come here." My answer pleased them all.

Since I was still standing at the door, they asked me to approach the table. As I came closer to them, they begin to examine me from every angle and spoke about me among themselves, saying that I was a handsome boy and smart but pitied me for wearing such poor clothing. I stood near the *gabbai* who questioned me. He wanted to know how I had come there, with whom, and, if I my parents were no longer alive, why had not a brother or a sister or some other family member brought me there?

I responded, imploring and sobbing. I told him that I did not have a brother, my sisters were terribly poor and did not have the means to travel to Odessa, and that if he would not accept me now into the yeshiva, I must throw myself into the sea.

He replied to me and to his family, who were pleading on my behalf, that one cannot simply admit someone on a whim, "Perhaps he's a thief or a crook?!"

These words seized my heart and I broke out crying in a voice not my own, "No, I'm neither a thief nor a crook, heaven forbid. I don't, God forbid, come from parents who might have had that type of offspring. I am an upright boy and want to study. I won't leave here, even if it means my death, until you admit me to the yeshiva. I don't have anywhere to spend the night, nor do I have a *kopek* to my name with which to buy a bit of bread. Don't you see how lost I am and how poor and alone I am? Don't you see that I'm orphaned?!"

My last words apparently touched their hearts, and I saw them wiping their eyes. Their faces showed both feelings of pain and sympathy. Finally, the *gabbai* addressed me and said that I should go to sleep in the yeshiva for the time being, and that tomorrow they would consider what was to be done. These few good words had almost a calming effect on me. With a glimmer of hope for the morrow, I wished them good night and went off to the yeshiva to sleep.

The next morning, the *gabbai* entered and asked me if I knew someone from Tiraspol named Nayman. I told him that I had never heard of a family by that name. "Well," he said to me, "if that's the case, then go and find me someone in Odessa who will be testify on your behalf. That's all I can do." My glimmer of hope disappeared, and I stood there as though my soul, too, had disappeared. What should I do?

Someone then spoke up and said that Shmiel Zeylinger was also from Tiraspol. Hearing that name, I said that I knew a family by that name there. "In that case," the *gabbai* said, "go and bring me a note from him testifying on your behalf. You don't need anything better than that, and you'll be admitted at once."

So, like the day before, I ran about the streets of Odessa, this time seeking the home of Reb Shmiel Zeylinger. After a long time of dashing about, to the point of exhaustion, I finally found his house and tried to enter. I was stopped at the door by a doorman who barred my way. When I tried getting by him, he said in Russian, "Get outta here!" and calmly took me by the hand and threw me out onto the street.

In my pain, I sat down at the gate and began to cry silently. Someone came out of the house and asked me, "Why are you sitting here, little boy?" I replied that I needed to see Reb Shmiel Zeylinger, and that I had to see him in person. He laughed loudly at my request and told me to leave here at once or else he would call the caretaker to deal with me. I became very frightened and began screaming so loudly that everyone in the house came running. Among them, too, was Reb Shmiel who asked me what I was screaming about and what I wanted here. I told him that I was from Tiraspol and needed to see him so that he could put in a good word for me in order that I would be accepted into the yeshiva. He told me to go into the house where he sat down and wrote a note to the *gabbai*. On my request that he go there in person, he replied that I would be admitted this way too and put the note into my hand. This was one of his visiting cards, though, at the time, I still did not know what it was called, so I called it a "note."

I ran back to the yeshiva and put it in the *gabbai*'s hands.

CHAPTER 13

In Odessa, Tiraspol, and Romanovke, 1863–1864

I was Admitted • An Important Student • *Zmires* for *Shobes* • A Cantor's Assistant • Praised to the High Heavens • Luckless • Dark Clouds • A Momentary Glimmer • Ending Up at New Places • A New Disaster • Out of the Yeshiva • In the *Bes-Medresh* • A Torah Reader • Half a Cantor • Back to Tiraspol • Darkness and Bitterness • In Romanovke • Surele • A Pretty Girl • Sisters and Brother Not Recognizing Each Other • Unfortunate Souls • Serving as a Rabbi's *Gabbai* • Saved • Wanted as a Son-In-Law • At The Cemetery • The Entire Family • A Desirable Meeting • "Everything That God Does Is for the Good"[1] • Shulem was Agitated

The *gabbai* could not but keep wondering how such a small, poor boy could obtain a visiting card from such an extremely wealthy man. He led me right into the yeshiva, where he met the other *gabbai*. He showed him the note, and the other *gabbai* was also impressed with it and he took a good look at me. They spoke among themselves and finally said to me, "You're ours now. You're remaining with us. You have a good guarantor for yourself." They led me to the table where the beginners studied and sat me down. "This is your table. Here you'll study, and we'll note your name in the enrollment book today." I studied at that table for only one day because they moved me the following day to a seat at a table where they studied at a higher level.[2]

---

1 Talmud (Brakhot 60b).
2 Rolnick (1954:70) recollects the separate tables designated for students of different capabilities in the yeshiva in Mir, Belarus when he studied there ca. 1894.

Thank God, I was in the yeshiva and studying diligently, and all was well with me. I had enough to eat and drink, and everyone liked me for my diligence and good conduct. Regarding the *gabbai* at whose door I had stood and pleaded for admittance, he now considered me to be quite important and dear, and I ate at his home every *Shobes*. Since he sang well, he really enjoyed singing, and he loved to hear me sing at the table on Friday night and *Shobes* day. At the conclusion of *Shobes* on Saturday night, he would keep me late and we would sing all the *zmires* and all sorts of cantorial pieces! The entire yeshiva was jealous of my high standing with the *gabbai*.

The *gabbai* was very learned and God-fearing. He was an outstanding person and an extraordinary individual. Though renowned in Odessa, he would have been considered outstanding even in Berditshev or Vilna.[3] He was the type of Jew considered to be "a distinguished individual among a distinguished people."[4] His name was Reb Shloyme-Itsye-Gershns, and who in those days did not know the name of Reb Shloyme-Itsye-Gershns?[5] His family, too, was pious and good-hearted, and they used to go out of their way to befriend me. Though there were many poor children in the yeshiva, I was cared for differently. I had clothes and food. And from day to day I improved in my studies. By the High Holy Days,[6] after studying over the course of the three summer months of *Tamuz, Av,* and *Elul*,[7] I was proficient in some forty complete folios of Talmud, including Rashi's commentary and select *Toysfes*, which we studied with the commentary of the *Maharsho*.[8]

Early in *Elul*,[9] the cantor of the *Shalashne Shul* came to the yeshiva.[10] He was seeking boys with good voices whom he could take on as assistants to

---

3 Berditshev and Vilna were prominent and established Jewish communities.
4 See Leviticus 19:5.
5 This nickname indicates either that his name was Shloyme and that he was the son, son-in-law, or close relative of someone named Itsye-Gershn or Itsye-Gershns (meaning Itsye, a close relative of Gershn), or that his name was Shloyme-Itsye, and that he was a close relative of someone named Gershn.
6 Rosh Hashanah began the night of September 13, 1863.
7 Mid-June until mid-September 1863.
8 *Toysfes* (*Tosafot* in Modern Hebrew), literally meaning "additions," are the commentaries (novella) by the medieval school of Talmudic scholars that are printed in all standard editions of the Talmud. *Maharsho* is an acronym for "Our Teacher, the Rabbi Shmuel Eideles" (1555–1631) who wrote a classic commentary on the Talmud.
9 August 1863.
10 *Shalashne shul* was the nickname of one of the synagogues in Odessa and denotes a tent-like synagogue. This nickname was perhaps a reference to an initial primitive structure, which was later replaced by something more permanent.

train them how to sing with the cantor.¹¹ The *gabbai*, Reb Shloyme, promptly pointed to me, and I was immediately taken along with another boy, but the other was quickly sent back and I was kept. I would go to the cantor every evening after my yeshiva studies. He praised me for learning quickly and said that I could become very adept if I performed with him for a couple of years. I actually made a hit in the *shul* with my fine alto voice and my emotional rendition. The *gabbaim* of the yeshiva took great delight in me.¹² Reb Shloyme-Itsye-Gershns and Reb Shie Tirbutin were interested in hearing me repeat the cantor's renditions of various prayers,¹³ such as the *Kedushah* and the *Mishebeyrakh*.¹⁴ And on *Shobes*, they would simply work me to death by having me sing the cantor's entire repertoire.

The cantor of the *Shalashne Shul* was also a pious Jew, not one of those cantors of the choral synagogues.¹⁵ Though his voice was well known and he was endowed with much musical knowledge, he led the services in a strictly traditional style.¹⁶ He followed in the path of his teacher, Reb Betsalel.¹⁷ Whoever had heard Cantor Betsalel in Odessa confirmed that my cantor prayed exactly like him. My cantor's name was Reb Berl-Dvoses.¹⁸

---

11 These musical assistants are called *meshoyrerim* (*meshorerim* in Modern Hebrew) in the original.
12 *Gabbaim* here refers to the administrators of the yeshiva.
13 Tirbutin may be a typographical error; the name may actually have been Triputin. See Beider (2008:1:896).
14 *Kedushah* (literally "holiness") is a passage in the public prayer service, with portions recited responsively by the cantor and the congregation.
15 Referring to the irreligious cantors who sang in choral synagogues (*khor shul* in Yiddish). Though still Orthodox, a choral synagogue differed from a traditional Orthodox synagogue in several important aspects: the cantor's piousness was of little or no regard; the cantor in such synagogues usually wore special vestments; the synagogue was large, architecturally beautiful, with good acoustics, and often designed with a special place for a male choir to stand; and often there was an organ, though it was not used on the Sabbath or Jewish holidays. Usually, the wealthy, more progressive element among the Jewish population attended such synagogues, and they could generally only be found in larger cities. Tsarist Russia never had any non-Orthodox synagogues as found in Germany or in the Hungarian-speaking regions of Europe. See Levin (2020).
16 Meaning that he led the prayers without the cantorial embellishments used by modern cantors.
17 Betsalel Shulzinger (ca. 1779–1873), called Tsalel Adeser (that is, of Odessa), was a renowned cantor whose compositions achieved wide appeal. His compositions were noted down by members of his cantorial assistants, many of whom later became well-known cantors. He left for Jerusalem in 1860 (Minkovsky, 1925:4:138–140).
18 Berl-Dvoses indicates that Berl was the husband, son, son-in-law, or close relative of a woman named Dvose.

After *Yontef*,[19] Reb Berl-Dvoses gave me ten rubles, meaning that he gave the money on my behalf to the *gabbaim* who provided me with new winter clothes. The new attire completely changed my appearance and lifted my spirits so that I began to really live and be happy. I thought that from now on things would be well with me, but given my bad luck could things really have gone well? Things would go well for me for only an instant. Soon, life would cloud over, and darkness was everywhere. I would then begin to meander once more and turn up in various places with brand-new troubles.

I did not study too long at the yeshiva. In midwinter, they began, on the government's order, to search out people without documents, which compelled me to leave the yeshiva and hide out in the *bes-medresh* called *Pas le'Orkhim*.[20] I lived off the few *kopeks* that the *shomes* would collect for me during prayers.[21]

Was that, then, a way to live one's life?

With Purim approaching, I learned the cantillation of the *Megilla*, and I read it in a couple of rich homes, earning two silver rubles.[22] On the following *Shobes, Parshes Pore*,[23] I led the prayers, for which the *gabbai* gave me a ruble. I led prayers again in a *shul* and began to earn money little by little and to live on what I myself had earned. Not long afterward, the police raided all the synagogues and caught some Jews who lacked permits, and I was miraculously saved by hiding under the stairs.[24] I then fled to Tiraspol. But for that matter, things were even worse in Tiraspol, so I traveled to my Uncle Idl in Groseles. I led the services there on Pesach and earned three rubles.[25] But Groseles did

---

19 Referring to *Sukes*, September 28–October 6, 1863.
20 *Pas le'Orkhim* literally means "Bread for Guests" in Hebrew. See footnote 24 below regarding internal passports.
21 *Shames* (the sexton of a synagogue) is pronounced as *shomes* in the author's sub-dialect of Southeastern Yiddish (see the Introduction to the Glossaries).
22 Purim occurred on March 22, 1864. *Megilla* literally means a "scroll" and refers to the Biblical Book of Esther handwritten on a scroll of parchment. The *Megilla* is read twice, once at night and once during the day, on the holiday of Purim.
23 *Parshes Pore* (*Parashat Para* in Modern Hebrew) corresponds to Numbers 19:1–22 and is the third of four additional Torah readings connected with the Hebrew months of *Adar* and *Nisan* (*Kitsur Shulkhan Arukh* 140:2–3). That *Shabes* occurred on March 26, 1864.
24 These Jews were either lacking internal passports, which would have allowed them to leave their permanent place of residence for a few months, or they had never registered with the Jewish community of Odessa. Internal passports were expensive, and Jewish communities would often only accept those who could afford to pay the poll-tax or who volunteered their sons for the conscription quota (Freeze, 1999:8). From the author's comments below regarding Romanovke, the danger in both Odessa and Tiraspol was from non-Jewish informants denouncing Jews who did not have proper documents. Such informants were monetarily rewarded by the authorities (Matthews, 1993:8). Being unregistered, the author would have been unable to obtain an internal passport.
25 Pesach occurred from April 21 to April 28, 1864.

not work out well either, and my uncle did not want to do anything for me. So right after Pesach, I traveled back to Tiraspol.

But in Tiraspol, it was the same story all over again—there was nowhere for me to stay. My sister Ite was a divorcée and lived in poverty with her son Itsele. She was still dependent upon Reb Zolmen-Kopls for his generosity, so I could only visit with Ite for an hour to share our sorrows. None of our other relatives was able to help. So I mounted a carriage and traveled to Kishinev and from there I traveled to Romanovke where my sister Surele lived with our late brother's father-in-law, Reb Ersh the *shoykhet*.[26] We understandably did not recognize each other after having been apart for so many years. The family welcomed me very warmly, and I remained there for quite a while, studying without fear at the *bes-medresh*. (Romanovke was a Jewish *shteytl*; no non-Jews could be found there.)[27]

During the years that we had been apart, they had married Surele off to a pious man from a good family, Leyb the *melomed*, the son of *Itsl-der-Bube-Ites*.[28] Leyb seemed to be a nice young man, a Hasid, and it seemed that she would have a good life with him. But, in truth, he was a simple young man, no more than a teacher's aide.[29] Being married to him, Surele, poor thing, had to struggle, live with her in-laws on *kest*, and her youth was buried forever.

Unfortunate souls, why did you have to be born?

---

26 Romanovke (Romanovka in Russian) was in the Tsarist Russian province of Bessarabia and is now called Basarabeasca, Moldova. It is not to be confused with Romanovka, Ukraine, formerly in the province of Kherson, where Rabbi Avróm-Dovid Lavut (ca. 1815-1890) served as rabbi and where a substantial community of Lubavitcher Hasidim resided. Rabbi Lavut, the author of several important halakhic works, was a maternal ancestor of the Lubavitcher Rebbe, Rabbi Menachem Mendel Schneerson (1902–1994). Though both Romanovkas began as Jewish agricultural colonies, they are some 200 miles apart.

27 As the author mentions above, residing in Odessa and Tiraspol had been difficult for him since he did not possess the proper documents. From his statement here, his fear was denouncements by non-Jews to the authorities, who monetarily rewarded such informants (Matthews, 1993:8).

28 In the original, Leyb Vaynberg's father is mistakenly referred to here as Idl instead of Itsl, though it is noted correctly in chapter 3, p. 108. See more details about his family there.

29 *Bahilfer* in the original, more commonly called a *belfer*. See chapter 4, pp. 131–132, for a description.

Ersh's son Shoyl was also a *shoykhet*.[30] He was very learned and was a Lubavitcher Hasid.[31] In the *shteytl* Romanovke were several people, Hasidim, who would travel to see the Rebbe, Reb Mendele of Lubavitch.[32] The leader of the group was the local rabbi, Reb Moyshe-Yosef,[33] of blessed memory, who had the opportunity to see the *Alter* Rebbe—the Hasidic Rebbe Rabbi Shneur Zalman of Lyadi.[34] There at the rabbi's, all of his devotees would gather for *Shaleshides*, and Ersh's son Shoyl took me there as well.[35] The rabbi befriended me and he took me along as his *gabbai* along with his ardent admirer Shoyl when he traveled into the surrounding towns and villages to earn money.[36]

---

30 The 1854 and 1859 additional revision lists (poll-tax censuses) of the Jews of Romanovke (aka Romanenko) indicate that Ersh's surname was Itskovitsh. It was identified by means of his son, Shoyl; the only Shoyl, son of an Ersh (Gersh in Russian), listed in the 1854 census of Romanovke, is a "Shoel Itskovitsh" (born ca. 1842), son of a Hersh Itschok (born ca. 1803). (The 1859 census refers to Shoyl as Shaya; perhaps he had two names.) The details on these censuses concerning Ersh Itskovitsh's daughter Mirye correspond with the known details about the unnamed widow and daughter, Freyde (born 1857), of the author's brother, Isruel (1837–1857): Mirye "Mirke" (born ca. 1840) is shown in April 1854 as being married (the name of the son-in-law is not mentioned in these censuses) but she is not mentioned as being married in 1859. Mirye's daughter, Freyde (born ca. 1856), is listed as being another daughter of her father Hersh. These censuses are housed at the Moldova State Archives in Chișinău (134/2/330, p. 73, registration no. 88, and 134/2/501, p. 30, registration no. 86). Transcriptions of these records were obtained from the JewishGen Romania-Moldova Database.
31 A Lubavitcher Hasid is a follower of the Rebbes of Lubavitch and their Chabad philosophy. The Chabad branch of the Hasidic movement, today synonymous with Lubavitch, was founded in the late eighteenth century by Rabbi Shneur Zalman (1745–1812) of Lyadi, the author of the *Tanya*, a seminal Hasidic work. He was a disciple of Rabbi Dov-Ber, the *Magid* (preacher) of Mezritsh, the heir to the Baal Shem Tov, the founder of Hasidism. Chabad is a Hebrew acronym for *Chochmah, Binah, Da'at*, meaning "Wisdom, Understanding, and Knowledge." It is known as the intellectual branch of Hasidism.
32 The author discusses the Lubavitcher Rebbe, Rabbi Menakhem-Mendl Schneerson (1789–1866), at greater length in chapter 16, pp. 247–251.
33 Reb Moyshe-Yosef did not necessarily travel all the way to Lyadi to see the *Alter Rebbe*, since he visited Mogilev-Podolsk, which was relatively close by, in the winter of 1809–1810 (Valershtein, 2015). In 2015, Yefim Kogan, the Bessarabian coordinator for JewishGen, arranged for the surviving tombstones in the Jewish cemetery in Romanovke (now Basarabka) to be photographed. Parts of the cemetery were destroyed by the Nazis during the Second World War. Reb Moyshe-Yosef's tombstone was not located.
34 Chabad Hasidim (also known as Chabadniks) refer to Rabbi Shneur Zalman (1745–1812) of Lyadi (Lyady, Belarus) as the *Alter Rebbe*, meaning "Old Rebbe" in Yiddish, since he was the first Rebbe of Chabad.
35 *Shaleshides* is the third and last meal of *Shabes* eaten before dusk on Saturday.
36 Reb Moyshe-Yosef was evidently the rabbi of Romanovke and the surrounding area. Such rabbis would often periodically travel to all the towns and villages under their jurisdiction and attend to communal and individual affairs, some of which required payment for their services.

The trip lasted a long time because we did not bypass a single *shteytl* or village. I created many problems along the way because I did not have any documents and we were miraculously rescued more than once.[37] And so we arrived safely at Mayak.

In Mayak, I remained with the *shoykhet*, Reb Leyzer, while the others continued on to Odessa and then to Kherson by boat, to meet with Reb Hilke, of blessed memory. It turned out that when they arrived in Odessa, Reb Hilke had died, so they sailed to Kherson for his funeral.[38] (I only learned of this later through people's reports.) And I stayed there and waited for them to return and pick me up, but I could not wait that long.

The *shoykhet* allowed me to stay with him, and I studied the entire time I was there. With the arrival of *Rosh-Khoydesh Elul*,[39] I returned to Tiraspol to try to find a position in a *shul* that would have me as a cantor for the High Holy Days.

I had noticed that Reb Leyzer's daughter Sheyndele had her eye on me and wanted me to marry her. And it seemed that the *shoykhet* himself wanted me as a son-in-law, but since I was not ready for that, I told him that I had to leave for Tiraspol to visit my parents' graves.[40] And I left.

I arrived in Tiraspol right on the day before *Rosh-Khoydesh Elul* and went off at once to the cemetery to cry my heart out at the graves of my parents, my brother Isruel, and my sister Khone.[41] I pleaded with my departed relatives to exert themselves to intercede for me and for my poor sisters who were suffering so pitifully and never had any rest. Suddenly, I saw my sisters Ite and Tsipe approaching. Tsipe had come from Bender (she was then already living in Bender). Since she had left her little daughter, Khayele, with a neighbor, she needed to return quickly. Ite and Tsipe came to the cemetery with my Aunt Ester, Shulem's mother, and his wife Khaye. Khaye had come to visit her parents' grave. We all left the cemetery and returned home together. They could

---

37 Subjects of Tsarist Russia needed an internal passport to travel beyond a radius of thirty *versts* (increased to fifty in 1894) from their permanent place of residence (Avrutin, 2010:91).
38 Rabbi Hillel Malisov (1794/5–1864) is commonly referred to as Hillel Paritsher; his first rabbinical position was in Paritsh (Parichi, Belarus) and afterward he became the rabbi of nearby Babruysk. He was one of the most outstanding and learned Lubavitcher Hasidim and was the author of a number of works on Hasidic thought. He died while staying in Kherson on *Shabes*, the 11th of *Av* 5624 (August 13, 1864), after having arrived there Friday morning from Nikolayev (Shmuel, 1994:57–83).
39 September 1–2, 1864.
40 It is customary for Jews to pray at their parents' graves during *Elul*, the month preceding Rosh Hashanah. See *Kitsur Shulkhan Arukh* (128:13).
41 This is the first time that the author has mentioned being in Tiraspol since learning of his sister Khone's death in the winter of 1860–1861 (ch. 10, p. 185).

not stop wondering at how I had grown and matured. Khaye told me that her daughter Beyle regretted persecuting me and asked me to forgive her. I told her that I had forgiven her long ago because everything had been for the best. We took our leave, and I went home with Ite.

Ite, the religious and long-suffering Ite, still lived in her apartment at Reb Zolmen-Kopls's and he helped her as much as he could while our relatives took no interest in her at all. I realized that there was no sense in expecting any help from our relatives in finding lodging, so I hired myself out to a cantor as one of his assistants for the High Holy Days. My payment was room and board, and some cash.

At that time I became acquainted with a Lubavitcher Hasid, a pious Jew, a scribe of Torah scrolls and *mezuzahs*, by the name of Olter, and we became very good friends.

I quickly left the cantor because his group of cantorial assistants did not please me, and I spent most of my time studying with Olter. I would often go to Reb Zolmen-Sukher-Kopls to see Ite and her little Itsele. If I arrived before a meal or during a meal, they would ask me to eat with them, which made me very uncomfortable.

I saw that strangers were apparently more concerned about our wellbeing than our own relatives.

It was almost the eve of Rosh Hashanah,[42] and people were coming from the surrounding villages, from Buter and from Tashlik for the High Holidays. Shulem and his family were among them. When Shulem spotted me, he was overjoyed; he kissed me and tears of joy welled up in his eyes. I told him that God had arranged it so that my unfortunate experience with him had driven me to a source of blessings. He was so excited that he did not know what to do first. He took me home with him to the inn where he was staying. There I saw Beyle, who was embarrassed to see me and surprised at how time can change a person. We all sat down and had a very friendly chat.

I said goodbye and started to leave, but they begged me to eat with them on Rosh Hashanah and they were quite persistent. Against my will, I agreed to eat with them, but only the mid-day meal—not at night under any circumstances.[43]

So I ate at Shulem's on Rosh Hashanah, and I noticed that he had mixed feelings toward me.[44] He was happy that I had turned out well but was pained

---

42 September 30, 1864.
43 The author evidently did not want to eat there because of Shulem's and Beyle's poor treatment of him in Tashlik.
44 The author uses the Hebrew word *va-yikhad* (Exodus 18:9), translated here as "mixed feelings," since Rashi's classic biblical commentary provides two contradictory interpretations

that he had not followed his neighbor Moyshe-Ersh's advice to take me as a son-in-law. It was too late now. Nonetheless, he did not rest and, without my knowledge, conspired to work out a match for me. His intention, of course, was to rescue me from my impoverished condition. He felt he owed it to me. So he worked on it and finally arranged it in a most ingenious way, and I did not have the slightest inkling that anything was going on.

---

of Jethro's reaction to Moses's news of Egypt's destruction. Rashi's first interpretation is the literal definition, "rejoiced," while his second is a midrashic interpretation, "felt sharp stinging sensations" because of his grief. Learned Yiddish-speaking Jews frequently include words and verses from the Torah as the author does here in this original description of his relative Shulem's ambivalence toward him.

Part II

ENGAGEMENT, MARRIAGE, AND SEEKING A LIVELIHOOD, 1864-1873

CHAPTER 14

My Unexpected Engagement, 1864–1865

That Yom Kippur, I spent all day in the *bes-medresh* in Tiraspol.[1] I stood there praying, sobbing, and asking God to take pity on me, for He is my father. I did not leave the *bes-medresh* for a moment the entire day, unlike the manner of some boys who would walk out of the *bes-medresh* during the Torah reading or during the breaks between prayers. I fasted, prayed, and studied the entire day. I studied the Mishnaic tractate of Yoma,[2] the rich pieces of poetic liturgy, and similar passages. At the close of Yom Kippur, after I had eaten a dry meager meal, I lay down to sleep because I was very tired from fasting and from exerting myself all day in prayer. As you can imagine, my pre-fast meal had also been quite meager. In short, I was so exhausted by the fast that I was satisfied with the meal that I ate and crawled onto the oven, my usual bed at Reb Olter's, and lay down to sleep. His wife and his aged mother were still sitting and chatting. I fell into such a deep hearty sleep that I did not begin to realize that I was being visited by distinguished guests. They were laughing at me for having gone to bed so early without being aware of the wonderful good fortune that awaited me. I was sleeping so soundly that when my sister Ite tried to wake me I did not hear her. It was not until they began poking me sharply that I realized something was going on and opened my eyes. I was about to turn over on my other side when I noticed my sister Ite and other people laughing, "Well, well. What a deep sleep!" said someone. "Apparently he's not aware of anything. He can't even imagine what's about to happen to him," said another.

I tore myself from sleep, particularly when my sister pestered me by saying, "Get up, sleepyhead. Aren't you ashamed? We're all waiting for you!"

---
1 October 10, 1864.
2 The Talmudic tractate Yoma discusses the laws of Yom Kippur.

"What is it," I asked, "and who is the 'all,' and what are you waiting for? And who is waiting for me?"

"Get up quickly," she repeated. "Get dressed and come down from the oven."

I awoke and began to dress, though all of this seemed to be a dream, and I did not understand what was happening. Coming down from the oven, I saw Reb Shimen, Zolmen-Sukher-Kopls's son-in-law, an upstanding, well-to-do young married man; our relative Shulem; and my sister Ite. Dressed up and with cheerful demeanors, they were all in Reb Olter's home and were laughing at my sleepy appearance. My good friend, Reb Olter, and his wife were also dressed up. So I asked them, "Well, won't you tell me already what's the meaning of all this, your coming here and your cheerfulness?" They said, "Wash up, put on your clothes, and go with your sister to Reb Zolmen's. From there you'll go with Reb Zolmen to the rabbi's because a large crowd is waiting for you there. We'll now go directly to the rabbi's to await your arrival. See that you don't delay, because the night is running out."

I went with my sister and Reb Shimen, Zolmen's son-in-law, to Reb Zolmen's, but still did not know why. I asked but was not told. "Why bother asking? When you get to the rabbi's, you'll know." I arrived at Reb Zolmen's and found his whole household there dressed-up and ready to go to the rabbi, Reb Shloyme. As soon as I came in, they all asked in unison, "Where did you find him?" And the group who escorted me related how they found me sleeping on the oven and how difficult it was to wake me. All laughed at the incident, but I still did not understand what was happening to me. Ite ordered me to put on the clothes that Reb Zolmen's young son-in-law Shimen handed me: one of his silk *kapotes*, a nice beaver hat, a silk vest, and a good pair of attractive shoes. After I dressed, I caught wind of what was going on. My sister Ite shouted, "See what a handsome groom he makes."[3] With those words, I understood that a match was in the works. So I said, "Since you're taking me to see a prospective match, you might at least tell me who she is." They replied, "Would it be so terrible if you found out later? Go, go, there's no problem. You can rely on us. We won't mislead you." "There's no time to waste," said Reb Zolmen, "we must go now." "Yes," said Shimen, looking at the clock, "it is already eleven. It took an hour for us to find him. Come on, then, come. It's already late."

We went off and everyone was whispering and speaking in low tones so that I could not hear. They avoided speaking to me, as though this had nothing to do with me. All this disturbed me, but there was nothing I could do. I could

---

3 In Yiddish, one becomes a groom upon becoming engaged.

not contradict Reb Zolmen and his wife or their son-in-law Reb Shimen. As for Ite, I was simply scared that she might strike me.

In short, I went with them until I entered the rabbi's house. At the rabbi's, I found a crowd of about sixty to seventy men, not including the women. All were already under the influence. When they saw me, a sudden shout went up, "He's here at last, the handsome groom. Look how he waited to be asked to come while such a large crowd, *kenehore*, was awaiting him." Some defended me while others blamed me, "Out of respect for the local rabbi, he shouldn't have delayed so long and waited for others to ask him to come." They grasped me and placed me next to the rabbi, Reb Shloymele. I began to look over the crowd, which included the very finest young married men in town and all my relatives and familiar tenant innkeepers from Tashlik and Buter, including the familiar tenant innkeeper, Reb Itsye, and his wife, Dvoyre. Reb Itsye was seated next to me and the rabbi, and Reb Shulem Tashliker was seated next to Reb Itsye and the rabbi, meaning between them. I looked and saw that the cantor Kolmen-Volf was also here with his cantorial assistants. The crowd was well imbibed, and the table was laden with wine. I knew that after Yom Kippur people drank at the rabbi's, but I never expected that they were about to write an engagement contract with me.[4]

"Hand over ink and a pen," said the cantor. I wondered why he needed ink and a pen all of a sudden, but I soon knew all. Reb Shulem, who had been speaking the entire time with Reb Itsye, while his wife Dvoyre stood nearby, suddenly addressed me, "You know, Pinkhes-Dov, you're now becoming engaged, and we're about to write the engagement contract." "How's that possible?!" I said. "What does it mean that I'm becoming engaged?! How can you write an engagement contract when I don't have the slightest idea with whom? Who's my father-in-law?"[5] Shulem said, "Yes, you're right about that. You need to know everything. So you should know that all of your friends are in agreement that you should become engaged to Reb Itsye's daughter. You know Reb Itsye and his wife well, and you know his daughter too. And if it's agreeable with all of us, it must be agreeable with you as well." The entire crowd became quiet and listened as Shulem spoke with me. Everyone gave their consent, and the rabbi also thought that it was a very good match. Everyone knew Reb Itsye to be an honest and virtuous Jew, particularly since he was ready to make the sacrifice to obtain a Torah scholar such as myself as a son-in-law, despite my poverty. Reb

---

4   After breaking the Yom Kippur fast, Jews customarily celebrate God's favorable judgment by drinking (*Kitsur Shulkhan Arukh* 133:29).

5   Until his actual marriage, the author refers to his prospective in-laws simply as his in-laws, as was customary in Yiddish.

Itsye simply wanted to make me happy, so he was willing to spend whatever was necessary to marry his daughter into a prestigious family and with a Torah scholar.[6]

They then began to list all the commitments undertaken by the father, namely a dowry of 300 rubles in cash, which was not to be given directly into my hands but to be deposited with a trustworthy person, and lifelong *kest*, which was possible because he did not have any other daughters, only a little boy. He must also clothe me from now on, especially for the wedding, with clothes for the Jewish holidays, for *Shobes*, and for weekday wear.[7] Since I had nowhere to live, he would pay for my room and board until the wedding, which must be delayed for at least two years because his daughter was still too young, having just turned thirteen.[8] And he undertook one more thing more important than all the other commitments: he must register me as his son. Since he was a former "Nikolayevian soldier," this would be my best protection from falling into the clutches of the antisemitic Russian military.[9] And the cantor was instructed to write all of this into the engagement contract.

I was torn and could not decide what to do. I never expected such a sudden development. All my relatives thought it was a fitting match, but what did they have to lose? This was such a sudden development for me. I pictured before me Reb Itsye's coarse house, the silly village girl, the shameful nickname "Soldier," which Reb Itsye was called, and many other issues. If I were to get up and leave, would they let me? Could I possibly contradict all the others, especially since they were all on my side and meant well for me. Shulem and the rabbi saw that I was very upset, so they persuaded me that this was truly a lucky break for me because who else would want to make a match with such a poor orphan who was not registered and therefore could not be allowed in one's home even just

---

6   Itsye Hershkovits was a *kohen*, which means that he was a patrilineal descendant of the sons of the Biblical Aaron, brother of Moses, who served as priests in the Temple in Jerusalem. The author's son Shloyme indicated this on a Page of Testimony on file at Yad Vashem, which he filled out on May 25, 1955 for his first cousin Itskhok (son of Mordkhe) Gershkovits (1888–ca. 1941), who perished in the Holocaust. Though many simple pious Jews desire to have a Torah scholar as a son-in-law, it is specifically mentioned in the Talmud (Pesakhim 49a) that a *kohen* should marry his daughter to a Torah scholar.

7   A Jew should have separate clothing for the Jewish holidays, apart from one's *Shabes* clothes (*Kitsur Shulkhan Arukh* 103:5).

8   Hence, Freyde was born around September 1851. The author was just shy of his sixteenth birthday. Dubnow (1918, 2:40,112) notes that though legislation was passed in 1835 in Tsarist Russia forbidding Jewish males from marrying younger than eighteen and females younger than sixteen under the pain of imprisonment, it was easy to evade this prohibition due to "the defective registration of births and marriages then in vogue."

9   Being a former soldier, Reb Itsye's sons were evidently exempt from military conscription.

to spend the night.¹⁰ The rabbi tried to convince me by telling me that Reb Itsye spent the Jewish holidays with him every year, that he already knew him for many years, and that he was truly a pious Jew who was meticulous in his observance of the Torah's commandments. The rabbi continued that Reb Itsye's having been a soldier made him even greater and more important.¹¹ And he had become even more honorable in the rabbi's eyes now that he was willing to give such a large dowry so as to obtain a Torah scholar for his daughter.

While the cantor kept on writing and the crowd kept on drinking, I kept thinking over what I should do. I finally decided to agree but dependent on the stipulation that Reb Itsye would register me as his son.¹² That commitment was more important to me than anything else, so everything was void if he would not do that. And that he should begin working on this right after signing the engagement contract. Everyone shouted, "Good! Good! The groom is right! That provision should be written in the most precise legal terms in the engagement contract stipulating that the registration must be completed within three months, without any excuses."¹³ In the end, the engagement contract was read, and I became, in a propitious hour, an unexpected fiancé.¹⁴

I did not see my fiancée then but she apparently wanted to see me, so she stood on the threshold of the door directly opposite me. When she stood up

---

10 Anyone harboring unregistered or unauthorized residents could be fined, and the authorities would monetarily reward informants who denounced such individuals (Matthews, 1993:7–8, Kofman, 1955:41 53). See ch. 13, p. 209, specifically footnote 27, regarding the author's fear of non-Jewish informants. Meir (2010:103–104) writes that the city of Kiev was unique in having nighttime roundups of Jews, but this because they lacked the requisite residency papers—not internal passports. Though the Jews had been forced out of Kiev in 1827, certain categories of Jews were allowed to live there beginning in 1855; many Jews would illegally lodge there on short business trips.
11 Since many such former soldiers were forcibly separated from many aspects of Torah observance for so many years, one who was very observant upon his return was to be particularly admired.
12 Reb Itsye's registering the author as his son would have provided the author with a second-level exemption from military service, which was for an only wage-earning son (though other sons were in the family) who assisted his father in supporting his family. (See the footnote regarding the three types of exemptions in chapter 24.)
13 Though translated as "in the most precise legal terms," the word used in the original is כפלן (*keyfln*). This word literally means "doubling" and refers to the need for conditions to be repeated in a contract in both their negative and positive forms, that is, if this condition will be fulfilled, the agreement is valid, and if the condition is not fulfilled, the agreement is not valid. See *Shulkhan Arukh* (*Even ha-Ezer* 38).
14 Itsye's full name was Shulem-Itsye (ch. 11, p. 191). His surname was Hershkovitsh (Gershkovits in Russian), as related by the author's granddaughter, Aliza (Goldenshteyn) Bernfeld in 2001 and as noted in the entry for the author's son Raphael Goldenstein in *Who's Who in American Jewry, 1926* (1927:207).

on her toes and raised her head to be able to see me over the heads of all the people, I saw her face and her blue eyes.[15] I recognized her as the Freydele who had begged me to play with her and her little brother and had not wanted me to go away for *Shobes*.

The crowd grew very lively. Dvoyre did not spare the liquor. She knew what needed to be done. The engagement contract had cost her a lot of money, but who considers money when one has the opportunity to fall in with such a prestigious family. Normally, they would never even have met them, and now they were actually in-laws![16] She had satisfied the rabbi and the cantor with a fine tip. The crowd was satisfied, too. At dawn, everyone left satisfied, but not I.

Though the engagement contract had been written, I was not excited about anything. I had not contemplated becoming engaged that quickly. Had I known earlier what was in the works, I would have left Tiraspol earlier. But apparently Shulem had understood well how I thought; therefore, he had worked it out in strict secrecy, so that I would not know of anything until all was prepared. He had deliberately gathered such a large crowd so that I could not wiggle out of it.

When I was about to leave, my father-in-law handed me a twenty-five-ruble note so that I could leave some hard currency for my bride-to-be. My future mother-in-law led her to me by the hand, and I bade her goodnight and gave her the money. In my state of surprise and distress, I do not remember whether I put it into my fiancée's hand or in my mother-in-law's hand for her to give to her.

In short, I left and took off the borrowed clothes and put back on my own. I lay down to sleep, but now I could not fall asleep so easily. My head was spinning, thinking of everything that had happened to me. Finally, I fell asleep until the morning. Upon waking up, I began to dress, to wash up, and ran to *shul* for prayers. When I arrived at *shul*, they had already finished prayers. Everyone wished me *mazel tov* and said that the match was a lucky one for me. In short, now I was lucky and was to be envied.

My heart was not joyful. All of this seemed like a dream to me. I did not want to know about anything except the registration. Were I to be finally registered and have a document attesting to that, I would know that I was alive, and I would be able to think about a future for myself. As long as I lacked such a document, my life was no life and I enjoyed nothing.

---

15 Freyde's granddaughter Aliza Bernfeld of Petakh-Tikva recalled her father Shloyme saying that his mother Freyde had striking royal-blue eyes.

16 Under normal circumstances, a member of the relatively simple and rural Hershkovitshes would not have been considered a suitable match for a Goldenshteyn, a family more sophisticated and learned, including being related to the rabbi of Tiraspol, Reb Shloymele.

Actually, that very day, Shulem left for his home in the village of Tashlik and took his leave of me in a friendly manner, promising me that he would see to it that they registered me right away. My in-laws also bade me farewell, and I cautioned them that the most important thing for me was being registered, and that until they registered me, I did not know whether I was engaged. They explained to me that this could not be rushed, since it did not depend on them and would require much laborious efforts with the authorities. They would start to work on it right after all the holidays,[17] and they hoped to God that by Pesach I would be registered as their son.[18] I believed them and bade them farewell. They gave me a few rubles and started to ride off to their village. They added that during the intermediate days of *Sukes* one of them would return to the city to arrange room and board for me, but, in the meantime, I had those few rubles. And with that, they rode off to their village.

After their departure, I thought that I should not depend on their arranging room and board for me. I did not want them to squander money on me because, as things might turn out, they might not be able to register me. Since this was my main concern and I would break the engagement if this was not done, why should I let them squander money on me and then have complaints against me? So I decided to leave for Romanovke and stay there with my late brother's father-in-law, Reb Ersh, and with my sister Surele. I would stay a bit here and a bit there until I would receive word from my future father-in-law that he had registered me. I could then obtain an internal passport and become a free person, the equal of all, and be able to travel to some yeshiva to study for a while.[19] And actually, the next morning, two days after Yom Kippur, I left Tiraspol for Romanovke.[20]

First of all, I traveled to Bender, which was on the way, to see my sister Tsipe because she deserved a *mazel tov*, having given birth to a son on Yom Kippur. Upon arriving there, I found her recovering from the birth. I happened to arrive when the midwife was bathing the baby, so I tossed a silver coin into the bathtub. Tsipe was very pleased that her brother could provide "bath money" for the midwife—and a silver coin at that.[21] The midwife, as well, certainly had

---

17 After *Sukes* and *Simchas Torah*.
18 Pesach was six months away. Though the engagement contract had specified three months, the author was evidently giving his first in a series of deadline extensions.
19 As mentioned in chapter 13, p. 211, footnote 37, one did not have the right to travel within Tsarist Russia without an internal passport. See also Avrutin (2010:91).
20 The author left Tiraspol on October 12, 1864.
21 Bath money is called *bodgelt* in the original and refers to the silver coins for the midwife thrown into the bathtub in which the child is bathed shortly after his birth. This passage is listed as one of the sources for this term in *Jewish Money* by Rivkind (1959:40–41).

not expected such great luck. "Oh," she cried with joy, "the child will be lucky!" She apparently foresaw this in the coin... I told my sister about my *mazel tov*— my engagement and my future in-laws. She asked me about my bride-to-be, so I told her that I knew her from afar and that I actually did not want to know her any better until I received my internal passport and would be registered. When that happened, I would truly know that I was engaged and would then also give her more thought.

The birth of this baby boy was quite significant since Tsipe had prayed for children for years and had barely lived to see the birth of her little girl, Ester-Khaye, born three years earlier, whom we already know.[22] And now God had provided her with a son, someone to say *Kaddish* for her. His birth was an answer to her tearful pleas before God by day and by night to grant her a son so that she could leave behind someone to say *Kaddish* for her in this world. Her great poverty mattered not to her, and she accepted it with love, as long as God would grant her a son to say *Kaddish* for her. And God heard her prayers and found her worthy of having a son whom she planned to name Duvid.

You can understand how joyful she was upon hearing that her brother had become engaged on the same evening as her son's birth, creating a double *mazel tov*. I bade her farewell and kissed her goodbye. Though she asked me to stay until the *bris*, I could not do so because I was in a hurry to leave for Romanovke and did not want my future in-laws to run into me somewhere during the intermediate days of *Sukes*. She said, "*Oy*, how I would love to meet your bride-to-be, dear brother." "You will meet her, God willing. When I come here for Pesach, I'll drive with you to my future father-in-law's, so you'll meet them all, God willing. Be well! Be well! Until we meet again, beloved sister." And with these words I left her home and headed for Romanovke.

It was about fifty *versts*, and perhaps more, to Romanovke, but what did that matter to me? The next morning, a day before the eve of *Sukes*, I arrived in Romanovke.[23] "A guest! A guest!" shouted everyone in Ershl's house, and they all greeted me. Shoyl the *shoykhet*, Ershl's son, asked me what was new with me since he had left me in Mayak with Reb Leyzer the *shoykhet* and felt sorry that I had left there. So I told him that it was precisely because Reb Leyzer had wanted me to marry his daughter that I left there, and that I was rescued from there only to fall into an even worse situation. I went on to tell him the entire story of my engagement. "Don't worry," he said. "It appears that you didn't do badly. Your future father-in-law is apparently rich, and you could have been stuck with a

---

22 For details regarding the birth of Tsipe's two children, see ch. 3, pp. 124–125.
23 October 13, 1864.

poor man as a father-in-law in Mayak. True, Reb Leyzer in Mayak has a more prestigious lineage, but that alone is not enough in life. You have it especially good since he's agreed to register you, which is more important than anything else. Be happy, Pinkhes-Ber, God is helping you and will help you. Don't worry. Stay with us over the winter. Study in the *bes-medresh*. I'll look after you and will study with you often and fellow Hasidim will also befriend you. You're a pious young man, and people like piety."

So I spent the entire winter at the home of our in-law Reb Ersh the *shoykhet*, until *Rosh-Khoydesh Nisan*.[24] My task was to study in the *bes-medresh* until eleven at night, wake up before dawn, and study until morning prayers. After prayers, I would go eat. When I would come to eat and did not find Reb Ersh at home, I would quietly seize a pen and pieces of parchment and practice writing on them the special Hebrew letters used in writing Torah scrolls and *mezuzahs*. Since Reb Ersh was also a scribe, these items were lying around. I wrote a small *Megilla*, and that is how I stealthily taught myself how to write these letters.[25] Once, Reb Ersh caught me writing, and I was afraid that I would be scolded. Instead, he was astonished at how well I had written and said. "When did you learn this?" When I confessed all my sins, he told me to show him all my work. When I showed him my little *Megilla*, he was even more astounded and said, "From now on, you don't have to be afraid of me. Actually, why don't I teach you myself. I'll give you *mezuzahs* to write, but first study the laws of writing *tefillin* and *mezuzahs*." I was delighted that I could finally earn the food he fed me, rather than eating the bread of charity, gratuitous bread. I learned the laws of Hebrew lettering used in Torah scrolls, *mezuzahs*, and so on.[26] Every afternoon, I would write one or two *mezuzahs* and was now honestly earning my food. On Fridays I would help him mark lines on the blank sheets of parchment of the Torah scroll that he was writing.[27] All in all, he received a lot of good help from me.

People in the *shteytl* thought that it was a pity that I had already become engaged, for there were many who would have been interested in having me as a son-in-law. Everyone inquired, "Is he already engaged?" I used to go to my sister Surele's every *Shobes*. As you already know, she was living with her in-laws, and her husband worked hard all week from morning to night trying to knock

---

24 March 28, 1865.
25 In his Hebrew ethical will from 1920, the author bequeathed this *Megilla* to his son Refuel. The current whereabouts of the *Megilla* are unknown. It is customary for those studying the art of writing Torah scrolls and *mezuzahs* to begin with the writing of a *Megilla*.
26 These laws can be found in Rabbi Shlomo Ganzfried's *Keset ha-sofer* (1835) and other similar works.
27 The *Shulkhan Arukh* (*Yoreh Deah* 271:5) requires that the blank parchment used for Torah scrolls be marked with horizontal lines with an awl-like tool.

some sense into his students' wooden heads. They lived nicely and quietly, and Surele got along with everyone, and everyone loved her for her goodness and piety. All in all, it appeared that everything was going well for me, but what was going on with my registration? Do you know? I knew as much as you. I had already sent letters to my future in-laws, to my sister Ite, and did not receive an answer. Around Purim,[28] I received a letter from my future mother-in-law telling me that there was no news yet, meaning that there had been no response since they applied for my registration. I understood from the letter that this was a lie, so I decided to travel to Tiraspol to put an end to the match. But due to the cold weather, I had to wait until *Rosh-Khoydesh Nisan*.[29]

When it grew warmer, I set out on foot for Tiraspol by way of Bender so that I could see my dear sister, Tsipe, and ask her advice. Upon reaching Bender, I went directly to the little house where my Tsipe lived and went right into the vestibule. I was about to open the front door of the house with the hope of seeing my sister and her child, puckering my lips to kiss my loved ones, when a woman stopped me and asked, "Who are you looking for?" I said, "What do you mean 'who am I looking for'? I'm looking for my sister Tsipe." She replied, "Who's Tsipe? What Tsipe? There's no Tsipe living here." I could not believe it, so I opened the door and saw that it was true—a strange woman was living there now. I stood there frozen. How could my sister have moved from there? Where had she gone? So I started to question her, "Perhaps you know the whereabouts of the former tenant?" She replied that she did not know who had lived there previously. When she moved in, she had found the place empty, and she has already been living there for two months. How could it be that my sister would move out of a dwelling in midwinter? What did that mean?

I ran off in shock to the owner of the house. I entered and asked if they knew where the previous tenant who had lived in the little house in their courtyard had moved. They said, "Why do you need her?" I said that she was my sister and that since her husband was a *melomed* he could not have left his *kheyder* in the middle of the winter term.[30] They did not know what to answer. At that, the landlord's daughter emerged. She had seen me on my visit to Tsipe when she was recovering from having given birth. She said, "*Oy!* Tsipe's brother, poor thing." Everyone motioned to her, and she retreated into the house. I then understood that something was amiss here. I began to plead with them to tell me the truth. They replied, "If you want to know where your sister is, go over

---

28 March 12, 1865.
29 March 28, 1865.
30 The winter term in a *kheyder* lasted from after *Sukes* in the fall until shortly before Pesach in the spring.

to Sluve, Nesonl the storekeeper's wife. She must know because they used to spend a good amount of time together." I immediately ran over to Sluve. As soon as Sluve saw me and heard that I was Tsipe's brother and was asking about her, she began to cry. And I too began to cry. "Tell me already, can it be that I don't have a sister anymore." "Yes," she said, "your sister has moved to her eternal resting place." Hearing those words, I fell to the ground and with the cry "My dear sister!" fell into a dead faint.

I do not know what happened to me then. I only know that when I came to and opened my eyes, I saw Nesonl the storekeeper standing near me, along with his wife Sluve and his children. They began to console me in the usual manner. I sat *shivah* for an hour and had a good cry.[31] I mourned her entire life. I asked where were her little children, where was her husband, and when did she die. They told me briefly that she had died two months after her son's birth.[32] The little girl had been taken in by someone locally by the name of Sender-Leytses,[33] and the little boy had been given to a wet nurse in Talmóz. The father himself, Reb Shloyme-Leyzer, had left right away to teach in order to make sure that he would not be asked to pay for the wet nurse. At that, they cursed him for being such an irresponsible father. I asked which wet nurse had the baby. They told me that my sister, Ite, had given him to a wet nurse in Tiraspol, "You'll learn everything from Ite." I wept profusely over the tragedy, particularly over the unfortunate children. From Sender-Leytses, I found out where Tsipe's oldest child Esther-Khayele was. Upon seeing her, I kissed and hugged her and grieved plenty. I thanked them for keeping her and left for Tiraspol.

In Tiraspol, I met with Ite, and then the real sobbing began. Ite told me all about Tsipe's illness, what Tsipe endured, and how she had tried to save herself by begging God to grant her the years to raise her little children. Tsipe's own death did not bother her as much as the fact that her little children would unfortunately remain alone and poor with an irresponsible father. That thought embittered her final moments even more than her own bitter life. Her life had been bitter, but her death was even more so.

Ite led me to a poor furrier's wife who was wet-nursing the baby Duvidl. The furrier's wife had her own child as well, and I found two babies in one

---

31 A Jew who hears of a close relative's death after thirty days only has to sit *shivah*, that is, in mourning, for one hour (*Kitsur Shulkhan Arukh* 206:2).

32 At the beginning of this chapter, on p. 223, the author writes that Tsipe's son, Duvid, was born on Yom Kippur (September 23, 1864). Hence, Tsipe died two months later, in November 1864. Being that she was twenty-four when her mother died in 1854 (ch. 1, p. 95, footnote 27), Tsipe was approximately thirty-four at the time of her own death.

33 Sender was either the husband, son, or close relative of a woman named Leytse, which is a nickname for Leye.

cradle. Both were lying there well soiled and in so many filthy rags that they could barely be seen. While looking at Duvidl, I said to Ite, "See how thin and bony he is." Ite said, "You should have seen what he looked like when I picked him up from the woman in Talmoz. He's now filled out somewhat. Right after our sister Tsipe's death, Shloyme-Leyzer found a wet nurse in the village of Talmoz for five rubles a month. When two months passed and he hadn't paid, she brought the baby back to Bender. Since the devoted father had gone into hiding, the wet nurse brought the baby to me. I traveled with the wet nurse back to Bender, found Shloyme-Leyzer, asked him for our sister's bedding, which he kept with our friend Sluve and I paid the wet nurse. I brought the baby here to Tiraspol and gave it to this poor but pious furrier's wife, where I can at least keep an eye on Duvidl. And now I don't know what's to be done. Shloyme-Leyzer doesn't want to have anything to do with his son, and I have to struggle to pay them. Do I have the means? But what should I do? Can I let the baby die, God forbid, now that this luckless soul is here in this world?"

My sister Ite told me all this while tears were streaming from her eyes. I said to her, "Don't cry. God will help. He's the father of orphans. Don't worry. The child will grow up. How that will happen is not up to us. Enough crying, my dear sister. Crying won't help at all." With these words we left the furrier's wife, and headed to Reb Zolmen-Kopls, where I spent *Shobes*.

On Sunday, I hired a coach at the marketplace and went to Tashlik to see my relative Shulem. He surely had to know the status of my prospective in-laws' struggles to have me registered. Since he got me engaged, let him get me unengaged if they would not register me. Sunday evening, I arrived in Tashlik exactly four days before Pesach.[34] I counted on spending Pesach with Shulem. When I arrived at Shulem's, I was welcomed as an honored guest. I could see that they were very glad to see me. His daughter and son-in-law had been married that winter, and Beyle, the young bride, hardly knew what to do for me. The young husband was also overjoyed that he would have a fellow city-dweller with whom to spend time, since he was a city dweller stuck in a village. In short, "Our relative Berele has arrived!" I pointed out to them that I should really be called Pinye-Ber rather than just Berl, and they promised to do so but soon forgot because they were used to calling me just Berele. Well, I forgave them for it.

The initial excitement passed. I was served food and we passed the time. I told them all that you know by now. They consoled me over my sister Tsipe's death and told me that they already knew about the tragedy. I asked if they heard anything about my prospective in-laws, and how things were going regarding

---

34 Pesach started the night of April 10, 1865.

my registration. They replied that they did not know and had heard nothing about it.

I hardly slept that night, and we sent a messenger the next morning to let them know that the groom-to-be was in Tashlik and wanted to meet his future father-in-law. In about an hour, my future mother-in-law Dvoyre arrived. She was overjoyed to see me and indicated that she was following up on the matter, but, she claimed, it was not yet finished. She would only know the outcome after Pesach. I made it clear to her that if she was fooling me, she was only fooling herself. I told her that as of now I believed her and would wait until after Pesach. She begged me to spend Pesach with her, but I did not want to. Nonetheless, she would not relinquish and proceeded to beg me and implore Shulem, Beyle, and her husband to pressure me to come until I finally had to promise her that I would come to her for Pesach. Shulem convinced me that my being right next to my future in-laws and not spending Pesach with them would be very embarrassing for them and others might deduce that I did not want the match. So I agreed that I would spend Pesach with them. She left Tashlik in great joy. In the late afternoon of the eve of Pesach, my father in-law's coach arrived and took me off to his home for *Yontef*. Twenty minutes later, I was at my father-in-law's home for it was only two *versts* away.

During the three days that I had spent at Shulem's, Beyle's husband and I passed the time amicably. He told me everything that was going on with him. I learned how little she tolerated him, poor fellow, and that this hurt him very much. I told him that she was a religious woman and that, therefore, with time she would probably reconsider and begin to appreciate him. I went on to say that she was still young, just a newlywed, and had not adjusted to him yet, while for his part he should bear the pain until they would have a child, when things would change. Beyle, being the same as ever, told me nothing, but her silence told me a great deal. And I understood from her sighing what was irking her: that such a simple girl as my bride-to-be, who was from common parents, could be so fortunate as to have such an accomplished fiancé—a learner and a singer, who was clever and had every desirable attribute. Her resentment was not out of jealousy, but it hurt her that she had committed such foolishness in rejecting me. Shulem also showed much regret over the foolishness that his fanaticism had caused in not taking me for his son-in-law. While sitting at the table, if the talk turned to Torah learning, I would always be proven right. For example, if I said that a certain topic or verse could be found in a particular source and they would argue and say it was in another source, it always turned out as I had said. So Shulem saw that my head was a lot better than his son-in-law's, though his son-in-law lived calmly while I was adrift and did not spend my nights where I spent my days. But it was a lost cause, and so it had to be. It was truly "a misfortune that was not to be rectified."[35]

We will leave these side matters and return to my father-in-law and see how I was doing at his house. As soon as I arrived at the house, my father-in-law, Reb Itsye, welcomed me in a very friendly manner, as did his wife. I was taken into the house with love and friendship. The house was clean and attractively decorated in honor of *Yontef*. The table was covered with a tablecloth, and the samovar was already steaming. I was quickly given tea to drink along with a bite to eat. My father-in-law had no time to spare, like any head of a household before *Yontef*, and his wife certainly had little time, so they did not have the leisure to keep me company.[36] I was left in the house with their little son, Leyzerke, whom you met earlier; he was the one who had stared with his eyes wide open.[37] Now he was older, so his eyes were larger and he stared even better. He came in and greeted me. I struck up a conversation and asked if he was applying himself in his studies. He told me that he was learning to read Hebrew and studying the *khimesh*, which was fine for a ten-year-old boy.[38] I said to him, "I'd like to know where my bride-to-be is." He replied that she was in the next room, at which point a pretty little girl, dressed up finely in a Jewish manner, entered the room.

I hardly recognized her since she had grown much taller over time and appeared far prettier. She entered silently and went over to a chest, took out an attractive *khalát* made from a simple material, and handed it to me,[39] "Here, *Mome* gave the material to the tailor to have this made for you, Berl." I asked her, "How could your mother have known my measurements?" She had no idea how to answer this question and said only, "I don't know," and sat down near her little brother. It was not so long ago that she had danced around me and had called me to play with her, but now she was embarrassed to say a single word to me and sat far away. Nonetheless, when I finished drinking the glass of tea, she came over and poured me another glass. Meanwhile, I began to study from a small Jewish religious book that I had brought from Shulem's. She said to me, "What are you reading in that little *sidur*?" (Among common folk, any Jewish

---

35 Ecclesiastes 1:15.
36 With all the many Jewish laws concerning major Jewish holidays, especially Pesach, the head of the household has many types of work that can only be done before the onset of the holiday at sunset. At the same time, the wife must prepare all the food needed for the meals that night, which in this case was the *Seder* meal.
37 For the author's first mention of Leyzerke, see ch. 11, p. 192.
38 The author is probably being sarcastic since such studies are generally under par for a ten-year-old boy such as Leyzerke.
39 In Yiddish, a *khalat* is a Jewish man's lightweight robe, often made of silk, worn by Hasidim as a housecoat, especially on *Shabes* and the Jewish holidays.

religious book is called a *sidur*.) "Drink your tea. It's getting cold." Her care for me had its effect since the tea had actually cooled off enough, and I finished the tea. She wanted to pour even more, but I did not let her. I thanked her and stood up to pray *Minkhe*.

After *Minkhe*, her mother came in to light the *Yontef* candles and her father returned to put on his *Yontef* clothes. Afterward we prayed *Marev*. After *Marev*, her father began to conduct the Pesach *Seder*. He donned a *kitl*, prepared the *Seder* plate, and sat down to read the Haggadah.[40] He read out loud from the Haggadah quite seriously. He counted the ten plagues so vigorously that by the time he reached their acronyms, "*Detsakh Adash Be'akhav*," there was no more wine in his glass and they had to refill his glass.[41] The *Seder* went very well and was in accordance with full Jewish tradition because he was a truly pious Jew, free of deception and guile. His wife, however, though a pious Jewish daughter and clever, was full of deceit and fraud, a babbler, and a swindler. She had a good heart, but tricking others was second nature to her. That is why I considered him to be a pure soul, and her to be a shrewd woman.

During the first days of Pesach, I had enough time to consider my in-laws in order to know with whom I would be dealing in my future life. I discovered that my fiancée had good Jewish character traits but had little upbringing. No one had taught her, and she had no one from whom to learn. It was not her fault. Her father was an honest Jew, pure and straight; whatever he said was sacred. Her mother was the opposite: whatever she said could not be believed. Her pure father informed me that all his wife had done about my registration was to inquire about what needed to be done, but that, in truth, she had not begun to do anything at all. This caused me to become very upset. I asked her the reason why nothing had been done, but she replied with false excuses. I understood that the fact that she was a swindler led her to believe that others certainly were too. So she had done nothing about this matter because she thought that if I were to become free by obtaining an internal passport, I would be off and would not return. So she wanted to delay my registration until the wedding. I gave her

---

40 The Haggadah is the text that sets forth the order of the Pesach *Seder*. Reading the *Haggadah* at the *Seder* table is a fulfillment of the commandment (Exodus 13:8) for each Jew to "tell your son" of the Jewish liberation from slavery in Egypt.
41 It is customary to dip one's finger in the cup of wine and tap the wine on the finger into a bowl (or pour out a little wine from the cup into a bowl) for each of the ten plagues, as mentioned in the Haggadah. Afterward, in the Haggadah, the initial letters of the Hebrew names of the ten plagues are divided into three acronyms, for which one also dips (or pours) for each acronym.

until *Shvues*.⁴² If I did not have my internal passport by *Shvues*, I would no longer be engaged...

On the first of the intermediate days of Pesach, I left them and went to Tashlik.⁴³ From there I left for Tiraspol. When I arrived in Tiraspol, I suddenly saw my mother-in-law Dvoyre there. Now, what was she doing there? She said that she wanted to really pursue the matter seriously; my words had finally moved her. She found a fixer and settled on a fee of 150 rubles. He promised her that all would be completed by *Shvues*. She explained to me that her husband was a good-for-nothing and that she had to take care of everything herself. That was why things had been delayed until now. "Now that I see that you are determined that it be finished quickly, I must pay a higher price so that it will be as you wish. Come with me to Bender. I have sisters there. You can eat at my sister Rukhl-Leye's, and you can study in the *bes-medresh* there." She gave the fixer, a Jew, twenty-five rubles for expenses and we left for Bender. I studied there in the *bes-medresh* and had my meals at her sister Rukhl-Leye's. Her husband was called Velvl Bidnezhid.⁴⁴ Their house was common but pious. He dealt in grain. They had three boys: Berl, Itsl, and Khayem.⁴⁵ Berl was to have become engaged to my fiancée, Freydele, but she chose me, a stranger named Ber, over her relative of the same name. "But that doesn't bother me," Rukhl-Leye said, "let the family grow larger."

Two weeks before *Shvues*, I traveled to Tiraspol and sought out that Jewish fixer to determine what was happening. He told me that he was waiting for my mother-in-law because she needed to give him money, but she was not even showing her face. I hired a coach for the round trip and went with that fixer to Perkon. I came to my father-in-law's so early that my bride-to-be was still asleep. His wife was astonished: why had I come suddenly with the fixer? So I told her why we had come, and she gave him another twenty-five rubles. We then drove back to Tiraspol.

Two weeks passed and the fixer was not to be found and the papers had certainly not been obtained; as it states, "We heard nothing and no one was

---

42 May 30, 1865.
43 April 13, 1865.
44 The words *bidne zhid*, originally from Russian, mean "miserable Jew." In chapter 14, p. 240, Velvl's wife is referred to as "Rukhl-Leye '*Bidne Zhid*,'" where (unlike here) the two words are within quotation marks, which evidently indicates that it was a nickname and not a surname. In fact, the surname Bidnezhid cannot be found in Alexander Beider's *A Dictionary of Jewish Surnames from the Russian Empire* (2008) or in any of the large databases of Jewish vital and census-like records from Eastern Europe. See ch. 18, p. 309, footnote 39, regarding another odd nickname, "Velvl the Nun's."
45 Khayem is referred to as Arn-Khayem in chapter 24.

responding."[46] I traveled to my father-in-law's to spend *Shvues* there and found that his wife was not at home but was expected to be returning from Tiraspol.[47] What does one do to while away some time on a summer day? Should I spend the time with my fiancée or with my father-in-law? I figured it would be more pleasant to go off to the banks of the Dniester River. There I found my old companions, the brothers Mordkhe and Avrum.[48] One of them was already married for six months and the other was engaged, though both were still children. They were bathing in honor of the approaching *Yontef*.[49] When they spotted me, they were overjoyed because they knew me to be a good and celebrated swimmer, and we swam together. Since it was the eve of *Yontef*, and greens are required for decoration on *Shvues*, we hired a boat, sailed across, and tore off greens for *Shvues*.[50] I tried to chop off as many large branches as I could and dragged them to the riverbank. My companions were already seated in the boat, and I was the last to arrive. So I clambered aboard in haste and threw down my branches, which pierced a large sieve that belonged to a Walachian who used it to remove debris from wheat kernels. The Walachian non-Jew who owned the boat we had hired set it in motion. The other Walachian, the one whose sieve I had pierced, was furious and incited one of his friends to go after me and beat me to death for the damage I had done. He demanded that I pay for the damaged sieve.

I understood that if these non-Jews were to beat me, the Jewish kids along the shore certainly would not stand on the side and permit my being trounced; I was afraid this would come to a very bad end, so I figured out a plan of action. Before my boat came ashore, I took off my shoes and *kapote* and held them in my hands. When my boat was about two meters from the riverbank, I jumped into the water and reached the shore before my boat did. Before the non-Jews had time to land their boat and disembark, I was already ten streets away from the shore. There was no way they could have caught me, even if they were on horseback. I ran right in to the *shoykhet*'s home because that's where I used to sleep—it was not far from my father-in-law's. I quickly asked them to hide me. They asked, "What? What?" I told them, "Don't ask. There's no time. But if

---

46   Kings I 18:26.
47   *Shvues* occurred on May 31–June 1, 1865.
48   Mordkhe and Avrum are mentioned in ch. 10, p. 183.
49   Certainly they went to bathe in honor of the *Yontef* of *Shvues* beginning that evening and, at the same time, took a swim, for "it is a mitzvah to bathe" on the eve of *Yontef* (*Kitsur Shulkhan Arukh* 103:2).
50   Many Jews have the custom to adorn their homes and synagogues with plants, flowers, and leafy branches to recall the greenery that suddenly blossomed on Mt. Sinai in the desert in honor of the giving of the Torah on its summit. See *Shulkhan Arukh* (*Orakh Khayim* 494:3).

someone asks for me, you should say that you haven't seen me and then go straight to my father-in-law's to see what happens there."

The *shoykhet* did not understand what was going on but he saw that I was extremely frightened. He hid me in a room and then walked over to my father-in-law's. An hour later, the *shoykhet* returned with my mother- and father-in-law. They told me, "The danger has passed, and you can *bentsh goyml* that you were saved from two such murderers who are the leading cutthroats in the village.[51] If they had caught you, they would certainly have killed you or permanently crippled you. But since they came over to us and found out that you are our son-in-law, we told them that we would pay for the damage, and they settled for two rubles. You can now go home." And I went home to my father-in-law's.

When the two days of *Shvues* were over, I decided it was time to complete the matter of my registration. I succeeded in having my mother-in-law give me twenty-five rubles so I could arrange for my own registration, though she did not have any desire to give me the money. Even after giving me the money, she still could not believe that I would be able to accomplish the task at hand. Noticing her reaction, I told her that she should consider it as if she had given the fixer another twenty-five rubles, but the difference was that the fixer would keep draining more and more money from her and would have done nothing, but I would make sure to succeed, using any possible means. She then asked me, "How will you do it and what will you do?" I answered, "It's not your concern. I won't say now what I'll do, but in a month you'll know what I did. Be well." And with that, I left for Tashlik.

Upon arriving in Tashlik, I told my relative Shulem about the twenty-five rubles that I received from my mother-in-law and that I hoped to register myself for that amount. He also did not believe that I could do it and said to me, "You think that you're a big shot, but you'll be cheated out of that money. If I would have been there, I wouldn't have let her give you the money." I then said to him, "What would you give me if within four weeks I'll be registered and have a passport?" He answered me, "If you accomplish that, I'd know that you're a fine young man, but I can't believe that you can do it."

Before I left, I saw that it was actually very difficult for him to part with me. He had by then grown to love me like a father loves a son and tears filled his eyes. I told him, "Don't worry. Everything will be fine. God Almighty will help

---

51 To *bentsh goyml* denotes making the blessing of deliverance from danger (*Kitsur Shulkhan Arukh* 61:1–2).

me." We kissed and bade farewell, and I left for Tiraspol by wagon. After being on the road for a bit, I noticed that Shulem was still standing on the road in the same place where I had left him and was still gazing at me. That parting was very difficult for him, which surprised me. But upon returning four weeks later, I learned the explanation for his behavior.

CHAPTER 15

Obtaining a Romanian Passport and Traveling to Lubavitch, 1865

Leaving Tiraspol • Stealing across the Border • Afraid for No Reason • Obtaining a Passport • Returning to Tiraspol • Sitting Down to Study Torah

Upon arriving in Tiraspol, I did not tell my sister Ite anything about my plans to obtain my own passport, and I traveled to Bender.[1] In Bender, I settled on a price with a wagoner to take me to Khotin near the border.[2] I found two additional Jews who would travel with me until Kishinev in my hired wagon; one had to pass through Kishinev on the way to Khotin.

One of the two understood that I was planning to steal across the border. Since he smuggled people across the border, he realized that I was a potential client. He struck up a conversation with me and over time revealed to me confidentially that he smuggles people across the border. He told me that he actually lives near the border in a village where the customs house was weak in its monitoring of the frontier. He explained that traveling via Khotin would cost me a lot of money and that I could still fall into the hands of crooks. He advised that it would be better for me to travel with him; it would be much cheaper for me, and I would be certain that I would not be cheated. He told me that I could ask about him in Kishinev where he was known as an honest person. He kept trying to persuade me to follow his advice. When we stopped at a tavern along

---
1   Early June 1865.
2   Khotin was near Tsarist Russia's border with Romania. The United Principalities of Moldavia and Walachia was only officially named Romania in 1866, and Romania gained its independence from the Ottoman Empire in 1877.

the way, everyone else got off the wagon and went into the tavern while we both remained sitting on the wagon talking quietly among ourselves. In short, I decided to stop off in Kishinev in order to inquire about him there. In Kishinev, I found out that he was an honest person and that he had children living there.

The next day, I traveled with him to his village, Beshtemák, where he kept me in his home for a week and then had me stay the next week at his neighbor's. With my bad luck, the border patrol became very strict then for they had caught a few people trying to cross illegally.[3] So we had to wait until it became a bit quieter. During that week and the next week, the excuse was that it was too light out—the moon was shining brightly—so we had to continue waiting. And do not forget that I did not even get to see the moon shine. Throughout my whole two weeks there, I was afraid of the slightest creak of the door.[4] I also did not have anything to eat and became miserably sick. But God helped and that man returned from his travels. He told me that it was not worth it for me to continue waiting here in his village because the monitoring of the border had become so intense and severe that I had to travel with him to Untsésht, a village near Kishinev. There he would hand me over to one of the locals, who would certainly smuggle me over the border into Romania. I had little faith in his words, but I was happy that I would at least be changing prisons.

I traveled with him that night to Untsesht, and he handed me over to a Jewish man who kept me at his home until after *Shobes*. On Sunday, he in turn handed me over to two non-Jews, Walachians, who took me on their wagon. At dusk, they took me to a village. As we arrived in the village, I heard another Walachian ask them, "Are you now bringing along a victim?" They burst out laughing and replied, "Yes." You can imagine how every one of my limbs trembled upon hearing that. I was terrified that they would kill me and take the eight rubles that remained from the original twenty-five. When we arrived in the village, the two non-Jews covered me over in the wagon and drove me to their home. They told me to immediately crawl into the attic to sleep for they were also afraid of being caught. One left while the other, evidently the master of the house, remained. I spent the night there in fright. In the morning, the master of the house left and told his wife that she should give me something to eat. She asked me what I was allowed to eat, so I told her to make a *pletsl* by mixing flour

---

3 Beshtemak was also on the border with Romania.
4 The author was hiding inside so as not to be noticed by any informants who were on the lookout for strangers in their border towns. The authorities would monetarily reward such informants (Matthews, 1993:8).

and water and then baking it and to roast some eggs, which she did.[5] I lay for two days in that attic.

On the third day, the other Walachian came. They led me on foot through valleys and over mountains. While walking, they heard footsteps. They became frightened and threw themselves into a gully. I also threw myself down because they had informed me earlier that I should immediately copy whatever I would see them do. We remained lying there until the danger passed. Such scares occurred often. More than once we had to throw ourselves into a hollow in the ground, and we were only able to climb out with great difficulty.

Suddenly we heard the clopping of horses and Russian song. The two non-Jews crossed themselves and lay down in the deep grass; they signaled me with their eyes that I should not even let a breath escape my mouth. While we were lying like that, I saw Cossacks riding on horses and singing to themselves. After the Cossacks passed and we were already quite a distance away, we crawled on our stomachs across the trail and reached a small forest safely. In the little forest, we again had a scare. The two non-Jews saw the shadows of people, so they hid behind a tree until the danger passed.

Finally, we came to a deep cavity in the ground. The non-Jews crossed themselves again, went in, and walked out on the other side. We kept going until we reached an open field. Now that we were past that little forest, we began to run downhill. After having run for about half a *verst*, we sat down to rest, smoked a cigarette, and spoke among ourselves normally, without whispering. They said to me, "You're already on the Walachian side and have nothing to fear."[6] In truth, I was much more afraid of them than of the Russian authorities. If they had killed me, who would have held them accountable for spilling my blood?

Once we rested, they led me to a tavern and told me that a Jew lived there. Upon hearing that, I was delighted. We knocked, and he opened up for us. I asked him to bring bread and cultured milk for me and liquor for the Walachians. We bade each other farewell, I thanked them, and they left.

A few minutes later, another four Jews and three Walachians came along. They had also just crossed the border. We all now realized that we had been afraid for no reason; we had been alarmed by each other's footsteps. Our previous fright now turned into joy. I soon hired a wagon for a ruble and arrived in Lyeve around ten a.m. That same day, I wrote to Iassy for a Romanian passport,

---

5   A *pletsl* is a flat onion bread.
6   The author sometimes refers to Romania as Walachia, since the United Principalities of Moldavia and Walachia were only officially named Romania in 1866.

and five days later I received it, written and sealed according to the law.⁷ On the way back, I now passed through the customs house in Beshtemak free as a bird. Exactly four weeks to the day, I returned to Tiraspol happy and registered with a Romanian passport made out in my own given name and surname.⁸ The whole of Tiraspol was now talking about my achievement—that a young fellow of sixteen should accomplish such a thing. Everyone was amazed.

My mother-in-law soon came to see me, and she was quite delighted. It also scared her because she thought, "Who knows if he'll stick around. Since he's now free to go where he wants, he'll leave and then who knows if we'll ever see him again." To find out my plans, her first question was, "What are you thinking of doing now?" I replied, "What should I think? I want to sit myself down and study Torah. Wherever you will arrange room and board for me is where I'll eat." She liked my answer. She was now sure that I had no thoughts of abandoning her daughter. She told me, "Travel to Bender to my sister, as you did before. You will stay there and study in the *bes-medresh*." I promised her that I would do so. Meanwhile, I asked her about my relatives and inquired about Shulem. She answered me that it was already two weeks since Shulem died! I exclaimed, "What? Shulem died? *Oy*, Shulem, Shulem!" It was not for naught that he had difficulty in parting from me when I left him last. He apparently felt it in his heart; he had a premonition that he would never see me again. I felt much sorrow over his death.

That same day, I traveled to Bender. I sat down to study Torah with great diligence in the Sadigórer *kloyz*.⁹ I stayed with my mother-in-law's sister Rukhl-Leye "*Bidne Zhid*," but did not last there long.¹⁰ Three weeks later, that is, after blessing *Rosh-Khoydesh Menakhem Av*, my situation changed drastically, and it was all my own doing.¹¹

---

7 The author wrote to Iassy, since it was the capital of Romania from 1859 to 1918. Many Russian-born Jews stole over the borders to Romania and Turkey, where they posed as native-born residents, applied for passports, obtained them, and then returned to Russia. Since foreigners were not conscripted into the Russian military, these passports helped them avoid conscription (Errera, 1894:34; Schoenfeld, 1946:9).

8 The author emphasizes that his passport was in his own name, since forged passports under false names were widespread in nineteenth-century Russia and Eastern Europe (Avrutin, 2010:127–132).

9 This *kloyz*, meaning a *bes-medresh*, belonged to the Sadigorer Hasidim, followers of Reb Avrúm-Yankev Fridman (1819–1883), the first Rebbe of Sadigor, Bukovina, Austria. He was a brother of two other Rebbes, the Lyever (ch. 17, p. 266, footnote 6) and the Shtefeneshter (ch. 17, p. 273, footnote 44).

10 See ch. 14, p. 232, footnote 44, regarding *Bidne Zhid*, meaning "miserable Jew."

11 The blessing of the new month was observed on the *Shabes* preceding *Rosh-Khoydesh Av*, which would have occurred on the 28th of *Av*, that is, July 22, 1865. *Menakhem Av* is another name for the month of *Av*.

Upon resting from my travels and from crossing the Romanian border, I looked around and saw that it was not a good plan to be supported on *kest* and to expect my mother-in-law to pay *kest* for me, especially since I knew that she had little capital—much less than she was thought to have. I reconsidered my plans to study Torah in the Sadigorer *kloyz* because the fellows there were not really interested in studying. Upon opening their volumes of Talmud, they would begin discussions about their Rebbe and the miracles he performed, sparing themselves the trouble of studying. Since I would not listen to their stories of miracles and I did not drink any liquor, I was not considered to be a Hasid and became detested by them. It was even worse in the Tolner *kloyz*.[12] The Tolner Hasidim did not study at all; no one even entered their *bes-medresh*.

Since I did want to study and was now a free person who could travel all over Russia, I decided that I would head out for the Hasidic yeshivas of Lithuania.[13] Since I had been among Chabadniks[14] and liked their style of Hasidism and their Lubavitcher Rebbe,[15] the Hasidic Rebbe, Reb Mendele,

---

12 The Tolner *kloyz* refers to a *bes-medresh* for the Hasidim of the Tolner Rebbe, Reb Duvid Tversky (1808–1882). He was a brother to the Lyever Rebbe's wife, Sheyndele, mentioned in ch. 17, pp. 288–289.

13 In Yiddish (particularly before World War I), Lithuania (*Lite* in the original Yiddish) does not correspond to the boundaries of today's independent Lithuania but refers to the areas in Eastern Europe where the northeastern dialect of Yiddish has traditionally been spoken, namely Lithuania, Belarus, northeastern Poland, northern Ukraine, Latvia, and Estonia (Jacobs, 2005:61, 64–65).

14 At that time, there was more than one kind of Chabad Hasid. With the death of the founder of Chabad Hasidism, Rabbi Shneur Zalman of Lyadi, in 1812, his son Rabbi Dov-Ber settled in Lubavitch where he became Rebbe. At the same time, Rabbi Shneur Zalman's disciple Rabbi Aaron Horovits (ca. 1766–1828) became the Rebbe in Shtrashelye (now Staraselye, Belarus). The latter was succeeded by his son Rabbi Khaym-Refoel Horovits, who died in 1842 (Bloy, 2008:122–154). By the time Pinye-Ber came to Lubavitch in 1865, Shtrashelyer Hasidism was waning. After the death of Rabbi Dov-Ber's son-in-law and successor Rabbi Menakhem-Mendl Schneerson in 1866, most of his sons became Hasidic Rebbes in various towns: Kopust (now Kopys), Lyadi, and Nyezhin (now Nizhyn, Ukraine). And the youngest son, Rabbi Shmuel, remained in Lubavitch where he assumed the mantle of leadership. After the First World War, Lubavitch remained the sole surviving branch of Chabad Hasidism, and a Chabadnik (Chabad Hasid) became synonymous with a Lubavitcher Hasid.

15 In the original, the author writes "Libavitsh," which is how the name of this town was traditionally pronounced in Yiddish, independent of Southeastern Yiddish's dialectal differences (since the vowel is unstressed, the /i/ pronunciation cannot be a function of the u>i shift). See Schaechter (1986:32–33), who lists a number of Yiddish writers, including Goldenshteyn, who spelled it this way. Schaechter also reproduces the personal stamp of the fifth Rebbe of Chabad, Rabbi Sholem-Ber Schneerson (1860–1920), which spells it as "Libavits"; a characteristic of many speakers of Northeastern Yiddish was the confusion of /ts/ and /tsh/. Though the Lubavitcher Rebbes generally wrote "Lubavitsh" or "Lubavits" before ca. 1900 (and "Lyubavitsh" afterwards), many pre-Second World War publications

of blessed memory, I decided to set out to see the Rebbe and ask him in which yeshiva I should study.[16] After all, no one was going to steal my fiancée from me, and I had no reason to rush and marry. For the time being, I needed to see to it that I studied Torah as long as I was free to do as I pleased. Since I was still unmarried and did not have the burden of supporting a wife, I felt I had to travel to Lubavitch.

But how would I get there? Where would I obtain money for the expenses involved? There was no way that I could tell my mother-in-law—or even mention to her that I had such an idea in my head—because she would think that I wanted to abandon their daughter and the rest of them. (As it turned out, her fear that I would run away somewhere as soon as I obtained a passport was not unwarranted.) Not only would she refuse to give me a single *kopek*, but she would also raise a huge storm about it. So I had to keep my travel plan a secret. My money issue remained unresolved, but since "nothing can stand in the way of a person's will,"[17] the question did not alarm me, and I left Bender with only one ruble.

Before leaving, I did not bid farewell to anyone. I did not even travel to Tiraspol to say goodbye to my dear sister Ite. I left Bender straight for Bolte with a wagoner to whom I gave the only ruble that I owned. From Bolte until Lubavitch was 150 *mayl* and it took me four weeks to cover the distance.[18] You can imagine what I endured and how much I had to undergo in my travels until I arrived in Lubavitch—and all without bringing along food for the road.

I obtained food for my travels in the following way: Upon arriving in Bolte, I went straight to the *bes-medresh* and confided in a young married man that I was traveling to study in a yeshiva and had no money for the road. I asked him if someone there could raise some funds for my expenses. They soon raised fifty

---

and letters by Chabad Hasidim, including Heilman's *Beit Rabbi* (1902), are replete with the spelling "Libavitsh."

16 Referring to the renowned Lubavitcher Rebbe Rabbi Menakhem-Mendl Schneerson (1789–1866), the third Rebbe of Chabad. He is posthumously referred to as the Tsemakh Tsedek after the title of his published volumes of rabbinical responsa and was generally regarded as one of the leading Torah scholars of his day. He was said to have had 600,000 Hasidim, who were primarily concentrated in Belarus and the Ukraine (Glitsenshtein, 1967). Goldenshteyn was in Lubavitch in August-September 1865, about seven months before the Tsemakh Tsedek's death.

17 A common saying based on *Zohar* 2:162.

18 The Yiddish *mayl* corresponds to the old Russian *milia*, which consisted of seven *versts* and is equivalent to 4.64 US miles. Hence, 150 *mayl* is the equivalent of 696 US miles. Since Lubavitch, via the author's route of Bolte, Kiev, Kozelets, and then Mogilev, is 508 miles north, as the crow flies, the author was probably including his diversion west from Uman to Chechelnik, which is at least 58 miles in each direction via the route described.

kopeks. After prayer services, I sought out a wagon going to Chechelnik and found a Jewish wagoner who would take me for thirty *kopeks* and bought some provisions for another ten *kopeks*, thereby having ten *kopeks* left over. To reach Uman,[19] I did not need to travel by way of Chechelnik, but I believed that I would be able to get some money from my relatives there.[20] But upon my arrival in Chechelnik, I did not find my Aunt Rosye; she had died some time before. Her children were poor, and I barely scraped together one ruble from all of them. Since no wagoners left there for Bershed, I went on foot to Bershed and then continued on to Teplik. From Teplik until Tirifke [*sic*], I walked along the highway, meaning on the thoroughfare going to Uman.[21] Was it actually worthwhile for me to take that detour to my relatives in Chechelnik and to make my life miserable all for one ruble? No, but go be a prophet. From there, the wagoners took me to Uman for a half ruble. In Uman, I found a Chabadnik, a Lubavitcher Hasid, who raised one ruble for my expenses, and I was able to travel to Kiev for a ruble and a half. From Kiev, it was a straight road to Mogilev, the capital of the province, and people traveled that road day and night.[22] In Mogilev, I went straight to the Lubavitcher *bes-medresh*, where I now found Lubavitcher Hasidim, who raised money for my expenses. From Mogilev, I went on foot to Kozelets [*sic*].[23]

On my way to Lubavitch, when a wagon would catch up with me, I would ride on it until it would stop. I would then resume walking on foot until another wagon would catch up with me, and that is how I traveled the entire way. I never waited for a wagon, and I never stopped anywhere, unless I did not have any money in my pocket or *Shobes* was approaching. Though I traveled in such haste, my journey still took me four weeks. If I had not rushed so, it would have taken six to eight weeks.

I believe that you now know how I managed to have food on the way and how my journey went. I barely ate or slept during those four weeks—I did not rest day or night. I was happy when I had a piece of dry bread and a piece of

---

19 The author pronounced Uman as Imen (with a palatalized "n"), as it was pronounced by all speakers of the Southeastern Yiddish dialect (Schaechter, 1986:47–48).
20 To reach Lubavitch, the author needed to travel north through Uman, yet he made a diversion west to Chechelnik with the hope that his relatives there would be able to provide him with some funds for his travel expenses.
21 Tirifke is evidently a typographical error since nineteenth-century maps of the area do not note any similarly named locale along the highway from Teplik to Uman. Perhaps it is referring to Topolefke (Topolivka, Ukraine) at 45°01'N, 34°53'E.
22 Mogilev, Belarus (now Mahileu) is referred to as Molev (with a palatized "l") in the original Yiddish—and as Groys Molev in chapter 21 (Schaechter, 1986:18).
23 The author did not pass Kozelets after Mogilev but rather passed Kozelets on his way from Kiev to Mogilev.

earth or a hard bench to sleep on. The saying of our sages, "This is the way of the Torah: Eat bread with salt, drink water in small measure, sleep on the ground . . ." was fulfilled in me.[24] One could ask, why did the Sages write, "This is the *way* of the Torah"? Why did they use the word *way*? It would have been better to say, "This is how one *studies* Torah," which would mean that whoever wants to study and acquire Torah needs to eat bread with salt and drink water in small measure. So why does it state, "This is the *way* of the Torah"? But I interpret our Sages' intentions as follows: Their words do not apply to those who are studying Torah but rather to those who want to study it by wandering off to a place of Torah, as it states, "Exile yourself to a place of Torah."[25] The way, the route, to a place of Torah has to be as follows: "Eat bread with salt, drink water in small measure, sleep on the ground . . . ," for you will fare no better along the way.[26] Better fare and accommodations are given to merchants conducting their business affairs, not to yeshiva students going to study Torah. Thank God, I survived everything along the way and arrived in Lubavitch safely on foot on *Rosh-Khoydesh Elul*.[27]

I remember that, upon seeing the city from afar, I began to dance for joy. I entered Lubavitch happily, with much praise for God Who had brought me safely to the place of my desire. I immediately rented a room in an inn where I ran into some young married men, Hasidim, whom I knew from Romanovke and Kishinev. I was very glad to have met up with them. They told me that more Hasidim from our region were supposed to be coming for the High Holy Days.

Over *Shobes*, I rested from my travels. On *Shobes*, I saw so many new things and was very pleased to observe the way everything was done at the Rebbe's court. All that I endured had been worth it just so that I could see such a Rebbe with such illustrious sons and such Hasidim, and to watch how they conducted themselves, as I will relate to you in the following account.

Right after *Shobes*, I went to the Rebbe with a *kvitl* as was the custom there.[28] They did not have many *gabbaim* there, only one *gabbai* who also

---

24 Mishna (Avot 6:4).
25 Mishna (Avot 4:14).
26 The Hebrew word *derekh* can denote either a "way" (that is, "manner") or a "route."
27 August 22–23, 1865.
28 A *kvitl* is a petitionary note forwarded to a Hasidic Rebbe with a donation. Chabad Hasidim use the word *tsetl* or *pan* (an acronym of the Hebrew words *pidyen nefesh*, that is, "redemption of one's soul") for such a petitionary note rather than *kvitl*, which the author uses since that was the term that he was accustomed to hearing among other types of Hasidim in the area of his native Tiraspol. Examples of such petitionary notes written by Chabad Hasidim are printed in Mondshine (1980:324–326).

FIGURE 6. A painting of the renowned Lubavitcher Rebbe, Rabbi Menakhem-Mendl Schneerson (1789–1866), the third Rebbe of Chabad. He is posthumously referred to as the Tsemakh Tsedek after the title of his rabbinical responsa. In August–September 1865, the author traveled to Lubavitch where he asked the Rebbe for his advice and blessings.

served as the Rebbe's personal attendant.[29] The *gabbai* did not necessarily write the *kvitlekh*—on the contrary, one had to write the *kvitl* on one's own.[30] Approaching the Rebbe was also simple; it was not noisy and there was no pushing in the line. When I entered, I wrote a *kvitl*, which stated my name and my request: that I wanted to study Torah and that I was a poor orphan from Tiraspol.[31] The Rebbe glanced at my *kvitl* and at me and asked me how long I had been an orphan. I told him briefly that I was five when I lost my mother, my parents had died in their forties, my brother died when he was twenty, a sister died when she was twenty-one, and another sister died when she was in her thirties.[32] When I finished, the Rebbe lifted his head, which he always kept

---

29 *Gabbai* is the singular of *gabbaim* and denotes here a Hasidic Rebbe's administrative assistant. In Tsarist Russia, the personal attendant or assistant to the Lubavitcher Rebbe was called a *meshores*—not a *gabbai* as among other Hasidim (Mondshine, 1986:61).
30 *Kvitlekh* is the plural of *kvitl*.
31 "In the Tsemakh Tsedek's old age, each person did not enter individually for a private audience with the Rebbe as had been customary; rather the Tsemakh Tsedek sat in a large room next to a table and each person, one after the other, would pass before him with a *tsetl* (note) in his hand. The Tsemakh Tsedek used to take the *tsetl* and give a quick response" (Kahan, 1990:2:44).
32 In chapter 1, p. 95, the author writes that his mother died at age thirty-eight. His brother Isruel died at age twenty (ch. 2, p. 105). The author's sister Khone died when she was twenty-one (ch. 3,

bent down because he had a tumor on his neck and also because he was a very elderly man.³³ He then supported his head with his hands and glanced at me through his thick eyebrows and said, "You shouldn't marry until twenty." I then said to the Rebbe that I had already been engaged for a year. He replied, "Well, you heard what I said to you. You should not marry until you are twenty." I then said, "Rebbe, I don't know where to be and I want to study in a yeshiva." He said, "Travel to Shklov. Sit yourself down there and study." Hearing these words, I left the Rebbe for the inn where I was staying and repeated all that had happened to me during my audience with the Rebbe. Everyone was amazed that the Rebbe had told a young man to study Torah and not marry until age twenty and commented, "Of course, he knows that by your doing this you won't die young."³⁴

I was very happy that God had given me the idea to travel to the Rebbe. Now that I heard that I had time until I was twenty to study Torah, things were certainly good. And if the Rebbe told me to travel to Shklov, I would fulfill his words. The next week, I made my way to Shklov. I simply went on foot traveling through Dubrovne, Kopust, and Orshe [sic],³⁵ and I arrived in Shklov in the middle of *Elul*.³⁶

Now I will briefly relate the ways and manners of the Lubavitcher Rebbe and of the Hasidim there.

---

p. 124) and his sister Tsipe died when she was about thirty-four (ch. 14, p. 227, footnote 32).

33 Brook (1987:67) writes that on the night before the Tsemakh Tsedek's death on March 29, 1866, "the doctor in Lubavitch commented that there was absolutely no change (as is known, he had a large wound on his neck)." Perhaps the wound was a result of the tumor having been removed.

34 They were amazed at the Rebbe's advice since according to Jewish law one should marry at the age of eighteen and preferably earlier. See *Shulkhan Arukh* (*Even ha-Ezer* 1:3). Mondshine (1986:61) mistranslated this sentence into Hebrew by writing, "He apparently knows that by your doing this you won't die young." The original states, "*Minastam* he knows that by your doing this you won't die young," which actually means, "Of course, he knows that by your doing this you won't die young."

35 The order should be Orshe and then Kopust.

36 Mid-September 1865.

CHAPTER 16

The Lubavitcher Rebbe and Studying in Shklov, 1865–1866

> At the Rebbe's *Tish* • The Rebbe's Ways and Manners • My Rebbe in Shklov[1] • The Great Enjoyment from Studying Torah • Suddenly Torn Away from Study • My Return to Exile • My Trip with the Polish Hasidim

Under no circumstances were women admitted to the Rebbe, Reb Mendele, of blessed memory.[2] He did not "conduct a *tish*" on *Shobes* or *Yontef*.[3] He would say words of Torah every *Shobes* and *Yontef*, but not at a *tish*, as is customary in Poland.[4] Here, the Rebbe would give a Torah discourse in a large empty hall without any furniture except a *bimah* in its middle, which was surrounded by

---

1   The author is referring to the head of his yeshiva of Shklov.
2   Perlov (1992:117, 119) also mentions that women were not admitted to the Tsemakh Tsedek. In fact, generally none of the Rebbes of Chabad met with women, with the notable exception of the Lubavitcher Rebbe, Rabbi Menachem Mendel Schneerson (1902–1994), of blessed memory. Nonetheless, many Hasidic Rebbes in Eastern Europe did address women directly when they asked for a blessing or advice. Though a few contemporary Rebbes do not address women, like the Gerer Rebbe, Rabbi Ya'akov Arye Alter, most Rebbes do.
3   "Conducting a *tish*" (*tish* denotes a table in Yiddish) is a Hasidic gathering led by the Rebbe on festive occasions usually accompanied by refreshments, drink, song, and words of Torah. Among non-Chabad Hasidim, the Rebbe does not speak at length, while some do not speak at all. In Chabad, these gatherings are called *farbrengens* and the Rebbe usually delivers a lengthy discourse. At this time in the Rebbe's life, there were no *farbrengens*; the Rebbe just gave a discourse.
4   Such formal Hasidic discourses delivered by one of the Lubavitcher Rebbes are generally referred to in Chabad circles as a *maymer* (*ma'amar* in Modern Hebrew). Jews in Tsarist Russia referred to the provinces of Volhynia, Podolia, and Kiev (in contemporary Ukraine) as Poland, and the Hasidic Rebbes who originated in those provinces were referred to as *Poylishe Rebbes* (Polish Rebbes). See ch. 3, p. 111, footnote 13, regarding the word "Poland."

benches.⁵ On *Shobes* and *Yontef*, all the local men and Hasidim who prayed in other *búte-medrúshim* would finish praying quite early in the morning and leave right after services for the hall where the Rebbe would be speaking.⁶ In particular, the visiting Hasidim from all over and those who regularly prayed with the Rebbe in his *bes-medresh* would hurry to the *zal* where the Rebbe would be speaking in order to seize the best spots.⁷

The Rebbe had five sons residing in town who were all great Torah scholars.⁸ Each had his own *bes-medresh*, and Hasidim prayed in each of them. All of those Hasidim also came after services to the Rebbe's *zal*. His illustrious sons, their own sons, and his sons-in-law also came and their places were on the benches around the *bimah*, while the entire crowd stood.

Even before the Rebbe entered, the *zal* was packed. So when the Rebbe came in, a pathway through the crowd was barely cleared for him to walk to the *bimah*. The Rebbe walked onto the *bimah* and was followed by the *khoyzer*.⁹ Sometimes the Rebbe would speak words of Torah for an hour or two.¹⁰ When the Rebbe finished speaking, they again would make a pathway for him so that he could leave, and then the Rebbe would depart. After him, all of his illustrious sons would leave, but a large crowd still remained to hear the Torah discourse once again from the *khoyzer* who had committed it to memory as it was being delivered. Not all remained to listen to the *khoyzer*. Many would leave right after the Rebbe finished. Often the local men would

---

5   *Bimah* here denotes the elevated platform traditionally in the center of a synagogue from which the Torah is read aloud.

6   "Local men" refers to the Hasidim who lived and had business in Lubavitch, while "Hasidim" refers those who had come to Lubavitch from out of town to be with the Rebbe. *Butemedrushim* is the plural of *bes-medresh*.

7   *Zal* literally means a "hall" in Yiddish and is used by Lubavitchers to refer to a Torah study hall (*bes-medresh*). Until today, Lubavitchers are the only Jews who refer to their yeshiva's study hall as a *zal*. The Tsemakh Tsedek would deliver a Hasidic discourse on *Shabes* sometimes before the morning services, at other times after the morning services, and still at other times after *Minkhe* (Bloy, 2020:41).

8   The Tsemakh Tsedek had a sixth son, Rabbi Yosef-Yitskhok Schneerson (ca. 1819–1875), who lived in the Ukraine and was the only one of his sons to become a Hasidic Rebbe during his lifetime. The Tsemakh Tsedek also had a seventh son, Yankev, who had died in 1848 in his early thirties (Oberlander & Shmotkin, 2021:564).

9   Among Lubavitcher Hasidim, the *khoyzer* was the Hasid who would memorize the Rebbe's discourses said on *Shabes* or *Yontef*, when Jews are not permitted to write. The *khoyzer* would usually repeat the discourse to the Hasidim for review and, after *Shabes* or *Yontef*, for transcription.

10 The author was in Lubavitch for the *Shabosim* of the Torah portions of *Shoyftim* (August 26, 1865) and *Ki Seytse* (September 2, 1865). Only the Rebbe's Hasidic discourse from *Shoyftim* survives, namely a discourse on the verse "I am my beloved's, and my beloved is mine" (Song of Songs 6:3), which is printed in *Or ha-Torah: Dvarim* (1994:2:721–725).

leave but the Hasidim would stay to hear the *khoyzer*'s repetition of the Torah discourse just given. After eating, each Hasid would go to one of the sons—Reb Yisroel-Noyakh,[11] Reb Leyb,[12] Reb Zalmen,[13] Reb Borukh-Sholem,[14] or Reb Shmulke[15]—and would then hear the Torah discourse repeated again by him. Like this, each Hasid could hear a repetition of the Torah discourse a number of times.

Each of the sons would say words of Torah, not only on *Shobes*, but whenever Hasidim would gather together and ask them to do so. The last time that the Rebbe's Torah discourse would be repeated that week was always at Reb Leyb's, after *Kabules Shobes* but before praying *Marev*.[16] Of course, the Hasidim were reviewing the Torah discourse the entire week from *Shobes* to *Shobes* until they knew it by heart. I was very pleased with this.

I also saw there that it was the custom to give arriving Hasidim who needed support and sustenance twenty-five *kopeks* for *Shobes* and seventy-five *kopeks* for the week (not including *Shobes*), with some being given one silver ruble for lodging and food. For example, I was given seventy-five *kopeks*—this did not include my *Shobes* expenses—which enabled me to afford lodgings, *krupnik*,[17] and bread every day. On *Shobes*, I ate at the home of Reb Zalman. Similarly, a different Hasid ate at the table of each son as a guest. The Rebbe would eat completely alone the entire week in the same small room in which he studied Torah, prayed, and received the Hasidim with their *kvitlekh*.

I found this out in the following way: I hid myself in the *bes-medresh*. After prayer services, the *shomes* did not see me hiding and locked up the

---

11 Shmuel-Noyakh is mistakenly printed in the original instead of Yisroel-Noyakh. Several years after his father's death, Rabbi Yisroel-Noyakh Schneerson (ca. 1816–1883) settled in Nyezhin (Nizhyn), Ukraine, where he became the Hasidic Rebbe (Bloy, 2020:159–185).

12 After his father's death in 1866, Rabbi Yehude-Leyb Schneerson (ca. 1809–1866) settled in Kopust, Belarus, where he became the Hasidic Rebbe. Most of his late father's Hasidim became his Hasidim. He died about seven months after his father and was succeeded by his son (Bloy, 2020:73–124).

13 After his father's death, Rabbi Khaym-Shneur-Zalman Schneerson (ca. 1814–1879) settled in nearby Lyadi where he became the Hasidic Rebbe (Bloy, 2020:125–158).

14 The author mentions Rabbi Borukh-Sholem Schneerson (ca. 1804–1869) more at length in chapter 17, pp. 271–273, when he met him in Iassy, Romania, in December 1866.

15 The author describes his visit to Rabbi Shmuel Schneerson (1834–1882), his father's successor as the Lubavitcher Rebbe, in chapter 21, pp. 376–380.

16 Pronounced *Kabalat Shabat* in Modern Hebrew, it literally means "Receiving the Sabbath" and refers to the part of the Friday evening service which precedes the regular evening prayer (*Marev*) and welcomes the Sabbath.

17 *Krupnik* was a soup made of potatoes and grains such as barley.

bes-medresh.[18] I wanted to see what the Rebbe was doing while alone in his room. At eleven a.m., I peeked in through the keyhole of the door. Since the Rebbe's table was facing me, I was able to see that he was still sitting and praying in his *talis* and *tefillin*.[19] From the Rebbe's room there was a door leading to the *bes-medresh* and another door leading to other rooms. After waiting a long time, I suddenly heard the Rebbe bang on the table. I again peeked through the keyhole and saw the *gabbai* come in, wrap up the Rebbe's *tefillin*, and lead the Rebbe away. I then heard water being poured, so I understood that the Rebbe was washing his hands. The *gabbai* then led the Rebbe to the table and left. The Rebbe began to write Hasidic discourses and continued writing for perhaps an hour. The Rebbe then again banged on the table, and the *gabbai* entered, folded the Rebbe's *talis*, and left. The Rebbe then sat down to study. About an hour later he finished studying and banged on the table once again. The *gabbai* entered, set the table, and passed him some water to wash his hands.[20] The Rebbe washed his hands and then said *Ha'moytse*.[21] The *gabbai* then brought him some soup along with either some meat or poultry. He ate a bit of each, and the *gabbai* took the leftovers away. Then the *gabbai* brought *mayim akhroynim* to the Rebbe,[22] and the Rebbe recited the blessings after a meal and resumed studying. The simplicity with which the Rebbe, the *tsadik* of the generation, conducted himself cannot be found in Poland.[23]

In that room where the Rebbe resided were two walls completely covered with holy Jewish books.[24] Along the third wall stood a little bed and a large chest, and along the fourth wall stood an armchair on which the Rebbe sat. Near the armchair were a makeshift table and two stools. You would not find such a

---

18   *Shomes* here refers to the sexton of the synagogue.
19   For an overview of accounts of Jews stealthfully observing their rabbis from the Talmudic era until the present, see the Introduction, pp. 35–38.
20   Before eating bread, Jews are required by Jewish law to wash their hands with water poured from a vessel (*Kitsur Shulkhan Arukh* 42:1–10).
21   *Ha-Motsi* in Modern Hebrew. This refers to the Hebrew blessing recited before eating bread (*Kitsur Shulkhan Arukh* 41:1–10).
22   *Mayim akhroynim* literally means "last waters" in Hebrew and refers to the washing of one's fingertips right before reciting the blessings after completing a meal eaten with bread (*Kitsur Shulkhan Arukh* 44:1–2).
23   *Tsadik* is the singular form of *tsadikim*. Among the Hasidic Rebbes with whom the author was familiar, even such mundane matters were conducted with much fanfare. For an example, see the author's account of his bringing an *esreg* to the Lyever Rebbe in ch. 17, pp. 279–289.
24   Levine (1993:42) notes that the accumulation of a large library of printed books in the Schneerson family chiefly began during the lifetime of the Tsemakh Tsedek. He mentions three sources that provide a physical description of that library, including this line from the author.

magnificently simple study in Poland either! "Fortunate is the eye that saw all of this."[25]

The Rebbe himself dressed in white. Even the crown of his *shtrayml* was made of white velvet or satin, and he looked like an angel of God.[26] Day and night he sat and studied Torah and prayed. He would only let Hasidim in to ask him for blessings or advice for two hours a day. Whatever money the Rebbe had received as *pidyoynes* was given away as charity to the poor Hasidim who came to study Torah and hear Torah from the Rebbe.[27] In other words, the Hasidim who lived close to Lubavitch and came just for a *Shobes* were given money only for their *Shobes* expenses, while the Hasidim who lived far away and came to spend weeks or months at the Rebbe's court would be given a weekly stipend.[28] If one of these out-of-town Hasidim was found not to be studying, they stopped giving him a stipend, which naturally resulted in his leaving. All of these Hasidim stayed in inns and not with the Rebbe. Hasidim would only gather together at the Rebbe's court or his sons' homes to hear or study Torah.

In short, the main aspects of Lubavitcher Hasidism was Torah study and prayer. Whoever did not know any Torah was not a Lubavitcher Hasid, which is exactly the opposite of the Polish Hasidim from whom no Torah is demanded. They do not need to be skilled in Torah study as long as they are dressed as Hasidim, travel to their Rebbe, recount and believe in miracles performed by their Rebbe and attribute every bit of wisdom to their Rebbe—such a person is considered a Hasid.[29] Even an uneducated woman can achieve the status of a Polish Hasid because one does not need to study Torah to do so—only

---

25 A verse from the *Musaf* service of the Yom Kippur liturgy describing the service of the *Kohen Gadol* (high priest) in the Holy Temple.
26 The Rebbe, the Tsemakh Tsedek, wore all-white garments on *Shabes* and Jewish holidays, which is how he is depicted in the well-known portrait of him (Rabbi M. M. Schneerson, 2006:248, 384). Only his sons Reb Yisroel-Noyakh and Reb Shmuel are documented as having worn white upon becoming Rebbes (Felshin, 1974:9; Rabbi M. M. Schneerson, 2006:167). The word used in the original for the crown of the *shtrayml* is *verekh*; Hasidim today, at least for those in the know, refer to the crown of a *shtrayml* as the *vyerekh*.
27 *Pidyoynes* (literally "redemptions" in Hebrew) is used by non-Lubavitcher Hasidim to refer to monetary donations given to a Hasidic Rebbe to redeem one's soul, which is accompanied by a petitionary note, known as a *kvitl*. Lubavitcher Hasidim use the word *pidyoynes* (or *tsetl* or *pan*, being an acronym for *pidyen nefesh*) to refer to the petitionary notes while they refer to the accompanying money as *moes pan* or *dmei pan*, both meaning "petition money" in Hebrew (Mondshine, 1986:62).
28 The original Yiddish refers to this weekly money as *vokhngelt*. In *Jewish Money*, Rivkind (1959:84) cites the author in his entry for this term.
29 There is some truth to this, though the author grossly exaggerates to emphasize his point. For some differences between Chabad Hasidism and other types of Hasidism, see Mondshine (1980:380–381).

to have complete faith. Now you have some sort of an idea of the holiness of the Lubavitcher Rebbe and the high quality of the Lubavitcher Hasidim, the Chabadniks.

Now we will return to our narrative. I arrived in Shklov in the middle of *Elul*, for I had spent two weeks at the Rebbe's court in Lubavitch.[30] Upon arriving in Shklov, I entered a Hasidic *bes-medresh*. There was also a yeshiva there in that *bes-medresh*, where they went to great lengths to make me feel welcome.[31] But the yeshiva was for students younger than me, so I switched to Reb Hillel's *bes-medresh*, which was a very fine yeshiva for older students, though they were *misnagdim*.[32] I had no choice because all of the *bute-medrushim* and yeshivas in Shklov were misnagdic, apart from that one Hasidic *bes-medresh*, which was not the right place for me to study since it was for younger students.[33] So I studied Torah in that misnagdic yeshiva for about three months, until I found out that at the *Poyeley Tsedek bes-medresh*,[34] not far from the large *shul*, there was a good rebbe[35] who was also the *magid* there.[36] Unfortunately, I have forgotten his name.[37] That *magid*

---

30 The middle of *Elul* was in mid-September 1865.
31 A *bes-medresh* is a study hall where people come to sit and study whenever they have the time, while a yeshiva offers an organized study program for boys or unmarried young men.
32 *Misnagdim* refers to non-Hasidic Eastern-European Orthodox Jews. Upon the emergence of the Hasidic movement in the mid-1700s, there was much opposition by the traditional Jewish community, i.e., *Misnagdim*. By the time of this episode, the intense antagonism between the two groups had subsided but they remained two distinct groups (Wilensky, 1970:15–16). In general, Hasidim stress joy in the study of Torah study and the performance of *mitzvahs* and enthusiasm in prayer, whereas *misnagdim* almost exclusively emphasize diligence in the study of the Talmud.
33 Luria (2009:186) mentions Goldenshteyn as support for his supposition that Chabad Hasidim did not specifically study at Hasidic educational institutions until the end of the nineteenth century. He refers to Goldenshteyn, whom the Lubavitcher Rebbe himself sent to study in Shklov, where the only yeshiva for those his age was a *misnagdic* one.
34 *Poyeley Tsedek* (*Poale Tsedek* in Modern Hebrew) means "righteous workers" in Hebrew. A *bes-medresh* or synagogue bearing this name indicated that it was attended by artisans (Marmor, 1959:186).
35 The term "rebbe" is referring here to the head of the yeshiva.
36 A *magid* is a preacher who speaks about moral and religious issues, often including much social criticism. Most *magidim* were itinerant, but large communities in non-Hasidic Lithuania and Belarus in the nineteenth and early twentieth centuries employed salaried *magidim* who preached every *Shabes*, while the rabbi only spoke twice a year—the *Shabes* before Yom Kippur and the *Shabes* before Pesach (Chitrik, 1985:344–345). When the author writes that the head of the yeshiva was a *"magid* there," it is not clear whether he was the *magid* of the entire town of Shklov or just of the *Poalei Tsedek bes-medresh*. See the next footnote.
37 Among those listed in the Hebrew-language Jewish communal death register of Shklov is a "Reb Ayzik, *m.m.* [that is, *magid meyshorim*]" who died in 1869 (Berman 1936:150). This entry might be referring to the author's rebbe, to whom he also refers in the original as a

and head of the yeshiva could explain the intricacies of the Talmud exceptionally well, and he devotedly taught his students the Talmud and Jewish legal codes. So I went to him and asked him to accept me into the yeshiva as one of his students. He immediately accepted me and grew to love me so much that apart from his teaching me in the *bes-medresh* during the regular study session with all of the students, I used to leave the *bes-medresh* at night and go to his home, where he would study privately with me until around twelve at night. He was so devoted to me—as if I was paying him a hefty tuition to teach me. He did all of this because he was virtuous and pious in his desire to disseminate Torah knowledge to the public. He liked me very much because he saw that I studied with great diligence. He had intended to turn me into a renowned Torah scholar, but his intentions for me were short-lived because I was quite unexpectedly torn away from his bosom and had to go into exile again.

But first I want to tell you how good it was for me in Shklov until my new troubles came along and mercilessly drove me from there and ripped me from the nest of Torah. I have lamented my entire life that I left such a place of Torah so quickly. I studied for a total of three months in Shklov, where I could have spent three years and have actually become a renowned scholar as my Rebbe had counted on.[38]

There in the yeshivas, the practice of *esn teg* was customary among young yeshiva students meaning that every family would take pains to have a young yeshiva student over to eat lunch one day a week.[39] Middle-class and wealthy families would have several yeshiva students over, with each one eating on a different day. The poorest, even the water carrier and the woodchopper, would also have a yeshiva student eat at his home once a week. If you had seen with what type of honor the poor man took a yeshiva student, you would say, "And who is like Your people, like the people of Israel?"[40] These poor people, who barely made it through the week on dry bread, managed to save food from their own portion to feed a young student for a day, making sure that on that day a piece of meat was cooked for lunch. They would also give the yeshiva student a few *kopeks* so that he would be able to buy something for breakfast and dinner. Everything was done with such honor and joy so that the yeshiva student marveled at how nicely he was welcomed by the poor man and particularly by the middle class, not to

---

"*magid meyshorim*," meaning a *magid*. Though the last line of the previous page of the list refers to an earlier *magid* of the *Poalei Tsedek bes-medresh* who died in 1826, no name of a synagogue or *bes-medresh* is mentioned regarding Reb Ayzik.

38 "Rebbe" here refers to the head of the author's yeshiva in Shklov.
39 *Esn teg* literally means "eating days."
40 Samuel II 7:23.

mention that the wealthy always honorably welcomed him with the best of foods, which was no wonder. But it was amazing to see how precious the *mitzvah* of strengthening Torah study and supporting Torah scholars was to the poor.

Now you can understand how good I had it there. When they found out that I was from Romania, from Iassy (for my passport was issued in Iassy), that I had cast myself so far just to study Torah, and that I sat and studied with such diligence, they all quarreled over me. Everyone wanted me to eat one meal a week at his house, and the person who hosted me considered it to be the greatest of honors. At the beginning, I ate all seven days of the week in the homes of poor people, but later, when people found out about me, the tremendously wealthy Reb Shloyme Moneszon took me to eat at his home. I ate at his and his children's homes the entire week, apart from one day a week, when I had to eat at the home of a certain poor person whom I could not abandon for two reasons. Firstly, I lacked absolutely nothing on the day I would eat at his home, even though he was poor. And secondly, he and his wife would have been greatly pained had I stopped going there.

I certainly lacked nothing when eating at the wealthy Moneszons. Similarly, his sons Reb Shmuel, Reb Monis, and Reb Bere, all treated me as if I were their own child.[41] The elderly Reb Shloyme Moneszon himself showed me the greatest affection. One could say regarding him that there was "Torah and wealth in one place."[42] On *Shobes*, after leaving *shul*, all of his sons, daughters-in-law, daughters, and grandchildren would go to the elderly couple's home for *Kiddush*, and I would also be among them. For *Shaleshides*, there was always a *minyan* of Jews at his home to sing *zmires* and to spend time there until late at night. I was the singer at the table.

Reb Shloyme and all of his children were Lubavitcher Hasidim. They also knew that the Rebbe had told me to study in Shklov until the age of twenty, for one of his sons had also been in Lubavitch at the Rebbe's court when I was there and had heard about it. So you can imagine how great was the affection that these Hasidim had toward me and how well-regarded I was by them, though I studied at the misnagdic yeshiva. Among the *misnagdim*, I was also well-regarded, since I sat and studied and wanted to learn.

I now began to come to life after the tremendous amount of hardship that I had until now. When I saw the bright shining sun beginning to shine for me,

---

41 Menakhem-Monish "Monye" Moneszon of Shklov was married to Rokhl, the granddaughter of the Lubavitcher Rebbe, the Tsemakh Tsedek, whom the author had just visited. She was the daughter of the Rebbe's son, Rabbi Yehude-Leyb Schneerson (mentioned earlier in this chapter on p. 249), later known as the Kopuster Rebbe (Heilperin, 1980:172).

42 Talmud (Gitin 59a).

I thought that it would shine for a very long time. But ultimately, the brightly shining sun, which I had just begun to enjoy, suddenly became clouded over with black, dark clouds so that none of its light could be seen any more. Only darkness and more darkness surrounded me, so that I thought my entire world was going under, as you will find out later.

After three months, I was supposed to exchange my Romanian passport for a Russian passport issued by the Governor General of the province. Once someone received his provincial passport, which was valid for one year, he only needed to exchange it every year and would be able to live many years on exchanged passports. I did as required by law, and, in order not to miss the deadline, as soon as my original Romanian passport became invalid, I sent it by means of the police to the Governor General of the province of Mogilev to be exchanged for a provincial passport. Through this I caused my own misfortune and created new troubles for myself, for who would have known that the Governor General would not want to exchange my passport and would actually tell me to return to Romania. If I had known that, I would have remained in Shklov without exchanging my passport because who would have done anything to me? And what type of punishment would I have received for remaining in Shklov for three years? At the most, I would have had to pay ten rubles. But go be a prophet and know that the Governor General of the province of Mogilev had never exchanged a foreign passport. A month later, he sent my passport to the police who let me know that the Governor General did not want to exchange it and that I must return home.

I became distraught and immediately traveled to the Governor General himself. I cried and pleaded, communicating through his translator. He answered me that it was already hopeless. Since he had not wanted to exchange my passport, he had already sent my passport to Kishinev, meaning to the Romanian border, with the comment that they should give me a permit allowing me to travel home to Romania. The Governor General gave me a permit allowing me to travel to Kishinev and did me a favor by lengthening by two months the amount of time I had before I was required to leave the country.[43] But he threatened that, should I stay longer, he would have me sent to Kishinev in chains. My crying and pleading were useless, and I returned to Shklov with the permit.

---

43 The author writes later in this chapter on p. 259 that on the day after Pesach (April 8, 1866), he had six days to reach Kishinev, meaning that he needed to be in Kishinev by April 14, 1866 (29th of *Nisan*). Since the entire journey to the border lasted two months, he left Shklov on approximately February 14, 1866.

I soon became dejected, and everyone sympathized with me in my plight. My rebbe, the *magid*, was very agitated over my situation and gave me a letter of recommendation to help me on my way. He was not able to help me financially as he was poor. The wealthy Reb Shloyme and his family also had great compassion for me but were unable to help me. In short, I still celebrated *Purim* in Shklov, and, right afterward, bade farewell to all of my dearly loved friends who had been so friendly to me.[44] At Reb Shloyme's, I received fifteen rubles for my expenditures. I thanked them very much and went on my way back home.

I first needed to travel to Mogilev. It was a total of three *mayl* to Mogilev, and I barely arrived there alive.[45] So how would I be able to travel such a long distance all the way to Kishinev in that extremely cold weather? How would I be able to travel in the winter dressed as scantily as I was? The wagon driver who was traveling from Mogilev to Homlye did not want to take me along because he was afraid that I would arrive frozen. So I decided that I had to buy some clothes with the twelve rubles I had left and would somehow manage to raise money along the way for my expenses. I planned to go a little of the way on foot and periodically catch a ride, as long as I would have some clothes and not be so scantily clad in such horribly cold weather. For six rubles, I bought a long fur coat of white lambskin covered with black material; for two rubles, a pair of large boots with leggings; and for one ruble, a warm hat. I then gave the 2.70 rubles that I still had left to the driver as wagon fare and traveled to Homlye.

On my way back, having lost all hope and feeling discouraged, I considered everything that I had undergone until I had been able to reach a place of Torah and how I ultimately had to leave so quickly. In addition, where would I find the renewed strength to endure the long, difficult, terrible road during the winter without any money? But I would constantly advise myself (because by nature I tend to take things in stride), "Such is the will of God, so it has to be good. And so it will be good. Don't worry. You don't need to have any heartache over this." And no matter how bad I was feeling then, I would calm down right away. Since I was seated next to the driver and not walking in the snow, I was happy and began to sing. When the driver heard my singing, he also showed his talent in singing, and we became very cheerful. The passengers became quite delighted and came to like me so much that they bought me some tea and a bit to eat at every stop.

---

44 Purim was on March 1, 1866.
45 Three *mayl* is the equivalent of 13.9 US miles, yet it is actually 20.4 US miles from Shklov to Mogilev.

Four days later, I arrived in Homlye, where I spent *Shobes*. Sunday morning, right after praying, I received a ruble for travel expenses.[46] I left town on foot, and a wagoner caught up with me on the way. I rode with him as far as my money would take me. And that is how I continued on. Whenever I was lacking money, I had to remain in a *shteytl* or a city until I was able to raise some money for my travel expenses. This is how I struggled on the road by day and by night.

I arrived in Kiev before the *Shobes* of *Parshes ha'Khoydesh*.[47] I spent *Shobes* in Kiev and left on foot on Sunday morning because it was not possible to ride on a wagon due to the great amount of mud on the road. Those traveling by wagon took longer to reach their destinations than those on foot. In short, you can now understand that from Kiev onward, I encountered a road where my suffering really began. On the way to Kiev, there had been two favorable factors that had eased my troubles: the roads had been frozen dry so there was no mud, or the roads were paved. This enabled me to be able to continue traveling, and when it would happen that I had no ride I was able to travel on foot. But from Kiev onwards the roads were not paved and no longer frozen. Instead, they were filled with mud and rivers of water. In addition, it rained nonstop. I left Kiev at a bad time and on poor roads. Under such poor conditions, I continued constantly for thirteen days without stopping or resting. At dusk on the eve of Pesach, I arrived in Uman.[48] I will not bother trying to convey to you the hardship and unnatural suffering that I withstood those thirteen days, though you can well imagine what it was like. But I will relate the miracle that happened to me while entering *Shvarts-Time*, which is called Bela Tserkov.[49] In fact, I had to *bentsh goyml* right afterward.[50]

When I was ten *versts* from *Shvarts-Time*, I came to a tavern owned by a Jew. Since it was already evening, an hour before nightfall, I decided to spend the night there. But somehow that tavern did not please me. Since it was still ten

---

46 As described in his account of his journey to Lubavitch (ch. 15, pp. 242–243), the author stopped in towns along the way and would ask the *gabbai* of the local synagogue to raise funds to cover his travel expenses for him after services.
47 That *Shabes* was March 16, 1866. *Parshes ha'Khoydesh* (Exodus 12:1–20) is the last of the four additional Torah readings connected with the Hebrew months of *Adar* and *Nisan*. It deals with the commandment to maintain a calendar and the commandments associated with Pesach.
48 March 30, 1866.
49 *Shvarts-time* (*shvartse-tume* in Northeastern Yiddish) literally means "black impurity" and refers to Belaya Tserkov, meaning "white church" in Russian. Under the tsars, Jews were often contemptuous of the church because its priests were frequently the instigators of violent antisemitism among the populace.
50 To *bentsh goyml* denotes making the blessing of deliverance from danger (*Kitsur Shulkhan Arukh* 61:1–2).

versts to the city, I figured I could walk the ten *versts* before nightfall. Even if I could not walk the entire ten, I could certainly walk at least eight and could then walk the remaining two at night. I began to walk and tried to move as quickly as possible so that I would not need to walk even the last two *versts* at night. But the road was so difficult that nightfall came by the sixth *verst*, though I had been walking quickly with all my strength. It became extremely dark. Simply put, "the darkness was palpable."[51] When I looked around me and saw how dark it was, I became frightened. All I heard was the plodding of the wagons in the mud. They had become stuck and remained trapped, and the riders were yelling, "*Oy-vey*."

You will certainly ask how I was able to see where to walk in such darkness. I will explain it to you. That road was a postal route, a dirt road. As is known, in Russia the postal routes have canals dug on either side. The pedestrians walk in the ditches. At that time the canals still contained water and bits of snow, which glimmered at night. Since I had been walking on the footpath in the ditch while it was still daylight, I continued walking there and was still able to see the glimmer of the footpath in front of me even though it was already dark. I followed the glimmer like this until I noticed the city lights in the distance and heard the barking of the dogs. I became happier and began to walk faster thinking that very soon I would be in the city and would go somewhere to rest a little.

But suddenly, the footpath disappeared from before me, and I no longer saw its glimmer. I stopped where I was and did not move, though I had not the slightest idea that I was saving my life in doing so. At the time I did not imagine the grave danger I was in. Had I taken, God forbid, just one more step, I would have been done for, God forbid. So I must say that I was stopped from on high by means of a miracle. Having stopped, I carefully used my walking stick to tap in front of me, which convinced me that I could not take another step forward. I tried moving the stick down to the right and to the left but found no ground there either. I was now certain that there was no ground around me. So I tried tapping behind me and realized that, yes, I could walk backward. How pained I was to see the city and not be able to approach it. Finally, I was able to walk back along the ditch. I walked and constantly tapped the path with my stick. In short, I walked back about two *versts*, and only then was I able to leave the ditch and walk on the road.

I walked until I emerged on a straight road leading over a bridge. By then I could see the houses at the edge of town. With my last bit of strength, I dragged myself to the first house of the city. Standing near the window, I listened to the language they were speaking, heard that they were speaking Yiddish and

---

51 Exodus 10:21, a description of the plague of darkness brought upon the Egyptians.

knocked. With fright they asked me, "Who's there?" and they came out to look me over. I asked them to let me sleep there and told them that the night had crept up on me while I was on the road, and I had barely arrived there alive. In short, they took me in, and I spent the night there. I told them what had happened to me. "*Oy*," they said, "this boy is lucky. He could've been killed. If he had taken one more step, he would have fallen off the mountain and his bones would have been scattered about like dust." When I arose early the next morning, it was only then that I saw where I had been and how it would have truly been like falling into an oil press with my remains being strewn about. More than one person had been killed at that spot. I saw the wonder that God had done for me, and I thanked Him.

I immediately went into town, where I spent *Shobes ha'Gudl*.[52] There, I went to the *bes-medresh*, where I *bentsht goyml*[53] for the miracle that happened to me. On Sunday, I left there and arrived in Uman on the eve of Pesach.[54] Upon my arrival, I immediately went to the Tolner *kloyz* where an exemplary Jew by the name of Rapaport invited me to spend Pesach with him. Though he was not a Hasid, he prayed in the Tolner *kloyz* since he lived nearby. I had a very fine Pesach with him. I ate, slept, and rested up during the eight days of Pesach. Right after Pesach, meaning on the following day, I set out on the road again to continue my journey.[55] I left my lambskin coat in the Tolner *kloyz* as a memento . . . I set out in the evening of that day and found out that I could spend the night with a pious Jew who lived at a watermill, four *versts* from the city. By nightfall, I arrived at that Jewish miller's and spent the night there. He welcomed me warmly and wanted me to remain there as a *melomed* for his children. I told him that I had to be in Kishinev in six days because the two months that the Governor General had given me were coming to an end.

First thing in the morning, I finished my prayers and set out for Bolte. I had to walk up a mountain and the incline stretched on for two *versts*. Upon reaching the top of the mountain, I noticed that in the valley from where I had come was a wagon speeding along and it was beginning to go up the mountain. I prayed to God that they would be Jews and that they would take me with them. Meanwhile, I sat down to rest until it came along. When it came a bit closer to me, I saw that it was a good britzka pulled by three horses and that

---

52 March 24, 1866. Pronounced *Shabat ha-Gadol* in Modern Hebrew. It is the *Shabes* before Pesach.
53 Past tense of *bentsh goyml*.
54 March 30, 1866.
55 The author set out on the road on Sunday, April 8, 1866.

it was carrying three Jewish men, a woman, and a driver who was also Jewish.[56] When the carriage was close by, I walked over to it and asked them to take me. I immediately recognized them as Hasidim from Tiraspol who were traveling back from seeing their Rebbe in Tolne. They also recognized me immediately and they all gave a shout, "Pinye-Berl! Is that you? How did you get here?" I then asked, "Firstly, I would like to know if you're going to take me with you or if you are going to leave me here." They replied, "What are you talking about? How can we leave you here? Even though we don't have any room, that's no excuse. Jump up, seat yourself wherever you can, and tell us how you got here."

I briefly recounted all that had occurred to me. They were amazed but then said, "You deserve it, you *Litvak*.[57] You're a Tiraspoler and have a Rebbe close to you in Tolne, but the devil carried you off to Lubavitch. You deserve it, you *Litvak* . . ." They laughed and made fun of me like this, but I did not reply to them because I was afraid that they would kick me off the wagon. They were extremely upset that I was a Lubavitcher Hasid, a Chabadnik, and not a Tolner Hasid, and that I would not drink liquor with them.[58] They intentionally began to relate miracles performed by their Rebbe, which impressed me so much that I dozed off. They noticed this, and one of them gave me a shake and said to me, "At least listen a bit to what is going on at the Rebbe's court, you *Litvak*!" I answered them, "I am keeping myself from listening because I know everything that goes on with the Polish *Gite-Yidn*."[59] That upset them, and they said to me, "Your luck is that you're from our city. If not, we would have thrown you out of the wagon, but we won't because of the respect we have for your sister Ite, though we can't stand you, you *Litvak*."[60] I replied, "If you continue to bother me, I'll get off your wagon myself as I would rather go on foot than listen to you." Then, the woman who was sitting there quietly the entire time said to her husband, "Yosele, do me a favor and bring an end to this talk." To the other two

---

56 A britzka (*britshke* in Yiddish) is generally a type of large four-wheeled carriage pulled by two horses, with a folding top over the rear seat and a rear-facing front seat.

57 A *Litvak* denotes a Jew speaking the Northeastern dialect of Yiddish, which was spoken in Lithuanian, Belarus, northeastern Poland, northern Ukraine, Latvia, and Estonia; this designation was particularly true until the First World War. Outside of these areas, the word *Litvaks* was often used pejoratively since non-Hasidic *Litvaks* were not considered to be particularly pious. Spector (1927:128–130) describes some severe and outlandish biases against *Litvaks* in his native Uman, Ukraine. Since the author had traveled to his Rebbe in Lubavitch where the Northeastern (Lithuanian) Yiddish dialect was spoken, he was called a *Litvak*.

58 The author's refusal to consume alcohol was clearly his own personal decision and unconnected to his being a Lubavitcher Hasid.

59 The author is referring to Hasidic Rebbes such as the Tolner Rebbe. Tolne was in the Podolia Province, which was also referred to as Poland in Yiddish (see ch. 3, p. 111, footnote 13).

60 As the author soon clarifies, one of them was his sister Ite's brother-in-law.

Jews, she said, "Leave him be. Why does it matter to you that he's a Lubavitcher Hasid. You won't change him, and he won't change you." Afterward, they did not pester me regarding my type of Hasidism, and I continued traveling with them until Bolte. Upon arriving in Bolte, the woman and her husband Yosele gave me two silver rubles for my expenses until I reached Tiraspol. From there, they traveled by themselves, leaving me in Bolte.

Now I will talk a little bit about those fervent Hasidim who brought me to Bolte. That Yosele was a wealthy Tiraspoler Hasid and a Torah scholar who held the lease to an estate. In town, they called him Yosele-Burekhls or Yosele-Spivakovs.[61] That Yosele had been one of my brother-in-law Shloyme-Leyzer's students. Yosele had studied under him when Shloyme-Leyzer had first arrived in Tiraspol and married my sister Tsipe. At that time, Yosele was already engaged, but not to the woman who was traveling with him now (she was his second wife and he did not have any children with her either). They had been traveling in their own britzka to Tolne to the Rebbe for Pesach because he was a devoted Hasid. He used to travel every *Yontef* to the Rebbe, and the Rebbe kept promising him children. Even though he began to take his wife along with him to the Rebbe, the Rebbe's blessing was never fulfilled.

The other two Hasidim on the britzka were simple and slovenly Hasidic *le'khaim*-sayers. They had also celebrated Pesach in Tolne, where they ran into the goodhearted Yosele and sat themselves on his britzka and naturally ate and drank at his expense. This very much pleased Yosele and his wife for they lavished their entire wealth on the Rebbe and the Hasidim. These two Hasidim were Ershl-Shie and Refuel-Mantses, who was married to the daughter of Reb Simkhe.[62] Refuel had become registered as Reb Simkhe's son so that he could

---

61 The Hebrew newspaper *Ha-Magid* (Lyck, East Prussia, October 23, 1857:4) mentions a "Burekh Spimakov, the merchant and dealer" of Tiraspol. Since this surname is not mentioned in Beider's *Dictionary of Jewish Surnames from the Russian Empire* (2008) and cannot be found in any other databases or sources regarding Ukrainian Jewry, it is likely a typographical error and should actually be Spivakov; the Yiddish representations of "m" (מ) and "v" (וו) often appear similar when handwritten. This Yosele was probably called both Yosele-Burekhls and Yosele-Spivakovs because he was either the son or son-in-law of this Burekh Spivakov. As mentioned in ch. 7, p. 163, footnote 18, regarding Itsye Erlikhman, businessmen and the wealthy were not yet referred to by their surnames in 1860; perhaps they were called by their surnames by the time this incident took place in 1866.

62 Referring to Simkhe Teplitsky, who was the father of Ershele (ca. 1835–1854), the first husband of the author's sister, Ite. Simkhe's daughter Sime was married to Refuel, whose surname was Kishinevsky, as noted in the Budiansky genealogical chart mentioned in ch. 2, p. 99, footnote 8. Refuel-Mantses denotes that Refuel was the son or close relative of a woman named Mants(y)e. The 1858 additional revision list (poll-tax census) of the Jews of Tiraspol indicates that Refuel Kishinevsky was the son of Ber (ca. 1821–1854) and Mashke; perhaps his mother had two names, most likely, Mashke-Mantse. (Note that the additional revision

take away the inheritance of my orphaned niece Ester-Khaye, the daughter of Ershele (Reb Simkhe's only son), whom you already know from part I.[63] This Ershl-Shie would have thought nothing of giving me a beating and then throwing me out of the wagon in the middle of road, but, thank God, I escaped his hands unharmed thanks to my goodhearted and kind sister Ite and Yosele-Spivakovs.[64]

I soon found out that one could travel until Rozdelnye by train for a small amount of money. Since the train line was just recently built, passage was free, but the conductor took a small fee. From Rozdelnye until Tiraspol was a total of thirty to forty *versts*. Since I had three rubles and some change on me, I permitted myself to buy some new clothes for that amount. I bought a brand new *kapote*—but without a winter lining—for 1.20 rubles, a pair of summer pants for fifty *kopeks*, and a vest for thirty *kopeks*, in other words an entire suit of clothes for two rubles.[65] Once I threw into the deal my old pair of boots, which in any case I had planned to throw out, I was also able to buy for fifty *kopeks* a nice pair of shoes and socks—in the Hasidic style of the time. I also bought a train ticket for thirty *kopeks*.[66] All totaled, I outfitted myself for 2.90 rubles. With the few *kopeks* that I had left over, I got a ride to the train station at Borshchi. From the Borshchi station, I traveled to Rozdelnye for twenty-eight *kopeks*.[67] Since I did not have the required thity *kopeks*, the good conductor let me ride

---

list incorrectly notes Refuel's father's name as Hersh in one place, and Sime is mistakenly referred to by the name of her niece, Etye-Khaye.) In his article about the Jewish community of Bender, David Carmel (1975:269) writes that this Refuel Kishinevsky, his great uncle, was a cantor in Tiraspol and came from a family of *shokhtim* in Tiraspol.

63 In fact, the 1858 additional revision list (poll-tax census) of the Jews of Tiraspol already shows the ten-year-old Refuel Kishinevsky as being raised (not officially adopted) by Simkhe Teplitsky; hence, this document makes it seem unlikely that Refuel's ascribed motivation was correct. After Refuel's father died in 1854 (see previous footnote), Simkhe took in Refuel, who was probably his blood relative, possibly to protect Refuel from being conscripted as a cantonist; the snatchers (*khapers*) preyed particularly on children from poor, fatherless homes, while the children of the middle-class Jews—like Simkhe—were largely exempt from conscription. (For more about cantonists, see ch. 6, p. 152, footnote 17.) Simkhe's original intent was for Refuel to marry his daughter Sime when they came of age.

64 Tsipe is mistakenly written in the original instead of Ite. The author is clearly referring to Ite since the two Tolner Hasidim said earlier that they would not throw him out of the wagon "out of respect for your sister Ite" and since Ite (not Tsipe) was Refuel's sister-in-law.

65 1.20 rubles denotes one ruble and twenty *kopeks*.

66 The author mentions above that passage was free, except for a small fee given to the conductor, yet he is purchasing a ticket. Perhaps the conductor would only issue a ticket once he was paid his small fee.

67 The author wrote above that his ticket cost thirty *kopeks* yet here he writes that it cost twenty-eight *kopeks*. Evidently, he had rounded off the price earlier.

FIGURE 7. The author's nephew Itsl (aka Isaac Goldstein) with his wife Khave (Ida) and two children Abraham (1884–1901) and Edith (1888–1953) in St. Paul, Minnesota ca. 1891. Itsl (1862–1907) was the son of the author's sister Ite. He and his family later settled in Portland, Oregon, where Edith married the author's son Yosl (aka Joseph Goldeen) in 1905. Courtesy of Nancy Merenbach Zuniga.

for less. At Rozdelnye, I found a familiar Tiraspoler wagoner who took me to Tiraspol at no charge.

Arriving in Tiraspol, I found my sister Ite with her little boy Itsele completely healthy, and he was now going to *kheyder*. I really enjoyed being with her son because he was such a clever and happy child. My sister Ite cleaned me up a bit and mended my clothes, and I then started to continue on toward Kishinev. I bade farewell to Ite and left for Kishinev.

I arrived in Kishinev and immediately went to the Governor General of the province of Bessarabia where I was given a permit to cross the border into Romania.[68] He was not able to exchange my passport because the Governor General of province of Mogilev had written an inscription on my original passport that I was only allowed to return home to Romania. It was practically the same for me whether I went to Romania or remained there, because I had nowhere to go in either place. The same type of Torah study was available in both places—and neither were places of Torah. The only drawback in going to Romania was that I had no money for my expenses, but I was already used to that, particularly since Kishinev is not far from Romania, a total of sixty to seventy *versts*.[69] I left Kishinev for Romania, and arrived at the customs house in Beshtemak, where I formally crossed the border. There I ran into Hasidim who were traveling to the Rebbe in Lyeve, and I went with them to a Jewish tavern, which was already on the Romanian side of the border.

---

[68] Bessarabia was a province in Tsarist Russia along the Romanian border. Most of Bessarabia is currently part of Moldova with the rest in Ukraine.

[69] Kishinev was the capital of the province of Bessarabia.

CHAPTER 17

Delivering an *Esreg* to the Lyever Rebbe, 1866–1867

The Trip with the Lyever Hasidim • The Hasidim in Distress • The *Rebetsn* • Cholera • Dancing and Playing on *Tisha B'Av* • King Karl Ludwig [*sic*] Kisses the Torah under the *Huppah*[1] • The King Visits the *Bes-Medresh* • Reb Borukh-Sholem in Iassy • In Shtefenésht with the Rebbe • Immersing in the *Mikveh* with Their Clothes On • Back to Russia[2]

From the tavern near the border, the Rebbe's Hasidim hired a wagon to travel to Lyeve. They decided to take me along, because I had told them I stood on a loftier level in Hasidism than they since I was going on foot while they were riding, a situation that they could not permit.[3] They barely managed to persuade me to come along in their wagon. In fact, I really did not want to travel in their company because the unpleasant trip in the carriage with the Tolner Hasidim was still fresh in my mind. But I figured that they would think I was a Lyever Hasid and not a Chabadnik and would therefore not hassle me. If they spoke to me, I would just make as if I was sleepy, and they could hold nothing against me. In any case, riding was better than going on foot, especially in a foreign country.

---

1   As explained on p. 270, footnote 24, the author is referring to Prince Karl of Romania.
2   This chapter summary covers less than half of this chapter.
3   Hasidim would consider someone walking on foot to their Rebbe to be on a higher level than someone traveling by coach or wagon. A Lubavitcher Hasid once explained his insistence on traveling on foot to his Rebbe by saying that he did not want to share his eternal reward for traveling to the Rebbe with the horses pulling the wagon (Rabbi Y. Y. Schneerson, *Igrot Kodesh*, 6:269–270). Walking on foot to one's Hasidic Rebbe has been compared to the Biblical obligation of "ascending on foot" (*aliyah le-regel* in Hebrew) to the Holy Temple in Jerusalem (Sadan, 1971:55).

To make a long story short, I traveled, suffered, and put up with everything because even though they did not know me, they realized that I was not a Lyever Hasid. They had some sort of knack or feeling for this type of thing, but I just kept quiet until I arrived in Lyeve.[4] Only there did I tell them that they had taken along a Chabadnik, a Lubavitcher Hasid. I thought, "At least let them be distressed over that!" And that truly grieved them, especially when I did not even go to visit their Rebbe's court since I heard that the Rebbe, Reb Bérenyu, did not "conduct a *tish*,"[5] and he did not meet with anyone.[6] Visiting Hasidim could only meet the *Rebetsn*, lodge in the Rebbe's court, and obtain responses from the Rebbe through her. This matter will be discussed later at greater length. My intent here is to explain the reason I did not go to the Rebbe's court, particularly since I was already in the city where the Rebbe lived. My failing to seek a blessing from the Rebbe really sickened the Hasidim who had taken me along in their wagon. Understandably, I made little of their ill feelings toward me, and soon left Lyeve for the nearby *shteytlekh* and villages looking for a position as a *melomed*. After all, what else was I able to do and how else could I earn a living? But I could not find even a miserable position so quickly since it was already two weeks after Pesach.[7] Nonetheless "finding only after toiling can be believed"![8] When one looks, one finds. I looked and inquired for a long time until I found a teaching position with a tenant innkeeper called Reb Shmiel Bruditshéshter, because the village was named Bruditshésht, which was not far from the city of Hish. I arrived exactly on Lag BaOmer.[9]

---

4   Since the author spent Pesach in Uman (ch. 16, p. 257) and Pesach ended that year on *Shabes*, he clearly left Uman on Sunday, April 8, 1866, and arrived in Lyeve later that same month.

5   See ch. 16, p. 247, footnote 3, for a description of a Hasidic *tish*. Wertheim (1988:248–251) provides a fuller explanation of a Hasidic *tish*. Isaac Even (1922:1:157–173) gives a detailed description of a *tish* conducted by the Lyever's brother, Rabbi Avrúm-Yankev Fridman of Sadigor (1819–1883).

6   The Lyever Rebbe, Rabbi Dov-Ber "Berenyu" Fridman (ca. 1821–1876), was a son of the great Hasidic Rebbe, Rabbi Yisruel Fridman of Rizhin (1797–1850), and a brother of the Shtefeneshter Rebbe, Rabbi Nukhemtse Fridman (mentioned later in this chapter, pp. 273–275), and of Rabbi Avrúm-Yankev Fridman of Sadigor (1819–1883). In October 1868, a year after Goldenshteyn's meetings with the Lyever Rebbe, as described later in this chapter, pp. 288–292, the Lyever became the center of conflict between the Hasidim of Sanz, led by Rabbi Khayem Halbershtam (1793–1876), and the Hasidim of Sadigor. Known as the Sanz-Sadigor controversy, it became one of the most controversial Hasidic episodes in the late nineteenth century. See Assaf (2012), Gutman (1952:3–17), and Refael (1991:248–260).

7   Since the new term begins right after Pesach, most teaching positions had already been filled in the two weeks since Pesach.

8   Talmud (Megilla 6b).

9   May 3, 1866.

Reb Shmiel had three boys, two small ones and one who was a young man of seventeen, already engaged to someone from Lyeve. Reb Shmiel really enjoyed my being there. Just as much as I had sought out a teaching position, he had similarly been looking for a good *melomed* but could not find one. He liked me very much, and I remained there until the end of the term, meaning until *Slikhes* time,[10] earning fifteen *rendlekh dikátn*.[11] At Reb Shmiel's I was now able to rest and started to come back to life. I ate, drank, and lodged at Reb Shmiel's under the best and most respectable conditions. In a separate little room, I would sit and teach his three children who liked me very much. From day to day, the family's appreciation of me grew, and they said that they had never had such a good *melomed*. Whenever someone visited and wherever he went, he would brag about me.

Over the hill from the village there was another village to which we would walk on *Shobes* to pray with a *minyan*. Once I led the prayers and they were elated. "Where did Reb Shmiel find such a *melomed*?" they asked. Reb Shmiel swelled with pride as he heard how envious the other tenant innkeepers were of him. He wanted to marry me off to a wealthy relative of his, but I told him that I was already engaged, thereby totally removing all thoughts concerning potential matches. In short, I felt that my position was very good and would remain so but, as usual, there were dark clouds on the horizon.

Around the month of *Tamuz*,[12] there was a very strong outbreak of cholera—may this never happen again—which wiped out entire villages of non-Jews around Brudıtshesht.[13] The outbreak was so severe that no one was left to bury the dead. Those who could flee did so, but no place would let them in because every city and village had quarantines. The fear that befell the living is impossible to describe, especially since the residents of the villages had no doctors or pharmacists and you could not travel to bring any unless it was from a place where the disease had not yet spread. But how could you go there if they would not let you in? So everyone remained at home awaiting death. You can

---

10 *Slikhes* (*Slikhot* in Modern Hebrew) are special penitential prayers that Ashkenazi Jews recite before and during the High Holiday season. Though *Slikhes* began that year on Saturday night, the 22nd of *Elul* (September 1, 1866), the author writes below that he finished teaching some nine days before *Slikhes*, which evidently would have been the 12th of *Elul*, 5626 (August 23, 1866).
11 A Yiddish name for Romanian ducats.
12 June–July 1866.
13 The fourth pandemic of cholera of the nineteenth century occurred from 1863 to 1875 and spread mostly in Europe and Africa (Evans, 1988:123). *Ha-Melits* (August 9, 1866, 448–449) has a report on this pandemic in nearby Kishinev. Kotik's memoirs (2002:383–385) describe this cholera epidemic in detail once it spread to Brisk, Belarus (now Brest) and nearby Kamenets from September to November 1866.

imagine what type of upheaval existed in Reb Shmiel's home and how depressing my life became. He would not let me teach his children, and I was not up to it either. The whole village was reveling and being cheerful, drinking, and playing music. That was the only cure—neither worrying nor being terrified, only being cheerful.[14]

Whenever people heard that someone had become sick, they immediately treated him by rubbing him down with vinegar and garlic.[15] A few were saved while others died while being rubbed down. We heard that a Jew not far away had become ill, so Reb Shmiel and I ran over there to treat him, which we did until he revived. And then someone else there became ill, but we could not save him, and he died while we were treating him. And woe to the deceased for the way they were treated during burial. And woe to the living who saw what was done with the deceased, because everyone was afraid that very shortly, perhaps in only a few hours, they would be treated similarly. This affected people more than death itself. But, thank God, I was able to survive unharmed, though the situation around Bruditshesht was catastrophic, as mentioned earlier. Many villages were left empty. It was pitiful to listen to the cries of the moaning cattle, crying and pleading for food; there was not a living soul in the village to care for them or water them. In our village, the situation was relatively bearable. No Jews were harmed, God forbid, and we got away with mere fright. The fear lasted only five weeks, and then came to a sudden end. I remember that on Tisha B'Av,[16] we were told neither to fast nor to say *kines*.[17] In the city of Hish, people went around playing music the entire day on the orders of the Rebbe, Reb Berenyu,[18]

---

14 In his description of the cholera epidemic in Yenakiyeve, Ukraine, ca. 1905, Gurwitz (1935:131–132) writes that the local Jews were lamenting loudly in the synagogue upon hearing that cholera had taken its first Jewish victims when the doctor arrived and told them to remain cheerful and return to their homes.

15 Ginsburg (1937:1:236) cites handwritten Yiddish documents from the 1830s in Tsarist Russia regarding curing cholera, which advise primarily treating the victims by rubbing them down with a warm mixture of good liquor and various spices using a piece of flannel on their "hands, feet, heart, entire stomach, and face—primarily the temples." See there for further details.

16 July 22, 1866.

17 *Kines* (*kinot* in Modern Hebrew) are special elegies recited on Tisha B'Av. Since the fast occurred on *Shobes* that year when one is not allowed to fast, it was deferred until Sunday, July 22, 1866. Since fasting and reciting *kines* for hours in the synagogue could have weakened the Jewish population, many of whom were already ill, these acts were forbidden that year.

18 Though Jewish law generally forbids playing music on Tisha B'Av, the Lyever Rebbe ordered it to be played to strengthen the spirits of people who felt so dejected and depressed from the cholera pandemic. Similarly, we are told that when large numbers of Jews left Spain in 1492 during the three weeks of mourning preceding Tisha B'Av, the rabbis "issued permission

who was himself in the city of Hish at that time.[19] Thank God, we survived and were finally able to travel from village to village and from town to town.

I continued teaching until the middle of *Elul*, and Reb Shmiel traveled with me to Hish so I could get myself some new clothes for *Yontef* with my newly earned money. I bought myself some good and expensive worsted wool to have made into a suit, and Reb Shmiel gave it to his tailor to sew and left me in town for a few days until the measurements were finished. He said when the suit was ready, he would come to pick me up. In the meantime, I went to the *bes-medresh* and sat down to study. A new cantor had been hired for the High Holy Days, and he was looking for cantorial assistants. I was eager to meet the cantor, and he was just itching to hire me as an assistant for the High Holy Days. The *gabbaim* of the *shul* and everyone in the *bes-medresh* asked me to remain in Hish with the cantor and assist him. I explained that I had a commitment to Reb Shmiel Bruditsheshter. "So what?" they replied, "Reb Shmiel himself prays in this *bes-medresh*, and we're sure that when we will ask him, he'll agree." And that is what happened.

When Reb Shmiel came to town to pick me up the next day, the *gabbaim*, the cantor, and other respectable townsmen surrounded him and asked him to let me off for the rest of the term to practice with the cantor since there were only eight days left before *Slikhes*, when the term ended. It did not take much to persuade Reb Shmiel and he readily agreed because he felt quite honored that everyone was pleading with him. And he was particularly inclined to agree since everyone would then know that I was his *melomed*. For my part, I promised him that I would teach his children the

---

to the exiles to march to the music of orchestras . . . in order to strengthen the spirit of the people, and to infuse hope and trust in God in them" (Kitov, 1978:3:288). Ginsburg (1937:1:237) quotes handwritten Yiddish documents from the 1830s in Tsarist Russia that recommend ways of preventing cholera especially by not becoming frightened or worried by thinking about the disease; and that a great means of prevention is a cheerful mood.

19 According to Gutman (1952:4–6), the Lyever Rebbe, Rabbi Dov-Ber Fridman, lived in Hish before moving to Lyeve, then returned to Hish in 1866 to flee the cholera epidemic, and only returned to Lyeve at the end of April 1867. These dates coincide with Goldenshteyn's account of arriving in Lyeve in April 1866 when the Rebbe was there, seeing him in Hish in the summer of 1866, and personally meeting him back in Lyeve in October 1867. Nonetheless, Dr. David Assaf, the author of *Hetsits ve-nifga* (2012) on the Lyever Rebbe and the subsequent Sanz-Sadigor controversy, wrote me in December 2009 that it is very difficult to determine exactly when the Rebbe moved around and is of the opinion that he served as Rebbe in both places, because he apparently continued to maintain a residence in Hish, which he frequented even after moving to Lyeve.

piyut and prayers for the High Holy Days, while he and his family were in town for *Yontef*.[20]

And so it was. I remained with the cantor as one of his cantorial assistants for the High Holy Days, and I received five *dikatn* plus room and board.[21] Three to four hours a day were spent singing with the cantor and rehearsing, and the rest of the time I spent in the *bes-medresh* studying. When Reb Shmiel arrived for the High Holy Days with his children, I taught them the prayers as I had promised. I was liked by all, and all the children of the wealthy people in town sought out my friendship since a pious person is well liked, particularly since I was dressed like a wealthy person. I had spent all of my earned money on clothing, particularly on that fine worsted wool suit. That suit could not be compared to the cheap suit which I bought in Bolte back in Russia, as you may recall.[22] This fine suit cost me ten *dikatn*, while the other one, together with a good hat and good shoes, cost me only a half *dikat*.[23] And don't forget that things are more reasonably priced in Romania than in Russia, and the merchandise is also of better quality. So those ten *dikatn* that I spent on myself in Romania were the equivalent of approximately fifty silver rubles. You can now imagine how well dressed I was then and how good I looked.

While I was in Hish, the new Romanian king, Karl Ludwig, who had been crowned king of Romania that summer, traveled through the country and came to Hish.[24] The Jews of Hish tried to surpass all other ethnic groups with their grandeur. They walked out of the town carrying *huppahs* of honor and Torah scrolls to welcome him. The Lyever *tsadik*, Reb Berenyu was under the *huppah* leading the way, holding a Torah scroll.[25] There were thousands of people there. I made a point of also being next to the *huppah*, so I was able to see King Karl descend from his carriage, go under the *huppah*, and kiss the Torah scroll. The

---

20 The *piyut* (usually used in plural form, *piyutim*, today) is a piece of liturgical poetry added into the High Holy Day prayer services. Jews who lived in villages would travel to the larger towns for the Jewish holidays.
21 *Dikatn* is a Yiddish term for Romanian ducats, which were also called *rendlekh* elsewhere in the author's autobiography.
22 See chapter 16, p. 262.
23 In chapter 16, p. 262, he did not mention that he had bought a hat for himself as well.
24 The author is referring to Karl Eitel Friedrich Zephyrinus Ludwig (1839–1914), a German prince of the house of Hohenzollern-Sigmaringen, who was elected *Domnitor* (that is, Prince) Karl of Romania, which was then still a vassal of the Ottoman Empire, in April of 1866. Only when Romania gained full independence from the Ottoman Empire in 1881 was he crowned its first king and assumed the royal title of King Carol I.
25 Welcoming royalty with a Torah scroll was standard practice among Jews through the ages.

Rebbe then said the Hebrew blessing recited upon seeing a monarch,[26] someone else delivered a nice speech, and afterward the king responded and offered his thanks. From there, the king went into town, where he first went into the church and then to the *bes-medresh*. Our cantor, along with all of his cantorial assistants among whom I was also included, made the *Mishebeyrakh* blessing in his honor, and the king departed the Jewish community very pleased.[27]

By then I did not want to return to Reb Shmiel in his village, so I was taken during the intermediate days of *Sukes* to a *shteytl* called Kodayésht to work as a *melomed*. There were two *shokhtim* in the *shteytl*.[28] One was a Lyever Hasid and the other was a Lubavitcher. Of course, I was drawn to the Lubavitcher Hasid, and it was specifically because of him that I went to that *shteytl*, for otherwise I could have also earned a living in Hish. In Kodayesht, I taught through the winter.[29] I was teaching five children, including one of the Rebbe's sons.[30] I really grew to love that Lubavitcher *shoykhet*, Reb Ber, and he also grew to love me. We lived like brothers. He was called Reb Berl Vasluyer because he was from Vasluy. He was a very pious Jew but poor, with a houseful of children. He was persecuted for not being a Lyever Hasid, as usual. The *shteytl* was filled with all types of Hasidim. Though boors, they were nevertheless fervent Hasidim, because the region in and around Romania was filled with Hasidic Rebbes.

Around Hanukah time,[31] we heard that Reb Mendele Lubavitcher's oldest son Reb Borukh-Sholem was coming to Iassy.[32] Reb Borukh-Sholem had a

---

26 A translation of the blessing is as follows: "Blessed are You, Lord, our God, King of the Universe, Who hast given of Your glory to a king of flesh and blood." See *Shulkhan Arukh* (*Orakh Khayim* 224:8–9).
27 A *Mishebeyrakh* is a special prayer of blessings.
28 *Shokhtim* is the plural of *shoykhet*.
29 The author is referring to his teaching there during the winter term, which began after the High Holy Days and lasted until shortly before Pesach, which began the evening of March 26, 1867.
30 Since no Hasidic Rebbe is known to have lived in Kodayesht, "Rebbe" was possibly mistakenly printed instead of "rabbi" (*ruv*), referring to the local rabbi overseeing halakhic matters. Perhaps this rabbi was Rabbi Menakhem-Nukhem Bokhner who was the rabbi of Kodayesht in the late nineteenth century and died before 1902. He was the author of a commentary on the Five Books of Moses called *Aniyat Amen* (Czernowitz, 1913).
31 Hanukah began on the night of December 2 and lasted until December 10, 1866.
32 Heilman (1903:3:24) also mentions Rabbi Borukh-Sholem Schneerson's trip to Romania in late 1866, as pointed out by Mondshine (1986:63). Based on their miscalculations of the author's year of birth, Bloy (2020:65) and Luria (2006:48) mistakenly conclude that the author was referring to an earlier trip to Romania made by Rabbi Borukh-Sholem Schneerson during his father's lifetime; Bloy gives the year as 1862 and Luria as 1861, at the latest. Mondshine (2000:34) comments that Rabbi Borukh-Sholem Schneerson's trip to Iassy, as mentioned here, may have been to visit his son-in-law, who lived there. Rabbi Borukh-Sholem Schneerson (ca. 1804–1867) was the only one of his father's surviving sons

deformed hand but was a tremendous Torah genius.³³ Reb Ber the *shoykhet* and I traveled to Iassy to spend *Shobes* of the Torah portion of *Mikets*.³⁴ The Rebbe, Reb Borukh-Sholem, himself served as the reader of the Torah portion of *Mikets* that *Shobes*. He raised a lot of money in Iassy because never before had Romania seen such a Hasidic Rebbe, such a *tsadik*, who was wise, a brilliant Torah scholar, a real genius, and also knowledgeable about medicine. He himself would write medical prescriptions, and so on. They had never seen the likes of such a Rebbe among their own Rebbes.³⁵ And to top it all off, he conducted himself so plainly, did not let anyone grab *shirayim*, and expounded on the Torah daily.³⁶

I asked Reb Borukh-Sholem the following question, which he answered extremely well. As you know, Reb Mendele Lubavitcher, of blessed memory,³⁷ told me not to marry until I turned twenty. At that time I had just entered my nineteenth year.³⁸ I was a fully grown young man with a large beard and was simply ashamed to pray in *tefillin* without a *talis*.³⁹ So I wanted to know whether I could marry at the beginning of my twentieth year.⁴⁰

---

who did not become a Hasidic Rebbe; he was the great-great-grandfather of the Lubavitcher Rebbe, Rabbi M. M. Schneerson (1902–1994).

33 Rabbi Borukh-Sholem Schneerson's right hand was deformed, without separate fingers and without a palm. When he became obligated to put on *tefillin* at the age of thirteen, the question arose as to which arm he should use for laying *tefillin*. His father, Rabbi Menakhem-Mendl Schneerson, wrote a rabbinical response regarding this matter, which is printed in his posthumous work, *Tsemakh Tsedek: Orakh Khayim*, sections 5–7. Mondshine (2012:151) notes that his deformed hand was also mentioned by another eyewitness, apart from his father, namely Goldenshteyn, as noted in his overview of Goldenshteyn's autobiography (Mondshine, 1986:63).

34 December 8, 1866, the sixth night of Hanukah. The Torah portion of *Mikets* constitutes Genesis 41:1 to 44:17.

35 Though the author refers to Rabbi Borukh-Sholem Schneerson as a Rebbe, in fact, he was the only one of his father's sons not to become a Hasidic Rebbe after his father's death. Nonetheless, being the scion of a Hasidic dynasty, he dispensed blessings and advice during his travels (Bloy, 2020:67–68).

36 Rabbi Borukh-Sholem Schneerson did not conduct himself with the pomp associated with many of the local Hasidic Rebbes. He also did not allow anyone to eat from his *shirayim*, literally meaning "leftovers" and denoting the custom among Hasidim to eat from the leftover food remaining on the platter after the Rebbe has taken his portion. See Wertheim (1992:252–254) for more details.

37 The author had been in Lubavitch in August 1865 (chs. 15–16, pp. 244–251), and the Lubavitcher Rebbe passed away on March 29, 1866 (13 *Nisan* 5626).

38 The author means that he had just turned eighteen.

39 Ashkenazi Jews (except for German Jews) traditionally begin wearing a *talis* (that is, a prayer shawl) upon marrying.

40 The author wanted to know if he could marry upon turning nineteen.

Reb Borukh-Sholem permitted this, using the Talmudic axiom, "up to but not including."[41] He said, "My father, of blessed memory, told you not to marry until your twentieth year, but he didn't mean to include your twentieth year. So as soon as you enter the first month of your twentieth year, you can marry."[42]

We spent about three days in Iassy and returned home very happy that we had merited seeing the Lubavitcher Rebbe's son.

I finished the winter term and earned seventy rubles, that is, thirty-four *rendlekh*.[43] Forty rubles went for clothes and trifles, and at the end of the term I was left with twenty-five rubles, because I had spent five rubles on the cost of traveling to the Rebbe in Iassy. I did not want to remain in Romania to teach the summer term. I figured I would have nothing to lose by teaching in Russia, so why should I remain in a foreign country? Therefore, I decided to return home, and I traveled to Iassy where I obtained a new Romanian passport to return to Russia.

In Iassy, I heard great praises about the Shtefenéshter Rebbe, Reb Nukheml, and that he had many Hasidim.[44] So I figured, "I have money. I also have nice clothes to wear. I'll travel to the Rebbe and ask him what I asked Reb Borukh-Sholem, the Lubavitcher Rebbe's son, and hear whether he also agrees."

In Iassy, I had bought myself a good box for my clothes, which made me look like a merchant. The wagoner figured that I must be an important person since I had a ruble in my pocket and was not stingy—these were different times for me. I started to live with the hope that there would be better days ahead and that I would only work as a *melomed* until my wedding. After my wedding, I would certainly be happy,[45] but you will still hear about my subsequent "luck." In the meantime, I traveled to Reb Nukhemtse. I arrived in Shtefenésht on the

---

41 The Talmud (Brakhot 26b) discusses whether an endpoint is included or excluded. As applied here, the Tsemakh Tsedek's ruling would refer to whether the author was to marry at the beginning of his twentieth year (upon turning nineteen) or at the end of his twentieth year (upon turning twentieth).

42 Meaning that the author could marry once he turned nineteen, thereby beginning his twentieth year.

43 The winter term ends shortly before Pesach which began the night of April 19, 1867. Romanian ducats were called *rendlekh* in Yiddish.

44 The Shtefeneshter Rebbe, Reb Menakhem-Nukhem Fridman (ca. 1823–1868), was a son of the renowned Rizhiner Rebbe, Reb Yisruel Fridman (1796–1850), and the brother of the Lyever Rebbe, Reb Berenyu Fridman, mentioned earlier. He settled in Shtefenesht in 1852. The author refers to the Shtefeneshter Rebbe as both Reb Nukheml and Reb Nukhemtse. He had an only son, Reb Avrúm-Motisyuhi Fridman (1847–1933), who succeeded him as Rebbe and left no heirs.

45 The author would be happy because he would then be coming into some money, meaning the dowry.

second day of the intermediate days of Pesach.[46] I found myself lodging and spent the last two days of Pesach at the Rebbe's court.

I asked the Rebbe, Reb Nukheml Shtefeneshter, about his thoughts on what the Lubavitcher Rebbe had said to me, since I wanted to return home and knew that once I arrived, my father-in-law would insist that we make the wedding right away. I wanted to know what to tell my in-laws whom I had avoided because I did not want them to pester me about marriage. This was a real issue, especially during that period when I could not tell them the reason, which only I knew and kept to myself. I did not even tell my sister Ite the reason. The Rebbe agreed to follow the Talmudic axiom "up to but not including," that is, that I may marry a few days after beginning my twentieth year.[47] He also wished me a long life.

I liked the Rebbe very much, but I did not like the Hasidim at his court. I had a major debate with them, and the Rebbe heard about it and sided with me.

This is what happened. On the Seventh Day of Pesach,[48] the Hasidim became so drunk that very early that morning they went off singing to the bathhouse and immersed themselves in the *mikveh* fully dressed.[49] They threw each other into the *mikveh* and, as a result, transgressed a number of Jewish laws such as the prohibition of squeezing water from one's clothing on *Yontef* and the like.[50] Furthermore, they looked so devilish. Then, during the prayer service, some of them who were *kohanim* wanted to *dukhn*.[51] I did not allow it, and they shouted, "Who are you? You old bachelor.[52] You have no respect for older Hasidim. Learn from us how to be a Hasid! You can't even drink any liquor..."[53]

Though I was certainly embarrassed by their comments, I nonetheless replied that I would drag away anyone daring to *dukhn* because the *Code of*

---

46 April 22, 1867.
47 Meaning that the author could marry as soon as he turned nineteen, thereby beginning his twentieth year.
48 April 26, 1867. There are eight days of Pesach. The first two and last two days are holidays with most of the same prohibitions as *Shobes*.
49 The Shtefeneshter Rebbe was known not only to have very learned Hasidim who reached lofty spiritual heights, but he also attracted coarse and unlearned Jews who became his Hasidim, as described by Agnon (1969:505). A *mikveh* is a specially constructed ritual pool containing at least 200 gallons of water into which Jews immerse for purification.
50 *Shulkhan Arukh* (*Orakh Khayim* 301:46).
51 *Dukhnen* is the *kohen's* recital of the priestly blessing (Numbers 6:24-26) in front of the congregation which is a part of the *Musaf* prayer service. For Asheknazi Jews living outside of the Land of Israel, it is generally recited in the *Musaf* prayer service on *Yontef*.
52 Though the author was eighteen, he looked older than he was because of his large beard, as stated earlier in this chapter, p. 272. Hence, he was teased for being an old bachelor.
53 By the author's refusing to drink, he appeared to these Hasidim to be conceited, holding himself aloof, and unwilling to be a part of their Hasidic brotherhood.

Jewish Law states that a drunk may not *dukhn*.⁵⁴ And in case the Hasidim followed a different *Code of Jewish Law*, I would go ask the Rebbe. You can just imagine the uproar made by those drunks. How so? They had already spent a half a year at the Rebbe's court and did not allow a single day to pass without *tikn*. (Every new guest visiting the Rebbe had to give money to this group of drunkards to buy liquor, which was called a *tikn*.) So now they asked me, "Where were you when we were busy with the splitting of the Red Sea all night long until the wee hours of the morning, until the time of the recital of the morning *Shma*—just as the tannaitic sages in Bnei Brak recounted the exodus from Egypt the entire night?⁵⁵ And we also immersed ourselves in the *mikveh* already. And along comes this *misnaged*, this overgrown kid, and gives us his opinion! You're about to get trounced!"⁵⁶

I went right to the Rebbe to at least let him know what was happening and to hear what he had to say about it because I saw that they could truly give me a beating. I was sorry that I had started the whole thing because everyone, as you can understand, was on their side. But when they saw that I was running to the Rebbe, they called me back telling me they would not *dukhn* as long as I did not say anything to the Rebbe. But the Rebbe himself was already aware of what had happened in the *shul* and sent a *gabbai* to tell them not to dare *dukhn* because the young man was, in fact, correct. At that, the *Musaf* prayer service ended, but they continued to drink. They had prayed earlier than the scheduled time since the congregation would assemble about two hours later, at ten a.m., while they had prayed at seven or eight. These were the ten or so permanent court Hasidim who stayed in the *shul* and ate at the Rebbe's table, while leaving their wives and children back in the towns from which they came. They stayed there, drank, and become real drunkards—the exact opposite of the Lubavitcher Hasidim.

---

54 The *Code of Jewish Law* (*Shulkhan Arukh*) is the standard code of law followed by Orthodox Jews. Though the *Shulkhan Arukh* (*Orakh Khayim* 128:38) forbids a drunk from *dukhnen*, many rabbinical authorities permit *dukhnen* when intoxicated by any alcoholic beverage other than wine.

55 It is a Jewish custom to remain awake the night of the Seventh Day of Pesach and to busy oneself with the study of Torah in honor of the anniversary of the splitting of the Red Sea (Kitov, 1978:2:384). In the city of Bnei Brak in ancient Israel, five great sages spent the entire night of Pesach discussing the exodus from Egypt until the time of reading the morning *Shma*, as mentioned in the Pesach *Haggadah* though its original source is in the Mishna (Brakhot 1:5). The *Shma* prayer is recited twice daily, morning and evening.

56 A *misnaged* denotes an opponent of Hasidism. The Hasidim there were certainly aware that the author was also Hasidic, but since they personally did not see him stay up the entire night of the Seventh Day of Pesach and since he was not drinking, they tried to insult him by calling him a *misnaged*.

On the day after Pesach ended, I traveled to the border checkpoint at Skulén, crossed into Russia, and arrived in Skulen, a very fine *shteytl*.[57] From there, I continued on to Kishinev. I happened to spend *Shobes* along the way in a *shteytl* called Kalarásh, where I arranged to work during the summer term as a *melomed* for three boys for fifty silver rubles.[58] I gave a handshake as an agreement on the condition that I would not be obliged to begin teaching them before my return from Tiraspol. Since I had not seen my sister Ite and her children for an entire year, I needed to find out everything that was necessary for me to know regarding my future in-laws and their preparations for the wedding. The person who had hired me agreed because, in any case, it was still before *Rosh-Khoydesh Iyar*, so I could start teaching in a couple of days.[59] I left my things there, only taking along some clothes, and set out for Tiraspol. Upon my arrival, they barely recognized me and thought that some foreign merchant had come to town. All marveled at me.

I brought a gift for my sister Ite's daughter, Ester-Khayke, and for her son, Itsele, too. Ite was extremely overjoyed that she had such a respectable brother but was sorry for me that I had become involved in such a worthless marriage prospect.

"Yes," I said, "what's going on at my in-laws?"

"*Oy!*" she replied, "what should I tell you, little brother? They were wealthy. They were not of prestigious ancestry, but at least they had money. But now they have neither prestigious ancestry nor money. The rest you can imagine yourself."

I replied, "If so, I still have time. I'll stay here for a few days and will then return to Kalarash. Don't tell them where I am. It makes no difference. Since they haven't heard from me in such a long time, they might even leave me alone and arrange another match for their daughter. I still have time, for I can't marry for the next half year."

"Why half a year?" asked Ite. I told her what the Lubavitcher Rebbe had said. Ite replied, "If so, then it's certainly proper to wait a half year. Travel safely. For God's sake, just make sure to visit Tsipe's little orphans who are now in Kishinev. Her widower, Shloyme-Leyzer, works there as a *melomed* and has his children stay with someone nearby."

---

57 Since the day after Pesach was a *Shabes*, the author meant that he left the next day, Sunday, April 28, 1867.
58 Since the author was headed toward Tiraspol, the easiest way there was via Kishinev.
59 *Rosh-Khoydesh Iyar* was on May 5–6, 1867. The summer term generally begins on *Rosh-Khoydesh Iyar*.

On my way back to Kalarash, I arrived in Kishinev and asked Shloyme-Leyzer the whereabouts of his children, and he led me to them. I went with him, and we came to an alley where poverty greeted us at every corner. He led me to a small hovel where many half-naked children in threadbare shirts were playing in the filth. We entered the house, and they brought two children to us—a three-year old boy and a six-year-old girl. They were naked, barefoot, and emaciated. The little boy, in particular, was lean and meager, just skin and bones, and so grimy that one could not make out his face. "Here they are," said Shloyme-Leyzer, "your sister's children. They cost me eight rubles a month. I slave over them plenty." I cried bitterly over their horrible misfortune. What could you expect from the impoverished Jewish woman when she only received a total of eight rubles a month for them and had her own six children to take care of? But what would be the fate of these children whose father could not even afford those eight rubles a month? You already know the great wage earner, Shloyme-Leyzer. For all you know, he could leave Kishinev shortly and stop paying the eight rubles. I asked, "Do the children have any clothes?" The Jewish woman replied, "No! That's why they're so unclean, poor things. If only they would at least have some shirts." One could not tell whether they were wearing shirts or just black rags. The little dress worn by the girl was torn to shreds and as brown as dirt. I cried my heart out, gave each one a *kopek*, and left, promising to be back the next morning with a gift for them. They were dancing for joy—their uncle had given them a *kopek*!

My brother-in-law went to *Minkhe*, and I went to look up his eldest daughter, Reyzl, who was living in Kishinev.[60] She, too, was quite impoverished but was trustworthy. She told me that were it not for her, the children would have been even worse off because she was the one who, with great effort, wrested the eight rubles out of their father each month. She put so much effort into helping them because, firstly, she was also a mother of children, and, secondly, she remembered how her stepmother, Tsipe, had treated her with compassion and took the trouble to help her marry. The third reason was because the children were her own sister and brother, so how could she not take pity on them and not look out for them. I promised her that as soon as I would marry, which would be within a year, God willing, they would be delivered from their poverty because I would make sure that they would be taken care of. They would then not have to struggle like this.

The next morning, I went shopping for the children and bought shirts, so that they would have a change of clothes, and little shawls and shoes for *Shobes*,

---

60 Reyzl was first mentioned in chapter 3, p. 124.

which I arranged to be made. They were shortly sewn and ready. The joy of the children was beyond description. They were washed up and dressed in their new little shirts and shawls. And the little boy was wearing his new little cap and shoes. The children's appearance was totally transformed. I spent two days in Kishinev on their behalf and then left for Kalarash for my new teaching position. I stayed there for the summer and studied devotedly with my students. I was pleased with them, and my employer was also satisfied.

While I was working there that summer, a great fire broke out in the month of *Tamuz*.[61] I saw how it happened, from its beginning, and how it would have been possible to extinguish it with one bucket of water. I was standing in the *bes-medresh* in the hallway and saw heavy smoke coming out of a shed. I let out a scream, "A fire!" and everyone ran out to take a look but did not put it out. Not only in the *bes-medresh* did they react this way, but even in that very courtyard they just yelled, "A fire!" and each person ran out to save his own belongings. No one ran over to first put out the fire, which could easily have been extinguished, as I said. Unfortunately, the fire spread throughout the entire *shteytl* and ruined some 100 families—a whole street of houses was burned down. My employer's house managed to survive, and the fire did not harm me, but my heart was torn to see the misfortune of those who had lost their property. People whom I had known as fine householders were now, unfortunately, wandering around the streets homeless. It was destined that I would not lack troubles and fright, but thank God for His kindness in sparing me that time.

Around the month of *Elul*, there were some new developments. My mother-in-law, Dvoyre, came to see me.[62] She had heard that I was in Kalarash and came to meet me to discuss the wedding. She reproached me. She wanted to know why I had left without seeing her and why I was hiding from her. She wanted to make the wedding! "How long are you going to wander around and stay away?"

I asked her if she was ready to make the wedding, if she was able to clothe me as we had agreed, and whether the dowry was completely ready. She replied to each question in the finest manner, "Everything is ready. There's no question. The dowry is ready. Not only that, but the clothes for you and the bride-to-be are also ready. I even prepared a *kitl* for you.[63] Nothing is missing. You only need to come, and I'll make the wedding!"

---

61 July 1867.
62 The author mentions twice (ch. 18, pp. 293 and 294) that his meeting with his mother-in-law in Kalarash occurred on *Rosh-Khoydesh Elul 5627*, which was September 1–2, 1867.
63 A *kitl* is a white robe-like garment traditionally worn by a Jewish groom at the wedding ceremony and at certain other times. See *Shulkhan Arukh* (*Orakh Khayim* 610:4).

We agreed that after *Sukes*, I would go to Tiraspol and decide upon a date for the wedding.⁶⁴ I would not be arranging a position as a *melomed* for the winter term. I asked her a thousand times whether everything was truly prepared, and she repeated her words with pledges and oaths that everything she said was true. I believed her and promised that after *Yontef* I would come to set a date for the wedding.

Soon after my mother-in-law left, I thought of the following plan. Since I would be left with fifty rubles at the end of the term, I would pay a visit to the Rebbe in Lyeve in Romania and ask his opinion whether I should follow the advice of those two *tsadikim* who said I should wait to marry "up to but not including" my twentieth year. If he should agree with them that I could marry once beginning my twentieth year, I would then have the approval of three great *tsadikim* and would then be certain that I could marry upon turning nineteen, otherwise I would be fearful of the Lubavitcher Rebbe's words telling me not to marry until age twenty. But since I could not travel before Yom Kippur because I had already promised the cantor in Kalarash that I would assist him on Rosh Hashanah and Yom Kippur,⁶⁵ I would travel to Lyeve to be at the Rebbe's court for *Sukes*.⁶⁶ I would set out for Kishinev the night after Yom Kippur and would be able to reach Lyeve by *Sukes*. In the meantime, I would obtain a Russian passport so that I could cross the border into Romania.

I carried out my plan and was busy with obtaining a passport up until Yom Kippur. As soon as Yom Kippur ended, I left Kalarash by wagon and was in Kishinev the next day. That year, Yom Kippur was on a Wednesday, so I needed to rush in order to cross the border on Friday or at least be at the border by *Shobes*.⁶⁷ Since I was already in Kishinev by Thursday at daybreak, I found a wagon that was to depart for Chimishliya two hours later. From Chimishliya, there were still twenty *versts* remaining until I would reach the customs house. While I was at the inn in Kishinev where we had stopped and were waiting for the wagon to take me on my way, four wealthy and dignified Jews came along and asked the innkeeper whether there were guests traveling to Lyeve to the Rebbe. He replied, "We have one such guest. There he is," and pointed to me. Hearing this reply from the innkeeper, all of them happily ran right over to me.

"Young man, are you traveling to Lyeve?"

---

64 *Sukes* ended on October 22, 1867.
65 Rosh Hashanah and Yom Kippur occurred on September 30–October 1, 1867, and October 9, 1867, respectively.
66 October 14–22, 1867.
67 In order to reach Lyeve by Sunday night when *Sukes* started, the author would at least have to spend *Shabes* somewhere near the border so that he could cross as soon as possible once *Shabes* ended.

"Yes," I said.

"Do you have a wagon, too?" they asked me.

"Yes," I replied

"Do you also have a passport prepared?"

"Yes, I do."

"Good, good," one said to the other. "It's a miracle from the Rebbe the way God has sent us a good emissary to help us."

I did not understand what was going on and why they were so happy. They sat down next to me and asked me, "Young man, will you take along an *esreg* for the Rebbe?"[68]

"Why not?" I replied. "What have I to lose?"

"Yes, you can't lose. You can earn the greatest merit, but you must know that you have to treat the *esreg* like a jewel because it cost a lot of money, and the Rebbe is looking forward to using this particular *esreg*."

"Don't worry about it," I said. "I'll take good care of it and bring it straight to the Rebbe."

"Who are you? What's your name?"

"I'm from Tiraspol," and I also told them my name.

They wrote everything down. Two of them soon left with a wagoner, and the other two stayed with me to explain the details of this privilege, which had come to me unexpectedly. They themselves could not have the privilege of bringing the *esreg* to the Rebbe since it was brought to Kishinev on the eve of Yom Kippur. The very well-to-do Mr. Perper, who had arrived from Trieste, had handpicked the *esreg* from among thousands and brought it back to Kishinev with him.[69] Hasidim had paid him seventy-five rubles for it. Nonetheless, there was no one with whom it could be sent to Lyeve since no one had a Russian passport at hand for travel abroad. In short, they decided to go around to all the inns to ask if perhaps some Hasid had already obtained a passport before Yom Kippur and was on his way to the Rebbe. "We looked and actually found someone, thank God." This was the story they told me excitedly and with joy. By the time they finished telling their story, the other two had already returned with a small box, which they gave me with their blessings. They said to me, "Young man, in the event that you want us to do so, we would pay the expenses of your

---

68 An *esreg* (*etrog* in Modern Hebrew) is the citron used as part of the *mitzvah* of the four species. Based on the Biblical commandment (Leviticus 23:40), the four species (citron, palm branches, willow, and myrtle) are taken by Jews each day of *Sukes* and are traditionally held together and waved in a prescribed manner (*Kitsur Shulkhan Arukh* 137).

69 After the rise of Napoleon in 1799, the city of Trieste took the place of Genoa as Europe's great market center for *esroygim* (plural of *esreg*) (Isaac, 1959:74). Part of the Austrian Empire for centuries, Trieste was annexed by Italy at the end of the First World War.

trip." I was offended by their words. "How could I possibly take money for bringing an *esreg* to the Rebbe, especially when I am traveling to him anyway for my own purposes? God forbid! Even if you gave me a fortune, I wouldn't take it!" "Ah! A fine young man! He seems to be very honest," said one to the other.

In the meantime, the non-Jewish wagoner harnessed the wagon, and I sat myself down. Those four Jews, and several other respectable Jews who suddenly appeared, all saw me off, wished me well, and shouted that I should mention them favorably to the Rebbe. They told me their names, and I then realized that that they were the finest and most elite residents of the city of Kishinev.

I left Kishinev with much celebration, thank God, and arrived in Chimishliya early Friday morning. I met my sister Sure there. She told me that she had been living there for a year. She was overjoyed to see me. She had not seen me in a while, and when she saw me as I looked now and heard what had become of me during the time we had not seen each other, she danced for joy and did not know what to do with me. She thought I had come to spend *Yontef* with her. But when she heard the story about the *esreg*, she was very happy, that is, she was happy that her own brother had the privilege of bringing an *esreg* to the Rebbe. Do not forget that my sister was a proper Hasidic woman, so this certainly gave her much joy. But it also grieved her that she could not detain me and have me stay with her during *Sukes*. Then again, as much as she loved me, no sacrifice was too great for the Rebbe's sake. At least she was consoled by my spending *Shobes* with her when everyone would meet her brother and know who her brother was and that he was bringing an *esreg* to the Rebbe. After all, it was no trivial thing to bring an *esreg* to the Rebbe. All the more so because it was the Lyever Rebbe, Reb Berenyu, whom everyone considered to be a holy man, especially from the time he began to confine himself to his room, not allowing Hasidim in to see him, no longer conducting a *tish*, and refusing to accept *pidyoynes*. This heightened reverence for the Rebbe began when Kishinev sent him a *pidyen* of 110 rubles, which he did not accept.[70] They then increased the sum by another 100 rubles, then by 200, and finally by 500 rubles, and he still refused to accept it. Since then, he was considered to be holy by all the various Hasidic groups, and definitely by his own Hasidim. So it was no wonder that my sister was so proud of her brother who merited to have such an honor.

You may now think that I was able to bring the *esreg* to the Rebbe quite smoothly and easily. No! The thought should not even enter your mind. I did

---

70 *Pidyen* is the singular of *pidyoynes*. The Hasidim of a certain town or city would often send a general *pidyen* to their Rebbe.

have the honor of actually bringing the *esreg* to the Rebbe, but I suffered plenty and endured much until I was able to do so. More than once did I say, "Neither them nor their reward!"[71] But it did not help me. I needed to suffer in every way on account of the Rebbe's *esreg*. If I had not met up with the *esreg*, what would I have been lacking if I would have spent the first two days of *Sukes* with my sister and arrived in Lyeve on the intermediate days of *Sukes*? Since apparently nothing was fated to come my way easily, listen to how it happened.

Before *Shobes*, I calculated that on Saturday night I would travel by moonlight a distance of twenty-five *versts* to the border, and then, on Sunday, I would cross the border. From the border to Lyeve is another twenty-five *versts*, a trip totaling two to three hours.

I would have the entire Sunday for this, so what did I have to worry about? But with my luck the clouds began to thicken, and a pouring rain began to fall on Friday at dusk. When I saw the rain, I felt miserable. How would I be able to travel that Saturday night? My hope was that the rain would stop, but it did not let up just to spite me; it kept raining the entire *Shobes*. It was already Saturday night, and it was still pouring with gusto.

The door of my sister's house was open the entire *Shobes* because everyone in the *shteytl* came to greet the young man who had the privilege of carrying the *esreg* to the Rebbe. All the Hasidim were envious of me, and all had to at least tap the box in which the *esreg* was kept. They were very eager for me to show them the *esreg*, but I swore to them that even I myself had not seen it, and I would not permit myself to open the box and have a look at the *esreg* before the Rebbe would see it.

Yes, all was fine and good, but how was I to reach the border? Where was I to obtain a wagon? And what type of crazy person would travel in such a rain? Not only was I in misery, but the entire *shteytl* was worried about it, and everyone shared my suffering. That entire *Shobes* we were hoping that the weather would clear up by Saturday night, in the Rebbe's merit, so that I could leave. It might have been expensive to hire a wagon, but I had to leave. As it turned out, the weather did not clear up on Saturday night, and the rain was not even thinking of stopping. By then I was truly miserable, but how would being miserable help?

We had to think of a solution, a means of traveling even though it was raining and the roads were very muddy. We thought and finally arrived at a solution. The town elite went with me to the postman, who was a Jew and apparently also

---

71   Talmud (Brakhot 5a–b) states that there are great rewards for accepting suffering and affliction with love. Nevertheless, several Talmudic sages are quoted as saying that they would rather forgo the suffering and its reward.

thought highly of the Rebbe. They told him about my misfortune and that it was obvious that he needed to tell his driver to harness the horses to the postal wagon and take me to the border. They explained to him that just like he would have to harness his horses if a nobleman came to him with a special ordinance commanding the use of his postal wagon, so too should he harness his horses now. Though he had no great desire to help, he, nonetheless, yielded and harnessed the three postal horses—for the sake of the Rebbe and the eight rubles he was offered to travel the twenty-five *versts*. He put a thick peasant coat on me to keep the rain from drenching me, and I was now on my way.

Believe me that trip was not worth just eight rubles. Not even fifty rubles would have been a fair price, because no sane human being would have undertaken to travel on such a pitch-black road in a drenching, pouring rain, which turned everything to mud. Only lunatics like us were traveling under such conditions. If it were not for the postal horses that knew the road well, and the driver who skillfully knew how to guide them, we would surely have been killed in some valley. Together they had to exert themselves to the utmost to save us from catastrophe. The driver repeatedly cursed himself and his boss for sending him out on a night like this. He guided those horses, step by step, otherwise we would have been unable to make the trip at all. The entire road was made up of hills and valleys forcing us to travel at a snail's pace.

Around midnight we came to a hamlet, and the driver approached a small house and knocked at the door. A trembling Jew opened the door. But when I greeted him in Yiddish by wishing him "*A gite vokh*," he and his family relaxed.[72]

Their fear was justifiable. The fellow did not run an inn; no one ever stopped off at his home. Then suddenly, late at night, out of the pouring rain and absolute darkness, a postal wagon with a bell ringing approaches his home. The ringing of the bell scared the souls out of them; they were sure it was some government officer, an excise tax official,[73] or another nuisance who would catch them red-handed with contraband or liquor.[74] But as soon as they heard Yiddish spoken, they realized that their fear was unfounded.

We had a good laugh at their expense, because why would anyone be afraid of us. In short, I rested for some two hours, paid for a drink of liquor for the driver, had a good bit to eat, and dried up a bit. We then continued on our way.

From there, we needed to travel eight *versts* to the customs house. We covered the distance before daylight and the driver led me straight to a rich Jew, to

---

72 "*A gite vokh*" means "A good week." This is the traditional greeting said after *Shabes* ends on Saturday night, which marks the beginning of the Jewish week.
73 Referring to the official in charge of the excise tax on alcohol. See Kotik (2002:192).
74 The production of liquor was strictly regulated in Tsarist Russia.

whom I was told to go. I went in to see him. Upon hearing that I was bringing an *esreg* to the Rebbe, he was overjoyed and said, "You should be happy that you have such a privilege."

I replied, "I would have passed up on the privilege if I had known that I would have such a journey!" "Oh, who cares about the difficulties," he said. "Everything is worth such a privilege!"

"Yes," I answered. "What will I do now? How do I cross the border? I still have twenty-five *versts* from the border to Lyeve."

"Don't worry," said that Jew. "I'll soon make sure that you get across the border. Just finish your prayers. For one ruble, I'll have a non-Jew harness up his wagon with horses, and I'll travel with you to the customs house. Though it's Sunday and they don't let anyone cross until two p.m., they will accommodate me if I request it. Don't forget, I got the Rizhiner, of blessed memory, across the border and with his blessing I became, thank God, a wealthy man, as you can see.[75] Therefore, it's no great matter for me to do something for one of his children." And so it was!

Soon after prayers, we went to the customs house. Though it was only nine a.m., the Russian gendarme drove me by wagon toward the border.[76] That Jewish fellow shouted after me, "Young man, don't forget to tell the Rebbe what I did for him," and he then told me his name and who he was. I thanked him

---

75 One of the most prominent Hasidic Rebbes in the history of Hasidism was the Rizhiner Rebbe, Rabbi Yisruel Fridman (1797–1850), who was the father of the Lyever (ch. 17, p. 266, footnote 6) and the Shtefeneshter (ch. 17, p. 273, footnote 44). Rabbi Yisruel Fridman was the great-grandson of the Baal Shem Tov's main disciple, Rabbi Dov-Ber (died 1772), known as the *Magid* of Mezritsh (Mezhirichi, Ukraine). In 1836, Russian authorities arrested the Rizhiner for allegedly having given the order to kill two Jewish informants who had been endangering their Jewish community. About fifty Jews were accused of hushing up the affair and were arrested and tortured. Among those convicted in 1840 were six community leaders who were sentenced to flogging and hard labor for life. The Rizhiner Rebbe was the only one of the accused to be acquitted and returned to Rizhin. Upon realizing that he would not be able to reestablish his court there because of harassment by the authorities, he asked to be relocated to Kishinev. The authorities granted his request, and he promptly moved there in July 1841. Since the Russian government wanted to exile him to inner Russia where he would be restricted from influencing other Jews, his Hasidim bribed the governor of Kishinev to provide the Rebbe with an exit visa to Iassy, Moldavia, which is the incident being referred to here by the wealthy Jew. The Rizhiner actually crossed the border into Moldavia at Ungen (now Ungheni in Moldova), which is fifty-eight miles northwest of Beshtemak (Vilf, 2017:213–214). Once in Moldavia, the Rizhiner quickly left for Austria when he learned that the Russian government was attempting to have him extradited. In Austria, he was authorized to reestablish his Hasidic court in the Bukovinian town of Sadigor (Assaf, 1997:167–173, 196–201).

76 The Russian gendarme drove the author from the Russian customs house to the bridge at the border.

too and proceeded to the border with the gendarme. The border was dry, that is, there was no flowing water, only a large ditch and a bridge. The gendarme drove me to the bridge. Russian soldiers stood on my side of the bridge, and Romanian soldiers stood on the other side. The gendarme handed me over to the Russian soldiers, and the Russian soldiers handed me over to the Romanian soldiers. One of the Romanian soldiers took me to the Romanian authorities in the government office. They signed my passport, took the customs fee, and released me. I would have been able to continue on my way if I had had a wagon, but obviously the Russian wagon remained on the other side of the bridge.

Earlier, when the gendarme was driving me from the Russian customs house to the bridge, which was a *verst* beyond the village of Beshtemak,[77] I thought to myself, "Yes, I'm crossing the border, but how will I obtain a wagon on the Romanian side of the border when the roads are so muddy? When it's dry, wagons come over from both the Russian and the Romanian sides. But what kind of a crazy non-Jew would drive to the border with a wagon in such weather? There's an inn across the border a *verst* away, but how will that help me? It appears that after all my troubles and suffering, I'm to remain stranded at this inn during *Yontef* with the *esreg*." Suddenly I noticed a wagon and a few horses at the inn across the border. I did not yet know whether I should rejoice: perhaps the wagon was not traveling where I needed to go or maybe they would not take me along. I was thinking, "who knows where that wagon might be traveling." As this was going through my mind, my wagon was moving closer and closer to the bridge. I saw three men running one after another approaching from the inn, and they were all making their way to the bridge that I was supposed to cross. I did not understand the meaning of this. In the meantime, as I was getting closer, I noticed that there were three horses harnessed at the inn apparently headed to Lyeve. I also noticed that the three men running to the bridge were Jewish—they were Hasidim.

By the time I got to the Romanian side of the bridge and to the Romanian soldiers, one of whom took my things and led me to the government office, the Hasidim had also managed to come closer.

At a distance, they started shouting, "Are you Pinkhes Goldenshteyn?"

"Yes," I replied.

And they shouted to each other, "He's here!"

"Are you Pinkhes?" shouted another.

"Yes," I said.

---

77 Though Peshtemák is written in the original Yiddish, its location clearly indicates that it is one and the same as Beshtemak, mentioned in ch. 15, pp. 238, 240, and 264.

"From Tiraspol? Are you taking the *esreg* to the Rebbe?"

"Yes," I said.

Upon hearing these words, they became tremendously joyful, and began dancing and leaping. Due to the rain, they were as wet as a drowned cat, but they could not care less as long as the young man with the *esreg* had arrived. I let them continue dancing as I signed the passport in the government office, where the officials looked over my things. They wanted to open the *esreg* box, but I asked them not to since there was only a lemon inside. I let them have a whiff of the box, and they believed me. In short, they charged me half a ruble and did not open the box. I left the government office and pandemonium broke out among the three Hasidim. One grabbed my bundle and the other wanted to take the box.

"But," I said, "I don't let this out of my hands."

"What are you afraid of?" he asked.

"I'm not afraid, but I won't let it out of my hands because I don't know you and I have no idea who you are."

"Ha, ha, ha ! Who we are, he asks! What a rat!"

This is how Hasidim talk even with other Hasidim whom they do not know. As long as he knows that he is talking to a Hasid, he refers to him as a rat or a lowlife or the like—the pure language of "Torah scholars."[78] I did not reply and headed straight for the inn. I asked where the wagon was and where it was headed. They broke into laughter and told me, "The wagon is going to Lyeve to the Rebbe. It is the Rebbe's wagon and horses. He dispatched them to the border to bring you back with the *esreg* because he knew well that no other wagons would be available at the border at this time. See what a holy Rebbe we have!" With that, they took a good drink of liquor. They gave me some also. I did not drink it.

"Bah!" they said. "He's no Hasid. He doesn't drink any liquor."

In short, we were now on our way, but the rain went right along with us. The mud was so deep and the road was so difficult that it took three such powerful horses until evening to travel the twenty-five *versts*.

During the trip, I had to battle the three Hasidim. Each one of them insisted that I give him the *esreg* box so that he could deliver the *esreg* to the Rebbe. The most insistent of them all was one fellow from Kishinev; he considered himself to be a well-to-do young man. This affair had cost him twenty-five rubles in cash, in addition to all that he suffered in traveling to the border, which had taken all night, and now he had to go all the way back to town. I realized that

---

78 Some Hasidim who lived in Tsarist Russia and eastern Romania used mildly offensive words on occasion. See Avtzon (1988:21).

this was the poor fellow's predicament upon hearing him complain, "It cost me blood and money. In the end, I won't even have the merit of delivering the *esreg* to the Rebbe with my own hands."

If they had been dealing with a weak person, they would certainly have succeeded in taking the *esreg* from him, but they ran into me; I was not afraid of all three of them. They first attempted to take the *esreg* by threatening me. But as soon as they realized that I had very little fear of them, they tried to convince me amicably. One of them said, "How's it possible? The Rebbe sent the three of us, and it personally cost me twenty-five rubles. Tell me, did it cost you that much money? Who did you pay?"

He told his story. "Last night, Saturday night, all the Hasidim were concerned that the *esreg* had not yet arrived. Many telegrams were sent to and from Kishinev. In short, everyone was upset since the Rebbe had no other *esreg*; he had been relying on this one. While this was going on, Sheyndele, the *Rebetsn*, came in. She said, 'The Rebbe is worried about the *esreg*. I assume that the person bringing the *esreg* must be at the border with no means of coming here. After all, what kind of driver would travel in such horrible weather? It would be a good idea to dispatch a wagon to the border. The wagon will surely find him and bring him here.' The Hasidim heard this and said that if this was the case then they should harness up a wagon from the Rebbe's courtyard and have two men travel to the border. Then the question arose—who should go? A noisy quarrel broke out. Each person shouted, 'I want to go.' In brief, when they saw that they could not come to an agreement, they decided that the privilege should be paid for. Whoever would offer the most money would go and have the right to take along two people to accompany him. They auctioned off the rights to the trip, and the price went up to twenty-five rubles. I had to pay cash to the Hasidim. They spent the entire night drinking and making merry while I and the two other Jews, whom I had taken along for company, were miserable all night. And we're not doing much better now. After all that, I run into this rude young man," he continued, "who doesn't want to hear what I have to say or my request that I give the *esreg* to the Rebbe."

I really understood his bitter heart, poor soul. I also understood quite well the Hasidic fanaticism that reigned in that country. But even after taking all that into consideration, I replied, "It's not my fault that it cost you money and you suffered for nothing. What would have been wrong if the Rebbe had dispatched a wagon with a common driver? Why did they have to send three Hasidim with the driver? First of all, it just made it more difficult for the horses and secondly it didn't serve any purpose. So I won't listen to you no matter what you say." And that is how we traveled the whole way until they tired and fell asleep.

As we approached the city, they woke up and started the discussion all over again. I informed them that it was futile and if they would continue to pester me I would jump off the wagon, continue on foot into town, go directly to the Rebbe, and tell him about this injustice against me. To make a long story short, we arrived in town. It was already evening. I saw everyone standing outside their homes and staring at us. People were running from their houses and telling each other the news. They were delighted and euphoric. At first, I did not understand what the commotion was about. As we came closer to the Rebbe's courtyard and onto the street where the Rebbe lived, I saw that all the inns were filled with Jews—guests who had traveled to Lyeve to be at the Rebbe's court on *Yontef* and *Shobes*. Everyone came running out into the streets shouting, "Here they are! Here they are bringing the *esreg*!" Each person ran to inform the other, and everyone ran to inform the Rebbe. It was then that I realized that the celebrating, excitement, and running around was all concerning us. Everyone had been waiting eagerly the entire day, so when they spotted us it created a tumult and commotion. In short, I traveled into Lyeve with pomp and fanfare like a groom being led into town.[79] When the wagon stopped at the inn and I got off the wagon, everyone besieged the inn. Everybody tried to get a look at the messenger who had brought the *esreg*. I took the box and wanted to head off to the Rebbe. The young man who had harassed me during the entire trip now appeared and asked that I let him carry the box because it had cost him money. I retorted, "Get away from me! If not, I'll hit you on the head with the box. Actually, why not let the people here tell us whether you have the right to take away my *mitzvah*. I've endured a lot since I left Kishinev, and I have had a lot of expenses because of it. Now he wants me to give it to him just because he paid for whisky for his friends." They all responded in unison, "The young man is correct. Stop harassing him."

I went straight to the Rebbe's court, which was the second courtyard past my inn. I entered the corridor where a *gabbai* was ready and waiting for me. He led me right away into an ornate parlor. The Rebbe entered, and I shook his hand and gave him the box with the *esreg*. The *gabbai* opened the box. The Rebbe took out the *esreg*, which was wrapped in oakum and took it into another room.[80] A quarter of an hour later, the Rebbe returned. The *Rebetsn* was also with

---

79 The custom of making a great to-do over the groom the night before the wedding when he came into town is mentioned in chapter 18, p. 297.
80 Oakum (*klyotshe* in the original Yiddish) is loosely twisted hemp or jute fiber impregnated with pine tar. For a long time, *esroygim* were traditionally wrapped in oakum to prevent damage, but by 2006 this natural fiber had been completely replaced by synthetic materials.

FIGURE 8. The Lyever Rebbe, Rabbi Dov-Ber "Berenyu" Fridman (ca. 1821–1876). The author was one of the few permitted to meet privately with this Hasidic Rebbe in his later years.

him. She asked him, "What's the story? Was it at least worth all the bother?" He replied, "It was all worth it! For such a beauty of an *esreg* is a rarity. This *esreg* is so fine that the other *esreg* I have is simple in comparison." He then turned to me, "I thank you, young man, for your efforts. I understand you have expended great effort." I replied, "My efforts would not have been so great had the road been a dry and good one. But even if you hadn't sent a wagon for me, I would have made the trip on foot just to bring the Rebbe this *esreg*." He then said, "Now it's already late, but if you ever need to see me about something, just tell the *gabbai*, who'll let you in at any time." He said goodbye to me and left.

All of the Hasidim looked at me with envy, as if to say, "How could it be that he had the privilege of bringing the celebrated *esreg* to the Rebbe. Not only that, but the Rebbe personally spoke to him because of it, something that no Hasid or wealthy person has had the privilege of experiencing since the Rebbe stopped allowing people in to see him," as explained earlier. In short, I was ecstatic.

After prayers, I returned to the inn where we ate in the *sukah*. We were a *minyan* of Hasidim, apart from those who ate inside because the *sukah* was wet.[81]

---

[81] Jewish law permits eating a meal outside of the *sukah* when it is raining, however, some Hasidim, like the author, have the custom to eat in the *sukah* regardless (Mondshine, 1995:302–306).

Everybody was talking about the *esreg*'s arrival, the young man who had brought it, and the miracles and wonders that had taken place.

So there you have it. How do you, my dear readers, like the whole story of the *esreg*? It cost a lot of money and health, and many people worked on its behalf—all because fanaticism reigned supreme...[82]

The *Seder* of the *esreg* has now concluded.[83]

---

82 The author thought that the great fanfare in Lyeve over the Rebbe's *esreg* was largely unnecessary and could have been done less pretentiously, more akin to his experience in Lubavitch as described in chapter 16, pp. 244–247.

83 With these words, the author is wittily alluding to the final words printed in most Haggadahs, "The Pesach *Seder* is now concluded," thereby signifying that he has completed a long and arduous ordeal.

CHAPTER 18

My Wedding and a Fiery Pursuit, 1867–1868

Permitted to Meet with the Lyever Rebbe • The Rebbe's Interest in Me • The *Shobes* Before My Wedding • My Wedding • My Suffering After the Wedding • My Perpetual *Kest* • Becoming a Storekeeper • A Fire Jumps from Place to Place

During the intermediate days of *Sukes*,[1] I went in to see the Rebbe with a *kvitl* despite the fact that no one had been allowed to see the Rebbe privately for two years, as I mentioned earlier. Nonetheless, I was let in, thanks to the *esreg*. Naturally, my main request was to know whether I could already marry even before I had completed my twentieth year because I would be turning nineteen after *Sukes*. The Rebbe questioned me extensively about my family—how long they had lived, what illness caused their deaths, and so on. I answered all his questions as best as I knew and could remember. The Rebbe was amazed that the Lubavitcher had so strongly warned me not to marry before the age of twenty. Nonetheless, he agreed to the Talmudic axiom of "up to but not including" like the two other opinions.[2] Now I had three opinions declaring that I could already marry.

    I was about to leave when the Rebbe said, "Listen, go to my doctor," and he mentioned his name. The Rebbe continued, "And you should tell him on my behalf that I sent you to him for an examination and that he should look you over well. And you'll see what he has to say." I left and found my way to the doctor. He promptly examined me, listened well to what I had to say, and told me the following, "You're completely healthy. You can marry without any

---

1   October 16–20, 1867.
2   See ch. 17, p. 273, footnote 41, regarding this Talmudic axiom.

fear." The next day, I told this to the Rebbe, and he wished me a long life and said, "You can marry already, and, God willing, you'll be healthy. Go home and marry." I told him about my match, how I became engaged to a girl from a very simple family which does not compare to my lineage, and how people were now proposing wonderful matches with wealthy girls of noble lineage. Then he asked, "Have you been engaged for a long time?" I replied, "About four years."[3] He responded, "Those other suggestions are not advisable! Don't look at a person's lineage. Our sages say, 'Go down a step to take a wife.'"[4] At that, I bade farewell to the Rebbe and left Lyeve that day for Iassy to obtain a new Romanian passport.

Arriving in Iassy, I figured that if the Rebbe had sent me to his doctor then apparently a doctor's opinion must have value. So I decided that it would not hurt to inquire with a prominent doctor in Iassy about this matter. I asked around until I located the most prominent physician, a Dr. Rozen, and gave him a *yirmilik*—a type of silver coin.[5] He listened well to what I had to say and then also told me the same thing—that I was completely healthy and could marry without any apprehension. By then I already felt reassured and decided to marry as soon as I returned home.

I obtained a new Romanian passport and left for home right after *Sukes*.[6] By *Rosh-Khoydesh Kislev*,[7] I was already in Kishinev and visited my orphaned niece and nephew, Esther-Khayele and Duvidl.[8] Once again I provided them with clothes and left for Tiraspol. Upon arriving in Tiraspol, I found my sister Ite and her dear, handsome son, Itsele, at the home of Zolmen-Sukher-Kopls, as expected. We were quite overjoyed to see each other. My sister was even more excited than me. Unbelievable! She had some brother—he was handsome, a learner, a singer, and well dressed. All that he was lacking was a wife. But marriage was definitely not a problem! Offers were coming from every direction. If he would just want one of them! She really wanted me to break my engagement because marrying into such a family was beneath her dignity. Apart from that, she knew that my prospective in-laws were poor and had no dowry or money to

---

3 The author had in fact been engaged three years and one month, as he had become engaged on October 10, 1864 (ch. 14, pp. 217–222).
4 Talmud (Yevamot 63a). The classic Talmudic commentator Rashi explains that a man should not marry a woman of a higher social status than himself because she may not be accepting of him.
5 A *yirmilik* is a type of Ottoman Turkish silver coin.
6 This is the author's third Romanian passport, since he had to obtain a new one every time he wanted to return to Russia from a visit to Romania. *Sukes* ended on October 22, 1867.
7 October 29–30, 1867.
8 They were the children of the author's late sister, Tsipe, and her husband, Shloyme-Leyzer.

pay for the wedding. At the same time, matchmakers were pursuing her brother with suggestions of matches with wealthy families of good lineage who had hefty dowries and beautiful girls with every virtue.

Certainly, my sister was displeased that I was engaged to a girl from a family of simple villagers, and she discouraged me from going through with the marriage. I told her that my future mother-in-law had visited me on *Rosh-Khoydesh Elul* and had said that the dowry was ready and everything was prepared, so it would be wrong for me to consider other marriage suggestions before I had thoroughly inquired into the truth.[9]

"Ah! So it's prestigious lineage that you want? Sister, you yourself are to blame for that. You woke me up after Yom Kippur and dragged me off to conclude the match.[10] So at that time my fiancée's family was suitable but now it's not?"

So I decided to travel to Tashlik to Shulem's daughter and son-in-law, Beyle and her husband Moyshe.[11] They were my relatives, were close neighbors of my prospective in-laws, and knew the inside story of my in-law's situation. Through them I would find out the complete and utter truth. I would also ask other residents of the village, and after the investigation I would meet with my in-laws because by then I would know what I had to do. There in Tiraspol I could not find out anything from my sister and could not come to any decisions. This is what I decided to do. So in the middle of the month of *Heshvan*, I traveled off to the village of Tashlik.[12]

When I arrived in Tashlik, my relatives did not recognize me because they had not seen me for approximately three years, during which time I had changed considerably and looked like a completely different person. They were overjoyed at the sight of me since they considered me a very special visitor, especially Beyle who could not have been more surprised to see what had become of me. She would never have believed it, she said, had she not seen me with her own eyes. She became very devoted to me, like a sister, and was quite sorry that I had fallen in with a poor family, and a simple one at that. Beyle told me the real truth—that my in-laws had become quite impoverished and did not even have enough to make it through each day. As to a dowry, there was nothing of which to speak since it did not exist. There were also no clothes for the bride-to-be, and obviously there would be no clothes for me, although they had promised

---

9   *Rosh-Khoydesh Elul* 5627 was September 1–2, 1867. See chapter 17, pp. 278–279, for details about this meeting.
10 See chapter 14, pp. 217–222.
11 The original mistakenly states "Shloyme's" instead of "Shulem's."
12 November 1867.

to furnish them. One can now begin to understand the type of "perpetual *kest*" that I would have at my in-laws following the wedding. My relative Beyle told me all of this, not out of hatred toward my in-laws, but out of loyalty to me so that I should know what to do.

Beyle even explained to me how they had become impoverished. It all happened because of my mother-in-law, Dvoyre. She had schemed, was greedy, and had made various types of business deals and lost money everywhere. Through all of this, she made many enemies in her village among both Jews and Christians, and they were all now impeding her from earning a livelihood. That's how she came to be in this situation. Beyle ended her narrative with these words, "I've no idea how she'll be able to make the wedding. How will you get married?" At this point, she burst into tears over my bitter fate. I thanked her for telling me the entire truth because my mother-in-law had deceived me when I met her in Kalarash on *Rosh-Khoydesh Elul*. At least now I knew where I stood. If only I had known this before *Yontef*, I would not have wasted the little bit of money I had.[13] By now I did not have a *kopek* to my name, and I was without a teaching position for the winter. But I had to decide what to do. So I resolved to renounce the match and leave town.

Afterward, I realized that I had not heard my in-laws' side of the story, so I sent notice to them that the groom-to-be had come either to marry or to end the match—an end to it! My in-laws came to me right away and claimed that they would hold the wedding the following week, that the bride-to-be had been provided with beautiful clothes, and that they would also provide as much clothing as was necessary for me, the groom. But they indeed had no dowry. Of course, since Dvoyre was the mother-in-law, he—the father-in-law—was silent.

This was very bad as far as I was concerned, but I did not know how to contend with the situation. I saw that everything was exactly the way Beyle had described it and that everything my mother-in-law said was a lie and false. But they still wanted to make the wedding and kept yelling that everything was ready, except that there was no dowry. Now how could one do such a thing—break an engagement because of money? But how does one get married without money? If I at least had money myself, I would not have had to seek money from such poor people. But since I also had nothing, how could I do this? How can two dead people dance? Any way you thought about it, it was bad! My conscience did not let me be so cruel as to renounce the match. But my financial situation prevented me from giving in to Dvoyre and thus causing my own misfortune.

---

13 The author decided before Rosh Hashanah that he would use his money to travel to the Lyever Rebbe during *Sukes*, as mentioned in ch. 17, p. 279.

I would have been justified in traveling off and leaving them standing in the mud into which they had led me, but my conscience gnawed at me.

Ah! How could religious people do this? Was it permissible for me to cause misfortune to an innocent child, the prospective bride? How was the girl, my fiancée, responsible for her parents' inability to fulfill their promises? If they had been able, they certainly would have provided what they had promised. What parents do not give to their children when they have the means? If I would be canceling an engagement with the daughter of a rich man, it would not be a catastrophe for the bride-to-be because her father would immediately find her some other groom. Money can buy anything, but my fiancée's parents were poor. Were they to have money, they would be able to find her a respectable match. But if I broke off the match now, when would they be able find a match for their child, and, being so poor, what kind of match would they find? They had neither prestigious lineage nor money, and since the girl had already been engaged for four [sic] years to a fine young man, she would not want to settle for just anyone and no one respectable would want her, especially not a learner or someone who studies Torah full-time in a *bes-medresh*.[14] So she would end up in one of two ways: either she would remain an old maid and cry over me forever or she would end up with someone coarse and unlearned and have no life. So after thinking the whole thing over and feeling sorry for my fiancée's situation, I decided that it was only proper for the wedding to take place the following week—without a dowry or new clothes for me. I would not cause anyone such misfortune because I considered it akin to killing a person. I relied on God; just as He had led me until then, so would He not abandon me in the future either. I told my in-laws, "Go and prepare the wedding, if you can. If you can't, then delay it for half a year because I won't break an engagement."

My in-laws replied, "We're ready to make the wedding right away. We don't want to postpone it. You've wandered around enough. We aren't wealthy people, but we'll provide you with *kest* and you'll be saved from wandering around for another half year. You'll be able to study Torah and be on *kest* as long as you yourself want." They left happily and proceeded zestfully with the wedding plans.

Though I told them that I would marry their daughter, the struggle in my heart was still great. One moment, I was completely resolute, and the next minute I was not so sure of myself. How could I possibly marry without my sisters Ite and Sure? I had only two sisters, should they not attend their brother's

---

14 The author had in fact been engaged three years and one month, since October 10, 1864, as related in chapter 14, pp. 217–222.

wedding? Yet how could I allow myself to invite them? After all, they would never allow me to marry without a dowry and without new clothes for the wedding. They would not allow me to fall into such a poor, coarse village home when they knew that their brother could obtain the greatest, finest, and wealthiest match. I also knew this but had my own understanding of the situation, an understanding they would not take into consideration. And since I would not listen to them, they were sure to disrupt the wedding, and it would really hurt my in-laws to hear my sisters complaining and lamenting. I also needed to refrain from inviting other relatives because they would also oppose my marrying into such a poor family and would consider me crazy for having more concern for another than for myself. That is how the struggle in my heart was raging back and forth.

In the meantime, *Shobes* arrived. I did not want to go to the *minyan* in the neighboring village, Buter, because I figured that my father-in-law would want to have the *ufruf* on *Shobes* so that the wedding would be held the following week.[15] So Beyle's husband and I remained in Tashlik to pray at home, while the other Jews in the Tashlik walked over to the *minyan* in Buter. Suddenly, I noticed that the entire congregation from Buter, including the Tashliker women and children, was arriving with a Torah scroll. "What's this?" I asked in fright. Similarly, Moyshe, Beyle's husband, and the entire family asked, "What's the meaning of this?" The arriving crowd explained that my in-laws figured that the groom had to have his *ufruf* this *Shobes*, so the *minyan* had waited for me. When the Tashlikers arrived for prayers and told them that we were not coming, my in-laws started to cry and asked everyone to go with the Torah scroll to Tashlik so that the groom could have his *ufruf*. So what do you think of my mother-in-law's idea? Perhaps you are thinking that I still did not have to let myself be called up to the Torah. But I could not avoid it, because I could not bear to see the pitiful state of my in-laws and I let myself be called up to the Torah. They considered it an *ufruf*, but I merely considered it being called up to the Torah.[16] After the prayer services, my in-laws served honey cake and liquor that they had brought with them. I realized that I was truly going to be married and that I had to accept the facts. So I told my relatives, Moyshe and Beyle, to stop feeling sorry for me and that they should realize, as I had, that this was the proper thing

---

15 On the *Shabes* preceding his wedding, a groom is customarily called up to the reading of the Torah to make the appropriate blessings. This is called an *ufruf* (Zinner, 1998:1:39–45). Since the author had mixed feelings about marrying, he wanted to avoid the synagogue that *Shobes* to delay the wedding, because without the *ufruf* his wedding would not take place that week.

16 In fact, eight Jewish men are called up to the Torah every *Shabes* morning to recite the appropriate blessings, and usually none of them are grooms. Due to his doubts about the match, the author was still somewhat hoping to avoid marrying.

to do because I saw that it was destined for me. After all, an entire community, consisting of perhaps two *minyanim*,[17] had allowed themselves to be convinced to take a Torah scroll to a groom who did not have in mind to have his *ufruf*. Coming to the groom, they insisted that he must, for the honor of the Torah and the community, have his *ufruf*. This means that it must be the way God willed it. If so, then we were forbidden to sin and go against God's will. "So from now on," I told Moyshe, Beyle, and her mother Khaye, "Start preparing for the wedding. You're the only relatives who'll be there. You—Beyle and Moyshe—will be my *interfirers*, and Khaye will be the groom's senior relative.[18] Bake honey cake for the wedding reception of the groom to make a poor wedding joyous."

My wedding was on Wednesday in the village of Buter. You may think that no musicians were there, but you are mistaken. In fact, important ones were brought from Bender—Reb Shie Poper and his company of musicians. You might think that many of my in-laws' relatives and plenty of villagers were in attendance and they really made merry. I can clarify how it really was: you already know how many relatives came from my side—a scanty three people. But you will be surprised to hear that from the other side came only five men and about ten women and girls. There should have been many guests from the villages. I do not know if it was the musicians' bad luck or my own, but a heavy snow began falling that Tuesday evening when I was traveling to Buter with my few relatives to the "groom's meal." Years ago, they used to make a meal at the groom's house the night before the wedding meal, which was called the "groom's meal."[19] So when we reached the village of Buter, the in-laws' family and friends and the musicians were supposed to be riding out of town to greet the groom as is the custom, but there was no crowd.[20] I was led to the large home of a Romanian where I was to be spending the evening and the night. No one showed up for the "groom's meal" because it would have been a sin to let even a dog out onto the street in such a winter storm, let alone people. So this was how the evening of my "groom's meal" passed—boring and undignified.

---

17 *Minyanim* is the plural of *minyan*. Two *minyanim* would be twenty Jewish men above thirteen years of age.

18 Both the bride and the groom each designate a married couple, often their parents, as *interfirers*, who lead the bride and group to the *huppah*. Either the groom's *interfirers* lead the groom and the bride's *interfirers* lead the bride, or, as is done among Hasidim, the two men lead the groom and the two women lead the bride (Zinner, 1998:1:107–113). Beyle's mother Khaye was not eligible for this honor since she was widowed. See also the Introduction, p. 21, footnote 40.

19 See Zinner (1998:1:51–53) for details and sources.

20 Some details and sources regarding the custom of friends and the musicians riding out of town to greet the approaching groom can be found in Zinner (1998:1:95). See the memoirs of Spector (1927:70–74) and Katsovits (1924:157–158) for detailed descriptions of this custom.

The following day, the day of the wedding, the storm had still not abated. Only two days later, the day after the wedding, did the weather become nice again and a sledding path was formed, and the beautiful weather was a pleasure to behold. Shie Poper complained bitterly about his bad luck. How could it be? He had expected to be able to coax a substantial amount of money from the Jewish villagers and the wealthy tenant innkeepers.[21] Ultimately, he struggled a lot in traveling back to Bender in the heavy snow and returned home with nothing, as it states, "If he comes in alone, he shall leave alone."[22]

The day before the wedding, I did not complain about my own situation, yet I could not feel any happiness because my heart was so embittered. I had spent that day at my lodgings, and no one came by until the evening, so I had had time for contemplation. I had enough time to contemplate my entire bitter life until then. My entire hope had rested on having to work as a *melomed* only until my wedding. I had thought that after my wedding I would be able to anticipate the greatest of joys.[23] Yet in the end, this hope vanished upon realizing that my in-laws had no money. So what could I still hope for? I had no money, and my in-laws were poor. Who knew whether I would even have enough bread to eat, and who knew what kind of wife my fiancée would be. So I prayed to the Master of the Universe, "Look at this act of loving kindness that I'm performing. I'm breaking my heart solely out of pity and common decency. I'm consenting to everything, and I'm marrying into such poverty, though I could have married the daughter of a wealthy family. So, You, Master of the Universe, please be merciful to me and let my intended wife be my 'helpmate' rather than my 'adversary.'[24] And may I merit having with her kosher, good, exemplary, and pious children. This would be the best reward for my current troubles and suffering." This was how I spent the entire day—fasting and praying with tears before God.[25] Afterward my heart felt lighter, and all my worry left me. It was as if all the stones lying on my heart until then had been removed. So I went to the

---

21 The wedding attendees used to tip the musicians for each additional song they requested to be played.
22 Exodus 21:3.
23 The author's greatest hope was to study Torah without any financial worries, as mentioned earlier in this chapter on p. 295.
24 Genesis 2:18 states, "God said, 'It is not good for man to be alone; I will make him a helpmate alongside him.'" The Hebrew word used for "alongside him," *kenegdo*, can also be translated as "against him." The Talmud (Yevamot 63a) comments on these opposing meanings, "If he is worthy, his wife will be his helpmate. If he is unworthy, she will become his adversary."
25 The Jewish groom and bride traditionally fast on the day of their wedding, which is generally considered to be similar to Yom Kippur (the Day of Atonement) as all of their sins are forgiven on that day (Kaplan, 1983:82).

huppah with strong trust in God that He had accepted my prayers. I was almost happy, and therein found a sign from God that He had accepted my prayers.²⁶

Now, my loved ones, it is already after my wedding, and I am about to start a new life that you will find even more interesting than everything until now. But we must stop here until the commotion of the wedding dissipates.

***

The village of Buter is thirty *versts* from Tiraspol, twenty-five *versts* from Bender, thirty-five *versts* from Kishinev, twenty-five *versts* from Dubisár, and lies next to the Dniester River. It is a large village divided into two parts. One part is alongside the base of the mountain. All the houses of that section are built along the base of the mountain. The second part is on the riverbank, along the length of the Dniester River. Between both parts of the village is a small empty field on which no houses can be built because, when it occurs that the Dniester overflows, the waters flow into this area. It was in that village that I got married at a propitious hour.

My wedding took place on a Wednesday, which was either the 22nd or 23rd of *Heshvan* in 5622 [*sic*], though I do not remember exactly.²⁷ I only remember that I was married in the third week of *Heshvan*. I know that it was no earlier than the 21st and no later than the 23rd of *Heshvan*, as just mentioned. You already know how joyful the wedding ceremony was. You know about the turnout, the guests who arrived, as well as the musicians. You can figure out on your own who my *interfirers* were. I had no relatives there from my side besides Beyle and Moyshe from Tashlik, Shulem's daughter and son-in-law.²⁸ So they were the *interfirers* from my side. The *interfirers* on the bride's side were her uncle from the village of Ternifke. His name was Yankev Ternifker, or, as he was called by others, "Yankev the Blind."²⁹ His grande dame of a wife was Rifke,

---

26 The Mishna (Brakhot 5:5) cites a tradition that a sign that one's prayers have been accepted is if they flow fluently from one's mouth. Apparently Goldenshteyn felt that his prayer met that criterion.

27 According to historical calendars, the Wednesday of the author's wedding corresponded to the 22nd of *Heshvan* 5628 (November 20, 1867). He was not married in 5622 (1861) as he writes here, which he calculated based on his mistaken notion that he was born in 1842. See the Introduction, pp. 67–70.

28 It mistakenly states "Shloyme's children" instead of "Shulem's children," which is how the author previously refers to Shulem's daughter Beyle and her husband Moyshe.

29 He is called Yankev Royzman in chapter 24. Yankev was certainly not completely blind, since the author does not mention such a severe disability in his description in chapter 25 of his

and she spoke with a bit of a nasal voice. These were the *interfirers* from the bride's side.³⁰

Early on the morning after the wedding, my relatives left. Shie Poper and his company also left, though dissatisfied because he had apparently expected larger earnings, but they had to move on. So too did all of the guests disperse, leaving behind only the members of the household. When I first began looking around, I realized that everything appeared to be as if it was all a dream. I was like someone who dreams that he finds a lot of money and in his sweet slumber is preoccupied with his money and his plans of what to do with it. Finally, in the middle of it all, he awakes and realizes that all of his plans were for naught and that his money is also gone. Everything had all been just a sweet dream. This was how it was for me as well! Until my wedding, I had dreamed that I would have money, live with my wealthy father-in-law, and have perpetual *kest*. In short, I had counted on falling into a pool of *shmalts*!³¹ Ultimately, the *shmalts* dried out and all that was left was an empty pit. All my plans were impeded, and I now awoke to what had thus far been a dream.

I had married, thank God, but had nothing else. All my assets amounted to fifteen rubles, two old and worn silver spoons, a silver saltshaker, which was also old, and two worn-out brass candlesticks.³² That was what I had received from my in-laws as a wedding gift—leftovers from their earlier days as wealthy people. True, my bride wore four strands of pearls, which were also considered mine because her mother had given them to her when she became engaged. Her wardrobe was the same as mine—she had almost nothing save a few simple stitched calico dresses and a few blouses. You could see the poverty in every corner of the house, and, in addition, there was almost no one to talk with because my wife was so rustic that there was simply nothing to discuss with her.

The next day, I began to feel so bad that I became quite nervous. I was not living as a groom after his wedding but was very gloomy thinking about my bad luck. I was idle all day and had no job apart from studying Torah, though I did

---

wandering around with him in Simferopol. Often someone blind in one eye was called "blind" in Yiddish, as in the case of "Shmiel the blind *melomed*," mentioned in chapter 4, p. 132.

30 Although the bride's parents are customarily the *interfirers* when both are living, the custom is that other relatives are asked to be the *interferers* when the mother of the bride is pregnant in order to avoid an evil eye (Zinner, 1998:1:112). Why should her parents draw attention to one's ample good fortune of being both pregnant and marrying off a child, thereby causing people to be jealous? Freyde's mother Dvoyre was evidently pregnant with her brother Mordkhe (see ch. 19, p. 335, footnote 30).

31 This Yiddish expression refers to striking it rich.

32 Though the author writes here that he had two silver spoons, he mentions later in this chapter on p. 309 that he had three silver spoons. In chapter 19, p. 322, he mentions that he had four old silver spoons as well as a small silver spoon.

not have any Jewish books to study. In his home, my father-in-law had a prayer book, a book of Psalms, a year-round holiday prayer book, and a thick volume in which all of the Five Books of Moses were bound together. Neither he nor the entire village had any other Jewish books, aside from the few that I had.

So what was I to do? I spent the first few days roaming around like a maniac. I had no job and also had no one to talk to. My in-laws were busy with earning their meager living, and I had nothing to do. My young wife was actually a very fine and pious person. She was lovely, quiet, and was glad to spend time with me. Nonetheless, she had been unfortunately raised to be very coarse and uncultured. She simply could not talk with anyone since there was no one with whom to socialize for she had never seen anyone let alone been around people. She only knew how to speak enough Romanian to a Romanian when one would come around to ask about buying or selling something. She actually did have a good head; when something was explained to her, she grasped it well—but everything seemed new to her as if it was the first time she was hearing it. The slightest thing she learned seemed to her as if she had just "discovered America!"[33] When it would happen that she had to reply to something, she would turn red, and every other color, from embarrassment—that is how difficult it was for her to reply let alone ask someone something! Such an underdeveloped child could only be raised by my in-laws, who never brought their children among other people and also never personally spent time speaking with them. They only had time to order them around when they needed to.

In short, I did not know what to do with myself for the entire day. One could just go crazy from lonesomeness. I managed to borrow a tractate of the Talmud and a volume of *Code of Jewish Law* from someone. I also borrowed some Jewish books from my Moyshe, Beyle's husband, in Tashlik and even from a tenant innkeeper from a village called Speye, not far from our village. Now I could sit down and study. When not studying, I made sure to teach my young wife how to begin speaking with others and about the world so that she would know that beyond the other side of the village was a big world with many, many people. I told her that a person needs to know everything that is happening in the wider world and needs to be able to get to know all types of people and how to get along with them.

Her only luck—or more correctly, my luck—was that her intelligence was good, and she understood things quite well, otherwise it would have been like living with a dumb beast, which I do not know if I would have been willing to do. If she had been foolish, she certainly would not have let herself be taught, because,

---

33 "*Andekt Amerike*" in the original Yiddish is a common expression of irony in Yiddish.

as they say, a fool is perpetual trouble. (As our sages write, when the Messiah will come, all the sick will be healed and anyone with a defect will be cured, because anyone with a sickness or defect will beseech the Messiah for help.[34] For example, if a person is missing an eye or if he limps, the Messiah will say, "You shall be able to see! You shall be able to walk straight like everyone else!" Since the Messiah will make a sick person healthy, all those who will beseech the Messiah because they are lacking something will be helped. But the fool will not come to ask the Messiah for help to become intelligent because the fool always considers himself smart, so how can he be discontented? Therefore, he will remain the same fool he was before, which is why they say that a fool is perpetual trouble.)

This is why I say that the luck was that she was actually not a fool. Her intelligence was not to blame for her inability to speak with others, for it was as if she had grown up alone in a forest without anyone to talk to. And so, as I began to engage her in conversation, her eyes began to open, and she really appreciated my making her aware of her flaws, thanking me time and time again. She followed everything I told her to do, since my words were precious and holy to her. Because of this, I acquired great affection for her and grew to love her more from day to day. Nothing was too difficult for me to endure as long as I was not parted from her, yet people thought that I would have to do just that. Despite her parents' poverty and my "perpetual" *kest*, which ended two months after our wedding, and despite the fact that my loss of *kest* was a financial blow, I did not want to abandon my beloved wife and head out into the bigger world. After all, I would not have wanted my wife to revert to her former crudeness for then all of my hard work with her would go to naught, God forbid.

I considered her my personal mission since she had been rescued and reborn due to my humane care for her. She reciprocated my love and appreciated me greatly, never ignoring anything I said. That is why our life together evolved with pure love from day to day because we always, even in our greatest poverty, considered ourselves happier than the happiest couple in the world. I always thanked and praised God for preordaining for me such a true partner who sweetened the bitter times that I lived through in my subsequent family life, as you will learn and know from my narrative.

I must, however, tell you that this uncultured village girl, this underdeveloped young wife of mine, was apparently lacking in basics that even any small child possesses. So whenever I went anywhere with her, I had to drill her in advance about what to say when she entered a house, whether it was "Good morning," "Good afternoon," or "Good evening," depending on the time of day. Similarly,

---

34 Talmud (Sanhedrin 91b).

when leaving, I had to make sure to prevent her from switching "Good night" for "Good day" and the like. You can imagine the level of her upbringing. But you should have seen what became of this young woman over time; she developed into the finest, most sophisticated lady, a person with whom it was a delight to spend time. Even her very own parents and family did not recognize her and could not believe that their little Freydele had grown up to be such a fine person. She was obviously their child, but how was it possible for her to use such refined language, understand matters so clearly, and have such fine manners. They indeed had other children, so why were they not as smart, refined, and so on? In short, she was unique in their family, someone with human sensibilities, and whoever did not know her wondered from which magnificent family she originated. Everyone treasured her, thought she was from the most refined family, and marveled at how an impoverished and distressed person like myself could find such a wife. Later on, when I became a *shoykhet*, people wondered how a *shoykhet* deserved such an impressive, intelligent wife. This shows that a person can work to develop himself over time if he only wants to and, in addition, has a good teacher.

But I have digressed far, and it is now already time to return to the narrative, to the subsequent events that happened to me after my wedding. Two weeks

FIGURE 9. A photograph of the author's first wife Freyde (1851–1896) with their daughter Rukhl (1887–1966) taken in the mid-1890s. Freyde is wearing a *sheytl*, as married religious Jewish women do as a sign of modesty. Courtesy of Shifra Bernfeld.

had passed since my wedding. My wife and I traveled into town, to Tiraspol, to introduce her to my sister Ite, and it was there that I received my comeuppance. When I entered Reb Zolmen-Sukher-Kopls's home where my sister always stayed, everyone welcomed me warmly. Everyone there—his wife and children—congratulated us with warm and friendly *mazel tovs*. Then, in came my sister and, disregarding the get-together, she ran straight over to me and gave me a slap and then another, "Here you are, Brother, for disgracing me by not inviting me to your wedding!" She then went over to my wife and embraced and kissed her, saying, "I have nothing against you. You are very precious to me because you are my only sister-in-law, my only brother's wife." At that, she burst into tears in recalling that she had not been at her brother's wedding. I stood there in shock the whole time. Though I could sense that her pain was great and that she was unfortunately deeply offended by my behavior, nonetheless, in truth, I was still in the right. But here, given our family relationship, she was also in the right from her point of view. So I accepted her entire reaction lovingly and apologized, and she finally had to forgive me.

The next day, my wife, sister, and I went around visiting all of our friends and relatives and we acquainted my wife with their fine families, which she appreciated very much and thanked me profusely. This was very useful in helping me teach her. I had much to show her regarding how she should conduct herself and speak in public without turning red from embarrassment every time she conversed with someone.

Eight days later—three weeks after our wedding—a guest came to visit me right in the village of Buter. She was a very precious but unexpected guest. Do you know who she was? It was the youngest of my sisters, Surele from Chimishliya, who had heard that her brother was getting married. She convinced her husband, the *melomed*, to send her to her brother's wedding using the following line of reasoning: How was it possible for her brother to get married and for her not to be there? After all, did she have that many brothers? How could she miss her only brother's wedding? She spent so much time weeping that her husband finally gave her the money for her expenses and permitted her to go. Now imagine her shock upon finding out that she arrived three weeks after the wedding. How horribly distressed she was, how great was her heartache, and how terribly she regretted making the trip at all. But my wife and I did not allow her to feel much hurt or pain. We consoled her and had a warm visit with her. She spent eight days with us, and I then hired a wagon and accompanied her until Kishinev.

I had plenty of time to talk to Surele about everything that had happened to me and why things had turned out the way they did, that is that neither of my sisters was invited to my wedding. I also explained that I only agreed to travel with her to Kishinev because I wanted her to take in one of our sister Tsipe's orphaned children, meaning that she should look after little Duvidl. He was a boy who already needed a *melomed*, aside from the fact that he needed a place to live.[35] I convinced her that with God's help I would take him to live with me at some later date. In short, she agreed to take the little boy, Duvidl.

Upon arriving in Kishinev, I discovered that the little girl, Khaykele, had already been placed with a relative, who was a fine person. He was an elderly man whose name, I think, was Khotskl Roytenberg, who lived in his own home on the main street. I located him and saw that she was doing well and looking very good and happy. But the little boy Duvidl's situation was the exact opposite; he was neglected, unclean, mere skin and bones, and totally dejected, as you can imagine. He did not even have the appearance of a child, having deteriorated from hunger and want . . . In short, we both cried bitterly over his condition, and we took him from the impoverished Jewish woman who was caring for him. She demanded the couple of rubles due her. I paid her and we took the little boy with us. By then Reb Shloyme-Leyzer had already left Kishinev and abandoned his daughter Khayele. But Reyzl, his daughter from his first wife, whom Tsipe had married off, as you know, took pity on the orphans. She had arranged for the little girl to be taken in by this Roytenberg relative, as already mentioned, and used to pay for the little boy as much as she could, though she herself was extremely poor. Of course, she could not have kept up much longer the struggle to pay for his upkeep ever since her father had gone. The third month since Shloyme-Leyzer's departure had just begun and had it continued a little longer, Reyzl would have been forced to stop paying, and the impoverished Jewish woman would have ousted the boy from her care, abandoning him. But divine providence had led me to come along with my sister Sure to take Duvidl. We saved Reyzl from distress and the boy from hunger.[36]

We brought Duvidl to our lodgings, where my sister washed him and changed his clothes. I hired a wagon to take her home to her husband in Chimishliya. It happened that on that day the clouds darkened and it began snowing. I sent them off well wrapped against the cold. But later in the evening, a blizzard began. *Oy!* I remember how I cried and spent the whole night

---

35 Since Duvidl was born in October 1864 (ch. 14, p. 223), he was three years old by December 1867.

36 In two letters to his daughter Nekhame dated the 21st of *Tamuz* 5686 (July 3, 1926) and the 18th of *Heshvan* 5690 (November 21, 1929), the author writes that Reyzl married a man named Kanter who had a tobacco store in Kishinev and was also a *moyel* and a cantor there and that she died young. Reyzl had a son named Shimen in New York and two daughters.

in tears: who knew whether my sister and nephew would arrive home alive and not freeze to death on the way, God forbid. And would the sturdy warm clothing that they had be enough? I blamed myself, worried myself to death, and constantly wrung my hands, until I received word—four days later—that they were both miraculously rescued and arrived home safely. They would have died from the cold had the driver not turned into a village and spent the night with them there. Had he kept going, they certainly would have frozen to death. But in the village, they warmed up overnight, and in the morning the wind died down and the weather became less cold. In that village, they gave them a lot of warm coverings, especially to the exhausted little boy who did not have a drop of warm blood left in him. In short, they arrived home, thank God. I only calmed down when I received the letter, and then returned to the tranquility of my home to live off of my perpetual *kest*.

It was on my return home to the village that I first started feeling my in-laws' poverty. During the first two or three weeks of my marriage when they still considered me a guest, they rallied their strength to make sure that I was not aware of their dire situation. But when I ceased being a guest, they stopped concealing their poverty and started to show their true destitution. They began eating bread and foods to which I could in no way become accustomed. It is possible that they did not eat any better previously, just that I was not aware of it. But once I ceased being a guest, they considered me one of their own. I, who was raised as a city boy, found the entire atmosphere and their coarse lifestyle unfamiliar and abhorrent. In particular, I could not tolerate their bread or their food. I just could not bear it. Not for a moment did I let go of the thought that I should leave them and be off . . . I thought that I would be justified in taking this step, but only one thing held me back—the pity I had for my young wife. Thinking about her situation and the suffering she would bear if I left was the one thing that prevented me from making that move. So I suffered and began to wane from day to day.

It was quite stressful for my young wife to see me suffer, but she was not capable of remedying the situation. Her parents asked me what was the matter, and I told them. They excused themselves passionately, claiming that their poverty was to blame, not they themselves. I admitted that they were correct, but I too was correct. I could not share a home with them and could not put up with their behavior or with their children who had no upbringing and were growing up as rustic boors, and so on.

"Here now, what do you want?" they asked me. "How can we do any better?"

"Yes, you won't be able to do any better," I replied. "But you definitely can improve my situation!"

"How so?" they asked astonished. "How can we improve your situation?"

"By doing the following—by parting from me."

"What do you mean?" they asked frightened. "How can we part from you? You don't even have your own business. How will you live?"

I replied, "Oh, that makes no difference! The same God who feeds the entire world will also feed both my wife and me. But we have to figure out how to persuade you to leave me the house and agree to let me have it as my own in lieu of a dowry. Once that occurs, I would remain in this house with my wife, your daughter, and would have absolutely no further demands of you. From that day onward, I would forgo your perpetual *kest* and anything else you promised. Just oblige me with this one thing."

"What are you planning to do?" they asked me. "Are you are planning to discard our daughter and leave her all alone?"

"Abandon your daughter? If I wanted to do that, I could just as easily do it to her now when she's with you. Why would I treat my wife so cruelly? How can you take me to be such a cutthroat? Why would I abandon her later when she would be left all alone? How can you suspect me of being such a murderer? No, you've made a grave error! I have nothing against your daughter. I'm more devoted to her than you are, though you're her parents. The proof of this is that I'm allowing you to end my *kest* so that I can do nothing less than remain living in this house with my wife, though I have nothing to support us apart from my trust in God that He won't abandon me. She agrees with me and trusts me more than she trusts you. She already knows your disloyalty to her. But I must say that if you don't oblige me, I'll have to leave everything and, reluctantly, also leave your daughter with you, only because of your disloyalty. Your daughter will then have something to cry about, though not about me, God forbid, but about you. I married her and want to live with her, but not with you, because I can in no way live together with you. If I had my own house, or at least some capital, I wouldn't leave her. But I will have to do this, albeit reluctantly. And who knows what calamity could later occur if I would leave moneyless to seek my fortune? And who among us would be to blame? You, of course! Only you, her disloyal parents."

Finally, after finishing all that I had to say and after many arguments, it was decided as I had wanted—that they, my in-laws, would move out of the house and leave it to me, as I explained above.

This was easier said than done. Though we agreed to this and it was so decided, the implementation of our plans could not be rushed because they first had to find themselves a place to live where they could open a tavern or a store. Since not every location was suitable for earning a living, my in-laws kept looking for a place of their own. In the meantime, a couple of months passed, during which time we all lived together and suffered. But I lived with the hope that I would not suffer much longer and would be relieved of them very shortly. These hopes made my bitter life easier, and finally my hope was realized when my in-laws were able to take over a wine and liquor tavern in Perkon, a Bulgarian village located next to the Dniester River near the city of Bender. The Jewish community of Bender leased out taverns in the surrounding villages to a lessee, who in turn set my in-laws up in a tavern under his authority and gave them good wages. Their new circumstances there worked out well for me. It was also good for them because, in any case, they had nothing to do in our village other than sit around and struggle to earn enough for a morsel of dry bread. Since they had no capital to set up their own tavern and there were no taverns available to be leased, this arrangement that came about in Perkon was a miracle. I do not know if this miracle occurred in my merit or in theirs, but however it happened it was actually a great miracle for all of us, and it saved us all from a desperate situation.

My in-laws left right away at the beginning of the new year, January 1, 1868, and my wife and I remained the residents of the house, the owners of a home with a good stone cellar.[37] As my in-laws bade us farewell, they cried much because they felt terrible that they were leaving us so poor and alone. They were especially concerned about their daughter. They were afraid I would abandon her and take off, God forbid. People had frightened them by putting such ideas in their heads: this young man has already been in the bigger world and will certainly not remain here in this village especially if he must live in such poverty. This was how their friends frightened them. It was not out of loyalty to my in-laws but rather out of envy, because they could not imagine that a young man falling into such a situation would not see to it that he save himself. If I had their corrupt morals, I would surely have done so, but I was prepared to endure anything before I would permit myself to deceive my wife who was destined for me by divine providence.

I calmed my in-laws' fears, telling them that they were sinning against God by thinking so badly about me. Their daughter also calmed them down by telling them that she implicitly trusted her devoted, beloved husband even more than she trusted them. She reassured them that they could go on their way

---

37 This date is according to the Julian calendar, which was used in Russia until 1918 and corresponds to January 13, 1868 in the Gregorian calendar. It is the first accurate year mentioned by the author. Its accuracy can be verified by the chronology of events until now and from the Hebrew date "the sixth or the eighth of the month of *Iyar* 5628" corresponding to April 28 or 30, 1868, mentioned later in this chapter on p. 312.

without concern for their daughter's wellbeing. They finally left, and we remained there alone.

Right after their departure, we began to contemplate what we needed to do. How would we earn our piece of bread? Under no circumstances was I going to run a tavern. I could not tolerate that line of work, which would involve associating with drunken non-Jews. Even though someone had offered me money to open a tavern in partnership with him, I thought that opening a small shop would be ideal. My wife was well suited for that work, and it would be a quiet way to earn a living. With God's help, a customer would enter, buy, and leave. Being near her, I would quickly learn how to sell, and we would earn our piece of bread. The location of the house was indeed too limited a place to support my wife's parents and their entire family, but it would certainly be sufficient for two people. Surely this was all true, but where would we find the money? With what means would we set up a store? I could not solve the question of money because I did not have from whom to borrow. No one would loan me any money because they knew that I was poor. And I did not want to go into partnership with someone who did have money, because I was afraid that the business could not sustain two families and the other person would claim that I had impoverished him, God forbid. As the Yiddish saying goes, "alone one's soul remains pure of sin." All in all, my situation was dire! I turned to everyone I knew. I brought up the subject of a loan with my relatives in Tashlik, but they naturally refused. After all, how could I ever permit myself to actually receive a favor from a relative? Only one single time in my life, and no more, did I ever obtain a favor from a relative, as I shall relate later.[38]

When I saw that a loan was unattainable, I took out all my assets, namely the fifteen rubles in cash that I had received as wedding gifts. I had held on tightly to that money and had miraculously saved it from the clutches of my in-laws, who had searched for it. They knew the exact amount I had received and that I had not given it over to them. In addition to these very well-guarded fifteen rubles, I took the three old silver spoons, which had also been a wedding gift, plus four strands of pearls that my wife wore around her neck—the sum total of her jewelry. With all of this, I traveled to Tiraspol to purchase merchandise for the new store, which I would be opening at an auspicious time.

Not far from our village lived my mother-in-law's sister, an aunt of ours named Blime. Her husband was called "Velvl the Nun's,"[39] or as others called

---

38   The author is apparently referring to the loan of three rubles that he obtained from a relative, as described in chapter 20, p. 363.
39   Velvl *der Monishkes* in the original. A *mnishke* (also *monashke*) denotes a nun in Yiddish. Perhaps he was called by such an odd nickname because his wife, mother, or mother-in-law

him, "Velvl the Lame."⁴⁰ Upon leaving, I asked Aunt Blime to send one of her children to my Freydele during the day and that Aunt Blime herself should spend the night with Freydele. Thus, I could travel into town whenever I needed.⁴¹

I came into town and pawned the items that I listed above. I received twenty-five rubles for them and now had a total of forty rubles. I spent thirty rubles on all sorts of groceries for our new store—I bought small quantities but of all types. I made purchases according to the list that my wife had put together. I bought a scale and weights for five rubles and all types of dishes: plates, spoons, glasses, bowls, a teapot, and so on—everything that we were lacking in our home. Three rubles were for the non-Jewish driver to take his wagon there and back, and I was still left with two rubles in my pocket to return home with.

I came home from town, and we set up our store. We set it up so skillfully that although all the groceries could have been tucked away in just one corner, it looked like almost all the shelves and two walls were full of merchandise.

We started selling, little by little, so that two weeks later I had to travel to bring more merchandise. We lived contently and calmly. Though we were not big spenders, we lived in great want. This is how we lived until Pesach,⁴² when we traveled to be with my in-laws in Perkon because our store was not earning enough to cover Pesach expenses. Right after Pesach, we returned home and continued to run our store. I saw that our little store was dying because there was neither merchandise nor money. What were we supposed to do?

I made use of the young cow that had just calved. When my in-laws left the village, they had given me a two-year-old cow, and I fed it the entire winter with the feed that my in-laws had left for it. And now that the young cow, which

---

was called "the nun," an indication of her stiffness. Or perhaps Velvl acquired this nickname due to his being close as a boy to his family's non-Jewish domestic helper who was called "the Nun" for her religiosity. Similarly, a Jewish man in Grodno, Belarus, was nicknamed "the priest" (Grodner, 1951:59), while another in Chernigov, Ukraine was nicknamed "the pope" (Schneersohn, 1968:224). Sometimes odd Yiddish nicknames have surprising origins, such as the case of "Zalmen *der Yid*" (Zalmen the Jew) as mentioned by Kopelov (1926:234) in his autobiography. Originally nicknamed "Zalmen *der goy*" (Zalmen the non-Jew) due to his tremendous ignorance of Judaism, Zalmen eventually had the rabbi issue a ban against calling him by that nickname only to have everyone begin calling him "Zalmen *der Yid*." Another such case mentioned by Rabbi Yitskhak Nissenbaum (1929:2) in his memoirs involves his childhood neighbor, a lumber merchant, who was called "Elye *der goy*"; when the non-Jewish wagoner would deliver the lumber every afternoon, Elye's wife would wake him up from his nap with the words, "Elye, *der goy*!" meaning "Elye, the *goy* [is here]."

40 Velvl *der krumer* in the original. *Krumer* can mean lame, squint-eyed, or crooked in Yiddish.
41 The author is evidently referring to Tiraspol.
42 April 7–14, 1868.

had just calved, had become a full-grown cow, we would be able to get milk and butter from it. But our store was dying, and I could not pay off the items I had pawned; the interest on those items would accrue and we would then lose those assets. So what was to be done? What was the best thing to do? I decided that we needed to sell the cow, so I sold it for thirty-five rubles and paid off the pawned assets. I bought some more goods and returned home. I bought a goat for three rubles. We had quite enough milk for our little family, and we had no reason to miss the cow. My Freydele was now wearing her pearls again, and we were now eating with our silver spoons. Meanwhile, the store continued to function, and we were managing. *Oy* and how did we manage? She ran our home, the household, and was the shopkeeper in the store, while I studied Torah and occasionally took her place in our little store. Time moved along, and, although sales did occur early in the day and at dusk, no one came around the rest of the day, not to mention after Pesach, when all the peasants were at work all day in the fields. Sales worsened from day to day. Aside from my not having anything to sell, I had no customers even for the little bit of merchandise that I did have. Instead of customers on two feet, four-footed customers came by to eat whatever remained . . .

At that time, I had to make a trip to my in-laws in Perkon. Being right in the middle of the working season, *Rosh-Khoydesh Iyar*,[43] it was not worth it for me to hire a wagon because of the expense. So I rented a horse from a Romanian for the day. Since I would be back that night, it was cheaper that way. In addition, by riding I would also have the opportunity to be in Tiraspol too. But something phenomenal and frightening happened to me. The fear has stayed with me until this day, and I still do not know what it means. Had I heard another person relate these events, I certainly would not have believed him. So too now, when I relate these events, there will be people who will not believe me and who will say it was all in my imagination, a dream or some other type of apparition. I have nothing against those who do not believe me, God forbid, because I just told you that I would have reacted the same way had I heard this from another person. But, since it happened to me, I know the truth. Since I know that it is a true story that happened while I was awake, not in a dream, and while completely alert, I can therefore relate everything that happened to me. Whoever knows me will certainly believe it. Whoever does not know me can say whatever he wants. I do not care whether he believes me or not, as long as I know that my conscience is pure and that I am relating the full truth without any exaggeration or falsehood, God forbid. I am recounting what happened in

---

43 April 22–23, 1868.

my life, and everything I endured and suffered, saw and heard. I am doing it all so that my children should know what occurred to their father and mother during their lives. Since I have digressed for too long, it is now time to return to our discussion of the frightening thing that happened to me.

On the sixth or the eighth of the month of *Iyar* 5628,[44] I recall that I left the village of Buter on horseback for Perkon, as mentioned earlier. By 10 a.m., I had covered the twenty-five *versts* to Perkon and stayed there for two hours. At 12 p.m., I left Perkon for Tiraspol. At 12:45, I arrived in Tiraspol, where I stayed until four. Then I left Tiraspol and at six in the evening I arrived in Molayésht, a village about fifteen *versts* from Tiraspol. I stopped there to visit a tenant innkeeper, a good friend of mine called Reb Arn Molayéshter, and spent half an hour with him while my horse rested. From there back home I still had another fifteen *versts* to ride because from Buter to Tiraspol is thirty *versts*, and Molayesht is exactly halfway between them. Since nighttime would soon be falling, the horse was tired, and I knew that I still had a distance to travel, I took a break for about half an hour and then continued on my way.

At this point, I have to stop and describe the road from the village of Molayesht to my home in the village of Buter. The road goes through four mountains and four valleys, with the four mountains following one after the other. From the first valley in which the village of Molayesht lies the road goes up the first mountain. Upon reaching the top of that mountain, the road goes right down into the next valley. From there, the road continues up and down that way until the fourth descent, where it goes down into a deeper valley where the village of Buter lies.

When I left the village of Molayesht and started traveling up the first ascent, which continues for about two *versts*, I began to pray *Minkhe* while on horseback, though it was still early. The horse was moving along leisurely, and I was praying slowly. By the time I reached the top of the first mountain, I had already finished the *Shimenesre* prayer.[45] I looked down into the valley and saw a fire burning on the side of the road, but it made no impression on me—it was just a fire in the valley. I figured it was either some shepherds cooking their dinner, a *chumak* stopping to graze his oxen, or peasants who had traveled onto the steppe to till the fields and were burning the tall weeds that grew there.[46]

---

44 April 28 or 30, 1868.
45 *Shimenesre* (*Shmona esre* in Modern Hebrew) refers to the silent Hebrew prayer consisting of nineteen blessings. It is the main prayer of each of the three Jewish daily prayer services.
46 *Bruyanes* is misprinted in the original instead of *buryanes*, a Russian loanword with the Yiddish plural ending "-*es*." *Buryanes* are the tall, wiry, and often thorny weeds that grow on the steppe. At that time, the burning of the vegetation on the steppe was the only kind of fertilizing to which it was ever subjected ("The Steppes of Southern Russia No. I," 1841).

Apart from the possibilities that I mentioned, I was not concerned about anything, though I could still see the little fire deep inside the valley while I was at the top of the mountain. It was of such little interest to me that it slipped my mind completely. I did not even think to later investigate the source of the fire when I would descend into the valley and approach the location where I saw it burning. I rode down into the valley, finished *Minkhe*, and was absorbed in my own thoughts. I traveled like this across the entire valley and had already started up the second ascent.

After riding a bit uphill, I heard something humming behind me. I turned around to look and saw that the humming noise was coming from the little fire I had seen earlier when I was on top of the mountain. Though I had passed it a while before, I had not noticed at all if it was still burning or who had made the fire. Now the little fire was moving swiftly. It was moving quickly from its position in the valley where I had first spotted it from the top of the first mountain. It was speeding right toward me with tremendous force and was screeching like a full-blown fire, God forbid. When I saw it, I became terribly frightened and started screaming *Shma Yisruel* and other verses with all my strength.[47] The fire started to diminish and recede, moving quickly back into the valley. I thanked God for saving me from the fire and prompted the horse to move as fast as possible, but it was tired and did not want to obey me.

In the meantime, I had already ridden up that mountain and was riding down the other side. I continued riding and thinking about what had happened to me in that valley. I started thinking and imagining all types of things about the fire. I was wondering to myself what I had just done. Perhaps it was actually a treasure and I was supposed to acquire it.[48] According to what I had heard, to acquire such a treasure you must throw a shoe or some other item you are wearing into the fire; the fire would immediately be extinguished and the treasure could be taken. So now I wondered why I had not done that. Then I changed my mind for how did I know there was a treasure there? Perhaps it was something spiritually impure, since I had seen written in holy books a description of a type of spiritual impurity called the "translucent shell,"[49] which appears to

---

47 Literally "Hear, O Israel," which are the first two words of the verse, "Hear, O Israel; the Lord is our God, the Lord is One" (Deuteronomy 6:4). Since this verse is considered a basic tenet of Judaism, the entire verse is traditionally recited at times of danger.
48 Stories of buried treasure emitting fires or lights can be found in Jewish folklore and—not dissimilarly—non-Jewish folklore. See, for example, Cahan (1938:163–167), Shvartsburg (1934:28–29), Feilberg (1895:297–298), and Walhouse (1894:295).
49 *Klipat noga* (as pronounced in Modern Hebrew) in the original. *Klipa* is a Kabbalistic term, literally meaning "peel," used to denote negative and evil forces which conceal the divine presence just as a peel conceals fruit. Literally meaning "bright *klipa*," the *klipat noga* gener-

humans and takes on the form of a fire jumping from place to place. So it might actually have been good that I had distanced myself from it and did not stop. Meanwhile, do not forget that I was riding and would periodically lash the horse to go faster. I was in the depths of the valley and started riding up the third mountain.

While absorbed in my above-mentioned thoughts, I again heard the fire humming louder than before. So I looked behind me and saw the fire racing down the mountain I had crossed. It was heading directly at me, only it was moving so rapidly and loudly that all my limbs began to tremble. Suddenly, the fire was upon me. It rose as high as a person is tall; it looked like a person burning in fire, and it was moving rapidly. I started screaming again, "*Shma Yisruel* . . ." and verses from the 91st Psalm with a voice not my own. I had no idea where I found the strength to scream like that. I then saw the fire begin to recede back into the valley. I struck the horse, and it was still barely moving along. I looked back to see the fire speeding back and becoming smaller and smaller until I could not see it anymore.

I again began to wonder what this meant. If it really was a treasure after all, then my good fortune was chasing after me while I was running away from it. Then I started thinking that, on the other hand, it could not be so, because if it really was a treasure and was coming because of my good fortune then it would appear in a way that would not frighten me. But since it appeared and caused me to be frightened, it was a sign that it was not spiritually pure, but rather a type of "translucent shell." I had all types of thoughts, one after the other, and was completely disoriented.

In the meantime, I had already ridden down into the third valley and had to ride up the fourth and last mountain—from its top one could already see the mills of the village Buter. The road to the mills is approximately two *versts* of straight road, that is, from the top of the mountain. Upon reaching the mills, there is an extremely deep valley descending straight into the village, which is located in the valley below the mountain.

I started up the last mountain as all sorts of confusing thoughts about this strange phenomenon were racing through my mind. I began to feel a little more comfortable since I was shortly approaching home. Four to five *versts* still remained, the moon was shining, the night sky was beautiful and studded with stars, the air was delightful, but my fear was intense. Seemingly, as if in spite, not even one human being was on the road and no wagons were passing by. I

---

ally indicates a type of negative force containing some good, which has the possibility of being transformed into holiness (Schochet, 1988:148–149). I have not found a source for the author's comments regarding it.

felt lonely in the silence of the night out in the countryside as if I were cut off from the entire world. I thought that if at least a wagon would overtake me, I would not be scared to stop if the fire appeared as it did before. Out of concern, I stopped the horse and tried to listen for a wagon moving on the road. As if to spite me, nothing could be heard. Though it was a postal route and a highway that never rested for a minute, now all human beings in the world had been banished from it, with only myself remaining here in the countryside. It was quiet all around me, and I continued riding, thinking only about other matters. I had almost completely forgotten about the fire and was almost finished going up the ascent.

I only had around three *versts* left until I would reach home. Suddenly, I once again heard the humming of the fire, which was screeching with an intensity even stronger than the first two times. I looked around and saw that the fire was not far from me. It began to rise, and I started screaming again, *"Shma Yisruel"* and other verses, but the fire rallied its strength and became stronger that the other two times. It was not speeding back, but rather it was moving forward in front of the horse and rose as tall as a large tree. When the horse noticed the fire, it became extremely frightened and started bucking so much that I thought I would be flung off and scattered about like dust. The fire chased after the horse like an arrow, and I feared that I would be killed either by the fire or by being thrown from the horse, God forbid. I screamed with all my strength and held onto the horse's mane. I now forgot about my fear of the fire and was more frightened of being killed together with the horse that was running down into the valley full of rocks below. If the horse fell or struck something, I would have been instantly killed, so I used all my strength to try to restrain the horse, but it was useless. Although earlier the horse had not wanted to move even when I hit it, it was now flying as fast as an arrow. I screamed, and the non-Jews living right in the valley saw a horse running with its rider screaming hysterically. They ran out to catch the horse, but the horse flew like an arrow shot from a bow, and they could not catch it. The horse was racing with me through the streets of the village, and the non-Jews hooked it from all sides and caught it. This took place not far from the house of my uncle, Velvl the Nun's, who also dashed out. His wife, Aunt Blime, shrieked, "What's the matter with you, Pinye-Ber?! Don't scream! What's wrong with you?" I could not stop screaming, *"Oy! Oy!"* and could not say anything more.[50]

---

50 William R. Corliss, the author of *Remarkable Luminous Phenomena in Nature* (2001), commented in a private letter to the translator that the fire described here is completely unlike any luminous phenomena found in nature (such as ball lightning, will-o'-the-wisps, and so on) particularly in its repetition and its intentional targeting of the author. Since its having

The non-Jewish villagers crowded around and wanted to know what had happened, but I could not say anything. I was speechless. They realized that it was caused by fright, and they tried to save me. They gave me some liquor. Although I never drink hard liquor, someone suddenly poured half a *shkalik* of liquor down my throat, and I could not even tell whether it was liquor or water.[51] They rubbed me down with spirits and laid me down to rest. Meanwhile, they informed my devoted wife, who immediately came running breathlessly. The poor thing did not know what to do; she was crying, she was dying. She wanted at least to hear me utter something. I heard and understood everything, but my tongue would not move, so I motioned that they should let me rest up and that she should stop crying. In short, I rested and only then did I feel better, thank God, and regain my ability to speak. When my wife finally heard me say something, "Freydele, come here. Thank God for His kindness in letting me live," only then did she calm down and take me home. Her relatives, her uncle and aunt, accompanied us to hear what had happened to me. They were astonished to hear the story that I have just described to you.

The non-Jewish owner of the horse came to complain to me that the horse was a wreck. He thought that I was at fault for having driven it that way, but

---

been a natural phenomenon has been ruled out, I propose that this episode is an example of a stress-induced hallucination. A striking example of how sheer stress can cause visual hallucinations is the frightened new recruit to the Israeli army who saw human-sized ants approaching him and then crawling on him; remarkably, the hallucinations were alleviated once he was allowed to express his fear of being unfit for military service (Feldman et al., 1998:166). Similarly, Goldenshteyn's experience was apparently induced by the tremendous stresses and grave disappointments recently experienced in his life. After a youth filled with hardship, he became engaged to a woman whose parents promised to support him for a few years so that he could fulfill his long-standing dream of studying Torah in peace upon marrying. As luck would have it, his future in-laws lost their wealth, but he went against his own best interests by marrying his fiancée out of concern for her. Upon marrying, he was so shocked to see the extent of his in-laws' poverty and coarseness that he went against his caring nature and told his in-laws to leave lest he divorce their daughter. After setting up a store for his wife to run while he studied Torah and seeing it fail, he now came to the bitter realization that his dream of studying Torah undisturbed was unattainable. Additionally, this incident with the fireball occurred upon returning from his in-laws, whom he blamed for his misfortune. Hallucinations are also called waking dreams and can be interpreted similarly; hence, it is no wonder that the pursuing fireball assumed the form of a person as it approached him, for it represented the long series of people, culminating in his in-laws, who had burned up his dreams of studying Torah in peace. (Although Goldenshteyn writes that his horse only became frightened upon seeing the fire, I posit that the horse finally bolted upon hearing its rider's scream and sensing his severe panic.)

51 A *shkalik* is an obsolete Russian unit of measurement equivalent to 2.08 ounces of liquid. In the original Yiddish, the word *shkol'nik* (a sexton in Russian) is mistakenly printed instead of *shkalik*.

when he heard from me what had happened, he no longer blamed me. The next morning many non-Jews, including the horse's owner, asked me to describe the exact direction from which the fire appeared the first time. I told them, and they replied that they wanted to go and dig up the ground because there was a treasure there. They ridiculed me and said, "A foolish Jew. A treasure appeared to him and he didn't have the brains to take it." They insisted that, "It was a treasure. Your good fortune was chasing you and you left it." I told them, "I'm not interested in such good fortune. May such good fortune be for you." To this very day I have no idea what those non-Jews did and what they found when digging, and I am not interested in knowing.

What I do know is that the fear I had then has remained with me ever since. Whenever I dream in my sleep, especially after a day of much hardship, or when I sleep alone in a room, I scream in my sleep out of fear, which frightens those who hear me. This can even happen to me a few times in one night, although by nature I do not shout and do not have any fears of walking or traveling alone at night. Nevertheless, this incident has left a lasting impression on me, and I still have nightmares from it. If whatever it was appears to me as a vision in my dream, I then start shouting like I did while being chased by the fire. My children know this, and they have heard me screaming in my sleep on many occasions.

After that trip, I lay in bed for three days until I recovered, and only after another three days did I become as healthy as before.

CHAPTER 19

In Search of a Livelihood, 1868–1869

Barley • A Grain Dealer • Fatherhood • No Longer a Dealer • Stuck in Debt • A Tavern Keeper • A Barrel of Wine at the Fair • The Wine Turned to Vinegar • In a World of Chaos • A Night on the Street • At the Home of the Malbim, of Blessed Memory • A *Melomed* in Sovitskis

It is now time to resume the discussion of our subsequent life. Our little store had breathed its last breath, and after *Shvues* we were left with neither an ounce of our merchandise nor any money.[1] There was not even a morsel of bread in the house. We were waiting until it was time to harvest the barley, since I had planted before Pesach a *desyatin* with barley seed, which had cost me six rubles.[2] We were now hoping that the barley would turn out well, and then we would have a few rubles.

Thank God, we endured until then. The barley was finally ready, so early one morning we both went to the steppe with two sickles and harvested the barley. My wife and I worked an entire day reaping it and tying up the sheaves. In the evening we returned home tired and exhausted, but there was nothing to eat. My wife borrowed some corn flour from a neighbor and cooked some *mamaliga* in milk from our goat. We ate it up heartily like someone eating the finest meal.

Three days later, I hired a wagon and brought the barley to the village, where I had it threshed. After selling it, I only had a clear profit of ten rubles due

---

1 *Shvues* was on May 27–28, 1868.
2 Pesach began the night of April 6, 1868. A *desyatin* is equivalent to 3.6 acres. The Yiddish word *desyatin* corresponds to the old-Russian unit of measurement *desiatina* and was used in measuring farming land. One *desyatin* was equivalent to 3.6 acres.

to the low price of barley at the time. We left ourselves a *mestl* of barley that we milled.[3] We had to be satisfied with the barley flour, which we cooked or baked, even though it was bad for our health. We had no other choice, since we could not afford any better without a source of income.

A short time later, God had mercy on us. Merchants from Tiraspol came to our village and suggested that I purchase grain (wheat, rye, oats, barley, and corn) locally on their behalf. They gave me a price for each type of grain and promised me a commission of ten *kopeks* for each *chetvert*. Even though it was a small commission, it was better than nothing. We agreed upon the terms, and they gave me 200 rubles to begin purchasing. They promised that as soon as I would have non-Jews transport the grain to them, they would send the balance of the money as calculated with the non-Jews. Or else they would come down personally to collect the grain. They told me that should I be lacking funds, I should write them, and they would send as much money as I needed.

In short, I became a grain dealer. I began buying and selling in our village. In a period of two months, I became the most able dealer. I bought all types of grains—better quality and larger quantities than the experienced dealers. Everybody was amazed, "Where did he acquire the skills of an experienced grain merchant who can accomplish so much in all of his business dealings?" I expanded my business, buying not only in my village but in others too. The merchants in Tiraspol were very happy with the results. I was buying a lot of grain, and they were profiting nicely, but I was working very hard and had nothing to show for it. Yet I valued the experience, which was good for me, and, after all, I did live off of that little bit of commission.

I managed decently until the High Holy Days and was even able to afford a few new articles of clothing in honor of *Yontef*. I arrived in Tiraspol for Rosh Hashanah and Yom Kippur all dressed for *Yontef*, like all the tenant innkeepers who always came into town for *Yontef*.[4] The costs of traveling to and from Tiraspol, lodging, and (not to be mentioned in the same breath) our seats in the *shul* added up to a pretty tidy sum. Nonetheless, I did not, God forbid, remain in debt to those merchants in Tiraspol whose 100-ruble notes were always on me. Many other merchants suggested that I also take their money and become a buyer for them since they all knew me to be an upright individual. When hiring

---

3 The author explains later that a *mestl* (literally "a small measurement" in Yiddish, plural *mestlekh*) is an eighth of the obsolete Russian unit of measurement of *chetvert* (pronounced *tshetvert*). An eighth of a *chetvert* was called a *chetverik* in Russian. Since a *chetvert* is equivalent to 126.39 pounds, a *mestl* (*chetverik*) is equivalent to 15.8 pounds.

4 Rosh Hashanah and Yom Kippur were on September 17–18, 1868, and September 26, 1868, respectively.

me, they raised my commission from ten to fifteen *kopeks* for each *chetvert*—a *chetvert* consists of eight *mestlekh*. That is how I dealt in grain that summer and the entire fall until well into the winter, and everything went smoothly.

I thought that since I was now earning a living, I would continue to support myself this way. But with my bad luck, it seems I was just not allowed to support myself. Things started to go wrong. Around the month of *Shvat*,[5] I was buying lots of *papshoy* (corn), which some call *kukeruze*. I had bought a large supply and was buying all types of grain: wheat, oats, rye, millet, and rapeseed. I had deposited some 800 rubles with several non-Jews as down payments, but the grain remained lying around; there was no way to have it delivered to the city because the roads were covered in heavy snow and mud. And those non-Jews were pestering me that I should pay the balance and take the grain away. So I had to pay more for its delivery in order to free myself from their pestering, but I now remained without any earnings.

Before Pesach,[6] the roads became worse, so that one could not even get a *pud* of grain delivered for fifty *kopeks*.[7] So I had to take much of the purchased grain and pour it into my own sacks.[8] Since it was impossible to transport, as already mentioned, much of the grain spoiled and lost its value, causing the merchants back in Tiraspol to suffer losses. Naturally, under the circumstances, I went totally broke. From the month of *Shvat* onward, I remained stuck with the grain and was not able to buy any more. Since the dealers were losing money, they did not pay me my commission, even though it was unfair.

Although my expenses were minimal and I lived meagerly, I had used up fifty rubles of the dealers' money on food for Pesach. In addition, a child was on the way, as my wife was due with her first child. I had to send her to Perkon to her parents for the delivery. Exactly eight days before Pesach, I became the father of my newborn first daughter.[9] Naturally, I could not prepare our home for Pesach on my own without my wife's assistance. So, as much as I disliked my in-laws' house, I was compelled to spend Pesach there for the sake of my wife and child.[10]

After Pesach, I traveled home, loaded up the remaining grain, and brought it to Tiraspol. I settled with the merchants and remained fifty rubles in debt. I consolidated my debt and saw to it that I should only owe one merchant, my

---

5   January–February 1869.
6   March 27–April 3, 1869.
7   A *pud* is equivalent to 36.11 pounds.
8   Evidently, the author had to pour the grain into his own sacks for storage purposes.
9   The author's first daughter was born March 19, 1869.
10 Pesach involves extensive preparations. See *Kitsur Shulkhan Arukh* (111, 112, 116, and 117).

wife's relative Shaye Ternofske, who had profited nicely the entire time we had worked together. He was not really satisfied but had no choice. He was aware that the losses were not my fault, as I had not, God forbid, squandered his money. And he also knew that as soon as I would have the means, I would repay him. He was even willing to give me more money to continue dealing in grain.

The merchants whom I had completely paid off felt sorry that I did not have a *kopek* to my name and suggested that I deal in barley at the beginning of the next season. Even though I was poor, they would loan me whatever I needed. I refused their suggestion as well as a similar suggestion from the merchant to whom I still owed those fifty rubles. I said that it did not pay for me to work so hard for others and remain with barely a profit for myself.

The merchant to whom I owed the fifty rubles, our relative Shaye Ternofske, urged me not to stop dealing in grain, "Yes, Pinye-Ber. What will be with the money that you owe me? If you continue to do business with me, I can hope to be repaid for I would deduct the debt from your commission. But now that you don't want to do business with me and you have no money, when will you be able to repay me?"

"Yes," I answered him, "Mr. Ternofske, you're right, but I can't do business like this because I know that I can't support myself on such a small commission and I can't afford to go into greater debt. Don't forget that I'm now a father of a little baby and my expenses have grown. In short, this business of working so hard so that others can profit is not advisable for me. I've come up with other plans for myself. And don't worry about the money I owe you. It may just take some time until I repay you, but it is not lost, God forbid!"

When I noticed that Mr. Ternofske doubted my holy word, I wanted to convince him how holy my debt to him was and that he should have no doubts about my honesty. So I ran home and took the little silver that I had, which consisted of a silver salt dish that came with a small silver spoon, and four old silver spoons. I took them from my house without my wife's knowledge, for she would not have agreed, and brought them to Tiraspol. As I gave them to him, I said, "Mr. Ternofske, please take these as security for the fifty rubles that I owe you. Though this security doesn't have the value of my debt, it is worth something—between twenty and twenty-five rubles. So now that I've paid half my debt, you can be assured of my complete honesty, and you can be sure that I'll pay the rest."

Naturally, he did not hesitate long and cheerfully took my security. He then said candidly, "Now I see that you're a most pious young man." With these words, he lifted ten stones from my heart, and I returned home extremely satisfied, feeling as if I had made the most fabulous business deal.

Upon returning home, I found my wife sad and teary-eyed. Frightened, I asked her why she was crying. She said that we suffered a great loss; the little bit of silver that we had in our chest was missing. Understandably, I calmed her down immediately, telling her that I myself had committed the crime and begged her forgiveness for causing her unnecessary pain. But she would not forgive me that quickly. And when I told her what I had done with the silver, she became quite angry that I had sold it without consulting her.

"How's it possible?" she challenged. Her voice was pained, and she had tears running down her cheeks, "Ternofske, he's a murderer! Didn't he earn good money through you? For an entire year, you bought him better grain and at a better price than any of the other buyers, and in the end, you earned a commission of ten *kopeks* per *chetvert* while he earned a ruble and two *kopeks*. So what if at the end of the season the last grain remained untransported? It was through no fault of your own. It only happened because at that time the roads were impassable, and it was impossible to obtain wagons. And even if you could have gotten wagons, they would have been way overpriced. So that murderer's 'conscience' and 'sense of fairness' compelled him to deduct his losses from your paltry commission. And now, thanks to his 'good heart,' you remain indebted to him. It should have been enough that you're honest and promised him that you'll repay him when God helps you. Had you gone to an arbitrator or to a rabbi, he would certainly have ruled that you don't need to pay him anything. Yet you went and took from our house your last few valuables, which could have saved you in a time of need, and you went and gave them to him behind my back so that I also had become frightened over their loss." She continued to complain and cry like this, and our baby joined her, crying for her mother's pain as if she understood the bitterness of her mother's lot.

And then my mother-in-law entered the scene, for this all occurred in her house in the village of Perkon. I had brought my wife to her parents' home to give birth to our child, and I had not yet taken her home to Buter. When my mother-in-law entered, things really became nasty. She sang a different tune, saying, "You had no right to give him the silver. It wasn't yours! Did you obtain it from your father? You had absolutely no right to take those things. They're mine. I'm going straight away to Ternofske to get them back. I'll take along a police commissioner." She shouted at me, yelling to the high heavens. Then my father-in-law came in, and he ranted on as well.

I sat in silence, tears flowing from my eyes. I was quite hurt. I knew that we were all in the right. More than anything, my heart ached for my dear wife, poor thing, who was suffering because of me. She had to nurse the baby and had to endure the provocation of her coarse, simple parents, who tried to turn her against me and incite her to treat me in a different manner, not refined and gentle but rough and crude. But she did not listen to them and did not use one harsh word, God forbid; she understood my position very well.

Eventually, my wife began to calm me down, saying, "Pinye-Ber, why are you so worried? Why are you crying?" I replied that I was brought to tears just by looking at her. "Here now," she said, "If so, I'm not going to cry anymore. Calm yourself down. So it's already done. It's too late. God will have to help us." Hearing these words from my wife, I immediately felt happy and calm. I then began to explain to her that an honest person must do as I did to convince another of his honesty, especially when he falls into the hands of an evil, dishonest person who believes that everyone is as bad and dishonest as he is. In dealing with such a person, one needs to convince him by any means possible that he is thinking incorrectly—that there are people who are the exact opposite and that the only thing that counts is a person's honesty and not the ruble. In short, my wife was convinced by my sound reasoning and supported my approach. From that time onward, we both shared the same opinion on how to deal with such people. Not once did she ever criticize my behavior toward such people, despite the fact that we encountered many such dishonest and bad people in our lives.

I know that you, my beloved readers, will be puzzled as to why I was only in debt to that Ternofske and not also to the other merchants. Well, I can clarify this. The other two merchants—one was Berl Ternofske, who was actually Shaye's brother, and the other was Refuel Bendersky—dealt honestly with me.[11] They covered the costs of the spoiled grain and of the additional delivery charges. They did not charge me for whatever I still owed them, saying, "We see that you're an honest person and aren't to blame for this. So we'll take the loss out of our previous earnings, meaning that we'll have earned twenty-five *kopeks* less per *chetvert*." But Shaye Ternofske charged me for everything, not leaving out any expense, although he should have done so out of a sense of fairness. So I remained in debt to him. My wife's claims were, unfortunately, true enough but arguing would not help.

Anyhow, it is now time to leave this conversation and begin to relate what happened to me further in my life. Then you will see how God helped me, how I paid back Ternofske, and how well Ternofske treated me for my having given him as security the little silver I had, as mentioned earlier. I think that only then will you have a concept of how "good and honest" Ternofske was . . .

---

11 Refuel (son of Nukhem) Bendersky was born ca. 1840, according to the 1858 additional revision list (poll-tax census) of the Jews of Tiraspol.

After my dealings with Ternofske, I remained without any money and without a source of livelihood. So it begged the question: What was I to do now? What line of work was I to take up now? I decided that in no way would I deal in grain, not because I did not like it, but because the only way to make money involved cheating when measuring it upon its delivery, which my sense of honesty made me unqualified to do. Also, I did not have any of my own money to invest, and it did not pay for me to work on a commission of ten to fifteen *kopeks*, because I would end up in debt again. Some grain dealers bought even less than I did at that same commission and earned a good living and lived the good life, but they only did this by measuring the grain dishonestly. But I did not know how to do such *shtik* or such misdeeds. I only knew how to take a straight commission of ten to fifteen *kopeks*, and for that reason dealing in grain could not support me.

In sum, I decided not to continue dealing in grain, and I needed to figure out what else I could do. But no matter how much I thought, I still could not come up with anything, because whatever idea I had was always hindered by my lack of money. There were many available options, but without money—I no longer had even the little bit of silver with which I could have borrowed twenty rubles or so—things were bad on two accounts. First of all, one could not begin to do anything without money. Secondly, I would soon not have enough money to purchase a *funt* of bread to quiet my hunger, unless I moved back in with my in-laws.[12] But for me, staying at their home would have been worse than death. As you know, I had not wanted to continue living with them since shortly after my wedding, so why should I return to them now, two years after my wedding, only to be mistreated after all my suffering in dealing with the grain? In short, things were bad! My brain became drained from all that thinking, and I could not come to a decision.

My mother-in-law came up with the following idea: I should move out of the village of Buter to Perkon where they lived, and they would seek out a means for me to earn a living. They decided that they would rent a place for us that had a cellar, and would arrange for me to get a barrel of wine; I would become a tavern keeper and would have to put up with a bunch of drunkards. I insisted that I did not want to do that, but they convinced me to do it. So I brought our few pieces of furniture from Buter to Perkon, rented a place that had a small cellar and obtained a wine barrel containing sixty buckets of wine. I began to wait, and I am still waiting.

---

12 The obsolete Russian unit of measurement of a *funt* is equal to 409.5 grams, which is slightly less than the current weight of a US pound (453.6 grams).

I was not fit for such an occupation. The drinkers would get one whiff of me and would not appear again, because the drinkers liked a tavern keeper to spend time with them, help them drink, and be chummy with them. But I was quite far from all those things, so they did not enjoy me at all. I could not bear their presence any more than they could bear mine. When two or three non-Jews would enter, sit down to drink, and begin to speak coarsely, I would immediately ask them to leave the premises. A clamor and a racket would ensue, and, of course, one drunkard would drag the other elsewhere, to a tavern where they would be appreciated and be far away from the foolish Jew who shunned them. I eagerly awaited customers who would buy some wine and then take it home, but that type was infrequent. So, I did little business and sold little.

My mother-in-law saw that I was not making any sales, my wine remained unsold, and the term of the wine was expiring, since the wine barrel cost sixty rubles, which were to be paid in three months. So she advised me to bring the barrel of wine to the Tiraspol market held outside the city on Ascension Day, rent a booth, and sell the wine there.[13] She claimed that during the eight days of the fair I would be able to sell the wine and pay it off, and I would also earn a small profit of about thirty rubles.[14] Such was her advice.

I was not practical in such matters, but I considered her to be so and I did as she advised. It ended with my having sixteen rubles in expenses and twenty rubles in sales over the eight days of the fair, where I endured a lot. At the fair, I did not eat, sleep, or rest day or night, and in the end I still had to have the wine barrel brought home because some of the wine in it remained unsold. After the barrel stood at the booth in the heat for the entire eight days, it turned over when it was carted back home, causing the wine to mix with the yeast, turning it into vinegar. With great difficulty, I had sold only a total of twenty-five buckets of wine out of the original sixty. I sold the remaining thirty-five buckets of wine, actually vinegar, for a total of twelve rubles. And now I was no longer a tavern keeper. Once again, I had no means of livelihood and not a *kopek* to my name. In addition, I still owed fifty rubles to a Bulgarian from whom I had bought the barrel of wine, which was reduced from sixty rubles since I had given him ten of the twelve rubles that I received for the vinegar.[15]

---

13   Ascension Day was on June 10, 1869, the fortieth day after Easter, which occurred on July 20, 1869. Note that the Eastern Church (including the Russian Orthodox Church) uses a different method of calculating the date of Easter than the Western Church.
14   In the Eastern Church, Ascension Day has an Afterfeast of eight days.
15   The village of Perkon, where the author's in-laws lived, was a Bulgarian colony ("Parkany," 1886).

I left our home and brought our few household possessions to my wife's parents, left her there too, and went off. Where to? I myself did not know, but I did know this: I had nothing to do there. Should I sit and eat at my in-laws and help them run their business and hear their opinions about me? No, I would not be able to bear that. More specifically, I could not bear to see the pain and suffering of my wife, who unfortunately suffered from all of us. My suffering hurt her, for everything grieved me. She was truly faithful and devoted to me but could not help me at all.

Though she knew me and my capabilities, she heard bad opinions expressed about her devoted husband along with "good advice," such as, "Ask him for a divorce because in the end he will leave you anyway and you'll be abandoned and unable to remarry. You don't have to feel sorry about divorcing him because he's a failure, a *schlimazel*. Nothing's working for him. You see how merry he is all the time and how he even makes others merry; he's always singing and dancing around. That's because nothing matters to him. Get divorced from him. You can easily get another 'big bargain' like him. He would certainly agree to divorce you. True, you might not be able to get a learner, but you'll have a breadwinner and a decent life." They kept hammering these ideas into her head, even though she did not want to hear any of it. Actually, she used to point out my virtues, justify my actions, and blame them. It was not enough that they did not understand me, but they disgraced me, hurt me, and considered all my merits to be flaws. You can now understand how taxing this was on her health.

My wife shed many tears because she felt miserable that she was able to eat breakfast and dinner and have a place to sleep while her devoted husband was unfortunately wandering around, not eating and not drinking. She knew my situation and was aware of the hunger I endured. Even when others heard me singing joyously, she knew that I was just singing to bring myself some relief. Only by exerting myself to be joyous was I able to cast away the horrible worry from my heart. From all of this, you can understand the pain that my wife endured on my behalf from her relatives and parents. Do not forget that after all was said and done, she was not able to live without them. Since they supported her and the baby, she could not make them feel too disgraced for their negative words about me. But it pained her not to be able to comment on their character flaws. Yet I could in no way agree to live with them and lead a life like theirs. For that reason, I left. I did not know where I was headed. I only knew that I was leaving there.

Now I entered a chaotic world. I took my *talis* and *tefillin*, two shirts, and said that I was going to Tiraspol to study Torah in the *bes-medresh*. I actually did not lie, for I went to Tiraspol, where I visited my sister Ite upon my arrival. She was overjoyed to see me and boiled some water and served me tea as soon as I walked in.

"I'm not interested in a glass of tea," I said.

"How can it be? How can a person not want tea?"

Ite, whose entire nourishment consisted of tea and a piece of bread, could not imagine how anyone could refuse a glass of tea. She insisted that I must drink, so I drank a glass. She was not lazy and poured me a second glass. I then said firmly that I would not drink any more. She then began to treat me high-handedly, saying that I had to obey her and oblige her because she ordered me to do so. I said to her that I was now no longer the same Berele from years ago who would get spanked if I did not do as I was told. I was now a grown-up Pinye-Ber and did not have to obey her. She pleaded with me with tears that I should drink it anyway because she received such pleasure from having her brother visit and enjoy something at her home.

I might have had to oblige her, but at that moment a cheerful and well-dressed, handsome little boy entered and wished his mother a good afternoon. This was her dear son, Itsikl, who had come home from *kheyder* to eat a hot meal. I took advantage of the occasion and began a conversation with him. I asked him what he was studying and some other questions, and my sister was beaming as he answered with confidence. She was thrilled with my praise for the child. She said, "But he needs a father or a mother who can support him and provide him with a good Jewish education." He asked for some food, and she gave him what she had prepared. Of course, by then she had forgotten me and my tea drinking, because the tea had already become cold. She told me her pile of troubles: how she struggled to get by with her son because the few sewing notions that she sold did not cover her meager expenses; how she managed on bread and tea the entire week and never ate her fill—and that was excluding the two days in the week, Monday and Thursday, that she fasted.[16] Though she was neglecting herself, she made sure that her precious child's needs, however much possible, were met: she dressed him well and also paid his tuition. But none of our relatives came to ask, "Ite, how are things going? Ite, how are you supporting yourself? What are you living on?" because they were afraid that it would cost them money. None of our relatives had any compassion for this poor unfortunate widow and her child.[17] "*Oy*, relatives, relatives!" I thought to myself, "That's what you call relatives? What good is your piety, your Hasidism, to me? Why are you running and traveling to your Rebbe three times a year?

---

16 Regarding fasting every Monday and Thursday, see ch. 2, p. 105, footnote 28.

17 Ite was widowed by her first husband and was divorced from her second, the father of her son.

Instead of traveling two or three times a year to your Rebbe, it would be better to donate the expense of one trip to your Rebbe to this impoverished widow and orphan, your own flesh and blood."

I figured that I had nothing to do there in Tiraspol. It was useless to study in the *bes-medresh* and wait for help from my relatives because I would not receive anything from them anyway. Therefore, it would be better for me to move on to another city where I would not have any financial assistance. And it would be better than in Tiraspol, for at least I would not feel resentful toward my uncaring relatives.

I spent three days in Tiraspol, where I slept in the *bes-medresh* on a hard bench and ate dry bread soaked in water and dipped in a bit of salt to give it some taste. On the fourth day, I set out on foot to Odessa, without any money and without a goal or purpose. I only knew that I was going to Odessa. "Why?" you may ask. I myself did not know. My impoverished and critical situation was driving me there. On the second day after leaving Tiraspol, I arrived in Odessa. I immediately went to the *Pas le'Orkhim bes-medresh* where I encountered old acquaintances from my yeshiva days, and I sat down to study.[18] They sustained me with two *funt* of bread a day and with five *kopeks* for something to spread on it. Meanwhile, I wanted to start working but could not find any work. There was always an issue; in one place it was my inability to speak or write Russian, in another they claimed that I had no experience, and in a third it was my *Shobes* observance. And then there was the job among vagrants which would have required me to spend time with them. In short, it was bad! I realized that Odessa was also not a good choice for me.

Since I had heard that there were salt lagoons in the Crimea and that many earned a living in salt production, I thought that it would be advisable for me to head out toward the Crimea. Had I any money, I would have been there in two days—I could have traveled by steamboat to Kakhovka, from which it is one day's travel on foot to the lakes. But since I did not have any money, I had to head out overland on foot until I reached the lagoons. There one did not need to know Russian nor have a secular education—one just had to have strength, and, thank God, strength I had. So that was the best plan for me.

In the morning, I took my bundle, and started making my way along the roundabout overland route to Kakhovka, which was actually quite frightening, but I had no choice. My route was: Nikolayev, Kherson, Aleshki,[19] and then

---

18   The author describes how he hid out in this synagogue during the winter of 1863–1864 in chapter 13, p. 208.
19   In the original Yiddish, Aleshiki is referred to as Aleshkis or Alyeshkis, which is perhaps a transcription error.

Kakhovka. I started out toward Nikolayev. Friday, during the day, I reached a small *shteytl* on the way to Nikolayev by the name of Kozlov, for I had left Odessa on Thursday quite early and that *shteytl* was midway between Odessa and Nikolayev. As I was accustomed to do, I went to the *bes-medresh* where I figured that I would rest over *Shobes*. But it was also destined for my *Shobes* to be disturbed. It just had to happen that way.

I talked quite a bit with the *shomes* of the little *shul*, who told me that a few *versts* from there lived a Jewish nobleman, an Orthodox Jew by the name of Yosef Kuperman, who had a little *shul* in his house and his own *minyan* composed of his employees. "Young man, there at his house you'll have a good *Shobes*, and you'll forget about your troubles for a while. And you may possibly earn some money from him." I did not think it over much because there was no time to think since it would soon be *Shobes*. I took my bundle and went straight to the Jewish nobleman.

For me, it would be a complete surprise to see a Jewish nobleman, especially since he conducted himself like a Jew and kept kosher.[20] I arrived in his courtyard exactly at sunset. I entered his courtyard—very beautiful and large—but they did not allow me to enter his house. They showed me to the little *shul*, where exactly a *minyan* of men had already gathered for Friday night services. There I learned that the rich man was not at home—he was supposed to come momentarily from Odessa. And actually right when we were in the middle of praying *Minkhe*, a three-horse carriage pulled in, and the rich man and two others stepped out. The rich man himself had a nice red beard and looked like a traditional Jew. Right afterward, we waited a bit to pray *Kabules Shobes*, and the rich man came in to pray. After services, everyone dispersed, and I remained there alone. No one invited me over for the traditional *Shobes* meal.

A servant entered and called me over. He led me straight to the kitchen and said to me, "Sit, young man. Here you'll be given something to eat, and you can go back into the little *shul* to sleep." I immediately felt despondent. Stunned, I remained seated. In the kitchen were two maidservants, who immediately served me some fish and also sat themselves down, which meant that we were eating together. "No," I said, "I first have to make *Kiddush*. And I need *khale* for the blessing of *ha'moytse*. Give me two whole *khales*."[21] One of them ran and brought me two *khales*, while the other brought wine. They were ready

---

20 The author is surprised that a Jew of his stature remained a practicing Jew, since many Jews in Tsarist Russia who "achieved significant economic mobility and success" apostatized (Stanislawski, 1987:196–197).

21 The blessing over bread, *ha'moytse*, must be made over two *khales* on *Shabes* (*Kitsur Shulkhan Arukh* 77:17).

to hear *Kiddush*, but I recited *Sholem Aleykhem* and then *Eyshes Khayil* slowly with an embittered heart. I started to make *Kiddush* and cried so loudly that the maidservants became frightened and did not understand what had happened to me. I was so depressed by my lowly standing. I had tried to keep my spirits up in order not to disturb the enjoyment of *Shobes* and accept all that had happened with love, but I could not contain myself at *Kiddush* and burst out crying, just like what happened to me during *Kiddush* in the village with the miller—when I was a child, if you remember—but those pains were less emotional then the ones I felt this time.[22]

Once I got back to myself and calmed down, they asked me, "What's wrong?" I said, "I don't like being put in the kitchen. The master of the house doesn't want to be ashamed by my presence at his table, God forbid. That's all right—so I say that I've decided not to eat anything."[23] They went to tell the rich man the entire story, and then the servant came and said, "The master of the house does this on principle. No poor person is allowed to eat at his table. They may eat only in the kitchen. What does it matter to you where you eat as long as you're given food?" I responded, "The table matters more to me than the food. I'm no vagabond, God forbid. I am a refined and learned person. If the master of the house is a pious Jew, then he should act like one." The servant went into the house and reported my words and returned with the following reply, "The lady of the house said that since the young man is insisting upon being let into the house to be seated at the table, she must conclude that he is a thief, a rogue. For that reason, she can in no way agree to this."

Understandably, I was greatly embarrassed. I washed my hands, ate some *khale*, and sang *zmires* but ate no other food.[24] Though the maidservants tried to comfort me and kept asking me to eat fish, soup, and meat, I only ate a dry piece of *khale* and snacked on *zmires* in honor of *Shobes*. I said the Hebrew blessings recited after a meal and went to sleep in the little *shul*. The next day, I did not want to set foot in the rich man's house and asked the servant to carry the *khale* for *ha'moytse* to me in the little *shul* where I ate. I did not set my eyes again on the rich man's kitchen or his cooks.

I spent the entire day studying Torah and looking into the Jewish holy books that I found there. I barely managed until Sunday morning, when I left

---

22 See chapter 8, p. 168.
23 Similarly, Abrahams (1953:95) also writes in his autobiography that he was unable to endure the shame of being served breakfast in the kitchen in someone's home in Shavl, Lithuania (now Siauliai) in 1897, thereby paying for his pride with hunger.
24 Before eating bread, Jewish law requires washing one's hands with a vessel (*Kitsur Shulkhan Arukh* 40:1–21).

that great philanthropist and hospitable landowner. I accepted everything with love and believed that afterward everything would begin to go well for me because I had already suffered enough.

I headed toward Nikolayev. In Nikolayev, I rested a day in the *bes-medresh*, where I was invited for lunch at the Rafalovitsh household, where I was warmly received.[25] We amiably spent some time together, and I was even given a half ruble. Such a difference between one rich man and the other, like night and day. I was ashamed to take their money, so they forcibly placed the money in my pocket, saying that it would certainly come in handy on the road.

I immediately left toward Kherson. That half ruble really came in handy for I was without a *kopek*. I bought bread on the way and arrived in Kherson in two days. I remember it as if it happened today. I arrived in Kherson at dusk and went straight to the little *shul*, where there was also a *bes-medresh*. But they did not let me spend the night in the *bes-medresh*, and I did not have money for lodgings. What did I do? I tried to entreat the *shomes* to at least let me leave my bundle at his house. He did not permit it, saying that there was a lot of thievery going on in town. One indigent had stolen valuable religious objects and *taleysim* from the *bes-medresh*. "And at my house too," said the *shomes*, "it just recently happened that someone asked me to let him keep his bundle here for a while, just like you're asking now. Ultimately, I almost had a tremendous misfortune befall me for inside it were stolen goods. So don't hold a grudge, young man." I saw that no amount of pleading would help here, so I went in to pray *Minkhe* and *Marev*, while keeping my bundle of troubles near me.[26]

After prayers, when everyone dispersed, I also left and remained standing in the street. I began to ponder my current situation. Tears began to flow from my eyes. Was I sinful—more sinful than anyone else? Apparently yes. I saw people before me—many men, women, teenage boys and girls, old and young—all well dressed and running and walking joyfully. One person was running to the theater, another was leaving it, while a third was going for a walk, and so on. But I was standing near the gate of the little *shul* and was alone, miserable, hungry, and exhausted from my journey, without a place to rest for the night. If I had to spend the night in the street, it would not have bothered me so much, but I was afraid that the night patrol would take me in the police station. My situation was awful.

Across the way, I noticed a house with a porch. I walked across the road to the house and thought that the porch might be a good place for me to be able to

---

25 The Rafalovitshes (also spelled Raffalovich) were Odessa's wealthiest Jewish merchants, who later branched into banking (Zipperstein, 1985:67).

26 *Minkhe* and *Marev* services are often prayed one right after the other.

spend the night. If I sat there, everyone would think that I was a resident of that house, and that way I would be able to rest there that night. "Yes," I thought, "it would be good if no one comes by, but what will happen if someone does come along?" Meanwhile, I sat and waited until they put out the lights in the house, when I would be certain that no one would disturb me. I sat like that until 11 at night. Then I heard someone approaching the door. I ran off the porch. The owner of the house came out and noticed me next to his house. Frightened, he asked me, "Who's there?" "A Jew," I said, "I just arrived in town. I'm a stranger. Let me in to sleep." He said, "Go away from here. I'm going to call a policeman right away, and you'll be taken to the police station."

I left and roamed the streets without strength in my feet, without a soul, and without a heart. I wandered around in circles until the middle of the night. I then noticed an inhabited house with a veranda in the back, which could be reached by going up some stairs. The veranda was surrounded by latticework, so that you would not be seen if you went up there, particularly at night. "Well," I thought, "here will be a good resting place. May God have mercy!" I carefully crawled up so that I would not be heard by those inside and not be spotted from the street. I leaned on the wall in a sitting position so that it would be impossible to notice me. I slept through the remainder of the night until it was day and then went to the small *shul*, prayed, and asked the *shomes* to raise a few *kopeks* for me so that I could buy something to eat. He raised thirty *kopeks* for me with which I bought bread for ten *kopeks*. I went straight to the Dnieper River and paid my remaining twenty *kopeks* to be ferried over to Aleshki.

I arrived in Aleshki and spent the night at the home of the *shomes* of the *shul*. Very early in the morning, I proceeded along on my journey. But I had entirely given up hope because the *shomes* had explained to me that all of my efforts were for naught; it was not advisable for me to work with the salt. He said, "You've got to have brute strength for that work, and you have to be a non-Jew too. After all, where is there anything Jewish there? What Jewish life is there?!"[27] And the wages are very small." In short, he dashed my entire plan to bits. I continued on, but I had lost my motivation because I believed him completely.

The heat that day was awful. On my way out of Kherson, I stopped at the edge of the city. I sat down to rest next to a Jewish house. The residents asked me where I was headed, and I told them. "*Oy!*" they said, "such a pity! You're going there for naught, young man. There's no work there. Workers are returning because there's no work there. Many workers are running away. Turn back!"

---

27 Evidently, the salt mines required working on Saturday, so no Jews worked there.

I did not listen to them because I felt that all my traveling until that point would have been for naught, so I continued walking in the sand, and the terrain began to look like a desert. I was barely dragging my feet through the sand. The sun blazed from above and the sand burned from below, making me feel like I was being cooked alive. I encountered no other living people.

I approached a tavern, where I met a coarse *Litvak* and his impoverished family. I asked, "Is the next village or tavern far away?" He replied that there was one twenty to twenty-five *versts* away where the sand ended, but it was all desert until then—sand and more sand. I sighed deeply and continued on. But the further I went, the heavier my heart felt. What was I pursuing? I realized that my entire journey until now had been for nothing and that I had to suffer because of my sin of being born without luck. That sin had chased me, but by now it was time to be saved. I had suffered enough. I was sick of the heat and becoming dirty from the sand. I spat, "Phooey on this! What type of misfortune is chasing me through such sand and in such heat at that?" Who knew if I would have the strength to drag myself all the way back to the train station in Kherson? I could also lose my way since no road was detectable. There were a thousand paths in that sand, because each person thought that he knew the better and easier way to travel, so each wagon made its own tracks. It was easy to stray, which was all that I needed! So I decided that no matter what happened to me, I would put an end to my exile and turn back toward Aleshki.

By nightfall, I was back in Aleshki. I again slept at the *shomes*'s house and told him that his words had convinced me and that I was listening to him because he had given me good advice. He raised fifty *kopeks* for me in the *shul* and I returned to Kherson. I was now able to stay at an inn because I could pay for it. At the train station, I learned that Itele was living in Kherson; she was a wealthy woman from Tiraspol, the widow of Meshilem Kashnitsky.[28] After his death, she married a rich man from Kherson. I asked where she lived and went there. She recognized me and welcomed me as an honored guest. She gave me food and drink for a few days, and I regained my strength somewhat.

Meanwhile, I found out that the Malbim was the rabbi in Kherson, so I went to have the privilege of meeting him.[29] He commiserated with me and wished me that God would ultimately remove all of my troubles. I told this to

---

28 The 1858 additional revision list (poll-tax census) of the Jews of Tiraspol lists a Meshilem (son of Nekhemye) Kashnitsky (born ca. 1815) and his wife Ite (born ca. 1823).

29 The Malbim (1809–1879) was a rabbi and a *magid*, whose famous commentary on the Bible continues to be widely esteemed. He is known by the acronym of his and his father's names, Meir-Leibush the son of Yekhiel-Mikhl, though his original surname was Wisser. The Malbim began serving as the rabbi of Kherson in the fall of 1868 and was asked to leave in the fall of 1869, a few months after the author met him there (Yashar, 1976:204, 209).

Itele, and it gave her great pleasure that her guest had become acquainted with the tremendous Torah genius, the Malbim.

She gave a note to the captain of her own steamship, which was leaving shortly for Odessa, allowing me free passage. She also gave me a couple of rubles and some food for the journey and sent me with one of her people to her steamship at the shore. In that manner, I traveled to Odessa and had money for travel expenses on my journey home which took me two days. I returned home after having suffered for eighteen days of so much hardship and so many indignities, as described above.

Arriving home, I was delighted for a short while to see my devoted wife and child. But I soon grew distressed at watching how my unfortunate wife suffered from her parents. Though she was their child, they did not know or understand her refined character. She could not bear to eat the bread of charity, even from her parents, and looked for every opportunity to work and earn her food. She helped in the store, in the tavern, and in the kitchen where she would cook and bake. And no matter how much she helped, they demanded more. It reached the point where they placed everything upon her—even the washing of clothes. Whatever work needed to be done in the house, she had to do it. Her parents figured that she owed it to them and that was the way it had to be. Their small children—her little brother and sister—also figured that, since Freyde was eating at their house for free, she had to work.[30] She worked especially hard when I came along, for they most definitely considered me to be a parasite, a freeloader. With my arrival, Freyde, poor thing, had to work strenuously to stop up their mouths from torturing her beloved husband, God forbid, during the short amount of time that he needed to be in their home. I say "needed" because only the One God knows the truth of how "pleased" I was to spend time with them and how "happy" I was to eat their lunch or dinner. One of their insults could penetrate me straight to the core. And Freyde also had to see and endure it all while still having to nurse the baby. Now how could I bear to see all of this and suffer like that?

Yet, all of my crying and pondering did not help at all! I had no means of extracting my beloved wife and child from that purgatory for I also had to be

---

30 Freyde's youngest brother Leyzerke was fifteen and her sister Tsipe Hershkovitsh was five (ch. 24). Since the author only makes reference to one younger brother here in 1869, Freyde's brother Mordkhe was evidently still an infant. See ch. 18, p. 300, footnote 30, which mentions that Mordkhe's mother was seemingly pregnant with him at the author's wedding in November 1867. (Mordkhe was seemingly born before 1869 since he had a son named Itskhok born in 1888, as indicated on his Page of Testimony on file at Yad Vashem filled out by the author's son Shloyme on May 25, 1955). See Appendix D4 for a genealogical chart of the Hershkovitsh family.

there. But I could not restrain myself and left again for Kishinev. From Kishinev, I went to Kalarash, where I once again began wandering around on foot for a few weeks. You may wonder what my goal was and why. I myself did not know. Something drove me. I had these thoughts that I should just continue walking until I would die from hunger or thirst, thereby putting an end to my troubles. But I was stopped by my strong trust in God that He would not abandon me forever and would ultimately have compassion on me and show me a way to earn a livelihood so that I could support my wife and child. I lived solely on hope and accepted everything with love, so when things were the worst they could possibly be I sang a lot and made myself happy. Outsiders thought that I had it good and that I sang out of contentment. Those who knew my bitter situation and saw me in such a happy mood very likely considered me to be out of my mind or an irresponsible husband whose family did not concern him.

After two weeks, I returned home to see how my devoted wife and beloved child were doing. When my Freyde saw how horrible I looked, she began to cry and wail for I had changed so dramatically in those two weeks that it was difficult to recognize me. "What happened to you," she asked. "Why do you look so bad? Why do you take everything so to heart? Where is this leading you?" With that, she cried profusely and shed bitter tears. In sympathy for me, rivers of tears poured from her eyes.

I explained to her that I had to flee to no place in particular so that I should not have to look at her parents who had doomed us forever. I particularly could not look at her mother who had swindled me and had caused me eternal misfortune. Since I was not skilled in any trade and had no money, what should I take up? I also received no encouragement from anyone, and I also could not just sit and eat, so I fled to no place in particular. Perhaps God would have mercy and I would come across something—perhaps a position of responsibility somewhere—such as a cashier or the like. But it was not yet time for that. In short, I now decided that I should continue putting up with my current situation until *Sukes*, when I would be able to become a *melomed*. I would then make a *kheyder* for a few little boys and would earn a living by teaching. I did not like teaching as a means of earning a livelihood, but it was better than nothing, God forbid. The only downside was having to endure my in-laws until the beginning of the new term.[31]

My new plan even met the approval of my mother-in-law, who commented to me, "Why didn't you do that until now?" I explained to her that I did not

---

31 The new term started after *Sukes*, which ended on September 22, 1869. For more details about the two terms in the Jewish school year, see ch. 3, p. 115, footnote 26.

want to do it because I did not care to earn a living by teaching, but I had to do it now out of necessity. So it was decided that I would live with my in-laws until *Yontef* when I would become, in a propitious hour, a *melomed*.[32] I could not stand staying with my in-laws, but nothing could be done about that since I had no other option. As they say, "necessity breaks iron." It was now the third week of *Tamuz*,[33] and, in total, only a few months remained until I could begin teaching. So I would probably spend more time in the *bute-medrushim* of Bender or Tiraspol, that way I would stay close to home.

A few days passed and my mother-in-law charged me with the following project. She was planning on purchasing a melon field, which already had ripe watermelons and cantaloupes from which one could earn some fifty or sixty rubles. One only had to put up fifteen rubles because it was in partnership with a non-Jew who was also putting up fifteen rubles. Soon they would have to take responsibility for the field, hire a guard, and bring the watermelons to the markets in the nearby villages. I accepted the project so that I would not be sitting empty-handed and eating the bread of charity.

The melon field was located twenty *versts* from Bender, ten *versts* from Kovishon, and twenty *versts* from Volontirovke. I left on foot with the non-Jewish partner and took along my *talis* and *tefillin* and some food for the road. In short, I suffered plenty for a month: sleeping on the steppe at night in the cold, enduring the heat during the day, and facing thirst and hunger. There were one or two days in which I was not able to obtain any bread. In addition, that non-Jew, together with two workers and myself, worked as hard as the devil. First of all, there was no profit because the expenses were so great, meaning that the wagons that transported the watermelons cost more than the sale price of the watermelons. For example, a wagon cost three rubles, but we sold each wagonload of watermelons for two or two and a half rubles. They were so cheap because there was a large harvest. In sum, it was time for me to leave the melon field and the watermelons. After all, how long did I have to toil like that for naught? For the non-Jew, it was certainly good business to stay there even another two months but not for me, particularly with the approaching High Holy Days.[34]

I was now also finished with the melons. Nothing was going right for me. I was as they said—a *schlimazel*! They were right about me. Meanwhile, I was

---

32 *Yontef* here is referring to *Sukes* (September 20–28, 1869).
33 The end of June of 1869.
34 It is unclear how it would have been profitable for his non-Jewish partner to stay, unless he could sell the melons locally, thereby avoiding the transportation costs, or the price of the melons rose over time. The author needed to return to a Jewish community for Rosh Hashanah, which began the evening of September 5, 1869.

summoned to Tiraspol to a Justice of the Peace because that Bulgarian had pressed charges against me for not paying him the remaining fifty rubles for the wine, as you may remember. I went to court and told the complete truth for I could not cheat like they did. I said, "It's true, I owe him money. But I don't have it. And he should demand less because the wine went sour." The Justice of the Peace asked him to reduce my debt a bit "for the reasons given" but he did not want to lower it at all. He said that it was not true that it had gone sour, but even if it was true, he did not care to hear about it. The Justice insisted that I pay fifty-two rubles—fifty for the wine and two for the court fees—but since I was poor, he gave me four months to gradually pay it off. As I left the courtroom, everyone laughed at me for acting so foolishly by incriminating myself when there was no written evidence or witnesses. "You could have gotten off easily. If you wanted to be honest, you should have said to him privately that you'd pay him whenever God would help you, but not in court, which will take away your soul when the time comes." I said, "That's the way I am, and I can't be different than I am. God will just have to help me because of my common decency."

Meanwhile, the High Holy Days—Rosh Hashanah and Yom Kippur—came along. I cried out my heart to God to have pity on me and bless me with a good year. But I soon had a tremendous calamity that knocked me senseless, so that I could not think about anything else.

Right after Rosh Hashanah, my precious, beloved child, Ester-Khaykele, became ill. The talk among the women was that it happened to her because of an evil eye.[35] She was such a beautiful and healthy child that the townswomen could not get their fill in looking at her. Ester-Khaykele was suffering from an eye infection. Naturally, I brought a *feldsher* and a doctor, but her situation did not improve.[36] After Yom Kippur, her eyes shut completely. In short, she had contracted the childhood disease known as the mumps. She died right on the first day of *Sukes* at dusk.[37] To my great pain, this was all that my summer suffering had lacked! Evidently, the amount of trouble I was to endure had not yet been filled.

After *Yontef* and *shivah*,[38] I left for the small *shteytl* called Sovitskis and set up a *kheyder* there for six young boys for seventy-five rubles a term including

---

35 In his memoirs of his grandmother, Max Apple (2000:213–217) adeptly describes how potent and powerful she considered the evil eye to be.
36 A *feldsher* was a kind of medical assistant who had often obtained some medical knowledge by being a medic in the army.
37 September 20, 1869.
38 Because Ester-Khaykele died on the *Yontef* of *Sukes*, *shivah* only began on September 28, 1869, the day after *Yontef* ended. Since *shivah* in such a case only lasts six days instead of the usual seven, the author stopped sitting *shivah* on the morning of October 4, 1869.

meals with their parents, each of whom was to provide a month of meals. Thank God, I was now a *melomed*. I had settled down to teach but do not think that it was easy for me at Sovitskis. Even though it was a small and poor *shteytl*, it was rich in Hasidism and fanaticism. Everyone went to a different Hasidic Rebbe, had his own particular approach to religious matters, and taught his child his ways. Naturally, each one sought a *melomed* who was disposed toward his Rebbe, to his ways, and to his own eccentricities. Here a *melomed* needed to use flattery, hypocrisy, deception, and—more than talent, pedagogy, and particularly Torah knowledge—he needed to know how to get along with all the different types of Hasidim.

I did not know any of this beforehand. I only knew that a *melomed* needed to know how to teach a child and possess the talent to impart the subject matter to his students. So in trying out for the position there, I gathered the boys together for half a day and tried teaching them the Torah portion of *Ha-Azinu* with Rashi's commentary.[39] Everyone admired my ingenuity and my clear presentation so much that they decided to give me 6 boys aged twelve and also promised me room and board. They did not ask me what type of Hasid I was and to which Rebbe I went, for they figured that since I was a Tiraspoler, I undoubtedly went to the *tsadikim* to which all the Tiraspolers went—Tolne, Sadigor, Lyeve, Behúsh, Chechelnik, Skvere, or the like.[40] How would they know that I was a Chabadnik? That did not even enter their minds.

I traveled home to retrieve my things and said goodbye to my family. I arrived in Sovitskis right on *Rosh-Khoydesh Heshvan*.[41] I came only to find utter havoc. They had found out that I was not a Hasid—some were saying that I was a Chabadnik while others said that I was not a Hasid at all, that I was a *misnaged*. In short, they had erred by quickly hiring someone who had appeared to be a good *melomed*. Because the intersession had already ended and they had already sealed an agreement with me, they could no longer change their minds, but they could still be displeased.

But I calmed them down by telling them that they had nothing to fear. I would not turn their children into Chabadniks, teach them any Hasidic

---

39 Deuteronomy 32:1–52.
40 The Sadigorer Rebbe is mentioned in ch. 15, p. 240, footnote 8. The Savraner-Chechelniker Rebbe is mentioned in ch. 7, p. 157. The first Behúsher Rebbe (aka the Bohusher Rebbe), Rabbi Itskhok Fridman (1834–1896), was a nephew of the Lyever (ch. 17, p. 266, footnote 6), the Shtefeneshter (ch. 17, p. 273, footnote 44), and the Sadigorer Rebbe (ch. 15, p. 240, footnote 9). The Skverer Rebbe, Rabbi Yitzchok Tversky (1812–1895), settled in Skvere (aka Skver) in the 1840s and was a brother of the Tolner Rebbe, Rabbi Duvid Tversky, mentioned at length in chapter 22.
41 October 5–6, 1869.

teachings, nor even bring up the subject. I would only teach them the material normally studied.[42] I explained to them that the fact that I did not drink any liquor may actually be a large deficiency in a Hasid but is a tremendous attribute in a *melomed*, for I would then teach with a clear head and not spend my time seeking out schnapps and celebrating all the minor Hasidic holidays. In general, I hoped that they would be more satisfied with me than all the *melomdim* they had had until then. I pointed out to them that I was more religious than the other *melomdim* there, for this one would come into the *bes-medresh* drunk, while the other would come late, and yet another tried not to miss out on any important *yurtsaytn*,[43] while I did not do any of these things and stuck to my work teaching the children. In short, I negated their concerns and the issue was muted. I finally settled down, at a propitious hour, to teach.

I rented a little room from a poor man, a grain broker called Yankev-Maryase-Frimes—because his wife was named Maryase-Frime—who was a neighbor and tenant to the owner of a five-room house with a straw roof. His landlord lived in one room, another tenant in another room, and a third room served as a common kitchen. These three rooms were on the right side of the house. The left side consisted of two rooms—a room and a kitchen (and a pantry for storing firewood)—and that was where the grain broker lived with his family of four little children, his wife's younger sister—a large girl—and his elderly mother. This family was all stuffed and squeezed together in that single room, while the kitchen—their second room—was rented out to me as a *kheyder*. In actuality, I was given only a corner of the kitchen to set up a table with benches for my students. The oven, the area in front of the oven, and the top of the oven were for Maryaske, the lady of the house.[44] You can imagine that I did not appreciate setting up the *kheyder* in such a tumultuous place where it was so hectic. But you can believe me that I had searched the entire *shteytl* and could not obtain a better room. I saw where the other *melomdim* were teaching, and they had worse places, meaning that the single rooms in which those *melomdim* lived with their wives and children served as their residences, kitchens, and classrooms. So I was now teaching in a corner of Maryaske's kitchen, where there was a table and two benches, which actually belonged to Maryaske.

---

42 In a typical *kheyder*, twelve-year-old boys would generally study the Talmud and the Five Books of Moses with Rashi's commentary.
43 Refers to the anniversaries of death of Hasidic Rebbes which would be commemorated with other Hasidim.
44 Maryaske is the diminutive of Maryase. Ovens then were not only for cooking but for warming the house. Maryase had her children sleep on top of the oven (see below).

At night, I would move the table aside and make a bed from the two benches, while her bunch of children slept on top of the oven.

Rent cost me ten rubles for half a year, meaning for the entire winter that I stayed there! I worked as hard as a donkey with those six dolts. I taught them from eight in the morning until nine at night. Trying to knock the subject matter into their heads was like chopping wood. I was able to take a short break for lunch, *Minkhe* and *Marev*, which totaled just about an hour and a half because it was not far to the homes where I ate. The *shteytl* was small and everyone lived close by. As soon as you walked out, you were at your destination. The local residents made sure, as best as they were able, neither to delay the *melomed* nor to distract him from Torah study. The arrangement of their tables was not elaborate, and there were also not many different types of food at their tables. A large bowl was put down and everyone stuck a spoon in and tried to eat as quickly as possible. In the bowl was cooked groats, beans, or rice with beans, which they called "soup." Once in a while you would come across a little piece of meat, but most of the time even that was not there. Naturally, with such a lunch, there were not too many reasons to stick around. The blessing after the meal lasted longer than the meal. Dinner was some cultured milk, potatoes, or a glass of milk. Each child brought breakfast to the *kheyder* for himself but not for his Rebbe. Their Rebbe did not need to eat anything but needed to teach a lot . . .

I had many people checking up on me, as you can just imagine: the homeowner, the neighbors, my landlord Yankev-Maryases, his wife Maryaske herself, and her younger sister too. Each was capable of spreading denouncements against the *melomed*—he spanked this and that boy today, he dozed off in the middle of the day, he took too long praying *Minkhe* and *Marev*, and so on. Apart from these people looking over my shoulders, the fathers themselves would come by to check up on me. When I would be teaching the children in the evening, the fathers would stand behind the door and listen. And how horrible it was when a father's son did not know what I had taught him and I called him a dolt, blockhead, or the like. The last thing that I needed at that moment happened: the boy's father would not be able to control himself and would burst into the room and begin yelling at me. Naturally, I justified everything, but I suffered a lot because of it.

On *Shobes*, do you think I had any rest? Certainly not. *Shobes* was completely disrupted because on *Shobes* the boys had to be tested, and the boy at whose house I was eating that month certainly had to be the first in line. The examination already began during the meal. The father would begin questioning his son. If he did not answer correctly, the *melomed* had to correct him and would not be served any food. So *Shobes* would also pass by in much anguish. In short, I survived the winter and it was now the month of *Nisan*.[45]

I collected the bit of tuition that I had earned, but some never paid. In addition to all my other woes, they were also poor payers. So I ended up with twelve rubles less than expected. After paying ten rubles for the room, I was left with a salary of fifty-three rubles. I had spent fifteen rubles during the winter on food because I never ate my fill at the meals provided me and could often not even eat their food. So I went home for Pesach with thirty-one rubles, because traveling expenses had cost me two rubles.[46] I gave the thirty-one rubles to the Bulgarian for my debt for his wine, and I was then finished with that problem.[47] I celebrated Pesach at my father-in-law's home in the village of Perkon. But the question arose again: What was I to do? I had already tried teaching, but it was not practical for me. I could contract consumption from such a profession and would then not be able to support my wife.[48] What, though, could I begin to do now? This was the crucial question that I could not resolve.

---

45 April of 1870.
46 Based on the figures above, it seems that the author returned home with thirty-six rubles.
47 Earlier in this chapter on p. 338, the author writes that the court ruled that he pay fifty rubles to the Bulgarian and two rubles in court fees. He probably had already paid the Bulgarian nineteen rubles and was now paying the remaining thirty-one.
48 The author apparently feared contracting consumption (tuberculosis) by staying indoors for many hours with so many children.

CHAPTER 20

Studying to Be a *Shoykhet* and Searching for Uncle Idl, 1870–1872

With Reb Shoyl the *Shoykhet* in Romanovke • With the *Shokhtim* in Tiraspol • Zlote the *Shoykhet*'s Wife • The Journey to Uncle Idl's Home • The Rain and the Cold Wind • The Non-Jew and the Dog • The Haystack and the Birds • Reciting *Vidui* and Bidding Farewell to the World • An Amazing Urge to Survive • Arriving at My Uncle's Home

I decided to begin studying *sh'khita*.[1] But a large obstacle stood in my way—money again. Where could I obtain some money for this purpose? I am not speaking about money to support my wife—she was suffering her purgatory at her parents' home—but I myself needed to stay somewhere. I was a living human being and needed food and lodging. After all, no one would be willing to give me that for nothing. And the *shokhtim* would not teach me for free either, and I needed slaughtering knives and whetstones to sharpen the knives. Where would I get money for all of that? All of these obstacles stood before me like huge mountains, which obstructed and disrupted my entire plan to study *sh'khita*. But since "nothing can stand against a person's will,"[2] I thought for a long time until I decided what to do. I would set out toward Romanovke to Shoyl the *shoykhet*, the son of my late brother's father-in-law. Perhaps he would have mercy on me and teach me *sh'khita* without asking for any payment. Food was only a small worry because I could survive on very little. After all, those who

---
1   The slaughtering of animals according to Jewish law.
2   The author mentions a popular Hebrew expression based on a passage in the *Zohar* (2:162).

frequented the *bes-medresh* there would not let me die of hunger, God forbid. All I would need would be enough to keep me alive. That was what I came up with and that was what I did. I said goodbye to my precious and beloved wife and left immediately on foot for Romanovke. No one besides her knew where I was going or what I was doing. Two days later, I arrived in little Romanovke.

I arrived on the Friday of the week in which the Torah portion of *Breyshis* was being read.[3] Shoyl welcomed me like family and accepted my plan and encouraged me to study *sh'khita*.[4] He undertook to teach me at no charge on the condition that I teach his little boy who was about to begin studying *khimesh*. He proposed that I also teach another little boy besides his, which would pay for my room and board. I liked his suggestion. I would be a part-time *melomed* and a *shoykhet* in training.

Shoyl gave me knives to sharpen. He explained that, in order for me to learn how to sharpen knives, he would give me old banged-up slaughtering knives to learn on. Of course, I sharpened them with great diligence and eagerness, but he did not let me work very long, saying, "But you need to teach the children. The day's passing by with your only having been involved with yourself—praying, studying the laws of *sh'khita*, learning how to sharpen the knives, and eating lunch. The day is passing you by. When will you teach the children?" It turned out that I had to teach the children more than I thought, and no time was left for me. Over the course of several weeks, I understood that I had made a mistake in my calculations. I thought that half a *melomed* was not a full one, but ultimately, it turned out that with these people it was all the same: when a *melomed* taught six children, he had to teach them an entire day, and when a *melomed* taught only two children, he also had to teach them an entire day. Actually, while I thought that half a *melomed* was not a full one, they thought the exact opposite! Since the costs for those who hire a *melomed* for two children were naturally higher, they wanted their children to make even more headway. They figured that the more they squeezed the *melomed*, the more they would see their children progress. Since Shoyl the *shoykhet* and the other father aspired for their children to greatly advance under my tutelage, they wanted me to devote myself the entire day to teaching their children and devote very little time to myself—only the

---

3   Friday, October 21, 1870. The Torah scroll is divided into weekly portions and is completed each year on *Simchas Torah*, after which it is started anew with the first Torah portion, *Breyshis*, constituting Genesis 1:1 until 6:8.

4   The original states "*sh'khita* and *bedika*." The latter denotes "inspection" and refers to the inspection for lesions in the lungs of the slaughtered livestock as required by Jewish law. Since the inspection of the lungs is an essential part of the slaughtering process (*sh'khita*), only the word *sh'khita* is used in the translation whenever the author writes "*sh'khita* and *bedika*."

time when the children were still asleep or when they were eating. I then saw that we had each fooled ourselves. In addition, since I had so little time to work on my own matters, I decided that, after making it through the winter, I would no longer take on any children as students.

Studying *sh'khita* here was not advisable because the two town *shokhtim* had so little work and so few animals were slaughtered. So how would I be able to learn how to slaughter animals, especially when the cow was wobbly and the impoverished butcher was terrified with worry that the *shoykhet* would determine that the cow was *treyf*, God forbid, when checking its lungs.[5] So how could he risk allowing an apprentice to slaughter the cow? Once, when merely a chicken became *treyf*, I observed the tremendous uproar the Jewish woman made in demanding to be paid for it.[6] How then would it be with a cow? And, if so, when would I ever become a *shoykhet*? And what type of *shoykhet* would I become with such meager experience? Therefore, like "one who sees the future,"[7] I immediately decided to abandon my "good fortune" in Romanovke and leave in due time. In order to avoid their complaints to me and so that Shoyl the *shoykhet* could not convince me to return and stay (because I could have easily been persuaded) I decided to leave there at dawn when everyone was still asleep and leave a note that I had left. It was better to be in a larger city, since my goal was to learn how to be a *shoykhet*—not to be a *melomed*, like they wanted.

I left Romanovke for Tiraspol, where I threw myself at the *shokhtim* there and pleaded with them to have pity on me. Reb Zolmen, who knew that I had no money, did not even want to speak with me. But Reb Shloyme had compassion on me and agreed to teach me *sh'khita*—not for free but for a little bit of money, no more than seventeen rubles.[8] I was to pay him when I would receive my certification papers permitting me to slaughter, which were required by Jewish law. This meant that he would not give me the certification papers until I would pay him. Where (you may ask) would I then get the money? I did not think about it—I relied on God. How and by what means (you may ask) would

---

5   The butcher would invest his own money in purchasing a cow, which cost him a large sum of money, but he could not afford to purchase a healthy animal. Hence, the butcher's money was at risk since certain types of lesions in the lungs render a cow *treyf* and prohibit it for kosher consumption. Of course, the *shoykhet* would only be able to determine this after the animal was slaughtered. If the animal was found to be *treyf*, the butcher would lose all of his money.
6   A slight pause or a slip of the *shoykhet*'s hand while slaughtering the chicken could render the animal to be *treyf*, i.e., prohibited for kosher consumption.
7   Mishna (Avot 2:10).
8   Reb Shloyme the *shoykhet* is mentioned (without a surname) on page 10 of the list of pre-subscribers from Treshpoli (that is, Tiraspol) to *Tehilim im ma'amadot* (Zhitomir, 1866).

I live? I did not think about that—God would certainly not abandon me. And I became apprenticed to study *sh'khita* in Tiraspol.

I took to my work quite diligently and did not let a spare moment go by. I spent the entire day, from five in the morning until ten at night, studying the appropriate laws, sharpening the slaughtering knives, and working in the slaughterhouse. From five until ten in the morning, I was busy studying the various laws.[9] From ten in the morning until ten at night I was busy sharpening slaughtering knives. During the shorter winter days, I would study the pertinent laws at night instead and in the early hours of the morning before dawn. I suffered like this for an entire year, from *Tamuz* of 5630 [*sic*] until *Tamuz* of 5631 [*sic*].[10]

I first received my certification from the *shokhtim* in the middle of *Tamuz* and was thereby rescued from my servitude in Egypt.[11] God apparently had pity on me and arranged a position for me as a *shoykhet* in the small village of Olt-Dubesár, where I was hired for twenty-five rubles including room and board for a period of two months, meaning until the High Holy Days.[12]

I know, my beloved, that you are interested in knowing how I managed to obtain food during my year in Tiraspol, how I managed with lodgings, and how I came up with the money to have my certification papers released from the *shokhtim* to whom I was obligated to pay seventeen rubles, as mentioned earlier. If this does interest you, I will tell it to you. You will also learn how a person can subsist for a year without anything—without a *kopek*.

You already know my daily work schedule. But I must explain to you that as I became more knowledgeable and experienced in this vocation—a holy vocation—I became busier and busier. I learned to sharpen a slaughtering knife on my own because no one assisted me or attempted to teach me or show me how. I gained experience by myself through a lot of work, because I understood that the *shokhtim* were not too interested in my progress and were not concerned

---

9   The classic work on the laws of *sh'khita* is *Simlah Khadashah* by Rabbi Aleksander Sender Shor, which was first printed in 1733 in Zholkve, Ukraine (now Zhovkva) and has since been reprinted numerous times. The author's great-granddaughter Cynthia Unterberg has in her possession a book on the laws of *sh'khita* called *Totsaot Khayim* (Pressburg, 1835) by Rabbi Khayim Toyber. The book belonged to the author and was probably purchased later in his career.
10 The author arrived in Romanovke on October 21, 1870, as indicated earlier in this chapter (p. 344, footnote 3). Hence, he left Romanovke and arrived in Tiraspol in *Tamuz* 5631 (July 1871), not in *Tamuz* 5630 (July 1870) as stated here, and he remained there for a year until *Tamuz* 5632 (July 1872), not in *Tamuz* 5631 (July 1871) as stated here. This dating is supported later in this chapter on p. 353 where the author writes that after a year in Tiraspol he set out for his Uncle Pinye's on Tuesday, the 10th of *Tamuz*, which indeed occurred on Tuesday, July 16, 1872.
11 End of July 1872.
12 Rosh Hashanah was on September 16–17, 1871.

with my living in the *bes-medresh* homeless, with only a little bit of dry bread to eat. They thought to themselves that perhaps I would finally quit this entire endeavor of mine and they would be rid of me. So I myself—alone with God's help—worked until I made those slaughtering knives look like new, and only then did those *shokhtim* show an interest in me and make use of my capabilities. I sharpened their slaughtering knives for them every day for the slaughterhouse, besides preparing a special knife for myself that I would use to demonstrate my skill when I would be tested for certification.[13]

Sh'khita was also a similar story. I had barely begun to slaughter poultry and livestock, when all the *shokhtim* began to use me. I did it willingly because I knew that the more I sharpened knives and slaughtered poultry and livestock, the more experience I would gain. In this manner, I worked like a mule yet received nothing for it. Not one of them asked me if I had eaten anything, for they were afraid to risk asking such a relevant question. After all, what would have happened if, God forbid, I had answered, "No!" What would they have done? Would they have asked me over to eat lunch? Not on your life! It was enough that out of pity they were letting me work with them. Could you really have expected them to give me something to eat? One should not have so much pity on a young married man who was not a fervent Hasid.[14]

So now you know a little about my work, but it would be impossible to write all the details. The only remaining unanswered question now is regarding food; where and how did I support myself? I will now write you all the details regarding my life during that year in Tiraspol.

Upon arriving in Tiraspol, I first went to a Jewish baker, whom I knew to be a pious Jew, and arranged for credit of a ruble and ten to twenty *kopeks*, meaning that he was to loan me bread for a month—one and a half *funt* of bread a day. Regarding sleeping arrangements, I could spend the night in any of the *bute-medrushim* that I wanted, so I chose the Tolner *kloyz* for my place of lodging. I slept there, used it as my living quarters, and studied there when I had the time. I picked a bench next to the furnace so that I would be warm in the winter. Near the bench was a table at which I studied and ate my dry morsel of bread. Before I went to sleep, I would prop a *shtender* under my head and

---

13   Certification in *sh'khita* requires a thorough knowledge of the following: the laws of *sh'khita*, inspection of one's slaughtering knife to make sure that it is perfectly smooth and sharp, and the slaughtering of a number of animals in the presence of the certifying rabbi or *shoykhet* (Berman, 1941:84–91).

14   Though the author was a Chabad Hasid, the other *shokhtim* did not consider him a Hasid since he was not a follower of their Hasidic Rebbes.

would rest on the hard bench and slept so soundly that I did not know where the night disappeared.[15]

I suffered a lot during my first two months in Tiraspol, so much so that I began to feel that my health was deteriorating. I began to feel weaker and weaker. Who knows what would have been the end result of my living such an austere existence? Do not forget that I had to work extremely hard sharpening knives, learning the laws of *sh'khita*, going to the livestock slaughterhouse in Tiraspol, and going to the poultry slaughterhouse in Bender every Friday, and being subservient—a slave—to all the *shokhtim* there, and enduring everything. Moreover, the dry morsel of bread that I ate did not satiate me and I had no bed, so I did not have restful nights as all other people had. With such a life, I could not guard my health, and, whether I liked it or not, my health deteriorated.

I know that you may be surprised that in all of Tiraspol, among all of my relatives, I was unable to find anyone to support me during that difficult period—during such an arduous time. I will explain it to you so that it will not be puzzling. Some relatives were so poor, so besieged by children, and lived in such narrow quarters that I had pity on them and avoided them so as not to cause them any pain. For example, I avoided my sister Ite for months at a time, and when I did see her I would not relate to her any of my sufferings; I could not let her know about my situation. If she would have realized my bitter plight, God forbid, she would not have been able to resist giving me the last bite of food from her and her child Itsele's mouths. For that reason, I had to make it sound as if things were wonderful and would not allow myself even a glass of tea at her home, though I really could have used a warm drink.

Regarding my relatives who were well-off and who could have helped me out, they feigned ignorance as if they never heard of my sorrows. They were ostensibly angry at me for having married a woman whose social class did not befit them. Since I had committed such a crime, they were exempt from helping me. Their treatment of me can be illustrated in the story told about a poor brother who was marrying off one of his children and went to see his wealthy brother. During his eight days on the road, the poor brother used up all his money to his last *kopek* until he reached his wealthy brother. He told his wealthy brother that he had to marry off one of his children and that absolute necessity had forced him to set out to request his brother's help. The wealthy brother asked him, "How old is your daughter?" He replied, "Thank God, she's twenty years old." The wealthy brother burst out laughing, "Ha-ha, What's going on? You don't have any time? She's but a young child.

---

15 A *shtender* is a lectern-like stand used for studying and praying by many Orthodox Jews.

My daughter is now twenty-three, and I'm not even thinking about marrying her off." The poor brother explained to him that a poor man's twenty-year-old daughter was considered a grown woman and that he would have married her off three years ago had he had the means. But at that time, the poor man had thought that perhaps God would help him so that he would not have to turn to his wealthy brother for help, so he decided to wait. And now, he could not and dared not wait, for if he would do so, perhaps she would never be able to marry. The poor man added, "My situation can't be compared with yours. A rich child does not have to worry about a match." "Yes," replied the rich brother, "just tell me with whom did you make the match. Who's the groom?" The poor brother told him that the groom was so-and-so who was a skilled laborer. When the rich brother heard this, he yelled, "Go away from here, you murderer! Don't you have any consideration for the honor of our family? How could you do a match with a skilled laborer and a poor person at that? Out of here! I don't want to look at your face. Murderer! I'm ashamed of this match. You're not getting one *groshn* from me." And with these words, the rich brother left and did not even listen to his brother's contentions. The poor brother was left to talk to the walls, receiving no response. He went home disappointed and empty-handed with a broken heart.

My wealthy relatives also refused to help me because they did not like the match I made. I perceived why they were angry with me, so I did not want to let them have the pleasure of seeing me sullenly plead before them. On the contrary, I pretended in their presence that everything was going well, though they could have easily found out the truth, especially in those times. My ragged clothes and my impoverished lifestyle were obvious, and others must certainly have told them about my predicament. But they had an excuse not to help me, "He has wealthy in-laws. Let them help him out. Since he made such a match, he deserves what he has. That match doesn't befit us."

After this short explanation, you are now aware of why none of my wealthy relatives assisted me. It only remains for me to explain and clarify where I obtained money to pay the baker for the month of bread that I owed him. When I noticed that the month was quickly coming to an end and that I seemingly had no hope of obtaining any money, I sought out and found—in time—a pious, young and well-to-do married man who loaned me one and a half silver rubles in cash, payable in a month to six weeks, which I found encouraging. At the end of the month, I paid the baker one silver ruble and ten *kopeks* for thirty pounds of bread, because I had only taken bread five days a week, from Sunday until Thursday. On Friday and *Shobes*, I was not in Tiraspol. Every Thursday, after finishing work in the livestock slaughterhouse, I would walk to Bender, where

I would arrive quite early on Friday morning to assist Reb Khayem-Ersh to slaughter chickens. Afterward, I walked to the village of Perkon to my wife and in-laws. And I would be back in Tiraspol by early Sunday morning and would take some bread from the baker. Naturally, the baker was quite satisfied that I had paid him on time and now heartily gave me bread, because during the first month he had given me the bread with fear and uncertainty, but now he gave it to me with complete trust.

I lived like this during the two months preceding the High Holy Days—Rosh Hashanah and Yom Kippur.[16] As usual, I spent *Sukes* in Bender,[17] because my wife and her parents would spend *Yontef* there, and I would be there together with them. From *kapores* I earned one ruble,[18] which the *shokhtim* gave me for working the entire day before Yom Kippur.[19] And I earned one ruble in Perkon.

After the Jewish holidays ended, I noticed that I was becoming weaker and weaker because of all that I was enduring: I was not eating any warm meals, only dry bread with salt.[20] Though not known for her kindness, Zlote, the wife of Reb Shloyme the *shoykhet*, was willing to have compassion on me. She allowed me some cooked food for lunch at her home. I only had to give her a small piece of meat. So every other day, I gave her a half *funt* of beef, and she would give me a bowl of her soup with a one-quarter *funt* piece of beef in it. Nonetheless, this was a great act of kindness that she did for me, and I can never forget this mitzvah, particularly when she would advance me soup on the days that I had no meat to give her, and she was willing to wait until I was able to do so. Truthfully speaking, she did not even want to accept any meat from me, but I would not agree to accept her soup otherwise; therefore, she had to give in to me, though she would have done me this favor in any case. What else did this fine Jewish woman do? She found out how I was suffering in the *kloyz* by lying on the bare benches, so she made a place for me to sleep in her kitchen, where I stayed until after the winter when I received my certification.

Not only was this Jewish woman kind to me, her husband, Reb Shloyme the *shoykhet*, was even kinder. From the moment we met, he showed his compassion for me, as described earlier. Apparently, he had prevailed upon his wife

---

16 September 16–17, 1871 and September 25, 1871, respectively.
17 September 30–October 8, 1871.
18 *Kapores* is a custom carried out by men, women, and children in the early morning of the eve of Yom Kippur or on the preceding days. Each male takes a live rooster and each female takes a hen. The live chicken is taken in the right hand and moved in a circular motion around the head three times, while reciting certain prayers. The custom is that the chicken is then slaughtered and given to the poor. The author was doing the slaughtering.
19 The author is evidently referring to the *shokhtim* of Tiraspol.
20 The last Jewish holiday of the season, *Simchas Torah*, occurred on October 8, 1871.

to do many favors for me. Be that as it may, I am indebted to and was profoundly impressed by Reb Shloyme and his wife Zlote for extending their friendship to me. God should bless them with long and happy years and with much pleasure from their only child Yekhiel, may his light shine.

Reb Shloyme was truly my primary teacher. He was genuinely devoted to me. He tested me in the laws of *sh'khita*, pointed out my mistakes, and always praised my ability to others. If not for his wife's kindness, who knows if I would have not, God forbid, become ill from my former onerous life. I led my life like this in Tiraspol until I received my certification papers. As for my creditors—I used to pay them monthly.

Shortly after Pesach,[21] I was ready to secure my certification papers, but the other *shokhtim* did not want to give me my papers until they were paid. Though Reb Shloyme was ready to give them to me regardless, and he had been my primary teacher and the only one to devote time toward my training, yet they all took charge when it came to receiving payment and did not want to let me go. After all, what did they care if Pinye-Ber was having a tough time? He was used to hard work. So I began to devise a plan to tear myself away from their hold on me by obtaining some money. Yet no matter how I tried, I could not find anyone to help me out with a loan...

Each week, meaning every Thursday when I finished my work at the slaughterhouse in Tiraspol, I would walk home for *Shobes* to Perkon, as you already know. I now stopped going directly home and walked through the village of Ternifke, where a few Jews lived.[22] I would go there every Thursday evening, spend the night, and slaughter some chickens and sometimes two or more lambs as well. I would then walk over to Perkon, which was only two or three *versts* from Ternifke, and would slaughter chickens and lambs for all the Jews there.[23] I was doing them a great service for otherwise they would have had to carry their chickens to the city, to Bender, to have them slaughtered, and it was even a greater service for me, because I was now earning some money, little by little. Right after *Shobes* on my way back to Tiraspol, I would do the same thing. Like this, I was making an income of one and a half rubles a week which provided me with the means of repaying my creditors to the last *kopek* and and still enabled me to put aside five rubles to pay the *shokhtim* to whom I still owed twelve rubles.

---

21   April 23–30, 1872.
22   In ch. 18, p. 299, the author briefly mentioned that his wife had an uncle in Ternifke.
23   Slaughtering before being certified would be problematic, since the Ashkenazic custom is not to slaughter without certification. See *Shulkhan Arukh* (*Yoreh Deah* 1:1). Perhaps he had oral permission from his primary teacher to practice *sh'khita*. As the author mentions, written certification was necessary for him to find a permanent position.

But by the time *Shvues* passed I still had not paid them the twelve rubles. I had no hope of obtaining it, but they still did not want to let me go.[24] You can understand how bitter my heart was. I was already a *shoykhet*, thank God, but I was tied down and not able to seek out a position anywhere. After all, what *shoykhet* could obtain a position without certification? In thinking over and over where I could obtain some money, I came up with an idea, but just listen to what a great idea it was.

My mother, of blessed memory, had two brothers, one of whom, Pinye Groseler, lived in Groseles. He was wealthy but would not acknowledge that he was my uncle as long as he felt that I needed his help. He was one of the highbrows who felt that the match I made was beneath his dignity, as illustrated in the parable mentioned above. In contrast, he had a brother by the name of Idl, who was his opposite. He was goodhearted, worldly, and a learned man. He had been poor but now was well-to-do. If only I could go to him, he would welcome me as an honored guest and would help me out and give me the entire twelve rubles. I would then be saved from my predicament. After all, for such a well-to-do person, twelve rubles would not be very significant to help out a relative, especially since my mother was his only sister and I had not taken a *kopek* from him in my entire life—I did not even know him. I was sure he would want to help me, especially when he heard that I hoped to repay him. So why should I think that he would not help me out? There was certainly no reason to think that he would not. How could I allow myself to think that such a wealthy, good person would not assist his impoverished nephew who was in such need? All of this went through my mind, and I decided to make the arduous journey to my uncle Idl's because I knew that I would be as good as helped as soon as I arrived there.

So I began to inquire about my uncle's whereabouts, and I found out that he lived in a village on the estate of a landowner which was fifteen *versts* from the train station in Rozdelnye. They did not know the name of the village but reassured me that it was no more than fifteen *versts* from Rozdelnye, that they knew him in Rozdelnye, and that upon my arrival I should inquire about his whereabouts and they would tell me where to go. In short, I decided not to even tell my wife about this trip to visit my uncle. I wanted to surprise her by coming home with the certification papers in my hands and only then tell her happily about the money I received on my trip. That was what I thought about doing and that was what I did. I remember that I readied myself for the trip on a Tuesday.

---

24 *Shvues* was on June 6–7, 1872.

***

Here begins my account of my horrible trip to visit my uncle.

I remember buying bread and some green cucumbers and then going to the train station to buy a ticket to Rozdelnye to travel to my Uncle Idl.[25] The train left Tiraspol at 2:30, and I arrived at Rozdelnye at four. I inquired among the inhabitants of Rozdelnye whether they knew where my Uncle Idl lived, and provided his description. They replied that they did indeed know such a person, that his name was Idl, and that his father-in-law was from Petótsk. He lived fourteen *versts* from there. I asked them for directions to his village, which they gave me and I began walking there.

It was very hot because it was midsummer, the 10th day of *Tamuz*, but it soon began to cool down.[26] I walked with gusto and strode cheerfully, hoping that I would arrive at my uncle's home momentarily and that he would help me out financially. Soon I would meet my uncle of whom I had only heard and never had the privilege of seeing, and I would meet my aunt and his household.[27]

After I had walked eight *versts*, the sun began to set and it now began to become cooler. My head was hurting from the heat, and my stomach also began to hurt a bit. I did not pay attention to my pains and went further with cheerful steps in order to arrive at my uncle's in time. I thought to myself that there I would be able to rest and that things would also take a turn for the good. In brief, the pain in my stomach did not want to stop. It became stronger and more painful, and it was accompanied by the pain in my head. It seemed as if those two pains had arranged between themselves to prevent me from arriving at my uncle's home in time to sleep there. Little by little, I became more and more exhausted until I could no longer continue. I dropped to the ground and rolled onto my stomach. I was now no longer thinking in terms of arriving at my uncle's in time to sleep there. I saw that I would not reach there before nightfall because, according to my calculations, it was still six *versts* away. I was now thinking of finding a nearby village or a tavern where I could spend the night and rest. Perhaps there my pains would pass. Remaining in the open fields overnight was not an option, for who knew what could happen to me there? I felt quite ill. I wanted to walk but could not. My stomach and head were aching, and I tried to figure out what could be the cause. I had not eaten anything that day;

---

25 Perhaps the author specifically refers to green cucumbers since yellow cucumbers were also frequently grown and sold.
26 Tuesday, July 16, 1872.
27 Though the author clearly did not know his Uncle Idl well, he does mention meeting him while in Groseles in the winter of 1857–1858 (ch. 6, p. 148) and 1864 (ch. 13, pp. 208–209).

nothing more than a green cucumber and some bread back in Rozdelnye. Now, this was not the first time I had eaten such fare, so why should it be harming me so? I could ponder this from today until tomorrow, but I was doing badly. I forced myself to continue walking as much as possible. Perhaps I would somehow manage to make it to a village or a tavern—as long as I did not remain outside. I came to the peak of a mountain and saw that in the valley below was a village. "Thank God," I thought to myself. So even if I would not be at my uncle's, at least I would be among humans. With all of my strength, I dragged myself into the valley toward the village and then to a Jewish tenant innkeeper where I spent the night.

The innkeeper and his family brought me back to life with some tea, with compresses for my head and stomach, and with a good bed. During the night, the pain eased and I felt optimistic, so much so that I did not wait a minute and, first thing in the morning, I resumed my journey to my uncle's. The members of the household pointed out the village where my uncle lived, which was exactly opposite their village in the same valley, which was split in two by a gully. Their village was at the bottom of one mountain, and my uncle's village was at the bottom of the opposite mountain. To go from one village to the other, one had to walk through the width of the gully. A stream flowed in the gully, which split the valley in two. The valley was four to five *versts* wide, but the other village appeared to be close and one could see it clearly. My uncle's house stood out from among the other houses because it was made of stone and had a sheet-iron roof, which made it appear like a nobleman's courtyard. Of course, just seeing his house restored my health and drove me to reach it as quickly as possible so as to be delivered from my financial woes. I took my bundle, thanked them for the lodgings, and went happily, full of hope.

I reached the small river, meaning the stream that flowed through the length of the gully. I washed myself so that I would be clean upon arriving at my uncle's. As I came closer to my uncle's house, my heart became joyful—even before I entered it. Since it was still before six in the morning, the members of the household were busy milking the cows. In the courtyard were a nice few cows. Since I realized that no one would be able to speak with me then, I decided to pray first. By the time I finished praying, they had already finished milking the cows and had driven them out to the steppe to graze.

The head of the household walked over, and I realized that he was not a member of our family. Something about him did not sit right with me. I began talking with him. Indeed, he was not the Idl that I needed. He was also named Idl but he was not my uncle. You can understand how dejected I felt. The only comfort I had was that this Idl said he knew where my uncle lived—some five *versts* from there. I needed to go up the mountain and then go down the other side, meaning that my Uncle Idl lived in the gully on the other side of mountain. "Your uncle," he said, "is also involved in milking cows, like me, and lives, as I do, in a similar house rented from a landowner." I bade him farewell and continued on my way, thinking about my "wonderful luck" and "joyful excursion." Who knew if I would find my uncle there? And who knew if I would be helped there?

Thundering and lightning began, and the sky became quite overcast. I hurried to walk faster but I was going uphill, and how quickly can one go uphill? It started to rain softly. I walked more quickly. It began to rain harder. I saw an earthen hut made for a watchman. I slipped into it to wait until it finished raining. The rain continued. It did not want to stop. The watchman, a Jew-hating Russian, came along and, noticing a Jew inside, became angry and wanted to hit me. I began to weep and asked him not to hit me for I did not come to steal anything but only to shelter myself from the rain. In short, he drove me into the pouring rain and sent his angry dog after me to escort me off the property in his dog language. Eventually, I was rid of that Russian and his dog and continued walking in the downpour.

I finally reached my destination, and I went into the house of the tenant innkeeper and found them churning butter. I asked, "Who lives here? What's the name of the head of the house?"

They gave me a completely different name—not Idl. I asked them about my Uncle Idl. They replied, "Actually, he lived here a few years ago. He maintained the nobleman's courtyard and his forty cows and used to deliver dairy products to Odessa. But we don't know where he currently lives." They continued, "We think that he now lives in Petotsk."

I asked with an embittered heart, "Is Petotsk far from here?"

They replied, "No, seven or eight *versts*."

I rested and thought to myself, "*Nu*, I have to keep going." Ignoring the continuing downpour, and the fact that I was thoroughly drenched, I went because I realized this was not just a patch of cloudy sky but that threatening clouds covered the entire heavens. Since the clouds were making the world dark, which was just like the feeling in my heart, it was not advisable to think about waiting until it stopped raining. I needed to make good time for who knew what else awaited me that day. It was as if my heart was telling me that something else would yet crimp my plans. I saw that my journey was not going well. I would have already headed home but it pained me to have endured so much without having reached my destination. In sum, I felt that I had to go on.

I walked and dragged myself along through the mud, and the rain fell on me and made mud out of me. Around noon, I arrived at the village of Petotsk. I began inquiring about my Uncle Idl and was directed to his wife's relatives from whom I could find out everything. I found his relatives who told me that my Uncle Idl did not live far from there—perhaps seven or eight *versts* away.

"Why do you need him?" they asked.

I only replied, "I need him regarding a certain matter," because I was ashamed to say that I was his relative. I did not want to embarrass him, God forbid. Incidentally, I now heard from them that he had come upon hard times and was poor. They apparently surmised that I must be his relative because I said that I was from Tiraspol, and they knew that he had relatives in Tiraspol. They now knew why I needed to speak with him. For my part, I also understood them well; they were making him out to be a pauper so that I should not exact any help from him. So I did not believe them and left using the road that they pointed out. They were apparently quite pleased that they were rid of me and that I had left their house because, when I began to leave, they did not even try to deter me for appearance's sake with such comments as, "What's going on? Where are you headed? Stay here. Perhaps the rain will stop."

I left them with a deep sigh. I continued on my way uphill as they had directed me. The road that led up to the mountain stretched out a long way, perhaps one and a half *versts*. It was a completely non-Jewish road; I did not run into a single Jew. The rain continued to pour down harder. The non-Jews were surprised to see a contemptible Jew walking in the rain. I decided that if I reached the end of the village and the rain did not stop, I would stop at the last house and not continue onward. Something frightened me, though I did not know what. I reached the last little cottage, and it was still raining. I asked the non-Jew there to let me into his home. He asked where I was going. I told him the name of the village. He told me that it was not far, six *versts* away on the other side of the mountain. I sat in his house; the stench was unbearable. It was full of filthy children, pigs, calves—all in one room—with me in the midst of it.

I waited impatiently for the rain to stop. Apparently the weather outdoors would not be clearing up so quickly. Indoors it seemed as if the night was quickly approaching, though according to my calculations it should have been quite early, something like three or four in the afternoon. What was six *versts* for me to walk? In one hour, I could be there—no matter how slowly I walked. In short, I had to continue because sleeping in that non-Jew's home was not an option. I would walk slowly and arrive there while it was still early. Once I arrived there, I would rest up. It seemed to me as if the weather was clearing up. Since the rain had lightened up a bit and I had already rested an hour, I decided to resume walking. I bade the non-Jewish family farewell and continued on my way.

I headed toward the mountain and began to walk uphill. The mountain was not steep. It rose gradually higher and higher. There were no steep inclines;

rather it rose slowly. Nonetheless, a mountain is a mountain, and it becomes more difficult to walk as one goes higher and higher, until one reaches the top when one naturally begins to walk downhill. At the bottom of the other side of the mountain was the village where my blessed uncle lived. I was still working my way up the mountain when I felt that my feet were giving way. For besides the rain—which, though sparse, had soaked me through and through—the wind was blowing at me, causing the rain to thrash me in the face and making it difficult to continue walking. I was walking against the wind, uphill in the rain. It was like swimming in a river against the current; even an excellent swimmer in such conditions would become exhausted and drown. Similarly here: though I was a healthy young man who could walk seventy to eighty *versts* a day, this walk had worn me out.[28] Do not forget what I had endured during the twenty-four hours since I had left Rozdelnye, including the night, and that I had not eaten anything that day. I could not beg for food, and I had no money to buy any. I was trudging along in the rain and mud in wet clothes that weighed a good amount, and the wind was blowing against me to boot. All of this together made it exceedingly difficult for me to walk up the mountain, especially since the higher I went, the more dangerous the wind became. It whipped at me and penetrated me to such an extent that I became chilled. Consequently, I began to cry to God that He should have pity on me and give me support. I felt that my strength was leaving me. I could no longer walk. Returning to Petotsk would take longer than it would to reach my uncle's because I had already almost prevailed over the mountain. Only a small distance remained until the mountaintop. I thought about where I could sit down to rest. I walked a bit more. I was now on the top of the mountain. The wind was gusting at top speed while howling and screeching. I was terrified. It was dark everywhere—as if it was nighttime. I noticed from afar, on the side of the road, a tall haystack. I did not think much and walked off the road toward the haystack. I thought that I would be able to protect myself from the wind in the haystack, which would also give me a break from the rain until I could gather my strength to continue on.

Upon approaching the haystack, I became petrified—a whole flock of black birds suddenly flew up like a black cloud with a tremendous racket. Actually, there was nothing to fear. It was the unexpected commotion and the noise of their caws that perhaps caused me to be frightened at first. But shortly afterward I calmed down as I realized that their situation was apparently no better than mine. They were also cold and wet, so they had perched themselves about the tall haystack as I had done. When I had come along, I had scared

---

28   Seventy *versts* is the equivalent of 46.4 miles.

them as they had scared me. We were all unfortunate. The birds quickly calmed down and found a place where they hid from the wind and rain, and I found a place where I covered myself completely. The wind continued to screech and wail but it had no power over my immediate surroundings or me. The rain also did not reach me, and I lay tucked away in the haystack. My situation seemed good, but then the cold started to penetrate me. It was as if I was trembling from a high fever, for my teeth were rattling and, in general, I did not feel well. I felt that my strength was leaving me.

I began to consider what I should do now. Night was falling. I had no strength to continue on. The wind and rain were not letting up. And what would become of me here? Would I be able to survive until morning? While thinking these thoughts, a chill seized me and made my entire body tremble. Afterward, I began to doze off. Then an idea struck me. Everyone who has frozen to death began by falling asleep. If so, I thought, did they in fact die easily? So I could also doze off and freeze to death in the middle of the summer! It would be amazing. My death would be a marvel—a young man freezes to death in the month of *Tamuz*.[29] But in my case, it was not only cold but hunger as well. But however it would be, I realized that my end was near.

I began to think of my beloved wife, who had never seen or known the wider world. Should she be left to be a young *aguna* on top of that?[30] No one knew where I had gone. I did not tell her where I was going. And the haystack in which my body would lie was off on the side some distance from the road. Who knew how long my body would lie around before being buried or how long it would be before someone would happen upon me? And who knew if the starving birds were not waiting to eat up my body? If so, no one would ever know who had died in this spot and whose bones were lying around. Being unable to remarry, my wife would then be miserable forever.

While having this frightening thought, I felt that my strength was leaving me and I began to say *Vidui*.[31] I cried, but no tears flowed. I spoke, but no words could be heard since my lips were not moving. But my mind was firm and sharp. I lifted my eyes toward the sky and began to bid farewell to it. Though the world had not shined for me—not during my life and not during my death—I cast my eyes toward the four corners of the earth and bade farewell to them.

---

29 *Tamuz* generally falls out in July and is considered the hottest month of the Hebrew calendar.
30 An *aguna* is a married woman who became separated from her husband and cannot remarry, either because she cannot obtain a Jewish divorce (known as a *get*) from him or because it is unknown whether he is still alive.
31 Jews recite the Hebrew *Vidui* confessional prayer before departing from this world to evoke God's mercy and bring great atonement upon the person (*Kitsur Shulkhan Arukh* 193:14).

Nonetheless, I did not feel like leaving this world so soon and so young. I was all of twenty-two years old and had not left any vestiges of myself.[32] But what does that matter, for when God wants something, it has to be as He wants. I started to doze off again forever. I began to see the horror of death before me. Oh, horrible, horrible—even now when I remind myself of it.

Suddenly the ravens screeched which caused me to wake up. I opened my eyes, and I felt like someone being pulled from the jaws of death. I noticed all the ravens jumping toward their roosting sites where I was lying. They apparently thought that I was already dead and would now have prey upon which to gorge themselves. This aroused in me the desire to live. I thought, "As long as even one of my limbs can still move, I must save myself. Even if I'm meant to die, God forbid, let me die on the road so that I can be found quickly. And perhaps God will have pity on me, and I'll be able to drag myself to someone's house—even a non-Jew's—as long as I am among people, so that they will be able to inform my wife what became of me." Then I said to the birds, "No, I cannot allow you to eat me alive. I must leave here by any means possible." With these words, I suddenly lifted myself up so that the birds became frightened and scattered, and I ripped myself away—literally out of the hands of death—and began running with my last bit of strength. I can honestly say that I did not have any strength left, and I myself do not know how or from where that bit of energy appeared. When I think back about this incident, I marvel at where I found the strength to move forward.

The wind made it almost impossible for me to run, and the rain thrashed all around as before. I tried to run in order to warm myself up because I was horribly cold. I figured I had nothing to lose—in any case I was soon going to die. So I would drop dead running—as long as I was closer to the road and closer to my uncle's village. Shortly afterward, the wind died down and I started going downhill as the wind became quieter and quieter. The rain no longer whipped against my face. I finally heard dogs barking and noticed cottages. I became steadfast and stronger in my hope of remaining alive. God had ultimately helped me. I dragged myself to the home of a fellow Jew and his family who lived in the village. They immediately revived my spirits and took me into their warm kitchen. I removed my clothes, and they gave me some of theirs until mine would dry. They gave me something to eat, and I was refreshed and invigorated. Do you think" to "Are you thinking that I may have possibly arrived at the house of my Uncle Idl and his family? God forbid! The time had not yet come for me to be with my blessed uncle. I was at the home of his neighbor, while my uncle lived

---

32   The author was actually a few months shy of his twenty-fourth birthday.

a *verst* from there. I became well acquainted with this neighbor, and when I let him know that I was his neighbor's nephew, he made me feel so welcome—may they live long lives because of that. They had rescued me from death itself. Nevertheless, after resting a bit, I put my dried clothes back on and asked him to have someone lead me over to my uncle's. I could not bear spending the night so close to my uncle, because I already wanted to be with him. Let me already see the person for whom I had suffered so much. I already doubted that I would ever see him. I was beginning to think that maybe this whole search had been one big blunder. In short, the Jewish neighbor did me the favor of sending over his non-Jewish worker, who led me to a well that stood at the bottom of a hill. I could see that on the hill were little peasant huts and a well where non-Jews were watering horses. His worker said to me in Ukrainian, "Go up the hill with the non-Jews who are carrying the water home. They'll then show you where Yudka lives."[33] With these words, he left.

I went up the hill and they pointed out to me the small hut of my blessed uncle. In that little hut, a candle was burning. I could not see the village because it was already dark, but I was able to make out the hut. I thought that I was walking into a living grave—a tiny house that was half underground. The windows were just above the ground. Outside, the roof was overgrown with green grass

FIGURE 10. A photograph of the entrance to a *zemlyanke*, dugout houses covered with earth or sod which were used by the poor. The *zemlyanke* of the author's Uncle Idl also had grass growing on its roof like the one in the photograph.

---

33 Yudka is referring to Idl.

and sloped to the ground. Upon entering the house, one had to go down two or three earthen steps where one entered a vestibule, which also served as a kitchen. Branching off from that vestibule was a room to the right and a room to the left—there were no other rooms. The floor was earthen. The family walked on the earth, and they lay and lived in the earth.

I entered the room, where a candle was burning, and I found nothing more than a woman and her helper, a non-Jewish girl. She was surprised to see a fellow Jew entering her home so late on such a rainy evening. She asked quizzically, "How is it that a Jew is coming here so late?" Apparently, no Jews ever came there. After all, what would a Jew be doing there? I tried to calm her by telling her why I was there, but I saw that she did not understand. I repeated myself but she asked me the same question again. I then understand that she could not hear me. I began to speak louder. She now understood and spoke to the point. I asked her what her and her husband's names were. She replied with the correct names that I needed. I asked her about her father, whether she was not Reb Yosef Pentshever's daughter from Petotsk.[34]

She replied, "Yes," and marveled, "How do you know my father?"

In return, I asked her if her husband was the son of Yankev Gredenitser of Groseles, the brother of Pinkhes.

She answered, "Yes."

"Don't you have relatives in Tiraspol?"

"Yes," she replied. "We have relatives there, but I don't know them."

I replied, "Well, I'm your relative—your husband's nephew by the name of Pinye-Ber."

Upon hearing the name Pinye-Ber, she cried out, "That's you, Pinye-Ber? I've heard so much about you. My Idl always mentions that when you were a child in Groseles you ran away one *Shobes* day."[35]

"Yes! Yes!" I said. "That's me."

"But what are you doing? What brings you here?"

"What am I doing? You see for yourself that I came here on foot and barely arrived alive at my uncle's. And what brings me here? Of course, I'll tell you after

---

34 Pentshever is not a surname but is a nickname denoting that her father had at one time lived in the hamlet of Pentshev. Though I have not found a hamlet by that name on any current maps, a 1942 German military map (G7010s100G4, L-36–38) shows a hamlet called Penkov (approximately 46'50" N, 30'50" E) about twelve miles east of Petotsk, Ukraine (now Severynivko). At that location, a Russian map from 1869 (G7010s126.R8, XXX-9) indicates an X. (The Russian letter X is pronounced as "kh" and is an abbreviation for the word *khutor*, meaning a rural settlement.)

35 The author had run away from Idl's brother Pinkhes in Groseles during the winter of 1859–1860 (ch. 7, p. 161). Perhaps Idl's wife did not remember the author well although they had met in 1857 (ch. 6, p. 148) and 1864 (ch. 13, pp. 208–209), or perhaps she was Idl's second wife.

I rest. But tell me, Auntie," I asked her, "where's my uncle? I've been here in your home for a half hour and have been waiting for my uncle to come in, but he's not here yet."

"Yes," she said, "he'll certainly come soon. He traveled out to the steppe to assess the damage caused by the wind and the rain to the barley and oats on the outdoor threshing floors and to the cut grain.[36] He's due to come home soon."

I was very tired. I would have gladly lain down, but I wanted to see my uncle.

In short, an hour passed before he finally arrived. I saw a person of average size enter. He was not unpleasant looking—but one could not have called him handsome—with a hoarse voice. He kissed me, like one would a close friend, and bombarded me with questions, "How did you get here? What are you doing? Where do you live? Do you have a wife?" and so forth—a lot of questions in one breath, all at once. I also asked him about everything. In short, I told him about my entire life until then, and about my travails in coming to him. In turn, he told me about his pack of troubles that practically made me forget about my own. We finished dinner and drank tea. He then went with me into the other room where they prepared a place for me to sleep. I lay down and, being so exhausted, immediately fell asleep. I did not know where the night disappeared.

In the morning when I awoke, the weather was completely different. It was now warm again—actually hot like it was supposed to be in *Tamuz*—and beautiful, as if there had never been any dark clouds, wind, or rain. Everything that had occurred the day before was apparently for my sake—to teach me a lesson about seeking out help from an uncle. I took a look at the village. There were ten little peasant huts and also *zemlyankes*, similar to the one in which my uncle lived.[37] This was not a village but a small hamlet belonging to a nobleman. My aunt asked me to slaughter a chicken for her so that she would have something to give me for breakfast; if not, we would have to eat a dairy meal. I did not wait to be asked twice and slaughtered the chicken for her because I had brought along a little slaughtering knife and also a whetstone, as if I knew it would come in handy.

My uncle was overjoyed to see me. One could see that his nephew's visit was like a breath of life to him. But he sighed from time to time and was very

---

36 For threshing floor, the author uses the word *arman*, which is a Turkish loanword in Romanian (Haspelmath & Tadmor, 2009:255). Since the Yiddish writer Peretz Hirschbein (1930:116) uses this word without defining it, *arman* was possibly also a loan-word in Southeastern Yiddish. Hence, the author did not necessarily learn it from Crimean-Tatar, a Turkic language which he heard upon moving to the Crimea in 1879 (ch. 23).

37 *Zemlyankes* denote dugout homes and are described in chapter 8, p. 168.

sorry that he could not help me out at all. Years ago, he had had good times, but now he was quite poor. Everything that he had was gone. He had been involved with agriculture for two years now, but he had yet to even recover his principal and it would not produce enough for him live on. Though he had a small family—only my uncle and his wife, as they had no children—it was not enough to support them. That year, he worked with partners and the crops had looked promising, but now the rain had caused a lot of damage, and who knew what else would occur until it was time for the grain to be poured into sacks? Like this, we spent time together exchanging stories and episodes until breakfast was ready, and we sat down to eat.

I asked my uncle to show me the way to Rozdelnye. He showed me the way and explained exactly how to go saying, "You have fifteen *versts* to walk until Rozdelnye." I told him how I had come, and he laughed and said, "You didn't go this way. You should've turned right from Rozdelnye and walked fifteen *versts*, but you turned left and walked fifteen *versts*. Afterward, you had to walk another fifteen *versts* to come to me. But now you have to walk only fifteen *versts* until the train station. Soon your aunt will come, and I will accompany you a bit of the way." I noticed that my aunt was running around from hut to hut. Finally, she came. They spoke between themselves, approached me, and handed me three rubles. "We're giving you a contribution toward having your certification papers released. We're not in a position to give more. Forgive us."

I understood that the three rubles were not theirs and that they, poor souls, had needed to seek out where to borrow them. I very much did not wish to take the three rubles because I had pity on them. But if I did not take the money, they might have thought that it was because I was not satisfied with the amount they were giving me; they would have been embarrassed and, in any case, they could not give more than that. I took the three rubles and said my goodbyes. I left the little hamlet and my uncle accompanied me on my way for a couple of *versts*. We walked while he talked and related incidents in his life, particularly of how his brother Pinele Groseler persecuted him and caused his permanent undoing.[38] My Uncle Idl and I kissed each other goodbye. He then gave me the last thirty *kopeks* from his pocket for a train ticket from Rozdelnye to Tiraspol, so that I would not have to break up the three-ruble bill, and we parted—my uncle to his hamlet and I continued to Rozdelnye.

As I walked alone on the road, I thought about what I had perpetrated—the type of punishment that I had incurred that week. I had made my life miserable for the sum of three rubles. Certainly God had given me the idea to

---

38 Pinele is a nickname for Pinkhes.

suddenly travel off to my uncle—and, oh, what an uncle, to my distress—in order for me to atone for some sin of mine so that things would be good for me afterward. I accepted everything with love, and thanked God for not letting the birds devour me in the haystack. Thinking these thoughts, I traversed the road until I was able to see the Rozdelnye train station. I arrived in Rozdelnye at three p.m. and a train arrived shortly afterward. By five, I was home in Tiraspol.

CHAPTER 21

Receiving Certification as a *Shoykhet* and Returning to Lubavitch, 1872–1873

My Frightened Appearance upon Returning Home • My Devoted Wife's Advice • Receiving Two Slaughtering Certificates • In Olt-Dubesar • In Grofinye with a *Shoykhet* • Leaving Stealthily for Lubavitch • The Postal Road • The Lubavitcher Rebbe's Answer • Falling Out of Favor with the Rebbe • Returning Home and Finding a Newborn Son • The Meeting in Petrovke After *Shobes* • Obtaining the Slobodzer *Shoykhet*'s Exclusive Slaughtering Rights

When I arrived in Tiraspol, everyone was very frightened. Whoever saw me was shocked and asked, "What happened to you, Pinye-Ber? Were you ill? Why have you changed so much? You practically don't look like yourself." I responded with all types of excuses. After all, what was the use of telling the whole story and how would that have helped my troubles? I tried to give the *shokhtim* the three rubles, but they did not want to take them; they would only accept the full twelve rubles. I had a difficult time persuading them to take those bloody three rubles from me and to give me a chance to find a means of obtaining the remaining nine rubles. I then went home to Perkon for *Shobes*.

When I entered the house and my precious, dear wife saw me, she cried out in fright, "*Oy*, Pinye-Ber! What happened to you? Why do you look so horrible? You certainly must have been sick the entire week, so why didn't you send me word? Why didn't you come home?" I calmed her down and began to tell her about my journey. We both cried bitterly over our bad luck and our poverty. As we worried about our questionable future, we comforted each other with the thought that we have a great and almighty God who would help us as long as we would place our trust solely in Him—and not in people.

That *Shobes*, my devoted wife did not let me walk to the *shul* in Bender to pray on *Shobes* morning, as I would do when I was home. She also did not let me go to Tiraspol after *Shobes*, saying, "Stay at home for a few days. Rest up, recover, and gather your strength so that you'll be able to endure fresh new afflictions that you wish you could avoid." I listened to her, she restored my health during those few days, and I recovered my normal appearance.

As I was leaving for Tiraspol, she said to me, "You know what I was thinking, Pinye-Ber?" "What?" I asked her curiously. She replied, "I have four strings of pearls that I wear ever since my mother gave them to me for my engagement. I was thinking of giving them to you to take along so that you could pawn them somewhere to obtain the nine rubles you need to give the *shokhtim*. Then you'll be able to obtain your certification papers and you'll be free from those *shokhtim*. After all, I'm afraid that you might make another journey like you did this week." I thanked her profusely for her generosity because I knew this was no small sacrifice for her. Of course, her parents were not allowed to know about it. I would never have dared to ask for them on my own, though I had thought about pawning her pearls already long before, especially since I saw that there was no other means of obtaining the money for the *shokhtim*. But how could I be so audacious as to ask her to give up her last few pearls for me to pawn? And when would I be able to repay the pawnbroker and recover them? The interest could accrue to more than their entire value, and then they would be gone forever. Consequently, I never dared to actually broach the subject. But now that she herself was suggesting it and was imploring me to do it—she was truly devoted to me—I expressed my enormous gratitude and blessed her for her piety and devotion to me in protecting me from any hardship that might come my way and in making my life as comfortable as possible.

I went to Tiraspol with the pearls and received ten rubles for them. I cheerfully went right to the *shokhtim* and asked them to release my certification papers. They gathered together and composed the document, to which all three *shokhtim* of livestock signed their names: Reb Shloyme, Reb Zolmen, and Reb Ershl.[1] I paid them the nine rubles, and it cost me an additional fifty *kopeks*

---

1   Kraus (1989:24–25, 27–28) includes facsimiles of seven certification papers for slaughtering received by Rabbi Shmuel Zalmanov (1888–1956), a Lubavitcher Hasid, in 1909–1912. The Central Archives for the History of the Jewish People in Jerusalem houses copies of 173 applications, including the applicants' *sh'khita* certification papers, for the position of *shoykhet* in Deutschkreutz (Tseylem in Yiddish), Austria, at the turn of the nineteenth century (Kunstlicher & Spitzer, 1989:289–320). Also see Appendix C3 for the text and translation of two certifications in *sh'khita* obtained by the author's son Refúel in 1904 and 1906.

extra for some liquor. All of my friends drank *le'khaim* and wished me success, blessings, and primarily that I should be a pious *shoykhet*.[2] I said goodbye to all the *shokhtim*, my friends, my sister Ite, and her darling child Itsele—with whom I left a *kopek* to give him a little encouragement—and left to go home. I planned to set out for Bender as soon as I arrived home so that I could show the *shokhtim* there my certification papers and have them endorsed. Upon arriving home, I did so, meaning that I only spent the night in Perkon and went in the morning to Bender, where I asked the *shokhtim*, Reb Itsele and Reb Shie, to endorse my certification papers. They said, "We know you well, know how impoverished you are, and know how much you struggle. You can just go with us to the slaughterhouse and slaughter a cow in front of us and then check its lungs. Tomorrow, bring us your sharpened slaughtering knives, and we'll look them over. Then we'll issue you certification papers without charging you even a *kopek*." That was so kind of them. They were so decent and generous to me; it was completely unexpected. I thanked them from the bottom of my heart and did everything that they requested. The next day, without delay, they gave me an extremely laudatory certification document, written and signed by them. I became quite demonstrative and spent my last half ruble on some liquor, which they drank to my health and wished me luck. They promised to let me know or recommend me if they heard of a village that needed a *shoykhet*, because they very much liked my work. I said goodbye and thanked them. Instead of giving them money, I gave them many blessings and returned home.

I was so happy that I could not wait to carry my joy home to my wife for I wanted to share my happiness with her. Naturally, she was overjoyed. Even my in-laws were happy when they saw the certification papers in my hands from the *shokhtim* of both Bender and Tiraspol. They used to constantly say that I had been fooled, that I would never be certified, and that I was deceiving all of them. Obviously, their daughter, my wife, was now happy, but even they were delighted, saying, "There's some hope now that our daughter can have a decent life with you. All you need to do is find a place to work as a *shoykhet*."

When times are good, they are really good. The next day, the 20th of *Tamuz*,[3] a Jew from Olt-Dubesar came to Bender and asked the *shokhtim* there if there were any apprentices available who could fill a position in his village for twelve rubles a month, including room and board. The *shokhtim* sent him to me. He arrived after I had just left for Tiraspol. He followed me by wagon to

---

2 A *shoykhet* is often tempted to pass off nonkosher meat as kosher due to pressure from the owners of the livestock, as the author describes in chapter 20, p. 345. Hence, the piety of a *shoykhet* is of utmost importance.
3 July 26, 1872.

Tiraspol, where he found me with the *shokhtim*. We agreed that I would work until *Slikhes*—a period of two months—for which I would receive twenty-five rubles and lodgings.[4] I would be eating all my meals at his home and would only have to slaughter chickens and small livestock, meaning lambs, because they did not slaughter any cattle there. He did not know if they would be able to continue to support a *shoykhet* during the winter, but he would make a written contract with me for two months. I was quite overjoyed with this turn of events, even though it was only a temporary position. At least for the time being, I had a livelihood that would enable me to rest from my troubles and enable me to eat my fill, sleep peacefully in a bed, have some money, and recover my wife's pearls. In short, I went home, took my bundle, and rode with him to his village, which was some thirty-five *versts* from Bender.

This fellow was known as Reb Isukher Olt-Dubesárer, and he was a gentle and refined person who came from a fine family and was somewhat of a Torah scholar.[5] He owned a butcher shop in Olt-Dubesar, from which the local Jews purchased their meat. When I would slaughter a chicken, they would not pay me anything, because Reb Isukher charged them a weekly fee for the *shoykhet*. He wanted to institute that each household should pay 50 *kopeks*, or at least 30 *kopeks*, which would then enable them to hire a permanent *shoykhet*. His intention was to bring a temporary *shoykhet*, thereby letting the residents become accustomed to the benefits of maintaining a local *shoykhet*. Like this, he tried to show them how they had been suffering by not having any meat during the week and by having red meat imported for *Shobes* from town.[6] In addition, they had to send their chickens to the *shteytl* of Tshornye [*sic*][7]—which was ten *versts* from Grigoriopol—to be slaughtered for *Shobes*. This cost them much more than the thirty *kopeks*—or even the fifty *kopeks*—a week they would be paying for a *shoykhet*. And sometimes, the chickens would suffocate and all the money paid to the courier would be lost. Besides, it was always difficult to find a courier; in the summer people were busy due to the harvest and in the

---

4 The word *slikhes* (*slikhot* in Modern Hebrew) literary means "pardons" and refers to special penitential prayers recited early in the morning from the days preceding Rosh Hashanah and afterward until Yom Kippur. *Slikhes* would have begun to be recited on September 29, 1872.
5 Olt-Dubesárer was his nickname in the surrounding area based on his place of residence, Olt-Dubesar.
6 "Town" is either referring to Grigoriopol, mentioned below, which had 832 Jews (11% of the population) in 1897, or Dubesár (Dubăsari, Moldova), which had 5,219 (43% of the population) in 1897. Olt-Dubesar is 7.8 km from Grigoriopol and 15 km from Dubesar.
7 Tshornye was evidently mistakenly printed instead of Tshornitse (aka Chornitsa and Chernitsa), which is now called Hirlop, Moldova (47°14'N 29°22'E) and is some ten *versts* northeast of Grigoriopol. It is not to be confused with Chornitsa (now Cernița, 47°02'N 29°31'E), currently in Moldova, which is about twenty *versts* southeast of Grigoriopol.

winter couriers were not available due to the snow and storms. Many times, they would pay for a courier to go to town only to have him return without any red meat because there just was not enough kosher meat. Despite this, Reb Isukher's arguments made no impression. He tried and tried but could in no way prevail upon them to pay for a permanent *shoykhet*. During the first two or three weeks after my arrival, they still paid the weekly fee but later they became weary, so Reb Isukher had to pay me out of his own pocket. I stayed there until *Slikhes*, as we had agreed, at which time he cheerfully gave me my twenty-five rubles. I traveled back home to Perkon and went with my wife and her parents to Bender for Rosh Hashanah and Yom Kippur.[8]

While in Bender, I earned several more rubles: three rubles helping the *shokhtim* slaughter the *kapores* for Yom Kippur, and three rubles for reading the Torah on Rosh Hashanah and Yom Kippur. So I now had a total of thirty-one rubles in cash earned with my own hands. Naturally, very little remained after I paid the pawn shop ten rubles to retrieve the pearls and spent ten rubles on myself. With another ruble being used up on trifles, I was then left with only ten rubles, which I hid away for a time of need. I stayed in Bender until after Yom Kippur.

On the day after Yom Kippur, I traveled off in search of a position to practice *sh'khita*. I first headed toward Kovishon, but there was nothing to be found there, so I traveled onwards to Grofinye. The first thing I did there was to walk straight to the *shoykhet*, because who would know where a *shoykhet* was needed in the surrounding area if not the *shoykhet* of the *shteytl*? In short, the *shoykhet* chatted a long time with me and related the following. He wanted to travel to his Rebbe in Tolne for *Sukes* but he could not unless he had another *shoykhet* take his place during his absence.[9] So he suggested that I remain there for a month until his return, and I would fill in for him while he travelled to his Rebbe for *Yontef*. We agreed that I would eat and also sleep at his house and would receive fifteen rubles for the month. He left that very night while I remained in the *shteytl*. I promptly let my wife know where I was so that she would not worry about me.[10]

Thank God, I had a very joyous *Yontef* because everyone in the *shteytl* was so overjoyed with me. They all grew very fond of me and wished that I would remain there as their permanent *shoykhet*. I learned "nice things" about their *shoykhet*; someone had one negative comment about him and another had some

---

8   October 3–4, 1872 and October 12, 1872, respectively.
9   *Sukes* was October 17–25, 1872.
10 The *shoykhet* of Grofinye left for Tolne on the night of October 13, 1872. *Sukes* was on October 17–24, 1872.

other negative comment. Since I had little experience in gossip against *shokhtim*, especially regarding *shokhtim* who were hated, I believed them. I figured that he was truly as bad as they portrayed him. I learned that he did not travel to his Rebbe out of pleasure or devotion as a Hasid but out of necessity. Being Tolner Hasidim, they told him to travel to their Rebbe to obtain certification papers for slaughtering or else they would not eat from his *sh'khita* and would harass him. Once he had left, they sent someone after him to inform the Rebbe that he should be checked out well to see if he was fit to be a *shoykhet*. They actually would have preferred to have their Rebbe drive him off. Because of their interference, the *shoykhet* had to spend five or six weeks in Tolne until he received the Rebbe's written approval that he could be a *shoykhet*.[11] The Rebbe also asked them to reconcile their differences for the world endures by virtue of peace.[12]

Upon the *shoykhet*'s safe return, we settled our accounts. As I was preparing to leave by wagon, the finest Jews of the *shteytl* gathered together and did not let me leave, saying "Young man, stay here and be *shoykhet*. That *shoykhet* won't be remaining here anyway, though the Rebbe sent word that he could be the *shoykhet* here. We know why the Rebbe did this. The Rebbe knows quite well that that *shoykhet* is a nothing, but he has pity on the *shoykhet*'s family. We, though, are going to take care of his family. We're going to take him to rabbinical court and you, young man, will remain here as our *shoykhet*. We like you very much. You're a good *shoykhet* and a good cantor." But I did not want to listen to them and left for Bender, meaning that I went home to Perkon and brought home the twenty rubles that I had earned in Grofinye.[13] I now had savings of thirty rubles.

Two days after my return home, I was summoned to appear before the Rebbe, Reb Itsikl, the rabbi of Bender.[14] I entered and saw the townsmen from Grofinye. They were taking their *shoykhet* to court and were asking the Rebbe to send another *shoykhet* there in the meantime. The Rebbe, Reb Itsikl, sent

---

11   The *shoykhet* of Grofinye returned in mid- to late-November 1872.
12   Based on a Mishna (Avot 1:18).
13   Though the author writes earlier that the *shoykhet* of Grofinye said he would pay him fifteen rubles for the month, the *shoykhet* was delayed in Tolne for "five or six weeks" and thus paid him twenty rubles.
14   The Benderer Rebbe, Rabbi Itskhok "Itsikl" Vertheym (ca. 1848–1911) was the son of Rabbi Shimen-Shloyme (1804/5–1864). Reb Itsikl was a second cousin to both the Chechelniker Rebbe, Rabbi Moyshe Giterman (ch. 7, p. 157), and his brother, the Savraner Rebbe, Rabbi Duvid Giterman (ch. 22). Rabbi Itskhok Vertheym served a dual role as both rabbi (that is, ruling on halakhic matters) and Hasidic Rebbe (that is, a spiritual mentor to his Hasidim) as did many Hasidic Rebbes. Of interest is that his *gabbai*, Nokhmen Kishinevsky, was a very learned Chabadnik (Grosman, 1989:67–68; Tamari, 1975:119–120, 263; Wertheim, 1975:299).

me there and said to me as follows, "Travel to Grofinye and be the substitute *shoykhet* there until this court case is resolved. I'm directing you to do so. And I'm giving you this directive in writing. Since I'm directing you to do this, you have nothing to fear." I then said, "If that's the case, Rebbe, since you're giving me this paper, I'm acting according to the dictates of a rabbinical court and I understand that this is permissible."[15]

In short, I traveled again to Grofinye, where I spent two weeks until the rabbinical court arrived at a decision regarding the case. The decision was that the *shoykhet* was to be paid 300 rubles for the exclusive rights to practice *sh'khita* there and that he must leave Grofinye. Since I did not have 300 rubles, I left right away, though the townsmen told me, "Don't leave. In any case, he'll no longer be the *shoykhet* here, and we won't allow the 300 rubles to be given to him." I understood that they were simply bad people who wanted to cause the *shoykhet*'s family to suffer. I told them to get lost and left for home.

I now had savings of forty rubles, because I was lucky enough to earn an additional ten rubles during those two weeks. Using ten rubles, I bought some good new slaughtering knives, whetstones, and some books dealing with the laws of *sh'khita*, which were necessary for my profession.[16] I also purchased a few articles of clothing for my wife, which cost twenty rubles. I was still left with ten rubles in cash in my pocket, which I was going to use for travel expenses in seeking out a place to practice *sh'khita*.

But since it was still destined for me to suffer and endure some more for a while and to wander around, I suddenly had the following idea: I had to travel to a Rebbe since I was a *shoykhet* and a Hasidic Jew. Once I would settle down somewhere where a position in *sh'khita* was available, I would not be able to travel to a Rebbe. So as long as I was free as a bird, I could carry out my plan. As long as I was planning on traveling, I certainly had to travel to Lubavitch. After all, I had been a Lubavitcher Hasid since my youth, if you recall.[17] What about my not having enough money to cover the expenses of the trip? And what about traveling such a long distance? All of that did not matter to a true Hasid, because

---

15 The author was making sure that his work in Grofinye as the temporary *shoykhet* would not be infringing on the rights of the permanent *shoykhet* there.

16 The author's great-granddaughter Cynthia Unterberg possesses the Hebrew book *Totsaot Khayim* by Rabbi Khayim Toyber printed in Pressburg in 1835, which bears the author's personal stamp from when he was a *shoykhet* in Bakhchisaray (chs. 24–29). Since it is devoted to the laws of *sh'khita*, perhaps it was one of the books he bought on that subject matter mentioned here in 1872.

17 The author's earliest mention of his identifying as a Lubavitcher Hasid was during his return trip from Shklov in April 1866 when he was eighteen, as mentioned in ch. 16, p. 260. He is now twenty-four.

nothing at all can deter a true Hasid from traveling to his Rebbe. From day to day, I became more determined to carry out my idea, though an important reason was preventing me—my dear wife was already in her seventh month and my traveling to Lubavitch meant that she would have to give birth without me. And in the event that, to spite me, the child would be a boy, then the *bris* would also have to be without me.[18] This thought deterred me for a couple of weeks. I struggled internally, debating all of this until, apparently, my idea got the better of me. I pushed away everything and resolved that I must travel to the Rebbe. The Rebbe could help me a lot. He could bless me that I should be a pious *shoykhet* and that I should not, God forbid, err accidently, thereby causing others to eat something *treyf*. In short, I overcame all reservations and decided to travel to the Rebbe.

I was now underway, meaning that I had made up my mind to go, made my plans, and started my journey exactly on the day that I had planned. Of course, my plans were kept top secret so that my wife's parents—and my wife herself—would not know, for they certainly would not have let me leave. In particular, my dear wife would definitely have disrupted my plan, and I would not have been able to go against her will because my compassion for her would have immediately stopped me. So even she did not know, though it grieved me greatly. I was almost sickened over the trip whenever I would remind myself of her and how much she would suffer from my absence during the birth. Yet something like a magnet was pulling me. In brief, early on a Sunday morning in the middle of *Kislev*,[19] I said goodbye to the rest of the household, only hinting that I would be gone for a long while, and parted the same way from my dear wife. I left for Tiraspol with just my *talis*, *tefillin*, and slaughtering knives as if I were traveling there for only a few days until *Shobes*. It did not even enter my wife's mind that I would do such a thing.

When I was already on the road leading to Tiraspol, I burst into tears over the crime I was perpetrating against my own dear wife. But how would crying help? On the other hand, if I backed out of my trip, I figured that I would always regret it, while my wife could be easily appeased once she that saw my trip to the *tsadik* resulted in God's helping us to have a sweet and calm life and our newborn child to have a long life with much happiness.[20] She would then always

---

18 *Bris* denotes circumcision, which the Jewish people are commanded by God (Leviticus 12:2), to perform on newly born males at eight days.
19 Sunday, the 15th of *Kislev* 5633 (December 15, 1872).
20 Since the Second World War, Hasidim generally no longer refer to a Hasidic Rebbe as "the *tsadik*," as in "We are traveling to the *tsadik*," though Chabad Hasidim never referred to their Rebbe in that manner.

give thanks that I had overcome this spiritual test. After all, I figured that God had given me the idea to make this journey. How could it have been otherwise? After having endured so much before becoming a *shoykhet*, finally living to see myself become one, and only lacking a place to work, which I could easily find, an idea had suddenly come to me and galvanized me and vanquished all obstacles. Certainly this idea was only sent to me to test me; once I had overcome all impediments, everything would go well for me from that point onward. Obviously my fanaticism at that time was spurring me on and making it so that I could not possibly have done anything but travel to Lubavitch, disregarding anything that might have disturbed my plan including my compassion for my wife.[21] Consequently, I continued traveling past Tiraspol and toward Bolte, meaning that my trip to Lubavitch was already underway. In Bolte, I bought a brass *menorah*, eight candles, and a little bottle of olive oil so that I could light and make the blessings for Hanukah.[22] I then traveled to Khashtshevote, because my sister Sure, of blessed memory, lived there. I spent *Shobes* there with my sister, who considered me to be quite a special guest for she had not seen me in a long time—not since a month after my wedding.[23] It was around Monday when she accompanied me for some of the way as I left.[24] She gave me some bread and three rubles in cash.

From Khashtshevote, I traveled by wagon until Uman, and from Uman until Kiev—all by means of oxen, that is, by means of catching rides on different wagons. From Kiev until Mogilev, I caught rides with postal wagons, on which I was able to travel both during the day and at night.[25] The difference was that during the day, I had to get off the postal wagon half a *verst* before the postal station so that the postmaster would not detect any unauthorized passengers that were officially forbidden. I also had to get on to the postal wagon in a similar manner so that I would not be noticed by anyone at the postal station.

---

21 Though the author left without telling his wife of his plans, he did send word to her that he had left for Lubavitch, as mentioned below in his conversation with her upon his return.

22 The author bought eight candles which he would use to light the appropriate number of wicks in his oil *menorah* (eight-branched lamp used on Hanukah) on each of the eight nights of Hanukah. Hanukah started the night of December 24, 1872 until January 1, 1873.

23 The author's wedding took place five years before on November 20, 1867 (ch. 18, p. 299).

24 The author apparently left Kháshtshevóte around Monday, December 23, 1872 (23 Kislev, 5633).

25 Mogilev is referred to here in the original Yiddish as Groys Molev, meaning Large Mogilev, and refers to Mogilev, Belarus (now Mahileu). Elsewhere, it is simply called Molev. The smaller Molev is Mogilev-Podolsk, Ukraine (now Mohyliv-Podilskyi), which is closer to Tiraspol. See also Schaechter (1986:18).

I can tell you that I once practically froze because I had never had any exceptionally good clothes, especially winter clothes, which one had to have here in Lithuania where the weather was freezing cold.[26] It happened one night when I was waiting at a postal station for a postal wagon, which was supposed to arrive shortly, so that I could catch a ride in it. I ended up waiting outside for some two hours and became so permeated by the freezing cold that I felt that my bones were breaking. I went into a non-Jew's house next to the station, and he had pity on me and let me warm up there. Meanwhile, before I had time to warm up, I heard a bell chime indicating that a postal wagon would be leaving in the direction that I needed. I looked through the little window and saw that a postal wagon was approaching. I told the non-Jew that I had to leave because I urgently needed to keep an eye on the postal wagon until it would depart. I told him that I urgently needed to travel with that postal wagon needed to wait for it. He shrugged his shoulders and let me out of his house.

I was once again standing in the freezing cold, which was now truly penetrating me. I kept running around and moving my feet so that the cold would not seep into my bones, but the wagon was not leaving the courtyard. I saw that it would soon be past midnight and the postal wagon was still not leaving. I felt that in a short while I would become frozen since I could barely move my feet by then. Realizing that I was putting my life in danger, I walked straight to the postal station and knocked on the door, which they opened.

I entered to warm myself up. I told them that I was traveling on foot, had lost my way until I arrived there but did not know where I was. I came up with good excuses answering all of their questions so that nothing about my story seemed odd to them. I let myself into the barracks where the drivers were. It was warm and "fragrant." Each one asked me about myself, each driver with sarcastic comments, and each one laughed at the Jew before them. Each driver made a joke about me and expressed his opinion about me. I pretended to be tired and lay down by the oven, clasping my shoulders to thoroughly warm myself up.

A few hours passed and I warmed up nicely. I could not sleep because I needed to make sure that the driver would not leave without me. If he did, then all of my suffering that night would have been for naught. Meanwhile, I saw that one of the drivers was preparing to leave. He put on his fur coat and took his whip in his hand. I understood that he was the driver I needed. I winked to him—a hint that I wanted to ride with him—and he responded with a similar gesture that he would take me and that I should leave with him. I obeyed him, naturally, and followed him. He showed me his little wagon and told me to be

---

26   See ch. 15, p. 241, footnote 13, addressing the reason the author refers to Belarus as Lithuania.

seated on it so that the building superintendent would not notice me. I traveled like this until daybreak. Now you have an understanding of the postal rides that I endured and the distress that I suffered on my crazy journey, which was fanned by my fanatical imagination.

You may possibly think that it entered my mind that I was not doing the right thing or that I regretted my actions. No, God forbid. On the contrary, I considered it to be a very worthwhile endeavor on my part. It was worth enduring such trials and bearing so much to go to a *tsadik*, to the Rebbe. And whenever I had a moment's rest, I would sing and be happy exactly as if everything was fine and good—I felt as lucky as could be. I traveled like this with the postal wagons, as just explained, until reaching the province of Mogilev, because there were highways until there. From Mogilev, I traveled once again by standard wagons on dirt roads, then again on foot, which involved suffering of a different kind. Finally, after a journey of three weeks,[27] I arrived in Lubavitch, to the Rebbe, Reb Shmulke, of blessed memory.[28]

Arriving in Lubavitch, I immediately asked the whereabouts of the *shoykhet*.[29] I decided that my lodgings would be there. Whether he was willing or not, it did not matter to me. I put down my bundle and lay down to rest.

"Hello! Where are you from?"

"From Bessarabia—from Kishinev." Since they did not know of Tiraspol, I had to mention a big city like Kishinev or Odessa.

"You're actually from Kishinev proper?" the *shoykhet* asked me.

"From a *shteytl* near Kishinev—Tiraspol."

"I know of Kishinev," he said, "but I haven't heard of Tiraspol. Why are you traveling from Tiraspol to the Rebbe? Are there Chabadniks there also?"

"Yes," I replied. "There are, but very few because it's so far."

---

27 The author arrived in Lubavitch after swiftly traveling for three weeks since leaving Kháshtshevóte (near Uman) and apparently arrived on Tuesday, January 14, 1873 (15 *Teyves* 5633). In 1865, he traveled to Lubavitch at a more leisurely pace; it took him twenty-nine days to reach Lubavitch from Uman (ch. 15, p. 243).

28 The fourth Rebbe of Chabad, Rabbi Shmuel Schneerson (1834–1882), known by the acronym Maharash (an acronym for *"Morenu ha-Rav* Reb Shmuel," meaning "Our Teacher, the rabbi, Reb Shmuel"), was the youngest child and successor of Rabbi Menakhem-Mendl Schneerson (1789–1866), the Tsemakh Tsedek, whom the author met in 1865 (chs. 15 and 16, pp. 244–251). Shmulke is a Yiddish nickname for Shmuel. In addition to leading his Hasidim, guiding and looking after their spiritual and material lives, and authoring many Hasidic discourses, the Maharash traveled throughout Europe to meet with government and business leaders to exert pressure on the Tsarist regime to halt its instigation of pogroms against its Jews (Glitsenshtein, 1986; Rubin, 2021).

29 A *shoykhet* named Meylekh is mentioned later in this chapter on p. 381. Perhaps it was referring to this *shoykhet* in Lubavitch.

"So why did you wind up at my house? Why don't you go to an inn?"

"Yes," I said to him. "I came here because I don't have any strength to walk further. I barely made it to your house."

"Why to my house? You could've reached ten other houses before mine particularly since you have no strength."

"There's another reason why I came to you. I don't have a single *groshn*, and one needs money to stay at an inn. In short, I must stay at a home where it won't cost me anything."

"If so, you can go to the *bes-medresh*. I have no lodgings here."

"It's possible that I'll rest here for an hour and then go to the *bes-medresh*—to the Rebbe—since only because of him have I suffered so much by traveling three weeks without enough food or sleep and suffering from the cold and hunger. Because of this, he must give me lodgings, at least in the *bes-medresh*. Only please let me rest here first for a few hours."

At that point he became a bit friendlier. His wife as well as his children had compassion toward me. They found my accent to be a novelty.[30] Meanwhile, they asked me to eat something. I willingly accepted their request. I washed for bread, and they gave me some barley soup. While eating, we began to speak. During our conversation, he realized that I was a *shoykhet*, and his attitude totally changed. "You're a *shoykhet*?" he asked. "Now I understand why you came to my house. If that's the case, stay with me for several days until you rest from your travels. Then we'll speak about matters regarding *sh'khita*." I thanked him for his offer and was made to feel right at home for the duration of my stay.

I arrived in Lubavitch on a Tuesday during the day. After resting the night, I washed up early in the morning and prepared myself to be received by the Rebbe in the *bes-medresh*. Naturally, I first prayed with the Rebbe in the *bes-medresh* and then prepared a *kvitl*.[31] Afterward I went in to have a private audience with the Rebbe. I had written a request asking him to bless me that I should obtain a position to practice *sh'khita* and that I should be a pious *shoykhet*, and so on. He glanced at me and said, "I would advise you to travel home right away. Don't delay and leave immediately... And God will most likely prepare for you a place to practice *sh'khita*." I stood there paralyzed. I stared but could not say a word out of fear. "Why are you standing there so terrified? I'm asking you to go home—nothing more." "What does this mean, Rebbe? How can I go home? I endured so much to get here. I made it here in such freezing cold weather and

---

30 The Northeastern dialect of Yiddish is spoken in Belarus where Lubavitch was located, and differs considerably from the Southeastern Yiddish spoken by the author. See the Introduction to the Glossaries.
31 The Rebbe evidently participated in the *Shakhris* prayer services held in his *bes-medresh*.

without a *kopek*, and now you're telling me to return immediately. The chill from my trip here still lies in my bones. I'd like to rest a bit and obtain some money for the trip back." I said all of this with tears in my eyes. The Rebbe replied, "Eh, no matter! God will help you. You'll make the trip home unharmed. But make sure you leave soon. And here's a ruble as a contribution toward your expenses. Now give me your hand and bid me farewell."[32]

Upon taking leave from him, I was in a frenzy. When I returned to my lodgings at the *shoykhet*'s, my confusion began to consume me like a fever. How could it be? How could I return before I rested for at least a few days? How could I leave the Rebbe so quickly, particularly when I barely made it here from such a far distance? And when would I again merit being with the Rebbe? After all, the entire purpose of my traveling to the Rebbe was only to spend time near him, to obtain his certification in *sh'khita* and to receive his blessings.[33] Instead, I ended up receiving such an unexpected directive from him. What had he discerned about me and how was I different from all the other visiting Hasidim that he singled me out to be sent home? These thoughts raced back and forth through my mind, and I could not hold back my tears.

The *shoykhet* and his family asked me, "Why are you crying like that?" I began sobbing even harder. He asked again, "What's going on?" to which I replied, "Why shouldn't I cry when even the Rebbe has no mercy on me and tells me to return home immediately?" He replied that the Rebbe did not intend for me to leave this minute but certainly meant that I should leave right after *Shobes*. "Today's Wednesday. You can stay until Saturday night.[34] I

---

32 Although ardent Chabad Hasidim would not shake their Rebbe's hand, nonetheless, the Rebbes of Chabad would at times offer their hands to newcomers and non-Chabad Hasidim. Zalmon Jaffe (2002:22–23) of England writes that upon his first private audience with the Lubavitcher Rebbe, Rabbi M. M. Schneerson, in 1959, the Rebbe offered him his hand, which he refused saying, "I am sorry, but Rabbi Shemtov said I must not shake hands with the Rebbe." The Rebbe then replied with a twinkle in his eye, "Never mind. We won't tell Rabbi Shemtov," and they then shook hands. Similarly, when the Belzer Rebbe, Rabbi Yisukher-Dov Rokeakh, visited the Lubavitcher Rebbe in 1981, the Belzer Rebbe's accompanying Hasidim stretched out their hands to bid farewell to the Lubavitcher Rebbe, who then said, "It's not our custom [for a Rebbe to shake hands]. This [my shaking your hands] is in honor of the guest. It is after all a Belzer custom" (Rabbi M. M. Schneerson, *Sikhot kodesh*, 5681, 2:819).

33 Though the author's intention was evidently to obtain certification in *sh'khita* from the Lubavitcher Rebbe, he does not indicate later whether he requested or obtained this from the Rebbe. In general, the Rebbes of Chabad did not give certifications in *sh'khita*.

34 The author evidently meant to write that the *shoykhet* told him, "You can stay until Saturday night," instead of, "You can stay until [next] Wednesday," as printed in the original. After all, the *shoykhet* said earlier that the Rebbe probably meant for him to leave right after *Shabes*, and the author states below that he would only be spending three more days (not a week) in Lubavitch from that Wednesday.

said, "From the Rebbe's words, I understood that he meant that I should leave immediately, even today, but you're saying that I can stay longer. I understand that staying an additional three days won't make a difference, but isn't it very painful to spend only three days with the Rebbe after such a journey?" "Yes," he said, "I admit that it's painful, but what can you do? When the Rebbe tells you to do something, you must certainly do it. But speaking between ourselves, I'm quite surprised that the Rebbe is being so stringent by forbidding you to remain here. I've yet to hear of him saying anything similar to the Hasidim who live in the area, let alone the Hasidim who come from afar. All of them spend as much time at the Rebbe's court as they can and desire. But regarding you, young man, something completely different has occurred. Amazing."

I did not understand the Rebbe's words to me and stayed there until after *Shobes*, because I did not feel that well before *Shobes* and especially since the Rebbe was going to "conduct a *tish*" that *Shobes*—a very rare occurrence. After all, the Rebbe did not conduct a *tish* every *Shobes* like the Polish *tsadikim*. Here in Lubavitch, it could happen that the Rebbe would "conduct a *tish*" only once a year and it was an exceptionally rare occurrence.[35] And such an occurrence was going to happen that *Shobes*, since that Friday his sister or niece would be married.[36] I don't remember her relationship to the Rebbe clearly because my mind

---

35   The Rebbes of Chabad did not exactly "conduct a tish" but rather held *farbrengens*, meaning Hasidic gatherings, as explained in ch. 16, p. 247, footnote 3. Though the Rebbe, Rabbi Shmuel Schneerson, would seldom hold a *farbrengen*, the subsequent Rebbes of Chabad would do so with increased frequency with each generation, with the last Lubavitcher Rebbe, Rabbi M. M. Schneerson (1902–1994), holding *farbrengens* every *Shabes* during his later years. In his memoirs, Gurwitz (1935:47–49) describes a *tish* conducted by Rabbi Mordkhe Tversky (1840–1906) of Loyev, Belarus (now Loyeu) in 1885.

36   Evidently, the the wedding of the Rebbe's niece occurred on Friday, the 19th of *Teyves* (January 17, 1873) and the author spent the *Shabes* of the Torah portion of *Shmos* (January 18, 1873) in Lubavitch. On that *Shabes*, the Lubavitcher Rebbe, Rabbi Shmuel Schneerson, recited a Hasidic discourse based on the verse in Songs of Songs (5:1), "I have come into my garden, my sister, my bride," apparently in honor of the wedding of the previous day; it is printed in his published Hasidic discourses for that year in *Likute Torah—Torat Shmuel . . . 5633* (1994, 1:101–111).

Mondshine (1986:64–65) mistakenly dates the author's visit to Lubavitch to December 1871—a year earlier than it occurred. He calculated it from the last year mentioned by the author, namely *Tamuz* 5631 (July 1871) appearing in ch. 20, p. 346, which is clearly an error, as explained in footnote 10 there, and should state *Tamuz* 5632 (July 1872). In turn, based on Mondshine's miscalculation, the Hasidic discourse heard by the author is incorrectly identified by the editors of the published Hasidic discourses recited by Rabbi Shmuel Schneerson (2003:218–219) in honor of weddings. (It states there that the author probably heard the discourses recited on the *Shabes* of the Torah portion of *Boi*, which was the 10th of *Shvat* 5632 (January 10, 1872). In any case, this is an implausible date since the author returned home on the 10th of Shvat.)

was dead by then. Meanwhile, a large crowd had convened with many dignified guests and rabbis including outstanding rabbinical personalities from the area. The Rebbe conducted a *tish* that *Shobes* afternoon, and after *Shobes* there was a *Melava Malka*.[37] The crowd there was comprised of distinguished Hasidim and the Rebbe's relatives by marriage. It was so crowded that you could not find a place to sit. You had to stand in a packed room and be grateful that you were standing inside instead of outside.

That *Shobes* made all my effort to come to Lubavitch worthwhile. In short, I spent *Shobes* at the Rebbe's court and attended the wedding ceremony and the *Kiddush* following *Shobes*-morning prayer services.[38] The Rebbe was not there—only the *rebetsn* and their distinguished relatives by marriage. Not everyone was allowed in, but I went in nonetheless—the strong hands of the *gabbaim* could not stop me. Later, I was also at the *tish* on *Shobes*. When the cantor began to sing a melody that I did not care for, I began to sing loudly, completely unsolicited. All eyes turned toward me as if to ask, "Who's that young man?" The Rebbe also noticed that I was there and glanced at me in astonishment. I became quite frightened and thought that he did not want to endure my singing, but he gestured with his hand motioning me to continue and said, "Sing, sing," and everyone repeated, "Sing, young man. You sing well—better than the cantor." This gave me courage, and I sang a lot. Everyone enjoyed my *Shobes zmires* and, when I stopped, I was compelled by them to continue on. The *shoykhet* with whom I was staying later told me that when the Rebbe noticed me at the *tish*, he asked, "He's still here?" It explained the look of amazement on the Rebbe's face when he saw me.

The meal after *Shobes* on Saturday night was very joyous. There was also a magnificent *badkhen*, who made the crowd laugh with his clever wordplays in

---

Rabbi Amram Bloy, the author of a series of articles on prominent members of the Schneerson dynasty, which were posthumously published in book form under the title *Bnei ha-Tsemakh Tsedek* (2020), pointed out to me in 2008 that the bride must have been one of the three daughters of the *Tsemakh Tsedek*'s late sister Rode-Freyde and her husband Rabbi Shneur Schneerson. The latter was the Rebbe's only relative mentioned by Heilman (1903:3:24) as residing in Lubavitch at that time. The three daughters' names are noted by Heilperin (1980:169).

37 A *Melava Malka* is a meal marking the conclusion of the Sabbath on Saturday after nightfall (*Kitsur Shulkhan Arukh* 96:13). This *Melava Malka* would have been particularly joyous since it would have been one of meals in honor of the bride and groom served every day of the week following the wedding, known as *Sheve-Brokhes* (*Kitsur Shulkhan Arukh* 149).

38 No doubt, the wedding took place on Friday afternoon, when Jewish weddings were traditionally held. See *Shulkhan Arukh* (*Even ha-Ezer* 64:3).

Hebrew—even the Rebbe was amused.[39] I was interested in all that was going on, but I could not see the Rebbe since it was very crowded and I happened to be at the opposite end of the long table at which he was seated. I thought of a clever means of getting closer. I bent down and crawled under the bench and then underneath the table. While remaining under the table, I crawled from one end of the table to the other until I was at the Rebbe's feet and could hear the Rebbe speaking words of Torah, mundane matters, and clever remarks among his inner circle.[40] This also made my entire trip worth all the effort. I lay there like that for a couple of hours until I could no longer breathe because of the stuffiness. I then moved myself backward until I came out, hot and sweaty, from under the table. I stayed until the *tish* was over—until the Rebbe left for his residence and the crowd began to go home. I then left for my lodgings.

Early the next day, I went to bid farewell to the Rebbe. He asked me what kept me from leaving before *Shobes*, and I of course explained. "*Nu*," he said, "travel safely and may God help you. You're a pious young man. No matter, God will help you." I immediately left on foot for home.[41]

I had to go on foot until Dubrovne, where I caught rides on various wagons as I made my way to Kopust, Orshe [*sic*], and then Shklov.[42] From Shklov to Mogilev, I struggled along—sometimes on foot and sometimes catching short rides. In short, I did not rest. On my way back home, I traveled even more hastily and quickly than on the way there as if I was simply being carried by the wind. After all, I was so anxious about having left my wife when she was due that I would have flown if I had wings. Who knew, God forbid, what had happened

---

39 A *badkhn* is a traditional Jewish performer specializing in making humorous and semi-improvised rhymes. Lubecki (2008:17) mentions that many *badkhonim* (pl. of *badkhn*) were present at the 1882 wedding of Rabbi Shmuel Schneerson's son Menakhem-Mendl (1867–1942) and describes the Rebbe's interactions with them. A *badkhn* existed in Lubavitch during the lifetime of Rabbi Menakhem-Mendl Schneerson (1889–1866), the third Rebbe of Chabad (Olidort, 2003:155–156). For additional references to *badkhonim* in Lubavitch, see B.S. Schneerson (2001:69) and Slutsky (1967:2:673–675). Lubavitchers no longer use *badkhonim* at their weddings though most other Hasidic groups do. The *badkhn*'s "clever wordplays in Hebrew" might be referring to his speaking in Hebrew, which was a novelty at the time, and was apparently a commonly used humorous device (Liberman, 1980:307–313).
40 A similar event occurred at the 1882 wedding of Menakhem-Mendl (1867–1942), who was the son of this Rebbe, Rabbi Shmuel Schneerson; a Hasid climbed under the Rebbe's table in order to hear the Hasidic discourse the Rebbe was giving (Lubecki, 2008:17). For several years prior to the 1992 stroke of the Lubavitcher Rebbe, Rabbi M. M. Schneerson, when the crowding became severe, several yeshiva students sat under the long main table at which the Rebbe would conduct his four- to five-hour-long *farbrengns* (Hasidic gatherings) every *Shabes* in order to be able to clearly hear all that the Rebbe said.
41 The author apparently left Lubavitch on Sunday, January 19, 1873 (29th of *Teyves* 5633).
42 In travelling south to Mogilev, Orshe comes before Kopust—not after.

to her in her confinement and whether she had given birth to a live child, and so on. The Rebbe certainly saw something with holy intuition, which was why he had urged me to go home like that. Everyone to whom I told my story on the way was of the opinion that the Rebbe had certainly foreseen something important, though we could not know what it was. So a lot of people asked me to write them immediately upon my return to let them know what had occurred. Naturally, their opinions caused me to become even more anxious about what was happening at home. I flew over valleys and mountains by day and by night until I arrived in Kiev.[43]

From Kiev, I was able to take the train. I could now travel quickly by purchasing a train ticket. So I traveled from Kiev to Kazatin for one ruble, which Reb Meylekh the *shoykhet* had raised for me.[44] I now still had one ruble left, but the conductor in Kazatin wanted two rubles to allow me to continue traveling to Rozdelnye. By some miracle, I ended up traveling to Rozdelnye by train; I crammed myself under a bench beneath some passengers who hid me out of pity. My trip from Kiev to Rozdelnye took me two days. The entire trip from Kiev to Rozdelnye and then home took me a total of three days—part of the way free and part with a ticket.

I arrived home and found my wife healthy and strong. She had prematurely borne me a beautiful, fine son—may his days and years be long—by the name of Isruel-Burekh, "he will also be blessed."[45] He was born on the 8th of *Teyves*,[46] and it was now already the 10th of *Shvat*.[47] Thank God, it had been a very nice *bris* but my wife had cried a lot over the absence of her son's father. She then began to tell me, "*Oy*, if you had only come three days earlier, we would have been provided with the means to earn a living." "How so?" I asked. She replied, "Just three days ago, two dignified Jews traveled here to our house and inquired

---

43 The author arrived in Kiev on February 3, 1873 (6th of *Shvat* 5633), as is clear from the narrative below.
44 Perhaps Meylekh was the name of the *shoykhet* by whom he stayed in Lubavitch (see pp. 375-376).
45 Genesis 27:33. With this quotation, the author is making a play on words since the verse includes the word "blessed" and his son's middle name was Burekh, also meaning blessed.
46 January 7, 1873. Metrical records of Bender record that Isruel-Burekh was born on December 14, 1871 (December 26, 1871, according to the Gregorian calendar). It is well known that the Jewish officials in charge of the recording of Jewish metrical records allowed fathers to record their sons' years of birth either a year earlier or later depending on their particular strategy to help their son eventually avoid Russian conscription, which was cruelly antisemitic and often forced its recruits to transgress the basic tenets of Judaism. He is later referred to by the nicknames Srul-Burekh, Srul-Burekhl, Srulik, and Srulikl.
47 The continuation of the author's narrative makes it clear that he arrived home on Thursday night, February 7, 1873.

about you. I told them that you were in Lubavitch with the Rebbe. They replied, 'All the way to Lubavitch? What a shame—both for him and for us. We live in the *shteytl* of Petrovke. Our *shoykhet* just died and we want Pinye-Ber as our *shoykhet*. The Benderer *shokhtim* praise him greatly, and the rebbe, Itsikl, also thinks highly of him.[48] So where can we find him? Will he be returning soon from the Rebbe's?' I replied that there was no way for me to know. 'If so,' they said, 'it's truly a shame,' and with these words they traveled off." My wife was left with a good heartache—apart from the pain she suffered from her parents, who pestered her with, "Where's your *schlimazel*?" This was what my wife told me and, with that, she began to cry over our not having any luck.

I comforted her and said, "Anything's possible for God. It could be that this was the reason that the Rebbe urged me to leave as quickly as possible, which is why I returned so quickly. If not for the Rebbe, I would not have returned until Pesach.[49] Since they visited you just three days ago, I have a feeling that the position is not yet lost. I'll rest up overnight and then travel there. 'Perhaps God will have mercy.'[50] Perhaps God will perform a miracle, and I won't lose this opportunity." And that is what I did. Ignoring my tired and worn body, I traveled to Petrovke which I reached in the late afternoon. I was informed that they already had a *shoykhet*. Those who had searched for me had found another *shoykhet* whom the Tiraspoler *shokhtim* had recommended. He had been the *shoykhet* in Slobodze, a large village near Tiraspol.

Their new *shoykhet* was middle-aged, a fervent Tolner Hasid, and everyone was excited over him. After *Shobes* ended, a meeting was to be held to sign a contract to hire him. I talked with him at length and saw that I could impede him greatly. He was afraid of me because he knew of my skill in *sh'khita* and my cantorial skills while his knowledge in such matters was lame.[51] His strength lay in the fact that he was a Tolner Hasid, and Tolner Hasidim played the leading role there. I said to him, "If you give me the exclusive slaughtering rights in Slobodze, I won't get in your way here."[52] He replied, "Give me 100 rubles, and

---

48 Referring to the Benderer Rebbe, Rabbi Itskhok "Itsikl" Vertheym, mentioned earlier in the chapter on p. 370.
49 Pesach began the night of April 11, 1873.
50 This phrase is part of a well-known refrain in Hebrew from a section of the *Slikhes* prayers.
51 The combination *khazn-shoykhet* (cantor and *shoykhet*) was a prominent feature of Jewish life in European villages and towns (see the Introduction, pp. 26–27). In many small towns and villages, the *khazn-shoykhet* was the only individual with formal religious schooling (Berman, 1941:137).
52 The exclusive rights to perpetually practice *sh'khita* in a town are called a *khazaka*, which the author uses as well. *Khazaka* is a halakhic term referring in general to the rights of possession. This privilege is obtained from the previous *shoykhet* or from the community (Berman, 1941:55–59; "Khazaka," 1998).

the slaughtering rights are yours." I said, "That's not bad, but you'll do better than that," to which he replied, "Well, we'll see."

He made sure that his Tolner Hasidic friends there would not give me any honors on *Shobes* so that I would not attract the attention of any of the Tolner Hasidim since many people, aside from those I had met earlier, noticed me and took a liking to me.[53] So *Shobes* passed with nothing but anguish. After *Shobes*, everyone gathered for the meeting. I also came to the meeting. Even though the *shoykhet* was a stubborn fellow and had a lot of supporters, I was certain that I would prevail and take his place in the village of Slobodze. And the truth is that in some ways Slobodze appealed to me more than Petrovke with its Tolner Hasidim. I actually did succeed in carrying out my plan and he had to give me the slaughtering rights in Slobodze at no charge—I only had to pay twenty rubles for his moving expenses.

I will relate all the details of how this occurred, and you will then see how God did not abandon me. Even though I lost Petrovke through my three-day delay, I did not return too late to miss getting the exclusive slaughtering rights in the village of Slobodze.

***

You already know that I remained in Petrovke over *Shobes* waiting for the meeting. The meeting was held after *Shobes* as planned, and all the men were in attendance. I was also there, though it was not to that *shoykhet*'s liking. Everyone sat around a table. The rabbi of the *shteytl* sat at the head of the table—as did the *shoykhet* and those Tolner Hasidim who supported him. I sat to the side—feeling totally out of place. You can understand how downhearted I was, but I soon rallied my strength and felt assured that God would not desert me. I decided that it would be a good idea to argue things out with the *shoykhet* in front of the entire community. And that is what I did. When the negotiations were winding down, and they finally came to a consensus that the terms needed to be put down in writing, I stood up and asked for permission to speak.

---

53 Honors on *Shabes* from which the author was excluded included leading one of the prayer services, receiving an *aliyah* to the Torah, and the like. The objective was evidently to make sure that the community did not hear the author's pleasant voice and thereby become more interested in him than in the other *shoykhet*. Kasdai (1926:4:223–224) notes in his autobiography that his fellow Ukrainian Jews were particularly drawn to music and traveled to their Hasidic Rebbes for the Jewish holidays to hear the latest Hasidic melodies composed by the cantors of their Rebbes' courts.

"Gentlemen!" I said. "Listen to the few words that I want to say to you—neither a sermon nor a reproof but a personal matter of life and death."

They responded in unison, "Speak, young man. We want to hear you."

I said, "Gentlemen! You know that the position that should have been mine fell to this fellow's lot. Apart from that, I have nothing of my own. Certainly my luck caused this to be so. God demands that I should still keep on struggling. This *shoykhet* arrived before me, and he appeals to you. That's his good luck. I won't even show you my skill in *sh'khita* or my talent in other matters so that I don't interfere with that fellow's position in this town. Fairness and Judaism dictate that I do so."

"Yes, yes," they nodded with their heads. "Very fine, you're really a gentleman. But what, young man, are you trying to accomplish with your speech?"

"Let me finish and you'll hear," I said.

"Speak!" yelled out the Tolner Hasidim, who were impatient as they wanted to know the intention of my speech.

"I've a request to ask of the *shoykhet*—and everyone should help me in obtaining his consent to this out of a sense of fairness and in the spirit of Judaism. That is to say that since he's remaining here as the *shoykhet* and is leaving his former position in Slobodze, he should give me his exclusive slaughtering rights there for free. Then I will also be helped, and he won't lose anything."

Everyone said that my request was just and that, in all fairness, that was how it should be. All turned to the *shoykhet* and asked, "So what do you say?"

The *shoykhet* replied, "I told him that I'd consider it."

"What do you have to think about," they said. "Say 'yes' and let it be done."

He said, "I'd give it to him if he gave me fifty rubles. From someone else I could get 100 rubles, but from him I am willing to take only fifty."

The crowd was ill-disposed toward his suggestion, and said, "You have to give it to him without charge because we aren't charging you anything for the slaughtering rights here. Suppose we charged you 100 rubles, would you pay it? So since you're paying nothing, it's worth it for you to give the slaughtering rights in Slobodze to this young man. He would have actually become the *shoykhet* here if we had found him at his home or if we had known that he would be arriving home in three days. Consequently, since he lost this position because of you, let him be helped through you. Give him the slaughtering rights at no cost."

The *shoykhet* wrinkled up his face since he did not want to consent to such an agreement. His reluctance did not appeal to the crowd, who were waiting for his answer—"yes" or "no"! He conferred with his Tolner Hasidic supporters. They decided that I should pay twenty rubles to at least cover the expenses of his and his family's move from Slobodze. But the crowd was unwilling to consent and said, "Better nothing than twenty."

I said, "Gentlemen! I'm willing to pay twenty rubles—not for the slaughtering rights, because it's not nice to write a document transferring such rights for twenty rubles. He should write in the document that he's giving it to me as a gift and that I'm giving him twenty rubles for his moving expenses. In return, he needs to assist me with the community in Slobodze. He should write a document letting them know that I would now be their *shoykhet* and would not be encroaching on anyone else's slaughtering rights, God forbid, and that this is with his complete agreement."

Everyone exclaimed, "Good, good. That young man is no fool. He makes a lot of sense."

So that is what was decided. The *shoykhet* made a contract with the Jewish men of Petrovke, who all signed it, and I made a written agreement with him regarding the slaughtering rights, that is, he wrote a document transferring the exclusive slaughtering rights of Slobodze to me. In return, I gave him a document stating that once I signed a contract with the community of Slobodze, I would then give him twenty rubles; if not, I was forbidden to use my slaughtering knife there and I would be encroaching upon his rights. Like this, everyone was satisfied. We snacked and drank *le'khaim*, especially the Tolner Hasidim, who were ecstatic.

I traveled home right away. I showed my wife and her parents the document and told them the good news—I was now delivered from my misery. In a week I would take my wife and child to my place of employment and would finally become, in an auspicious hour, the head of my own household. Naturally, everyone was overjoyed, especially my young wife. She was beside herself with joy. How was it possible? Help had now come her way.

But I still had to find a way to raise the twenty rubles that I had obligated myself to pay. "This must be taken care of!" I said to my wife, "We need to resort to your few strings of pearls again." She responded willingly, "I'll give them to you, and you can even sell them. Do whatever you want as long as we'll finally be able to earn our own modest livelihood and you'll be saved from this purgatory." I responded, "Sell them I won't—I'll only pawn them." "Do as you think is best," she answered.

I took her pearls and went back to the person who had lent me ten rubles for them in the past, but this time I asked him to loan me twenty rubles. He said, "I can't lend you twenty rubles, but I'll lend you fifteen." I told him why I needed the money—that he would be keeping me alive by lending me twenty rubles—and that he had nothing to fear for I would not leave him stuck with the pearls, God forbid. I would soon be earning a living, thank God, and I hoped to God that I would pay him off and take the pearls back. He could not bear to see my pain and understood that he was doing a tremendous thing. His wife also urged him to do this mitzvah. In short, he lent me twenty rubles, which was due in three months. Apart from the pearls, he also had me write a promissory note in case I could not repay him or did not want to repay him. So I now had the twenty rubles in my hand. There was joy and jubilation at home.

The next day, I received a letter from the *shoykhet* informing me that he was traveling to Slobodze and asking me if I wanted to meet him there. Naturally, I traveled to Slobodze right away and found him there already. He went with me to the men of the Jewish community so that I could become acquainted with them and ask them for their approval of me. Many of them knew me since I was a child, and I knew them too. Though many had only heard of me, all were willing since I was a local *shoykhet* whom the Tiraspoler and Benderer *shokhtim* held in high esteem and praised tremendously in their certifying papers. In short, together we prepared a contract, which we signed, stating the following: they were taking me on as their *shoykhet*; the exclusive slaughtering rights were mine with the agreement of the community and the former *shoykhet* who gave me them to me as a gift; and that I was bound by the same terms of agreement used with the previous *shoykhet*.

Once I had the contract in my hand, I went with the *shoykhet* to his home in Slobodze and paid him the twenty rubles, and he returned my previously mentioned promissory note. We agreed that the next day he would move to Petrovke while I would move from Perkon to Slobodze, where I would live in the same dwelling that he had lived in. I had already agreed with his landlord that when he left, I would move in and pay the same rent.

And that is how it was. I immediately left for Perkon. My in-laws rented a wagon at their expense, and the next day I, my wife and child, and all of my furnishings were on the wagon, which nonetheless remained practically empty. The non-Jewish driver charged one ruble for transportation and in three hours we were in Slobodze. We were taken to our rented home, from which the previous *shoykhet* had just moved out some three hours earlier.

We unloaded our possessions and immediately went about putting everything in order in our home. Naturally, it did not take us long to be finished. My entire household possessions consisted only of a large old chest that had been given us—and it was older than my great-grandmother—an old bed that was held together with metal brackets, a poker, a noodle board, two little stools, a couple of plates, a bowl, and a couple of wooden spoons and the like. I did not have a table, a sofa, or any chairs. Our landlord was astonished that we had nothing. I told him my situation—how I had struggled until now. He lent me a small table and two boards with which I could make a bed. My wife was overjoyed. Poor as we were, we were nonetheless on our own in peace and quiet, without any harassment and without having to watch her parents' business dealings.

You are certainly puzzled as to why I did not have any furnishings since we had once been on our own for a bit. So what happened to my previous possessions? You should know that there is nothing to be puzzled about because I did not have too much furniture and what I did have was old, worn, and had been handed down to us by my in-laws. In short, I was once again the head of my own household and now, thank God, a *shoykhet* with a decent income. I could now grow and be a man among men. It appeared to us then that no one was as fortunate as we were.

I worked day and night. I brought everything I earned home, and everything I brought home was cherished by my wife. When we sat down to eat, we felt that we were living off our hard-earned money and that no one could disturb us now. The community gave me as much support as possible. People could now come to our home, and we would not feel ashamed, just like everyone else. I thought that it would always be like this and that no one was as fortunate as we were.

But quiet, my dear readers. Do not think that I had it good, God forbid. Do not think that it was quiet for long for the new *shoykhet* in Slobodze and that Pinye-Ber had more luck there than all the previous *shokhtim*. It was a fantastic dream to believe that they were truly good people and that they would always treat their *shoykhet*, who truly appreciated them with his entire heart, so well. No, my dear readers! The quiet and good treatment did not last long—only half a year—meaning until after *Shvues*, and the quarreling already began by the middle of *Sivan*.[54] They caused my family and myself such aggravation and bitterness that I had to start fighting back. The war between us lasted three years without respite. Of course, such a life was not a happy one. I found out that I was not the only one they had fought with. They had quarreled with all the previous *shokhtim* they had hired. The *shoykhet* who was hired in Petrovke, that is, the *shoykhet* who gave me the slaughtering rights, was overjoyed that he was rid of them for they had persecuted him greatly. So it should not be a surprise that they persecuted me. Why should they treat me any better than their previous *shokhtim*? They did not even give me the respect they would a stranger,

---

54 *Shvues* is on the 6th and 7th of *Sivan*, which was on June 1–2, 1873. Hence, the middle of *Sivan* was around June 10, 1873.

especially because I was young and some of them had known me as a child. Apart from that, I had not yet learned how to conduct myself with such men, each of whom thought the *shoykhet* existed for his sake alone. I did not understand the life of a *shoykhet* in a small town, which is why I was persecuted and my life again became gloomy. I lived three and a half years [*sic*] in a sea of troubles until I was free of them.[55] I find it necessary to now describe what I endured during that time.

With this, I am ending the second part of my work. If you are interested, please read the third part and you will see how God constantly guarded me from all enemies through tremendous miracles because my trust in God was strong, as it states, "and those who put their trust in You shall never be disgraced."[56]

---

55 The author lived in Slobodze for over two and a half years, as he later correctly mentions in chapter 22. He lived there from March 1873 until early 1876, as noted at the beginning of chapter 23.

56 Excerpt from the prayer *Shoshanat Ya'akov* recited after the reading of the *Megilla* on Purim.

Volume Two

Part III: My Forty Years as a *Shoykhet* and Moving to Palestine, 1873–1929

Chapter 22: As the *Shoykhet* of Slobodze, 1873–1875

Chapter 23: The Nobleman's Attack and Moving to the Crimea, 1876–1880

Chapter 24: Corruption in Bakhchisaray and Ungrateful Relatives, 1880–1889

Chapter 25: The Threat of Banishment from Tsarist Russia, 1881–1884

Chapter 26: Persecution in Bakhchisaray, 1884–1889

Chapter 27: Raising My Children and My Wife's Death, 1884–1897

Chapter 28: Remarrying and My Children's Departure from Russia, 1896–1910

Chapter 29: Preparing to Leave for Palestine, 1910–1914

Part III—Addendum: My Life in Palestine, 1913–1928

Chapter 30: The World War and the Death of My Second Wife, 1913–1916

Chapter 31: Marrying Off My Niece and Writing a Torah Scroll, 1916–1917

Chapter 32: Exile to Kfar-Saba, 1917–1918

Chapter 33: Suffering in Exile and Returning to Petakh-Tikva, 1918

Chapter 34: Completing the Torah Scroll, the Arab Attack, and My Children Join

Me in Palestine, 1919–1929

Appendices:

Appendix A: The Author and His Relatives

   A1. The Author's Final Years in Petakh-Tikva

      His House, His Property, and the Local Synagogue

      Memories From Those Who Knew Him

      His Demise

      His Chabad Legacy

   A2. The Author's Children

      His Son Isruel (aka Israel Goldenstein in France, 1873-1946)

      His Daughter Nekhame Brakhtman (Noami "Nadya" Brockman, 1877-1955)

      His Son Itskhok-Yosef "Yosl" (Joseph Edward "Joe" Goldeen, 1880-1954)

      His Son Yankev "Yankl" (aka Jacob "James" Goldeen, 1882-1948)

      His Son Refuel (aka Raphael Goldenstein, 1885-1933)

      His Daughter Rukhl (aka Raissa "Raya" Goldinstein Oulianoff, 1887-1966)

      His Son Shloyme Goldenshteyn (Shlomo, 1889-1962)

   A3. His Nephew Itsl (Isaac Goldstein, 1862-1907)

   A4. His Second Wife Feyge (ca. 1854-1916)

   A5. Bashe's *Tsores* —The Story of the Author's Third Wife

   A6. Salomon (Shlomo) Bernstein, Relative and Portraitist of the Author

   A7. The Printing of The Author's Autobiography

Appendix B: Translations of Documents Written by the Author

   B1. Hebrew Engagement Contract for His Daughter Nekhame (1897)

   B2. Hebrew Ethical Will (1920)

   B3. Family Letters

    January 23, 1914 Postcard From the Author's Son Isruel in Feodosiya

    June 1926 Letter From the Author

    July 3, 1926 Letter From the Author

    October 10, 1926 Letter From the Author

    January 27, 1927 Letter From the Author

    March 14, 1929 Letter From the Author

    April 1929 Letter From the Author

    November 21, 1929 Letter From the Author

    July 15, 1930 Letter From the Author

    October 30, 1930 Letter From the Author

    August 28, 1939 Letter From the Author's Son Isruel in France

Appendix C: Translations of Additional Documents

    C1. Hebrew Letter from Rabbi Medini (Sdei Khemed) Regarding the Author (1879)

    C2. Episodes Related by the Author about Rabbi Medini (Sdei Khemed)

    C3. Two Certificates in *Sh'khita* Obtained by the Author's Son Refuel (1904 and 1906)

Appendix D: Genealogical Charts

    D1. The Author's Ancestors and Siblings

    D2. The Extended Family of Ershl Teplitsky, the Author's Brother-in-Law

    D3. The Author's Children and Grandchildren

    D4. The Extended Hershkovitsh Family, the Family of the Author's Wife Freyde

Bibliography

Glossaries:

    Introduction to the Glossaries and the Romanization/Transliteration Schemes

Glossary 1: Foreign Terms

Glossary 2: Jewish Personal Names

Glossary 3: Geographic Locations in Eastern Europe

Index

"This is a remarkable book, brimming with much information about East European traditional Jewish life in the second half of the nineteenth century. Its author, Pinkhes-Dov Goldenshteyn, describes his experiences in a most direct, straightforward way, with great attention to detail. His is the story of a simple Jew who writes with disarming openness, honesty, simplicity and naivité, with absolutely no pretense, no airs, no filter, and no agenda. What emerges is a remarkable first-hand description of his experiences, both challenging and joyous alike. Special commendation goes to Michael Rotenfeld for providing an excellent translation, comprehensive introduction and detailed notes for this volume which, for him, is clearly a labor of love. This book contains a treasure trove of information for the scholar and will provide hours of reading pleasure for the layman."

— *Rabbi Dr. Jacob J. Schacter, University Professor of Jewish History and Jewish Thought, Yeshiva University*

"Autobiographies offer a unique window into history. This is particularly the case when the author is a nineteenth-century traditional Jew, as we do not have many such works. Pinkhes-Dov Goldenshteyn's lengthy memoir is thus of great significance as he takes us with him throughout his journeys in East European Orthodox society. Here we meet many fascinating personalities up close, including the famed rebbe of Lubavitch, the *Tzemach Tzedek*. Originally written in Yiddish, we can thank Michoel Rotenfeld for his wonderful translation—a true labor of love— and his learned introduction and notes that allow us to get the most out of this fascinating work."

— *Marc B. Shapiro, Weinberg Chair in Judaic Studies, University of Scranton*

"This autobiography's importance is indisputable. It is a rare example of an ego-document written by a 'simple,' ordinary Jew, someone who never belonged to the elite circles of the maskilim, but instead lived far from their centers and influences; moreover Pinkhes-Dov Goldenshteyn never experienced any kind of 'conversion' or loss of faith—a central motif in nineteenth-century Jewish autobiographies. Thus, his writings may represent a 'silent voice' of the majority of orthodox or conservative Jews, who did not take part in the big debates of the era. Goldenshteyn's seemingly mundane life may represent the lives of many others who chose not to write. For historians of the period seeking to draw a fair and balanced portrait of the times, Goldenshteyn's voice is an important one."

— *David Assaf, Professor of Jewish History, Tel Aviv University*

"A rare journey deep into the Hasidic world of nineteenth-century Tsarist Russia. Goldenshteyn, a Lubavitcher Hasid, conveys his daily struggles and fleeting joys in a manner unencumbered by the nostalgia and alienation so typical of secularist Jewish memoirs. He is not uncritical; yet his story radiates Old-World charm. *The Shochet* is meticulously edited, and is essential reading for an understanding of everyday Hasidic Eastern Europe."

— *Glenn Dynner, author of* The Light of Learning: Hasidism in Poland on the Eve of the Holocaust

Printed in the USA
CPSIA information can be obtained
at www.ICGtesting.com
JSHW011550010724
65693JS00005B/119